THE**GREEN**GUIDE
Dordogne
Berry Limousin

Vineyards of Sancerre, A. Cassaigne/MICHELIN

General Manager Cynthia Clayton Ochterbeck

THEGREENGUIDE **DORDOGNE BERRY LIMOUSIN**

Editor	Jonathan P. Gilbert
Principal Writer	Paul Shawcross
Production Manager	Natasha G. George
Cartography	Stephane Anton, John Dear
Photo Editor	Yoshimi Kanazawa
Interior Design	Chris Bell
Layout	Therese Schneider, Michelin Apa Publications Ltd.
Cover Design	Chris Bell, Christelle Le Déan
Cover Layout	Michelin Apa Publications Ltd.

Contact Us
The Green Guide
Michelin Maps and Guides
One Parkway South
Greenville, SC 29615
USA
www.michelintravel.com

Michelin Maps and Guides
Hannay House
39 Clarendon Road
Watford, Herts WD17 1JA
UK
✆01923 205240
www.ViaMichelin.com
travelpubsales@uk.mi chelin.com

Special Sales
For information regarding bulk sales, customized editions and premium sales, please contact our Customer Service Departments:
USA 1-800-432-6277
UK 01923 205240
Canada 1-800-361-8236

HOW TO USE THIS GUIDE

PLANNING YOUR TRIP

The blue-tabbed PLANNING YOUR TRIP section at the front of the guide gives you **ideas for your trip** and **practical information** to help you organize it. You'll find tours, practical information, a host of outdoor activities, a calendar of events, information on shopping, sightseeing, kids' activities and more.

INTRODUCTION

The orange-tabbed INTRODUCTION section explores Dordogne Berry Limousin's **Nature** and geology. The **History** section spans from prehistoric man to the modern day. The **Art and Culture** section covers architecture, art, literature and music, while the **Region Today** delves into the modern region.

DISCOVERING

The green-tabbed DISCOVERING section features Principal Sights by region, featuring the most interesting local **Sights, Walking Tours**, nearby **Excursions**, and detailed **Driving Tours**. Admission prices shown are normally for a single adult.

ADDRESSES

We've selected the best hotels, restaurants, cafes shops, nightlife and entertainment to fit all budgets. See the Legend on the cover flap for an explanation of the price categories. See the back of the guide for an index of hotels and restaurants.

Sidebars

Throughout the guide you will find blue, orange and green-colored text boxes with lively anecdotes, detailed history and background information.

☺ A Bit of Advice ☺

Green advice boxes found in this guide contain practical tips and handy information relevant to the sight in the Discovering section.

STAR RATINGS★★★

Michelin has given star ratings for more than 100 years. If you're pressed for time, we recommend you visit the ★★★, or ★★ sights first:

★★★	**Highly recommended**
★★	**Recommended**
★	**Interesting**

MAPS

☺ Regional Driving Tours map, Places to Stay map and Principal Sights map.

☺ Region maps.

☺ Maps for major cities and villages.

☺ Local tour maps.

All maps in this guide are oriented north, unless otherwise indicated by a directional arrow. The term "Local Map" refers to a map within the chapter or Tourism Region. A complete list of the maps found in the guide appears at the back of this book.

4

CONTENTS

Welcome to Dordogne Berry Limousin

The Dordogne, Berry and Limousin regions together include some of the most and the least visited areas in France. The Dordogne and the Quercy, with their characteristic castles, caves and river valleys are well known. The unspoiled verdant countryside and plateaux of the Berry and Limousin are much less familiar.

Lascaux II, Périgord Noir

©Patrick Somelet/Photononstop/Tips Images

DORDOGNE

The modern Dordogne coincides roughly with the old province of the Périgord, each with its own character-istic colour. The Périgord Noir (Black) owes its name to its high density of trees; the Périgord Blanc (White) for it's outcrops of chalky limestone; the Périgord Vert (Green) for the verdant countryside of the north and the Périgord Pourpre (Purple) for the vines that are grown there.

The Romans were here, of course, and remains of their presence can best be seen in Périgueux. Following incur-sions by Vandals, Visigoths, Franks, Moors and Vikings, the area finally came under the control of the English in 1152. Later, during the Hundred Year's War, it was much contested and like most of France suffered during the Wars of Religion. In recent years the area has suffered yet another invasion, this time peaceful, as many northern Europeans have flocked to live here.

- *Périgord Noir (p96–137).*
- *Bergerac and the Périgord Pourpre (p138–159).*
- *Périgueux, the Périgord Vert and Périgord Blanc (p160–181).*

BERRY

One of the oldest agricultural regions of France, the province of Berry was unified due to its shared heritage rather than its geography. It corresponds approximately with the modern départements of Cher and Indre and lies between the Paris Basin and the Massif Central.

The region consists of a low-lying plateau rising, in the north east, to the famous wine producing Sancerre Hills and tilting westwards towards the Brenne nature park.

A relatively quiet region set in the heart of France, Berry has always been resolutely French. In fact, during the Hundred Years' War, the capital of the Berry–Bourges, an important town since Gallo-Roman times–was the seat of the French King. The region has also produced some extremely colourful characters; Jean de Berry, patron of the arts and even more so, Jacques Coeur, the financier.

- *Boischaut and La Brenne (p354–377).*
- *Bourges and the Champagne Berrichonne (p378–405).*
- *Sologne, Pays Fort, Sancerrois (p406-417).*

Landscape of La Brenne

Jacass/MICHELIN

Château de Belcastel,
Upper Dordogne Valley

J. Damase/MICHELIN

LIMOUSIN

The unspoiled countryside of the Limousin has it all: medieval villages, hills, gorges, verdant green meadows and moorland ideal for breeding horses. In fact, the Anglo-Arab horse originated at Pompadour. The Limousin Region on the western slopes of the Massif Central is comprised of three *départements*: Creuse, Haute-Vienne and Corrèze. The Creuse borders the Berry in the north; the Haute-Vienne is adjacent to the Poitou-Charente and the Dordogne in the west and southwest respectively, while the Corrèze borders the Quercy to the south and the Auvergne to the west.

Inhabited by a Gallic tribe known as the Lemovices, from which the area took its name, the region became part of Roman Aquitania following the conquest of Gaul. After the Romans, the Franks eventually gained control before the area came under the suzerainty of the English crown in 1152. Like its neighbours, the Limousin was the scene of fierce fighting during the Hundred Years' War, before it was eventually taken back under French sovereignty.

- *Upper Dordogne Valley (p238–269).*
- *Upper Vézère and Corrèze Valleys (p270–301).*
- *Limoges, the Vienne and around (p302–333).*
- *Marche and the Upper Creuse (p334-353).*

QUERCY

Quercy stretches from the Massif Central in the east to the plains of Aquitaine in the west and from the Limousin in the north to the Midi-Pyrénées in the south. No longer an administrative entity, the region has a strong historical unity and in the Middle Ages Quercy belonged to the province of Guyenne or Aquitaine. Today, Quercy comprises all of the Lot and part of Tarn et Garonne départements.

The region was first occupied by the Cadurques or Cadurci a Celtic tribe. From the mid 1C BC it was part of Roman Gaul until it succumbed to the barbarian invasions of the 5C. Part of the Duchy of Aquitaine in the Middle Ages, the region was heavily involved in the Hundred Years' War; Later the region was again ravaged by warfare as it was heavily involved in the Wars of Religion and also the French Revolution. Although less well known to tourists than its neighbour the Périgord, tourism is of increasing importance with more than 1 million visitors per year visiting Rocamadour and 400,000 exploring the cave systems.

- *Rocamadour and Northern Quercy (p182–199).*
- *Lot Valley and Southern Quercy (p200–237).*

Figeac,
Southern
Quercy

©bobroy20/Fotolia.com

Canoeing on the River Lot
S. Sauvignier/MICHELIN

Michelin Driving Tours

⟐Explore the areas highlighted on the driving tours map overleaf.

1 THE HEART OF BERRY
235km/146mi starting from Bourges.
If you like variety, this itinerary is made for you. From Bourges and its magnificent cathedral, drive to Mehun-sur-Yèvre at the heart of porcelain country, then on to Reuilly, Quincy and, further on, to Châteaumeillant, where local wines will delight wine-lovers. Stop to contemplate the medieval gardens at Notre-Dame d'Orsan, then continue to the feudal castle of Culan. The Renaissance château of Ainay-le-Vieil is less austere, as are the richly decorated Château de Meillant and the elegant Château de Jussy-Champagne. Also on the tour: the vast and inspiring Noirlac Abbey and the more humble but very interesting abbey church of Plaimpied.

2 GEORGE SAND COUNTRY
210km/130mi starting from La Châtre.
Journey through the landscapes which inspired George Sand's novels from the Vallée Noire to the Creuse Valley, from Nohant Château to Gargilesse, from the Crozant ruins to La Motte-Feuilly.

3 DECORATIVE ARTS AND CONTEMPORARY ART
250km/155mi starting from Limoges.
This itinerary offers an insight into the artistic wealth and variety of the Limousin region. The Creuse Valley inspired two Impressionist painters, Claude Monet and Armand Guillaumin (some of their works are on display in Limoges and Guéret). The other fine arts and crafts to see on this tour include: the famous Aubusson tapestries, woodcarving (stalls in Moutier-d'Ahun) and stone carving (in the village of Masgot), contemporary art on the island of Vassivière and, of course, Limoges porcelain and enamel work.

4 WHERE RIVERS START THEIR JOURNEY
230km/143mi starting from Ussel.
Several rivers start their journey in the Limousin mountains. From Ussel, it is only a short way up the Monédières massif (splendid panorama from the Suc-au-May viewpoint); then up again onto the Plateau de Millevaches, the rooftop of Limousin. Rugged winters and plenty of rain have turned it into a reservoir feeding the many rivers that run from it, including the Creuse, the Vézère and the Corrèze. The pastoral Site du Rat, the remote Tourbière du Longéroux and the enigmatic Site des Cars are ideal for rambling. A stroll through the old town of Meymac will offer a welcome contrast.

5 DOWN THE RIVER DORDOGNE
210km/130mi starting from Argentat.
In bygone days, traditional gabares were moored along the River Dordogne. Today, you can take a trip aboard one of these boats, once intended for cargo, from Pont-

Ruines de Crozant at the confluence of the Creuse and the Sédelle

A. Cassaigne/MICHELIN

de-Chambon or Spontour. Dams (Chastang and l'Aigle) bar the Dordogne below the spectacular Orgues de Bort and the route is dotted with viewpoints.

6 THE GATEWAY TO PÉRIGORD

195km/121mi starting from Brive-la-Gaillarde.
Brive and its foie gras market, Aubazine and its monastery, Tulle and its lace, Gimel and its waterfalls, Sédières and its castle and the leisure park in Marcillac…and that is just the beginning of the region the French region know as Périgord. Follow the Gorges de la Cère then drive on to Beaulieu-sur-Dordogne and admire the proud outline of Curemonte castles before reaching the red-sandstone village of Collonges-la-Rouge and the nearby Château de Turenne.

7 FORESTS, VINEYARDS AND BASTIDES AROUND BERGERAC

230km/143mi starting from Bergerac.
Montaigne and his legendary wisdom, and Cyrano de Bergerac (and his sharp wit) form the historic background of this itinerary, which meanders through picturesque vineyards producing wines with enchanting names like Pécharmant, Rosette, Montravel and above all Monbazillac (the cellars are open to visitors). Picturesque castles can be seen along the way and the itinerary goes through the former bastide (fortified town) of Beaumont-du-Périgord.

8 PÉRIGORD NOIR

185km/115mi starting from Montignac.
The Vézère and Dordogne valleys have revealed 30 000 years of mankind's history. Drive from Lascaux to Le Bugue via Les Eyzies, the European capital of prehistory. Continue your journey forward into medieval times from Monpazier to Domme: fortresses, bastides and abbeys tell the terrible story of the Hundred Years War. Leave the Dordogne Valley to reach the heart of Périgord Noir in Sarlat-la-Canéda which has retained the charm of a fine Renaissance city and upholds the region's gastronomic traditions (foie gras and Bergerac wines).

9 LIMESTONE PLATEAUX OF HAUT-QUERCY

125km/78mi starting from Padirac.
This amazing journey starts more than 100m/110yd underground, inside the fascinating Gouffre de Padirac; next comes the extraordinary site of Rocamadour with its sheer cliff crowned by ramparts. The route then leads you to the borders of Périgord Noir, through the towns of Souillac and Martel, along the Dordogne Valley hemmed in by high cliffs and on to St-Céré among green hills overlooked by the castles of Castelnau and Montal.

10 THE LOT AND CÉLÉ VALLEYS

120km/75mi starting from Figeac.
The two rivers have carved their way through the limestone plateau between St-Cirq-Lapopie and Figeac, meandering across a varied and picturesque landscape of sheer cliffs alternating with undulating meadows. Of particular interest are the Pech-Merle cave, the hilltop village of St-Cirq-Lapopie, the castles of Cénevières and Laroque-Toirac and the churches of St-Pierre-Toirac and Marcilhac.

11 THE LOT VINEYARDS AND QUERCY BLANC

185km/115mi starting from Cahors.
The wide and imposing River Lot meanders through the Cahors vineyards, lined with picturesque towns and villages such as Luzech, Belaye (perched on top of a cliff) and Puy-l'Évêque, leading you straight to Bonaguil, an amazing fortress standing on the border of Périgord and Quercy. Beyond the Lot Valley and its vineyards lies an area known as Quercy Blanc dotted with bastides and windmills, with a definite southern flavour.

Driving Tours

For descriptions of these tours, turn to the *Planning Your Trip* section following.

30 km

1. The heart of Berry
2. George Sand country
3. Decorative arts and contemporary art
4. Where rivers start their journey
5. Down the River Dordogne
6. The gateway to Périgord
7. Forests, vineyards and bastides around Bergerac
8. Périgord Noir
9. Limestone plateaux of Haut-Quercy
10. The Lot and Célé valleys
11. The Lot vineyards and Quercy Blanc

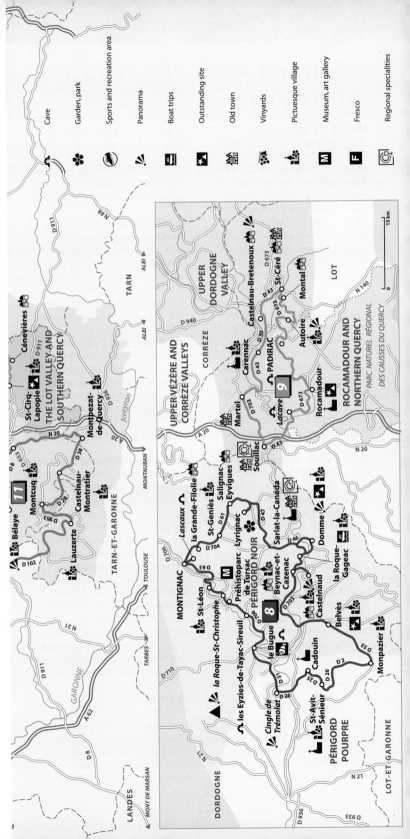

When and Where to Go

WHEN TO GO

This inland region is open to oceanic influences from the Atlantic. The climate on the whole is mild, winter frosts are limited, spring is early and warm and summer is hot. Rainfall is evenly distributed throughout the year. In Berry however, several micro-climates make for small, distinct weather systems within the region. For example, the Champagne Berrichonne, with its vast fields of grain crops, is often dry and gets very hot in the summer, while the humidity keeps things cooler in the Boischaut, the Brenne wetlands and the high forests of the Motte d'Humbligny.

The climate in Limousin is also variable, in particular with regard to altitude. The prevailing south-west winds blow hard against the foothills of the Massif Central mountain range, provoking significant rainfall (1 200-1 700mm/47-67in per year) – although summer droughts are not unusual. Winter on the high plateaux (Millevaches, Gentioux, Monédières, Combraille) is long and harsh, with low temperatures and chill, stiff winds. Elsewhere in the region, winters are milder, with less rain, but crops are often damaged by freezing temperatures in the spring and fall.

The Dordogne is more clement on the whole, beginning with the Brive basin. While the climate is nearly Mediterranean, there is enough water to keep the landscape green and crops prosperous throughout the summer. A blanket of flowers soon covers the countryside, as the region quickly warms to the new season.

The **summer** holidays bring many tourists to enjoy the delights of the beautiful natural settings, towns and monuments and the many festivals and activities organised for visitors. In Dordogne in the summer, rain often falls in torrential storms, in the wake of a hot wind blowing steadily from the west. In the **winter**, snow is infrequent; frosty nights and foggy mornings come with the spring. **Autumn** is quieter and a lovely time to appreciate the flowering heather, the browns and golds of the changing leaves, the colourful markets with an abundance of harvest produce, or the delights of wild mushrooms served with game from the forest.

DORDOGNE

Weekends away -Bergerac, the capital of the Périgord Pourpre, has its own airport. As the name of the area suggests, wine is the main interest here and a visit to the Maison des Vins is a must. Don't forget about Cyrano - his statue can be found in the main square!

One week - There are enough castles and bastide towns in the Périgord to keep the visitor busy for at least a week! The impressive fortresses of Beynac and Castelnaud keep an eye on each other across the Dordogne River and the unusual bastide of Domme are just some of the splendours of the region.

Second week - The Cave systems and prehistoric rock paintings at Lascaux and Les Eyzies are world famous and visits to these together with the outstanding gardens such as those at Marqueyssac, rounded off with a trip in a gabarre (or a canoe!) on the Dordogne, will complete a very pleasant and fulfilling stay in the area.

QUERCY

Weekends away - Cahors is the capital of the Lot and can easily be reached from Toulouse. The famous black wine of Cahors can be sampled here but the impressive medieval towers of the Pont de Valentré should be not be missed.

One week - The Lot Valley in either direction is fascinating and provides much interest. To the east, the hilltop village of St-Cirq-Lapopie is a splendid sight (best visited early morning or evening to avoid the crowds) while to the west, where the vineyards are located, the meanders of the River Lot lead to the fascinating small towns of Luzech and Puy l'Évêque.

Second week - The Parc Naturel des Causses du Quercy is well worth spending some time exploring. This dry moorland contains many surprises and the town of Martel on the Causse de Martel is no exception. On the Causse de Gramat, the Gouffre de Padirac and the spectacular site of Rocamadour invite further exploration. South of Lot the Causse de Limogne is drier again and while there are few settlements there are dolmens, megaliths and white truffle oaks.

LIMOUSIN

Weekends away - Limoges is the capital of the Limousin Region and famous for its porcelain. There are plenty of porcelain shops and a visit to the round kiln of the Four de Cassoux, just out of the centre, is fascinating.

One week - There is much of interest both in and around Limoges. The city itself has enough to interest the visitor for a few days and locally the commemorative site of Oradour-sur-Glane, the village destroyed by the Nazis in WW2, the Église Abbatiale de Solignac and the Parc Zoologique at the Parc Reynou are all within easy reach.

Second week - The Limousin is a best explored in sections, perhaps starting with the Upper Dordogne Valley in the south, being sure to visit the plus beau villages of Beaulieu-sur-Dordogne and Collonges-la-Rouge, followed by the adjacent Upper Corrèze and Vézère Valleys . In the north, the Marche and Upper Creuse have fewer sights but be sure to include the Basse Marche.

BERRY

Weekends away - Bourges the capital of the Berry, and briefly the capital of France, can be reached from Paris (Orly) in 2.5 hours. This gem of a city has a splendid Cathedral, half-timbered houses and the well-appointed 15C residence of Jacques Coeur.

One week - Much of the Berry can be visited from Bourges and the wine region of the Sancerrois to the north of the city is of interest to the wine lover. Slightly to the west lies the Sologne and Aubigny-sur-Nère.

Second week - The area to the west of Bourges includes the old town of Issoudun which has associations with Richard the Lion Heart and further west again the Château de Valençay is reminiscent of those in the Loire

THEMED TOURS

Travel itineraries on specific themes have been mapped out to help you to discover the regional architecture and the traditions that make up the cultural heritage of the region. As you drive through this region, you are likely to see signs posted for the routes listed below: go to the nearest tourist office for more information, or just detour and follow along!

PREHISTORY, HISTORY

Prehistoric Périgord-Quercy

Below is a list of the main prehistoric caves of the Périgord and Quercy areas mentioned in this guide; they all contain paintings or engravings: **Bara-Bahau** (Périgord), **Bernifal** (Périgord), **Combarelles** (Périgord), **Cougnac** (Quercy), **Font-de-Gaume** (Périgord), **Lascaux II** (Périgord), **Pech-Merle** (Quercy), and **Rouffignac** (Périgord).

HISTORIC ROUTES

Routes historiques are signposted local itineraries following an architectural and historical theme, accompanied by an explanatory booklet, available from local tourist offices.

♦ **Berry**
*La Route des Dames de Touraine,
La Route François I,
La Route Jacques Cœur.*

♦ **Limousin**
*La Route des Plantagenêts,
La Route Richard Cœur de Lion,
La Route de St-Jacques.*

♦ **Dordogne**
La Route des mille et un Châteaux en Périgord, La Route des Marches du Quercy.

TRADITIONS AND CULTURAL HERITAGE

These thematic routes have been created by regional associations; contact the local tourist offices for details and maps.

Dordogne

◆ **Sentiers Romans en Quercy Blanc**
Romanesque churches in the Quercy Blanc area.
☎ 05 65 21 84 39.

◆ **Route des Métiers d'Art en Périgord**
The itinerary includes 60 workshops of traditional craftsmen; www.cm-perigueux.fr.

◆ **Route des Metiersd'Art dans le Lot**
45 workshops of traditional craftsmen. www.rm-art46.org.

◆ **Vallée de la Dordogne**
8 short itineraries from Souillac across the Périgord Noir and Quercy areas.
www.tourisme-souillac.com.

◆ **Route des Vins**
Discovering local wines in the Bergerac area.
www.vins-bergerac.com.

Berry

◆ **Chemin des Lavoirs dans le Cher**
15 waterside wash-houses to discover in the Germigny Valley, maintained by the association Nos villages en Berry.

◆ **Ronde des Champs d'Amour**
Fields of love in the Champagne Berrichonne region around Issoudun.

◆ **Route des Vignobles du Cœur de France**
A tour of the vineyards of the Berry region, Quincy, Reuilly, Menetou-Salon, Sancerre, Coteaux du Giennois and Châteaumeillant, producing fine AOC wines; information on www.vins-centre-loire.com.

◆ **Route de la Porcelaine**
Factories, museums, workshops and shops devoted to porcelain between Vierzon and St-Amand-Montrond.

◆ **Vallée des Peintres**
In the footsteps of Guillaumin, Monet and other artists along the Creuse Valley from Argenton to Glénic.

Limousin

◆ **Circuit du Châtaignier**
A day trip in chestnut country, where the crafting of hoop-wood strips for barrel-making is traditional; May–Nov.
☎ 05 55 78 49 92.

◆ **Parcs et Jardins du Limousin**
The tour includes over 30 parks and gardens selected by the association Découverte du Patrimoine Paysager et Botanique.

COOKERY COURSES

If your favourite recreation takes place with pots and pans for equipment, why not spend 2 or 3 days in a French kitchen for a holiday? In Dordogne, the season for preparing foie gras is generally from October to mid-December and from mid-January to April. A number of farmhouse-inns offer sessions which include lessons on preparing foie gras, confits, cou farci and other delights, as well as lodging and board. Generally, you must buy your own duck or goose.

For information, contact:

☞ **Loisirs-Accueil Corrèze**
Quai Aristide Briand,
19000 Tulle. ☎ 05 55 29 98 70.

☞ **Loisirs-Accueil Dordogne**
25 rue du Président-Wilson,
BP 2063, 24002 Périgueux.
☎ 05 53 35 50 24, or 05 53 35 50 50.

☞ **Loisirs-Accueil Lot**
Place François-Mitterrand,
46000 Cahors. ☎ 05 65 53 20 90.
www.reservation-lot.com.

Beyond mere learning, two family-run operations specialising in goose and duck respectively, take the visitor right into the heart of local matters. Excellent cooking and facilities and a warm welcome await at:

🍲 **Ferme du fort de la Rhonie**
Coustaty Family, Boyer,
24220 Meyrals.
📞 05 53 29 29 07.

🍲 **La Maurinie**
Alard Family, Eyliac,
24330 St-Pierre-de-Chignac.
📞 05 53 07 57 18.

Sessions open when enough participants have enrolled. You are also welcome to stay and eat as a regular guest, without cooking, and just enjoy the food, the company, and farm life.

EQUESTRIAN TOURS

Horse-drawn caravans
Savour the countryside at a gentle pace aboard a horse-drawn caravan. At 4kph/2.5mph, you will have ample time to look around the back roads and lanes you are travelling. This nomadic life can last for 2-7 days, according to the itinerary.

Équitation et Roulottes du Périgord
Métairie du roc, 24560 Faux.
📞/Fax 05 53 24 32 57.
http://metairieduroc.free.fr

Les Roulottes du Quercy
46700 Sérignac. 📞 05 65 31 96 44.

Château d'Aynac (Castel SARL)
Château d'Aynac, 46120 Aynac.
📞 05 65 11 08 00.
www.castel-aynac.fr.

Horse-drawn carriage rides
These last 1hr, half a day or a day (with picnic).

Calèche de Dordogne
Ferme de Charmonteil, 24350 Lisle.
📞 05 53 03 58 35.

Les Attelages du Haut Repaire
Haut Repaire, 24390 Coubjours.
📞 05 53 50 32 79.

Le Périgord en calèche
Le Bourg, 24550 Mazeyrolles.
📞 05 53 29 98 99.

Donkey-trekking
If you plan a long walking tour, a donkey is a useful companion for carrying your luggage (up to 40kg/88lb), and children usually feel motivated by its presence.

The **Fédération nationale ânes et randonnées (FNAR)**, 16 route de Canlers, 62310 Ruisseauville
📞 03 21 41 21 97, www.ane-et-rando.com, will provide general information. You can rent a donkey for a day or a week with or without a guide from:

Arcâne
"Ravary", 24250 Cenac.
📞 05 53 59 63 79 or 06 07 75 90 84.
www.arc-ane.com.

Brahmâne
Cazillac, 82110 Cazes-Mondenard.
📞 05 63 95 84 61.

PORCELAIN
♿ *See the Introduction.*

Limoges is synonymous with fine china, and there is no dearth of shops selling it, including factory outlets (*vente directe d'usines*) just outside of town. Many workshops (*manufactures*) and showrooms (*magasins*) are also open on the road between Vierzon and Bourges. The larger outlets often have interesting museums, video presentations and demonstrations. Limoges is also a historical and contemporary centre for the production of enamelware (*émaux*). Look for shops around place Wilson in town, or stop in one of the many workshops scattered around the region.

Limoges teapot

©Rabbitsfoot/Dreamstime.com

Porcelaine à pâte dure

True porcelain (hard-paste) or china: Resonant when struck, translucent, made from ground feldspathic rock and kaolin clay.

Porcelaine tendre

Artificial porcelain (soft-paste): Softer than true porcelain, it can be cut with a file, whereas true porcelain cannot. Dirt accumulated on an unglazed base can only be removed with difficulty; on true porcelain it comes off easily.

Porcelaine phosphatique

Bone china: A translucent ware, neither hard-paste or *Porcelaine hybride* nor soft-paste porcelain, that contains kaolin, petuntse and bone ash.

Faience fine

White earthenware, opaque porcelain or creamware: A generic term for a fine, hard earthenware of high strength and durability.

Grès or Grès céramique

Stoneware: Glassy in appearance, or semi-vitreous, with a fine texture, stoneware is always hard and is always fired in a high temperature kiln; the non-porous clay does not require a glaze.

Terre Cuite

Terra Cotta, redware: This clay is fired at a low temperature to a rather soft and porous body ranging in colour from pinkish-buff to brick-reds and reddish browns.
As a rule it is covered with a soft lead glaze.

RAIL-BIKING

Pedal away along disused railtracks aboard specially adapted rail trucks:

Les cyclodraisines d'Aubigny
Route de Clémont, 18700 Aubigny-sur-Nère, ℘02 48 81 50 07 (weekdays), ℘02 48 58 35 81 (weekends and holidays), May 1–Sept 30. 5€ per hour, 15€ per half-day, 25€ per day. www.aubigny-sur-nere.fr

Cycling path in the Lot Valley

M.-H. Carcanague/MICHELIN

Vélo-rail de Bussière
Plan d'eau des Ribières, 87230 Bussière-Galant, ℘05 55 78 86 47, www.velo-rail.com; open Apr 1–Jun 15 and school hols, Sat departures, 2 and 4.30pm, Sun and Public Holiday departures, 10am, 12.30pm, 3pm and 5.30pm. Jun 15–Aug 31 open daily exc Sat, departures 10am, 12.30pm, 3pm and 5.30pm. Sept, Sat departures 10am, ipm and 4pm (Chalus only) 24€ (2hr 30min maximum).

RIVER CRUISING

Houseboats

For a weekend or a week, enjoy the pleasant pace of life as you cruise the River Lot, where new sections of locks have been opened for pleasure craft. No license is required; the captain must be an adult, and go through a brief course given on board before departure. The rental agent explains, in particular, the methods for going through a lock and for docking, which is about all you need to know to operate these holiday barges.

Babou Marine
Port St-Mary, 46000 Cahors. ℘05 65 30 08 99; www.baboulene-jean.fr

Crown Blue Line
Le Moulinat, 46140 Douelle. ℘05 65 20 08 79. www.crownblueline.com.

Lot Navigation Nicols
Le Bourg, 46330 Bouziès. ℘05 65 24 32 20. Route du Puy-St-Bonnet, 49300 Cholet. ℘02 41 56 46 56. www.nicols.com

Maps and guides are available from:
Éditions Grafocarte-Navicarte
125 rue Jean-Jacques-Rousseau,
BP 40, 92132 Issy-les-Moulineaux
Cedex. ℘01 49 93 22 53.
Éditions du Plaisancier
43 porte du Grand-Lyon,
01700 Neyron. ℘04 72 01 58 68.

Boat Trips

For a shorter trip, and without the
responsibility of the helm, take a
cruise on the Lac de Vassivière, or
the Lac de Val at Bort-les-Orgues,
or enjoy a ride in a traditional gabarre
on the Dordogne from Chalvignac,
Spontour, Pont du Chambon, Barrage
du Chastang, La Roque-Gageac,
Vezac-Beynac, Bergerac.
Gabarres de Beynac
24250 St-Martial-de-Nabirat.
℘05 53 28 51 15.
www.gabarre-beynac.com.
Apr–Oct, 10am–12.30 and 2–6pm.
7.50€ Departures every 30 mins
in season. (no charge for children
in the morning).
Gabarres Norbert
La Roque-Gageac.
℘05 53 29 40 44; www.norbert.fr.
Apr–Oct: 1hr trips with
commentary. Departures every hr.
(Oct pm only) 8.50€.

TOURIST TRAINS

In the **Limousin**, different routes are
travelled by vintage, 1930s trains,
with a steam engine leading the way.
Visit the Haute Vallée de la Vienne
(Limoges-Eymoutiers-Limoges);
the Millevaches Plateau (Limoges-
Meymac-Limoges); the Vienne Gorges
(Eymoutiers-Châteauneuf-Bujaleuf-
Eymoutiers) or the Realm of Ventadour
(Meymac-Ussel-Meymac).
🛈Contact local tourist offices, ℘05
55 34 46 87 (Limoges) or 05 55 69 27
81 (Eymoutiers) or **Vienne Vézère
Vapeur**, www.trainvapeur.com.

In the **Dordogne, Autorail
Espérance** offers a guided tour and
a taste of regional cooking, travelling
from Sarlat to Bergerac in one hour

(reservation required: ℘05 53 59
55 39). **Quercyrail** runs trains from the
1950s along the old Cahors-Capdenac
line, where passengers get a good
look at the Lot Valley:
For further information call ℘05 63
40 11 93 (reservations recommended).

The **Chemin de fer touristique
du Haut-Quercy "**

Le Truffadou" runs full steam ahead
between Martel and St-Denis-près-
Martel along the top of 80m/262ft
cliffs overlooking the Dordogne
Valley; ℘05 65 37 35 81.
www.trainduhautquercy.info.

TAKE TO THE SKIES

Several options are available for a
bird's-eye view of **Périgord**:
hot-air balloon, light aircraft, glider,
microlight…
Montgolfière du Périgord
Clos St-Donat, 24250 La Roque
Gageac. ℘05 53 28 18 58; www.
montgolfiere-du-perigord.com.
Preparation and flight (3hr
minimum) daily morning and late
afternoon spring and autumn, the
rest of the year once per day pm;
prices start at 190€.
The **Aéroclub de Brive**
Aéroport de Brive-Laroche
℘05 55 86 88 37. Open daily
9am–noon, 2–6pm; excl. Mon am.
Offers introductory flights aboard
a plane or a glider.
The **Aéroclub du Quercy**
Aérodrome de Cahors-Lalbenque,
46230 Cieurac. ℘05 65 21 05 96.
Offers flights over the area.
The **Aéroclub du Sarladais**
Aérodrome de Sarlat-Domme,
24250 Domme. ℘05 53 28 32 95.
Tours on a plane or microlight.
The **Association
Rocamadour Aérostat**
Hôtel de Ville. ℘05 65 33 71 50.
Proposes year-round 45min flights
over Rocamadour. Reservation
required. 150€ per person.

What to See and Do

OUTDOOR FUN
WATER SPORTS

This inland region is awash with man-made lakes, many well-equipped for swimming and boating, and the rivers and streams are inviting, too. The region's leading water sports centre is the **Lac de Vassivière** (*970ha/2 397 acres*), which offers beaches suitable for youngsters as well as opportunities for sailing and wind-surfing. (♿*see Lac de VASSIVIÈRE*).
For general information on water-skiing, contact the **Fédération française de ski nautique**, 27 rue Athènes, 75009 Paris, ℘01 53 20 19 19; www.ffsn.fr. The village of Trémolat, on the Dordogne, also has an international water sports centre (℘05 53 22 81 18).

CANOEING AND KAYAKING

Canoeing is a popular family pastime on the peaceful waters of the region. In fact, on some weekends, in Dordogne, there seem to be more people on the water than on the road! **Kayaking** is practised on the lakes and, for more experienced paddlers, rapid sections of the rivers. For beginners, the River Dordogne and River Lot are not only ideally calm, but also offer splendid views. The Corrèze, Elle, Auvézère, Céou and the upper parts of the Dronne, Isle and Célé rivers are more of a challenge. In all cases, be

Auvézère Valley

J. Malburet/MICHELIN

sure to wear the buoyant life jacket the rental agent is obliged to provide. For general information contact:

◆ **Fédération française de canoë-kayak**
  87 quai de la Marne, BP 58 – 94344 Joinville-le-Pont.
  ℘01 45 11 08 50.
  www.ffck.org.
◆ **Ligue régionale de canoë-kayak du Val de Loire-Centre**
  Maison des Sports, 1240 rue de la Bergeresse, 45160 Olivet.
  ℘02 38 49 88 80.
  www.canoe-regioncentre.org
◆ **Ligue régionale de canoë-kayak du Limousin**
  Base de la Minoterie, 13 rue Jean-Moulin, 19140 Uzerche.
  ℘05 55 73 02 84.
◆ **Comité régional de canoë-kayak d'Aquitaine**
  Route de Hon, 40380 Gamarde-les-Bain. ℘05 58 98 50 06.
◆ **Comité régional de canoë-kayak de Midi-Pyrénées**
  Allées du Duc-de-Ventadour, 31810 Venerque. ℘05 61 08 74 40.

Or, try the **Comité départemental de canoë-kayak** of the following départements:

◆ **Corrèze**
  23 bis Sajueix, 19130 Voutezac.
  ℘05 55 84 19 03 or 06 78 59 03 44.
◆ **Creuse**
  La Chassagne, 23320 Gartempe. ℘05 55 81 30 22.
◆ **Dordogne**
  Philippe Vallaeys, 83 rue du 8-Mai-1945, 24430 Marsac-sur-l'Isle.
  ℘05 53 04 13 00.
◆ **Haute-Vienne**
  1bis rue de la Caraque, 87700 Aixe-sur-Vienne. ℘05 55 70 35 62.
◆ **Lot**
  314 route de Laroque, 46000 Cahors. ℘05 65 35 91 59.

Most canoeing/kayaking centres welcome all comers, experienced or not, renting boats and in some cases

Trout

Carp

Pike

R. Corbel/MICHELIN

providing guides; a pick-up point downstream carries boaters and boats back to the base. Mountain bikes are sometimes available at the same sites.

FISHING

The rivers, lakes and streams are a joy for those who love to fish. A *Carte de Pêche* (fishing permit) is required; it may be purchased for a day or for the year in sports clubs, tourist information centres, and cafés where a sign so signifies. Local regulations are enforced; crayfish are protected in most areas, and anglers should seek information on which fish are in season. Frogs are a speciality of the Brenne wetlands.

For further details, contact the **Conseil supérieur de la pêche,** Immeuble "Le Péricentre", 16 avenue Louison-Bobet, 94132 Fontenay-sous-Bois Cedex, ℘ 01 45 14 36 00, or the **Fédération départementale de pêche** of the following départements:

🖙 **Cher**
103 rue de Mazières, 18000 Bourges. ℘02 48 66 68 90.

🖙 **Corrèze**
Place Abbé-Tournet, 19000 Tulle. ℘05 55 26 11 55. www.peche-correze.com.

🖙 **Creuse**
60 avenue Louis-Laroche, 23000 Guéret. ℘ 05 55 52 24 70.

🖙 **Dordogne**
Jacques Laguerre, 16 rue des Prés, 24000 Périgueux. ℘05 53 06 84 20.

🖙 **Haute-Vienne**
31 rue Jules-Noël, 87000 Limoges. ℘05 55 06 34 77.

🖙 **Indre**
17-19 rue des Etats-Unis, 36000 Châteauroux. ℘02 54 34 59 69. www.unpf.fr/36.

🖙 **Lot**
182 quai Cavaignac, 46000 Cahors. ℘05 65 35 50 22. www.pechelot.com.

HIKING

There is an extensive network of well-marked footpaths in France which make hiking a breeze. Several Grande Randonnée (GR) trails, recognisable by the red and white horizontal marks on trees, rocks and in town on walls, signposts etc, go through the region. Along with the GR exist the Petite Randonnée (PR) paths, which are usually blazed with blue (2hr walk), yellow (2hr 15min-3hr 45min) or green (4-6hr) marks.

To use these trails, obtain the Topo-Guide for the area published by the **Fédération Française de la Randonnée Pédestre**, ℘01 44 89 93 93; www.ffrp.asso.fr. Some English-language editions are available as well as an annual guide (Rando Guide) which includes ideas for overnight itineraries and places to stay together with information on the difficulty and accessibility of trails.

Local tourist organisations also provide maps of itineraries. In Sarlat the tourist office publishes *Promenades et Randonnées en Périgord Noir*, a series of

LAKES AND PONDS	Dép.	Acreage	Swimming	Water Sports	Fishing
Argentat (Lac de Feyt)	19	198	swimming	–	fishing
Aubazine (Plan d'eau du Coiroux)	19	59	swimming	–	Cat. 1
Bessais (Étang de Goule)	18	334	swimming	water sports	fishing
Bort-les-Orgues (Lac de Val)	19	3459	swimming	water sports	Cat. 2
Bourges (Lac du Val d'Auron)	18	203	–	water sports	Cat. 2
Bujaleuf	87	198	swimming	water sports	fishing
Carsac-de-Gurson (Lac de Gurson)	24	27	swimming	–	fishing
Compreignac (Lac de St-Pardoux)	87	815	swimming	water sports	Cat. 2
Egletons (Lac du Deiro)	19	32	swimming	–	Cat. 1
Éguzon (Lac de Chambon)	36	741	swimming	water sports	–
Gimel (Étang de Ruffaud)	19	49	swimming	water sports	fishing
Guéret (Étang de Courtille)	23	30	swimming	water sports	–
Lissac-sur-Couze (Lac du Causse)	19	222	swimming	water sports	Cat. 2
Luzech (Base de Caix)	46	371	swimming	–	fishing
Marcillac (Barrage de la Valette)	19	568	swimming	–	Cat. 2
Meymac (Lac de Sechemailles)	19	104	swimming	–	Cat. 2
Mézières (Étang de Bellebouche)	36	247	swimming	water sports	fishing
Neuvic (Lac de Triousoune)	19	1013	swimming	water sports	fishing
Seilhac (Lac de Burnazel)	19	79	swimming	–	–
Sénaillac-Latronquière (Lac du Tolerme)	46	17	swimming	water sports	Cat. 1
Sidiailles (Lac de)	18	222	swimming	water sports	fishing
St-Estèphe (Étang de)	24	74	swimming	water sports	fishing
Trémolat (Barrage de Mauzac)	24	247	swimming	water sports	fishing
Treignac (Lac de Bariousses)	19	247	swimming	water sports	Cat. 2
Vassivière (Lac de)	23	2471	swimming	water sports	Cat. 2
Viam (Lac de)	19	467	swimming	–	Cat. 2
Videix (Plan d'eau de Lavaud)	87	99	swimming	–	Cat. 1
Vigeois (Lac de Pontcharral)	19	35	swimming	–	–

Dép means **département:** 18 Cher; 19 Corrèze; 23 Creuse; 24 Dordogne; 36 Indre; 46 Lot; 87 Haute-Vienne. ♦ *Lac* means **lake**. *Étang* means **pond** or **small lake**. *Barrage* means **dam**. ♦ *Plan d'eau* means a **flat body of water**.

Category 1: Fish from the Salmonidae family (trout),usually the upper portion of major rivers. **Category 2:** Cyprinidae (carp, barbels, tench, bream, chub, dace, shiners).

Guidelines for Hikers

Choosing the right equipment for a hiking expedition is essential: flexible hiking shoes with non-slip soles, a rain jacket or poncho, an extra sweater, sun protection (hat, glasses, lotion), drinking water (1-2l per person), high energy snacks (chocolate, cereal bars, banana...), and a first aid kit. Of course, you'll need a good map (and a compass if you plan to leave the main trails). Plan your itinerary well, keeping in mind that while the average walking speed for an adult is 4kph/2.5mph, you will need time to eat and rest, and children will not keep up the same pace. Leave your itinerary with someone before setting out (innkeeper or fellow camper).

Respect for nature is a cardinal rule and includes the following precautions: don't smoke or light fires in the forest, which are particularly susceptible in the dry summer months; always carry your rubbish out; leave wild flowers as they are; walk around, not through, farmers' fields; close gates behind you.

If you are caught in an electrical storm, avoid high ground, and do not move along a ridge top; do not seek shelter under overhanging rocks, isolated trees in otherwise open areas, at the entrance to caves or other openings in the rocks, or in the proximity of metal fences or gates. Do not use a metallic survival blanket. If possible, position yourself at least 15m/15yd from the highest point around you (rock or tree); crouch with your knees up and without touching the rock face with your hands or any exposed part of your body. An automobile is a good refuge as its rubber tyres ground it and provide protection for those inside.

70 itineraries ranging from 2km/1.2mi to 24km/15mi. The **Comité départemental du tourisme du Lot** publishes *Promenades et randonnées*, which contains over hiking and biking routes.

USEFUL ADDRESSES

- **Comité régional de la randonnée pédestre en Aquitaine**
  153 rue David Johnston, 33000 Bordeaux
  ℘05 58 40 04 22.
- **Comité régional de la randonnée pédestre en Midi-Pyrénées**
  Maison des Sports, rue Buissonière, BP 81908, 31683 Labège Cedex. ℘05 62 24 18 77. www.randonnees-midi-pyrenees.com.
- **Comité régional de la randonnée pédestre du Val de Loire-Centre**
  La Vilaise, 36370 Bélâbre.
  ℘02 54 37 61 73 or 06 81 30 94 86. www.rando-centre.com.fr

Information is also available from the **Comité départemental de la randonnée pédestre** of the following départements:

- **Cher**
  4 rue Didier-Daurat, 18000 Bourges. ℘02 48 67 05 38.
- **Corrèze**
  45 quai Aristide Briand, 19000 Tulle. ℘05 55 27 89 40.
- **Dordogne**
  46 rue Kléber, 24000 Périgueux.
  ℘05 53 45 51 21.
- **Haute-Vienne**
  Maison des Sports, Mme Texier, Présidente du CDRP 87, 35 rue Jean-Louis Paguenaud, 87100 Limoges. ℘05 55 10 93 87.
- **Indre**
  Maison départementale des Sports, 89/22 allée des Platanes, 36000 Châteauroux.
  ℘02 54 35 55 63. http://rando-centre.fr/36/index.htm
- **Lot**
  BP 7, 46100 Figeac.
  ℘05 65 34 34 19. www.randonnees-lotoises.net

CYCLING

For general information, write or call the **Fédération Française de Cyclotourisme** (12 rue Louis-Bertrand, 94200 Ivry-sur-Seine Cedex, ℘01

56 20 88 88; www.ffct.org). Off-road enthusiasts, contact the **Fédération Française de Cyclisme** (5 rue de Rome, 93561 Rosny-sous-Bois Cedex, ✆01 49 35 69 00; www.ffc.fr) and request the Guide des centres VTT.

OTHER USEFUL ADDRESSES

- **Ligue régionale de cyclotourisme du Limousin**
  6 rue Léon-Tolstoï, 87100 Limoges.
  ✆05 55 38 26 11.
- **Ligue régionale de cyclotourisme de Midi-Pyrénées**
  7 rue André-Citroën, 31130 Balma.
  ✆05 61 99 86 46.

You can also contact the **Comité départemental de cyclotourisme** of the following départements:
- **Corrèze**
  45 quai Aristide-Briand,
  19000 Tulle. ✆05 55 20 71 46.
- **Creuse**
  M. Jean-Louis Jagot, Lycée professionnel Roussillat, 23320 St-Vaury.
  ✆05 55 80 13 69.
- **Dordogne**
  Hubert Prévost, 46, rue Kleber,
  24000 Périgueux ✆05 53 53 73 33.
- **Haute-Vienne**
  5 rue Georges-Bizet, 87170 Isle.
  ✆05 55 38 26 11.
- **Lot**
  46120 Leyme. ✆09 52 29 46 00.
  www.randocyclovtt46.com.

Local tourist offices have a list of cycle hire firms, which include SNCF train stations in St-Amand-de-Montrond, Uzerche, Bergerac, Le Bugue, Cahors, Gourdon, Gramat, Rocamadour-Padirac, Sarlat and Souillac. Maps and suggested itineraries are provided.

HORSEBACK RIDING

There are numerous itineraries suitable for horseback riding through forested areas, across the causses and along the main river valleys.
The **Comité National de Tourisme Équestre** (41600 Lamotte Beuvron, ✆02 54 94 46 80; www.tourisme-equestre.fr) is a useful source of information if you want to plan a riding holiday. It publishes the brochure *Cheval Nature, l'Officiel du tourisme équestre*, where you will find the addresses of riding centres (Centres de Tourisme Equestre) region-by-region, and practical tips on holidays for kids, insurance and more.

OTHER USEFUL ADDRESSES

- **Association régionale de tourisme équestre d'Aquitaine**
  Hippodrome du Bouscat, BP 95,
  33110 Le Bouscat Cedex.
  ✆05 56 28 06 74.
- **Association régionale de tourisme équestre de Midi-Pyrénées**
  Jean Bergraser, 31 chemin des Canalets, 31400 Toulouse.
  ✆05 61 14 04 58.
- **Association régionale de tourisme équestre du Val de Loire-Centre**
  A.R.T.E. Val de Loire-Centre,
  34 rue de Villebrême, BP 50, 41914 Blois Cedex 9. ✆02 54 42 95 60 (Tue-Thu, 1.30-5.30pm).

Information on local conditions and opportunities is available from the various **Comité départemental de tourisme équestre:**
- **Cher**
  61, ave de Pré le Roi, 18230 St Doulchard. ✆02 48 24 04 38.
- **Corrèze**
  Ferme Équestre de l'ecurie, 19260 Treignac. ✆05 55 98 02 92.
- **Creuse**
  7 ave de l'Abattoir, 23700 Auzance.
  ✆05 55 83 92 22.
- **Dordogne**
  25 ave Wilson, BP 2036 24002 Périgueux.✆05 53 56 05 04.
  The Comité publishes the map *Sentiers et relais équestres du Périgord*.
- **Haute-Vienne**
  La Maurie, 87150 Oradour-sur-Vayres.
  ✆05 55 78 77 52.
- **Indre**
  L'Ébaupin, 36330 Velles.
  ✆02 54 36 38 48.

🐎 **Lot**
quai Cavaignac BP7 46001 Cahors
Cedex 9. ☎05 65 35 80 82.
www.cheval-lot.com.
The map *Carte départementale de
la randonnée,* showing GR footpaths and riding tracks is available
at this address.

EXPLORING CAVES

The Dordogne attracts many speleologists; its limestone relief is pitted with
caves and caverns. Contact any of the
following organisations for further
information:

- **Fédération française
  de Spéléologie**
  23 rue Delandine, 69002 Lyon.
  ☎04 72 56 09 63.
  www.ffspeleo.fr.
- **Comité régional
  de spéléologie d'Aquitaine**
  Maison des Comités, 46 rue Kléber,
  24000 Périgueux.
  ☎05 53 02 65 06.
- **Comité régional de spéléologie
  de Midi-Pyrénées**
  7 rue André-Citroën, 31130 Balma.
  ☎05 61 11 71 60.
  http://comite-speleo-midipy.com.
- **Comité départemental de
  spéléologie de la Dordogne**
  46 rue Kléber, 24000Périgueux
  ☎05 53 02 65 06.
- **Comité départemental
  de spéléologie du Lot**
  391 rue Anatole de Monzie, 46000
  Cahors. ☎05 65 35 43 22 (M. Bon-
  net). www.ffspeleo.fr/cds/46.

GOLF

The Michelin map *Golf, les parcours
français* (French golf courses) will help
you locate golf courses in the region
covered by this guide.

For further information, contact:
Fédération française de golf
68 rue Anatole-France,
92300 Levallois-Perret Cedex.
☎01 41 49 77 00. www.ffgolf.org.

These events may be held at different
dates, depending on the year. It is
best to inquire at the tourist office for
precise details.

ACTIVITIES FOR CHILDREN

This region of France has a lot to
offer children from boat trips aboard
traditional gabarres to visiting caves,
châteaux, museums and sights of
special interest. In this guide, sights
of particular interest to children are
indicated with a KIDS symbol (👥).
Some attractions may offer discount
fees for children.

Dordogne:
- Le Bugue, Village of Bornat and
  Aquarium *p150.*
- Castelnaud, Museum of Warfare of
  the Middle Ages *p103.*
- Les Eyzies; Prehisto Park *p113.*
- Jardins de Marquessac *p133.*
- Le Thot, Espace Cro Magnon *p118.*
- La Roque St. Christophe *p119*
- Neuvic, Parc Botanique *p169.*
  and Grand Étang de la Jemaye
  p170.

Berry:
- Aubigny-sur-Nère, Witchcraft
  Museum *p409.*
- Nancay, Planetarium and Ciel
  Ouvert *p411.*
- Neuvy-sur-Barangeon, Le Hameau
  des Automates and the Maison
  de l'Eau *p403.*

Limousin:
- Eymoutiers, Insect City *p306.*
- Gueret, Parc Animalier *p348.*
- Limoges, Planète Aquarium and
  Parc Zoologique et Paysager du
  Reynou *p309.*
- St-Léonard-de-Noblat, Historail
  p328.
- Ydes, Insects of the World
  exhibition *p250.*

Quercy:
- Martel, Reptiland and Chemin de
  Fer Touristique du Haut Quercy
  "Le Truffadou" *p257.*
- Gouffre de Padirac *p190.*

- Rocamadour, Féerie du Rail and Fôret des Singes and Parc Animalier de Gramat ⚓ *p192.*

The towns and areas labelled **Villes et Pays d'Art et d'Histoire** by the Ministry of Culture (Bourges, Cahors, Figeac, Pays Monts et Barrages, Pays de la Vézère et de l'Ardoise, Périgueux, Sarlat, Souillac and Vallée de la Dordogne) offer activities for 6 to 12-year-olds. More information is available from local tourist offices and from www.vpah.culture.fr

SHOPPING
MARKETS

The souvenir of choice is edible, but remember that foie gras and truffles are expensive, even here at the source! Dordogne is also famous for its red fruit and nut liquors (especially in Villamblard and Brive), pork and duck preserves, and wines from Cahors and Bergerac. The wines of Sancerre in Berry deserve their fine reputation. Many of the specialities can be purchased directly from the producer – look out for signs along the road side (dégustation – vente for wines, produits de la ferme for preserves). Fresh food and plants may not be carried home, and for Americans this includes non-pasteurised cheeses, nuts and fruit. It is acceptable to carry tinned products or preserves.

Main markets in the region:
Périgueux
Livestock and flowers, Wednesday and Saturday.
Brive-la-Gaillarde
Local farm produce, preserves and confits etc Tuesday, Thursday and Saturday. Flower market Tuesday.
Sarlat
Chestnuts and walnuts, Saturday in October and November; foie gras and truffles, Saturday mornings from December to March; weekly markets on Wednesdays and Saturdays with a wide choice of local specialities.
Brantôme
Chestnuts, walnuts and foie gras, Friday in the winter months; local farm produce, Tuesday mornings, Clothes and general products every Friday all year. Fri Jul–Aug, Farmer's Market.

BOOKS
Eleanor Of Aquitaine

Eleanor of Aquitaine, queen of France and England, a 12C divorcée, patroness of poets, source of inspiration for chivalry and Courtly Love, ruler of a kingdom that spanned Scotland to the Pyrenees, mother of 10 children (including Richard the Lion Heart), lived her 82 years as few women in history before or since. The fascinating story of her life is a good introduction to regional history:

Eleanor of Aquitaine: The Mother Queen, Desmond Seward, NY, Dorset Press, 1978.
Eleanor of Aquitaine and the Four Kings, Amy Kelly, Cambridge MA, Harvard University Press, 1950.
Beloved Enemy: the Passions of Eleanor of Aquitaine: a Novel, Ellen Jones, NY, Simon and Schuster, 1994.

For young readers:
A Proud Taste for Scarlet and Miniver, EL Konigsburg, NY, Atheneum, 1973 (illustrated).
Queen Eleanor: Independent Spirit of the Medieval World, Polly S. Brooks, NY, Lippincott, 1984 (illustrated).

George Sand
George Sand was a prolific novelist and correspondent, and many of her works have been translated (⚓*see her biography under NOHANT).* Her rustic tales of country life are suitable for younger readers, too, in particular 'The Story of My Life' and 'Tales of a Grandmother'. Among the many biographies, the following are especially recommended:

*Infamous Woman: the Life of
George Sand,* Joseph Barry, 1977.
*The Double Life of George Sand,
Woman and Writer,*
Renée Winegarten, 1978.
For a closer view of the author's life:
The Intimate Journal of George Sand,
Chicago, Cassandra Editions, 1988.
*The George Sand –
Gustave Flaubert Letters,* Chicago,
Academy Chicago LTD, 1979.

Alain Fournier

Alain-Fournier was the pen name
of Henri-Alban Fournier. His only
completed novel has been published
in English as *Le Grand Meaulnes*,
or 'The Lost Domain'.

Josephine Baker

Josephine Baker's life of scantily
clad artistry, wartime heroism, social
idealism, bankruptcy and triumphant
stage returns makes for good reading.
There was more to this woman than a
banana skirt, as you will learn in these
excellent biographies:
*Jazz Cleopatra: Josephine Baker in Her
Time*, Phyllis Rose, NY,
Doubleday, 1989.
*Naked at the Feast: A Biography of
Josephine Baker*, Lynn Haney, NY,
Dodd-Mead, 1981.
Josephine, Josephine Baker
and Jo Bouillon (Translated
by Mariana Fitzpatrick), NY,
Harper & Row, 1977.

Gastronomy

To whet your appetite:
The Wine Regions of France,
Michelin APA Publications, 2007.
An in-depth guide for touring the
wine regions of France.
The Wines of France,
Alexis Lichine, NY, Knopf, 1965.
A classic that ages well.
Enjoying Wine, Don Hewitson, London,
Elm Tree Books, 1985. Friendly,
no-nonsense approach to one of
life's great pleasures, with useful
explanations and illustrations.

The Wine Lover's Guide to France,
Michael Busselle, London,
Pavilion Books, 1986.
At Home in France, Ann Barry,
NY, Ballantine, 1996.
An American journalist explores
happiness in Carennac.

FILMS

Jacquou le Croquant 2007.
The story of Jacquou, a 19C rebel
peasant boy from the Périgord,
seeking revenge for the death of
his parents from the evil Count
of Nansac, which evokes the
perennial struggle between the
peasantry and the ruling classes.
Timeline 2003
This film is set in the Dordogne
during the Hundred Years War and
recounts how a group of archeol-
ogy students, led by actor Paul
Walker, are zapped back through
a wormhole to the 14C to rescue
their time-travelling Professor,
played by Billy Connolly, who is
unable to return to the present.
Le Souffle 2003
A rather dark film set in the Limousin, dispelling the myth that rural
life in France is always a bucolic
paradise, by following a day in the
life of a boy invited to join the adult
males of the village for a feast.
Le Boucher 1969.
A murder mystery filmed in the
town of Trémolat in the Périgord,
Claude Chabrol's film featuring his
wife, actress Stéphane Audran, as
the schoolmistress who meets the
local butcher and begins an affair
with him against the background
of an outbreak of serial killings in
the town.
Jour de Fête 1949.
Jacques Tati's first film, set in a
small village in the Berry, about a
postman who is impressed by the
efficiency of the US Mail system
and tries to introduce these methods locally with hilarious effects.

Calendar of Events

Many Regional Tourist Offices publish brochures listing local fêtes, fairs and festivals. Most places hold festivities for France's National Day (14 July) and the 15 August, also a public holiday.

FESTIVALS

JANUARY-FEBRUARY
Limoges
Danse Emoi. Dance festival (even-numbered years). ℘05 55 34 45 49 (Jean-Gagnant cultural centre).

APRIL
Bourges
Printemps de Bourges. International festival of popular contemporary music and songs. ℘02 48 27 28 29. www.printemps-bourges.com.

MAY-JUNE
Bourges
Synthèse. International festival of experimental music (first two weeks in June). ℘02 48 20 41 87. www.imeb.net.

Nohant
Fêtes romantiques (3 weekends in June). ℘02 54 48 46 40. www.festival-george-sand.com.

Solignac
Rencontres photographiques. (Second week of June) Photography festival, ℘05 55 32 30 78. www.culture.fr

MID-JUNE–MID-SEPTEMBER
Bourges
Un été à Bourges. Classical music and jazz in various venues. ℘02 48 24 93 32.

Bellac
Festival national de Bellac. Jean Giraudoux theatre and music festival. ℘05 55 60 87 61. www.theatre-du-cloitre.fr.

JULY–SEPTEMBER
Coussac-Bonneval
Moments Musicaux. Music festival. ℘05 55 75 27 40.

JULY
Noirlac
Festival de Noirlac. International singing festival (second week of July). ℘02 48 48 00 27.

Cahors
Blues Festival. ℘06 45 71 75 60. www.cahorsbluesfestival.com.

La Châtre
Rencontres internationales Frédéric-Chopin. Piano festival (third week of July). ℘02 54 48 46 40. www.festivals-chopin.com.

Montignac
Danse et musique du Monde (end of July). ℘05 53 50 14 00.

Périgord
Fête de la Félibrée. Regional folklore festival hosted by a different town every year. First Sun in July. ℘05 53 29 90 80.

Souillac
Jazz festival. ℘05 65 37 04 93. www.souillacenjazz.net.

Argenton-sur-Creuse
Mercuria. European folklore festival.℘02 54 01 11 53 or 06 85 78 11 53. contact@festivalmercuria.fr.

Gourdon
Chamber music festival (end July). ℘05 65 41 20 06.

JULY-AUGUST
Aubusson
Musique au cœur de la tapisserie. Organ and chamber music concerts. ℘05 55 66 32 12. www.orgue-aubusson.org

Biron, Bergerac, Cadouin, Monpazier, Abbaye de St-Avit-Sénier
L'été musical en Bergerac. ℘05 53 74 30 94.

Bourges
Très Riches Heures de l'Orgue en Berry. Organ festival. ℘02 48 20 57 66. www.grandorguebourges.org.

Brive-la-Gaillarde
Festival de la Vézère. Various cultural events in selected venues.
☎ 05 55 23 25 09.
www.festival-vezere.com.

Castelnau-Montratier, Lauzert, Montcuq
Festival de musique du Quercy Blanc (early August).
☎ 05 65 31 83 12. www.tourisme-montcuq.com

Domme
Festival de la chanson. Song festival (mid-July to early August).
☎ 05 53 31 71 00.

La Borne
Rencontre internationale de la céramique. International ceramics festival.mid-July–early Aug.
☎ 02 48 26 96 21. http://ceramicla-bourne.org

Sarlat
Festival des jeux de théâtre. (mid-July to early August).
☎ 05 53 31 10 83.
www.festival-theatre-sarlat.com.

St-Léonard-de-Noblat
Été musical de St-Léonard. Classical and traditional music concerts.
☎ 05 55 56 25 06.

St-Céré
Festival de Musique (late July to mid-August). ☎ 05 65 38 28 08.
www.festival-saint-cere.com.

AUGUST

Belaye
Cello festival (early August).
☎ 05 65 36 27 90.

Audrix, Le Bugue, Les Eyzies, St-Cyprien
Musique en Périgord (1st two weeks of August). ☎ 05 53 30 36 09.

Bonaguil
Theatre festival. ☎ 05 53 71 17 17.

Brive-la-Gaillarde
Orchestrades universelles Festival of youth orchestras (mid-Aug). ☎ 04 78 35 87 14.
www.orchestrades.com.

Gargilesse-Dampierre
Festival musical d'été. Harp workshops (second half of August).
☎ 02 54 47 83 11.

St-Léon-de-Vézère, Montignac and St-Amand-de-Coly
Festival musical du Périgord Noir.
☎ 05 53 51 95 17.

SEPTEMBER-OCTOBER

Brantôme, Chancelade, Périgueux
Sinfonia en Périgord. Baroque music festival (late August-early September). ☎ 05 53 09 51 30.

Tulle
Festival Les Nuits de Nacre. Pearly nights festival (3rd weekend in September). ☎ 05 55 20 28 28.
www.accordeon.org.

OCTOBER-NOVEMBER

Châteauroux
Lisztomanias. International Franz Liszt Festival. ☎ 02 54 34 10 74.

SON ET LUMIÈRE

Sound and light shows are a great way to spend a summer night outdoors and give new perspectives on the monuments they highlight. There are a lot of variations on the theme, from living history plays through costumed pageantry and creative combinations of lighting effects and music that bring out the details of architecture. Check with the local tourist office for details; in some cases you may need to bring your own blanket and chairs; in others, visitors stand and walk around the site. These shows are held in July and August, and generally start at nightfall, which may mean after 10pm.

TRADITIONAL FESTIVALS, FAIRS AND MARKETS

JANUARY

Brive
Epiphany fair (early January).

Périgueux
Epiphany fair (first Wednesday after 6 January).

EASTER WEEKEND

Reuilly
Wine fair. ☎ 02 54 49 24 94.
www.ot-reuilly.fr.

APRIL
Aubazine
Goat fair. ℘05 55 25 79 93.

MAY
Beaulieu-sur-Dordogne
Strawberry fair (2nd or 3rd Sunday of the month). ℘05 55 91 09 94.
Turenne
Foire aux Chèvre et aux Chevaux (early May) ℘05 55 85 59 97.
www.fete-et-foires.com

MAY-JUNE
Lignières
Donkey and mule fair (Whit Sunday). ℘02 48 60 20 41.
Rocamadour
Cheese fair (Whit Sunday – Pentecôte). ℘05 65 33 22 00.
www.rocamadour.com.
Domme
Fête de la Saint-Clair. Folklore festival and concerts (1st weekend of June). ℘05 53 31 71 00
Sarlat
Fête de la Ringuetta. Traditional games (even-numbered years). ℘05 53 31 45 45.

JULY
Martel
Wool fair (late July).
Aubigny-sur-Nère
Franco-Scottish Festival. Historical tableaux, parades, folk dancing and music (mid-month). ℘02 48 81 50 07.
www.aubigny-sur-nere.fr.
Aubusson
Cheese and wine fair (penultimate Saturday of the month).

AUGUST
Argentat
International ceramics fair (1st weekend of the month). ℘05 55 85 58 38.
Gourdon
Medieval pageant in the old town (1st weekend and Monday of the month). ℘05 65 27 52 50.
Belfort-du-Quercy
Brocante/Vide -Grenier (Aug 15).

Bué-en-Sancerre
Foire au sorciers. Village fair and folk festival (1st Sunday of the month). ℘02 48 54 06 61.
Duravel
Wine and produce fair.
Arnac-Pompadour
Annual Horse festival.(mid Aug) ℘05 55 98 55 47.
www.pompadour.net.

SEPTEMBER
Rocamadour
Annual pilgrimage (2nd wk Sept).
Issoudun
Foire du tout et de la curiosité. "A-bit-of-everything" fair: second-hand market, entertainment, tasting of local specialities (1st Sun of the month). ℘02 54 21 13 53.
Brive-la-Gaillarde
Bird fair (mid-month). ℘05 55 23 73 37.

OCTOBER
Limoges
Frairie des petits ventres (3rd Friday of the month). Regional festival for food and wine lovers.

NOVEMBER
Brive-la-Gaillarde
Book fair (first weekend).

SPORTS EVENTS
JUNE
Argentat
International de canoe-kayak rally (mid-June). ℘05 55 28 86 45.

AUGUST
Chambon-sur-Voueize
International de pétanque. International boules competition (1st weekend of the month). ℘05 55 82 29 04.
Aubusson
Creuse Valley rally. Swimming, running, kayaking, shooting and mountain biking (14-15 Aug). ℘05 55 66 32 12.
www.raid23.org.

Know Before You Go

USEFUL WEBSITES

www.ambafrance-us.org

The French Embassy in the USA has a website providing basic information (geography, demographics, history), a news digest and business-related information. It offers special pages for children, and pages devoted to culture, language study and travel, and you can reach other selected French sites (regions, cities, ministries).

www.franceguide.com

The French Government Tourist Office/ Maison de la France site is packed with practical information and tips for those travelling to France. The home page has a number of links to more specific guidance.

www.FranceKeys.com

This sight has plenty of practical information for visiting France. It covers all the regions, with links to tourist offices and related sites. Very useful for planning the details of your tour in France!

www.fr-holidaystore.co.uk

The French Travel Centre in London has gone on-line with this service, providing information on all of the regions of France, including updated special travel offers and details on available accommodation.

www.visiteurope.com

The European Travel Commission provides useful information on travelling to and around 27 European countries, and includes links to some commercial booking services (ie vehicle hire), rail schedules, weather reports and more.

TOURIST OFFICES

Visitors may also contact local tourist offices for more precise information, to receive brochures and maps. The addresses and telephone numbers of tourist offices in the larger towns are listed after the symbol 🄸, in the *Discovering Dordogne Berry Limousin* section of the guide. The following addresses are for local tourist offices of the départements and régions covered in this guide.

REGIONAL

Four regional tourist offices are concerned with the area covered by this guide; address inquiries to the **Comité Régional de Tourisme** (C.R.T.):

- **Aquitaine**
  Cité Mondiale, 23 parvis des Chartrons, 33074 Bordeaux Cedex. 𝒫05 56 01 70 00.
  www.tourisme-aquitaine.info.

- **Limousin**
  27 boulevard de la Corderie, 87031 Limoges Cedex. 𝒫05 55 45 19 00.
  www.tourismelimousin.com.

- **Midi-Pyrénées**
  54 boulevard de l'Embouchure. 31022 Toulouse Cedex. 𝒫05 61 13 55 55.
  www.tourisme-midi-pyrenees.org.

- **Centre-Val de Loire**
  37 avenue de Paris, 45000 Orléans. 𝒫02 38 79 95 28.
  www.visaloire.com

DÉPARTEMENTS

For each département within the region, address inquiries to the **Comité Départemental de Tourisme** (C.D.T.), unless otherwise stated:

- **Dordogne**
  25 rue du Président-Wilson, BP 2063 24002 Périgueux. 𝒫05 53 35 50 24.
  www.perigord.tm.fr/tourisme/cdt.

- **Cher**
  Maison Départementale du Tourisme, 5 rue de Séraucourt, 18000 Bourges. 𝒫02 48 48 00 10.
  www.berrylecher.com.

- **Haute-Vienne**
  Maison du Tourisme, 4 place
  Denis-Dussoubs, 87000 Limoges.
  ℘05 55 79 04 04.
  www.tourisme-hautevienne.com.

- **Corrèze**
  Maison du Tourisme,
  45, quai Aristide Briand,
  19000 Tulle.
  ℘05 55 29 98 78.
  www.vacances-en-correze.net.

- **Indre**
  1 rue Saint-Martin, BP 141, 36003
  Châteauroux Cedex.
  ℘02 54 07 36 36.
  www.berrylindre.com.

- **Creuse**
  43 place Bonnyaud,
  BP 243 23005 Guéret.
  ℘05 55 51 93 23
  www.tourisme-creuse.com.

- **Lot**
  107 quai Eugène-Cavaignac, BP 7
  46000 Cahors Cedex 9.
  ℘05 65 35 07 09.
  www.tourisme-lot.com.

- **Tarn-et-Garonne**
  7 boulevard Midi-Pyrénées, BP 534
  82005 Montauban Cedex.
  ℘05 63 21 79 09.
  www.tourisme82.com.

MAISONS DES PAYS

These regional promotion centres
provide a whole range of information
including special events, mapped-out
tours of the area and places to stay.

- **Maison Aquitaine**
  21 rue des Pyramides, 75001 Paris.
  ℘01 55 35 31 42.
  http://maison.aquitaine.fr.

- **Maison du Limousin**
  30 rue Caumartin, 75009 Paris.
  ℘01 40 07 04 67.

VILLES ET PAYS D'ART ET D'HISTOIRE

Nine towns and areas, labelled **Villes
et Pays d'Art et d'Histoire** by the
Ministry of Culture, are mentioned in
this guide *(Bourges, Cahors, Figeac,
Pays Monts et Barrages, Pays de la
Vézère et de l'Ardoise, Périgueux, Sarlat,
Souillac and Vallée de la Dordogne).*
They are particularly active in promot-
ing their architectural and cultural
heritage and offer guided tours by
highly qualified guides as well as
activities for 6 to 12-year-olds.
🛈 More information is available from
tourist offices and www.vpah.culture.fr.

FRENCH TOURIST OFFICES ABROAD

🛈 For information, brochures, maps
and assistance in planning a trip to
France travellers should apply to the
official French Tourist Office or Maison
de France in their own country:

Australia – New Zealand
Sydney – Level 13, 25 Bligh St, Sydney,
New South Wales 2000.
℘(02) 9231 5244.
Fax (02) 9221 8682.
info. au@franceguide.com.

Canada
Montreal – 1981 Avenue McGill Col-
lege, Suite 490, Montreal QU H3A
2W9. ℘(514) 288-2026.
Fax (514) 845 4868.
canada@franceguide.com.
Toronto – 30 St Patrick's Street,
Suite 700, Toronto,
Ontario M5T 3A3.
℘(416) 593 6427.

Ireland
Dublin – 10 Suffolk Street, Dublin 2.
℘1560 235 235 (€0.95/minute).
Fax (01) 679 0814.
info.ie@franceguide.com

South Africa
P.O. Box 41022, Craig Hall 2024.
℘(011) 523 8292.
info.za@franceguide.com

United Kingdom
London Maison de France
178 Piccadilly, London WIJ 9AL.
℘(09068) 244 123 (60p/minute).
Fax 020 793 6594.
info.uk@franceguide.com.

United States
East Coast
New York – 444 Madison Avenue,
16th Floor, NY 10022-6903.
℘(212) 838-7800.
Fax (212) 838-7855.
info.us@franceguide.com.

West Coast
Los Angeles – 9454 Wilshire
Boulevard, Suite 715, Beverly Hills,
CA 90212-2967. ℘(310) 271-6665.
Fax (310) 276-2835.
info.losangeles@franceguide.com.

Request further information from:
France on Call ℘(410) 286-8310.

INTERNATIONAL VISITORS
EMBASSIES AND CONSULATES
Australia Embassy
4 r. Jean-Rey, 75724 Paris Cedex 15.
℘01 40 59 33 00.
Fax: 01 40 59 33 10.
www.france.embassy.gov.au.

Canada Embassy
35 avenue Montaigne, 75008 Paris.
℘01 44 43 29 00.
Fax: 01 44 43 29 99.
paris@international.gc.ca.

Ireland Embassy
4 r. Rude/12 ave Foch, 75116 Paris.
℘01 44 17 67 00. www.embas-syofireland.fr
Fax: 01 44 17 67 60.
paris@dfa.ie.

New Zealand Embassy
7 ter rue Léonard-de-Vinci,
75116 Paris. ℘01 45 01 43 43.
Fax: 01 45 01 26 39.
nzembassy.paris@fr.oleane.com

South Africa Embassy
59 quai d'Orsay,
75343 Paris Cedex 07.
℘01 53 59 23 23.
Fax: 01 53 59 23 68 .
info@afriquesud.net.
www.afriquesud.net

UK Embassy
35 rue du Faubourg St-Honoré,
75383 Paris Cedex 08.
℘01 44 51 31 00.
Fax: 01 44 51 31 27.
www.britishembassy.gov.uk.

UK Consulate
18bis rue d'Anjou, 75008 Paris.
℘01 44 51 31 02 (visas),
or 01 44 51 31 00.
www.amb-grandebretagne.fr.

USA Embassy
2 avenue Gabriel,
75382 Paris Cedex.
℘01 43 12 22 22.
Fax: 01 42 66 97 83.
www.amb-usa.fr.

USA Consulate
2 rue St-Florentin,
75382 Paris Cedex.
℘01 43 12 22 22.
www.amb-usa.fr.

ENTRY REQUIREMENTS
Passport
Nationals of countries within the European Union entering France need only a national identity card. Nationals of other countries must be in possession of a valid national **passport**. In case of loss or theft, report to your embassy or consulate and the local police.

Visa
No **entry visa** is required for Canadian, US or Australian citizens travelling as tourists and staying less than 90 days, except for students planning to study in France. If you think you may need a visa, apply to your local French Consulate. US citizens should obtain the booklet *Safe Trip Abroad* (US$2.75), which provides useful information on visa

requirements, customs regulations, medical care etc for international travellers. Published by the Government Printing Office, it can be ordered by phone – ☎1 866 512-1800 – or consulted on-line (www.access.gpo.gov). General passport information is available by phone toll-free from the Federal Information Center (item 5 on the automated menu), ☎1-877-487-2778. US passport application forms can be downloaded from http://travel.state.gov.

CUSTOMS REGULATIONS

Apply to the Customs Office (UK) for a leaflet on customs regulations and the full range of duty-free allowances; available from HM Customs and Excise, Thomas Paine House, Angel Square, Torrens Street, London EC1V 1TA, ☎08450 109 000. The US Customs Service offers a publication *Know Before You Go* for US citizens: for the office nearest you, consult the phone book, Federal Government, US Treasury (www.customs.ustreas.gov). There are no customs formalities for holidaymakers bringing their caravans into France for a stay of less than six months. No customs document is necessary for pleasure boats and outboard motors for a stay of less than six months but the registration certificate should be kept on board.

Americans can take home, tax-free, up to US$800 worth of goods (limited quantities of alcohol and tobacco products); Canadians up to CND$300;

Australians up to AUS$400 and New Zealanders up to NZ$700.

Residents from a member state of the European Union are not restricted with regard to purchasing goods for private use. *For recommended allowances for alcoholic beverages and tobacco see the chart on this page.*

HEALTH

First aid, medical advice and chemists' night service rotas are available from chemists drugstores (pharmacie) identified by the green cross sign. All prescription drugs should be clearly labelled; it is recommended that you carry a copy of the prescription.

It is advisable to take out comprehensive insurance coverage as the recipient of medical treatment in French hospitals or clinics must pay the bill. **Nationals of non-EU countries** should check with their insurance companies about policy limitations. Reimbursement can then be negotiated with the insurance company according to the policy held.

UK citizens should apply to the Department of Health before travelling for a **European Health Insurance Card** (EHIC), the replacement for Form E111, which entitles the holder to urgent treatment for accident or unexpected illness in EU countries. ☎0845 606 2030; log onto www.ehic.org.uk or obtain an application form from a Post Office. A refund of part of the costs of treatment can be obtained on application in person or by post to the local Social Security Offices (Caisse Primaire d'Assurance Maladie).

Americans concerned about travel and health can contact the International Association for Medical Assistance to Travelers, which can also provide details of English-speaking doctors in France: ☎(716) 754-4883; www.iamat.org.

The **American Hospital of Paris** is open 24hr for emergencies as well as consultations, with English-speaking staff, at 63 boulevard Victor-Hugo, 92200 Neuilly-sur-Seine, ☎01 46 41 25 25; www.american-hospital.org.

DUTY-FREE ALLOWANCES	
Spirits (*whisky, gin, vodka etc*)	**10 litres**
Fortified wines (*vermouth, port etc*)	**20 litres**
Wine (*not more than* *60 sparkling*)	**90 litres**
Beer	**110 litres**
Cigarettes	**3200**
Cigars	**200**
Smoking Tobacco	**3 kg**

The British Hospital is just outside Paris in Levallois-Perret, 3 rue Barbès,92300 ℘01 46 39 22 22; www.british-hospital.org.

ACCESSIBILITY
The sights described in this guide that are easily accessible to people of reduced mobility are indicated in the admission times and charges information by the symbol ♿ (*see Discovering section*). On TGV and Corail trains operated by the national railway (SNCF), there are special wheelchair slots in 1st class carriages available to holders of 2nd-class tickets. On Eurostar and Thalys, special rates are available for accompanying adults. Web-surfers can find information for slow walkers, mature travellers and others with special needs at www.access-able.com. For information on **museum access** for the disabled contact La Direction, Les Musées de France, Service Accueil des Publics Spécifiques, 6 rue des Pyramides, 75041 Paris Cedex 1, ℘01 40 15 80 72.

The Michelin Guide France and the **Michelin Camping France** guide indicate accessible hotels and camp sites with suitable facilities.

Getting There Getting Around

BY AIR

Choose between scheduled flights on Air France or commercial and package-tour flights with rail or coach link-ups or fly-drive schemes. The following airlines operate flights from the UK to the Dordogne and Limousin regions, as well as to neighbouring regions in south-west France:

- **Ryanair**
  www.ryanair.com
  (flights to Limoges, Bergerac, Poitiers and Rodez).

- **EasyJet**
  www.easyjet.com (flights to Toulouse and Bordeaux).

- **Bmibaby**
  www.bmibaby.com (flights to Toulouse and Bordeaux).

- **British Airways**
  www.ba.com (flights to Bordeaux and Toulouse).

- **Air France**
  www.airfrance.com (flights to Toulouse and Bordeaux).

It is very easy to arrange air travel to one of Paris' two airports (Roissy-Charles-de-Gaulle to the north, and Orly to the south). Contact airline companies and travel agents for details of package tour flights with a rail link-up or fly-drive schemes.

Visitors arriving in **Paris** who wish to reach the city centre or a train station may use public transportation or reserve space on the **Airport Shuttle** (27€ for one person; 19.90€ each for 2-3 persons and 17€ each for 4 or more persons) 5am–8pm (Roissy-Charles-de-Gaulle or Orly) ℘0033(0)825 09 20 92, www.paris-airport-shuttle.com). Air France operates a coach service into town with frequent departures (℘01 41 56 89 00). The cost and duration of a taxi ride from the airport to the city centre varies with traffic conditions. From Charles-de-Gaulle: about 1hr, 45€; from Orly about 30min, 35€. There is an extra charge (posted in the taxi) for baggage; the extra charge for airport pick-up is on the meter; drivers are usually given a tip of 10-15%.

In addition, Brit'AirLimoges operates flights from Paris and Lyons to **Limoges**, ℘05 55 43 30 30, www.aeroportlimoges.com. Four daily connections (Mar 25–Oct 27) with Paris-Orly, one daily connection with

Paris-Charles-de-Gaulle) and three daily connections with Lyon-Saint-Exupéry. The other main airports in the region are:

🛧 **Aéroport de Périgueux-Bassillac**
9km/5.6mi E of Périgueux.
24330 Bassillac.
℘08 92 70 77 37.

🛧 **Aéroport de Bergerac-Roumanière**
5km/3mi SE of Bergerac.
Route d'Agen, 24100 Bergerac.
℘05 53 22 25 25.

🛧 **Aéroport de Brive-Souillac**
Planned opening Spring 2010.

🛧 **Aéroport de Bourges**
SW of Bourges. 18001 Bourges.
℘02 48 67 80 80.

Private planes can land at the Bourges airfield. Limoges airport is linked daily to 18 French towns and five European ones. Daily flights are scheduled from Limoges-Bellegarde Airport to Paris and Lyon.

BY SEA

There are numerous **cross-Channel services** (passenger and car ferries), from the United Kingdom and Ireland, as well as the rail Shuttle through the Channel Tunnel (**Le Shuttle-Eurotunnel**, ℘08705 35 35 35 or 08000 969 992; www.eurotunnel.com). To choose the most suitable route between your port of arrival and your destination use the Michelin Tourist and Motoring Atlas France, Michelin map 726 (gives travel times and mileages) or Michelin maps from the 1:200.000 series.

🚢 **P & O Ferries**
Reservations for all UK routes:
℘ 08716 645645.
www.poferries.com.

🚢 **LD Ferries**
In the UK: ℘0844 576 8836.
In France: ℘02 35 19 78 78.
www.ldlines.co.uk

🚢 **Brittany Ferries**
In the UK: ℘0871 244 0744.
In France: ℘0825 828 828.
www.brittany-ferries.com.

🚢 **Irish Ferries**
In the UK: ℘08705 17 17 17.
In Ireland: ℘0818 300 400.
In France: ℘01 70 72 03 26.
In the US: ℘(772) 563 2856.
www.irishferries.com.

🚢 **Seafrance**
In the UK: ℘0871 2222 500.
In France: ℘08 25 08 25 05
(Mon–Fri, 9am–6.30pm) or
www.seafrance.fr.

BY TRAIN

Eurostar runs via the Channel Tunnel between **London** (St.Pancras) and **Paris** (Gare du Nord) in 2hr 15mins (bookings and information ℘08705 186 186 in the UK; ℘888. EUROSTAR in the US). Trains leave from Paris (Gare d'Austerlitz) for Bourges, Limoges, Brive and Cahors. You can take the high-speed TGV train to Bordeaux or Angoulême and change for Périgueux.
Eurail Global Pass, Eurail Select Pass, Eurail Regional Pass, One Country Pass are some of the travel passes that may be purchased by residents of countries outside the European Union. In the US, contact your travel agent or **Rail Europe** ℘1 888 382 7245or **Europrail International** ℘1 888 361 7245. If you are a European resident, you can buy an individual country pass, if you are not a resident of the country where you plan to use it. In the UK, call Rail Europe at ℘08700 841 410. Information on schedules can be obtained on websites for these agencies and the **SNCF**, respectively: www.raileurope.com; www.eurail.on.ca; www.sncf.fr. At the SNCF site, you can book ahead, pay with a credit card, and receive your ticket in the mail at home.
There are numerous **discounts** available when you purchase your tickets in France. These include discounts for using senior or youth cards (the

nominative cards with a photograph must be purchased, and for 2-9 people travelling together (no card required, advance purchase necessary). There are a limited number of discount seats available at peak travel times, and the best discounts are at off-peak periods. Tickets must be validated *(composter)* by using the orange automatic date-stamping machines at the platform entrance (failure to do so may result in a fine). The French railway company SNCF operates a telephone informa-tion, reservation and prepayment service in English from 7am to 10pm (French time). In France call *✆08 36 35 35 39 (✆when calling from outside France, drop the initial 0).*
Accessibility facilities for rail travel in Europe ✆212 838 7800.

BY COACH/BUS

♦ **Eurolines (National Express)**
Ensign Court, 4 Vicarage Road, Edgbaston, Birmingham,B15 3ES. ✆0871 818181. www.national express.com/eurolines. Helplines: for disabled people: t0121 423 8479 and for deaf or hard of hearing people:✆0121 455 0086

♦ **Eurolines (Paris)**
Ave du General de Gaulle 93177 Bagnolet. ✆892 89 90 91. www.eurolines.fr

♦ **www.eurolines.com** has information about travelling by coach in Europe.

BY CAR
PLANNING YOUR ROUTE

The area covered in this guide is easily reached by main motorways and national routes. **Michelin map 726** indicates the main itineraries as well as alternate routes for avoiding heavy traffic during busy holiday periods, and gives estimated travel times. **Michelin map 723** is a detailed atlas of French motorways, indicating tolls, rest areas and services along the route; it includes a table for calculating distances and times. The latest Michelin route-planning service is available on the Internet at,

www.ViaMichelin.com.
Travellers can calculate a precise route for free using such options as shortest route, route avoiding toll roads, Michelin-recommended route and tourist information (hotels, restaurants, attractions).
The roads are very busy during the holiday period (particularly weekends in July and August) and, to avoid traffic congestion it is advisable to follow the recommended secondary routes (signposted as Bison Futé – itinéraires bis). The motorway network includes rest areas (aires de repos) and petrol stations (stations-service), usually with restaurant and shopping complexes attached, about every 40km/25mi.

DOCUMENTS
Driving licence
Travellers from other European Union countries and North America can drive in France with a valid national or home-state **driving licence**. An **international driving licence** is useful because the information on it appears in nine languages (keep in mind that traffic officers are empowered to fine motorists). A permit is available (US$10) from the **National Automobile Club**, 1151 East Hillsdale Blvd., Foster City, CA 94404 ✆ 650-294-7000 or www.nationalautoclub.com; or contact your local branch of the **American Automo-bile Association**.

Registration papers
For the vehicle, it is necessary to have the registration papers (logbook) and an approved nationality plate.

INSURANCE
Certain motoring organisations (AAA, AA, RAC and the Caravan Club) offer accident insurance and breakdown service schemes for members. Check with your current insurance company in regard to coverage while abroad.

ROAD REGULATIONS
The minimum driving age is 18. Traffic drives on the right. All passengers must wear **seat belts**. Children under

the age of 10 must ride in the back seat. Headlights must be switched on in poor visibility and at night; dipped headlights should be used at all times outside built up areas. Use side-lights only when the vehicle is stationary. In the case of a **breakdown**, a red warning triangle or hazard warning lights are obligatory as are reflective safety jackets. In the absence of stop signs at intersections, cars must **give way to the right**. Traffic on main roads outside built-up areas (priority indicated by a yellow diamond sign) and on roundabouts has right of way. Vehicles must stop when the lights turn red at road junctions and may filter to the right only when indicated by an amber arrow.

The regulations on **drinking and driving** (limited to 0.50g/l) and **speeding** are strictly enforced – usually by an on-the-spot fine and/or confiscation of the vehicle.

Speed limits
Although liable to modification, these are as follows:
Toll motorways (autoroutes) 130kph/ 80mph (110kph/68mph when raining); Dual carriageways and motorways without tolls 110kph/68mph (100kph/ 62mph when raining);
other roads 90kph/56mph (80kph/ 50mph when raining) and in towns 50kph/31mph;
Outside lane on motorways during daylight, on level ground and with good visibility – minimum speed limit of 80kph/50mph.

Parking regulations
In built-up areas there are zones where parking is either restricted or subject to a fee; tickets should be obtained from the ticket machines (horodateurs – small change necessary) and displayed inside the windscreen on the driver's side; failure to display may result in a fine, or towing and impoundment. In some towns you may find blue parking zones (zone bleue) marked by a blue line on the pavement or road and a blue signpost with a 'P' and a small sqare underneath. In this case a cardboard disc (ask for a disque de stationnement, available from supermarkets, petrol stations) must be displayed with times indicated on it.

Tolls
In France, most motorway sections are subject to a toll (péage). You can pay in cash or with a credit card (Visa, Mastercard).

PETROL/GASOLINE
French service stations dispense:
- sans plomb 98 (super unleaded 98)
- sans plomb 95 (super unleaded 95)
- diesel/gazole (diesel)
- GPL (LPG).

Petrol is considerably more expensive in France than in the USA, but cheaper than in the UK. Prices are listed on signboards on the motorways; it is usually cheaper to fill up after leaving the motorway; check the large hypermarkets outside of towns. If you run out of petrol on the highway, pull over onto the hard shoulder, and call 112, or walk to the nearest emergency phone.

RENTAL CARS – CENTRAL RESERVATION IN FRANCE	
Avis:	08 20 05 05 05 www.avis.com
Europcar:	08 25 358 358 www.europcar.com
Budget France:	08 25 00 35 64 www.budget.fr
Hertz France:	01 39 38 38 38 www.hertz.fr
SIXT-Eurorent:	08 20 00 74 98 www.e-sixt.com
National-CITER	08 25 16 12 20 www.citer.fr
Ada	08 25 16 91 69. www.ada.fr

CAR RENTAL

There are car rental agencies at airports, railway stations and in all large towns throughout France. Drivers must be over 21; It is relatively expensive to hire a car in France. There are many on-line services that will look for the best prices on car rental. Nova can be contacted at www.rentacar-worldwide.com or ☎ 0800 018 6682 (freephone UK) or ☎ 44 28 4272 8189 (calling from outside the UK). All of the firms listed below have Internet sites for reservations and information. 🖔*In France, you can call the numbers in the chart opposite.*

MOTORHOME RENTAL

- ◆ **Worldwide Motorhome Rentals**
  Offers fully equipped camper vans for rent.
  ☎888- 519-8969 *US toll-free.*
  ☎530-389-8316 *outside the US.*
  www.mhrww.com.

- ◆ **Auto Europe.**
  Wide range of recreational vehicles.
  ☎888 223 5555 *US (Toll free).*
  ☎+1 207 842 2000 *outside the US.*
  www.autoeurope.com.
  ☎888- 519-8969 *US toll-free.*
  ☎530-389-8316 *outside the US.*
  www.mhrww.com.

Where to Stay and Eat

WHERE TO STAY

We feature hotels throughout this guide. Use the **Places to stay map** to identify recommended places for overnight stops. For a wider selection, use **The Michelin Guide France**, with its famously reliable star-rating system and hundreds of establishments all over France. **The Michelin Charming Places to Stay** guide contains a selection of 1 000 hotels and guest houses at reasonable prices.

SELECTION

The Legend on the cover flap explains the symbols and abbreviations used in this guide. We have reported the prices (double occupancy) and conditions as we observed them, but of course changes in management and other factors may mean that you will find some discrepancies. Please feel free to keep us informed of any major differences you might encounter.

BOOKING

Be sure to book ahead to ensure that you get the accommodation you want, not only in tourist season, but year round, as many towns fill up during trade fairs, arts festivals etc. Some places require an advance deposit or a reconfirmation. Reconfirming is especially important if you plan to arrive after 6pm.

For further assistance, **Loisirs Accueil** is a booking service that has offices in some French départements – contact the local tourist offices for further information or for internet booking log onto: *www.loisirsaccueilfrance.com www.resinfrance.com.*

A guide to good-value, family-run hotels, **Logis et Auberges de France,** is available from the French Tourist Office, as are lists of other kinds of accommodation such as hotel châteaux, bed-and-breakfasts etc.

Relais et châteaux provides information on booking in luxury hotels with character: 15 rue Galvani, 75017 Paris, ☎0823 32 32 32 (within France) ☎0800 2000 00 22 (from the UK) ☎1 800 735 2478 (from the US) or go to: www.relaischateaux.com.

ECONOMY CHAIN HOTELS

These can be useful if you need a place to stop en-route, as they are inexpensive (30-45€ for a double room) and generally located near the main road. While breakfast is available, there may not be a restaurant; rooms are small, with a television and bathroom. Reservation numbers:

- **Akena**
  📞 01 69 84 85 17.
  www.hotels-akena.com.
- **B&B**
  📞 01 72 36 51 06 (11am-5pm).
  www.hotel-bb.com.
- **Etap Hôtel**
  📞 08 92 68 89 00
  www.etaphotel.com
- **Mister Bed**
  📞 01 46 14 38 00.
  www.misterbed.fr
  (No on-line reservation).
- **Première Classe**
  📞 01 64 62 59 70
  www.louvrehotels.com
- **Villages Hôtel**
  📞 03 80 60 92 70.
  www.villages-hotel.com.

The hotels listed below are slightly more expensive (from 60€), and offer a few more amenities and services. Central reservation numbers:

- **Campanile, Kyriad**
  📞 0 825 003 003 (in France);
  From abroad: 📞+33 1 64 62 46 46.
  Within France: 📞01 64 62 46 00.
  www.louvrehotels.com or
  www.envergure.fr.
- **Ibis**
  📞 0 892 68 66 86.
  www.ibishotel.com.

RURAL ACCOMMODATION

The **Maison des Gîtes de France** is an information service on self-catering accommodation in France. Gîtes usually take the form of a cottage or apartment decorated in the local style where visitors can make themselves at home, or bed and breakfast accommodation (chambres d'hôtes) which consists of a room and breakfast at a reasonable price.
For a list of Chambres d'Hôtes contact the **Gîtes de France** office at 59 rue St-Lazare, 75439 Paris Cedex 09, 📞01 49 70 75 75, or their representative in the UK, **Brittany Ferries** (⏷see Getting There and Getting Around).

The Internet site, www.gites-de-france.fr, has a good English version. From the site, you can order catalogues for different regions illustrated with photographs of the properties, as well as specialised catalogues (bed and breakfasts, chalets in ski areas, farm stays etc). You can also contact the local tourist offices, which may have lists of available properties and local bed and breakfasts.
You can also contact: www.bed-breakfast-france.com, which has a good selection of accommodation throughout the region.
The **Fédération Française des Stations Vertes de Vacances,** 6 rue Ranfer-de-Bretenières, BP 71698, 21016 Dijon Cedex, 📞03 80 54 10 50, www.stationsvertes.com, is able to provide details of accommodation, leisure facilities and natural attractions in rural locations selected for their tranquillity.
The **Centre permanent d'initiation à l'environnement** (CPIE, Environment awareness centre), 35 rue Hersent-Luzarche, 36290 Azay-le-Ferron, 📞02 54 39 23 43, Fax 02 54 39 25 12, has been entirely renovated and now offers 76 beds (including 6 for disabled travellers) to those who wish to explore the Parc naturel regional de la Brenne. Entertainment for adults and children is organised at weekends. Equipment used for observation is available on location. There are various activities centred on nature and astronomy.

FARM HOLIDAYS

The guide *Bienvenue à la ferme* is published by and available from the Assemblée Permanente des Chambres d'Agriculture, Service "Agriculture et Tourisme", 9 avenue Georges-V, 75008 Paris, 📞01 53 57 11 44, www.bienvenue-a-la-ferme.com. It includes the addresses of farmers providing guest facilities who have signed a charter drawn up by the Chambers of Agriculture. *Bienvenue à la ferme* farms, vetted for quality and meeting official standards, can be identified

Places to stay

Spa

Spas ‡ are classified according to the quality and range of facilities offered.

Popular holiday destination

Short break

Overnight stop

by the yellow flower which serves as their logo.

HIKERS

Hikers can consult the guide, *Gîtes d'Étapes et Refuges* by A and S Mouraret, which can be ordered from: www.gites-refuges.com.
This guide, which lists 4000 places to stay, also contains much information to help with planning itineraries and is intended for those who enjoy hiking, cycling, climbing, skiing and canoeing-kayaking holidays.

HOSTELS, CAMPING

To obtain an International Youth Hostel Federation card (there is no age requirement, and there is a senior card available too), you should contact the IYHF in your own country for information and membership applications (US ☎ 00(1) (301)495 1240; England ☎ 01707 324170; Scotland ☎ 01786 891400; Canada ☎ 00(1) (613) 2377 884, Toll free 1-800-663-5777; Australia ☎ 61-2-9283-7195).
There is a new booking service on the Internet (www.iyhf.org), which you

may use to reserve rooms as far as six months in advance.

The main youth hostel association (*Auberges de Jeunesse*) in France is the **Ligue Française pour les Auberges de la Jeunesse** (67 rue Vergniaud, 75013 Paris, ℘01 44 16 78 78; www.auberges-de-jeunesse.com). Annual membership costs 15.25€ (15€ for under-26-year-olds).

There are numerous officially graded **camp sites** with varying standards of facilities throughout the Region. The **Michelin Camping France** guide lists a selection of camp sites. The area is very popular with campers in the summer months, so it is wise to reserve in advance. An International Camping Carnet for Caravans is useful but not compulsory; it can be obtained from motoring organisations or the Camping and Caravanning Club (www.campingandcaravanningclub.co.uk) or The Caravan Club (www.caravanclub.co.uk)

WHERE TO EAT

We feature hotels throughout this guide. Restaurants usually serve lunch between noon and 2pm and the evening meal between 7.30-10pm. It is not always easy to find something in-between those two meal times.

Eating out

Restaurants are found in all towns and cities and usually only open at traditional meal times, that is, between noon and 2pm for lunch and 7pm–10pm for dinner. Food ranges from regional cooking to *nouvelle* and *haute cuisine* – expect to pay anything from 12€ upwards for a main course, depending on the type of food on offer. Many restaurants offer good value-for-money set menus at lunch times. You'll find restaurants specialising in fish (*poisson*), only but vegetarians will be disappointed to know that there are few places that cater exclusively for their needs.

Café-Restaurants are where to have a coffee or breakfast.

Brasseries – Brasseries, found in cities and towns, often serve food 24/7.

Relais Routiers – These places, mainly frequented by lorry drivers, can be found on A roads.
Go to: www.relais-routiers.com.

Auberges – Usually found in the countryside and can be a good option to both eat and stay. Regional produce is served.

Créperies – There are thousands of *créperies* across Brittany serving the region's traditional dish. A *crêpe* is made with sweet batter and a *galette* is made with salty batter – both usually available with a choice of fillings.

L'assiette de pays

This simple menu option, initiated by the Fédération nationale des pays touristiques, consists of a reasonably priced single course, prepared from local produce and accompanied by a drink. Restaurants taking part have a small sticker in their window (a plate with a knife and fork and the mention "l'assiette de pays."

Tipping

In French restaurants and cafés, a service charge is included. Tipping is not necessary, but French people often leave the small change from their bill on their table, or about 5% .

Sites remarquables du goût

Among places in the Périgord-Quercy region that have been awarded the special distinction of *site remarquable du goût* (first-class gourmet shopping sites) are Brive-la-Gaillarde (fairs and markets), Sarlat (foie gras and poultry market), Martel-en-Quercy (walnut oil) and Monbazillac (sweet white wine). You can find out more at: www.sitesremarquablesdugout.com.

Michelin Guide

For an extended selection, see **The Michelin Guide France**, with its famously reliable star-rating system and hundreds of establishments all over France, for an even greater choice.

Useful Words and Phrases

Sights

	Translation
Abbaye	Abbey
Beffroi	Belfry
Chapelle	Chapel
Château	Castle
Cimetière	Cemetery
Cloître	Cloisters
Cour	Courtyard
Couvent	Convent
Écluse	Lock (Canal)
Église	Church
Fontaine	Fountain
Halle	Covered Market
Jardin	Garden
Mairie	Town Hall
Maison	House
Marché	Market
Monastère	Monastery
Moulin	Windmill
Musée	Museum
Parc	Park
Place	Square
Pont	Bridge
Port	Port/harbour
Porte	Gate/gateway
Quai	Quay
Remparts	Ramparts
Rue	Street
Statue	Statue
Tour	Tower

Natural Sites

	Translation
Abîme	Chasm
Aven	Swallow-hole
Barrage	Dam
Belvédère	Viewpoint
Cascade	Waterfall
Col	Pass
Corniche	Ledge
Côte	Coast, Hillside
Forêt	Forest
Grotte	Cave
Lac	Lake
Plage	Beach
Rivière	River
Ruisseau	Stream
Signal	Beacon
Source	Spring
Vallée	Valley

On The Road

	Translation
Car Park	Parking
Driving Licence	Permis De Conduire
East	Est
Garage (For Repairs)	Garage
Left	Gauche
Motorway/highway	Autoroute
North	Nord
Parking Meter	Horodateur
Petrol/gas	Essence
Petrol/gas Station	Station Essence
Right	Droite
South	Sud
Toll	Péage
Traffic Lights	Feu Tricolore
Tyre	Pneu
West	Ouest
Wheel Clamp	Sabot
Zebra Crossing	Passage Clouté

Time

	Translation
Today	Aujourd'hui
Tomorrow	Demain
Yesterday	.......hier
Winter	Hiver
Spring	Printemps
Summer	Été
Autumn/fall	Automne
Week	Semaine
Monday	Lundi
Tuesday	Mardi
Wednesday	Mercredi
Thursday	Jeudi
Friday	Vendredi
Saturday	Samedi
Sunday	Dimanche

Numbers

	Translation
0	zéro
1	un
2	deux
3	trois
4	quatre
5	cinq
6	six
7	sept
8	huit
9	neuf
10	dix
11	onze
12	douze

13	treize
14	quatorze
15	quinze
16	seize
17	dix-sept
18	dix-huit
19	dix-neuf
20	vingt
30	trente
40	quarante
50	cinquante
60	soixante
70	soixante-dix
80	quatre-vingt
90	quatre-vingt-dix
100	cent
1000	mille

Shopping

	Translation
Bank	Banque
Baker's	Boulangerie
Big	Grand
Butcher's	Boucherie
Chemist's	Pharmacie
Closed	Fermé
Cough Mixture	Sirop Pour La Toux
Cough Sweets	Cachets Pour La Gorge
Entrance	Entrée
Exit	Sortie
Fishmonger's	Poissonnerie
Grocer's	Épicerie
Newsagent, Bookshop	Librairie
Open	Ouvert
Post Office	Poste
Push	Pousser
Pull	Tirer
Shop	Magasin
Small	Petit
Stamps	Timbres

Food and Drink

	Translation
Beef	Bœuf
Beer	Bière
Butter	Beurre
Bread	Pain
Breakfast	Petit-déjeuner
Cheese	Fromage
Chicken	Poulet
Dessert	Dessert
Dinner	Dîner
Fish	Poisson
Fork	Fourchette
Fruit	Fruits

Glass	Verre
Ice Cream	Glace
Ice Cubes	Glaçons
Ham	Jambon
Knife	Couteau
Lamb	Agneau
Lunch	Déjeuner
Lettuce Salad	Salade
Meat	Viande
Mineral Water	Eau Minérale
Mixed Salad	Salade Composée
Orange Juice	Jus D'orange
Plate	Assiette
Pork	Porc
Restaurant	Restaurant
Red Wine	Vin Rouge
Salt	Sel
Spoon	Cuillère
Sugar	Sucre
Vegetables	Légumes
Water	De L'eau
White Wine	Vin Blanc
Yoghurt	Yaourt

Menu Reader

	Translation
Ballottine	Turkey and foie gras moulded in aspic
Jambon	Ham
Bréjaude	Soup with rye bread
Langue de bœuf	Beef tongue
Cabecou	Quercy goat's cheese
Lapin	Rabbit
Canard	Duck
Lièvre	Hare
Cèpes	King bolete mushrooms (Boletus edulis)
Magret	Filet (cutlet) of duck or goose
Chabrol	Broth with wine
Marcassin	Young wild boar
Champignons des bois	Wild mushrooms
Noix	Walnut
Châtaignes	Chestnuts
Œufs au vin	Eggs in wine sauce
Clafoutis	Cherry pie/flan
Oie	Goose
Confit	Duck or goose preserved in its own fat
Petit salé	Salt pork
Crottin	Small, round goat's cheese

Picard	Potato pâté
Dinde	Turkey
Pommes de terre	Potatoes
Écrevisse	Crayfish
Potée	Boiled dinner with cabbage, potatoes, meat, sausage, and the cook's secret
En conserve	Preserved
Poulet en barbouille	Chicken in thick wine sauce
Enchaud or Anchaud	Pork confit
Pounti	Pork and prune loaf, served sliced
Farcidures	Potato dumplings
Pruneaux	Prunes
Foie de veau	Calf's liver
Rognons	Kidneys
Foie gras	Fattened liver
Sanciaux	Honey doughnuts
Fraise	Strawberry
Tourain blanchi	Garlic soup
Galantine	Cold cuts in jelly
Truffe	Truffle
Gibier	Game
Truffiat	Potatoes in pastry crust
Girole	Chanterelle mushroom (cantharellus cibarius)
Truite	Trout
bien cuit/ à point/ saignant/ cru	well-done/ medium/ rare/ raw

Personal Documents and Travel

	Translation
Airport	Aéroport
Credit Card	Carte De Crédit
Customs	Douane
Passport	Passeport
Platform	Voie
Railway Station	Gare
Shuttle	Navette
Suitcase	Valise
Train/plane Ticket	Billet De Train/d'avion
Wallet	Portefeuille

Clothing

	Translation
Coat	Manteau
Jumper	Pull
Raincoat	Imperméable
Shirt	Chemise
Shoes	Chaussures
Socks	Chaussettes
Stockings	Bas
Suit	Costume
Tights	Collant
Trousers	Pantalon

Commonly used words

	Translation
Goodbye	Au Revoir
Hello/good Morning	Bonjour
How	Comment
Excuse Me	Excusez-moi
Thank You	Merci
Yes/no	Oui/non
I Am Sorry	Pardon
Why	Pourquoi
When	Quand
Please	S'il Vous Plaît

Useful Phrases

Do you speak English?
Parlez-vous anglais?

I don't understand
Je ne comprends pas

Talk slowly
Parlez lentement

Where's...?
Où est...?

When does the... leave?
À quelle heure part...?

When does the... arrive?
À quelle heure arrive...?

When does the museum open?
À quelle heure ouvre le musée?

When is breakfast served?
À quelle heure sert-on le petit-déjeuner?

What does it cost?
Combien cela coûte?

Where is the nearest petrol/gas station?
Où se trouve la station essence la plus proche?

Where can I change traveller's cheques?
Où puis-je échanger des traveller's cheques?

Where are the toilets?
Où sont les toilettes?

Do you accept credit cards?
Acceptez-vous les cartes de crédit?

Basic Information

BUSINESS HOURS

In Paris and much of Northern France, banks are normally open from 9am- 4.30 or 5pm. Some close 1–3pm and some are open Saturday morning.

In the Provinces the banks open from 10am–1pm and 3–4.30 Tue–Sat (they often close early the day before a Public Holiday). Post Offices are open from 8pm or 8.30am–5pm or 6pm Mon–Fri and Sat from 8am–noon. In the Provinces they often open at 9am–4.30pm with two hours for lunch. If a holiday falls on a Tuesday or Thursday then the nearest Monday or Friday will be taken as well.

SHOPPING HOURS

Most of the larger shops are open Mondays to Saturdays from 9am to 7pm or 7.30pm. Smaller, individual shops may close during the lunch hour. Food shops – grocers, wine merchants and bakeries – are generally open from 7am to 7pm or 7.30pm; some open on Sunday mornings. Many food shops close between noon and 2pm and on Mondays. Bakery and pastry shops sometimes close on Wednesdays. Hypermarkets usually stay open non-stop from 9am until 9pm or even later. People travelling to the USA cannot import plant products or fresh food, including fruit, cheeses and nuts. It is permitted to carry tinned products or preserves.

COMMUNICATIONS

Internet access is widely available. Most public phones in France use prepaid phone cards (télécartes), rather than coins. Some telephone booths accept credit cards (Visa, Mastercard/Euro-

EMERGENCY NUMBERS	
Police (Gendarme)	17
Fire (Pompiers)	18
Ambulance (SAMU)	15

INTERNATIONAL DIALLING CODES	
Australia	(00+) 61
Eire	(00+) 353
United Kingdom	(00+) 44
Canada	(00+) 1
New Zealand	(00+) 64
United States	(00+) 1

card). *Télécartes* (50 or 120 units) can be bought in post offices, branches of France Télécom, *bureaux de tabac* (cafés that sell cigarettes) and newsagents for national and international calls. You can receive calls at phone boxes with the blue bell sign; the phone won't ring, so watch the message screen.

NATIONAL CALLS

French numbers have ten digits; around Paris these begin with 01; 02 in NW France; 03 in NE France; 04 in SE France and Corsica; 05 in SW France.

INTERNATIONAL CALLS

To call France from abroad, dial the country code (33) + 9-digit number (omit the initial 0). When calling abroad from France dial 00, then dial the country code and area code.

International information (US/Canada): ℘00 33 12 11
International operator: ℘00 33 12 + Country Code
Local directory assistance: ℘12
Toll-free numbers: In France these begin with 0800.

MINITEL

France Télécom operates a system offering directory enquiries (free of charge up to 3min), travel and entertainment reservations, and other services (cost per minute varies). These small computer-like terminals can be found in some post offices, hotels and France Télécom agencies and in many French homes. 3614 PAGES E is the code for directory assistance in English (turn on the unit, dial 3614, hit the connexion button when you get the tone, type in PAGES E, and follow the instructions on the screen).

CELLULAR PHONES

In France these have numbers that begin with 06. Two-watt (lighter, shorter reach) and eight-watt models are on the market, using the Orange (France Télécom) or SFR networks. Mobicartes are prepaid phone cards that fit into mobile units. Mobile phone rentals:

- **Euro Exaphone**
  📞 01 44 09 77 78
- **Rent a Cell Express**
  📞 01 53 93 78 00.
- **World Cellular Rentals**
  www.worldcr.com.
- **Ellinas Phone Rental**
  📞 01 47 20 70 00.

ELECTRICITY

The electric current is 220 Volts. Circular two-pin plugs are the rule. Adapters and converters (for hairdryers, for example) should be bought before you leave home; they are on sale in most airports. If you have a rechargeable device (video camera, portable computer, battery recharger), read the instructions carefully or contact the manufacturer or shop. Sometimes these items only require a plug adapter, in other cases you must use a voltage converter as well.

DISCOUNTS

Significant discounts are available for senior citizens; students; youths under age 25; teachers; and groups, for public transportation, museums and monuments and for some leisure activities such as movies (at certain times of day). Bring student or senior cards with you, as well as passport-size photos for discount travel cards. The **International Student Travel Conference** (www.istc.org), global administrator of the International Student and Teacher Identity Cards, is an association of student travel organizations around the world. ISTC members collectively negotiate benefits with airlines, governments,

and providers of other goods and services for the student and teacher community, both in their own country and around the world. The non-profit association sells international ID cards for students, youth under age 25 and teachers (who may get discounts on museum entrances for example). The ISTC is also active in a network of international education and work exchange programmes. The coorporate headquarters address is Keizersgracht 174-176, 1016 DW Amsterdam, The Netherlands 📞 31 20 421 28 00; mailbox@istc.org. ⓘ See Getting There: By Train for other discounts on transportation.

MAIL/POST

Main post offices open Mondays to Fridays, 8am to 7pm, Saturdays, 8am to noon. Smaller branch post offices often close at lunchtime between noon and 2pm and in the afternoon at 4pm.

✉ AIRMAIL POSTAGE RATES TO:		
UK	Letter	(20g) 0.60€
North America	Letter	(20g) 0.85€
Australia	Letter	(20g) 0.85€
New Zealand	Letter	(20g) 0.85€

Stamps are also available from newsagents and tobacconists. Stamp collectors should ask for timbres de collection in any post office. *Poste Restante* (General Delivery) mail should be addressed as follows: Name, Poste Restante, Poste Centrale, post code of the département followed by town name, France. ⓘ *The Michelin Guide France gives local post codes.*

MONEY
CURRENCY

There are no restrictions on the amount of currency visitors can take into France. Visitors carrying a lot of cash are advised to complete a currency declaration form on arrival, because there are restrictions on currency export.

The European currency unit, the **euro**, went into circulation as of 1 January 2002, and since 17 February 2002, euros are the only currency accepted as a means of payment. Notes in francs will be accepted by the Banque de France until 2012; coins in francs were accepted until 2005.

BANKS

For opening hours see Business Hours, above.

A passport is required as identification when cashing travellers cheques in banks. Commission charges vary and hotels usually charge more than banks for cashing cheques.

One of the most economical ways to use your money in France is by using **ATM machines** to get cash directly from your bank account (with a debit card) or to use your credit card to get a cash advance. Be sure to remember your PIN number, you will need it to use cash dispensers and to pay with your card in shops, restaurants etc. Code pads are numeric; use a telephone pad to translate a letter code into numbers.

Pin numbers have four digits in France; inquire with the issuing company or bank if the code you usually use is longer. Visa is the most widely accepted credit card, followed by Mastercard; other cards, credit and debit (Diners Club, Plus, Cirrus etc) are also accepted in some cash machines. American Express is more often accepted in premium establishments. Most places post signs indicating which card they accept; if you don't see such a sign and want to pay with a card, ask before ordering or making a selection. Cards are widely accepted in shops, hypermarkets, hotels and restaurants, at tollbooths and in petrol stations.

Before you leave home, check with the bank that issued your card for emergency replacement procedures. Carry your card number and emergency

phone numbers separate from your wallet and handbag; leave a copy of this information with someone you can easily reach.

If your card is lost or stolen while you are in France, call one of the 24-hour hotlines listed below.

American Express ☎01 47 77 72 00	
VISA ☎01 42 77 11 90	
MasterCard/Eurocard ☎01 45 67 84 84	
Diners Club ☎01 47 62 75 75	

You must report any loss or theft of credit cards or travellers cheques to the local police who will issue you with a certificate (useful proof to show the issuing company).

PRICES

As a rule, the cost of staying in a hotel and eating in restaurants is significantly higher in Paris than in the French regions. Nevertheless, reserve a hotel room well in advance and take advantage of the choice of restaurants to make the most of your money.

Restaurants usually charge for meals in two ways: a menu, that is a fixed price menu with 2 or 3 courses, sometimes a small pitcher of wine, all for a stated price, or à la carte, the more expensive way, with each course ordered separately.

Cafés have very different prices, depending on where they are located. The price of a drink or a coffee is cheaper if you stand at the counter *(comptoir)* than if you sit down *(salle)* and sometimes it is even more expensive if you sit outdoors *(terrasse)*.

PUBLIC HOLIDAYS

See the chart to the left for days when public services, museums and other monuments may be closed or may vary their hours of admission.

National museums and art galleries are closed on Tuesdays; municipal museums are generally closed on Mondays. In addition to the usual

1 January	New Year's Day (*Jour de l'An*)
March/April	Easter Day and Easter Monday (*Pâques*)
1 May	May Day (*Fête du Travail*)
8 May	VE Day (*Fête de la Libération*)
Thurs 40 days after Easter	Ascension Day (*Ascension*)
7th Sun-Mon after Easter	Whit Sunday and Monday (*Pentecôte*)
14 July	France's National Day (*Fête de la Bastille*)
15 August	Assumption (*Assomption*)
1 November	All Saint's Day (*Toussaint*)
11 November	Armistice Day (*Fête de la Victoire*)
25 December	Christmas Day (*Noël*)

school holidays at Christmas and in the spring and summer, there are long mid-term breaks (10 days to a fortnight) in February and November.

SMOKING

In February 2007, France banned smoking in public places such as offices, universities and railway stations. The law will become effective for all enclosed public spaces (including restaurants, cafés etc...) in January 2008.

TIME

France is 1hr ahead of Greenwich Mean Time (GMT). France goes on daylight-saving time from the last Sunday

WHEN IT IS NOON IN FRANCE, IT IS	
11am	in London
7pm	in Perth
11am	in Dublin
9pm	in Sydney
6am	in New York
11pm	in Auckland
3am	in Los Angeles

in March to the last Sunday in October. In France the 12-hour clock is not used.

TIPPING

Service charge is automatically included in the prices of meals and accommodation in France. However, if the service in a restaurant is especially good or if you have enjoyed a fine meal, an extra tip (this is the *pourboire*, rather than the service) will be appreciated. Usually 1.5 to 3.5 euros is enough, but if the bill is big, leave 7 to 8 euros or more.

VAT

There is a Value Added Tax in France (*TVA*) ranging from 5.5% to 19.6% on almost every purchase. However, non-European visitors who spend more than 175€ (figure subject to change) in any one participating store can get the VAT amount refunded. Usually, you fill out a form at the store, showing your passport. Upon leaving the country, you submit all forms to customs for approval (they may want to see the goods, so if possible don't pack them in checked luggage).

The refund is usually paid directly into your bank or credit card account, or it can be sent by mail. Big department stores that cater to tourists provide special services to help you; be sure to mention that you plan to seek a refund before you pay for goods (no refund is possible for tax on services). If you are visiting two or more countries within the European Union, you submit the forms only on departure from the last EU country.

The refund is worth while for those visitors who would like to buy fashions, furniture or other fairly expensive items, but remember, the minimum amount must be spent in a single shop (though not necessarily on the same day).

The Region Today

The region's economy has long depended on its agricultural activities, as the scarcity of mineral wealth and raw materials prevented the development of major industrial centres as in northern and eastern France. More recently, investment in a wider range of sectors, including high-tech industries, tourism, and the development of high-quality culinary and craft products, have expanded the region's economic potential. The region's communication infrastructure has also improved, making the countryside less isolated. And of course, the region's trademark products continue to fly the region's flag, in particular Limoges porcelain, foie gras and truffles.

LIFESTYLE

The lifestyle of the population in the area covered by this guide is much the same as elsewhere in France except, perhaps, that there is a greater emphasis on good food and wine, especially in the Dordogne and Quercy where the French paradox of long life and a rich diet is very apparent. Life begins earlier in the day than in the UK and the two hour lunch break signalled by the klaxon at 12 noon is still common in rural areas. People may start the day earlier but they also retire earlier in the evening - most small towns and village become quiet after 9 or 10 pm.

ECONOMY
AGRICULTURE

Berry

Agriculture has long been the mainstay of the Berry's economy, although improvements to the road network have enabled industrial development. Mechanisation and the use of fertilisers reaped rewards in **Champagne Berrichonne**, which has become France's second-largest grain-producing region. However, there are few processing plants to handle the harvest, and this impedes growth. In the Indre *département*, another handicap is the ageing of the farming population.

Limousin

As elsewhere, small farms have decreased in number over the years, to be replaced by larger, more modern operations. In the north, fields are planted with grain crops, whereas southern areas specialise in orchards, mostly apple.

Périgord-Quercy

Alongside the Lot-et-Garonne, the Dordogne *département* is the number one producer of **strawberries** in France, with almost 20 000t harvested annually. The protective plastic coverings visible in spring protect the young plants from bad weather and enable them to flower and grow in a controlled environment. The fruit ripens under these sheets before it is picked and packed off to the large markets of the Paris region and the north of France, where the Périgord strawberry is particularly appreciated.

Although on the decline, **walnuts** are another local speciality harvested in large quantity (5-7 000t per year). Several varieties are produced locally: Marbot walnuts ripen early and are often sold fresh; Grandjean are produced around Sarlat and Gourdon, accounting for most of the green walnuts; Corne is a small nut of good quality; while Franquette has increased in popularity in recent years. In 2002, the four varieties were awarded Appellation d'Origine Controlée (AOC) *Noix du Périgord* status.

Conditions in the Périgord and the Quercy, and southwest France as a whole, are favourable to the growing of **tobacco**, a hardy plant imported from America in the 16C and initially used for medicinal purposes (*see BERGERAC: Musée du Tabac*).

The traditional dark tobacco that long gave French cigarettes their strong, distinctive flavour and aroma now grows side-by-side with lighter varieties such as Virginia tobacco, which have increased in popularity. Nowadays, there are around 3 000 planters in the region, mostly in family-run operations. The Dordogne is France's leading tobacco-producing *département* with 1 300 growers producing 15% of the country's crop.

Perhaps the most evocative of all the region's products, however, is the rare and secretive fungus known as the **truffle**, which grows underground, at the base of a tree, where it is sniffed out by specially trained pigs or dogs. Exchanged at market for fabulous sums which seem incongruous with their lumpy, dusty appearance, these subterranean "black diamonds" are not as plentiful as in the past and are threatened by imports from countries such as Italy, Poland and China. Whereas a century ago hundreds of tonnes would have been harvested every year, today this figure has dwindled to around 4t. To encourage production, oak trees continue to be planted in areas where conditions favour growth of these *diamants noirs*.

STOCK-RAISING

Each region has developed its stock-raising in line with the natural fertility of its soil, with rich pastureland given over to the grazing of cattle, and more arid plateaux set aside for the rearing of sheep.

SHEEP

In bygone days sheep-rearing was the only way of earning a living when a lack of money and materials were major obstacles on the plains of the Berry.

The Berry breed is declining in numbers and is being replaced by the Charmois and the English Southdown. Much prized for their meat, they are now reared in sheepfolds and no longer roam the open pastureland. Goat herds are also increasing, particularly as a result of the rise in popularity of goats' cheese.

The *causses* continue to play an important role in sheep-rearing: the plateau sheep or Gramat species is known as the spectacled breed, due to their white fleece and black rings around their eyes. These hardy, prolific animals bear fine

Limousin cattle

S. Sauvignier/MICHELIN

wool, but are especially prized for their meat, which contains very little fat.

LIMOUSIN CATTLE

Limousin beef-cattle, with their short withers and distinctive russet hides, were already widely known in the 17C and 18C. Improved by culling and better feeding, the breed now produces some of the finest meat in the world. To supply market demands, Limousin farmers have turned to the production of young calves for white veal.

Natural features have transformed the Limousin into a leading area for the production and export of both the breed and its meat. Indigenous meadowland has been complemented by specially sown pastures where grass grows more profusely.

CRAFTS AND INDUSTRIES

The presence of metallic oxides, which could be used in producing enamelware, resulted in the establishment of an **enamelling industry** in Limoges.

After three centuries of decline, the last 50 years have seen the re-establishment of Limoges' reputation, which is now as high as it was in the days of such master-enamellers as the Nardon Pénicauds, the Limosins and the Nouailhers.

The discovery of important deposits of kaolin near St-Yrieix at the end of the 18C was the catalyst for the development of the **china industry**. The first factories were scattered in the southern part of the Haute-Vienne, otherwise the wood needed for the kilns would have been liable to the payment of a toll upon entering the city of Limoges. By the end of the 19C, due to improvements in the production process, porcelain had become a major industry in the city.

Another traditional manufacturing activity is centred around Aubusson, famous for its **tapestries**.

The **leather** industry and its many ancillary sectors developed thanks to abundant water supplies, tanning resins from the forests and hides obtained from large-scale stock-raising. In the early 19C, some 50 tanneries were established in the region. Today, shoes are made at Limoges and St-Amand-Montrond, and St-Junien is famous for its gloves. While this industry seems to be past its heyday, the forest holds promise for the development of the **paper industry**, which is on the upswing.

The area around Limoges has seen a steady increase in new **high-tech** businesses as a result of the development of national institutes (industrial ceramics, engineering, biotechnology, optical and microwave communication etc) and leading industries such as Ariane Espace and Airbus Industrie. Many smaller businesses have started up and experienced considerable international growth.

Prospection of the old Limousin granite massifs led to the discovery of the first uranium deposit near Crouzille in 1948, which became the largest processing centre in Western Europe. These mines are now closed. The very last **gold** mine, of its kind in France, in Bourneix, closed in 2002; the economic environment had become unfavourable and viable reserves were exhausted.

FOLKLORE AND TRADITIONS

The regions of the Berry, Limousin and Dordogne are home to age-old rural civilisations. Traditional costumes and time-honoured crafts have been preserved in all three areas and are actively on display and promoted in the many local festivals (&see Calendar of Events). Legends, superstitions and folk tales have continued to flourish alongside religious events in which the lives and legends of saints play an important role. In addition, alchemists, sorcerers and werewolves, and creatures such as toads, owls, and wolves, to name but a few, have long fuelled the imagination of the region's inhabitants.

Local accents trace the boundaries of the different regions as clearly as a line drawn on a map. Regional patois (provincial dialects) are seldom heard nowadays, although interest in preserving the traditions of the langue d'Oc is reviving.

LANTERNS OF THE DEAD

The earliest known reference to **lanterns** of the dead is found in a 12C text, De Miraculis, by Pierre le Vénérable, abbot of Cluny. The legend recounts how a young novice from the Abbaye de Charlieu (Loire) received a visit from his uncle Achard, the monastery's former prior, who had been dead for some years. The apparition led the youth to the cemetery, where wrapped in concentric circles of glowing light, a group of holy persons had gathered. "In the middle of the cemetery, a stone edifice rose up; on the top, there was a small compartment for holding a lamp which, nightly and in honour of the faithful resting there, lights this sacred place. Steps lead to a platform where two or three people can stand or sit down." This definition is similar to one given in a study written in 1882 by a local

Lantern of the Dead, Feletin

R. Corbel/MICHELIN

abbot and scholar. Mostly built between the 11C and the 13C, in cemeteries near Romanesque churches, many of the lanterns were later destroyed, moved or converted to other uses.

These structures, dubbed lanterns of the dead in the 19C, seem to be the expression of ancient ideals. Their form, with a height equal to six or eight times their diameter, complies with ancient Roman canon. The vertical design is symbolic of prestige, but also designates security, and indeed no reference to mourning or suffering seems apparent in the decoration or the exultant skyward movement. Experts still question the use made of the stone dais: perhaps a movable altar was placed upon it, or perhaps it was used to indicate the East, the direction of the Holy City of Jerusalem, thus serving to define the alignment of the graves in the cemetery. People have long believed that the spirits of those who have passed away seek out the light which death has extinguished for them.

Although the early Christian church condemned the practice of lighting candles on tombs, the symbol of the eternal flame soon came to be totally assimilated.

THE LIMOUSIN OSTENSIONS

Every seven years the **Haute-Vienne** and **Creuse** *départements* honour their saints: St Martial, the apostle of the Limousin; St Valérie; the Good St Eligius, founder of the monastery at Solignac; St Stephen of Muret; hermits who lived in the forests of the Limousin and Marche; and St Junien, St Victurnien and St Leonard, founders of monasteries scattered in the region's valleys.

The *ostensions*, or solemn exhibition of relics to the faithful, date back to the 10C. One of the earliest of these festivals was held at Limoges when a terrible epidemic of ergotism, also known as St Anthony's fire, was raging. To combat the malady, the relics of St Martial were brought out. A visitation – whether in the form of a plague or an illustrious personage – became an occasion for holding these ceremonies, which were later repeated at regular intervals.

Each town has a traditional ceremony of its own, hosting religious festivals also based on local folklore. The blessing of the banner, which is solemnly hoisted to the belfry pinnacle, marks the opening of the *ostension*. Once the festival has been opened on the Sunday after Easter, the relics are presented to the faithful for veneration in their shrines or reliquaries which, in some cases, are masterpieces of the gold and silversmith's art. Colourful processions pass through bunting and flower-decked streets in towns and villages, accompanied by fanfares, drums and banners and escorted by guards of honour, representatives of different craft guilds, and other groups in rich finery. Neighbouring parishes often participate in these events; as an example, 50 parishes come together in Le Dorat for the closing ceremonies. The next ceremony is in 2016.

THE FÉLIBRÉE

In July every year a different town in the Périgord hosts the Félibrée, a meeting of a society of poets and writers set up in the late 19C with the aim of preserving the **Provençal language**. The windows and doors of the chosen town are decorated with thousands of multicoloured paper flowers, and trees and shrubs are illuminated to form triumphal arches. The people of the Périgord flock from all corners of the *département* decked out in traditional costume: lace headdresses, embroidered shawls and long skirts for the women, and wide-brimmed black felt hats, full white shirts and waistcoats for the men.

The queen of the Félibrée, surrounded by a member of the Félibrige society committee and the guardians of local traditions, receives the keys of the town and makes a speech in the local dialect. The assembled gathering files off in procession to Mass, accompanied by the sound of hurdy-gurdies, before sitting down to a sumptuous feast. Traditionally, the meal begins with *chabrol*, a soup of wine and clear stock typical of the southwest, which is served in dishes made especially for the occasion, and bearing the year and the name of the

History

PREHISTORY IN THE DORDOGNE

The Quarternary Era is relatively young, since it only began about two million years ago. Nevertheless, it is during this short period that human evolution has taken place. There is no definitive evidence of life having existed on Earth in the Pre-Cambrian Age; reptiles, fish and tailless amphibians appeared in the course of the Primary Era, mammals and birds during the Secondary Era. Primates, the most ancient ancestors of mankind, appeared at the end of the Tertiary Era and were followed in the Quarternary Era by ever more advanced species.

The slow pace of human progress during the Palaeolithic Age is quite extraordinary: it took people nearly two million years to learn to polish stone. Yet, the few thousand years that followed saw in the Middle and Far East the development of brilliant civilisations which reached their zenith in the construction of the pyramids in Egypt. A few centuries later bronze was discovered, followed, in approximately 900 BC, by that of iron.

RESEARCHERS

The study of prehistory is a science essentially French in origin which began in the early 19C. Until that time only the occasional reference by a Greek or Latin author, a study by the Italian scholar Mercati (1541-93) in the 16C and a paper by Jussieu, published in 1723, gave any hint of the existence of ancient civilisations. In spite of the scepticism of most learned men – led by Cuvier (1769-1832) – researchers pursued their investigations in the Périgord, Lozère and the Somme Valley. **Boucher de Perthes'** (1788-1868) discoveries at St-Acheul and Abbeville were the catalyst for an important series of studies, but it was **Paul Tournal** who in 1831 first used the term **prehistory** to describe the evidence of ancient human culture that was emerging at the time from certain caves in France. Among the pioneers who laid modern archaeology's foundations are: **Édouard Lartet** (1801-71), who undertook many excavations in the Vézère

Valley and established a preliminary classification for the various eras of prehistory; **Gabriel de Mortillet** (1821-98), who undertook and completed the classification, adding the names Chellean, Mousterian, Aurignacian, Solutrean and Magdalenian to correspond with the places where the most prolific or most characteristic deposits were found: **Chelles** in the Seine-et-Marne, **Le Moustier** in the Dordogne, **Aurignac** in the Haute-Garonne, **Solutré** in the Saône-et-Loire and **La Madeleine** in the Dordogne.

Excavations can only be performed by specialists with knowledge of the geological stratigraphy, the physics and chemistry of rock formations, the nature and form of stones and gravels, and the ability to analyse fossilised wood, coal and bone fragments.

In rock shelters and the entrances to caves, prehistorians have discovered hearths (accumulations of charcoal and kitchen debris), tools, weapons, stone and bone furnishings and bone fragments. These vestiges are collected in layers; during excavations each of these different layers is uncovered and the civilisation or period is reconstructed.

PREHISTORY IN THE PÉRIGORD

The Périgord has been inhabited since Palaeolithic times. The names **Tayacian** (Les Eyzies-de-Tayac), **Micoquean** (La Micoque), **Mousterian** (Le Moustier), **Perigordian** and **Magdalenian** (La Madeleine) are evidence of the importance of these prehistoric sites. Nearly 200 deposits have been discovered, of which more than half are in the **Vézère Valley** near Les Eyzies-de-Tayac.

THE PALAEOLITHIC AGE

Our most distant ancestors (some three million years ago) were the early hominids (ie the family of man) of East Africa, who, unlike their instinctive predecessors, were rational thinkers. They evolved into *Homo habilis*, followed by *Homo erectus*, characterised by his upright walking (Java man or *Pithecanthropus erectus*, discovered by E Dubois in 1891, with a cranial capacity midway between that of the most highly developed ape and the least developed man): and Peking man or *Sinanthropus* (identified by D. Black in 1927), who made rough-hewn tools, tools for chopping from split pebbles and heavy bifaced implements.

Neanderthal man appeared c 150 000 years ago. In 1856, in the Düssel Valley (also known as the Neander Valley, east of Düsseldorf, Germany) portions of a human skeleton were discovered with the following characteristics: a cranial capacity of approximately $1\,500\text{cm}^3$/ 91.5in^3 an elongated cranium (dolichocephalus), a sharply receding forehead, prominently developed jawbones and a small stature (1.60m/5ft 3in).

Skeletons with similar characteristics were found in France at La Chapelle-aux-Saints (Corrèze) in 1908, at **Le Moustier** (Dordogne) in 1909, at **La Ferrassie** (Dordogne) in 1909 and 1911, and at **Le Régourdou** (Dordogne) in 1957. The Neanderthal group completely disappeared without descendants 35 000 years ago; at the same time the first burial sites started to appear.

Homo sapiens were flourishing in France about 40 000 years ago. Their essential characteristics – perfect upright stance, raised forehead, slightly projecting eyebrows – showed them to be highly developed and comparable to people today (*sapiens* means intelligent). Several races have been traced as belonging to this same family. Cro-Magnon individuals must have been quite similar in appearance to the present *Homo sapiens*.

Cro-Magnon man (named after skeletons found in the rock shelters of Cro-Magnon in the **Dordogne** and **Solutré** in the Saône-et-Loire) was tall – about 1.80m/5ft 11in – with long, robust limbs denoting considerable muscular strength; the skull was dolichocephalic in shape. These people lived in the Upper Palaeolithic to the Neolithic Ages.

Chancelade man (from a skeleton discovered in 1889 at **Chancelade**, near Périgueux) appeared in the Magdalenian Period; these people had a large cranium of dolichocephalic form, a long, wide face, pronounced cheekbones and a height of not more than 1.55m/5ft 1in.

CULTURE AND ART IN THE PALAEOLITHIC AGE

The oldest skeletons belonging to Neanderthals, found in the **Périgord** and the **Quercy**, date from the Mousterian Culture (Middle Palaeolithic).

Later, during the Ice Age, tribes are thought to have come from Eastern Europe and settled in the **Vézère** and **Beune** valleys. Bordering these valleys were cliffs and slopes pitted with caves and shelters offering many natural advantages which flatter landscapes were unable to provide: protection from the cold, nearby springs and rivers abundant in fish, and narrow ravines used for intercepting game as it passed through. There were, however, several dwelling huts found in the **Isle Valley**, upstream from Périgueux.

The Palaeolithic Age (*palaeos* means ancient, *lithos* means stones) covers the period in which people knew only how to chip flints. An intermediate age, the Mesolithic (*mesos* means middle), separates it from the Neolithic Age (*neos* means new), when they learnt to polish stone. The first group were predators (hunting, fishing and gathering), whereas the last group were farmers and breeders. Skill in flint-knapping evolved very slowly and, therefore, the Palaeolithic Age is subdivided into three periods: the Lower, Middle and Upper.

LOWER PALAEOLITHIC

This began about two million years ago. People living in this period in the Périgord knew how to use fire and hunted big game. The earth suffered three successive ice ages known as the Günz, the Mindel and the Riss (after the tributary valleys of the Danube where they were studied). Between each ice age, France and Britain had a tropical climate.

Flint-knapping began with a cut made by striking two stones violently one against the other, or by striking one against a rock which served as an anvil.

MIDDLE PALAEOLITHIC

This began about 150 000 years ago. Neanderthal society brought with it better finished and more specialised tools. Mousterian industry used both bifaced implements and flakes. New methods enabled triangular points to be produced, also scrapers, probably used for working skins, and flints adapted to take a wooden handle and serve as hunting clubs (bear skulls pierced by such weapons have been found).

During the Mousterian Culture some cave entrances were used as dwellings, others were used as burial places. More sophisticated weapons were developed and used to hunt big game and animal skins provided protection from the cold.

UPPER PALAEOLITHIC

This began about 35 000 years ago. Cro-Magnon and Chancelade individuals replaced Neanderthals. During this period there was a constant improvement in the production of tools; living conditions were made easier with the perfecting of new hunting methods, resulting in more leisure time and, therefore, artistic expression.

Perigordian and Aurignacian cultures

These two cultures, following the Mousterian and Levalloisian cultures and preceding the Solutrean culture, were contemporary but parallel.

The **Aurignacian** stone industry produced large blades, stone flake tools, burins (a sort of chisel) and points made from antlers (early ones have a split base). Cave decoration, applied to blocks of limestone (**La Ferrassie** near Le Bugue) and at times in tiny caves, consisted of engraved animals, painted or partially carved, or female figures.

At the end of the Perigordian culture, Gravettians made burins and points; these people decorated their shelter walls (**Le Poisson**, Laussel), and carved Venus figurines (small female statues with exaggerated curves evoking fertility).

Burial places contain some ornaments and jewellery, such as shells and bead necklaces. The first examples of wall decoration appear as hands placed flat against the rock and outlined in black or red; these can be found at **Font-de-Gaume** and **Le Pech Merle**, although the animals depicted are sketched in a rudimentary fashion. By the end of this period, people had truly discovered their artistic nature, as the sculptures at the Abri du Poisson (Fish Shelter) and the engravings and paintings found at **Font-de-Gaume** and **Lascaux** show. The **Grève** cave with its engraved bison in turned profile dates from between the late Perigordian and early Solutrean periods.

Solutrean Culture

Very well represented in the Dordogne, this period is distinguished by exquisite low-relief sculptures carved out of limestone slabs, such as the **Devil's Oven**, found near Bourdeilles and now exhibited in the National Museum of Prehistory at Les Eyzies.

The stone-cutting industry also underwent a brilliant period during the Solutrean culture. Flint blades, following a method of splitting under pressure, became much slimmer, forming blades in the shape of laurel or willow leaves. Shouldered points were used as weapons, after they had been fitted with wooden shafts. It was during this period that needles with eyes appeared.

Magdalenian Culture

It was in this period that bone and ivory craftsmanship reached its peak. The existence of herds of reindeer, which is accounted for by the very cold climate that occurred at the end of the Würm Glacial Period, encouraged carvers to work with bone and antler, producing perforated batons, sometimes engraved, which were used as armatures for points and harpoon heads; projectile tips, sometimes engraved, used as spears; and decorated flattened points.

This is also the period when cave wall art, depicting essentially animal subjects, reached its peak. To protect themselves from the cold, people of the Magdalenian culture lived in the shelter of overhanging rocks or at the mouths of caves; inside, these caves were underground sanctuaries, at times quite some distance from the cave entrance.

They used the shelter (as at the **Cap-Blanc** Shelter) and sanctuary walls to express their artistic or religious emotions by low-relief carving, engraving and painting. This period introduced a very sophisticated style compared to the more rudimentary outline drawings of the Perigordian and Aurignacian cultures. However, due to the juxtaposition or superimposition of the figures drawn and deterioration (only a few Magdalenian caves are open to the public due to the difficulty in preserving the art), the study of these paintings is not easy.

After **Lascaux**, numerous cave-sanctuaries appeared during the Middle and Upper Magdalenian periods. Portable art, manifested through smaller objects, is another form of expression developed in the shelters. Animals are much less stylised and increasingly realistic in the details of their anatomy and their movements, as well as the faithful and detailed rendering of their physical aspects: coat, tail, eyes, ears, hoofs, antlers and tusks.

Nonetheless, the style is more ornamental. The perspective of the animals in profile, non-existent in the beginning, was pursued and even distorted during Lascaux's last period. New graphic techniques appeared: stencilling, areas left intentionally without colour, polychrome colours etc. Towards the end of the Magdalenian culture, art became more schematic and human figures made their appearance. Animal art then disappeared from France and Spain, as the herds of reindeer migrated northwards in search of lichen, which was disappearing during the climatic warming at the end of the Würm Glacial Period.

GAULS AND ROMANS

BC   The Périgord is inhabited by the **Petrocorii** and the Quercy by the **Caduici**.

6-5C The **Bituriges Cubi** people settle in the Berry.

59-51 Conquest of Gaul by **Caesar**. The last Gaulish resistance to

Venus of Laussel

©World Illustrated/Photoshot

Caesar is at **Uxellodunum**, which historians believe to be in the Quercy.

16   **Emperor Augustus** creates the province of Aquitaine. The capital of the land of the Petrocorii is **Vesunna** (Périgueux) and of that of the Caduici, **Divona Cadurcorum** (**Cahors**).

AD

1-3C **Pax Romana**. For three centuries towns develop and several public buildings are built. In the countryside around the towns new crops are introduced by the Romans: walnut, chestnut and cherry trees and above all vineyards.

late 3C The Berry and the Limousin are incorporated into primitive **Aquitaine**; Bourges is its capital.

235-284 **Alemanni and Franks** invade the region. In 276, several towns are razed. Vesunna defends itself behind fortifications hastily built from the stones taken from Roman public buildings.

313   **Edict of Milan**. Emperor Constantine grants Christians the freedom of worship.

476   End of the Roman Empire.

MEROVINGIANS AND CAROLINGIANS

486-507 **Clovis**, king of the Franks, conquers Gaul and Aquitaine.

8C The Quercy and Périgord become counties under the kingdom of Aquitaine.

800 **Charlemagne** is crowned Emperor of the West in Rome.

9C The Dordogne and Isle valleys and Périgueux are laid waste by **Vikings**.

10C **The four baronies** of the Périgord – Mareuil, Bourdeilles, Beynac and Biron – are formed as well as the overlordships of Ans, Auberoche, Gurson etc.
The County of Périgord passes to the house of Talleyrand. Powerful families rule the Quercy.

c 950 Beginning of the **pilgrimage** to St James' shrine in Santiago de Compostela, Spain.

12C Many **influential abbeys** are founded in the region (Noirlac, Chancelade, Cadouin, Rocamadour etc). Construction started on the cathedral in Bourges.

WARS BETWEEN ENGLAND AND FRANCE

1152 **Eleanor of Aquitaine** marries **Henry Plantagenet**, bringing as her dowry all of southwest France. In 1154 Henry Plantagenet becomes King Henry II.

1190 The Quercy is ceded to the English with the exception of the abbeys of Figeac and Souillac.

1191 **Richard the Lionheart** dies at Châlus.

early 13C Albigensian Crusade. Simon de Montfort raids the Quercy and Périgord.

1234 **Louis IX** buys the Berry from the Count of Champagne.

1259 By the **Treaty of Paris**, St Louis cedes the Périgord and the Quercy to the English. The treaty puts an end to the constant fighting and enables the

Charles V and du Guesclin

in 1253

at the start of the Hundred Years War

after the treaty of Brétigny (1360)

after Charles V and du Guesclin's reconquests (1380)

people of the region to live in peace until the Hundred Years War.

1273 Construction is started on the cathedral in Limoges.

1324 **Bourges Cathedral** is consecrated.

1337 French king **Philip VI** declares the English-held duchy of Guyenne confiscated.

1340 **Edward III** of England proclaims himself king of France.

1345 Beginning of the **Hundred Years War** in Aquitaine.

1346 Edward III defeats the French at Crécy.

1355-1370 Edward the Black Prince begins his campaign, ravaging the Berry and Limousin. Edward defeats and captures **King Jean II** (Battle of Poitiers 1356).

1360 The **Treaty of Brétigny** cedes Aquitaine to the English as part of the ransom for Jean II's liberty.

1369 The Quercy and Périgord are won back by the king of France (Charles V). **Du Guesclin**, constable of France, is active in the liberation of the Périgord. During the period that follows the lords of the north of Périgord owe allegiance to the king of France; the lords of the south of Périgord to the English. Many regularly swap sides in unabashed support of their own interests.

1415   **Henry V** defeats the French at *Azincourt* (**Ajincourt**).

1420   Henry V of England is recognised as king of France under the **Treaty of Troyes**. France is divided into three parts controlled by Henry V (Normandy, Guyenne, Paris area); **Philip the Good**, duke of Burgundy (other parts of the area in and around Paris, Burgundy); and the Dauphin (Central France and the Languedoc).

1444   **Truce of Tours** (Charles VII and Henry V); the English retain Maine, the Bordelais region, parts of Artois and Picardy and most of Normandy.

1449   The French begin a campaign in Guyenne, but the people of the region are hostile to the French from years of loyalty to the English crown; Bergerac falls in 1450, Bordeaux in 1451.

1453   Defeat of **John Talbot**, earl of Shrewsbury, at the **Battle of Castillon**, which marks the end of the Hundred Years War.

1463   University of Bourges founded.

2nd half of 15-early 16C
Towns and castles are rebuilt during this period of peace.

1558   **England loses Calais** to the French.

WARS OF RELIGION

1562   **Massacre of Protestants** at Cahors.

1572   **St Bartholomew's Day** massacre (20 000 Huguenots die).

1570-90   War is declared; Bergerac and Ste-Foy-la-Grande are **Huguenot** bastions whereas Périgueux and Cahors support

Hidden Agenda?

Eleanor's eagerness to go to the Crusades may have been coloured by the fact that her uncle Raymond of Poitiers was aleady in the Holy Land. Some chroniclers maintain that they had an affair and this led to her estrangement from Louis.

the **Catholic League**. **Vivans**, the Huguenot leader, scours the Périgord; Périgueux falls in 1575 and Domme in 1588.

1580   Cahors is taken by Henri de Navarre (Henri IV).

1589   **Henri IV** accedes to the throne, converts to Catholicism in 1593 and is crowned in 1594.
Under Henri IV, the County of Périgord becomes part of the royal domain.

1594-95   **Croquant** peasant revolt.

1598   **Edict of Nantes** grants Huguenots freedom of worship and places of refuge.

1607   Viscounty of Limoges comes under the French crown.

1610   Henri IV is assassinated; **Louis XIII**'s reign begins.

1637   Croquants' revolt against Louis XIII's government and Richelieu's taxes.

1643-1715 Louis XIV's reign.

1685   Revocation of the Edict of Nantes. Huguenots flee France.

18C TO 20C

1743-57   **Tourny**, administrator of the Treasury of Bordeaux, instigates a number of town planning projects in the southwest (Allées de Tourny in Périgueux).

1763   **Peace of Paris** ends the French and Indian War (1754-63), marking the end of France's colonial empire in America.

1768   Kaolin is discovered in St-Yrieix-la-Perche.

1789   **Storming of the Bastille** and the beginning of the French Revolution.

1790   Creation of the Dordogne *département*.

1792   Proclamation of the **French Republic** after the Battle of Valmy.

1812-14   Périgord is a Bonapartist fief; several of Napoleon's generals and marshals (Murat, Fournier-Sarlovèze, Daumesnil) are natives of the region.

1868   **Phylloxera** destroys the vineyards of Cahors and Bergerac, causing a rural exodus. Discovery of Cro-Magnon cave skeletons.

1914-18   **World War I**.

1940   Discovery of Lascaux Cave.

1942-1944 The French Resistance movement intensifies in the Limousin during the **World War II**.

1944   Massacres at Tulle and Oradour-sur-Glane.

20C   Marked by a continued rural exodus, the depopulated regions live essentially from agriculture and tourism.

1963   The first **Maison de la Culture** opens in Bourges, an initiative of André Malraux.

1964   Limousin *Région* is created.

1977   Le Printemps de Bourges music festival holds its first concerts.

1994   **Channel Tunnel** links England and France's rail networks.

1995   Jacques **Chirac** President.

1989   The **Parc Naturel Régional de la Brenne** is established. A new motorway is opened from Paris to the centre of France, via Bourges.

1999-2002   **euro** replaces the franc.

2000   Construction begins on the A89 motorway linking Bordeaux to Clermont-Ferrand, cheduled for completion in 2008.

2005   European Constitution rejected in referendum of French electorate.

2007   **Nicolas Sarkozy** elected President.

KEY HISTORICAL FIGURES

Over the centuries, three key figures have left an indelible mark on the region, sparking the imagination and bringing to life the history of this part of France.

ELEANOR OF AQUITAINE

In 1122, a daughter was born to William X, duke of Aquitaine and count of Poitiers, who was to become heiress to one of the largest domains in France (more extensive than that of the king's). In 1137, Eleanor wed **Louis VII**, who succeeded his father to the throne just one month later. The young queen of France was beautiful and influential, though some historians have criticised her juvenile frivolity. Eleanor accompanied her husband on the Second Crusade, where her capricious enthusiasm fired Louis' jealousy, and the marriage was annulled in 1152, shortly after their return to France. Thanks to feudal customs, she regained possession of Aquitaine, and two months later married Henry Plantagenet, count of Anjou and duke of Normandy. When her second husband became king of England (1154) as **Henry II**, England, Normandy and the west of France were united under one crown. In addition to her two daughters from her first marriage, Eleanor bore eight more children, including **Richard the Lionheart**, John Lackland, Eleanor (who married the king of Castille) and Joan (who married the king of Sicily and later the count of Toulouse). No wonder some have called her the grandmother of Europe!

Eleanor was both a political and cultural force to be reckoned with. She turned the court at Poitiers into a centre of courtly life and manners, celebrated by the troubadours; she also promoted the historical legends of Brittany, romantic songs in the Celtic tradition. She supported her sons in a failed revolt against their father; afterwards, Henry had her kept guarded under close watch in England until his death. Released at last, she

14C chronicle of St Denis depicting the marriage of Eleanor of Aquitaine and Louis VII in 1137 (left) and the departure of Louis VII for the Second Crusade in 1147 (right)

became an invaluable advisor to her son Richard, keeping the kingdom intact and administering it during his long absences. She was 80 years old when she set off across the Pyrenees to fetch her granddaughter Blanche of Castille for marriage to the son of the French king, hoping thus to cement peace between the Plantagenets and the Capetians. Her influence was felt even after her death: following the loss of Normandy (1204), her ancestral lands, and not the old Norman territories, remained loyal to England. She died in 1204 in the monastery at Fontevrault where she had retired. The nuns of Fontevrault described this exceptional queen as "beautiful and just, imposing and modest, humble and elegant".

JEAN DE BERRY

In the 14C, when its population was about 350 000, the Berry was plunged into the turmoil of the Hundred Years War following the Black Prince's raids. The region had strategic importance as a potential base for the conquest of Poitou and Aquitaine. King **John the Good** elevated the Berry and Auvergne to the rank of duchies, and granted them to his third son; thus, in 1360, Jean de Berry came into control of at least one-third of the territory of France.

After a period of captivity in England, the young duke was in urgent need of funds. He taxed his lands heavily for the defence of the kingdom, and also spent lavishly on the arts. His military career was marked by a triumphant march on Limoges, which brought the local bourgeoisie and clergy into the Valois camp, but also led to terrible English reprisals. Pursuing his campaign with **Du Guesclin** and the duke of Anjou, he took control of Poitou in 1373.

Meanwhile, his brother, by then King Charles V, passed away, and his nephew, the young **Charles VI**, took the throne. As a member of the regency council from 1380-88, Berry shared royal powers while Charles was too young to rule. He thus gained control of the Languedoc. In conflict with the royal family, Berry also struggled against the peasants' revolt (1381-84), which resulted from his oppressive fiscal policies and opulent lifestyle. The king, although beset by fits of insanity, announced his determination to rule alone, but soon earned the surname Charles the Mad. Still bent on power, and always ready to take advantage, Berry handled negotiations between the conflicting factions of John the Fearless, duke of Burgundy, and his own brother Louis, duke of Orléans, and even promised the English to deliver the province of Guyenne (1412). The end result was the siege of Bourges by royal troops. Berry capitulated and died four years later, at the age of 76.

Throughout his life, he showered his fortune on the arts and artists, building palaces and fine residences in his cities, so much so that at his death there was not enough in the coffers to pay for his funeral. History has recognised his importance as a supporter of the arts, and the treasures he commissioned remain as his monument: paintings, tapestries, jewellery and illuminated manuscripts, including the world-famous Très Riches Heures du Duc de Berry.

JACQUES CŒUR

Born the son of a furrier in Bourges, Cœur's life is exemplary of the spirit of enterprise and the rise of the merchant classes in the period of prosperity that followed the Hundred Years War. His generation was perhaps the first in Europe to aspire to honours, noble rank, wealth and property, without being born into the aristocracy. If he may be said to have represented the rise of the merchant class, his downfall signifies how difficult it was for such social changes to take root.

Jacques Coeur before Charles VII from a copy of 15C miniature, Chroniques of Monstrelet

Gifted with an uncanny flair for business opportunities, Cœur gained the confidence of Charles VII, and became his argentier, managing the royal funds like a modern-day investment tycoon. His power and fortune grew simultaneously as he became a member of the king's council, the tax collector for the Languedoc and the inspector general of the salt tax. He diversified his affairs, stocking all kinds of merchandise – cloth, spices, jewels, armour, wheat and salt – from around the world in his vast stores in Tours. He had a large staff of salesmen, shipowners (he himself owned seven ships) and negotiators, as well as 40 manor houses and a beautiful palace in Bourges, one of the finest examples of lay Gothic architecture in Europe. Cœur set up individual companies for each branch of trade, and sought political support from all quarters. His prosperity was held up by a delicately spun web of bills of exchange, credit, and fiscal receipts issued by the king. A creditor for many of France's aristocrats and the king himself, Cœur was the object of intense jealousy.

His rocketing career plummeted on 31 July 1451, when he was arrested on trumped-up charges of poisoning Agnès Sorel, the king's mistress. His enemies came forth with more accusations: currency fraud, trading arms with the infidels, returning a Christian slave to a Muslim master, running ships with slave crews, and abuse of power. Found guilty on all counts except the poisoning, he was banished, ordered to relinquish all of his goods and property, and pay an impossibly high fine for his release.

Meanwhile, French troops, paid with the confiscated funds, won the final battle of the Hundred Years War. Cœur, the financial adventurer and proto-bourgeois, escaped and fled to Italy before setting out on a Papal naval expedition against the Turks. He is believed to have died on the Aegean island of Chios in 1456. The following year, in an attempt to make amends for his father's treatment of Cœur, King Louis XI returned his unsold property to his sons and revived some of his old companies.

Art and Culture

ART AND ARCHITECTURE

The Vézère Valley, the prehistoric sites of Les Eyzies and the caves of the Quercy contain some of the finest known examples of prehistoric art (♨ see HISTORY), the earliest manifestations of art in France. Since that time, art and architecture have evolved in close connection with the region's turbulent history. The significant periods of construction took place in periods of peace: the Pax Romana, the 12C (many monasteries date from this century) and the period spanning the end of the 14C to the 16C. During times of war – the Hundred Years War, the Wars of Religion – the main concern of the local population was its protection, hence the fortification of towns, castles and churches.

GALLO-ROMAN ARCHITECTURE

Only a few buildings constructed by the Romans have withstood the test of time, although vestiges of the Gaulish period do still survive.

Excavations undertaken at **Drevant**, near St-Amand-Montrond, have established that a large Gallo-Roman centre developed on the site of a small Gaulish market town; a theatre, baths and a vast walled area which may have been a Gallo-Roman forum or temple have been uncovered here.

In **Limoges**, an amphitheatre was built on the northwest outskirts of the old town; however, it was razed to the ground in the 16C and its ruins are now hidden beneath the Jardin d'Orsay.

In Périgueux, traces have been discovered of the ancient **Vesunna**, capital of the Petrocorii. The finds include the Vesunna tower, the arena and the perimeter wall. The Puy d'Issolud near Vayrac is believed to be the site of the **Uxello-**

ST-LÉONARD-DE-NOBLAT – Church belltower (12C)

Belltower with 4 storeys of square design surmounted by 2 receding storeys on an octagonal plan; characteristic of Romanesque gabled belfries in Limousin.

Double window divided into two compartments by a slender **column**.

Octogonal stone spire

Blind arcading

Gable: the decorative, vertical triangular portion of the top of the tower, above the windows.

Belfry

Pilaster or **attached pier:** rectangular support projecting partially from a wall and treated architecturally as a column, with a base, shaft and capital.

Ogee moulding

Angle: projecting corner with a recessed rib formed by the meeting of two walls.

Twin bays: a set of two bays

Corbel Arch: spans an opening by having successive courses of masonry project farther inward (cantilever), thus relieving stress on the load-bearing wall.

R. Corbel/MICHELIN

BEAULIEU-SUR-DORDOGNE – East end (chevet) of St-Pierre (early 12C)

Lantern

Octagonal bell tower

Polygonal roof

Limousin Moulding: slender columns set in the embrasure of the bay.

Dosseret: a sort of pier without base or capitals which supports a column.

Engaged column: partly embedded in or bonded to the wall.

Modillion: a horizontal bracket or console; here the decorative scrolling recalls wood shavings.

Stringcourse moulding with **billets:** a series of cylinders disposed alternately with notches in rows.

Axial chapel or **Lady chapel**

Talus wall: the sloping face of the buttress.

Apsidal or **radiating chapel**

Plinth: visible projecting base of the wall.

R. Corbel/MICHELIN

dunum encampment – this was the last bastion of the Gauls in their resistance against the all-conquering Caesar. At Luzech, traces of the Impernal encampment which commanded a bend in the River Lot have been unearthed; the ruins of the Murcens oppidum have also been discovered near the Vers Valley.

ROMANESQUE ART AND RELIGIOUS ARCHITECTURE

In the Berry

Though characteristics of the Poitou School are widely represented across the region, most Romanesque churches in the Berry have a precise plan with certain features peculiar to the area: the chancel generally consists of two bays flanked by aisles which communicate with the choir through arches resting on columns adorned with historiated capitals; the apse is semicircular; the transept has a dome on squinches above the crossing and barrel vaulting above the arms; the nave is wider than the transept crossing and communicates with the arms of the transept by narrow passages known as **Berrichon** passages.

The abbey churches are based on the Benedictine design, for the Order of St-Benedict spread throughout Berry and built abbeys at **Fontgombault**, **Chezal-Benoît** and at **Châteaumeillant**, where the church of St-Genès has an unusual arrangement of the chevet with six parallel apsidal chapels.

Noirlac was created by the Cistercians, **Plaimpied** and **Puy-Ferrand** by the Augustinian Canons Regular. One church in the Bourges diocese is designed quite differently: the basilica of **Neuvy-St-Sépulcre** was built in the form of a rotunda and was inspired by the church of the Holy Sepulchre in Jerusalem.

The Limousin School

The Limousin School combines many of the characteristics of its neighbours: the Auvergne School, whose chief feature is the semi-barrel vaulting of the aisles or the galleries above the nave **Beaulieu-sur-Dordogne**); the Poitou School, whose influence can be seen in the collegiate church of **St-Pierre in Le Dorat** – a blind nave with broken-barrel

CARSAC-AILLAC – Vaulting in Saint-Caprais (12-16C)

Stellar vault (16C) covering the nave

Cell: a compartment formed by the ribs of a vault

Tierceron or **secondary rib:** emanates from a main springer or central boss and leads to the ridge-rib

Key-stone

Rib arch or **wall rib:** the side arch of a vault, also called an **arc formeret**

Arch band: a narrow elongated surface forming or connected to the arch

Impost: projecting bracket-like moulding atop a support (no capital)

Chancel entrance covered by a dome on pendentives

Oven-shaped vault over the apse

Pointed arch with a double row of **arch stones**

Pendant bracket: sculpted in the form of a **bust**

R. Corbel/MICHELIN

vaulting and aisles with groined vaulting; and the Périgord School – the domes on the church at **Solignac**.

Nevertheless, certain elements can be considered as purely Limousin. Firstly, the use of granite, which is found throughout the region and whose colour, while usually grey, sometimes verges on a golden tone.

Secondly, in the peculiar design of some belfries: the octagonal spire which crowns them is joined to the square tiers that form the base of the tower by one or two octagonal storeys; and the gables that stand on the upper square tiers are not only ornamental but play a part in the overall construction, since they divide and balance the weight of the upper octagonal tiers.

The best examples of this style are the **belfries** at **St-Léonard**, **Collonges**, **Uzerche** and **Brantôme** (in the Périgord). The belfry at **St-Junien** was probably planned to follow this pattern as the beginning of a steeply sloping gable can be seen above the second square tier.

Lastly, the façades present a more or less uniform style: massive belfry-porches adorned with blind arcades of various sizes and forms (**Le Dorat**, St-Junien); doorways with recessed elongated arcades on either side (St-Junien); a first storey flanked by bell turrets which are pierced at Le Dorat and encircled by a corbelled gallery at St-Junien; and doorways with twin doors framed by recessed covings, which in some cases are scalloped, showing the influence of Islamic art (Mozarabic style).

In the Dordogne

The plain, almost severe appearance of the area's many Romanesque churches was enhanced by the use of fine golden sandstone. The exteriors are startling for the extreme simplicity of their decoration: the doorways without tympana were embellished with recessed orders, and carved with rounded mouldings and festoons in a saw-tooth pattern. Inside, the churches are equally plain, with apsidal chapels opening off the chancel, which is usually flat. Only a few churches were built with side aisles; as a general rule the nave stands alone.

The originality of the **Périgord Romanesque** style is in its vaulting and dome. Some specialists believe that this shows eastern influence, others that it is a French invention.

The **dome** offers several advantages over cradle vaulting, which requires the use of powerful buttresses. The dome on pendentives allows the support of the weight of the vault to be divided between the side walls and the transverse arches of the nave. Often set over the transept crossing, the domes also vault the nave when they follow one after another in a series (such as at **St-Étienne-de-la-Cité**, **Périgueux**).

The nave is thus divided into several square bays vaulted with a dome on pendentives.

The pendentives serve as a transition from a square base to the circular dome. The cathedral of **St-Front in Périgueux** (see illustration: PÉRIGUEUX) is unique, with its five domes erected above a Greek-cross plan. However, some of the region's numerous Romanesque churches illustrate different designs: as an example, in **St-Privat-des-Prés** and **Cadouin** the naves have aisles with rounded and pointed barrel-vaulting. Some façades are adorned with rows of arcades; this reflects the influence of the Saintonge and Angoumois regions.

The neighbouring **Quercy** has a slightly different Romanesque style, characterised by richer sculptural embellishment (influence of the Moissac and Languedoc schools). Inspired by Byzantine art, illuminations and Antiquity, some of the carved doorways and tympana in this region are stunning: **Cahors**, **Carennac**, **Martel**, and **Collonges-La-Rouge**, on the border with the Limousin.

Decorative Arts

The **Abbaye de St-Martial**, **in Limoges**, with its many dependent priories, was the principal centre in the Limousin for the development of enamel, gold and silverwork. From the 10C onwards, the monks here produced shrines, episcopal rings and statues in gold and silver. The skill of the Limousin gold and silversmiths and their proven technique paved the way for the subsequent development of **enamelwork**.

Using methods practised from the 6C onwards by Byzantine enamellers, the Limousin workshops at first undertook cloisonné ware (in which the colours are kept apart by thin outline plates). But in the 12C they turned entirely to champlevé enamelware (in which a thick sheet of copper is hollowed out in certain areas and the cavities are filled in with enamel). Towards the end of the Romanesque period, colours became more subtle and often the cavities were filled with two or even four col-

CADOUIN – Ground plan of the abbey church (1119-1154)

This ground plan is characteristic of the Aquitaine school of ecclesiastical architecture with aisles flanking the nave and chancel on both sides, forming a Latin cross with short arms.

Transept arm, slightly protruding

Bay

Apsidal chapel

Doorway

Pillar flanked by engaged columns

Nave

Chevet: the east end of the church, outside; inside this end is called the apse

Aisle

Transept crossing, covered by a dome

R. Corbel/MICHELIN

12C champlevé enamel and gold jewel case
from Limoges depicting the assassination and the burial of St. Thomas Becket

©DeAgostini/World Illustrated/Photoshot

ours, placed one on top of the other. The folds of garments were rendered by the use of a highlight – white, light blue or yellow – around areas of dark blue and green.

Most of the work was inspired by the art of illuminators, by manuscripts, ivories and Byzantine and Oriental silks. From the beginning of the 12C, small enamelled figures were represented on a background of smooth gilded copper. From 1170 onwards this background was chiselled with decorative foliage motifs, with fantastic fauna intermingled with religious symbols. The compositions, although often naïve, show a very strong artistic sense. Of the many objects produced in this way, the most remarkable are the reliquary shrines of **Ambazac**, **Gimel** and **Bellac**. The municipal museums of **Limoges** and **Guéret** contain rich collections of enamelwork.

GOTHIC ART AND ARCHITECTURE

Religious architecture

The essential elements of Gothic art – quadripartite vaulting based on diagonal ribs and the systematic use of the pointed arch – underwent various regional modifications. Diagonal ribs revolutionised construction and archi-

tects became masters of the thrust and balance of a building. Through the use of pointed arches, piers and flying buttresses, they freed the inner space so that a church could be lofty and light, illuminated by stained-glass windows.

The Berry

The most important Gothic building in the region, recognised worldwide as an architectural masterpiece inscribed on UNESCO's World Heritage List, is **Bourges Cathedral**. It bears no resemblance to any of the other great cathedrals of France; its high nave covered with sexpartite vaulting, its double side aisles which extend round the chancel and the absence of a transept make it unique.

The Limousin

The simultaneous influences of the Languedoc School (southern Gothic) and the schools of northern France were in play in the region. The passion for building in the 13C and 14C is illustrated in the **cathedral of St-Étienne** and the churches of **St-Pierre-du-Queyroix** and **St-Michel-des-Lions at Limoges**, in the nave of the church of **St-Martin at Brive**, the collegiate church at **St-Yrieix**, and the belfry-porch of **Tulle Cathedral**.

The Dordogne

Sarlat Cathedral is an example of the influence of both southern and northern Gothic styles: the nave has wide side aisles and soaring flying buttresses typical of the north, whereas the side chapel shows southern influence. Another commonly found aspect of the Languedoc School is the nave's shape, almost as wide as it is high, with side chapels but no aisles (**Gourdon**, **Martel**, **Montpezat-du-Quercy** and **St-Cirq-Lapopie**). In the Berry, Limousin and Dordogne, many **monasteries** were built during this period, although few have emerged intact from the ravages of time. In **Cadouin** and **Cahors**, there are still cloisters built in the Flamboyant style, and in **Périgueux** the cloisters were built between the 12C and the 16C.

During the 13C-14C, **fortified churches** were built in the region in response to unrest, in particular during the Hundred Years War. The sanctuaries provided villagers with a safe place of refuge from marauders and the churches and abbeys were like fortified castles in appearance, with crenellations, watch-paths, and sometimes even protective moats.

Sculpture and painting
The Berry

Art in stained glass reached its climax in Bourges with the completion in the 13C of a remarkable series of windows.

Around the middle of the 14C, under the guidance of Duke Jean de Berry, the Berry developed into a great intellectual and artistic centre. As an example, the stained-glass window known as the *Grand Housteau* in the cathedral at Bourges was a gift from the duke.

The duke assembled excellent artists but most of the masterpieces created in the studios and workshops in Bourges have unfortunately disappeared: only a few fragments of Berry's tomb remain in the cathedral crypt (originally placed in the **Sainte-Chapelle in Bourges**, since demolished). The greater part of the statuary, however, dates from this period and has survived. At **Issoudun**, in the chapel of the former **Hôtel-Dieu**, there is a fine carved Tree of Jesse.

The Limousin

In **Limoges**, two tombs executed in the purest 14C style can still be seen in the ambulatory around the chancel in the cathedral of St-Étienne; the village of **Reygade** in the Corrèze possesses an Entombment dating from the 15C which resembles the one at Carennac; and the church at **Eymoutiers** is ornamented with interesting 15C stained glass.

Limousin enamelwork which flourished in the Romanesque period was transformed in the 15C with the appearance of painted enamels produced under the direction of such famous mastercraftsmen as Monvaerni and Nardon Pénicaud.

The Dordogne

From the second half of the 13C until the 15C, several remarkable works were produced: the tomb of St Stephen at **Aubazine**, a magnificent shrine carved in limestone in the second half of the 13C; the Entombment (15C) at **Carennac**; the tomb of the Cardaillacs at **Espagnac-Ste-Eulalie**; and the recumbent figures of Cardinal Pierre des Prés and his nephew Jean in the church at **Montpezat-du-Quercy**.

Frescoes, mural paintings produced with water-based paint on fresh plaster (a technique which allows the colours to sink in), were used to decorate many chapels and churches. The west dome of **Cahors Cathedral** is entirely covered with 14C frescoes. Naïve 14C and 15C polychrome statuary and certain frescoes give a good idea of how peasants and nobility dressed at the time. In **Rocamadour**, the interiors of chapels are painted, with further embellishment on the façades.

CIVIL AND MILITARY ARCHITECTURE

A few Gothic residences remain in the region, the most noteworthy example of which is the **Palais Jacques Cœur** in **Bourges**, one of the finest Gothic palaces in Europe. Built on the vestiges of a Gallo-Roman wall, the building is a combination of massive, forbidding towers and a lively, sculpted façade.

Villefranche-de-Lonchat Vergt
Ste-Foy-la-Grande
Bergerac Lalinde
La Bastide
Puyguilhem Molières
Fonroque Roquépine Beaumont-du-Périgord
Eymet Monpazier
Castillonnès Villeréal Villefranche-du-Périgord
Montcabrier
N

Sarlat-la-Canéda
Bretenoux
Domme
Rudelle
Labastide-Murat
Cahors
Vézère
Dordogne
Drupt
GARONNE
Lot

BASTIDES OF PERIGORD AND QUERCY

| Domme | : | French foundation |
| *Montpazier* | : | English foundation |

Castelnau-Montratier
Beauregard
Lauzerte
Puylaroque

Inside, the architecture seems to hint at the approaching Renaissance in its graceful lines and fanciful motifs.

BASTIDES

These new, fortified towns (in the *Oc* language: *bastidas*) appeared in the 13C; their fortified aspect was further developed during the course of the following century.

Foundation

The principal founders of *bastides* were Alphonse de Poitiers (1249-71), count of Toulouse and brother to St Louis, and, from 1272 on, seneschal lords under Philip the Bold, Philip the Fair and King Edward I of England, who also held the title of duke of Aquitaine.

Development

Their construction satisfied economic, military and political needs, with founders taking advantage of the growth of the population and encouraging people to settle on their land, in turn rationalising its use and cultivation. In return, inhabitants were granted a charter, guaranteed protection, exempted from military service and given the right to inherit. The bailiff represented the king, dispensed justice and collected taxes, whereas the consuls, elected by the people, administered the town; towns flourished under this system. After the Albigensian Crusade, when the count of Toulouse, Raymond VII, built about 40 *bastides*, and with the outbreak of hostilities between the French and the English over the Périgord, Quercy and the Agenais, the political and military advantages of the *bastides* were confirmed. Alphonse de Poitiers built **Eymet**, **Catillonès** and **Villeréal** along the River Dropt as well as **Villefranche-du-Périgord** and **Ste-Foy-la-Grande**. The king of England responded with the construction of **Beaumont**, **Molières**, **Lalinde** and **Monpazier**, while in 1281 Philip the Bold founded Domme.

All of the *bastides*, French and English, were built to the same plan – a square or rectangle – and yet they differed because of the terrain, the type of site, the potential for population growth, and their defensive plan. Occasionally, the *bastide* was built around a pre-existing building such as a fortified church (Beaumont) or a castle.

The design of Monpazier is most characteristic: it is built according to a quadrilateral plan with straight streets crossed at right angles by alleys known as **carreyrous**; narrow spaces, **androns**, stand between the houses and serve as fire breaks, drains or even latrines. In the centre of town, the main square is surrounded by covered arcades or **cou-**

Architecture of the bastides

DOMME – Porte des Tours (late 13C)

In the 13C, the new towns known as bastides, often fortified, became common in Périgord and Quercy. This was the most important defensive gateway in the ramparts of Domme.

Crown of the tower, raised and fitted with loop-holes in the 14C

Two **circular towers**

Gable-wall

Curtain wall: an enclosing wall between two towers or bastions

Bartizan: a small overhanging turret with lookout holes and defensive loops

Balistraria: a cruciform loophole through which a crossbow could be fired.

Fortified gate: protected by two portcullis and a deadfall

Bossage: projecting, rough-finished stone; until the 15C, used only in military architecture

Arrow-loop

Moat (filled in)

R. Corbel/MICHELIN

MONPAZIER – Central square in the bastide (late 13C and 14C)

The most typical and best preserved of the Périgord bastides, it is designed around a central rectangular area, bordered by a covered market on the southern side.

The church in a bastide is generally placed near the central square

Spire: the pitch on the lower section is different

Andron: (regional term) narrow passage for fire protection, used as a sewer

Arcade or **cornière**

Covered market (timber)

Basket arch

Gothic house (13C): Originally, all of the residential buildings in the bastide were the same size

In the corner, an **opening** provides access to the square

Couverts: covered galleries

Footstall: the plinth or base of a wooden post, protecting it from ground water

R. Corbel/MICHELIN

verts (also known as **cornières**). The covered market or **halle,** also stands in this square. The church and the cemetery stand nearby, and the outer walls are punctuated with towers and gateways. The best-preserved *bastides* are today found in **Monpazier**, **Domme** and **Eymet**.

THE BERRY AND LIMOUSIN

The fortresses of **Turenne**, **Merle**, **Ventadour**, **Châlus**, **Montbrun** and **Chalusset** all existed in the Limousin in the 13C. The ruins of **Crozant** overlooking the valley of the Creuse evoke what was once the powerful stronghold of the counts of Marche.

Numerous castles were built in the Berry during the Middle Ages: on Henry II's accession to the throne of England in 1154, the English controlled Aquitaine and threatened the neighbouring Berry. The local lords therefore improved the fortification of their castles to resist the enemy. The **Château de Culan**, taken by Philip Augustus in 1188, was rebuilt in the 13C but retained its severity of appearance emphasised by its three round towers topped by a wooden hoarding. **Ainay-le-Vieil** is protected by its perimeter wall with nine towers, while Meillant still possesses its seven haughty feudal towers.

THE DORDOGNE

There are few traces left of the civil architecture of the Romanesque period. The feudal fortresses erected in the 10C and 11C were greatly altered in later centuries and can scarcely be said to have withstood the warfare and destruction of the times. The only remaining buildings of this period are the square keeps – the last refuge of the defensive system. **Castelnau-Bretenoux** in the Quercy, with its strongly fortified keep, is a good example of feudal construction built on a hilltop site.

In the Périgord, parts of the castles of **Biron** and **Beynac**, **Bourdeilles**, **Commarque** and **Castelnaud** date back to the Romanesque period.

Public building and civil engineering

FIGEAC – Hôtel de la monnaie (late 13C)

Probably a market place for money-changers, the "Oustal de lo Monédo" is representative of the urban architecture of Haut Quercy built during the Gothic period.

Relieving or discharging arch: an arch built over a lintel to relieve or distribute the weight of the load-bearing walls

Solellho: (regional term) open attic space used for drying laundry or storing wood, etc.

Chimney stack: (the part of a chimney which projects above a roof) the stack is one of the distinctive features of Figeac's architecture

Quatrefoil: a circular design made up of four converging arcs

Double window divided into two compartements by a slender column

Cornice

Mezzanine: small square windows light the upper part of a high-ceilinged room

Arcade of Gothic arches: this is typically found in commercial buildings in Quercy

Oculus: a circular bay

R. Corbel/MICHELIN

75

Military and Civil Architecture

Château de MONTBRUN (12C and 15C)

Machicolation: an overhanging defensive structure with floor opening for dropping boiling oil, missiles, etc on attackers

Corbelling supporting an overhanging **hoarding** (wooden gallery)

Stair turret built around a spiral staircase

Square keep

Merlons separated by crenels

Batter slope: the inclined plane on the outer surface of the wall

Curtain wall: an enclosing wall between two towers

Gun-loop: a slit or hole for firearms

Arrow-loop: a slit through which bowmen fired

R.Corbel/MICHELIN

Château de MEILLANT – Western side (early 14C)

End-ornament: a decorated upper part of a buttress, a gable, etc.

Imperial roof

Lantern

Hip knob: a pointed finial or other ornament in ceramic or metal

Crockets

Dormer window

Gable: a triangular-shaped ornamental piece above a door or window

Flamboyant-style open-work railing

Mullion windows: the mullions are the vertical parts of the tracery, separating and supporting the window

Interlacings in a heart-shaped pattern

R.Corbel/MICHELIN

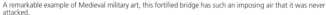

CAHORS – Pont Valentré (14C)

A remarkable example of Medieval military art, this fortified bridge has such an imposing air that it was never attacked.

Rectangular tower (length greater than width)

Trefoil arch

Mantelet: a movable cover protecting a crenel

Bartizan

Square tower

Straight-stair: a steep stairway built against a fortification

Cut-water: the angular edge reinforcing the pier, facing upstream

Chatelet controlling the bridgehead

Arch

Abutment: end support of mansonry that relieves the thrust of the arches

Crenelation

Deck

R. Corbel/MICHELIN

Many of the castles in the Périgord and Quercy were constructed during the Gothic period, as is visible in their architectural detail; examples of these are at **Bourdeilles**, **Beynac-et-Cazenac**, **Castelnaud** and **Castelnau-Bretenoux**. **Bonaguil** is unique in that although it was built at the end of the 15C and in the early part of the 16C, it has all the features of a medieval fortress.

A considerable boom in **town** building occurred after the Hundred Years War with Sarlat, Périgueux, Bergerac, Cahors, Figeac, Gourdon and Martel all benefiting from this. The façades of town houses were decorated with large pointed arches on the ground floor (where small shops were set up), flattened arches or rose windows adorned the upper floors, with turrets crowning the roof. Among the finest examples of this period, note the Hôtel de la Raymondie in **Martel**, the Hôtel de la Monnaie in **Figeac**, the Hôtel Plamon in **Sarlat** and the famous Pont Valentré in **Cahors**.

THE RENAISSANCE

At the beginning of the 16C the artistic movement in France was revitalised by the influence of Italy. King François I and the aristocracy were moved by the desire to copy Italian architecture and sculpture and introduced new styles by employing Italian artists. In the space of a century, hundreds of châteaux were built or restored, as financial resources boomed with the end of the Hundred Years War.

Other factors encouraging this artistic movement in the region included improved returns on farm estates (thanks to the development of sharecropping), increased freedom of trade, the mining of iron ore, low labour costs and the advent of ready credit.

ARCHITECTURE

The Berry

At least half of the châteaux in the Berry were rebuilt in the years between 1430 and 1550, and most of the urban centres were transformed. Yet it took a long time for the Italian influence to be felt in the Berry where Gothic art was so strongly implanted. Generally, the Italian styles were interpreted, rather than copied. In **Bourges**, which was ravaged by fire in 1487, the most notable examples of Renaissance architecture are the Hôtel Lallemant, the Hôtel Cujas and the Hôtel des Échevins. In the countryside, **defensive castles** became more comfortable residences, as was the case with Ainay-le-Vieil, Meillant, La Verrerie and Villegongis.

The Limousin

In Limoges, the Renaissance influence can be seen on the St John's doorway (Portail St-Jean) – the monumental entrance to the cathedral. In Tulle, the Maison de Loyac is a manor house dating from the 16C. Châteaux which were built or transformed in what is considered a transitional style include those at **Rochechouart**, **Coussac-Bonneval**, **Pompadour** and **Sédières**.

The Dordogne

The new style flourished in **Montal** and **Puyguilhem**, which are similar in appearance to the châteaux of the Loire Valley. Most of the other 16C châteaux incorporate significant defensive features besides the windows, dormers, chimneys and other purely Renaissance elements; this is particularly evident in **Monbazillac**. In **Cénevières**, **Bourdeilles**, **Languais**, **Les Bories** and **Rouffignac** (church), buildings were partially transformed; the **Château de Biron** is graced by a marvellous Renaissance chapel.

Civil architecture was also influenced by the Italian style, as witnessed in the Maison de Roaldès in **Cahors**, the Maison Cayla (or Maison des Consuls) in **Périgueux**, the Hôtel de Maleville in **Sarlat**, and the Hôtel Labenche in **Brive**.

SCULPTURE AND OTHER ARTS

The Berry and the Limousin

In the **Marche**, **tapestry-making** developed rapidly. Throughout the 16C the **Aubusson**, **Bourganeuf** and **Felletin** workshops profited from the growing demand for tapestries and hangings as part of contemporary furnishings.

Aubusson and Felletin continued to take pride in making tapestries and even as late as the Revolution produced *verdures* (greeneries) in which plants and fantastic animals appeared against a background of foliage.

Sculpture can be best admired in the cathedral in Limoges, where the magnificent rood screen, erected between 1533 and 1535, and the tomb of Jean de Langeac, are considered outstanding works of art.

Following the exceptional developments of the 12C to 14C, Limousin enamelwork found new favour in the 15C-16C through the Pénicaud, Nouailher and Limosin families. Léonard Limosin reached new artistic heights through the use of innovative techniques.

In **Bourges**, the art of making stained-glass windows was revived through the work of the artist Lescuyer.

The Dordogne

The inner court of the **Château de Montal** is an outstanding example of the Italian style, with its busts in high relief – superb works of art which are both realistic and refined. Inside, the remarkable staircase rivals those of the Loire Valley châteaux. In the chapel at **Biron**, the recumbent figures of the Gontaut-Biron family are decorated with figures influenced by the Italian Quattrocento (15C).

FROM THE 17C TO THE 20C

By copying the styles of Paris and Versailles, art lost all its regional character in the 17C.

In the Berry, **François le Vau** - brother of the architect who designed the Louvre, Vaux and Versailles - planned the Château de Lignières in the style of the *Grand Siècle*: the frontons are supported by pilasters, and the main buildings are reflected in sheets of water, with French-style gardens extending beyond.

The **Château de Hautefort**, on the border of the Limousin and Périgord, is a very good example of Classical architecture in its planning and unity of design; although it was ravaged by fire in 1968, it has since been completely restored. The **Château de Rastignac** was built at the end of the 18C: the purity of its lines and the harmony of its proportions place it among the most interesting buildings of that period.

In architecture, the 19C was largely devoted to the restoration and renovation of old buildings. Painting and tapestry, however, saw the introduction of numerous innovations. **Auguste Renoir** and **Suzanne Valadon** both heralded from the Limousin, although both left the province at a young age. Corot, on the other hand, was born in Paris and came to the region often to paint. His student, **Berthe Morisot**, a native of Bourges, was influenced by Renoir and Manet. **Claude Monet** was inspired by the ruins at Crozant, and painted 30 versions of the site in 1889. **Ingres** and **Bourdelle**, both from Montauban, are considered the most eminent representatives of the Quercy from this period.

The art of tapestry-making was revived in the 20C thanks to the new ideas and techniques introduced by **Lurçat**, **Dufy**, **Marc Saint-Saëns**, **Gromaire** and the Association of Tapestry Cartoon-Painters. Modern art is now displayed in many regional and municipal museums as well as at the Centre National d'Art et du Paysage at the Lac de Vassivière.

TRADITIONAL RURAL ARCHITECTURE
THE BERRY

Limestone, sandstone and cob are the traditional building materials of the Berry countryside, yet distinctive differences in style exist between one area and the next. For example, in the **Champagne Berrichonne**, large farm buildings are set around a courtyard. The low roof is covered in flat, brown tiles (or slate closer to the Loire); inside, where a big communal room is heated by a stone chimney, the floor is also tiled. The farms of the **Pays Fort** are more modest, with walls made from cob (clay and straw). Thatched roofs have gradually been replaced with tiles, with the extension of the eaves protecting the walls from wet weather. Around **Sancerre**, farms have a long façade of white limestone crowned with a roof punctuated with dormer windows; the living area is often flanked by a barn or stable. Other types of houses are found near the **Sologne** region and in **La Brenne**. Some features, however, are shared by all; these include ceramic finials, weathercocks or other ornaments placed on the ridge of the roof or at the apex of a gable, and plain interior furnishings.

THE LIMOUSIN

Most of the houses in the Limousin countryside date from the 19C and are made of local granite. In the area known as the **Montagne**, the low-built dwellings are attached to the barn and stable. The double-sloped roofs used to be predominantly thatch, but have been mostly replaced by slate. Many houses have lean-to additions next to the garden or orchard, and in the past each farm had its own well or spring.

In the **Xaintrie**, the barn dwellings are often built into a hillside and the rough-cast walls are biscuit-coloured. In the south of the area, half-timbering appears, along with upper storeys in the form of wooden terraces protected by overhanging *lauze* roofs.

The granite houses of the **Haute-Marche** are usually built with a door and a small window on the ground floor, two small windows on the floor above, and an attic used for storing grain on top.

In the **Bas-Pays Corrézien**, the ground floor is used for storage, whereas the dwelling rooms are located above. The sandstone houses are covered with a four-sided sloping roof; an outer stairway links the two storeys by way of a landing and the cellar entrance is at the bottom of the steps.

Higher up on the **plateau**, the box-shaped buildings in blue or ochre granite have small windows and round-tiled roofs. In addition to the stables, where the hay is stored above the animals, many farms have a special room for drying chestnuts, or a dovecot. Every farm is served by its own well.

THE DORDOGNE

The most typical type of house found in the **Périgord Noir** is a sturdy, block-like construction in golden limestone, topped with a steeply pitched roof covered with flat, brown tiles or *lauzes*. The *lauzes* are neither slate nor layered schist tiles, but small limestone slabs. Set horizontally, their weight is such (500kg per m^2/about 102lb per sq ft) that they require a strong, steeply pitched timberwork roof to distribute the weight. Towers or dovecots adjoin the houses of larger houses.

In the **Périgord Blanc**, low houses in grey or white limestone are lit through windows topped with bull's-eyes (*œils-de-bœuf*). The flat roof covered with Roman-style terracotta tiles already reflects the more southern style.

In the forested area known as the Double, houses were traditionally built of cob and half-timbering.

In the vineyards of **Bergerac**, the houses of wine-growers are understandably organised around the activities of pressing grapes and making wine; generally they form a U shape or else have two adjoining courtyards. The tumble-down cottages in the surrounding vineyards are used as dwellings for labourers etc. The houses of the **Quercy** are built in blocks of white limestone mortared in lime, and display a range of shapes, additions, towers and windows. The lower level is partly below ground and called the *cave*; it was here that the stable, shed and storerooms were traditionally located. The floor above was reserved for the living quarters; the two levels are connected by an outside staircase above a terrace protected by a porch supported by stone or wood columns.

Dovecots

The region is dotted with numerous dovecots, many of which are particularly elegant. Some are no more than small towers attached to the main building; others stand alone, either resting on a porch or supported by columns. Before the French Revolution, the right to keep pigeons was generally reserved for large landowners, although the Quercy and Périgord (where the right could be purchased for a fee) were exceptions. Dovecots were built mainly for collecting pigeon droppings – the value of these droppings is evident in the fact that when a property was divided up after a death, they were shared out between heirs in the same way as the livestock. Not only was it excellent manure, but it was also prized by bakers (for the aroma it gave their bread) and by pharmacists as a relief for goitre – the swelling of the thyroid gland – among other conditions. The appearance of chemical fertilisers after 1850 led to a decline in production.

The oldest types of free-standing dovecots were arcaded (so-called hanging dovecots), built on small columns to protect them from the damp. The stubby capitals (*capels*) created overhangs to deter would-be predators from climbing up the columns.

Drystone Huts

These small constructions are dotted around the region, and can be found either standing in isolation in a field or, more rarely, grouped together (💰*see SARLAT: Cabanes de Breuil*). They are built entirely of dry stones and crowned with conical roofs of stones supported by joggles (notches in each new layer are fitted into notches of the layer below to stop the roof from slipping, and the whole roof is fixed at the top by a sort of keystone). They are known as *gariottes*, *caselles* or *bories*, but it is not known precisely what their function used to be, nor exactly when they were built. Today's farmers may speculate about the mysterious origins of these surprisingly solid huts; meanwhile, they are happy to use them as tool sheds and storage space and proudly show them off to visitors.

Food and Drink

CUISINE
THE BERRY

The **cuisine** of the Berry is plain and simple and makes full use of farm produce. While vegetable, salt pork or bread soup blended with a little cream combine to produce the typical regional soup known as *mique*, the true Berry speciality is *poulet en barbouille*. This chicken dish is flambéed with brandy, cut into pieces and cooked with a blended sauce of blood and cream, an egg yolk and chopped liver. Dishes featuring a wine or cream sauce appear frequently on the tables of the Berry.

Also look out for traditional staples such as pumpkin pâté, *truffiat* (potatoes covered in pastry), stuffed rabbit, eggs in wine, ox-tongue au gratin, kidneys, calf's liver, game and fish, often garnished with fresh mushrooms. For dessert, try specialities such as plum flan, *sanciaux* (honey fritters) and *millats* (stewed black cherries).

THE LIMOUSIN

The hearty **cuisine** of the Limousin is typified by the traditional dish known as *bréjaude*, a pork rind and cabbage soup garnished with rye bread.

Patés made from truffles or wrapped in pastry and garnished with a mixed veal and pork stuffing (especially the pâté de foies gras from Brive-la-Gaillarde), are deservedly famous.

Although the region is most renowned for its excellent beef, other delicious local dishes includes *lièvre en chabessal*, a dish made from hare stuffed with fresh pork and ham, and seasoned with salt, pepper, spices and condiments. Cabbage is a traditional Limousin ingredient and is served with partridge, in heart-warming *potées* (country stews) or braised with chestnuts. For a long time, chestnuts (*châtaignes*) were a staple of the farmer's diet, and can still be found garnishing turkey, goose, black pudding, veal and pork stew, or served as a purée with venison. Perhaps the dish most closely associated with Limousin is clafoutis, a creamy flan with cherries.

Truffe

S. Sauvignier/MICHELIN

THE PÉRIGORD AND QUERCY

Cuisine in the Dordogne (which the French invariably refer to as the Périgord when speaking of gastronomy) is one of France's culinary jewels. For centuries, the region has been synonymous with delicacies such as truffles, foie gras and confits. Sit down to a traditional meal here and you may never want to eat any other way again: perhaps start with *tourain blanchi* – a white soup made from garlic, goose fat and eggs, sometimes with sorrel or tomato added; next comes the foie gras or pâté de foie (a general term for liver pâté); the third course might perhaps be a delicious omelette made with cèpes (wild mushrooms) or delicately sliced truffles. For the main course, enjoy *confit d'oie aux pommes sarladaises* (goose preserved in its own fat, fried until brown, with potatoes fried in goose fat and garlic, and garnished with mushrooms). A refreshing salad drizzled in a light walnut oil dressing is then followed by the cheese platter. To round things off, why not indulge in a slice of walnut cake or plum pie?

The **truffe** (truffle) is the elegant name of a knobby, black fungus which weighs about 100g/3.5oz, and imbues all it touches with its unique aroma. A truffle must be fresh or very carefully preserved and their rarity and price make them a gourmet luxury. It is found in delicate black specks in foie gras, pâté, poultry dishes, *ballotines* (white turkey meat and liver moulded in aspic) and *galantines* (cold cuts); it is also sliced thinly into salads and omelettes. A truffle wrapped and cooked whole over an open fire – *à la cendre* – is a supreme extravagance.

FOIE GRAS

Foie gras is certainly the pride of the Périgord. Once their feathers have grown in (after approximately 1 month), ducks and geese are put outdoors.

To prepare for force-feeding, they are nourished with grains and alfalfa, which help expand the digestive system. After three months in the open air, the birds are placed in individual cages for 15-18 days. Progressively over-fed, they are given ground meal then whole corn with a funnel-like feeding device known as the *gaveuse*. A duck thus absorbs 10-15kg/22-33lb, a goose up to 20kg/44lb of corn, tripling or even quadrupling the weight of its liver to achieve an ideal weight: 450-500g/1lb for a duck; 800-900g/2lb for a goose.

Foies gras can be preserved with excellent results, and are labelled according to content; read the label or menu carefully to know what you are getting.

Foie gras entier is sliced from a whole liver, the nerve fibres removed, seasoned and sterilised (*mi-cuit* livers must be kept refrigerated and eaten fresh).

A **bloc de foie gras** is reconstituted, made from bits of liver chopped and mixed at high speed and emulsified with water. Other forms of foie gras are *parfait* (75% liver), *mousse, pâté, médaillon* and *galantine* (50% liver). Foie gras should be served chilled (allow 50grams/2oz per person), and cut with a knife rinsed in hot water.

Enjoy a glass of cool, sweet Monbazillac wine with your foie gras.

CONFITS

Confits are the traditional base of the region's cuisine. Confit was first used as a method of preserving various parts of the goose, before the advent of the freezer. Now regarded as a gourmet dish, it is still prepared using traditional methods. The pieces of goose are cooked in their own fat for 3hr and then preserved in large earthenware pots (*tupins*).

This procedure is also used to preserve duck, turkey and pork (pork confit is called *enchaud*). Goose grease is used instead of butter in local cooking, for example in *pommes de terre sarladaises*.

STUFFINGS AND SAUCES

Stuffings and sauces, often comprising liver and truffles, are used frequently to garnish poultry, game, suckling pigs and in a favourite regional dish – *cou d'oie farci* – stuffed goose neck.

The most commonly used sauces are the *rouilleuse*, which is used to give colour and to accompany poultry fricassee, and *sauce Périgueux*, a Madeira sauce made from a base of chicken stock, to which fresh truffles are added.

WINE
APPELATIONS

French wines are classified according to a system which provides a rough guide to price and quality, although there is plenty of room for overlapping, especially where small growers are concerned. The lowest category is simply labelled **Vin de table**. Such wines may have been elaborated using any variety of grape from any country in the EU (although this must be stated on the label). While generally to be avoided in shops and restaurants, you may buy satisfactory table wine from a local producer or cooperative (bring your own container). Next comes the **Vin de Pays**, which bears a label identifying the place of origin and possibly the grape variety (if not a blend) and the year. The category following is the **VDQS**, *Vin Délimité de Qualité Supérieure*, which also shows place of origin and may show variety and year. The superiority comes from the fact that the grape varieties are approved and the district of production clearly defined; in addition, these wines pass a yearly taste test to confirm their quality.

The top 20% of French wines are labelled **Appellation d'Origine Contrôlée** (abbreviated AOC or simply AC). These wines come from designated vineyards, use approved grape varieties and are vinified in a manner specific to each one. The system is controlled by the Institut National des Appellations d'Origine, and it is a serious business indeed. The AOC label is a reward for years of continuous merit and lobbying. Similar systems are now being used for other produce.

THE REGIONS

The renown and popularity of **wines** from the region date way back to the Middle Ages. **Cahors** wine was transported by barges (*gabares*) to Bordeaux and from there by ship to the capitals of Europe. A deep-red colour, with a robust flavour to match, Cahors accompanies hearty foods including game, roast meats and strong-flavoured cheese. The bouquet only achieves subtlety and loses its rather harsh presence on the tongue after ageing two to three years in the cask and another dozen in the bottle.

The vineyards of **Bergerac**, largely planted with Sauvignon grapes, produce reds as well as whites. Among the latter, **Monbazillac** holds pride of place. Golden and smooth, and with a heady aroma, this syrupy wine is served as an aperitif, with foie gras or with dessert. Like other sweet, highly alcoholic wines (notably Sauternes), Monbazillac depends on the effects of the noble mould (*Botrytis cinerea*), a highly beneficent mould which forms on the skins of the ripening grapes, bringing about a concentration of sugar and flavour and a vast improvement in the quality of the resulting wine, without imparting any trace of this on the palate. The process has been employed since the Renaissance. The grapes are harvested in several batches as they reach the desired state. Monbazillac develops its full flavour after two to three years and will keep for up to 30 years.

Dry white wines such as **Montravel** and Bergerac, vigorous and fruity, go well with seafood and fish; sweeter wines like **Côtes de Bergerac**, **Côtes de Montravel**, **Rosette** and **Saussignac** are good as aperitif wines or with white meats. Red Bergerac wines are firm, with a fruity bouquet, and can be enjoyed soon after bottling. **Pécharmant** is fuller-bodied, more complex, and must be left to mature before its charms can be fully appreciated.

Wines from the Berry are generally clean and crisp and of good quality. Sancerre is a well-known appellation known more readily for its white wines, although red and rosé are also produced here. Many small growers are scattered around outlying villages, with some of the best wines produced in **Bué**, **Chavignol**, **Ménétréol** and **Fontenay** - the expressive characteristics of these wines are best enjoyed young. A good companion for local dishes and cheeses is **Ménétou-Salon**, a quality wine produced in limited quantities which is hard to come across elsewhere. Grown in the same chalky soil as Sancerre, many find it to be fuller and more rounded than its illustrative neighbour.

Sancerre

The wines of Sancerre are commonly classified as Eastern Loire Valley wines. The upper reaches of the Loire are mostly planted with the Sauvignon Blanc grape, which produces two of the finest wines in France: **Sancerre** and **Pouilly-Fumé**. These wines are produced within 8km/5mi of each other, on different sides of the river, and yet their taste is, to the connoisseur, leagues apart. Mostly white wines are produced; the term fumé is in reference to the smoky bloom that forms on the skin of the fruit rather than to the resulting flavour. Sancerre is reputed for its full, round finish, whereas Pouilly-Fumé is considered a more complex, flowery wine.

In addition to these famous labels, some of the other wines in the region are delightful discoveries for the traveller. Certain wines, produced in small quantity and difficult to find outside

Sancerre wine with local cheese

S. Sauvignier/MICHELIN

the region, make for a memorable and unique experience. It is worth a visit to the wine-growers of Bué, Chavignol, Ménétréol and Fontenay to savour the regional savoir-faire.

Mostly white, but also some rosé and red AOC wines are produced in the villages of **Ménétou-Salon**, **Quincy**, and **Reuilly**. Reds and rosés are drawn from Sauvignon Blanc, Pinot Noir, Pinot Gris and Meunier grapes.

Sancerre is a beautiful wine town, surrounded by hillside vineyards which sweep away from the town like striped skirts on a lovely lady. The signposted wine route meanders around back roads and through the village of Chavignol, famous for its crottin de Chavignol goat's milk cheese. The Sancerrois is not a very big region, but visitors will have plenty of temptation to stop and sample local wines and cheeses and to enjoy a slower pace of life.

Bergerac

Another leading wine-producing centre in the region covered in this guide is Bergerac, which has 12 different types of AOC wines. There is a well-marked wine route around the vineyards (information at the Maison des Vins, Cloître de Récollets, in Bergerac). The varieties grown are Cabernet Franc, Cabernet Sauvignon, Merlot, Cot, Semillon and Sauvignon Blanc. Bergerac, Côtes de Bergerac and Pécharmant are strong red wines; the rosés are less enticing, and the white wines are sweet (moëlleux) or if dry, bottled under a separate AOC, **Bergerac Sec. Ambrosial Monbazillac** white wines, very sweet, are often served with foie gras. The flavour is similar to Sauternes, and the wine keeps for about four years, although a good year may age better. Rosette is a less sweet white wine produced in small quantity and not found elsewhere; enjoy it as an apéritif wine. Montravel vineyards are in the Dordogne, but also on the far edge of Bordeaux territory. The white wines (from dry to sweet) are bottled as Montravel; reds are sold as Bergerac.

🏛 **Maison des vins de Bergerac**
Quai Salvette, 1, Rue des Récollets
24104 Bergerac Cedex.
☎ 05 53 63 57 57.
www.vins-bergerac.fr.
Wine tasting, tour of selected vineyards and cellars.

🏛 **Cave coopérative de Monbazillac**
Route de Mont-de-Marsan,
24240 Monbazillac.
☎ 05 53 63 65 00. www.chateau-monbazillac.com. Wine tasting.

Cahors

The deep-red wines of Cahors are made from Malbec, Merlot and Jurançon grapes, grown in ruddy soil scattered with limestone pebbles. Start a tour of the regional vineyard right at the famous Pont de Valentré across the River Lot. From here you can go to Pradines and Douelle, where wine was once loaded onto flat-bottomed boats for transportation. The wine road is a beautiful route through the countryside and along the river; many of the vineyards have been producing wine for centuries. During the Roman occupation, the Emperor Dolmitian ordered the vines uprooted as punishment for an uprising, thus temporarily (for 200

Bergerac vineyards

0   20 km

CÔTES DE MONTRAVEL

ROSETTE   BERGERAC

PÉCHARMANT

MONTRAVEL   Bergerac

SAUSSIGNAC   MONBAZILLAC

BERGERAC

N

Red wine   White wine   Red and white wine

years) halting production, which is now back in full swing. The AOC label was awarded to regional wines in 1971.

To earn the name **Cahors**, the hearty red wines must have at least 70% Malbec, and at most 20% Merlot and Tannot; the remaining 10% is Jurançon. While they are known for their dark colour bordering on black, and their robust and tannic flavour, Cahors wines are evolving to suit modern tastes and now more subtle vintages are coming to light. Labelled vieux (old), it has aged three years or more in a wooden cask.

Locally made Coteaux de Quercy, red and rosé wines from the Lot Valley, are Vins de Pays.

Union interprofessionnelle du vin de Cahors
430 avenue Jean-Jaurès, BP 61 46000 Cahors. ☎05 65 23 22 24. www.vindecahors.fr. Publishes a booklet listing winegrowers' addresses (also available from local tourist offices) but does not sell wine.

Les Vignerons du Query -Cave Coopérative
82270 Montpezat-de-Quercy. 05 63 02 03 50. www.montpezat-de-quercy.fr. Wine tasting and sales throughout the year. Guided tours for groups by appointment.

Nature

LAND DIVISION

The *région* (there are 22 in France) is the largest administrative division in the country, followed by the *département* (96, excluding overseas territories), which is sub-divided into communes run by an elected mayor. In total, there are 36 394 mayoral districts in France.

Berry (formerly Berri) is the name historically and popularly applied to the area south of the Paris basin, comprising the *départements* of Cher and Indre in the Centre *région*. This old county, later a duchy, came under the crown in the 13C.

Limousin is the name of an administrative *région* comprising three *départements*: Corrèze, Creuse and Haute-Vienne. For a long time an Anglo-Norman fief, it was united to the French throne by Henry IV, and later administered by appointed Intendants.

Dordogne is a *département,* which is part of the larger *région* of Aquitaine. The French *départements* were created in 1790 and were generally given the name of the main river within the territory, hence the Dordogne, named after the two rivers (the Dore and the Dogne) which combine to form this famous waterway. Before that time, the same area was known as **Périgord** (named after the Petrocorii who occupied the area at the time of the Gauls), a free county dating back to the 11C, which fell into the possession of the Albret family. Henry IV, its last feudal lord, brought it under the authority of the French crown. Many French people still use the old appellation to refer to this popular holiday destination, especially when describing its culinary delights.

LAND FORMATION
PRIMARY ERA

This began about 600 million years ago. It was towards the end of this era that an upheaval of the earth's crust took place. This upheaval or folding movement, known as the Hercynian fold, the V-shaped appearance of which is shown by dotted lines on the map, resulted in the emergence of a number of high mountains, notably the Massif Central, formed by crystalline rocks which were slowly worn down by erosion.

SECONDARY ERA

This began about 260 million years ago. Towards the middle of this era, there was a slow folding of the Hercynian base, resulting in the flooding of the area by the sea. Sedimentary deposits, mainly calcareous, accumulated on the edge of the Massif Central, forming the Quercy causses (limestone plateaux) during the Jurassic period and then beds of Cretaceous limestone in the Périgord region. Similar formations are found in Champagne Berrichonne, Boischaut and Sancerre.

TERTIARY ERA

This began about 65 million years ago. During this period siderolithic deposits (clay and gravel, rich in iron) originating from the Massif Central covered some parts of the Quercy, such as the Bouriane region, whereas clay-rich sands accumulated to the west of Périgord, creating the heathlands of the Brenne, Sologne, Double and Landais regions, with their numerous lakes.

QUATERNARY ERA

This began about 2 million years ago. It was during this period that human evolution gathered pace. By this time, the effects of erosion had given the region its present-day appearance. Rivers with their source in the Massif Central created the Vézère, Dordogne and Lot valleys.

THE COUNTRYSIDE TODAY

Regions totally different in character lie side by side in the area between the Berry and the plains of the Agenais. This region of contrasting countrysides is one of great natural beauty: the wide horizons of the Berry succeeded by the green mountain country of the Limousin; the limestone plateaux of the Quercy stretching out in stark silhouette; and the wooded plateaux of the Périgord divided by picturesque valleys and bountiful orchards. The area has many visible traces of its earliest settlers and

Chestnut tree

M. Janvier/ MICHELIN

is rich in prehistoric sites. Charming churches, the imposing religious sanctuaries of the Limousin and the hundreds of fortresses, castles, manors and mansions in a variety of architectural styles all bear witness to the region's rich historical past. In addition, the region' is renowned for its delicious traditional cuisine and excellent local wines, offering the perfect accompaniment to your voyage of discovery.

DORDOGNE
PÉRIGORD VERT

The Green Périgord, located between the Nontronnais and Excideuil, comprises fragments of the old massif, small basins scoured out of the soft Lias marl, and the occasional table of limestone. Its landscape of woodlands, well-tended farms and patches of bright sunflowers echoes the neighbouring Limousin. The handful of towns scattered across this lush borderland act as centres for light industry and the marketing of locally produced farm products.

Contrasting colours are provided by pastures grazed by dairy cattle and calves (for veal), especially around **Ribérac**, and fields of cereal crops. Numerous agricultural markets are held in local towns.

PÉRIGORD BLANC

The White Périgord takes its name from the frequent outcrops of chalky limestone that illuminate this open landscape.

The countryside of hills and slopes around Périgueux consists of meadows interspersed with coppices of oak and chestnut. This region is drained by the River Beauronne and River Vern, whose valleys are covered with pasture and arable land; the extensive **Vallée de l'Isle** is dotted with small industrial towns, its alluvial soil used as pasture, or for growing maize (corn), tobacco and walnuts.

South of Périgueux, around **Vergt** and **Rouffignac**, the iron-rich siderolithic deposits covering the limestone have proven to be ideal for the cultivation of strawberries, which are exported to all parts of France.

To the northeast of the town, Central Périgord meets the **Périgord Causse**. This block of Jurassic limestone, scored by the **Isle**, **Auvézère and Loue valleys**, is characterised by its sparse vegetation, although its stunted oak trees harbour the famed, yet elusive truffle.

The **Double,** lying to the west, between the River Dronne and the River Isle, is an area of forests where tall oak and chestnut trees predominate; the clay soil here favours the formation of ponds. The **Landais**, to the south of the Isle, is a less rugged region abundant in fruit orchards. The maritime pine is more common here than the chestnut; meadows are also more abundant than to the north of the river.

PÉRIGORD POURPRE

The Purple Périgord around **Bergerac** is divided into several areas, all of which share a mild climate favourable to the cultivation of crops more commonly associated with more southerly parts of the country. The Dordogne Valley, which is particularly wide here, is divided into plots of land where tobacco, maize (corn), sunflowers and cereals all flourish in the rich alluvial deposits.

Timber production predominates to the west of Bergerac, in an area whose slopes are covered with the vineyards of Bergerac and **Monbazillac**.

The town of Bergerac itself is an important centre for the tobacco and wine industries.

PÉRIGORD NOIR

Dissected by the Vézère and Dordogne valleys, the Black Périgord owes its name to the high density of trees growing in the sandy soil covering the limestone areas, and to the predominance of the holm oak, with its dark, dense foliage, particularly in the area around **Sarlat**. The alluvial soil of the valleys, whose river courses are lined with screens of poplar or willow, supports a variety of crops, including wheat, maize (corn), tobacco and walnuts. The bustling and colourful local markets all sell excellent nuts, mushrooms, truffles and foie gras. Springs, chasms and prehistoric caves

and shelters with sculpted or painted walls offer further attractions for visitors to this area. Along the River Dordogne the landscape is gentle and harmonious, as can be seen from the viewpoints at Domme, and the castles of Beynac and Castelnaud. The former capital of Périgord Noir, **Sarlat-la-Canéda**, with its *lauze* roofs and medieval atmosphere, is a lively tourist centre and popular holiday base.

Vast stretches of gently undulating molassic hillside, with the occasional limestone outcrop and terrace extend beyond the wine-producing slopes of Monbazillac. Small farms interspersed with woodlands are planted with cereal crops, vineyards (AOC Bergerac) and plum trees. To the east, in an area of transition with the Bouriane region in the Quercy, the dense **Forêt de Bessède**, a forest which continues to flourish on the millstone or siderolithic sands, has hardly been disturbed by the foundation of *bastides* and abbeys during the Middle Ages.

QUERCY

Quercy corresponds to a region that stretches from the Massif Central to the plains of Aquitaine and was occupied by the **Cadurques** who made **Cahors** their capital. The region has a strong historical unity: in the Middle Ages Quercy belonged to the province of **Guyenne**; under the Ancien Régime two regions were recognised – the Haut-Quercy, centred on Cahors and seat of the main administrative departments, and the Bas-Quercy, governed from **Montauban**. During the Revolution they were reunited as part of the Lot *département*. However, in 1808 **Napoleon** separated them once more, creating the *département* of the Tarn-et-Garonne, which covers most of the Bas-Quercy, and parts of Rouergue, Gascony and Languedoc.

THE CAUSSES

This dry land, dissected by dry valleys known locally as *combes*, forms a protected area known as the **Parc Naturel Regional des Causses du Quercy**. Flocks of sheep graze on the sparse

Lot Valley

S. Sauvignier/MICHELIN

grass of the pastures which are subdivided by drystone dikes. Stunted oaks and maple are the only trees growing here. The more fertile valleys are a mix of pasture, vineyards and other crops.

The **Causse de Martel** is a vast, arid, stone-covered plain, dissected by a relatively fertile zone. The numerous drystone walls here were built by shepherds as they cleared stones from the ground to allow sheep to graze and marked out boundaries. The area takes its name from the nearby agricultural town of Martel.

The **Causse de Gramat**, an extensive limestone plateau at an average altitude of 350m/1 150ft is home to a number of sites of natural interest (&see Gouffre de PADIRAC) and unusual landscapes: to the north lie the **Ouysse** and **Alzou** canyons (the spectacular village of **Rocamadour** clings to the cliff face); to the south the much longer **Célé Canyon**. Between the narrow gashes of the Alzou and the Célé lies the waterless **Braunhie**, an arid region riddled with caves and ravines. Like many of their neighbours, the local towns of Gramat and Labastide-Murat have suffered from serious depopulation in recent decades.

The low-lying plateau of the **Causse de Carjac** is hemmed in by the banks of the River Célé and River Lot, the banks of which are particularly fertile.

The **Causse de Limogne**, with its drier climate, takes on a very different appearance. Bordered by the Lot Valley, the plateau is dotted with dolmens and megaliths, which appear amid clusters of white truffle oak, juniper bushes and fields of lavender. Dotted around this landscape are unusual shepherds' shelters built of flat stone with strange conical roofs, known as *garriottes*, *cazelles*, or *bories* (&see SARLAT: Cabanes de Breuil). There are few big towns in this area, although Limogne-en-Quercy and Lalbenque remain busy centres for the **truffle trade**.

THE VALLEYS

Cutting a wide swath through limestone, the region's rivers have carved out their valleys, shaping meanders which enlarge as the valley broadens, to the point that they become ever-widening loops *(cingles)* in the course of rivers. The valleys of the **Dordogne**, **Célé** and **Lot** have been inhabited since prehistoric times. During the Roman era, settlers lived in fortified *oppidums*; castles and châteaux bear witness to the role of these valleys in the region's later history. Today, they are richly covered with crops, vineyards and orchards. The main centres of population in this area today are **Souillac** (Dordogne Valley), **Figeac** (Célé) and **Cahors** (Lot).

HAUT-QUERCY

The major part of the Haut-Quercy comprises limestone plateaux or *causses* with an average altitude of 300m/1 000ft. The fertile areas of the **Limargue** and **Terrefort** extend across flat basins and vast plains; the soils of the area favour the production of a variety of crops including greengage plums and strawberries *(between Carennac and St-Céré)*, grapes, walnuts and tobacco. The eastern part of the Haut-Quercy includes the **Châtaigneraie**, an area with a cold, damp climate and poor soil. This plateau, at an altitude of 700m/2 300ft, tilts eastwards and is cut by deep gorges. The widely cultivated chestnut tree has given the area its name; cereal crops are grown on lowering hilltops, while cattle are raised on small farms. The **Bouriane** is blanketed in heath, coppices and woods, and bears more resemblance to the Périgord than the Quercy. In this area, timber, chestnuts and walnuts are harvested, maritime pines are tapped for resin, and livestock is raised and sold. The capital of this area is the bustling town of **Gourdon.**

QUERCY BLANC

Southwest of the Lot Valley and the town of Cahors, the Jurassic limestone disappears under tertiary limestone to create unusual landscapes known as *planhès* – vast undulating areas of white which have given the region its name (White Quercy). These plateaux are cut into narrow ridges *(serres)* by the rivers. The crests of the *serres* are levelled off into plains which are covered with pastures used for grazing sheep, oak forest and, occasionally, fertile fields of crops. Between the *serres*, the valleys are fertile corridors, spreading between the sandstone as they get closer to the Garonne. Pastures lined with poplars produce abundant crops of fruit, cereals and tobacco, in addition to wine from local vineyards. The lively market towns of **Montcuq**, **Lauzerte**, **Castelnau-Montratier**, and **Montpezat-de-Quercy** are all situated on rocky hilltops known as *puechs.*

LIMOUSIN

This vast region of crystalline rocks forms the western bastion of the Massif Central. The area takes its name from the Lemovices, the large tribe which occupied the country at the time of the Gauls. The individuality of the region is emphasised by its wet winter climate and verdant countryside. Limousin has been aptly described by Jérôme and Jean Tharaud in their novel La Maîtresse Servante:

"Before us unrolled a green and ever-changing countryside, silent and impenetrable, cut by thick hedges, filled with dark shadows and watered by running brooks. No rivers, only streams; no lakes, only pools; no ravines, only valleys."

LA MONTAGNE

This vast series of plateaux, at altitudes no higher than 977m/3 205ft, has been levelled by erosion. The "Mountain" is the source of many rivers and streams which filter across the rest of the region. The weather on these highlands is rugged, the rains heavy, the winds strong and snow has been known to lie on the ground for four months at a time. Farms are few and far between and stony wastes and moors are more common than ploughed land, particularly on the Plateau de Millevaches (*see MEYMAC*) and in the Massif des Monédières (*see TREIGNAC*). As you pass through this eerily quiet landscape, your eyes are drawn to a landscape of meadows, moors and woodlands of beech and pine, dotted with the ever-present sight of grazing sheep.

THE PLATEAUX OF HAUT-LIMOUSIN

The plateaux to the northwest are undulating in appearance – the **Monts d'Ambazac** and the **Monts de Blond** – with alternating escarpments and deeply incised valleys. The bocage is a patchwork of woods and fields. Trees thrive in this wet climate, with oak and beech on the uplands and chestnut trees at lower levels. Quickset hedges surround fields and meadows. The pastures enriched by manure and artificial fertilisers make good cattle-grazing country. Farther north, the drier, less-wooded **Marche** area is a marshland between the Massif Central and the Pays

de la Loire. The **Haute-Marche**, drained by the Creuse, is an area of stock-rearing, whereas arable farming is more prevalent in the **Basse-Marche**, particularly around Bellac.

To the west, the **Confolentais** is the name given to the green and forested foothills of the Massif Central, which are dissected by the River Vienne.

THE PLATEAUX OF BAS-LIMOUSIN

This area, where the influence of Périgord and Quercy is already evident, is characterised by its wonderful light, milder climate and fertile basins. The **Xaintrie** is an area dotted with woods of pine and silver birch – this granite plateau is deeply incised by the Dordogne, the Maronne and numerous smaller rivers.

The depression of the **Bassin de Brive** straddles the Lower Limousin and the northernmost part of the Périgord. The *Nontronnais* is also partly in the Limousin and takes on a similar appearance, with its grassy fields, chestnut trees, heather, gorse and isolated farmhouses.

BASSIN DE BRIVE

The depression of the Brive Basin is a sunken zone between the crystalline escarpments of the **Uzerche plateau** and the limestone ridges of the **Causses du Quercy**. It is an area of sandstone and schist, drained by the River Vézère and River Corrèze. In its green valleys demarcated by screens of poplar, the gentle south-facing slopes are given over to orchards. Today, Brive is an important centre for the fruit and vegetable canning industries.

South of Brive, the **Causse Corrèzien** is covered with large farms devoted to the rearing of geese and sheep, and truffle oak plantations.

BERRY

This province is one of the oldest agricultural regions in France, with a unity that is the result of its shared heritage, rather than of its geography. The geological position of the Berry lies at the contact point between the Paris Basin and the Massif Central. The area consists of a vast low-lying plateau, rising in the northeast to the Sancerre Hills (highest point: the Motte de Humbligny at an altitude of 434m/1 424ft), tilting westwards in a series of steps towards the Brenne depression. To the south, the countryside is more undulating with numerous isolated hills and escarpments. The River Cher and River Indre are part of the Loire drainage system, whereas the Creuse is a tributary of the Vienne.

NORTHERN BERRY

The **Pays Fort** and **Sancerrois** are transitional areas bordering the Pays de la Loire. The former, characterised by its marl and clayey soils, slopes towards the Sologne, whereas the vine-covered, chalky slopes of the Sancerrois rise above the river banks. This once-forested landscape has been remodelled as bocage (wooded farmland). The Forêt d'Allogny, the last remaining area of primitive forest cover, overlooks the vast orchards of St-Martin-d'Auxigny.

The **Northern Boischaut**, meanwhile, is an area of rich pasture.

The **Southern Berry – Champagne Berrichonne** is a region of plateaux and limestone soil extending between the Loire to the east and the Indre to the west, and is covered in the main by scattered woods and forests. Manure and rich fertilisers have transformed this light, sandy soil into excellent farm land. In addition to grain crops, sheep

Beech

and Normandy dairy cows are bred indoors and fed on beetroot pulp; beekeeping is also an important economic activity around Châteauroux. Away to the east, the **Val de Germigny** is a long depression, formerly marshland, which runs along the foot of the escarpments crowned by the Bois de Meillant. The pastures here are grazed by Charolais cattle.

BOISCHAUT

This district lies between the Cher and the Creuse, its clay soils overlapping the neighbouring Marche province. This is an area of small farms where the emphasis is on livestock rearing, in particular the Charolais breed, and sheep.

The countryside, crisscrossed with many rivers, farms and gardens, is much the same as when described by the novelist George Sand (*see NOHANT*).

BRENNE

This vast sand and clay depression, characterised by its abundant marshes, is predominantly covered with heather, pine trees and broom. Once the exclusive haven of hunters and fishers, the Brenne is now a nature park, popular with visitors interested in observing its exceptional flora and fauna (*see La BRENNE*).

FLORA AND FAUNA
WATER

The region has a dense network of rivers and streams. In the Limousin, the rivers tumble through picturesque valleys, whereas in the Berry they tend to flow more peacefully. With a few exceptions (near urban areas), the waters are pure and clean, harbouring myriad species of fish. The region is home to numerous ponds and wetlands, man-made lakes, as well as abundant flora and fauna.

La Brenne

This nature park is part of the region's commitment to the preservation of wetlands and their ecosystems, and to the development of green tourism. The hundreds of ponds and the diversity of habitats make it an ideal refuge

M. Janvier / MICHELIN

for many species, including a host of migrating birds. (👆See La BRENNE for details and illustrations of local wildlife.)

Wetlands

These ecosystems, characterised by the presence of slow-moving water or saturated soil, are vitally important in maintaining the region's ecological balance. The protection of these often fragile areas has led to a better understanding of their morphology.

Wet Meadows

The outer ring of the pond system, these meadows of variable size are often rich with wildflowers in springtime. The flora is diverse and in La Brenne includes as many as 50 species: marsh violets, gentian, orchids etc.

Swamps

The waterlogged banks of the region's ponds are invaded by willows which develop into groves extending from the water's edge to firmer ground. Trees provide nesting for green-winged teal; the branches dipping in the water protect paddling ducks; while the grey heron and the black-crowned night-heron gather beneath them. The muddy banks are teeming with mollusks which attract waders such as black-tailed godwits, curlews, crested lapwings and snipe. Partially submerged plant life includes perennial herbs, quillwort, clovers and ferns.

Marshes

Plant life in the mineral-rich soil is dominated by grasses in many forms, including sedge, reeds, cattails and bulrushes. Impenetrable and considered undesirable for fish hatcheries, these grassy areas are essential to the survival of certain rare species. Waders such as bitterns and other members of the heron family build their nests in these protected zones alongside marsh harriers, millerbirds, swamp sparrows, reed-buntings etc.

Ponds

Floating plants make good nests for crested grebes. Many species of duck are also found here (such as mallard, pintails (with their wide, spatula-shaped bills), canvas-backs and grey ducks). Osprey choose the region's ponds to rest during their annual migrations, while black and striped terns are a regular sight gliding over the water.

European pond turtles are shy creatures, living off water-lilies and sunbathing by the reeds. Insects are everywhere, with as many as 600 to 1 000 species identified. Snakes, frogs, toads, newts and some rare mammals have also been spotted, including a remarkable sighting of the European mink, at the Etang Ricot (Réserve Naturelle de Chérine) in 1982.

The abundant **lakes and rivers** of the Limousin are popular with fishing enthusiasts: the **Creuse** is a favourite for trout; the **Gartempe** is popular for carp; while the river's oxygen-rich rivers are the domain of trout, grayling and salmon. In still waters, look out for freshwater fish (carp, barbel, tench, bream, goldfish, chub, dace and shiner). Several species of fish, in particular pike and perch, can grow to a considerable size.

MOORS AND FORESTS

Moorland and Peatland

The **Brenne** is poor in pastureland and has been gradually abandoned by its rural population; as a result, the few tilled fields have mostly given way to idle, uncultivated land. The humid ground is covered with besom heather, a tall bushy plant with greenish-white flowers. On drier ground, gorse, Scotch broom and bracken grow beneath a few isolated trees. The skies here are populated with birds such as the kingfisher, harrier and hawk, while the undergrowth provides a natural habitat for hare, boar, deer, badger and genet.

In the Limousin, the high plateaus with their vast granite depressions (**Millevaches**, **Gentioux**) have highly acidic soil where sphagnum moss flourishes; consequently, parts of the countryside have developed into peat bogs. Near Meymac, the **Tourbière du Longéroux**, harbours the source of the Vézère.

Peat is made by the slow decomposition of organic materials (especially sphagnum) in cold, acidic water and is a process that takes centuries. In **Longéroux**, where the average thickness of the peat is 2m/6.5ft, the analysis of fossilised pollen shows that the deposits began forming 8 000 years ago. The bog's inhabitants include lizards, snakes, toads, frogs, newts and the birds who prey on them, as well as the elusive otter, whose presence can often only be deduced by its spoor.

The granite hills around the site are drier, and are covered with common heather, fuzzy broom and scattered bilberry bushes. Over the decades, however, indigenous deciduous trees such as birch and ash have been disappearing as a result of unchecked development.

FORESTS

In the 19C, state-owned forests began operating a coppice-with-standards system, whereby selected stems are retained, as standards, at each felling to form an unevenly aged canopy which is then harvested selectively. The forest is managed so that part of the growth is natural and part of seedling origin, together forming a composite forest. The Indre *département*, one of the first to use this method, has become a leading producer of oakwood for panelling. The **Forêt de Châteauroux** (5 04 ha/13 000 acres) and the **Forêt de Bommiers** (4 470 ha/11 000 acres) are remarkable examples of successful forestry. The dark, low-acidic soil has produced a seedling forest of English oak growing alongside plantations of hornbeam and ash, with ferns growing low to the ground. Boar, deer, martens, skunks, squirrels and wild cats wander the reserve, where the bird population includes wood pigeons and woodpeckers.

To the north, the acidic, wet soil of the Boischaut is home to birch *(Forêt de Gâtine)*; oak and beech are found in the Marche; while pubescent oak grow on the limestone plateaux in the southwest of the Indre *département*. On the highest plateaux of the Limousin, conifers have multiplied, with spruce, larch and pine replacing meadows of heather and fields of grain crops. To the south, and on the borders of the Périgord, deciduous hardwood forests prevail on the sunny slopes, and chestnut trees, which are native to the region, are cultivated for their nuts.

At certain times of the year, the region's woods become the haunt of mushroom-hunters searching for varieties including king bolete *(Boletus edulis)*, bay bolete *(Boletus badius)*, chanterelle *(Cantharellus cibarius)* and yellow morel *(Morchella esculenta)*. In rural France, pharmacists are able to identify edible mushrooms, so if you are unsure of what mushrooms you have picked, take them to the local *pharmacie* before taking them home.

FIELDS AND BOCAGE

The **Champagne Berrichonne**, an open land of large, ploughed fields which attracts numerous birds, is the most northerly area covered in this guide. South of this area, the **Boischaut-Sud** and parts of **La Brenne** are completely different, with a more secretive feel. The *bocage* landscape here is one of hedges and hedgerows, groves of trees, small plots of land and protected pastures. This maze of vegetation is further marked by *chemins creux* – tunnel-like pathways laid out between high banks topped with vegetation. These deep-sided lanes, many now overgrown and too narrow for tractors, prevented erosion; prickly bushes held climbing vines tight together to keep the animals safely enclosed; trees provided wood for cooking and making tools; and the leaves of elm trees could be used as fodder (*see* ST-AMAND-MONTROND).

CAVES AND CHASMS IN THE DORDOGNE

Although dispersed throughout the region, the arid *causse* slices through the otherwise luxuriant landscape of the Périgord. In the Quercy, the limestone plateaux roll away to the horizon, stony, grey and deserted. The dryness of the soil is due to the calcareous nature of the rock which absorbs rain like a sponge.

Water Infiltration

Rainwater containing carbonic acid dissolves the carbonate of lime found in the limestone. Depressions form, known as **cloups**, which are usually circular in shape and small in size. When the *cloups* increase in size, they form large, closed depressions known as **sotches**. Where rainwater infiltrates the countless fissures in the plateau more deeply, the hollowing out and dissolution of the calcareous layer produces wells or natural chasms which are called **igues**.

Underground Rivers and Resurgent Springs

Infiltrating water eventually reaches the impermeable layers (marl) of the earth, developing into rivers which sometimes flow for miles. The waters merge into more powerful streams, widening their beds and tumbling over falls. In zones where the impermeable marl comes close to the surface of a hillside, the water bubbles up to the surface, sometimes with great force, in the form of a **resurgent spring**.

The circulation of water underground through chasms and galleries follows an unpredictable course, for the cracks in the rock continually affect the underground drainage. There are many dry river beds underground, where waters have sought out deeper domains.

When water flows slowly, as at Padirac, small lakes are formed by natural dams called **gours**. The walls holding back the waters are built up by the deposit of lime carbonate. Dissolution of limestone continues above the water level, with blocks of stone falling from the roof, resulting in the creation of domes. As the dome pushes upwards and its roof grows thin, it may cave in, opening the chasm to the surface above. The *Gouffre de Padirac* is such a dome, with the top of its ceiling just a few feet beneath the surface.

Cave formations

As it circulates underground, water deposits the lime it carries, building up concretions of fantastic shapes which

Spruce

M. Janvier/ MICHELIN

seem to defy the laws of gravity. The seeping waters deposit calcite (carbonate of lime) to form a series of stalactites, stalagmites, pendants, pyramids, draperies and eccentrics.

Stalactites are formed on the roof by water dripping down. The concretion builds up slowly as drops deposit calcite on the surface.

Stalagmites are a sort of mirror image, rising up from the deposits of dripping water from the ceiling above, eventually meeting the stalactite to form a pillar. Such concretions form very slowly: the rate of growth in temperate climates is about 1cm/0.5in every 100 years.

Eccentrics are very delicate protuberances, formed by crystallisation, which seldom exceed 20cm/8in in length. They emerge at odd angles, as slender spikes or in the shape of translucent fans.

Modern exploration

The caves and chasms of the Dordogne were initially inhabited by animals and then by people, who abandoned these natural shelters c 10 000 years ago.

At the end of the 19C, the methodical and scientific exploration of the underground world led to the discovery of a number of caves and their subsequent conversion into tourist attractions.

Yet, despite significant research, many mysteries remain beneath the earth's surface.

PÈRIGORD NOIR

This beautiful region, the heart of which lies between the River Vézère and River Dordogne, is called the Black Périgord due to the dark colour of its forests, which consist mainly of oaks, chestnut and sea pines. This is the most visited part of the Perigord, with Sarlat at its centre, full of ancient villages to wander, stunning cave systems to explore and castles to admire.

The alluvial soil of the valleys supports a variety of crops, including wheat, maize, tobacco and walnuts, all of which are sold in colourful local markets. Its river courses are lined with screens of poplar or willow, while chasms, prehistoric caves and shelters explore man's prehistory.

Along the River Dordogne the landscape is gentle and harmonious, as can be seen from the viewpoints at Domme, and the castles of Beynac and Castelnaud. The former capital of Périgord Noir, Sarlat-la-Canéda, with its lauze roofs and medieval atmosphere, is a lively tourist centre. The Saturday market here extends through the whole town and is justifiably famous.

The Vézère River meanders westwards through the region, passing the amazing prehistoric sites at Lascaux, La Roque St-Christophe and Les Eyzies, before flowing into the Dordogne at Limeuil, not far from the Cingle de Trémolat with its wonderful views of the mighty river.

To the south, beyond the perched bastide of Domme—constructed by Philip the Bold in 1283 to keep a watchful eye on the English—is an area of transition with the Bouriane region in the Quercy and in the south west, near Belvès, the dense Forêt de Bessède. The forest continues to flourish on the millstone or siderolithic sands, all hardly disturbed by the foundation during the MIddle Ages of bastides such as Monpazier and abbeys such as Cadouin (see *Périgord Pourpre*).

The Périgord Noir is a gastronomic highlight of the region, well-known for the high quality of its produce, which can be seen at the many local markets in the area. There is a profusion of exceptional produce such as foie gras, truffles, mushrooms, cheese, soft fruit, wine, a variety of preserves derived from duck and goose, abundant vegetables not to mention the delicious breads and pastries.

Belvès★

and around

Perched on a limestone promontory on the site of a Gallo-Roman castrum, Belvès enjoys a marvellous position overlooking the Nauze Valley. The surrounding rolling countryside is renowned for its wild mushrooms and chestnuts.

◄—TOWN WALKING TOUR

Plaques identify the town's major monuments (a town plan is available at the tourist office).

The 11C bell tower and 15C covered market (*halle*) with stone and wooden supports stand on **place d'Armes**, at the centre of the village. A complex of nine underground rooms situated in the medieval moat, beneath place d'Armes, gives an insight into the daily life of the families who lived in the **troglodyte dwellings** (☾*open mid-Jun to mid-Sep; ◄—guided tours (45min) at noon, 3.45pm, 6pm; mid-Sep to mid-Jun, tours at 11am and 3.30pm. ◄—4€; ℰ05 53 29 10 20*) between the 12C and 18C.

Take the covered passage to the right of the Archbishop's House, which leads to **rue Rubigan**. This attractive street leads to the Tour de l'Auditeur (Auditor's Tower), the former castrum keep. The Maison des Consuls (tourist office), is located along rue des Eiffols. Follow the street to the western edge of town,

- ▶ **Population:** 1 503
- ◔ **Michelin Map:** 329: H-7
- ◑ **Location:** 65km/40.5mi S. of Périgueux. Approach from the southwest along the D 53 (the Monpazier road) for a charming view of the town with its old turreted houses, bell towers and leafy garden terraces.
- ◄— **Guided Tours:** In season, guided tours of Belvès take place daily (except Sun) in Jul and Aug at 6pm. **Tours of local area**: Guided tours by car on Tue and Thu (full day) in Jul and Aug.

where you can admire the Gothic church of Notre-Dame-de-Montcuq (13C-15C), which used to be a Benedictine priory. Walk towards place Croix des Frères: the castle is on your right and a 14C octagonal keep, all that remains of a former convent, on your left.

Near the Place d'Armes on rue J.-Manchotte is the **Musée Organistrum et Viellesà Roues du Périgord Noir** (*no. 14; ☾open by prior arrangement; ◄—no charge; ℰ05 53 29 10 93*), which houses a small collection of reconstructed lutes, hurdy-gurdies and other medieval instruments.

Belvès

B. Kaufmann/MICHELIN

🚗 DRIVING TOUR

*60km/37mi round tour – allow half
a day. Drive S out of Belvès along the
D 710; turn left onto the D 54 after
1km/0.6mi, then right 2km/1.2mi farther
on. The road runs through fields and
woodland dotted with charming
small villages.*

Orliac

This tiny village, buried in the hollow of
a valley occupied by a pine forest, has a
fortified church in which the nave served
as a protective keep; the Renaissance
doorway provides the only decorative
touch.

Prats-du-Périgord

The Romanesque **Église St-Maurice**★,
fortified in the 15C, has an unusual
appearance, with its nave framed by a
tall apse and a graceful belfry wall.

▷ *Leave Prats to the south
along the D 60.*

Villefranche-du-Périgord

This *bastide* was founded in 1261 by
Alphonse de Poitiers. An enormous
covered market, with its heavy stone pillars, and part of the covered arcades are
still standing. A chestnut market takes
place here on Saturdays from late September to November.

Maison du Châtaignier, Marrons et Champignons

🕐*Open Jul–Aug, Tue–Fri, 9.30am–
13.30pm and 2–7pm, Sat and Sun
9.30am–1.30pm; Apr–Jun and Sept,
9.30am–1pm and 2.30–7pm, Sat
9.30am–1.30pm; Oct–Mar 10am–
12.30pm and 2.30–5.50, Sat 10am–
12.30pm. Closed Wed and Sun.* ⊛*1€.*
✆*05 53 29 98 37.*

This ecological museum is devoted to
mushrooms and the chestnut. 🚶 The
1km/0.6mi nature trail (allow 30min) is
particularly popular. A chestnut market
is held here every Saturday morning
during the harvest season.

▷ *Drive NE along the D 57.*

Église de Besse

This church is famous for its remarkable
carved **doorway**★ in the west front, dating most probably from the 11C. Such
features are rare in the architecture of
the Périgord region, and this particular
example is exceptional. The sculptures
on the archivolt depict the Redemp-
tion, including images of Adam and
Eve before and after the Original Sin, St
Michael slaying the dragon and Isaiah
being purified by a glowing coal.

▷ *Continue NE along the D 57.*

St-Pompon

This old village contains many houses
typical of the Périgord region with its
attractive dormer windows surmounted
with shell ornamentation and framed
with spiral scrolls. Cross the small bridge
by the town hall to reach the **fortified
doorway**★, all that remains of a fortress
built here by the English in the 15C.
Beyond the church, you will see the
ruins of a castle dating from the same
period. Farther east, on the road to Daglan, stands **Notre-Dame-de-Bedeau**, a
chapel dating from the 13C and 17C and
a place of pilgrimage for hunters at the
start of the hunting season.

▷ *Drive NW out of St-Pompon along
the D 60 towards Prats. After 1km/0.6mi,
turn right onto the D 52 to St-Laurent
then follow the D 51 back to Belvès.*

ADDRESSES

🛏 STAY

⊜⊜⊜ **Le Branchat** ♿♨*24170 Sagelat.
3km/1.8mi S of Belvès on the D 710
towards Fumel and a secondary road to
the left.* ✆*05 53 28 98 80. www.lebran-
chat.com. Closed Nov–Mar. 8 rooms.*
A sheepfold, stable, barn and farmhouse have been wonderfully restored
and turned into charming guestrooms.

⊜⊜ **Chambre d'Hôte La Grande
Marque** – *24220 Marnac. 9km/5.4mi NE
of Belvès on the D 703 and to the right.*
✆*05 53 31 61 63.*🚳 *5 rooms.* The view

from this 17C hill-top house will take your breath away. Under the eaves, three pretty rooms have recently been redecorated.

⚲/ EAT

🍽🍽 **Auberge de la Nauze** – *Fongouffier - 24170 Sagelat - 1km/0.6mi N of Belvès on the D 53. ℘05 53 28 44 81. Closed Jun 20–29, Nov 29–Dec 14, Mon eve (exc Jul & Aug), Tue eve and Sat lunchtime Sept–Jun.* This typical regional house stands above the picturesque town of Belvès. Large bay windows and warm colours brighten the dining room.

🍽🍽 **Chambre d'Hôte Maison Vanille,** *rue du Priolat – 24220 St-Cyprien. 12km/ 7.5mi NE of Belvès on the D 703 just after entering village from S. ℘05 53 59 13 98.*

jennieatlgm@wanadoo.fr.🛏 *2 rooms.* This imposing house with an interesting history has just two special en-suite bedrooms. Dinner available. Tea Garden. The owner is a former award winning chef.

🛒 SHOPPING

Markets in Belvès – Traditional market in on Sat morning. Local growers' market Wed 4pm in Jul–Aug. Walnut market Wed morning Oct–Dec.

Markets in Villefranche-du-Périgord – *23km/13.8mi S of Belvès on the D 660.* Chestnut market Sat morning Oct–Dec. Mushroom market (cèpes) weekdays from 4pm and Sun all day (depending on the growing conditions).

Beynac et Cazenac★★

The **Château de Beynac stands on a remarkable site**★★ **crowning a rugged rockface. From this strategic position, it overlooks the beautiful Dordogne Valley as it winds its way between hills and castles.**

CHÂTEAU★★

Climb to the top of the village.
🕐*Open Jun–Sept, 10am–6.30pm; Jan–Feb and Dec, noon to dusk; Mar–May, 10am–6pm; Oct–Nov, 10am to dusk.*
🎟*7€. ℘05 53 29 50 40.*

A formidable stronghold - In the Middle Ages Beynac, Biron, Bourdeilles and Mareuil were the four baronies of Périgord. The castle was captured by Richard the Lion Heart and used as a base by the sinister **Mercadier**, whose bands of men pillaged the countryside. In 1214, Simon de Montfort seized the castle and demolished it. The castle was later rebuilt, as we see it today, by a lord of Beynac. During the Hundred Years War, the Dordogne marked the frontier between the English and the French, and there were constant skirmishes between Beynac and Castelnaud (👁*see Ch. de CASTELNAUD).*

▸ **Population:** 511
⏱ **Michelin Map:** 329: H-6; or see SARLAT
ℹ **Info:** La Balme 24220 Beynac-et-Cazenac. ℘05 53 29 43 08.
📍 **Location:** 64km/40mi SE of Périgueux and 12km/7.5mi SW of Sarlat. For a great view of the river and surrounding area, head up to the castle.
😊 **Don't Miss**: The view from the castle or a lazy boat trip on the Dordogne.

The castle is in the form of an irregular quadrilateral with a bastion on the south side. The austere crenellated keep dates from the 13C. A double curtain wall protected the castle from attack from the plateau; on all the other sides there is a sheer drop of 150m/492ft to the Dordogne. The main building, dating from the 13C and 14C, is extended by the 15C seigneurial manor house to which a bartizan was added in the 16C.

The castle was abandoned from 1798 until 1961. The present owner has launched a vast renovation programme

Château de Beynac

J. Damase/MICHELIN

due to last a century. The kitchens, the drawbridge, the guard-room and the keep have already been restored.

Visitors enter the dark 13C guard-room and proceed to the next floor where the 14C kitchen and its two fireplaces can be admired. Above the kitchen is the great Hall of State; note the carvings decorating the fireplace from Italy. The oratory is adorned with Gothic frescoes. The grand 17C staircase, leads to a drawing room furnished in Louis XIII style; note the paintings on wood decorating the ceiling. One last staircase leads to the watch-path and the south bastion, which overlook the Dordogne: there is a wonderful **panorama**★★ of the valley. On the way down, visitors go through the 13C kitchen and across the drawbridge before leaving via the barbican.

VILLAGE★
Rue Tibal Lo Garrel★
This steeply sloping footpath leads from the bottom of the village, through rows of houses dating from the 15C to the 17C, to the castle. All along the climb the architectural decor exudes elegance and the prosperity of Renaissance Beynac. There are gabled doorways, façades decorated with coats of arms or discs, ornate dormer windows, and small, beautifully laid out squares.

A *calvaire* (wayside cross) stands on the cliff edge, at the end of rue Tibal Lo Garrel. A **panorama**★★ as wide as the one from the castle watch-path can be seen from this point.

Parc Archéologique
La Tour du Couvant (at the foot of the Château)

🕐*Open Jul to mid-Sep, daily except Sat and Sun, 10am-7pm.* ⬜*5€.*
📞*05 53 29 51 28.*

This includes about 10 reconstitutions based on the discoveries of archaeological research, mainly living quarters from the end of the Neolithic period, a fortified gateway and a Gallic potter's oven.

ADDRESSES

🍽 EAT

⬤⬤ **La Petite Tonnelle** – *La Balme, 24220 Beynac.* 📞*05 53 29 95 18. Closed Wed, Nov–Apr except school holidays at Christmas.* This family restaurant offers a unique twist on traditional cuisine by spicing up dishes with an Asian flare (the chef is a native of Vietnam). In the winter, sit by the fireside; in the summer, sit beneath the arbour covered in Virginia creeper.

🛒 SHOP

Markets - A local producers' market is held every morning from mid-Jun-mid Sep in place de la Balme.

LEISURE

Gabares de Beynac – *24250 St-Martial-de-Nabirat - 📞05 53 28 51 15. www.gabarre-beynac.com. Open Jul-Aug, 10am-12.30pm and 2-6pm, departures from the car park (1hr) - boats leave every 30mins; May-Jun and Sept, 10.30am-12.30pm and 2-6pm; mid-Mar to Apr and Oct: by prior arrangement. 7.50€.*
Boat trips along the Dordogne on traditional flat-bottomed *gabare* boats.

Aux Canoës Roquegeoffre du Port d'Enveaux – *Enveaux Rive Droite - 24220 St-Vincent-de-Cosse. 📞05 53 29 54 20. www.canoe-roquegeoffre.com. 🕐 daily 9am–pm. Prices start at 9. 50€.*
This recreation centre on the banks of the River Dordogne also offers guided canoe and kayak trips.

Château de Castelnaud★★

The impressive ruins of the Château de Castelnaud stand on a wonderful site★★ commanding the valleys of the Céou and the Dordogne. Right opposite stands the Château de Beynac (see BEYNAC-ET-CAZENAC), Castelnaud's implacable rival through the Middle Ages conflicts.

CASTLE

In 1214 Simon de Montfort (c 1165-1218, father of the English statesman and soldier) took possession of the castle, whose occupants had taken the side of the Cathars. In 1259 St Louis ceded the castle to the king of England who held it for several years.

During the Hundred Years War the castle constantly changed hands between the French and the English. When at last peace was declared the castle was in terrible condition.

During the whole of the second half of the 15C the castle was under reconstruction. Only the keep and curtain wall have kept their 13C appearance. In the 16C the castle was once again transformed in various ways, and the artillery tower was added. In 1969 a major restoration program was undertaken which has enabled most of the buildings to be rebuilt. Castelnaud is a typical example of a medieval fortress with its powerful

- **Michelin Map:** Michelin map 329: H-7; or see SARLAT.
- **Info:** Le Bourg - 24250 Daglan. ℘05 53 31 30 00. www.castelnaud.com.
- **Location:** 69km/43mi SE of Périgueux and 13km/8mi SW of Sarlat. Take a boat trip on the Dordogne to get a good view of the castle.
- **Museum:** Open Jul–Aug, 9am–8pm; Apr–Jun and Sept, 10am–7pm; Feb–Mar and Oct to Nov 11, 10am–6pm; Nov 12–Jan, 2–5pm; Christmas school hols, 10am–5pm, Dec 25 and Jan 1 2–5pm. 7.80€. Jul–Aug, reduced rate after 1pm, 6.80€.
- **Kids:** Musée de la Guerre au Moyen Âge.
- **Don't Miss**: The view from the terrace.

machicolated keep, curtain wall, living quarters and inner bailey. Nonetheless, certain parts of the castle – artillery tower, loopholes – which were added later reflect the evolution of weapons in siege warfare. Reconstructed hoarding, later replaced by machicolations, and audio-visual presentations offer an insight into siege warfare tactics in the

Château de Castelnaud

J. Damase/MICHELIN

Middle Ages; housed in a small room, a model illustrates the siege of Castelnaud in 1442, when Charles VII attempted to finally expel the English from France. The castle is entirely devoted to medieval warfare. A great variety of weapons and objects connected with warfare are on display: 15C and 16C guns in the artillery tower; bows, crossbows and defensive weapons used by bowmen in the lower part of the keep; catapult, battering ram and trebuchet in the siege-warfare room; 15C-17C swords in the sword room. Another room houses the reconstruction of an armourer's workshop. One room on the ground floor contains a wide choice of comic strips and books about the Medieval period. Reconstructions of siege apparatus, including a 12C mangonel, or ballista, and other stone-casting devices are displayed in various parts of the castle. In the 15C, these weapons, which were difficult and dangerous to operate, were replaced by artillery.

From the ward the view extends southwards over the Céou Valley. From the east end of the terrace there is an exceptional **panorama**★★ of one of the most lovely views of the Dordogne Valley. In July and August, visitors can also visit the castle at night (◯*open Mon–Fri, from 8.30pm*). A new play, based on historical figures, is performed every year in the torch-lit rooms.

WALNUT MUSEUM
Écomusée de la Noix du Périgord – *Ferme de Vielcroze, 24250 Castelnaud. ℘05 53 59 69 63. ecomuseedelanoix@ wanadoo.fr. - fhttp://ecomuseedelanoix. site.voila.fr. Open Easter–1 Nov, 10am– 7pm. Closed 12 Nov–early Apr 1* ⇔*4€.*
A restored farm is home to this museum entirely devoted to walnuts, in which exhibits and educational displays explain the cultivation and uses of this precious local product. On-site shop, plus a scenic path through the huge walnut grove surrounding the museum.

Château de Commarque★

The impressive remains of Commarque castle stand on the south bank of the River Beune. Commarque was built as a stronghold in the 12C and 14C and for a long time it belonged to the Beynac family. In 1968, Hubert de Commarque, a descendant of the original owners, commenced a long term restoration project.

VISIT
◯*Open Jul–Aug, 10am–8pm (last entrance 1hr before closing); May–Jun and Sept, 10am–7pm; Apr & Nov schoolhols, 10am–6pm.* ⇔*6.40€. ℘05 53 59 00 25. www.commarque.com.*
The tour of the fortified village begins with the well-preserved chapel; next come four mansions once occupied by noblemen. The *Maison à contreforts* (buttressed house) illustrates the successive building periods: a troglodytic base,

- ♿ **Michelin Map:** Michelin local map 329: H-6; or *see Les Eyzies-de-Tayac.*
- ▷ **Location:** 9km/5.5mi E of Les Eyzies and 14km/9mi W of Sarlat. From the castle keep, there is a fine view of the valley and of the elegant 15C-16C Château de Laussel perched on a cliff across the river.
- 🅿 **Parking**: Situated 600m (650yds) from the Château.

a 10C-11C wall, a 15C fireplace and 16C murals. Along a narrow street, separate entrances indicate that each household was independent.
The double keep comprises the 14C great hall covered with a five-rib vault: the carved pendant brackets are well preserved and the keystone represents a helmet bearing the arms of Pons de Beynac.

Domme★★

Domme, the Acropolis of the Dordogne, is remarkably situated on a rocky crag overlooking the Dordogne Valley. This exceptional site inspired many artists including the writer Henry Miller.

A BIT OF HISTORY

A royal bastide – Domme was founded by Philip the Bold in 1283 in order to keep watch on the Dordogne Valley and check the desire for expansion of the English established in Gascony. The king granted the town important privileges including that of minting coins and Domme played an important role during the Hundred Years War. In the 17C, its wine-growing and river-trading activities were thriving and its markets were renowned throughout the region.

Captain Vivans' exploit– While the struggles of the Reformation were inflaming France, Domme kept up resistance against the Huguenots who were overrunning Périgord. Yet, in 1588, the famous Protestant Captain **Geoffroi de Vivans** captured the town by cunning. One night he and 30 of his men climbed along the rocks of the cliff face known as the *Barre*, a place so precipitous that it had not been thought necessary to protect it, and entered the sleeping town. Vivans and his men created an

- ▶ **Population:** 1086
- **Michelin Map:** 329; or *see SARLAT.*
- **Info:** Pl. de la Halle, 24250 Domme. ✆05 53 31 71 00. www.ot-domme.com.
- ▶ **Location:** 74km/46mi SE of Périgueux and 13km/8mi S of Sarlat.
- **Parking**: A number of car parks are available within the walls of the bastide (*see town plan*). You can also park outside of the walls and catch a tourist train to the centre.
- **Don't Miss**: The view from the Belvédère de la Barre.

infernal racket and during the ensuing confusion opened the tower doors to their waiting army. The inhabitants were too sleepy to resist, and Vivans thereupon became master of the town for the next four years. He installed a garrison, burned down both the church and the Augustine priory and established the Protestant faith.

However, noting the increasing success of the Catholics in Périgord, he sold the *bastide* to his rivals on 10 January 1592. The unwary purchasers found nothing but ruins.

In the village of Domme

©Denis Badet/Fotolia.com

༈࿊ BASTIDE★ WALK

Domme is far from presenting the perfect rectangular plan of the bastide; it is more in the form of a trapezium. The surrounding fortifications have been adapted to the terrain; inside the fortified town, the streets follow a geometric plan, as far as possible.

▷ *Start from the tourist office and follow rue Mazet (running parallel to Grand'Rue) then rue Porte Delbos.*

Porte del Bos

This gateway, which has a pointed arch, was once closed with a portcullis. Walk inside the ramparts to the 13C **Porte de la Combe**.

▷ *Walk toward the town along rue de la Porte-de-la-Combe.*

The street is lined with many fine houses. The beauty of the gold stone and the flat brown tiles is often enhanced by the addition of elegant wrought-iron balconies and brightened by climbing vines and flower-decked terraces.

▷ *Rue de la Porte-des-Tours on the right leads to the Porte des Tours.*

Porte des Tours

🕐༈࿊*Open Jul–Aug, guided tour at 10.15am, 2pm and 4pm. Sept by prior arrangement* ༄*6.50€.* ℘*05 53 31 71 00.* This late-13C gateway is the most impressive and best preserved of the town's gateways. On the side of place des Armes, the wall is rectilinear but on the outside, the gateway is flanked by two massive semicircular rusticated towers, built by Philip the Fair and originally used as guard-rooms. Between 1307 and 1318 Knights Templars were imprisoned there and left their mark with graffiti.

▷ *Turn left.*

Rue Eugène-le-Roy

During the period he spent in a house along this street (*plaque*), Eugène le Roy wrote two of his master-works: *L'ennemi de la mort* (The Enemy of Death) and *Le moulin du Frau* (Frau Mill).

Place de la Rode

This is the place where the condemned were broken on the wheel. The *Maison du batteur de monnaie* (Money Minter's House) is decorated in fine Gothic.

Grand'Rue

This shopping street is lined with shops displaying many of the culinary specialities of Périgord. Note the elegant mullioned windows of the house standing on the corner of rue Geoffroy-de-Vivans.

▷ *Walk to rue des Consuls via rue Geoffroy-de-Vivans.*

Rue des Consuls

The Hôtel de Ville (town hall) is located in a 13C building, which was once the Seneschal law courts.

▷ *Walk along Grand'Rue to the town centre.*

Place de la Halle

In this large square stands an elegant 17C covered market (*halle*). Facing it is the 15C **Maison du Gouverneur** (Governor's House) flanked by an elegant turret. It now houses the tourist office. Destroyed during the Wars of Religion, the **church** was rebuilt in the 17C and the belfry-porch was added in the 19C.

Grottes

🕐༈࿊*Open Jul–Aug, guided tour (30min), 10.15am–6.30pm. Feb–Jun, Sep to mid-Nov and Christmas hols, 10am-noon and 2–5.30pm.* 🕐*Closed the rest of the year and Sat in Feb, Mar, Oct and Nov.* ༄*8€.* ℘*05 53 31 71 00.* The entrance is in the covered market converted into an entrance hall. The panoramic lift which brings visitors up at the end of the visit offers a magnificent view of the Dordogne Valley. These caves served as refuge for the townspeople of Domme during the Hundred Years War and the Wars of

DOMME
0   200m
D 46
CÉNAC
BELVÉDÈRE DE LA BARRE
PROMENADE
DES FALAISES
Jardin public du Jubilé
MOULIN
DU ROY
Forteresse de
Domme-Vieille
N
Pl. de
la Halle
Hôtel
de ville
Musée d'Art et
Traditions populaires
Grottes
des Consuls
R.
R. Mazet
Grand'Rue
R. G. de Vivans
Pl. d'Armes
R. E.-Le-Roy
D 46ᴱ
Porte
des Tours
R. Porte Delbos
Porte del Bos
Pl. de
la Rode
R. de la Porte-
de-la-Combe
Promenade des Remparts
Porte de la Combe

WHERE TO STAY	
Esplanade (Hôtel de L')	①
Guérinière (Hôtel La)	④
Touille (Chambre d'hôte La)	⑧

WHERE TO EAT	
Colombier (Auberge Le)	①
Plume d'Oie (Auberge La)	③
Prés Gaillardous (Les)	⑤

Religion. So far about 450m/490yd of galleries have been cleared for the public to visit; the chambers are generally small and are sometimes separated by low passages.

The ceilings in certain chambers are embellished with slender white stalactites. There are also places where stalactites and stalagmites join to form columns or pillars. The Salle Rouge contains some fine eccentrics.

Bison and rhinoceros bones, discovered when the caves were being prepared for tourists, are displayed precisely as they were found.

Musée d'Art et Traditions Populaires
🕐 *Open Jul–Aug, 10.30am–7pm; Apr–Jun and Sep, 10.30am–12.30pm and 2.30–6pm. 4€. ☎05 53 31 71 00.*
In an old house on place de la Halle, this museum presents a retrospective of every day life in Domme, with displays of furnishings, clothing and farm tools. Amid the archives and photographs, note the royal missives according special privileges and exemptions to the inhabitants of Domme.

Belvédère de la Barre
From the promontory, the **view**★★★ embraces the Dordogne Valley from the Montfort meander in the east, to Beynac in the west. Changing with the time of day – hazy in the early morning mist, bright blue between lines of green poplars in the noonday sun, a silver ribbon in the evening light – the Dordogne winds its way through the carefully cultivated fields dotted with villages and farms. Of all the creative artists who have come here seeking inspiration, Henry Miller was perhaps the most affected, describing the area as the nearest thing to Paradise on earth. The esplanade at the end of the Grand'Rue offers the best panorama of the valley below.

▶ *Follow the Promenade des Falaises, a cliffside walk along the promontory.*

Jardin Public du Jubilé
These attractive gardens (*viewing table*), are situated between the town and the tip of the promontory, on the site of the entrenched camp installed here in 1214 by Simon de Montfort. He had just beaten the Cathars and razed their fortress **Domme-Vieille**, leaving but a few ruins standing.

ADDRESSES

🏠 STAY 🍴 EAT

⊖ **Chambre d'hôte la Touille** – *Route de l'Eglise. ℘06 76 92 28 62. www.chambres-hotes-sarlat.fr. 3 rooms.* Simple but cheery colourfully decorated rooms in a modern house 1km from town. Pleasant small garden.

⊖⊖ **Hôtel de L'Esplanade** – *℘05 53 28 31 41. www.esplanade-perigord.com. Closed 6 Nov–1 Mar. 20 rooms.* This typical Périgord property offers stunning views of the Dordogne Valley and refined traditional cuisine.

⊖⊖ **Chambre d'hôte La Guérinière** – *"Baccas", D 46 towards Gourdon - 24250 Cénac-et-St-Julien. ℘05 53 29 91 97. www.la-gueriniere-dordogne.com. Closed Nov 2–Apr. 16 rooms.* This 18C building, set in parkland, has an unbeatable view of Domme; attractive individual bedrooms, and friendly atmosphere

⊖⊖⊖ **Auberge La Plume d'Oie** – *Le Bourg - 24250, La Roque Gageac. ℘05 53 29 57 05. www.aubergelaplumedoie. com. Closed 15 Nov–20 Dec, 10 Jan– beg. Mar. Tue lunch off season and Mon except dinner July–Aug.* Pleasantly restored old residence with stylish rustic restaurant. Modern cuisine. Four comfortable guestrooms (⊖⊖⊖).

⊖⊖ **Les Prés Gaillardou** – *24250 La Roque Gageac. ℘05 53 59 67 89. www. lespresgaillardou.com Closed Wed.* Farm converted into a restaurant.with stone walls and beams,enclosed garden with a pleasant terrace. Local cuisine served.

⊖⊖ **Auberge le Colombier** – *24250 Rocque-Gageac - ℘0553 28 33 97. Closed Mid-Oct to Easte. Res. required.* This inn is renowned for its convivial atmosphere; the canard and its homemade patisseries are the picks of its farm-fresh fayre.

EVENTS

Fête de la Saint-Clair - Folklore and concerts first weekend in June.

Eymet

On the border of the Bergerac and Agen regions, Eymet is a small Périgord town famous for its gourmet food factories, which preserve goose and duck liver (foie gras), galantines and ballottines, and local specialities in the window of the many *charcuteries* **selling cold-cuts.**

▶ **Population:** 2 541
🕐 **Michelin Map:** 329: D-8
ℹ **Info:** Place de la Bastide, 24500 Eymet.
℘05 53 23 74 95.
😋 **Don't Miss:** Thur market.
🕐 **Also See:** Bergerac and the Pèrigord Pourpre

BASTIDE

Founded in 1256 by Alphonse de Poitiers, the *bastide* was ruled by several seigneurial families who were alternately in allegiance with the king of France and the king of England. Consequently, it had an eventful history during the Hundred Years War and the Wars of Religion. All that remains of the castle is the 14C **keep.** Villagers that wished to live within the fortifications were originally offered 200sqm per family for building a house, which they had to construct within two years or pay a fine. Villagers kept plots of land outside the encircling walls for agricultural production.

In town, head for **Place Centrale** first, an arcaded square lined with old half-timbered or stone houses, some of which have mullioned windows. In its centre is a 17C fountain. It was once accessible by three gates, two of which had towers.

Eymet has an interesting **church**, built on the site of a former Benedictine church of Moissac Abbey. The church often played a defensive role.

The lower parts of the **mill** date from the 13C. Up until 1902 when the river traffic stopped altogether, boats were moored along the quays situated downstream.

Les Eyzies-de-Tayac★★

the Beune and Vézère

The village of Les Eyzies occupies a grandiose setting on steep cliffs crowned with evergreen oaks and junipers at the confluence of the River Vézère and River Beune. The poplar-lined River Vézère winds between meadows and farmland, sometimes narrowing to flow between sheer, vertical walls of rock 50-80m/164-262ft high. Shelters cut out of the limestone base served as dwelling places for prehistoric people; caves located higher up on the cliff face were used as sanctuaries. The discovery within the last 100 years of many such dwellings within a limited radius of Les Eyzies, has earned the town the title, 'European Capital of Prehistory.'

- ▶ **Population:** 848
- **Michelin Map:** 329: H-6
- **Info:** Pl. de la Mairie, 24620 Les Eyzies-de-Tayac. ℘05 53 06 97 05. www.leseyzies.com.
- ▶ **Location:** 45km/28mi SE of Périgueux and 21km/13mi W of Sarlat.
- **Kids:** Roc de Cazelle; Préhisto Parc.
- ⏱ **Timing:** Allow a day for the archaeological sites in the Beune and Vézère valleys.
- **Don't Miss:** Musée National de la Préhistoire; Grotte du Grand Roc; Grotte de Font-de-Gaume.

A BIT OF HISTORY

The capital of prehistory – During the Second Ice Age prehistoric people abandoned the northern plains and headed for the warmer areas of the south. The lower Vézère attracted the migrants because of its easily accessible natural caves and overhanging rocks, which could be hollowed out into shelters without much difficulty.

People used these cave dwellings for tens of thousands of years and left in them traces of their daily tasks such as bones, ashes from their fires, tools, weapons, utensils and ornaments.

As their civilisation evolved, so did animal species: after elephants and cave bears came bison, aurochs, mammoths and, later still, musk-oxen, reindeer, ibex, stags and horses.

The archaeologists' paradise – Methodical study of the deposits in the Les Eyzies region has considerably increased our knowledge of prehistory. The Dordogne *département* has greatly contributed to the study of prehistory with more than 200 deposits discovered

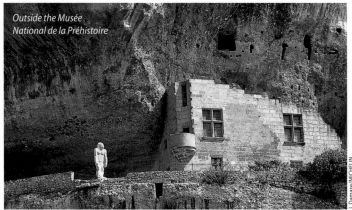

Outside the Musée National de la Préhistoire

J. Damase/MICHELIN

there, of which more than half are in the lower Vézère Valley. Following these discoveries, two great periods of the Paleolithic Age were defined and named – Mousterian and Magdalenian.

MUSÉE NATIONAL DE LA PRÉHISTOIRE★

Open Jul–Aug, 9.30am–6.30pm; Jun and Sep, daily except Tue, 9.30am–6pm; Oct–May, daily except Tue, 9.30am–12.30pm and 2–5.30pm. 5€, No charge 1st Sun of the month. 05 53 06 45 45. Guided tours. 05 53 06 45 65.
www.musee-prehistoire-eyzies.fr

The museum is in a new purpose-built building near the old castle of the barons of Beynac. The 13C fortress, restored in the 16C, clings to the cliff half way up, beneath a rocky outcrop, overlooking the village. From the terrace, there is a good **view** of Les Eyzies and the valleys of Vézère and Beune.

The museum collection illustrates the evolution of flint-cutting from around 2.5 million years BC and the successive civilisations through displays of tools dating from the major Paleolithic periods; anthropology and funerary rituals are also covered.

The impressive collection of modern man's first works of art, includes a low-relief carving known as the **Devil's Furnace** (around 20 000 BC). Other carved stone blocks (36 000-26 000 BC) depict animals and various symbols. The newer acquisitions illustrate the quaternary fauna found in palaeontological sites.

DRIVING TOURS

◻ SITES ALONG THE D 47

Grotte de Font-de-Gaume★

Leave the car by the road to St-Cyprien opposite a cliff-spur. A path takes you up 400m/440yd to the cave entrance.
Guided tours by arrangement mid-May 15–Sept 15 (45min, last entrance 1hr 30min before closing), daily except Sat 9.30am–5.30pm; Sept 16– May 14, daily except Sat 9.30am–12.30pm and 2–5.30pm.(From Nov 1–May 15 by prior arrangement with the reservation service). Closed Sat, Jan 1, May 1 & 11, Nov 1, Nov 11 and Dec25. 7€. 05 53 06 86 00.

The cave runs back in the form of a passage 120m/130yd long with chambers leading off it. Beyond a narrow passage, known as the Rubicon, are many multicoloured paintings, often superimposed on one another; all the drawings of horses, bison, mammoths, reindeer and other deer indicate great artistic skill and, after Lascaux, form the finest group of polychrome paintings in France. The frieze of bison, painted in brown on a white calcite background, is remarkable.

Abri Pataud *(Pataud Shelter)*
Open Jul–Aug, daily 10am–7pm; Apr–Oct 10am–noon and 2–6 exc Sat;mid Nov–Mar 10am–12.30pm and 2–5.30pm. 6€. 05 53 05 65 65.
A museum on site shows objects and bones discovered during excavation work; note in particular two large stratigraphic sections and 14 archaeological layers where bones, flints and the fireplace remains can be seen in place.

Abri de Cro-Magnon
(Cro-Magnon Shelter)
This cave was discovered in 1868 and it revealed, in addition to flints and carved bones of the Aurignacian and Gravettian Cultures, five adult skeletons which were studied by Paul Broca, the surgeon and anthropologist who founded the School of Anthropology in France. The discoveries made in this cave were of prime importance for prehistoric studies, since they were the first remains of *Homo Sapiens* to be found. A commemorative plaque is all that is left of the site today.

Église de Tayac
Open Jul–Aug, Sun 3–6pm, arrange with the tourist office. 05 53 06 97 05.
The warm, gold-coloured stone enhances this 12C fortified church. Two towers roofed with *lauzes* frame the main body of the church.
The doorway is intriguing; the first scalloped arch gives it an Eastern air whereas the two outermost columns, with Corinthian capitals of white marble, show Gallo-Roman influence.

Musée de la Spéléologie
Open Jun 15–Sept 15, daily except Sat–Sun and public hols, 2–6pm. 3€. 05 53 06 97 05 or 05 53 06 97 15.
The museum is installed in the rock fortress of Tayac, which overlooks the Vézère Valley. The four chambers, cut out of the living rock, contain a selection of items pertaining to speleology: caving equipment, exhibits describing the geological formations and plant and animal life in local caves as well as several models.

Abri du Poisson
(The Fish Shelter)
Open May 15 to Sept 15 daily. 9.30–5.30pm and Sept 16–May 14 9.30am-12.30 and 2–5.30pm . Closed Sat, Jan 1, May 1 & 11, Nov 1, Nov 11 and Dec25 3€ 05 53 06 86 00. http://eyzies.monuments-nationaux.fr/fr/bdd. Tickets from Font de Gaume office.
A 1.05m/3.3ft-long fish has been carved on the roof of a small hollow. It is a species of salmon which was very common in the Vézère until quite recently. It dates from the Gravettian Period (about 23000 years BC), and is one of the oldest cave sculptures yet discovered.

Grotte du Grand Roc ★★
(*Grand Roc Cave***)*
Open Jul–Aug, guided tour (35min) 10am–7pm; Low season 10am–6pm. 7.50€, (9.50€ combined ticket with shelter and caves). 05 53 06 92 70. www.grandroc.com.
There is a good **view** ★ of the Vézère Valley from the stairs leading up to the cave (discovered in 1924) and the platform at its mouth. The length (40m/45yd) of tunnel has, within chambers, an extraordinary display of stalactites, stalagmites and eccentrics resembling coral formations, as well as a wonderful variety of pendants and crystals.

Abri Préhistoriques de Laugerie Basse
(Lower Laugerie Deposit)
Open daily Easter to Oct. Jul–Aug, 9.30am–7pm; Apr–Jun and Sept–Oct 30, 10am–6 pm. 6€, (9.50€ combined ticket for cave and shelters). 05 53 06 92 70. www.grandroc.com.
Prehistoric bones, stone tools and other artefacts were discovered in this deposit, downstream from the Upper Laugerie Deposit. They are in various museums and private collections, but an exhibition centre here contains reproductions of the best of them.

Gisement de Laugerie Haute
(Upper Laugerie Deposit)
Open daily except Sat, guided tour (1hr), by prior arrangement only.

LA VALLÉE DE LA BEUNE

May 15–Sept 15, 9.30am–5.30pm;
Sept 16–May 14, 9.30am–12.30pm,
2–5.30pm.Contact the Grotte de Font-
de-Gaume. ⊜3€, ℘05 53 06 86 00.
Scientific excavations going on for over a
century in a picturesque spot at the foot
of high cliffs have revealed examples of
the work and art of prehistoric people at
different stages of civilisation.
Note the drip stones or channels cut in
the rock in the Middle Ages to prevent
water from running along the walls and
entering the dwellings.

Gisement de la Micoque
(La Micoque Deposit)

🕐*Open daily except Sat, guided tour
(1hr), by prior arrangement only. May
15–Sept 15, 9.30am–5.30pm; Sept 16–
May 14, 9.30am–12.30pm, 2–5.30pm.
Contact the Grotte de Font-de-Gaume.
℘05 53 06 86 00.*
This deposit revealed many items
belonging to periods known as the
Tayacian, Micoquian and Mousterian
Ages. Some of the finds are exhibited
at Les Eyzies National Museum of
Prehistory.

② ALONG THE RIVER BEUNE AND RIVER VÉZÈRE
50km/31mi round-trip – allow one day.

▶ *Drive E out of Les Eyzies along the D 47.*

Grotte des Combarelles

🕐*Open mid-May to mid-Sept,
guided tour (1hr), daily except Sat,
9.30am–5.30pm; mid-Sept–mid-May,
9.30am–12.30pm and 2–5.30pm. By
prior arrangement only. 🕐Closed 1
Jan, 1 May, 1 and 11 Nov, and 25 Dec.
⊜6.50€. ℘05 53 06 86 00.*
A winding passage 250m/275yd long
has many markings on its walls for the
last 120m/131yd of its length, some
of which are superimposed one upon
another. The drawings include nearly
700 representations of animals (horses,
bison, bears, reindeer and mammoths
can be seen at rest or in full gallop) and
human caricatures. The cave, discovered
in 1901, demonstrated the importance
of Magdalenian art at a time when some
scholars were still sceptical about the
worth of prehistoric studies.

▶ *Continue along the D 47
towards Sarlat.*

Grottes du Roc de Cazelle

♿🕐*Open Jul–Aug, 10am–8pm;
May–un and Sept, 10am–7pm; Mar–Apr
and Oct–Nov: 10am–6pm; Dec–Jan and
Feb, 11am–5pm. ⊜6.80€ (5–12 years
3.20€℘05 53 59 46 09.
www.rocdecazelle.com.*
👥 This cliff site offers an insight into
our ancestors' life from the Paleolithic

J. Damase/ MICHELIN

Cliff dwellings at the site de la Madeleine

period to the mid-20C. A marked path leads visitors past scenes of prehistoric daily life to the monolithic dwelling occupied until 1966 by a farming couple. Children will appreciate the sound effects and the animals hidden in the forest as well as the adventure trail.

Grotte de Bernifal

10min on foot. ◷☞☜*Open Jul–Aug, guided tour (1hr), 9.30am–6.30pm; Jun and Sept, 10am–12.30pm and 2.30–6.30pm.* ☜*5€.* ☏*05 53 29 66 39.*
Cave paintings and delicate carvings from the Middle Magdalenian period (16000-13000 BC) are spread over about 100m/330ft. They include mammoths, horses, human figures, a bear and shapes suggesting dwellings.

◖ *Continue along the D 47, which follows the River Petite Beune and turn left 2km/1.2mi farther on. Beyond Sireuil, drive N to join the D 48 on the right.*

Abri du Cap-Blanc

(Cap-Blanc Shelter)
◷☞☜*Open May 15–Sept 15, guided tour (45min) 9.30am–5.30pm; Sept 16–May 14, 9.30am-12.30pm, 2-5.30pm.* ◷*Closed 1 Jan, 1 May, 1 and 11 Nov, and 25 Dec* ☜*8€. Contact the Grotte de Font-de-Gaume* ☏*05 53 06 86 00 / 05 53 59 60 30.*
Excavation of a small Magdalenian deposit in 1909 led to the discovery of

carvings★ in high relief on the walls of the rock shelter. Two bison and in particular a frieze of horses were carved in such a way as to use to full advantage the relief and contour of the rock itself.

◖ *Drive on along the D 48 for 1.5km/0.9mi and turn left onto the D 6 to Moustier; 9km/5.6mi farther on, turn left again onto the D 706 towards Les Eyzies.*

Préhisto Parc

👫👪♿◷*Open Jul–Aug, 10am–7.30pm; Apr–Jun and Sept, 10am–6pm; Feb 15–Mar and Oct–Nov, 10am–6pm.* ☜*6.20€(child 3.10€).* ☏*05 53 50 73 19.*
In a small cliff-lined valley, carpeted with undergrowth, a discovery trail reveals about 20 reconstituted scenes of Neanderthal and Cro-Magnon daily life.

◖ *Continue along the D 706 for 500m/547yd then turn right onto a minor road which soon crosses the River Vézère. Turn left in Lespinasse.*

Site de la Madeleine★

◷☞☜*Open daily Jul–Aug, guided tour (50 mins), 9.30am–7pm; Easter–Jun & Sept–Oct, 10am–6pm; Nov–mid-Feb, 11am–5pm.* ☜*5.50€.* ☏*05 53 46 36 88. www.village-la-madeleine.com.*
The location of the site of La Madeleine *(access from Les Eyzies via Tursac and the bridge to L'Espinasse)* stands out

very clearly, from the point where the wooded plateau meets the Vézère's alluvial plain below. The terrain is formed by the river's narrowest and most distinctly shaped meander. On the rock above stand the remains of a medieval castle. Located midway up the cliff, this village was probably occupied from the end of the 10C (Viking invasions) to the 20C. The village consists of some 20 dwellings, capable of accommodating about 100 people, carved out of the rock near a spring and protected by a narrow fortified entrance. A chapel consecrated to St Mary Magdalene, which was enlarged and had ogive vaulting added to it in the 15C, gave the site its name.

At the foot of the cliff lies the **prehistoric deposit** which established the characteristics of the Magdalenian cul-

ture which predominated during the last 60 centuries of the Upper Paleolithic Age (15000-9000 BC). The richness and quality of the items discovered here in 1863 is remarkable. The majority of the objects are exhibited in the museums at Les Eyzies and St-Germain-en-Laye.

▶ *Turn back then right onto the D 706.*

Tursac

The **church** is dominated by a huge, forbidding bell-tower. There is a series of domes, characteristic of the Romanesque Périgord style, covering the church. The road once more scales the cliff, giving good views of Tursac village and the Vézère Valley.

▶ *The D 706 leads back to Les Eyzies.*

ADDRESSES

🛏 STAY

🍽 **Le Panoramique** – *Beune, 24620 Les Eyzies de Tayac - 3.9km/2.3mi SE of Les Eyzies on the D 47 towards Sarlat then the D 48 towards St-Cyprien.* ℘*05 53 06 98 82.* 🛏*4 rooms.* A pleasant park with trees forms an oasis of quiet around the three regional-style houses. The decor of the guestrooms is plain; two have panoramic terraces overlooking the site of Les Eyzies.

🍽🍽 **Hôtel Le Moulin de la Beune** – ℘*05 53 06 94 33. www.moulindela beune.com. Closed Oct 31–Apr 8. 20 rooms.* The guest rooms at this former mill on the River Beune are traditional and comfortable. Wood and stone are the predominant themes in the dining room, where you can admire the mill's old waterwheel mechanism. Waterfront terrace.

🍴 EAT

🍽🍽 **Hostellerie du Passeur** – *Place de la Mairie, 24620 Les Eyzies-de-Tayac.* ℘*05 53 06 97 13. www.hostellerie-du-passeur.com. 19 rooms.* This handsome house covered in Virginia creeper stands in the heart of Les Eyzies. Stylish, cheerful rooms all sporting bright

colours, some overlooking the cliffs. At dinner, choose from the classical dining room with its stone fireplace, the bright conservatory or the shady terrace facing the Vézère. Traditional cuisine.

🍽🍽 **Auberge de l'Étang Joli** – *4km/ 2.5mi S of Les Eyzies on the D 706 and a minor road.* ℘*05 53 35 29 87. http://aubergeetangjoli.com. Reservation required in winter.* Far from the tourist crowds, this peaceful Périgord inn has an attractive flower garden and terrace. Regional cooking, prepared with care by the exuberant *patronne.*

🍽🍽 **La Métairie** – *On the D 47 - 7km/ 4.3mi E of Les Eyzies-de-Tayac.* ℘*05 53 29 65 32. bourgeade@wanadoo.fr . Closed Dec 1–Feb 28, Sun eve out of season, Mon, and Wed lunchtime.* This farm once belonged to the Château de Beyssac and is built around a courtyard-terrace. The old feeding troughs in the dining room are an appropriate reminder of the building's past history!

🛒 SHOPPING

The farmers' market is open daily in the summer season, selling a range of local crafts and produce.

Grotte de Lascaux★★

Lascaux Cave ranks among the finest prehistoric sites of Europe by dint of the number and quality of its paintings.

- **Michelin Map:** 329: I-5
- **Info:** Pl. Bertran-de-Born, 24290 Montignac. ℘05 53 51 82 60. www.bienvenue-montignac.com
- **Location:** 2km/1.2mi south of Montignac, and 26km/16mi north of Sarlat.
- **Kids:** Régourdou.

A BIT OF HISTORY

Discovery of the cave – The cave was discovered on 12 September 1940 by four young boys looking for their dog, which had fallen down a hole. They found an extraordinary fresco of poly-chrome paintings on the walls of the gallery they were in.

In 1949 the cave was officially opened to the public. Over 15 years, more than a million people came to admire the famous Lascaux paintings. Unfortunately, in spite of all the precautions taken, carbon dioxide and humidity resulted in two damaging effects: the green effect (the growth of moss and algae) and the white effect (less visible but much more serious as it leads to a build-up of deposits of white calcite).

In 1963, in order to preserve such a treasure, it was decided to close the cave to the public. Ten years later, a project was put forward to build a replica; Lascaux II was opened in 1983, under the care of the Dordogne Tourist Administration. As early as 1966, The National Geographic Institute (*Institut Géographique National – IGN*) had accomplished a precise photographic survey of Lascaux using three-dimensional scenes of the cave and stereo images. This survey enabled a shell to be constructed in reinforced concrete. Once the cave walls were reproduced, the painter Monique Peytral copied the cave paintings using slides and the results from numerous surveys she had made. She used the same methods and materials (pigments, tools etc) as the cave artists.

THE CAVE

The cave, carved out of Périgord Noir limestone, is a relatively small cavity, 250m/820ft long. It is made up of four galleries, the walls of which are covered with more than 1 500 representations, either engraved or painted. These works were created from around 17000 BC, during the Magdalenian Culture, a period when the climate was relatively mild. At that time the cave was open to the outside air. Some time after the cave artists had decorated the cave, the entrance collapsed and a flow of clay tightly closed the cave.

The airtight entrance and the impermeable ceiling are the reasons for the lack of concretions and the perfect preservation of the paintings fixed and authenticated by a thin layer of natural calcite. The simplified scene of a wounded bison and a falling man offers one of the rare representations of a human figure. This collection of paintings is truly unique in the history of prehistoric art, in regard to the state of preservation, the number of works created over a long time span, and the precision of execution.

A wide range of fauna is depicted on the cave walls, mainly animals hunted during the early Magdalenian period: aurochs, horses, reindeer, bison, ibexes, bears and woolly rhinoceroses appear side by side or superimposed, forming part of extraordinary compositions.

The Lascaux style – There is a definite Lascaux style: lively animals with small, elongated heads, swollen stomachs and short legs, and fur illustrated by dabs of coloured pigment. The horns, antlers and hoofs are often drawn in three-quarter view at times even full face while the animal itself is drawn in profile; this procedure is known as the turned profile. In addition, the artists used the wall contours to give relief to the subject matter. The most impressive feature is the conveyed movement, where the animals seem to leap around visitors.

LASCAUX II★★

Open daily Jul–Aug, guided tour (40min), 9am–8pm; Apr–Jun and Sept, 9am–6.30pm; Oct–Nov 11 10am–12.30pm and 2pm–6pm; Feb 4-Apr and Nov 12 - Jan 1 10am-12.30pm and 2-5.30pm. Closed anually Jan. From Apr-Sep, tickets are sold in Montignac, under the arcades next to the tourist office. Tickets go on sale at 9am and are sold until 2,000 have been issued (allocation can sell out very quickly). 8.20€. 05 53 51 95 03/ 05 53 05 65 65.

Located some 200m/219yd from the original cave, the facsimile reconstitutes two galleries from the upper part of the cave; the Bulls' Hall and the Axial Gallery, which contain the majority of the cave paintings at Lascaux. Airlock antechambers retrace the cave's history in explanatory exhibits and present items discovered in the cave's archaeological strata (tallow lamps, coloured powders, flints used by the engravers); a model of the scaffolding used; an explanation of the dating methods used; and displays on flint and bone knapping.

In the **Bulls' Hall** (La Rotonde), the paintings are on the calcite-covered upper part of the wall and the vaulting, so that the animals seem to be running along the natural rim as if along the horizon line. The second animal, the only imaginary animal figure painted at Lascaux, has been nicknamed the unicorn because of the odd-looking horns above a bear-like muzzle, on a body not unlike that of a rhinoceros. Among the other animals represented there are some magnificent black bulls, red bison, small horses and deer.

The **Axial Gallery** (Le Diverticule axial) contains a vault and walls covered with horses, cows, ibexes, bison and a large deer. A charming frieze of long-haired ponies, a great black bull and a large red pony, seeming to sniff at a branch, bear witness to a developed style of art.

EXCURSIONS
Régourdou

500m/550yd from Lascaux. You are advised to leave your car in the Lascaux car park. Open Jul–Aug, guided tour (1hr), 10am–7pm; Sept–Nov and Feb–Jun, 11am–6pm. Closed Dec–Jan. 5€. 05 53 51 81 23. www.regourdou.fr.

Older than Lascaux this prehistoric site, which goes back to the time of Neanderthal man was discovered in 1954; numerous objects and bones were brought to light, including a skeleton, Régourdou Man (70000 BC) and now displayed in the Périgord Museum in Périgueux.

A **museum** presents various elements found on the site and elsewhere, which help to illustrate the evolution of man from the Stone Age to the Iron Age.

Château de
Montaigne

Lovers of literary history will find the spirit of the great essayist Montaigne in the tower library of this château, where he was able to meditate and write in peace.

Michelin Map: 329: B-6
Location: 9km/5.5mi NE of Castillon-la-Bataille.

A BIT OF HISTORY
A Renaissance man

The essayist **Michel Eyquem de Montaigne** (1533-92) was born and died in this château; in his lifetime he served as a member of the Parliament of Bordeaux, was twice elected mayor of that city, and participated in high-level diplomatic negotiations during the Wars of Religion.

In 1571, at the age of 38, Michel de Montaigne took refuge in his family home in Périgord to reflect and write, as well as to care for his property. He continued to

"…I myself am the matter of my book."

Montaigne's *Essays* have been widely read and highly influential in the world of letters. Among his Anglophone readers were John Webster, William Shakespeare, Lord Byron, Ralph Waldo Emerson, Virginia Woolf, TS Eliot and Aldous Huxley. He is recognised as the inventor of the essay form. The original title of the works, *Essais*, signifies attempts, which reveals his penchant for exploration of the mind: *"to follow a movement so wandering … to penetrate the opaque depths of its innermost folds, to pick out and immobilise the innumerable flutterings that agitate it."* Many readers have been charmed by Montaigne's unassuming self-portrait of a doddering country gentleman (*"I want death to find me planting my cabbages"*), full of contradiction. In fact, he was active in public life, following a tradition begun by his grandfather, and viewed public service as a noble duty. Today's readers will find him remarkably timely in his defence of cultural relativism and tolerance, personal dignity and fidelity to nature.

perform civic duties when called upon, and travelled throughout Europe (his travel journal was published posthumously in 1774). His personal life was saddened by the loss of his one great friend (Étienne de la Boétie, to whom the essay *On Friendship* is dedicated), an uninspiring marriage, and the death in infancy of five of the six daughters he fathered.

TOUR HISTORIQUE DE MONTAIGNE

Times vary throughout the year, but the tour is always available 10am–noon and 2–5.30pm. Closed Dec 25, Jan 1 and Jan 7–Feb 8. 6€. 05 53 58 63 93. www.chateau-montaigne.com.

The main building was rebuilt after fire ravaged it in 1885; the **library tower**, Montaigne's domain, was saved. From his room above the chapel, the philosopher attended services by means of an opening in the wall (he died while hearing Mass thus). On the top floor, his famous **library**, is lined with books and decorated with Greek and Latin inscriptions.

Outside, visitors can admire a landscape little changed since the author's day: wooded hillsides, vineyards which produce a popular white wine, the outline of the feudal keep of Gurson on the horizon.

Montignac

and the Vézère

The old town of Montignac consisted of a group of houses around a tower, a last reminder of the fortress that once belonged to the counts of Périgord. In only a few years, this pleasant hamlet has become a busy tourist centre, thanks to the nearby Lascaux Cave. The small town spreads out on both banks of the River Vézère: on the west bank lies the "feudal village" with its network of narrow medieval lanes, and on the east bank lies the "suburb", once a trade centre and river port.

- **Population:** 2,888
- **Michelin Map:** 329: H-5
- **Info:** Place Bertran de Born. 05 53 51 82 60. www.bienvenue-montignac.com
- **Location:** On the banks of the Vézère, just 2km/1.2mi from the Lascaux caves and 25km/15km NW of Sarlat.
- **Kids:** La Roque St-Christophe.
- **Timing**: Allow a full day to explore the Vézère valley.
- **Don't Miss**: Grotte de Lascaux.

A BIT OF HISTORY

Man's presence here can be traced back to the Paleolithic era. The site was later occupied by the Romans and the fortress, built in the early part of the Middle Ages, turned Montignac into a stronghold. Taken and dismantled several times during successive wars, the castle was finally destroyed in 1825.

OLD TOWN

Start at the tourist office (east bank), housed in the former St John's hospital dating from the 14C (note the gallery). Église St-Georges, an extension of the hospital chapel, now houses temporary exhibitions. Follow **rue de la Pègerie**★ opposite: it is lined with medieval houses, including a fine 13C timber-framed house at the end of the street. Continue towards the river and admire, on the opposite bank, the houses built on piles and their wooden galleries. Walk to the old stone bridge and cross the river to Pautauberge square, where there is a bust of Eugène Le Roy, the "novelist of Périgord" who spent the last years of his life in Montignac. Exit the square opposite the 17C Hôtel de Bouillac, turn left then right onto rue des Jardins offering a fine **view**★ of Montignac. Continue along rue de la Tour which skirts the 11C castle and walk down towards the church. Note the fine house with its wooden gallery on the left. Return to the old bridge along the quays.

EXCURSIONS

La Grande Filolie

5km/3mi E on D 704; ⌁ *Closed to public.*
Set in the hollow of a small valley, this charming castle dating from the 14C and 15C consists of a group of overlapping buildings and towers linked together. This building, part-castle, part-farm, is built in golden-coloured limestone and covered with a superb roof of *lauzes*.

Fanlac

7km/4.3mi west.
This charming village was chosen by Eugène Le Roy as the setting of his most famous novel, *Jacquou le Croquant.*

🚗 DRIVING TOUR

VALLÉE DE LA VÉZÈRE★

55km/34mi round-trip – allow one day
From Montignac to Les Eyzies the road closely follows the course of the river, which is lined with magnificent poplars. This is the most attractive part of the valley.

▷ *Drive SW out of Montignac along the D 706 towards Les Eyzies.*

Le Thot, Espace Cro-Magnon★

🕐*Open Jul 5–Sept 2, 10am–7pm; Apr 4–Jun 30 and Sept, 10am–6pm; Oct 1–Nov 4, 10am–12.30pm and 2–6pm; Feb 4–Apr 3 & Nov 5–Jan 3, daily except Mon, 10am–12.30pm and 2–5pm.* 🕐*Closed Jan 3–Jan 31, 25 Dec.* ⊚*6€ (child 3.70€).* 🕾*05 53 50 70 44.*
👪The museum displays a large overview of the expression of prehistoric people through painting, sculpture, graffiti etc; prehistoric cultures are placed in the historical context of civilisation, its evolution and driving forces. These topics are developed with the aid of modern technology; re-creations, enormous slide shows, film and so on.
The **park** is especially well-designed, and is home to a number of species which inhabited the area in prehistoric times, such as aurochs and Prjewalski's horses. Species which no longer roam the planet, the mammoth and the woolly rhinoceros, are represented by animatronics.

▷ *Continue along the D 706.*

Château et Jardins de Losse★

🎧*Open Jun–Aug, guided tour (40min) of the grand logis, 12am–7pm; May and Sept, noon–6pm.Closed Sat exc Pub Hol weekends.* ⊚*7.50€.* 🕾*05 53 50 80 08. www.chateaudelosse.com*
This elegant 16C building set amid terraced gardens is perched high on a rock above the right bank of the River Vézère. A terrace adorned with a balustrade, supported by a fine basket-handled arch, projects in front of the main building, which is flanked by a round tower

at one corner. A fixed bridge, which has replaced the original drawbridge, gives access to the main courtyard past a fortified gatehouse.

A walk along the ramparts offers a good overall view of the fortifications; from the **Tour Sainte-Marguerite**, now a dovecote (*video presentation of period costumes*), an alleyway lined with boxwood hedging leads to the **Tour de l'éperon** housing a bath and resting room. Look down on the **Jardin bas**: a restored garden planted with lavender, santalina and rosemary bushes, separated by a small canal. Nearby is an **outbuilding** presenting a film describing the castle and stone-slab roofing methods. Farther on are the **Jardins en terrasse** inspired by 17C bowers.

Splendid furnishings make in particular **tapestries** make for fine decoration. Note the fresh colours of the Flemish tapestry, illustrating the traditional preparation for a tournament, and the Florentine tapestry depicting the Return of the Courtesan; both are 17C.

▷ *Drive onto Thonac then turn right onto the D 45.*

Plazac

The Romanesque church, in the centre of a churchyard planted with cypress trees, stands on a hillock overlooking the village. The 12C belfry-keep is roofed with *lauzes* and embellished with blind arcades resting on Lombard bands.

▷ *Drive S along the D 6.*

Le Moustier

This village, at the foot of a hill, contains a famous prehistoric shelter (**Abri du Moustier** – ◷ *open daily except Sat by reservation only (minimum 2 weeks in advance)*. ◷*Closed 1 Jan, 1 May, 1 and 11 Nov, and 25 Dec.* ◉*2.50€.* ℘*05 53 06 86 00.* The prehistoric finds made here include the skeleton of a Neanderthal man and many flint implements. A culture in the Middle Paleolithic Age was named Mousterian after the finds. An interesting 17C carved confessional can be seen in the village church.

▷ *From the village, drive towards Chabans passing Côte de Jor, which affords a panoramic view of the Vézère and St-Léon-sur-Vézère.*

Château de Chabans

☞ *Closed to the public*

An avenue lined with ancient trees leads to this imposing castle still protected by defensive walls. The round tower dates from the 15C whereas the remainder of the edifice was rebuilt in the 16C and 17C. The castle was tastefully restored at the end of the 20C.

▷ *Return to Le Moustier. Cross the Vézère then turn left onto the D 66.*

La Roque St-Christophe★

◷☞ *Open Jul–Aug, guided tour (1hr, last entrance 45min before closing), 10am–8pm; Apr–Jun and Sept, 10am–6.30pm; Feb–Mar and Oct–Nov 11, 10am–6pm; Nov12 –Jan 31, 12–5pm.* ◷*Closed 1 Jan and 25 Dec.* ◉*7€ (child: 3€).* ℘*05 53 50 70 45. www.roque-st-christophe.com*

👥 This long and majestic cliff rises vertically (80m/262ft) above the Vézère Valley over a distance of more than 900m/0.5mi. It is like a huge hive with about 100 caves hollowed out of the rock on five tiers. Excavations along its foot have shown that the cliff dwellings were inhabited from the Upper Paleolithic Age onwards.

In the 10C the cliff terraces served as the foundation for a fortress which was used against the Vikings and during the Hundred Years War (accommodating up to 1 500 people), and then subsequently destroyed during the Wars of Religion, at the end of 16C. The drainage channels and water tanks, the fireplaces, the stairways and passages hollowed out of the rock all show that St Christopher's Rock was the site of continued, lively human activity. A house leaning against the cliff was reconstructed according to methods used in the 10C and 13C; in the **Cuisine de l'an mil** (the AD 1000 kitchen) are displayed replicas of archaeological finds. On the **Grande terrasse**, visitors can see a reconstruction of a medieval building site and a model of the whole site. From this terrace, admire the **view**★ of the green Vézère Valley.

▶ *Continue along the D 66.*

Peyzac-le-Moustier

The **Musée du Moustier** illustrates the evolution of living beings as well as technical progress from the first creatures going back to some 600 million years to the Gallo-Romans. The park contains the sculpture of a dinosaur (11m/36ft long and 5m/16.5ft high) and several megaliths. ♿ *open mid-Jun to mid-Sep, 10am–6.30pm; mid-Sep to mid-Jun, by prior arrangement (2 weeks in advance); contact Mr Quinsac-Mandeix. 3€. 05 53 50 81 02. or 05 53 04 86 21. (out of season).*

▶ *Leave Peyzac S and join the D 65.*

St-Léon-sur-Vézère★

See ST-LÉON-SUR-VÉZÈRE.

▶ *Return to Peyzac, follow the D 65.*

Sergeac

This village is pleasantly situated beside the Vézère at a spot where tall cliffs follow the line of the valley.
The village which has an interesting and delicately carved 15C cross standing at its entrance, also contains old houses roofed with *lauzes* and a turreted manor house, the remains of a commandery, which once belonged to the Knights Templars. The restored Romanesque **church**, still retains a fortified appearance with its loopholes, machicolations and bell-tower.

Castel-Merle

This site, which is well-known to the specialists, was for a long time closed to the public. Some of the finds – bones, flints, headdresses – are exhibited in the museums of Les Eyzies, Périgueux and St-Germain-en-Laye (west of Paris).
Near the site, a small local **museum** exhibits a number of interesting artefacts from the Mousterian Age to the Gallo-Roman era. ♿ *guided tours (1hr), by prior arrangement, one day in advance; contact Mr Castanet, le Bourg, 24290 Sergeac. 05 53 50 77 45.*
Several shelters *(abris)* can be visited, one of which contains wall sculptures (bison, horses) from the Magdalenian Age (*open Jul–Aug, guided tour (1hr), 1–7pm, closed Sun; Apr–Jun & Sept, 2–5pm, closed Sat–Sun. 5€. 05 53 50 79 70).* In the Souquette shelter a section of strata is shown with levels from the Aurignacian Age to the modern era.

▶ *Return to Montignac on the D 65.*

ADDRESSES

🛏 STAY

🍴 **Relais du Soleil d'Or** – *16 R. du 4-Septembre. 05 53 51 80 22. soleil-or @wanadoo.fr. Closed Jan 31– end Feb. 32 rooms.* This former coaching inn is an ideal base from which to visit nearby Lascaux. Rooms overlooking the garden are preferable. The dining room-veranda faces the swimming pool and outdoor terrace. Traditional cuisine. Bistro menus at lunchtime.

🍴 **Hôtel de la Roseraie** – *Pl. 05 53 50 53 92. www.laroseraie-hotel.com. Closed Nov 1–Easter. 14 rooms.* A large old house on a quiet square, with attractive rooms decorated with floral fabrics and painted wooden furniture. The dining rooms and terrace overlook a charming rose garden. Swimming pool.

🍴 EAT

🍴 **Hotel le Lascaux** –*109, ave Jean Jaures 24290 Montinac. 05 53 51 82 81. www.hotel-le-lascaux.fr. Closed Nov 20– Jan 20.* In the the heart of Périgord Noir this family run Logis offers traditional cuisine served in the spacious dining room or on the shaded terrace overlooking the garden.

🛒 SHOPPING

Markets - Walnut and chestnut market on Wednesdays in October and November.

La Roque-Gageac★★

The village of La Roque-Gageac, huddled against a cliff which drops vertically to the River Dordogne, occupies a wonderful site★★ – one of the finest in this part of the valley, in which Domme, Castelnaud and Beynac-et-Cazenac are all within a few miles of each other. At the top of the cliff there are clear traces to remind visitors of the tragic day in 1957 when a huge block of rock came away from the cliff face, killing three inhabitants.

THE VILLAGE

Attractive little streets run tightly along the rocky bluff. One of them, leading off to the right of the Carrier hotel, climbs through luxuriant plant life to reach a kind of oasis backing onto the cliff face. It has taken Gérard Dorin 30 years to develop his exotic garden: the micro climate favours the growth of Mediterranean vegetation (olive, lemon and banana trees thrive here together with 20 varieties of palm trees).

Walk back down the street towards the troglodytic fort opposite. On your way, take a look at the **Manoir de Tarde**. Two pointed gabled buildings, with mullioned windows, stand next to a round

▶ **Population:** Dordogne Population 420

Michelin Map: 329: I-7; or *see SARLAT*.

Info: La Balme" F-24220 Beynac-et-Cazenac ℘05 53 29 43 08

Location: 69km/43mi SE of Périgueux and 12km/7.5mi S of Sarlat. The best view of La Roque-Gageac is from the west: the late afternoon sun highlights the tall grey cliff face covered with holm oaks, while the houses, with their stone slab (*lauzes*) or tile roofs, are reflected in the calm waters of the river below.

Don't Miss: A boat trip.

tower. This charming manor house is associated with the Tarde family, whose most famous member was canon Jean Tarde, a 16C humanist, historian, cartographer, astronomer and mathematician. The impregnable **troglodytic fort** (*open Jun–Aug, 10.30am–7pm; Apr–May and Sep to mid-Nov, 11am–5pm; 5€; ℘05 53 31 61 94*) was built in the 12C and reinforced in the 17C before being dismantled in the 18C. A 140-step climb will take you within sight of what remains of the defensive system and the beautiful view will reward your efforts (*note the outline of the Château de la Malartrie on the right*).

ADDRESSES

STAY

Auberge La Plume d'Oie ℘05 53 29 57 05. laplumedoie@wanadoo.fr. *Closed Jan 8–Feb 13, Nov 20 to Dec 20, Sun evening, Mon, Tue lunchtime. Reserv. required.* 4 rooms. A little village inn in an old renovated house, typical of the region. The dining room is bright and cheerful with blonde wooden beams, stonework and large bay windows. A few rooms with views of the Dordogne.

La Roque-Gageac

J. Damase/MICHELIN

Rouffignac-St-Cernin-de-Reilhac★

▸ **Population:** 1 484
▸ **Michelin Map:** 329: G-5
▸ **Information:** Place de la Mairie ℘05 53 05 39 03
▸ **Location**: 18km/11mi north of Les Eyzies de Tayac.

Rouffignac lies at the heart of a region rich in archaeological and historic sites, including the splendid prehistoric cave of the same name. The church is all that escaped when the Germans set about burning the village in March 1944 as a reprisal; it has since been rebuilt and is now a peaceful holiday resort and the ideal starting point of excursions in the area.

CHURCH

The **church** entrance is through an interesting belfry-porch with an early Renaissance door. It was built in 1530 and is decorated with Corinthian capitals.

GROTTE DE ROUFFIGNAC★

5km/3mi S along the D 32. 🚹🕐*Open Jul–Aug, 9–11am and 2–6pm; Apr–Jun and Sept–Nov 1, 10–11.30am and 2–5pm.* 🚶*Guided tour (1hr).* ✆*5.90€. Limited number of daily visitors.* ℘*05 53 05 41 71. www.grottederouffignac.fr.* This dry **cave**, also known as Cro de Granville, was already well-known in the 15C. The galleries are over 8km/5mi long. An electric train carries visitors to the main galleries and this is one of the few prehistoric sites in the area which is fully accessible to persons of limited mobility. In 1956 Professor LR Nougier called attention to the remarkable group of paintings marked with black lines and **engravings**★ produced during the middle or upper Magdalenian period (around 13000 BC). These engravings are of horses, ibexes, rhinoceroses, bison and a great number of mammoths, among which may be seen the Patriarch and an amazing frieze depicting two herds locked in combat. There is an outstanding group of drawings on the ceiling of the last chamber.

ADDRESSES

🛏 STAY

🍴🍴🍴🍴 **Les Glycenes** – *rte Périgueux Les Eyzies de Tayac. 16km/10mi S of Rouffignac on the D31 & D 47.* ℘*05 53 06 97 07. www.les-glycines-dordogne.com*: 🛏*14€. 27 rooms.* Former post house (1862) in a verdant setting near the Vézère. Impressive grounds and wisteria clad arbour. Renovated guest rooms with four at garden level. Restaurant with view of hotel grounds, a pleasant tranquil terrace and up-to-date cuisine.

Painting of rhinoceros, Grotte de Rouffignac

©World Illustrated/Photoshot

Sarlat-la-Canéda★★★

and the Dordogne

At the heart of Périgord Noir, Sarlat-la-Canéda (Sarlat for short) was built in a hollow surrounded by wooded hills. Its charm lies in its preservation of the past; it still gives the impression of a small market town – the home of merchants and clerks during the Ancien Régime (period before the Revolution) – with narrow medieval streets, restored Gothic and Renaissance town houses (*hôtels*). Such is the aesthetic allure of the town that it has been used as the setting for two Hollywood films and has featured in several others.

A BIT OF HISTORY

From abbey to bishopric – Sarlat grew up around a Benedictine abbey founded in the 8C in which the relics of St Sacerdos, bishop of Limoges, were kept. The abbots were all powerful until the 13C when internal strife and corruption caused their downfall. In 1299 the Book of Peace, an act of emancipation signed by the community, the abbey and the king, stated that the abbot might continue in his role of lord but that the consuls should be given all administrative power concerning the town itself. In 1317, however, Pope John XXII divided the Périgueux diocese and proclaimed Sarlat the Episcopal see of an area which extended far beyond the Sarladais region. The abbey church therefore became a cathedral.

Sarlat's golden age – The 13C and early 14C had been a prosperous time for this active market town, but the Hundred Years War left it weakened and depopulated. Therefore, when Charles VII bestowed numerous privileges upon Sarlat and its population to thank them for their loyalty and strong resistance against the English, the people of Sarlat began reconstruction. Most of the town houses to be seen were built between 1450 and 1500. This has created an architectural unity which is appreciated by

- ▶ **Population:** 9 432
- **Michelin Map:** 329: I-6; or *see SARLAT*.
- **Info:** R. de Tourny, BP 144, 24200 Sarlat-la-Canéda. ℘05 53 31 45 45. www.sarlat-tourisme.com.
- **Location:** 52km/32.5mi south of Brive-la-Gaillarde, 60km/37.5mi north of Cahors and 74km/46mi east of Bergerac.
- **Parking**: There are a dozen car parks in Sarlat, four of which are free of charge (*see town plan*). In summer, traffic is banned from the town's historical quarter.
- **Don't Miss**: Old Sarlat; Place du Marché aux Trois Oies; Hôtel Plamon; Hôtel de Maleville; Maison de la Boétie; Saturday and Wednesday markets.

the townspeople and tourists alike. The magistrates, clerks, bishops, canons and merchants formed a comfortable bourgeois class which included such men of letters as Étienne de La Boétie.

The true and faithful friend - Étienne de La Boétie, who was born in Sarlat in 1530 in a house that can still be seen (*see below*), became famous on many counts. He proved himself to be a brilliant magistrate in the Bordeaux Parliament as well as an impassioned writer – he was only 18 when he wrote the compelling appeal for liberty, *Discourse on Voluntary Subjection or Contr'un* (Against One), which inspired Jean-Jacques Rousseau. He formed a lifelong friendship with **Michel de Montaigne** and which has been immortalised by posterity. Montaigne was at La Boétie's bedside when the young man died in 1563; with his friend in mind, Montaigne wrote his famous *Essay on Friendship* in which he formulated the excellent sentiment: "If I am urged to explain why I loved him, I feel I can only reply: because he was himself and I am myself."

OLD SARLAT★★★WALK

Sarlat's old district was cut into two in the 19C by the Traverse (rue de la République). The town houses are quite unique: built with quality ashlar-work in a fine golden-hued limestone, with interior courtyards; the roofing, made of heavy limestone slabs (*lauzes*), necessitated a steeply pitched framework so that the enormous weight (500kg per m^2 – about 102lb per sq ft) could be supported on thick walls. Over the years new floors were added: a medieval ground floor, a High Gothic or Renaissance upper floor and Classical roof cresting and lantern turrets.

This architectural unit escaped modern building developments and was chosen in 1962 as one of the new experimental national restoration projects, the goal of which was to preserve the old quarters of France's towns and cities. The project, begun in 1964, has allowed the charm of this small medieval town to be recreated.

▷ *Start from place du Peyrou.*

Cathédrale St-Sacerdos

St Sacerdos' Church was built here in the 12C. In 1504 Bishop Armand de Gontaut-Biron had the church razed, in order to build a cathedral.

However, when the bishop left Sarlat in 1519, the construction work ceased for

more than a century and completed during the 16C and 17C.

Inside, the most striking features are the elevation and harmonious proportions of the nave, which has ogive vaulting, and of the chancel surrounded by an ambulatory.

Ancien Évêché

To the right of St Sacerdos' Cathedral, is the former bishopric. Its façade has windows in the Gothic style on the first floor, Renaissance on the second floor and an Italian Renaissance loggia above, added by the Italian bishop Nicolo Goddi, friend of Catherine de' Medici. *The tourist office is on the ground floor.*

Maison de la Boétie★

This house, built in 1525, is the birthplace of Étienne de La Boétie.

A large arch on the ground floor used to shelter a small shop; the two upper floors of Italian Renaissance style have large mullioned windows, framed by pilasters carved with medallions and lozenges.

On the left of the house is **passage Henri-de-Ségogne**, between Hôtel de Maleville and La Boétie's House. The alleyway leads visitors through an arch, a passageway and a covered passageway.

Picturesque half-timbered buildings have been restored and, in summer, craft shops do a swift business.

Hôtel de Maleville★

This edifice is also known as the Hôtel de Vienne after the man who built it, Jean de Vienne. Born of humble parents in Sarlat in 1557, he successfully climbed the social ladder to become financial secretary under Henri IV.

Later, the town house was bought by the Maleville family; a member of this same family, Jacques de Maleville (♿ *see DOMME*), helped write the French *Code Civil*, the general rules of law.

Three existing houses were combined in the mid-16C to form an imposing mansion. In front of the tall, narrow central pavilion, like a majestic tower, is a terrace under which opens the arched

Distinctive roof line of the Maison de la Boétie

J. Damase/MICHELIN

VIEUX SARLAT

0   100m

WHERE TO STAY

Abbys (Hôtel).................................. ①
Altica (Hôtel).................................. ②
Clos-Vallis (Chambre d'hôte Le)...... ③
Filolies (Chambre d'hôte Les)......... ⑦
Jardin de Clélia (Hôtel Le)............... ⑨
Mas de Castel (Hôtel)..................... ⑫
Montaigne (Hôtel).......................... ⑬
Récollets (Hôtel des)...................... ⑮

Rhonie (Ferme-auberge de la)......... ⑰

WHERE TO EAT

Bistrot de l'Octroi (Le)................... ⑩
Garrigue-Haute
  (Ferme-auberge La).................... ⑫
Jardins d'Harmonie (Les)................ ⑬
Rossignol.. ⑮
Quatre saisons (Le)......................... ⑰

---

main doorway surmounted by medal-lions depicting Henri IV and Marie de Medici.

The right wing, overlooking place de la Liberté, has a late Renaissance gable.

◐ *Take the covered passage to the left of the entrance, then take rue du Minage opposite, follow rue de la République and turn right onto rue des Consuls.*

Rue des Consuls

The town houses in this street are beau-tiful examples of Sarlat architecture from the 14C-17C.

◐ *On the right after the bend.*

Hôtel Plamon★

As identified by the shield on the pedi-ment above the doorway, this town house belonged to the Selves de Plamon

Sarlat from above

J. Damase/MICHELIN

family, members of the cloth merchants' guild. Because it is made up of a group of buildings built in different periods, it is a particularly interesting illustration of the evolution of the different architectural styles used in Sarlat construction.

Left of the town house is the very narrow Plamon Tower with windows which get smaller the higher up they are; this architectural ruse makes the tower seem much taller than it is.

On the corner of the street is a rounded overhanging balcony supported by a squinch. Go into the courtyard to admire the elegant 17C wooden **staircase**★.

Fontaine Ste-Marie

Opposite the Hôtel de Plamon, the fountain splashes in a cool grotto.

Place du Marché aux Trois Oies★

Appropriately called Goose Square, this is the place where on Saturdays from December to March people come from far and wide to haggle over the price of geese and, of course, *foie gras.*

The square is an elegant architectural collection of turrets, pinnacles and corner staircases.

Hôtel de Vassal

Located on a corner of place des Oies, this 15C town house consists of two buildings at right angles flanked by twin corbelled turrets. Beside it, the **Hôtel de Gisson** (16C) is made of two buildings joined by a hexagonal staircase tower with a remarkable pointed roof.

Place de la Liberté

Many pavement cafés liven up Sarlat's main square. The 17C **town hall** stands on the east side and the disused **Église Ste-Marie,** now converted into a covered market, on the north side.

▷ *Leave place de la Liberté and walk along rue de la Salamandre.*

Hôtel de Grézel

Built at the end of the 15C, the town house straight ahead has a half-timbered façade with a tower and a lovely Flamboyant Gothic ogee-arched doorway. Continue onto rue Présidial, then rue Landry (as far as no 7), until you can see the 17C tower of the **Présidial**, former seat of royal magistrates (now a restaurant).

▷ *Retrace your steps and turn left onto rue d'Albusse.*

At the corner of the dead end (where the old post house can be seen) stands the **Hôtel de Génis**, a massive, plain 15C building with an overhanging upper storey supported by seven stone corbels.

▷ *Follow rue Sylvain Cavaillez and enter the garden.*

Lanterne des Morts

Built at the end of the 12C, this myste-rious cylindrical tower topped with a cone and split into tiers by four bands contains two rooms. The room on the ground floor has domed vaulting held up by six pointed arches; the other room is in the cone part of the tower, which was inaccessible.

A number of hypotheses have been put forward concerning the lantern's function: was it a tower built in honour of the visit of St Bernard in 1147; a lantern of the dead; or a funerary chapel?

◐ *Go down the stairs and walk around the Chapelle des Pénitents Bleus (12C). Go into cour des Chanoines then cour des Fontaines. Rue Munz and rue Tourny lead back to place du Peyrou.*

✿◐ WEST SIDE TOUR★

This part of town, on the opposite side of rue de la République (the so-called Traverse), is currently under renewal. Its steep and winding lanes are quieter, off the main tourist track, and offer another image of Sarlat.

◐ *Walk along rue de la République and turn left onto rue J.-J.-Rousseau.*

Chapelle des Pénitents Blancs

Used by the Order of Pénitents Blancs, the chapel (1626) was part of the religious establishment of the Pères Récollets.

Rue Jean-Jacques Rousseau

This is the main street in this part of town, and many attractive old houses grace it. At no 9, on the corner of Côte de Toulouse, there is an admirable 18C façade (Hôtel Monméja); at the intersection with rue de la Boétie, you can see the bartizan which marks the site of **St Clare's Convent**, a vast 17C building once occupied by the Poor Clares, and today provides low-rent housing.

◐ *Continue along rue du Siège then turn left onto rue Rousset.*

Typical house in old Sarlat

S. Sauvignier/MICHELIN

Tour de Guet

Overlapping the buildings, the watch-tower is crowned by 15C machicolations and flanked by a corbelled turret.

◐ *Turn right onto rue du Cordil.*

Rue des Trois-Conils (des Trois Lapins)

This street bends sharply left around the foot of a house flanked by a tower, which once belonged to relations the La Boétie family.

Tour du Bourreau

The Executioner's Tower, which was part of the ramparts, was built in 1580.

◐ *Walk along rue du Siège leading back to rue de la République.*

EXCURSIONS

Marquay

11.5km/7mi NW along the D 47 and D 6.
This sought-after holiday resort sur-rounded by important Paleolithic sites has an unusual 12C church.

Tamniès

15km/9.3mi NW along D 47 and D 6.
The 12C village church and former priory overlook the Beune Valley. There is a lake with leisure facilities nearby.

🚗 DRIVING TOURS

THE DORDOGNE TO THE BEAUNE★

60km/37.3mi round-trip – half a day.
This route is not marked on the map.
After Beynac this route follows the Dordogne Valley to St-Cyprien. From here it takes the backroads past sleepy hamlets through the unspoiled Périgord Noir.

▶ *Drive SW out of Sarlat along the D 57; turn right onto the D 703 shortly after Vézac.*

Beynac-et-Cazenac★★

See BEYNAC-ET-CAZENAC.
Continue on the D 703 to St-Cyprien then turn right as you leave the village.

Cazenac

This hamlet possesses a 15C Gothic church with a lovely view of the valley.

▶ *Turn back and rejoin the D 703.*

St-Cyprien

See Le BUGUE: Excursion.

▶ *Drive NE along the D 25.*

Chapelle de Redon-l'Espi

This remote Romanesque chapel is flanked by the ruins of a small monastery, destroyed during the Wars of Religion. The Virgin Mary is said to have appeared to a young shepherdess in the 19C, giving rise to a pilgrimage that still takes place in September.

▶ *Rejoin D 25 (right); left on D 47 beyond Allas; right 1.5km/0.9mi on.*

Cabanes du Breuil

🕐♿*Open Jun–Sep, 10am–7pm; Mar–May and Oct to mid-Nov, 10am–noon and 2–6pm; mid-Nov to Feb, Sat–Sun, 10am–noon, 2–5pm.* 🎫*5€.* 📞*06 80 72 38 59. www.cabanes-du-breuil.com.*
The hamlet of Breuil has the richest collection of drystone buildings known as *caselles* (or *gariottes*) in Périgord. There are five huts, forming an architectural grouping unique in the region.

▶ *Turn back and turn left onto the D 47 towards Sarlat; turn left again 3km/1.9mi farther on.*

Château de Puymartin★

🦆*Open Aug 10am–6.30pm; Jul 10am–noon and 2–6.30pm; Apr–Jun & Sept, 10am–noon and 2–6pm; Oct to Nov 11, 2–5.30pm.* 🎫*7€.* 📞*05 53 59 29 97. www.chateau-de-puymartin.com*
Constructed in the 15C and 16C, considerably remodelled in the 19C, the castle consists of several buildings linked to towers, and protected by a curtain wall. The **interior decoration**★ is impressive: period furnishings, Aubusson tapestries, painted beams and paintings.

▶ *The D 47 takes you back to Sarlat.*

ROUND-TRIP FROM SARLAt★★

75km/47mi – allow one day.
See map opposite.
The houses, castles, châteaux, manor houses and churches along this route have walls of golden-coloured local limestone and steeply pitched roofs covered with lauzes or small flat tiles in a warm brown hue. These architectural elements, combined with the rolling, wooded countryside, make a harmonious picture.

▶ *Leave Sarlat travelling SE along the D 704 towards Gourdon. As you leave town, turn right to La Canéda.*

Site de Montfort★

Occupying an advantageous site on the River Dordogne, Montfort has given its name to one of Périgord's most famous meanders.

Cingle de Montfort★

From the cliff road (D 703 – car park), there is a splendid **view**★ of this meander in the river, known in French as the *Cingle de Montfort*, encircling the Tursac peninsula and its walnut tree plantations; the château clings to its promontory.

Château de Montfort★

The castle stands in a grandiose **setting**★, which aroused the envy of those who wished to rule Périgord; its history consisted of a long series of sieges and battles. Seized by Simon de Montfort in 1214 and razed to the ground, it was rebuilt and then later destroyed three times – during the Hundred Years War (1337-1453), under Louis XI (1461-83), and again by order of Henri IV (1562-1610). The renovation work carried out in the 19C gives it the whimsical look of a stage setting for light opera.

◯ *Drive NW along the D 703.*

Carsac-Aillac

The modest but delightful church of Carsac, in lovely golden stone, is set in countryside near the Dordogne. The porch has five recessed arches resting on small columns. The massive Romanesque bell tower and the apse are roofed with *lauzes*. The nave and the lower aisles had stellar vaulting decorated with elegant discs or bosses added to them in the 16C.

◯ *Leave Carsac travelling S along the D 704 to St-Rome and follow the signposts to the Jardins d'eau.*

Jardins d'Eau★

🕐 *Open May–Oct, 9am–8pm (Sept 20–Oct,10am–6pm)* ⊜5.5€. ℘*05 53 28 91 96 or 06 08 92 37 82. www.jardinsdeau.com.*
This 3ha/7.50-acre water garden was laid out along the riverside. The reception area is surrounded by a pond covered with exotic water lilies; it is home to a colony of frogs and five different kinds of dragonflies. The great white-water-lily pond, spanned by a Japanese bridge, evokes one of Monet's paintings, whereas the five varieties of iris bring Van Gogh to mind. The largest lotus flowers (2m/6.5ft high with leaves 70cm/28in in diameter) grow near the fountain, next to six varieties of white lilies. Take the footbridge wending its way above the lotus pond then touch and smell the water lilies floating on the tiered ponds among smaller water plants. You can buy plants in the nursery.

◯ *Rejoin the D 704, cross the River Dordogne and turn left onto the D 50.*

Château de Fénelon★

🕐*Daily Jul–Aug 10am–7pm; May, Jun & Sept 10.30am–12.30pm, 2.30–6pm; Mar & Oct 2–7pm; Apr 10.30am–12.30pm, 2.30–7pm; Feb & Nov Sat–Sun only 2–7pm. Closed Dec–Jan and Tue exc Jul & Aug.* ⊜*7.50€.* ℘*05 53 29 81 45.*
François de Salignac de Lamothe-Fénelon, later to become the duke of Burgundy's mentor and author of *Télémaque*, was born here on 6 August 1651 and spent his early childhood within these walls. His family had been feudal lords since the 14C and remained so until 1780.
Built near Ste-Mondane village, on a hill overlooking the Dordogne and the Bouriane Forest, the 14C castle underwent substantial alterations in the 17C. Its triply fortified walls give it the appear-

Jardins d'Eyrignac

J. Damase/MICHELIN

ance of being a very powerful fortress. The residential buildings and towers are still covered with *lauze* slate roofs. A beautiful **staircase** with two bends gives access to the main courtyard. From the terrace, there is a fine view of undulating countryside.

Inside, the bedroom where Fénelon was born, the Louis XVI and Empire rooms, the kitchen hollowed out of the rock and a collection of medieval military miscellany are all open to visitors.

▷ *Follow D 50 to St-Julien-de-Lampon; cross to the north bank via the D 61.*

The crossing of the Dordogne is guarded by the **Château de Rouffillac**; its attractive outline can be seen rising out of the green oak trees.

Carlux

Overlooking the valley from its commanding position, the village still has some old houses and a small covered market. Two towers and an imposing curtain wall are all that remains of the large castle, which once belonged to the viscounty of Turenne.

From the castle terrace, there is a lovely **view** of the valley and the cliffs, which were used as the castle foundations.

▷ *Take the road behind the castle and follow the signposts for "Jardins de Cadiot."*

Jardins de Cadiot★

Ⓞ*Open May–Oct, 10am–7pm.* ⊚*5€.* ℘*05 53 29 81 05.* This private 2ha/5-acre garden is surrounded by an oak wood. The tour starts with the vegetable garden and continues through 10 areas of different colours: the peony garden, the hornbeam maze, the rose garden containing 500 species of roses, the poetry garden, the English garden and the French garden, each having its own attraction.

▷ *Continue along the D 61 towards Salignac and turn left onto the D 47 3km/1.9mi farther on. Turn right in Ste-Nathalène and drive towards Proissans.*

Moulin de la Tour

♿Ⓞ*Open daily 9am–noon and 2–6pm.* 🗣*Guided tours (30min) on some days; contact or see website for more information.* Ⓞ*Closed 1 Jan, 1 Nov, 25 Dec and Sun.* ⊚*4.40€.* ℘*05 53 59 22 08. www.moulindelatour.com.* The 16C watermill, driven by the flow of the River Enea, continues the traditional manufacture of walnut and hazelnut oils. There used to be many grain mills in Périgord which were also adaptable for the production of walnut oil during the winter. The mechanism of this mill is 150 years old.

▷ *Return to Ste-Nathalène. Shortly before reaching the village, turn left towards the hamlet of La Tour.*

Jardins d'Eyrignac★★★

♿Ⓞ🗣*Open daily guided tour only (1hr), May–Sept , 9.30am–7pm; Apr 1–Apr 30, 10am–7pm; Oct–Mar, 10.30am–12.30pm and 2.30pm to dusk.* ⊚*9.50€.* ℘*05 53 28 99 71. www.eyrignac.com.* Laid out in the 18C by the Marquis de la Calprenède, these gardens were remodelled many times during the 19C and finally given their present aspect in the 1960s by Gilles Sermadiras de Pouzols de Lile. Five gardeners work full time to look after the 4ha/10-acre gardens. The result is a happy compromise between the French-style garden and Tuscan topiary art, rich in evergreens which make for year-round delight. The grassy paths are bordered with yew, creating little green chambers; there are apple trees in quincuncial arrangements (four trees in the corners and a fifth in the middle); cypress groves, urns, pools and dainty pavilions ornament the grounds of the 17C mansion, built in pale Sarlat stone. The latest addition to this enchanting place is the **Jardin blanc** (white garden); alleyways lined with white roses lead to five ornamental pools representing the five senses against a background of white rambling roses.

▷ *Rejoin the D 61 and turn left.*

Salignac-Eyvigues

The market square, the façade of the 13C convent (Couvent des Croisiers), and the neighbouring streets, in particular rue Sainte-Croix, are a charming sight, just a few yards away from the entrance to the castle.

Château

⚬┅ *Closed for restoration.*
There is a good overall view from the D 60, east of the village, of this medieval fortress which still belongs to the family of the archbishop of Cambrai, François de Salignac de la Mothe-Fénelon.
The castle, which was built between the 12C and 17C, is encircled by ramparts. Mullioned windows lighten the façade of the main building, which is flanked by round and square towers. The whole building is enhanced by the warm colour of the stone and the lovely stone slab (*lauzes*) roofs.

▷ *Drive W along the D 60 (Sarlat) and turn left as you leave the village.*

Carlucet

The church of Carlucet has an unusual 17C cemetery. Some of the tombs have been set in carved recesses in the curtain wall.

▷ *Drive SW out of Carlucet along a small winding road.*

St-Crépin-et-Carlucet

The charming **Château de Lacypierre** (&⚙┅*Open Easter to 1 Nov, guided tour. Tue and Fri 3.30pm, unaccompanied tour of the park and the exhibition on the restoration of the castle;* ⊜*5€;* ℘*05 53 29 39 28),* was built at the end of the 16C on the spot where a fortified building had once stood. The square main building is entirely roofed in lauzes and framed by turrets. .

▷ *Continue N along the D 60 to Salignac and turn left onto the D 61 2km/1.2mi farther on.*

St-Geniès★

This is one good example of the Périgord Noir's many beautiful villages with its golden limestone houses covered in *lauzes,* the ruins of a Romanesque keep and the 15C castle next to the church. Located at the top of a mound behind the post office, the **Chapelle du Cheylard**, a small Gothic chapel, is decorated with lovely 14C **frescoes**★ depicting the life of Christ and lives of popular saints.

▷ *Leave St-Geniès travelling S along the D 64 towards the D 704 and follow signs for Sarlat. Turn left at Les Presses.*

Temniac

The chapel of Notre-Dame, set on a hill overlooking Sarlat, offers a good **view**★ of that town. Once a pilgrimage centre, this 12C structure has certain Romanesque Périgord School characteristics: a nave vaulted with two domes and a pentagonal chancel.
Near the chapel stands the curtain wall of a castle which was once a commandery of the Knights Templar before it became the residence of the bishops of Sarlat.

▷ *The D 57 leads back to Sarlat.*

DORDOGNE IN THE PÉRIGORD★★★

Round tour from Sarlat – 70km/44mi – allow half a day. See map opposite.

Château des Milandes

J. Damase/MICHELIN

Drive S out of Sarlat on D 46, cross the Dordogne; turn right onto the D 50. Soon after Vitrac, Domme comes into view on its rocky promontory.

Domme★★
👣 *See DOMME. Continue on the D 50.*

Cénac
The only remaining evidence of the large priory built in Cénac in the 11C is the small **Romanesque church** which stands outside the village. Even the church did not escape the Wars of Religion, and only the east end escaped the depredations of the Protestants serving under Captain Vivans in 1589.

Go into the churchyard to get an overall view of the east end with its fine stone roof and its column buttresses topped with foliated capitals. Inside, in the chancel and the apse, there is a series of interesting historiated capitals.

▷ *Continue along the D 50 to St-Cybranet then follow the D 57 towards Sarlat and turn left before the bridge.*

Château de Castelnaud★★
👣 *See Château de CASTELNAUD.*

▷ *Rejoin D 57 (left) then D 53, which follows the south bank of the Dordogne.*

Château de Fayrac
The castle is tucked amid the greenery on the south bank of the Dordogne

opposite Beynac-et-Cazenac. A double curtain wall surrounds the interior courtyard, which is reached by two drawbridges.

▷ *Continue along the D 53.*

Château des Milandes★
🕐 *Daily Jul–Aug 9.30am–7.30pm; Apr & Oct 10am–6.15pm (Closed Sat); May, Jun & Sept 10am–6.30 (Sat from 1.30pm).* ✎8€. ✆05 53 59 31 21. *www.milandes.com*

Built in 1489 by François de Caumont, the estate remained the property of this family until the Revolution and was eventually purchased by the well-known American singer, Josephine Baker or *La Perle Noire* as she was known in her Paris cabaret heyday in the 1920s and 1930s. It was here that she sought to create a world village, gathering together and adopting children of different races, religions and nationalities and bringing them up to promote mutual understanding.

Joséphine Baker adapted the interior decoration to her own taste as visitors can gather from walking through various rooms devoted to the different periods of the singer's life.

An unrelated addition to the tourist attraction are the falconry demonstrations staged in the gardens surrounding the château. Visitors may also stroll through the park beyond.

AU SUD DE SARLAT-LA-CANÉDA

LES EYZIES-DE-TAYAC-SIREUIL · MONTIGNAC

SARLAT-LA-CANÉDA ★★★

LES EYZIES-DE-TAYAC-SIREUIL ★ ★ Beynac-et-Cazenac
St-Vincent-de-Cosse
Allas-les-Mines
★ Les Milandes
Fayrac
La Cavalerie
★ Castelnaud
La Malartrie
Marqueyssac ★ ★
La Roque-Gageac ★ ★
Pont-de-Cause
St-Cybranet
VILLEFRANCHE-DU-PÉRIGORD · CAHORS
★ Montfort
★ Cingle de Montfort
Vitrac
DORDOGNE
Cénac ★
★ Domme ★ ★
CAHORS

▶ *Rejoin the D 53 then turn right onto the D 50 and right again 4.5km/2.8mi farther to Allas-les-Mines. Cross the Dordogne and turn right onto the D 703 which follows the north bank.*

Beynac-et-Cazenac★★
See BEYNAC-ET-CAZENAC.
Continue along the D 703; turn left past the railway line onto the D 49 towards Sarlat then right onto the D 57.

Jardins de Marqueyssac★★
*Daily Jul–Aug 9am–8pm; Apr–Jun & Sept 10am–7pm; Feb, Mar, Oct–Nov 11 10am–6pm; Nov 12–Jan 2–7pm.*7.20€ *(10-17 years old: 3.60€) or 13.40€(10-17 years old: 6.70€) for a combined ticket with Castelnaud. Candlelight nights Jul–Aug every Thur 7pm 10€(10-17 years old: 5€)* 05 53 31 36 36. www.marqueyssac.com.
Situated at the tip of a rocky promontory, the splendid 22ha/54-acre park offers a pleasant mixture of natural vegetation, essentially holm oaks, and hand-trimmed box shrubs forming patterns, and includes a terrace, a waterfall as well as three walks leading to a belvedere. The shaded paths wending their way through the gardens are lined with panels detailing the local flora, fauna and history and there is a playground. From the belvedere, there are striking **views**★★ of nearby villages and castles: La Roque-Gageac, Beynac, Castelnaud and the Dordogne meanders.
Rejoin the D 703 (on the left).

Note, on your left, the **Château de la Malartrie**, a castle built in the 20C, greatly influenced by the 15C style.

La Roque-Gageac★★
See La ROQUE-GAGEAC.
Drive 2km/1.2mi on the D 703 and turn left onto the D 46 back to Sarlat.

Josephine Baker
1906, St Louis, Missouri – 1975, Paris, France

An early symbol of the beauty and vitality of artistic expression in the American black community, Josephine Baker was also an honoured hero of the Second World War, winning the Croix de Guerre for her work as a member of the Free French forces and the Résistance. She began her theatrical career in her early teens, eventually earning a place as a chorus girl in the revue *Shuffle Along*, which brought her to New York City.

Still a very young woman, she stirred sensation in Paris with her *danse sauvage*, playing on colonial fantasies and high-octane sexuality, while learning much about the world, her art, and herself. She got star billing for her performance at the Folies-Bergère, clad in the famous banana skirt. Baker became a French citizen in 1937. When war broke out, she used her special position as an entertainer (albeit one who had caused much scandal in more conservative cities than libertine Paris) to carry secret messages and to spirit friends out of France to safety. She retired at age 50, but, short of funds and determined to continue building her dream and her family at Les Milandes, she returned to the stage within a few years, and worked tirelessly up until the day of her death.

ADDRESSES

🛏 STAY

⬤ **Hotel Abbys** – *Vialard, 24201 Sarlat.* ☎*05 53 30 85 50. www.abbys-hotel.com.* Modern single-storey hotel with simple functional en-suite rooms, a few kilometres east of the centre of Sarlat.

⬤ **Hôtel Altica** – *Av. de la Dordogne.* ☎*05 53 28 18 00. altica-sarlat@altica.fr. 50 rooms.* This hotel (part of a chain) near the centre of Sarlat is conveniently located for those who wish to visit one of the prettiest towns in Périgord. The rooms are satisfactory for the price.

⬤⬤ **Hôtel des Récollets** – *4 r. Jean-Jacques-Rousseau.* ☎*05 53 31 36 00. www.hotel-recollets-sarlat.com. 18 rooms.* This unique hotel is in a former convent (17C). The rooms are not large, but they are quiet and all have been renovated with contemporary furniture, original beams and walls. Enjoy breakfast in a vaulted room or on the patio. Staff will help you carry your bags from the public parking lot.

⬤⬤ **Mas de Castel** – *3km/1.8mi south of Sarlat via the D 704 and C 1.* ☎*05 53 59 02 59. 13 rooms.* An attractive hotel occupying an old farm in a peaceful rural setting. Pastel tones and rustic furniture in the bedrooms, some of which are on garden level. Swimming pool.

⬤⬤ **(from €52) Arcantis Hotel Montaigne** – *Place Pasteur, Sarlat la Canéda. 28 rooms.* 150 metres from the cobbled medieval centre of Sarlat and housed in a beautiful historical building, the hotel offers comfortable and well-equipped rooms with free Wi-Fi internet access.

⬤⬤ **Chambre d'hôtes Gite Filolies** – *24200 Saint André d'Allas.* ☎ *05 53 30 31 84. www.lesfilioles.com.* This lovely rustic 18C relais de poste (former coaching inn), a few kilometres north west of Sarlat, is run by an Anglo-French couple, Adrienne and Pat. Bedrooms, with exposed rough stones, are beautifully decorated in local rustic style and there is a lovely garden with pool.

⬤⬤ **Ferme Auberge de La Rhonie** – *Boyer - 24220 Meyrals.* ☎*05 53 29 29 07. www.hotel-sarlat-en-perigord.com. 12 rooms.* Although this hotel was built in 1976 it feels much older with lots of exposed stone and wood and is very traditional in style with beautifully decorated characterful bedrooms and public areas. The lovely gardens include a covered pool and an outdoor pool. The food too is excellent.

⬤⬤ **Hôtel Le Jardin de Clélia La Vigne du Foussat** – ☎*05 53 28 56 32. www.le-jardin-de-clelia.com.* Set in what was an old stone tobacco drying warehouse, the hotel is situated above the town in a tranquil setting, just 1km (0.6mi from the medieval centre. Bedrooms are colourful, simple and (lightly) themed according to countries (Italy, Egypt, India etc..). Outdoor pool and home cooking with the hosts.

⬤⬤ **Chambre d'hôte Le Clos-Vallis** – *Chemin de Peyrigna (3.5km/2mi east of Sarlat)- 24200 Sarlat la Canéda.* ☎*05 53 28 95 64. www.leclosvallis.com. 4 rooms.* Beautifully restored stone farmhouse with lovely simply furnished exposed-stone-and-wood bedrooms. Outdoor swimming pool surrounded by gardens and fields

🍴 EAT

⬤⬤ **Rossignol** – *15 r. Fénelon -* ☎*05 53 31 02 30 - closed Thu.* A simple, central, family-run restaurant, with one rustic-style dining room. Copious and unpretentious local cuisine, including fish.

⬤⬤ **Ferme Auberge Garrigue Haute** – *24370 Prats De Carlux.* ☎*05 53 29 80 08. www.lagarriguehaute.fr.* Set in the countryside, a few kilometres north east of Sarlat, in an imposing late-19C farmhouse, this large restaurant specializes in rich local home-made foods such as goose, duck and paté de foie gras. (chambres d'hôtes from €52)

⬤⬤ **Quatre Saisons** – *2 Côte de Toulouse.* ☎*05 53 29 49 59. http://4saisons-sarlat-perigord.com.* Charming small restaurant set in the old town off a steep stairway in a 14C building with one dining room at street level and one below in an atmospherically lit vaulted cellar. The menu, like the decor, is a contemporary twist on the traditional.

⬤⬤ **Le Bistro de l'Octroi** – *111, av. de selves (600 m north of town centre).*

05 53 30 83 40. www.lebistrodeloctroi. fr. Enjoy fine local and regional cuisine in the old tax office, dating from 1830. Choose from upstairs, downstairs or the outdoor terrace.

⊜⊜ **Les Jardins d'Harmonie** – *Pl. André Malraux. *05 53 31 06 69. www.lesjardinsdharmonie.com. Closed Mon–Tue.* Very attractive little restaurant set in the old cobbled part of town, spilling out onto the streets beneath its awnings. Try one of their speciality salads or steaks or maybe foie gras. They also have a Salon de Thé.

🛒 SHOPPING

Markets – Traditional market in the streets of the old town on Saturdays, plus a smaller market in place de la Liberté on Wednesday morning. Covered market in the former Eglise Sainte-Marie, daily (except Monday and Thursday from early-Nov to Feb). Truffle and duck and goose product market on Saturday mornings from December to March. Walnut and chestnut market on Saturday mornings in October and November.

St-Amand-de-Coly★

and around

Tucked away in the fold of a small valley off the Vézère Valley is St-Amand-de-Coly, its old *lauze*-roofed houses clustering round the impressive abbey church, where concerts take place during the Festival du Périgord.

CHURCH★★

This church of fine yellow limestone is perhaps the most amazing of all Périgord's fortified churches. The Augustinian abbey it once belonged to saw its spiritual activity reduced during the Hundred Years War: consequently, it was transformed into a fortress. The elaborate defence system was designed to keep enemies at a distance, but also to drive them away should any forays be made

Chez le Gaulois – *3 r. Tourny - *05 53 59 50 64. Open daliy, Apr–Oct, 9am–midnight; rest of the year: Tue–Sat, 10am–10pm.* The Gauls in the Asterix comic books were known for their love of good food, and here the tradition is maintained. You can savour some fine products of the region, and from other regions of France, including a great variety of *jambons crus* (the hams are hanging from the ceiling) , chestnut preserves and ice creams.

HORSE RIDING

L'Étrier de Vitrac – *Pech de Pech. *05 53 59 34 31 / 06 87 76 90 34.* An equestrian centre in a pleasant wooded area.

TOURS

Guided tours – *Tours (1hr 30min) led by qualified local guides. Jun–Sept Wed 11am (In Engish) 5€.*

Evening visits – Organised by the tourist office, these fascinating visits provided a different perspective of this delightful town. *Sat 9pm mid-Aug & early Sept. 8€.*

▸ **Population:** 394
Michelin Map: 329: I-5
Location: 58km/36mi SW of Perigueux and 22km/ 14mi N of Sarlat.
Don't Miss: Village church.

into the church. The Huguenots occupying the church in 1575 were able to hold out for six days against 20 000 soldiers of the Périgord seneschal, who had powerful artillery backup. An impression of tremendous strength is created by the **tower keep**, indented by the enormous pointed arch of the doorway which supports a defence room intended to prevent anyone approaching. The harmony of the apsidal chapels is a contrast to the severity of the high walls of the nave and transept. A watch-path runs around the building beneath the *lauze*-covered roof. Purity of line and simplicity of **decoration**, typical of Augustinian architecture, contribute to the beauty of the lofty space inside. The concern for protection also affected the interior design; remains of the defence system include a narrow passage enclosing the chancel, small look-out posts in the pillars of the crossing and the loopholes in the base of the dome.

The **Point Accueil-Information** opposite the church presents an audio-visual show on the abbey and its history. It is also the starting point of guided tours and a "Topo-guide" detailing eight local rambles is on sale. ○➜Guided tours leave from here. For information, call ℰ05 53 51 04 56 or 05 53 51 67 50 (town hall).

EXCURSION
Terrasson-Lavilledieu
15km/9.3mi E along the N 89.
Terrasson, built beside the Vézère, has old districts stretching in tiers up the side of a hill overlooking the south bank of the river. It is a busy little town with a prosperous trade in truffles and walnuts. A walk through the narrow streets will enable you to discover many half-timbered houses, the 15C church overlooking the town and the valley, the 12C cutwater bridge etc. There is an interesting **historical tour** *(free map available at the tourist office, ☎05 53 50 37 56)* of the town lined with explanatory panels.

Jardins de l'Imaginaire★
&○➜Open daily Jul–Aug, guided tour (1hr 10min) every 30 mins, 10am–noon, 2–6.20pm; Apr 9.50–11.20; May–Jun, 10–11.30am and 2–5.30pm; Apr 11, Sept and Oct 11–11.30am and 2–5pm.Closed Tue exc Jul–Aug ➤7€. ℰ05 53 50 86 82.

This 6ha/15-acre terraced garden overlooking Terrasson and the valley, a contemporary creation, guides visitors to the realm of fantasy through its holy wood, its forest alive with elves and imps, its water garden, its rose garden (2 000 rose bushes), its arbour, its iris garden and its greenhouse lined with vegetation. A night show takes place in the garden every year, in summer.

ADDRESSES

🛏 STAY

➤ **Hostellerie La Commanderie** – *24570 Condat-sur-Vézère. 11km/6.6mi NW of St-Amand on the D 62 and D 704. ℰ05 53 51 26 49. www.hotel-lacommanderie. com. 7 rooms.* In the heart of the village, this charming house was once a waystation on the road to Compostela. The pretty rooms under the vaulted ceilings of the upper floor are king size. Quiet garden.

➤ **Château de la Fleunie** – *24570 Condat-sur-Vézère. 11km/6.2mi NW of St-Amand via the D 62, D 704 and a secondary road. ℰ05 53 51 32 74. lafleunie@ free.fr. Closed Oct 31–Apr between 5 & 10, and Sun eve, Mon in Oct–Nov & Mar–Apr. 33 rooms.* A great place to relax. The 12C and 15C château with its four round towers sits in the middle of a 100ha/247-acre park. The rooms in the castle have old-fashioned furnishings, whereas those in the annex are more modern.

In the dining room, admire the embellishments on the exposed beams and the fireplace.

➤ **Manoir d'Hautegente** – *24120 Coly. 3km/1.8mi N of St-Amand on a secondary road. ℰ05 53 51 68 03. www.manoir-hautegente.com. Closed Nov–early Apr. 15 rooms.* In the summer, when the Virginia creeper covers the façade, this 14C mill seems to melt into the landscape. Quiet nights in cosy rooms overlooking the park, with the sound of the river flowing nearby to sweeten your dreams. Three vaulted dining rooms; fireplace.

🍴 EAT

➤ **L'Imaginaire** – *Pl. du Foirail - 24120 Terrasson-Lavilledieu - ℰ05 53 51 37 27. www.l-imaginaire.com. Closed last week Feb–first week Mar, 11–31 Nov, Sun eve, Mon and Tue lunchtime from Sep to Apr, and Mon lunchtime from May–Aug.* This former 17C hospice is the setting for this elegant restaurant with a charming vaulted room.

St-Léon-sur-Vézère★

Built in a picturesque loop of the River Vézère, this charming village overrun by greenery possesses two castles and one of the finest Romanesque churches of the Périgord. It comes to life in August during the Festival Musical du Périgord Noir.

12C Romanesque church

J. Damase/MICHELIN

▶ **Population:** 434
◉ **Michelin Map:** 329: H-5
▶ **Location:** midway between the Grotte de Lascaux and Les-Eyzies de-Tayac.

openings, known as passages *berrichons* as they are a feature of churches in the Berry region in particular.

The apse and south radiating chapel are decorated with parts of Romanesque frescoes, in which red is predominant.

◯ *Walk along the river on the left.*

Château de Clérans
This elegant 15C and 16C palace, flanked with machicolated towers and turrets, stands on the banks of the river.

◯ *Go into the village.*

Château de la Salle
Standing on the square, this small castle built of dry-stone has a fine 14C square keep crowned with machicolations.

Chapelle du Cimetière
This small 14C chapel in the cemetery is roofed, like the church, with *lauzes*. An inscription in the *Oc* language above the door harks back to an extraordinary event; in 1233, a servant who had let fly an arrow onto the crucifix guarding the entrance to the cemetery dropped dead on the spot, with his head turned back-to-front. In 1890, the blasphemer's grave was excavated, and a skeleton with its skull back-to-front was unearthed.

✷ VILLAGE WALK
Church★
The church was part of a Benedictine priory which was founded in the 12C. It was built on the ruins of a Gallo-Roman villa and the remains of one of the villa's walls can be seen on the river-side.

From the square, the apse, the perfectly smooth radiating chapels and the fine square two-storey arcaded bell tower form a harmonious unit. The church is roofed with the heavy limestone slabs (*lauzes*) of Périgord Noir.

Inside, the transept crossing is vaulted with a dome, whereas apsidal chapels are connected to the apse by narrow

ADDRESSES

🛏 STAY

☞ **Camping Le Paradis** – *4km/2.5mi SW of St-Léon-on-Vézère along the D 706. ✆05 53 50 72 64. www.le-paradis.com. Open Apr–Oct 19. Reserv. recommended. 216 pitches. Restaurant.* "Paradise" is a good name for this campsite. Former farm buildings serve as facilities and the sites are attractively landscaped.

Modern and comfortable. Pool, tennis court and play areas.

🍽 EAT

☞☞ **Le Petit Léon** – *✆05 53 51 18 04. Closed Sun eve, Mon lunchtime and Sept –Jun.* This garden restaurant is a real find! White parasols shade the wooden tables under the apple trees. The dishes are inventive and tasty.

The Périgord Pourpre, or Purple, around Bergerac, owes its name to the wine produced here. The region is at the south western corner of the Dordogne and shares a border with the Lot-et-Garonne *département* in the south and the Gironde *département* in the west. The appellations associated with the region are legendary: Bergerac, Montravel, Haut-Montravel, Pécharmant and Saussignac, not to mention the famous sweet wine of Monbazillac.

The Périgord Pourpre is divided into several areas, all of which share a mild climate favourable to the cultivation of crops more commonly associated with more southerly parts of the country. The Dordogne Valley, which is particularly wide here, is divided into plots of land where tobacco, maize (corn), sunflowers and cereals all flourish in the rich alluvial deposits. Timber production predominates to the west of Bergerac, in an area whose slopes are covered with the vineyards of Bergerac and Monbazillac and the town of Bergerac itself is an important centre for the tobacco and wine industries.

Many people associate Bergerac and the surrounding area with Hector Savinien de Cyrano de Bergerac (1619–1655) the playright and soldier with the rather large nose. You'll find an unusual, coloured statue to the great man in Bergerac.

Cyrano has become Bergerac's adopted son, although there are no connections other than his name and no indications that he ever visited.

The Périgord Pourpre like the rest of the Dordogne and much of Aquitaine was part of the Guyenne region which was dominated by the English crown during the height of the Middle Ages.

Outside the fortified walls of the its medieval towns, or bastides, vineyards alternate with orchards of plum trees, pastures and woods, where there always seems to be a good place to enjoy a meal and a fine bottle of the local wine.

🚗 DRIVING TOUR

1 BERGERAC WINE COUNTRY
130km/80mi round-trip.

The Bergerac vineyards are the most extensive of the whole southwest, both in volume and area. They stretch some 50km from west to east along the north bank of the Dordogne, briefly crossing over to the hillsides on the opposite bank, south of Bergerac. Sweet or extra sweet white wines long dominated production but, for the past 25 years, the volume of red wines has been double that of white wines. All 93 municipalities in the Bergerac area are entitled to the **Bergerac** AOC which includes around twelve local classifications.

Drive northeast out of Bergerac along N 21. On the outskirts of town, the **Pécharmant** vineyards, exclusively devoted to the production of rich red wines, climb up the hillsides framing the Caudau Valley. Return to Bergerac and follow D 933 S for the beginning of the **Monbazillac** appellation, reserved for sweet white wines. It covers a hillside area extending over 2 500ha on the south bank of the Dordogne and includes the region's oldest vineyards, appreciated by the Dutch as early as the 17C because the wines travelled well. Monbazillac wines are made from grapes affected by what is called "noble rot" and collected manually through successive harvests.

The process is the same as at Sauternes. The buildings of the **Monbazillac cooperative** are about 4km from Bergerac. Turn left onto D 14 then right onto D 13 for the **Château de Monbazillac★** and its **Musée du Vin**. Several renowned estates are situated west of the château, among them **Clos l'Envège**. Continue to Monbazillac then turn right onto D 14E, which joins D 933; turn right then immediately left onto D 17. The road runs through **Pomport**, a small municipality of the Monbazillac area, which produces some of the best Monbazillacs such as those of **Domaine de Pécoula**. From here, drive to **Sigoulès** via D 17, which has the most important **cooperative** in the Bergerac region. Drive northwest out of Sigoulès along D 15 then turn left onto D 14 and left again onto D 4 to **Saussignac**. This village, camped on a hillside, is surrounded by vineyards of the same name. The Côtes-de-Saussignac vines produce only sweet and extra sweet white wines. The **Côtes-de-Saussignac** AOC was "revived" by a handful of Britons among the many who have settled in the region.

Drive back along D 4 then turn left onto D 14, pass the former bastide of **Sainte-Foy-la-Grande**, now a wine-growing centre, and continue on D 936 to Tête Noire and turn right to pass through **Montcaret** with its Gallo-Roman villa, and continue north towards St-Michel-de-Montaigne, home to the current 19C **Château de Montaigne**. From here continue northwest along D 9 then turn right onto D 21 and right again onto D 10 to Montpeyroux. Between St-Michel-de-Montaigne and Fougueyrolles in the east, the hillsides produce dry white **Montravel** wines as well as sweet and extra sweet white wines classified as **Haut-Montravel** and **Côtes-de-Montravel**. The whole district also produces red and white Bergerac and Côtes-de-Bergerac wines. From **Montpeyroux** leave northeast towards **Carsac-de-Gurson**, surrounded by vineyards, with a fine Romanesque church.

La Grappe de Gurson Cooperative offers a selection of local wine.

Leave Carsac E on D 32, then, 2km further on, turn right onto a minor road leading to **St-Vivien**, where you can buy wine from the **St-Vivien et Bonneville Cooperative**, housed in an unusual neo-medieval building.

Drive on to Vélines, then turn left onto D 32E2 towards Fougueyrolles and Le Fleix. Running on top of the plateau, the small road winds through vineyards, past some of the finest estates in Bergerac country, such as **Château Roque-Peyre** *(accommodation)* in **Fougueyrolles**. Its owner is one of the wine-growers who initiated the recent red **Montravel** appellation, produced from small yields and fully matured in barrels. Continue past the small town of **Le Fleix** and drive east to Prigonrieux along D 32. In spite of its name, the tiny **Rosette** appellation, located on the hillsides overlooking **Prigonrieux**, only produces sweet white wines with a strong bouquet.

Beaumont-du-Périgord

local bastides and mills

Beaumont was built as a bastide in 1272 by the Seneschal of Guyenne in the name of Edward I, king of England. Today, a few traces of its fortifications are preserved, such as the 13C fortified Porte de Luzier, a gateway that provides access to the town.

BASTIDE
Église St-Front

Built after 1272 in the Early Gothic style with four huge towers connected by a rampart walk, this church was the last place of refuge for the inhabitants of the town during periods of siege. The asymmetry of the towers on the main façade reflects their different functions; the lower was a bell tower until 1789, and the higher a crenellated keep armed with machicolations. The towers frame a doorway, which has five archivolts and is supported by clustered columns, and a **gallery**★ with a beautifully decorated balustrade and an illuminated frieze underneath it. The elegant south porch has a trefoil arcade dominated by a lancet dais. It is protected by a brattice. Major restoration work during the 19C has significantly altered the church's originally military character. Inside the church in the bell tower to the left, the enormous keystone (weighing 450kg/992lb) of the chancel vault can be seen. Decorated with carved figures of faces, it includes that of the church's patron, St Front. In the same side aisle towards the middle of the nave, note the chapel of St Joseph, almost certainly the remainder of a much older church.

EXCURSION
Dolmen de Blanc

3km/1.9mi S along the D 676.
According to a strange legend, a young girl lost during a storm stopped near the megaliths and prayed to be rescued. She then saw the stones move to show her the way.

▶ **Population:** 1 145
⟳ **Michelin Map:** 329: F-7
✦ **Don't Miss:** The opportunity to explore this typical fortified *bastide*.
🕐 **Timing:** Allow a full day to visit the bastides and water mills of the area to the south of the River Dordogne.

🚗 DRIVING TOUR

BASTIDES AND MILLS★
110km/69mi round-trip – allow one day

▷ *Leave Beaumont travelling N along the D 660.*

Château de Bannes

Perched on a rocky spur, the château was built at the end of the 15C by the bishop of Sarlat, Armand de Gontaud-Biron. What is so incongruous in this château is that the military features – machicolated towers – are tempered by the carved doorway and richly decorated dormer windows surmounted by finials and pinnacles in the Early Renaissance style.

▷ *Continue along the D 660.*

Couze-et-St-Front

Located at the mouth of the Couze Valley, this active small town has specialised since the 16C in the manufacture of Dutch paper, which was sold as far away as Russia. It was the most important paper-making centre in the Aquitaine, and, at its peak, 13 mills were in operation here.

Out of the three remaining mills, only two, the **Moulin de la Rouzique (Ecomusée du Papier)** (🕐*Open Jul–Aug,* ⟶*guided tour (1hr, last entrance 1hr before closing), Daily 10am–7pm, Sun, 2–7pm; Apr–Jun and Sept–Oct 15, 2–6.30pm;* ⊛*6€ (under 8 years old; no charge);* ✆*05 53 24 36 16)* and the **Moulin de Larroque** *(workshop open*

Église St-Front

B. Kaufmann/MICHELIN

Mon–Fri, 9am–noon and 2–5pm; craft gallery open Mon–Fri, 9am–noon and 2–5pm, Sat 10am–noon, 2–5pm. guided tours only in summer; closed public hols and 24 Dec-1 Jan; 4€; ℘05 53 61 01 75. www.moulin delaroque.com) are still making filigree paper using traditional methods.

> Drive W out of Couze along the D 37.

Château de Lanquais★
Open Jul–Aug, guided tour (1hr) 10am–7pm; May–Jun and Sep, daily except Tue, 10.30am–noon and 2.30–6.30pm; Apr and Oct, daily except Tue, 2.30–6pm. 8€ (child: 3.50€). ℘05 53 61 24 24.

The 14C and 15C main building, with all the defensive characteristics of a **fortified castle**, had a **Renaissance building** added to it during the Wars of Religion, and was extended further in the 19C. In the courtyard, the elegant **façades**★ are divided into vertical registers. Inside, the blue drawing room with its finely carved **chimney**★ and the reconstructed Renaissance kitchen are worth noting. Concerts and shows are staged here in summer.

> Continue along the D 37 and cross the Dordogne 1.5km/0.9mi farther on. Turn right onto the D 660 in St-Capraise-de-Lalinde, then right again in Lalinde, crossing the Dordogne once again.

St-Front-de-Colubri
Built in the 12C on top of a cliff overlooking the Dordogne, the chapel sheltered sailors venturing along the Saut de la Gratusse rapids. This passage was the most difficult of the river's middle section; specialised river-hands were needed to guide sailors through it until the mid-19C, when the Canal de Lalinde canal was built.

There is a marvellous **view**★ of the valley and the rapids up-river.

> The D 29 follows the river.

Badefols-sur-Dordogne
The village occupies a pleasant site beside the Dordogne. The country church stands close to the foot of the castle ruins perched on the cliff. This fortress served as the hideout for local

Bastides

These fortified towns (in the *Oc* language: *bastidas*) first appeared in the 13C. They were usually built to the same plan (a square or rectangle) according to a grid sytem with streets built around a main square, often arcaded, and with a covered market hall at its centre. Depending on their location, bastides were often surrounded by walls to offer increased protection.

BASTIDES ET MOULINS

mitory has been transformed into a regional **Museum of Geology and Archaeology** (*Open Jul–Aug, guided tours available daily except Sat, 10am–6pm. ℘05 53 57 52 64*).

> Continue along the D 25 and turn left onto the D 26 2km/1.2mi farther on.

Ste-Croix

This village has a charming Romanesque church surrounded by the half-ruined buildings of what used to be a priory. This 12C church has a clear, uncluttered outline. The nave is covered in round tiles, in contrast to the apse and side chapel which are covered in *lauzes* – the small limestone slabs typical of the region. A gabled belfry adorns the top of the façade.

> Leave Ste-Croix to the E and turn right onto the D 26.

Montferrand-du-Périgord

The main feature of this pretty terraced village above the Couze is the half-ruined château with its 12C keep.
The old houses, dovecotes and 16C covered market with its beautiful columns all add to Montferrand's charm.
In the cemetery above the village, the Romanesque chapel (accessible along a marked path starting from the foot of the castle) is decorated with a lovely collection of mural frescoes dating from between the 12C and the 15C.

> Return to the D 26, then turn right onto the D 2.

Monpazier★
See MONPAZIER.

> Drive W from Monpazier on D 660 back to Beaumont-du-Périgord.

thieves and robbers who used to ransack *gabares* as they sailed downstream.

> Continue along the D 29, then turn onto the D 28 4km/2.5mi farther on.

Cadouin★ See CADOUIN.

> Drive SE out of Cadouin along the D 25. After 2km/1.2mi, turn right onto the D 27.

Molières

This unfinished English bastide, founded in 1284, has a Gothic church with a façade flanked by a tall two-storey square defensive tower and the ruins of an old castle to the north.

> Turn back and rejoin the D 25 on the right.

St-Avit-Sénieur★

This small village is dominated by its massive **church** and monastic buildings, vestiges of a former Benedictine abbey constructed in the 11C in honour of Avitus Senior, a soldier in the service of the Visogoth king Alaric II who later became a hermit. The fortifications on the church date from the 14C. The dor-

Bergerac★
and the Vallée du Caudau

Spread out on both banks of the Dordogne where the river tends to be calmer and the valley widens to form an alluvial plain, this distinctly southern town is surrounded by prestigious vineyards and fields of tobacco, cereals and maize. A project to restore the old quarter has seen the embellishment of a number of Bergerac's 15C and 16C houses.

> ▶ **Population:** 27,716
> 🛆 **Michelin Map:** 329: D-6
> 🗎 **Info:** 97, rue Neuve-d'Argenson, 24100 Bergerac. ☏05 53 57 03 11. www.ville-bergerac.com.
> ◖ **Location:** 49km/30.5mi S of Périgueux.
> ◈ **Don't Miss:** Old Town; tobacco and wine museums.

A BIT OF HISTORY

Intellectual/commercial crossroads – The town's expansion began as early as the 12C. Benefiting from the town's situation as a port and bridging point, the local merchants profited from successful trade between the Auvergne and the Limousin and Bordeaux on the coast. This flourishing city and capital of the Périgord, became one of the bastions of Protestantism as its printing presses published pamphlets which were widely distributed. In August 1577 the Peace of Bergerac was signed between the king of Navarre and the representatives of King Henri III; this was a preliminary to the Edict of Nantes (1598). Despite this, in 1620, Louis XIII's army took over the town and destroyed the ramparts. After the Revocation of the Edict of Nantes (1685), the Jesuits and Recollects tried to win back their Protestant disciples. A certain number of Bergerac citizens, faithful to their Calvinist beliefs, emigrated to Holland, a country where they had maintained commercial contacts. Bergerac was the capital of Périgord until the Revolution, when the regional capital was transferred to Périgueux, which also became Préfecture of the Dordogne *département*.

In the 19C, wine-growing and shipping prospered until the onslaught of phylloxera and arrival of the railway.

Bergerac today – Essentially an agricultural centre, Bergerac is the capital of tobacco in France and, as a result, the Experimental Institute of Tobacco and the Tobacco Planters Centre of Advanced and Refresher Training are located here.

In addition the 12 000ha/29 650 acres of vineyards surrounding the town produce wine with an *appellation d'origine contrôlée* (which means it is of an officially recognised vintage) including: Bergerac, Côtes de Bergerac, Monbazillac, Montravel and Pécharmant. The Regional Wine Council, which establishes the *appellation* of the wines, is located in the Recollects' Cloisters (🛆*see Old Bergerac*). The main industrial enterprise of the town is the powder factory producing nitro-cellulose for use in such industries as film-making, paint, varnish and plastics.

Famous citizens – Oddly enough, the Cyrano of Edmond Rostand's play was inspired by the 17C philosopher **Cyrano de Bergerac** whose name had nothing to do with the Périgord town. Not discouraged in the slightest, the townspeople took it upon themselves to adopt this wayward son and erect a statue in his honour in place de la Myrpe.

☙ OLD BERGERAC★★WALK

Start in the **Ancien port**. The *gabares* of yesteryear moored here to drop off goods from the upper valley.

◖ *Turn left at the end of quai Salvette.*

Rue du Château
An unusual balustraded balcony overhangs a sharp bend in the street.

◖ *Cross rue de l'Ancien-Port; turn left.*

Rue St-Clar
The walls of the corbelled half-timbered houses lining this charming street are a mixture of cob and small bricks.

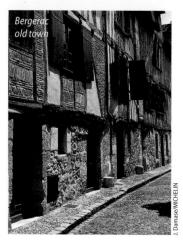

Bergerac old town

J. Damase/MICHELIN

▷ *Turn left into rue des Rois-de-France and right into rue de l'Ancien Port.*

Maison Peyrarède★

Also known as the French Kings' House, this elegant building dating from 1603 is ornamented with a corbelled turret.

Rue d'Albret

At the end of this street to the right is the town hall, the former convent of the Sisters of Faith. On the left, on the corner of place du Feu, is a vast building with pointed arched doorways.

▷ *Walk to place du Docteur-Cayla.*

Place du Docteur-Cayla, Place de la Myrpe

The 13C chapel adjacent to the former Couvent des Récollets became a **Protestant temple** in the 18C. The charming shaded place de la Myrpe is lined with half-timbered houses. In the middle of the square stands the statue of Cyrano de Bergerac swathed in his cape.

▷ *Follow the narrow street leading off the square and turn right.*

Rue des Conférences

This street's name recalls the conferences held before the Peace of Bergerac. It is bordered by half-timbered houses.

▷ *Turn left.*

Place Pélissière

This large square was opened up after the demolition of some run-down houses. Spread on different levels around a fountain it is overlooked by **Église St-Jacques** (○*open Jul–Aug, noon–7pm; Sep–Jun, 2–7pm, Wed 2–6pm, Sat 2–5pm; ∞no charge; ✆05 53 63 57 55*), once a centre for pilgrims on their way to Santiago de Compostela; it now houses contemporary works of art.

Underneath the **Église St-Jaques** in the Place de la Petite Mission is the **Musée Costi** (○*open every day in July and Aug; ∞2€ (free under 18); ✆05 53 63 04 13*), which contains the bronze and plaster sculptures of Constantin Papachristopoulos also known as 'Costi'. From the north end of the square, you can divert from the route marked on the map and follow Grand'Rue some distance north then cross boulevard de la Résistance to reach place de Lattre-de-Tassigny and **Notre Dame**. Built in the Gothic style, this 19C church has a slender bell tower. In the west chapel is an immense **Aubusson tapestry** portraying the Bergerac coat of arms.

▷ *Return to St Jacques and the marked route.*

Rue St-Jâmes

There are 15C, 16C and 17C half-timbered houses with mullioned windows all along this street.

▷ *Turn right.*

Rue des Fontaines

The Vieille Auberge at the corner of rue Gaudra has well-preserved moulded arcades, 14C capitals, and pointed arched windows.

MUSEUMS
Musée du Tabac★★

Rue de l'Ancien-Port. ♿○*Open Tue–Fri 10am–noon and 2pm–6pm; Sat 10am–12noon and 2pm–5pm; Sun 2.30–6.30pm.* ○*Closed public hols, Sat afternoon and Sun mid-Nov to mid-Mar.* ∞*3.50€ (combined ticket with*

BERGERAC
plan I

0   200 m

LIMOGES
PÉRIGUEUX

N 21

D 709 MUSSIDAN

D 32

BORDEAUX D 936
MONT-DE-MARSAN D 933

N 21
AGEN

D 660 SARLAT-LA-CANADA
CAHORS

WHERE TO STAY	
Agrybella (Chambre d'hôte L')	①
Europ Hôtel	④
Verotel (Hôtel)	⑨

WHERE TO EAT	
Méli-Mélo (Le)	①
Table du Marché (La)	⑦

BERGERAC
plan II

WHERE TO EAT

Imparfait (L') .... ①

0   50m

Cloître des Recollets

J. Damase/MICHELIN

the Musée du Vin and the Musée Costi below, 5€). ☎ 05 53 63 04 13.
This remarkable and beautifully presented collection, which includes satirical engravings, traces the history and evolution of tobacco through the centuries. On the **second floor** works of art depicting tobacco and smokers are displayed. *Two Smokers* from the 17C Northern French School, *Three Smokers* by Meissonier and the charming *Interior of a smoke den* by Teniers the Younger, are among the works exhibited.
A section is devoted to the cultivation of tobacco (planting, harvesting, drying etc) with special reference to the Bergerac region. Another room is set aside to display the techniques used to manufacture smoking accessories both in the past and throughout the world.

Drying tabaco

S. Sauvignier/MICHELIN

The Tobacco Industry

Until the 15C tobacco was used only by the American Indians, who believed it possessed medicinal properties. After the discovery of the New World, tobacco was introduced to Europe. Jean Nicot brought it into France in c1560; he sent snuff to Catherine de' Medici to cure her migraines.
Use of tobacco was controversial from the very start: Pope Urbain VIII ordered the excommunication of nicotine fiends and Louis XIII forbade its sale (before hitting on the idea of taxing it). In those days, tobacco was sold as a carrot-shaped lump which was grated into powder. The familiar diamond-shaped orange sign, Tabac, which hangs outside of shops licensed to sell tobacco products, is still called a carotte today. At the end of the 18C snuff was sold directly as a powder. The next step in the art of smoking was the pipe. The pipe had been in use in Holland since the early 17C, but its use was considered vulgar and common. Officers of the First Empire started the fashion and were quickly followed by the Romantics, including George Sand. Finally in the mid-19C, the cigarette arrived on the scene, with accessories including elegant ivory cigarette holders.

Musée Régional du Vin et de la Batellerie★

5 rue des Conférences. &. *Open Tue–Sun 10am–noon, 2–5.30pm, Sat 10am–noon, Sun 2.30–6.30pm. Closed public hols and Sun mid-Nov to mid-Mar.* 2.50€. *05 53 63 04 13.*

This museum is located at the end of place de la Myrpe. On the first floor, the importance of barrel-making to the Bergerac economy is explained. The section on wine shows the evolution of the Bergerac vineyards over the centuries and the type of houses the wine-growers lived in. On the second floor there are models of the various kinds of river boats, *gabares*, flat-bottomed boats sometimes with sails.

Maison des Vins – Cloître des Récollets

The former Couvent des Récollets is reached via quai Salvette. Open all year (exc. Jan) mid-Jun to Aug, every day 10am–7pm; Sept to mid-Jun, daily except Mon, 10.30am–1pm and 2–6pm; No charge. 05 53 63 57 55.

Go through the corridor into the vaulted wine cellar where the meetings of the Bergerac wine society, Conférence des Consuls de la Vinée, are held. There is an audio-visual presentation on the Bergerac vineyards.

The brick and stone cloister building was built on 12C foundations. The interior courtyard has a 16C Renaissance gallery beside an 18C gallery where exhibitions devoted to wine are staged.

There is a fine view of the Monbazillac vineyards from the sumptuously decorated great hall on the first floor.

The wine-testing laboratory includes the wine-tasting room (*open to visitors*), where all the Bergerac wines are tasted annually to determine whether they are worthy of the *appellation d'origine contrôlée* – the AOC mark on the label.

The AOC system is a method of ensuring the quality of wine and here one can learn how it works. The vineyards on the banks of the Dordogne cover 12,000 hectares/29653 acres, producing wine for the 13 local appellations like Bergerac and Montravel.

🚗 DRIVING TOUR

VALLÉE DU CAUDAU
60km/37mi – allow half a day

▷ *Leave Bergerac travelling NE along the N 21 to Les Pélissous, then turn right onto the D 21E1.*

Lamonzie-Montastruc
Perched on a rock to the left of the road is Château de Montastruc, a handsome building in the Classical style.

▷ *Continue along the D 21.*

Château de la Gaubertie
Built in the 15C, this castle was completely restored in the early 20C. The large main building, its façade overlooking the Caudau Valley, is flanked by a square tower on one side and a round corbelled tower on the other side. The 17C chapel is nearby.

▷ *Return along the D 21.*

Vergt
This large agricultural town has become one of the main strawberry centres. The sandy soil of the region is perfect for the cultivation of this fruit. (*Daily market Open mid-Apr to mid-Nov*).

▷ *Rejoin the D 8 and drive towards Bergerac taking the second road on the left 1.5km/0.9mi farther on.*

Lac de Neufont
This is a pleasant recreational lake with swimming beaches and pedal boat rental. Go through **St-Amand-de-Vergt**, which has a pretty Romanesque church surmounted by a dome.

▷ *Continue S.*

Château de St-Maurice
The castle is partly hidden by the trees in its grounds, but its 14C and 15C buildings, pierced with Renaissance windows and crowned with machicolations, are nonetheless an attractive sight.

ADDRESSES

🏠 STAY

🛏️ **Europ Hôtel** – *20 r. du Petit-Sol* ℘*05 53 57 06 54. www.europ-hotel-bergerac.com. 22 rooms.* 🍽️*7.5€* Close to the train station, this hotel, has the feel of the countryside about it, especially if relaxing under the trees around the pool. The rooms are ordinary but well kept and the price is right.

🛏️ **Verotel Hôtel** – *9 rte d'Agen, Domaine de Lespinassat.* ℘*05 53 24 89 76 www.hotelverotel.fr.* Modern 3-star hotel located at the entrance of Bergerac, 2km (1.25mi) from town in a tranquil pleasant setting. Cheerful rooms, pleasant pool

🛏️🛏️ **Chambres d'hôtes Agrybella** – *Place de l'Eglise 24560. St Aubin De Lanquais (11km/7mi SE of Bergerac).* ℘*05 53 58 10 76. www.agrybella.fr.st.* A lovely 18C mansion, completely renovated with cosy charming bedrooms and all mod cons. The lounge includes an open fireplace for chilly evenings. The peaceful park-style gardens include an outdoor pool.

🛏️ **La Flambée** – *49 av Marceau-Feyry.* ℘*05 53 57 52 33. http://laflambee.com. 21 rooms.* 🍽️*8€* This recently renovated country house enjoys an attractive leafy setting. Spacious bedrooms, some with their own terrace. An elegant restaurant where the emphasis is on regional cuisine.

🛏️🛏️🛏️ **Château Lespinassat** – *Rte d'Agen - 3km/1.8mi SE of Bergerac along the N 21* ℘*05 53 74 84 11. 5 rooms.* 🍽️*15€.* The fine lines of this 18C château are mirrored in the reflecting pool in the centre of a grand park. The rooms are very spacious and perfectly fitted out. Pool.

🍴 EAT

🍽️🍽️ **Le Méli-Mélo de la Marquise** – *2 r. Ste-Catherine.* ℘*05 53 57 10 86 www.bergerac-traiteur-lemelimelo-dordogne.com . Closed evenings, Sun lunchtime and Mon. Reserv. recommended.* Big bay windows fill this cosy little place with light. Breakfast daily, brunch Wed and Sat; market-fresh lunch-hour specials plus afternoon tea.

🍽️ **Le Plat dans l'Assiette** – *18 r. du Mourrier -* ℘*05 53 24 25 26. - Closed 2 wks*

in May, Sun (open lunch in season) and Mon. Reservations recommended. This Lyon-style bistro is a happy surprise in the land of foie gras and duck filet. The typical decor is a mix of bistro tables, knick-knacks, old advertising signs, paintings and a piano. Lyon meets Périgord on friendly ground here.

🍽️🍽️ **L'Enfance de Lard** – *Pl. Pélissière -* ℘*05 53 57 52 88.l enfancedelard@ yahoo.fr. Closed lunchtime and Tue Reserv. required.* This old house stands on a pretty square in old Bergerac. An intimate atmosphere prevails in the tiny, country-style dining room.

🍽️🍽️ **L'Imparfait** – *8 r. des Fontaines* ℘*05 53 57 47 92 www.imparfait.com. Closed Dec 20–Jan 20, Sun and Mon.* Set in a medieval building in the heart of the old town this quirkily-named restaurant serves local specialities, and has an open fire for grilling meats.

🍷 BARS AND CAFES

🍽️ **La Table du Marché** – *21 pl de la Bardonnie (Place du Marché couvert).* ℘*05 53 22 49 46. Closed Wed dinner, Sun.* Enjoy local and creative cuisine with fresh produce straight from the nearby Covered Market in this bright and modern but traditional little restaurant.

La Désirade – *Rue des Conférences* ℘*05 53 58 27 50. - Open Jun–Sep, daily, 10am–midnight; May, 9am–7pm Closed Oct–Apr.* With a terrace in front of a lovely fountain, this café is a cool and refreshing place to take a break. The friendly couple who run it offer old-fashioned ice cream and alcohol-free cocktails.

La Treille – *12 Quai Salvette -* ℘*05 53 57 60 11. Open daily in summer, 8am–2am; rest of the year, 9.30am–1am. Closed Tue eve and Wed.* This is the only café terrace in townthat overlooks the River Dordogne. Its arbour is an inviting place to escape the heat while its cosy interior beneath a vaulted ceiling is especially popular for romantic winter tête-à-têtes.

🛒 SHOPPING

Markets – Farmers' market Wed and Sat morning in pl. du Marché Couvert, Fri morning in pl. de la Madeleine, Wed morning in pl. Doublet. *Marché au gras* (market selling duck and goose products) Sat from Oct-Feb.

Château de
Biron★

From its strategic position on top of a rock, the massive bulk of the towers and walls of the Château de Biron commands this area on the borders of the Périgord and Agenais regions. The Dordogne *département* bought the castle in 1978 and began a massive restoration programme; an art centre was also established here, organising exhibitions every summer.

A BIT OF HISTORY

From the Capitol to the Tarpeian Rock – Among the many celebrated men of the Biron family, **Charles de Gontaut** met with a particularly memorable fate. Friend of Henri IV, he was appointed first Admiral and then Marshal of France. In 1598 the Barony of Biron was created for him and he eventually became Governor of Burgundy. Even these honours did not satisfy him and, in league with the Duke of Savoy he plotted against France. Biron, his treason exposed, was pardoned but he was soon involved in further intrigue Again exposed, the king agreed to pardon him if he confessed. He refused and was beheaded at the Bastille on 31 July 1602.

From medieval fortress to the present building – This castle is made up of buildings of very different styles. An 11C medieval fortress was razed by Simon de Montfort. Rebuilt in the 13C, it changed hands constantly during the Hundred Years War. In the late 15C and 16C, Pons de Gontaut-Biron, decided to transform his castle into a Renaissance château. He altered the buildings east of the main courtyard and had the Renaissance chapel and colonnaded arcade built. Work was interrupted, however, and not resumed until the 18C.

CHÂTEAU
Outer courtyard

Surrounding the castle's living quarters on three sides, the outer courtyard includes the caretaker's lodge, chapel, the receiving house and the bakery. The guards' tower, now the **conciergerie**, is an elegant building in which crenellations, a watch-path and Renaissance decoration are juxtaposed.

The **chapel** was built in the Renaissance style in the 16C. A pierced balustrade runs round the base of the roof. The lower chamber once served as a parish church for the village; the upper chamber or seigneurial chapel has remarkable pointed vaulting. It shelters **two tombs with recumbent figures**: Armand de Gontaut-Biron, bishop of Sarlat, and his brother Pons (d 1524)

Cour d'honneur (main courtyard)

Access is by a staircase and a pointed vaulted corridor. On the right, the 16C seigneurial living quarters, with Renaissance windows, lead to the large 13C polygonal keep redesigned in the 15C. On the left, the 16C-18C main building has an elegant remodelled staircase, which ascends to the Great Hall of State.

In the basement, the kitchen, the former garrison's refectory, is a vast room (22x9m/72x30ft) with barrel vaulting. A portico leads to the castle terraces; from there, the **view**★ extends over the rolling countryside and the Birons' other fief, the *bastide* of Monpazier.

ADDRESSES

STAY

Camping Le Moulinal – *24540 Biron 4km/2.5mi S of Biron on the Lacapelle-Biron road. ℰ05 53 40 84 60. lemoulinal@perigord.com. Open Apr 1–Sept 16. Restaurant on-site.* This campsite comes complete with a lake and swimming beach. There is also a pool, and a play area and organised activities for children. Canvas bungalows and mobiles homes available.

Michelin Map: 329: G-8
Location: 57km/35.5m SE of Bergerac.

Le Bugue

the Vézère to the Dordogne

This busy agricultural centre is situated at the gateway of the Périgord Noir, on the north bank of the Vézère, near its confluence with the Dordogne. A wide variety of leisure and cultural activities are available in and around the town, including museums, caves, castles etc.

- ▶ **Population:** 2 762
- **Michelin Map:** 329: G-6
- **Info:** rue Jardin Public - 24260 Le Bugue. ℘05 53 07 20 48.
- **Location:** 47km/29.4mi E of Bergerac.
- **Kids:** Aquarium du Périgord Noir; Maison de la Vie Sauvage-Musée de Paléontologie; Village du Bournat.
- **Don't Miss**: Gouffre de Proumeyssac; Cingle de Trémolat; Aquarium du Périgord Noir; Village du Bournat; Les Grottes de Maxange; Limeuil.
- **Timing**: Allow a full day to explore the Vézère and Dordogne valleys.

A BIT OF HISTORY

Le Bugue, located on the banks of the Vézère, has been inhabited since pre-historic times. A Benedictine monastery was founded here in the 10C, but the settlement didn't enjoy prosperity until the mid-12C when Périgord came under English control. The town was often disputed for by the French and English crowns. One of Le Bugue's famous sons is the chemist and physician **Jean Rey** (1583–1645) who discovered the Law of the Conservation of Mass over a century before Lavoisier confirmed the hypothesis in 1789. The law states that the mass of a closed system will remain constant over time regardless of processes acting within it.

MARKET TOWN

A charming small market town with winding streets and traditional Périgordien houses and is a convenient base for the many attractions of the area.

Aquarium du Périgord Noir★

rue de la République 🛝♿🕐*Open daily from mid-Feb–mid Nov. Times vary.* ⊜*9.90€ (children aged 4-16: 7.20€).* ℘*05 53 07 10 74. www.parc-aquarium.com* This aquarium has been designed to make visitors feel as if they were moving below the surface of the river. The open-topped aquariums have natural lighting and open onto large windows. They contain fresh water fish, crustaceans and invertebrates from various parts of Europe. Of particularly impressive dimensions are the gleaning catfish, originating from the centre and east of the continent (some of the larger specimens are over 1.5m/5ft long), white and silver grass carp and sturgeons. There is a separate display on the breeding cycle of the salmon. Fish feeding by the touch pools with the biologists (see website)

Maison de la Vie Sauvage-Musée de Paléontologie

9, Rue de la République. Open daily Jul–Aug & Sept 10am–1pm, 3–7pm; Apr–Jun Tue & Sat 10am–noon, 3–6pm. Rest of year telephone for times. ⊜*4€ (child 3€). 05 53 08 28 10.*
Vie Sauvage 🛝 *The focus of this section is birds, including a collection of stuffed and mounted specimens, their habits and habitats in Europe.*
The displays explains about feathers, beaks, and song; techniques for flying, hunting and fishing. Migratory routes and their many dangers are described. In the **Musée de Paléontologie** a collection of over 3 000 items are grouped together in families: ammonites, trilobites etc.

Village du Bournat★

Follow the rue de la République SW from town centre and take first right. ♿🕐*Open Mar–Apr, 10am–5pm; May, Jun & Sept 10am–6pm. Guided Tour July and Aug*⊜*12.90€ high season;*

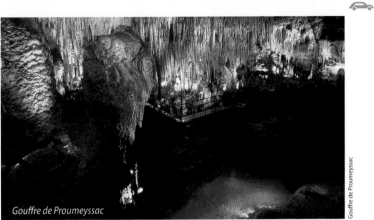

Gouffre de Proumeyssac

Gouffre de Proumeyssac

8.90€ low season. ℘05 53 08 41 99.
www.lebournat.fr

👥 A reconstitution of a regional village-farm at the turn of the last century with its school, chapel, town hall, washhouse, wine cellar. In each of the buildings, figures stage the joys and chores of the past: harvest supper, a wedding celebration, washerwomen at work. Bakers, smithies and other craftsmen perpetuate their traditional tradecraft, also highlighted by the collection of farm tools and machinery. Fun Fair.

CAVES

Caverne de Bara-Bahau
1km/0.6mi W of Le Bugue via D703 .
🕐*Open Jul-Aug.* 👥*guided tours (35min, last tour 30min before close).*
💶*6.40€.* ℘*05 53 07 44 58.*
The cave, which is about 100m/300ft long, ends in a chamber blocked by a rock fall. On the roof of the chamber may be seen drawings made with sharpened flints and fingers (Early and Middle Magdalenian Culture) discovered in 1951 by the Casterets; they depict horses, aurochs, bison, bears and deer.

Gouffre de Proumeyssac★★
3km/2mi S via the D 31E. 🕐*Open Jul-Aug.* 👥*guided tours (45min).*
💶*8.40€. Descent via lift by reservation: 16.50€.* ℘*05 53 07 27 47.*
www.perigord.com/proumeyssac.
A tunnel drilled into a hill, overlooking the Vézère, leads to a platform built half way up the chasm. This platform offers a view of this underground dome which is decorated, particularly at the base of the walls, with fine yellow and white concretions. Water seeps through abundantly, adding to the stalactites which, in some places, are very numerous and form draperies, pure coloured stalagmites and fantastic shapes such as the eccentrics and triangular crystallisations that are building up from the floor of the caves. All these concretions are revealed in turn by a *son et lumière* presentation. A short film explains the formation of the cave and a second *son et lumière* presentation takes place after the descent into the depths of the chasm.

The minute basket suspended in mid-air was until 1952 the only way of getting into the chasm. The 52m/171ft descent in complete darkness at the mercy of the fluctuations in temperament of the mule which was working the winch must have been an unforgettable experience for the four tourists allowed down each time with their guide. This primitive lift is available once more (*apply in advance*). Outside, a landscaped area dotted with explanatory panels offers visitors an insight into the geological features of the site. In summer, concert and shows are organised inside the chasm.

A woodland trail (30min there and back) leads to a spot overlooking the Vézère which offers a fine panorama of the river.

🚗 DRIVING TOUR

VÉZÈRE TO THE DORDOGNE
80km/50mi round tour – allow one day. Drive SE out of Le Bugue along the D 703.

Campagne
At the opening of a small valley stands a small Romanesque church preceded by a belfry. The **castle** of the lords of Campagne, built in the 15C, was restored in the 19C. The towers with crenellations and machicolations which flank the living quarters and the neo-Gothic elements give the castle the appearance of an English manor house. The last Marquis de Campagne gave the castle to the State in 1970.

▷ *Continue E along the D 35.*

St-Cyprien
St-Cyprien clings to the side of a hill near the north bank of the Dordogne, in a setting of hills and woodlands characteristic of the Périgord Noir. It is dominated by the massive outline of its **church**, the old houses of the village clustered close around. The large church was built in the 12C and restored in the Gothic period; the belfry keep is Romanesque. Inside, the enormous main body of the church has pointed vaulting. A wealth of 17C furnishings include altarpieces, a pulpit, stalls, an organ loft and a wrought-iron

balustrade. Close to the village are the carefully restored ruins of the **Château de Fages**.

▷ *Leave St-Cyprien travelling SW along the D 703E. The road skirts the north bank of the Dordogne. Turn left onto the D 703.*

Siorac-en-Périgord
This small village, sought after for its beach, has a restored 17C castle, home of the Comte de Vivans, and a small Romanesque church.

▷ *Return to the D 703E and continue to follow the River Dordogne.*

Coux-et-Bigaroque
This village consists of two formerly independent parishes. Note the carved doorway of the Romanesque church of Coux and the picturesque streets of Bigaroque.

▷ *Continue your journey along the Dordogne via the D 51 then turn left onto the D 51E to Le Buisson-de-Cadouin. Turn left beyond the railway line then left again and drive on for another 1.5km/0.9mi.*

Les Grottes de Maxange★
🕐*Open Jul–Aug, 9am–7pm; Apr–Jun and Sept, 10am–noon and 2–6pm; Oct–Nov, 10am–noon and 2–5pm.* 💶*7.20€.* 📞*05 53 23 42 80.*

Eccentric concretions, Grottes de Maxange

Les Grottes de Maxange

DE LA VÉZÈRE À LA DORDOGNE

These caves, discovered in a quarry in 2000, consist of galleries dug out of the yellow limestone by the sea when it withdrew, and later obstructed by alluvial deposits which it was necessary to clear away. The different deposit strata can be seen in the lower gallery, whereas the upper gallery contains a great variety of concretions (including stalactites and stalagmites), some of them with strange shapes and colours.

▷ *Return to the D 51.*

Limeuil★

Walk up the main street. Built on a steep promontory, this old village, arranged in tiers overlooking the confluence of the River Dordogne and River Vézère, occupies a picturesque **site**★. Its two bridges, unusually set at right angles and spanning each of the rivers, mark the confluence. Traces of its past as a fortress town can be seen on climbing up the ancient narrow streets to the site of the old castle and church.

Limeuil's role as arsenal and watchtower established itself quite early on, thanks mainly to its strategic position, which aroused desire and envy in those who saw it. At one point the militant peas-ants known as *Croquants* gained control of the town during an uprising. Limeuil was also for many centuries a port and safe haven for heavy barges (*canoes for hire*).

The village has retained traces of the former walled town along the pedestrianised streets leading up to the church. The imposing house with mullioned windows situated next to the 16C fortified harbour gate was the seat of the boatmen's guild. Immediately to the left, the town hall is housed in a former convent. The Grand Rue leads to the Récluzou gate with a pointed arch on the outside and a rounded one on the inside. From the **Parc du Château** (a former mansion remodelled in the early 20C) there is a fine panoramic view of the confluence of the Dordogne and Vézère. ◔*Open Jul-Aug, ⟲ guided tour daily except Sat, 10am-7pm; at other times between Easter and early Nov. ◒5€ ℘05 53 57 52 64.* The cliff road (D 31) overlooks the Limeuil meander.

▷ *2km/1.2mi, then right onto the D 2.*

Paunat

This modest village has retained an imposing church, once part of a monastery under the control of the powerful abbey of St-Martial in Limoges.

The austere-looking **Église St-Martial** was built in the 12C and remodelled in the 15C. The fortified belfry-porch, featuring two domed storeys, is an unusual example of Romanesque architecture in the Périgord.

▶ *Turn back and take the D 31 on the right.*

Trémolat

Built on a meander in the Dordogne, this charming village was made famous by the shooting of Claude Chabrol's film *The Butcher*. It has a 12C Romanesque church which represents a condensed version of all the religious architectural features of the Périgord region: heavy fortifications are combined with a vaulting system supporting a row of three domes and a huge defensive chamber covering the whole of the interior; the latter served as a refuge for the entire village.

▶ *Continue NW and follow the river.*

Cingle de Trémolat★★
(Trémolat Meander)

At the foot of a semicircle of high, bare, white cliffs highlighted by clumps of greenery, the river coils in a large loop, spanned by bridges of golden stone and reflecting lines of poplars. Beyond the wonderful stretch of water, which is often used for water sports and rowing regattas, on the convex bank lies a vast mosaic of arable fields and meadows (Trémolat Water Sports Centre).

▶ *The road offers fine glimpses of the valley. Just before Mauzac, turn right onto a minor road leading to the D 703 which takes you back to Le Bugue.*

ADDRESSES

🛏 STAY

🛶 **Camping St-Avit Loisirs** – *24260 St-Avit-de-Vialard. 7km/4.3mi NW of Le Bugue on the D 710 and a minor road.* ℰ*05 53 02 64 00. www.saint-avit-loisirs.com. Open Apr 1 to Sept 26. Reserv. recommended. 350 pitches.* Large pitches, comfortable facilities and a range of services at this campsite in a lovely location near a 100-year-old farm surrounded by oak and chestnut trees. Several pools, one of which is covered.

🛶💷 **Maison Oléa** – *La Combe de Leygue, 24260 Le Bugue. 5km/3mi E of Le Bugue on the D 703 towards Sarlat and then a minor road to the left.* ℰ*05 53 08 48 93.* 🛏 *5 rooms.* A peaceful stay is assured in this modern building which takes its inspiration from local architecture. The ground floor is embellished with Moorish touches and a lovely veranda which is used as a winter garden.

🍽 EAT

🛶💷 **Cygne** – *2 le Cingle.* ℰ*05 53 06 01 16. www.lecygne-perigord.com. Closed Dec 15–Jan 15, Fri eve, Sun and Mon.* This old family home on the edge of town has been converted into a hotel with a country feel. Plain but well-kept rooms, a warm dining room with a stone fireplace, plus a veranda and shady terrace.

🛶💷 **Le Chai** – *Pl. du Port. 24510 Limeuil.* ℰ*05 53 63 39 36. Open every day.* This former wine storehouse at the confluence of the Vézère and Dordogne has been converted into a restaurant. Pleasant garden terrace. Salads, crêpes and pizza feature on the menu.

🚶 LEISURE ACTIVITIES

Canoës des Courrèges – ℰ*05 53 08 75 37.* Canoes for hire on the Dordogne and the Vézère.

A Canoë Raid – *Campeyral. 24170 Siorac-en-Périgord* ℰ*05 53 31 64 11. www. a-canoe-raid.com. Open daily, Easter–Oct.* Full-day and overnight canoe and kayak trips on the Dordogne and the Vézère.

Canoë Rivière Loisirs – *Maisonneuve 24510 Limeuil.* ℰ*05 53 63 38 73. www. canoes-rivieres-loisirs.com. Open 9am-5pm.* Canoe, touring and mountain-bike hire. Boat trips from Limeuil (at the confluence of the Dordogne and the Vézère) exploring the superb lan

Cadouin★

The Abbey of Cadouin, founded in a narrow valley near the Forêt de Bessède in 1115 by Géraut de Sales, was occupied soon after by the Cistercians and was extremely prosperous during the Middle Ages, particularly as a place of pilgrimage. A small village, with its old covered market, has grown around the church and cloisters, which were restored after the Revolution. On 14 October 1890, the cinematographer and film critic Louis Delluc was born in a house on Cadouin's market square.

▶ **Population:** 335
Michelin Map: 329: G-7
Location: 41km/25.5 W of Sarlat
Don't Miss: Abbey church and cloisters.

A BIT OF HISTORY

The Holy Shroud of Cadouin – The first written mention of the Holy Shroud appeared in 1214 in an act decreed by Simon de Montfort.

This linen cloth adorned with bands of embroidery had been brought from Antioch by a priest from the Périgord and was believed to be the cloth that had been wrapped around Christ's head.

The shroud became an object of deep veneration and attracted large pilgrimages, bringing great renown to Cadouin. It is said that Richard the Lion Heart, St Louis and Charles V came to kneel before it in reverence. Charles VII had it brought to Paris and Louis XI to Poitiers.

Tradition versus Science – In 1934, two experts attributed the Holy Shroud of Cadouin to the 11C, as the embroidered bands bore Kufic inscriptions citing an emir and a caliph who had ruled in Egypt in 1094 and 1101. The bishop of Périgueux therefore had the pilgrimage to Cadouin discontinued.

ABBEY

The **church**★ building, completed in 1154, presents a massive, powerful west front divided horizontally into three sections: the middle section, opened by three round-arched windows which light the church's interior, divides upper and lower arcaded sections.

This austere architectural plan, where decoration is limited virtually to the play of light on the stone, emphasises the ornamental effect brought about by the gold colour of the Molières stone.

The finely proportioned building broke away from Cistercian architecture with its interior plan: a chancel with an apse between two apsidal chapels, a dome at the transept crossing capped by a

Abbaye de Cadouin from above

J. Damase/MICHELIN

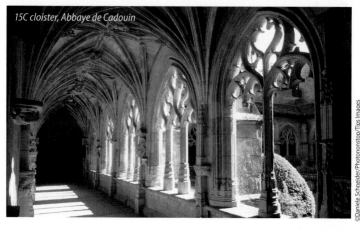

15C cloister, Abbaye de Cadouin

©Daniele Schneider/Photononstop/Tips Images

pyramidal bell tower roofed with chestnut shingles, and a more elaborate interior decoration (windows surrounded by mouldings, carved capitals). Nonetheless, the harmonious proportions and the grandeur of the construction emanate a spirituality entirely in keeping with Cistercian sanctuaries.

Thanks to the generosity of Louis XI, the **cloisters**★★ (&⊙*Daily 10am–12.30pm and 2–6.30pm; ☞guided tours; ⊙closed Jan and 25 Dec. ☞5€. b0800 891 991*) were built at the end of the 15C in the Flamboyant Gothic style. The work, in fact, continued to the middle of the 16C, as the Renaissance capitals of some of the columns bear witness. Despite the damage suffered during the Wars of Religion and the Revolution, the cloisters were saved and restored in the 19C, owing to the enthusiastic attention they were given by historians and archaeologists alike. Fine doors, adorned with coats of arms, pendants carved into people and lively little scenes and a large fresco of the Annunciation make it a fascinating visit. Four small columns cast in the form of towers are decorated with themes from the Old and New Testaments (Samson and Delilah, Job etc). The chapter house and two other rooms have been set up as a **Musée du Suaire** (Shroud Museum), where the restored relic is on display, forming the centrepiece of an exhibition to mark the eight centuries of pilgrimage and religious fervour that it provoked.

ADDRESSES

⌂STAY

⊜ **Camping La Grande Veyière** – *24480 Molières. 4km/2.5mi W of Cadouin along the D 25 and D 27. ☏05 53 63 25 84. www.lagrandeveyiere.com. Open Apr 1– Nov 2. Reserv. recommended. 44 pitches.* This hilltop campsite is next to an attractive traditional farm, whose outbuildings have been converted into a shop and bar. Spacious, well-shaded pitches.

⊜⊜⊜⊜ **Le Vieux Logis** – *Trémolat. 13km/8.1 NW of Cadouin via D28/D29/D31 ☏05 53 22 80 06. www.vieux-logis.com. 26 rooms.*

A former 16-17C priory, this house tells the story of the 450 year old family of the present owners. Cosy rooms, comfortable sitting rooms and asuperb garden.Unusually located ina former tobacco drying building. Terrace and a tempting classic menu.

♀/EAT

⊜⊜ **Bistrot d'en Face** – *24510 Trémolat. 13km/8.1 NW of Cadouin via D28/D29/ D31 ☏05 53 22 80 69. In the heart of the village where Chabrol filmed Le Boucher (1970).* Old stonework, beams and tasty country cuisine including andouillette and confit de Canard.

Château de Monbazillac★

Emerging from the undulating vineyards, this château rises proudly on the edge of a limestone plateau overlooking the Dordogne Valley. It is owned by the Monbazillac Wine Cooperative, which restored and refurbished it. Monbazillac, like Bergerac, actively supported the Reformation and supplied wine to Protestants who had sought refuge in the Netherlands.

CHÂTEAU

This relatively small château was built in 1550 and is surrounded by a dry moat. Its elegant silhouette is eye-catching, the architectural style half-way between a defensive castle and a Renaissance château. There are machicolations and a crenellated watch-path around the main building, which is flanked at each corner by a massive round tower.

The façade is pierced by a double row of mullioned windows and a doorway with Renaissance-style ornamentation. Two tiers of dormer windows can be seen above the machicolations. The grey patina of the stone blends well with the brown tiled roofs of the turrets and pavilions. From the north terrace there is a good view of the vineyard and of Bergerac in the distance.

The **Great Hall**, its painted ceiling decorated with gilt foliated scrolls, has a monumental Renaissance chimney-piece, 17C furnishings and two beautiful Flemish tapestries of the same period. Several rooms are open on the first floor; note in particular the viscountess of Monbazillac's **bedchamber** furnished in Louis XIII style.

Partly hollowed out of the rock, these cellars house a small wine museum displaying harvesting and winemaking equipment used in the past, as well as a **Musée du Protestantisme et du Meuble périgourdin** (Museum of Protestantism and of Furniture from Périgord). There is also a restaurant giving onto the main courtyard.

Michelin Map: 329: B-7; or see Bergerac map.

Location: 10km/6.25mi S of Bergerac.

Info: ℘05 53 63 65 00. or ℘05 53 61 52 52 (weekends). www.chateau-monbazillac.com.

Don't Miss: The tour inside the castle and a visit to the wine museum.

Times and Charges: Open Jul–Aug 10am–7pm; Jun and Sept, 10am–12.30pm and 2–5.30pm; May and Oct, 10am–12.30pm and 2–7pm; Nov–mid-Jan and mid- Feb–Mar 10am–noon and 2–5pm; daily except Mon. ⏱Closed mid-Jan–mid-Feb. ≈6.10€.

🚗 DRIVING TOUR

Vignoble de Monbazillac

Round trip of the wine-growing area surrounding the Château (15km/9.3mi – allow 1hr). Leave Monbazillac heading north on the D 13. Turn left onto the D 14 then left again onto the D 933 1.5km/0.9mi farther on. Drive over 2km/1.2mi along this road then turn left for the **Moulin de Malfourat**. The mill, now without its sails, stands on top of a hillock. From the viewing table there is a **panorama**★ of the Monbazillac vineyard and Bergerac and the Dordogne Plain to the north.

Château and vineyards at Monbazillac
S. Sauvignier/MICHELIN

Monpazier★

Monpazier was one of the **bastides** built to command the roads going from the Agenais region to the banks of the Dordogne. The square, surrounded by arcades, the **carreyrous** (alleyways), the old houses, the church and the ruined fortifications make it the best preserved of all the Périgord *bastides*.

▷ **Population:** 533
◔ **Michelin Map:** 329: G-7
▤ **Info:** Place des Cornières.
  ✆ 05 53 22 68 59.
▷ **Location:** 46km/29mi northeast of Villeneuve-sur-Lot and 50km/31mi southwest of Sarlat-la-Canéda.
◉ **Don't Miss:** Place des Cornières.

A BIT OF HISTORY

A difficult start – The *bastide* of Monpazier was founded in 1284 by Edward I, king of England and duke of Aquitaine. This *bastide* was designed to complete the process of defence and colonisation of Périgord begun in 1267 with the founding of Lalinde, Beaumont, Molières and Roquépine. To this end Edward I allied himself with Pierre de Gontaut, lord of Biron. Many difficulties soon arose: delays in the building, disagreements between the lord of Biron and the people of Monpazier and renewed hostilities between the king of England and Philip the Fair.

Monpazier receives royalty – The Reformation, in which the marshal of Biron played a prominent part, marked the beginning of a violent era. In 1574, the town was betrayed and fell into the hands of the Huguenot leader, Geoffroi de Vivans, who later won fame with the capture of Domme.

Buffarot the Croquant – After the Wars of Religion were over, the peasants rose again in revolt. The rebels, known as *croquants*, held a great gathering at Monpazier in 1594. The revolt flared up again in 1637. Led by a man named Buffarot, a local weaver from Capdrot, 8 000 peasants plundered castles across the countryside.

The soldiers of the duke of Épernon pursued them and, after some difficulty, captured Buffarot. He was brought back to Monpazier, tortured and broken on the wheel in the main square.

☞☞TOWN WALKING TOUR

Bastide

⏱☞*Guided tours, Jul–Aug, Wed and Fri, 11am; Sept–Jun by prior arrangement. ⊙4.60€. Contact tourist office. The general layout of the bastide is still in evidence, as are three of its original six fortified gateways. Several houses still have their original appearance.*

The town is in the shape of a quadrilateral (400×220m/1 312x722ft), the main axis running north-south. Streets

Distinctive geometry of the bastide

J. Damase/MICHELIN

are laid out from one end to the other, parallel with the longer sides, and four transverse roads run east to west, dividing the town into rectangular blocks. Originally all the houses had the unique characteristic of being of equal size and separated from each other by narrow spaces or *androndes*, to prevent the spread of fire. There is a panoramic view of the Dropt Valley from the Jardin des Franciscains to the SE of the *bastide*.

Place des Cornières★

The main square's rectangular shape echoes the *bastide* itself. On the south side stands a covered market housing the antique weights and measures. Round the edge, the arcades or covered galleries are supported on arches, some of which are pointed, and have angle irons (*cornières*). The houses overlooking the square date from the Middle Ages to the 17C.

▶ *Leave the square via a cut-off corner in a wall to the left.*

Église St-Dominique

This interesting church was built in the 13C and remodelled several times: the doorway dates from the 14C, the rose window and the gable were all rebuilt in the 16C. The wide nave has pointed vaulting and extends into a polygonal east end.

▶ *Turn right as you come out of the church.*

Chapter house

This 13C house stands near the church. It was used as a tithe barn. Paired windows light the upper floor.

Atelier des bastides

◔*May–Sept: 10.30am–12.30pm, 4-6.30pm.* ✎*No charge.* ℘*05 53 22 60 38. Behind the church.*
This centre, devoted to *bastides*, offers extensive information: photos, models, archaeological evidence. Temporary exhibitions are organised in summer.

ADDRESSES

🏠 STAY

⌂ **Camping Le Moulin de David** – *3km/1.8mi SW of Monpazier on the D 2.* ℘*05 53 22 65 25. http://moulindedavid. village-center.com. Open mid May–early Sep. Reserv. recommended. 160 pitches. Restaurant.* This popular campsite is set around an old mill in a pretty valley with a brook. Friendly, quiet, comfortable, well maintained, good sports facilities and a wide range of services.

⌂🍴🍴 **Edward 1er** – *5 r. St-Pierre.* ℘*05 53 22 44 00. www.hoteledward1er. com. Closed mid Nov–mid Mar. 12 rooms.* The building's towers give this manor house the appearance of a small castle. Cosy, English-style interior, quiet rooms, plus a swimming pool and small garden.

🍽 EAT

⌂⌂ **Privilège du Périgord** – *58 r. Notre-Dame.* ℘*05 53 22 43 98. www. privilegeperigord.com. Closed Dec–Feb and Tue. Reserv. recommended.* This 18C coaching inn covered in Virginia creeper has an attractive rustic-style dining room. In warm weather dine amid the greenery in the courtyard. Traditional dishes from the southwest.

🛒 SHOPPING

Markets and fairs – Traditional market on Thursday morning in place des Cornières. Large fair on third Thursday of the month as well as July 8 and August 6. Wild mushroom market in October (depending on harvest) under the *halle* from 3pm onwards.

Verrerie d'Art de Monpazier (M. Pascal Guernic) – *13 r. St-André -* ℘*05 53 74 30 82. www.artisans-d-art.com/guernic. Opening times vary. Closed Dec 25, Jan and Mar.* This glass-blower displays an interesting collection of original works in his workshop.

Périgueux is the main town of the Périgord Blanc, or White, region to the west of the Dordogne département and is, in fact, its largest city. The Périgord Blanc is so called due to the frequent outcrops of chalky limestone that illuminate the open landscape and, in effect, it is sandwiched between the Périgord Vert to the north and the Périgord Pourpre to the south. The Périgord Vert, or Green, stretches in a crescent across the north of the département from the Limousin in the east to the Gironde in the west and was first named by no less a figure than the author Jules Verne for the woodlands, the green pastures of the farms grazed by dairy cattle and the abundant fields of cereal crops.

Périgueux used to be two cities, one with its landmark Byzantine style Cathedral of St.Front, now a UNESCO World Heritage site, founded in the 11C, vying with the other, older, district of the Cité to the west. The Cité was all that was left of the old Roman town of Vesunna, with the church of St-Etienne at its centre and the roman amphitheatre and Temple de Vésonne nearby. Now of course Périgueux is the thriving Préfecture of the Dordogne with nearly 30,000 inhabitants.

Périgord Blanc

Many visitors are drawn to the Périgord Blanc in order to visit Périgueux and, fascinating though the city may be, there is much more more to the area than that. The valley of the River Dronne, which flows through the picturesque village of Aubeterre-sur-Dronne with its monolithic church just over the border of the Charente département, past the impressive Château de Bordeilles where the chronicler Pierre de Bordeilles, better known as Brantôme, was born in 1538

and magnificent Abbey at Brantome, where he was later to become commendatory abbot, to the magnificent Renaissance Château of Puyguillhem.

Périgord Vert

The Périgord Vert is the most rural of the two with few settlements of any size. Nontron, the main town, can barely muster 3500 souls but this is part of the charm of this region. Green valleys with large tracts of forest and granite landscape mean that it has more in common with the neighbouring Haute-Vienne and Corrèze départements to the north than it does to the Dordogne. This similarity, and a desire on the part of the regional authorities to promote sustainable tourism and encourage the economic and cultural development of the area, has led to the establishing of the Parc Naturel Régional Périgord-Limousin in the northern part of the Périgord Vert and the south west of the Haute-Vienne département of the Limousin.

Aubeterre-sur-Dronne★

Located halfway between the Charente and the Aquitaine, the village of Aubeterre overlooks the Dronne Valley amid a landscape of verdant pastureland. With its picturesque, steep, narrow streets fronted by houses adorned with wooden balconies, it is one of the prettiest villages in the whole region and takes its name from the local white chalk (*alba terra* in Latin, which translates as "white land"). It is centred around place Travieux, and the bust in honour of Ludovic Travieux, born in Aubeterre, who founded the League for the Defence of the Rights of Man.

- ▶ **Population:** 418
- ⓘ **Michelin Map:** 324: L-8.
- ⓘ **Info:** Place du Chateau, 16390. ☏05 45 98 57 18. www.aubeterresur dronne.com
- ▶ **Location:** 53km/33mi W of Périgueux via D710/D20. The centre of the village is place Travieux.
- ⓘ **Don't Miss:** Aubeterre is famous, first and foremost, for its impressive churches, in particular the monolithic church.

MONOLITHIC CHURCH★★

From pl Travieux descend rue St Jean and church is below the Chateau.
🕘*Open daily, 9.30am–noon, 2pm–6pm. (Jun–Sept till 7pm).*🕘*Closed Dec25, Jan 1* ⊕*4.5€.* ☏*05 45 98 65 06.*
This church is a rare example of a building hewn from a single block of rock. A corridor bordered with niches leads to a vast cavity cut into the rock; the inner surface is bare and rough.

A baptismal font from the 5C or 6C, sculpted in the shape of a Greek cross, testifies to the presence of a primitive church and evokes the practice of baptism by total immersion. The crypt must have hosted followers of Mithras, a god worshipped by members of a mystery cult which was one of early Christianity's most serious rivals. The present church was probably started in the 12C to house relics brought back from the Holy Sepulchre in Jerusalem. During the Revolution, the church was used as a saltpetre works and later as the local cemetery.

The 20m/65ft-high nave is flanked by a single aisle where a small spring venerated by early pilgrims still filters. The apse surrounds a monolithic Romanesque monument, carved from a block left in place when the church was hollowed out. In it, a shrine holds the relics of the Holy Sepulchre.

At the other end of the nave is a primitive 6C chapel, transformed into a necropolis in the 12C after work on the church was completed. In the higher part of the nave, a gallery above the ambulatory overlooks this place of primitive worship.

Monolithic church, Aubeterre-sur-Dronne

J. Damase/MICHELIN

Bourdeilles★

and the Boulou Valley

The impressive castle of Bourdeilles, with the village clustered at its foot, stands imperiously above the River Dronne. It was here that the chronicler, Brantôme, was born in 1540.

A BIT OF HISTORY

A coveted spot – In 1259 St Louis ceded Périgord and Bourdeilles, his most important barony, to the English. This incredible desertion made the country rise in revolt and divided the Bourdeille family: the elder branch supported the Plantagenets, and the Maumonts, the younger branch, the Capetians. A while later, after plots and lawsuits, Géraud de Maumont, Counsellor to King Philip the Fair, who urged him on, seized the castle of his forebears. He turned it into a fortress. Then, to show his strength in Périgord, Philip the Fair set up a strong garrison within the fief of his enemies, the English.

The Renaissance touch – Credit for the plans for the 16C château must go to Jacquette de Montbron, wife of André de Bourdeille and sister-in-law to Pierre de Brantôme, with her active and informed interest in geometry and architecture. Building was started in haste at the promise of a visit by Catherine de' Medici, but was abandoned when the visit was cancelled.

▶ **Population:** 777
◔ **Michelin Map:**329: E-4
▤ **Info:** Place des Tilleuls, 24310 Bourdeilles. ℘05.53.03.42.96. www.bourdeilles.com.
▷ **Location:** On the river Dronne, 9.2km/5.7mi southwest of Brantôme.
◈ **Don't Miss**: The village's medieval and Renaissance châteaux.
◔ **Timing**: Allow a couple of hours to explore the churches of the Boulou Valley.

CHÂTEAU★

◔*Open Jul–Aug,* ◞*guided tour (1hr) 10am–7pm; Apl–Jun and Sept–Nov, Wed–Mon, 10am–12.30pm, 2–6pm; Feb. Mar and DecMon, Wed, Thur and Sun 10am–12.30pm, 2–6pm.*
◔*Closed Jan, Tue in Jul–Aug and 25 Dec.* ◉*5.80€.* ℘*05 53 05 65 65.*
Cross the first fortified curtain wall, pass under the watch-path to get inside the second wall and enter the outer courtyard, in which there is a fine cedar.
The 13C **castle**, built by Géraud de Maumont is an austere building surrounded by a quadrangular curtain wall. Inside the main building, exhibitions are held in a great hall. A 35m/115ft-high keep

Castle above the village of Bourdeilles by the Dronne

dating from the early 14C, towers above it. From the upper platform there is a good overall view of the castle and a sweeping view of the River Dronne.

Sober and elegant in appearance, the 16C **château** houses remarkable **furnishings**★★ collected by two patrons who donated their collection to the Dordogne *département*.

Do not miss the **salon doré**★★, a sumptuously decorated room built to accommodate Catherine de' Medici, and above all the dining hall with its 16C carved **chimney-piece**★★★. From the watchpath there is a lovely **view**★ of the castle and its setting, a Gothic bridge with cutwaters and an attractive 17C seigneurial mill.

Salon doré,
Château de Bourdeilles
©A. J. Cassaigne/Photononstop/Tips Images

 DRIVING TOUR

CHURCHES OF THE BOULOU VALLEY
Round trip of 22km/14mi – allow 2hr

▷ *Leave Bourdeilles N on the D 106E2 towards Brantôme. Pass the rock formation known as the Forge du Diable (Devil's Forge), and take a small road on the left.*

St-Julien-de-Bourdeilles
In this modest hamlet is a small Gothic church with two lovely statues in polychrome wood and parts of a 17C altarpiece.

▷ *Continue N to Boulouneix.*

Boulouneix
A Romanesque chapel with a domed bell-tower stands in a cemetery. In the chancel, 17C murals represent Mary Magdalene and St Jerome.

▷ *About 100m/109yd after the church, bear left towards Au Bernard.*

The road descends through the woods (hornbeam and filbert) to the marshy Boulou Valley.
Numerous prehistoric sites have been discovered in the region.

Paussac-et-St-Vivien
Several 16C houses and a 13C-15C fortified church are of interest in this village. The south wall is decorated with arcades. Inside, note the capitals decorated in low relief with naïve carvings, a large Christ in polychrome wood and a Louis XV-style pulpit.

▷ *Take the C 2 towards Brantôme; at Les Guichards turn right towards Les Chauses, leaving the road to Puy-Fromage on the left.*

From the road you will soon see Bourdeilles and its tall keep.

ADDRESSES

STAY

Chambre d'hôte Le Pigeonnier de Picandine – *24350 Lisle - 5km/3mi SE of Lisle - leave Lisle on the D 1 towards Périgueux, then take the 3rd road on the right.* ✆*05 53 03 41 93. www.picandine. com. Closed Nov 15–Feb 15 .- 5 rooms.* A pair of two-hundred-year-old chestnut trees stand in front of the half-open courtyard of this 17C home. The rooms are plain but comfortable, and are contained within the old barn or the main building. Two pleasant suites are a good option for families.

Brantôme★★

and around

Brantôme lies in the charming Vallée de la Dronne. Its old abbey and picturesque **setting**★ make it a delightful place to visit.

BANKS OF THE RIVER DRONNE★★

The former abbey buildings, located at the foot of the cliff, overlook the island upon which the village has been built.

Clocher (Belfry)★★

Boulevard Charlemagne. &. ①*Open Jun 15 to Sept 15 daily except Sun and Tue from Jun 15–Jun 30 and Sept.,* ⁀*guided tour (1hr 15min), 11am-7pm, Sun 2.30-6pm;* ⊚6€. ℘*05 53 05 80 63.*
The bell tower was built apart from the church upon a sharp rock towering 12m/39ft high, beneath which are vast caves. It was erected in the 11C and is the oldest gabled Romanesque bell tower in the Limousin style. It was made of four storeys, each stepped back and slightly smaller than the one below, and topped with a stone pyramid.

Abbey

Boulevard Charlemagne.
Brantôme Abbey, which was founded by Charlemagne in 769, under the Benedictine rule, to house the relics of St

▶ **Population:** 2 112
⏾ **Michelin Map:** 329: E-3
ⓘ **Info:** 24310 Brantôme. ℘05 53 05 80 52. www.ville-brantome.fr.
⊙ **Location:** 27km/17m N of Périgueux via D939. 93km/58mi NW of Sarlat. A boat trip on the river is the perfect way to discover this charming town. There is a traditional market on Friday mornings. Farmers' market on Tuesday morning in Jul-Aug. Marché au gras (selling duck and goose products) Friday mornings from Nov-Feb. Truffle market from Dec-Feb.
⌐ **Boat trips:** (45min) with on-board commentary operate May-Sep from quai du Pavillon Renaissance. ⊚6.50€.

Sicaire, attracted a multitude of pilgrims. Sacked by the Normans, it was rebuilt in the 11C by Abbé Guillaume. In the 16C, it became a commandery headed by Pierre de Mareuil as abbot and later his nephew, Pierre de Bourdeille, became the administrator.

Brantôme on the banks of the Dronne

J.P. Clapham/MICHELIN

The Chronicler Brantôme

The literary fame of **Pierre de Bourdeille**(1538-1614), better known as Brantôme, brought renown to the abbey of which he was commendatory abbot He began life as a soldier of fortune and courtier, went to Scotland with Mary Stuart, travelled to Spain, Portugal, Italy and the British Isles and even to Africa. Wild adventures brought him into contact with the great and famous in an era rich in scandal.
After fighting at Jarnac in 1569, he withdrew to his abbey and began his famous chronicles. He returned to court as chamberlain to Charles IX.
In 1584 a fall from his horse crippled him, he then left the restless and impetuous Valois court to retreat to the peace of his monastery and finish his chronicles.
Brantôme, famous for his *Les vies des hommes illustres et grands capitaines* (Lives of Illustrious Men and Great Leaders), was a witty and sometimes cynical historian.

The present buildings were remodelled in the 18C by Bertin, administrator of Périgord and extensively restored in the 19C.

Angevin vaulting, a compromise between cross-ribbed vaulting and a dome, replaced the two original domes of the **abbey church** in the 15C. The nave is plain and elegant; a bay in the form of a cross and three depressed-arched windows below it illuminate the flat east end. Near the main doorway, go into the 16C cloistral gallery from where it is possible to get a glimpse of the former chapter-house.

The **convent buildings** now house the town hall and an art museum (&*see the Fernand-Desmoulin Museum*) A monumental staircase leads to the former monks' dormitory where temporary exhibitions are regularly held.

Du Creusé au Construit (Troglodyte tour)

Boulevard Charlemagne (behind Abbey)
&Open Jul–Aug, 10am–7pm; Apr–Jun and Sept, daily except Tue 10am–12.30pm and 2–6pm; Oct–Mar, daily except Tue, 10am–noon and 2-5pm.
Closed Jan and 25 Dec. 4€.
(Combined ticket with Musée Fernand Desmoulin) 05 53 05 80 63.
The hermits who had converted the fountain of the rock, originally a place of pagan worship, to Christianity were succeeded by monks, who initially occupied the caves in the rock face.
Later on they continued to use the caves as outbuildings, or as refuges when the

abbey buildings came under attack (in the 11C, 12C, 14C and 17C). The tour shows the monks' calefactory and the lavacrum, the remains of the abbey mill and the troglodyte dovecote.

Pont Coudé

Boulevard Charlemagne.
Walk through the gardens adorned by the Fontaine Médicis towards the Renaissance house with mullioned windows.
A 16C elbow bridge with asymmetrical arches gives access to the **Jardins des Moines** (Monks' Gardens).

"VENICE OF THE PERIGORD"

On leaving the Jardins des Moines, cross the bridge to reach quai Bertin where the old houses with their flower-covered balconies and trellises are reflected in the tranquil mirror of water.
Follow the numbered panels marking the tour of the town and providing information about the different architectural styles (*a map is available at the tourist office*).

Musée Fernand Desmoulin

Abbaye 05 53 05 80 63 Open Feb –Dec daily (exc. Tue) 10am–7pm in July and August; 10am–12.30pm and 2pm –6pm at other times. Closed Jan exc school hols and Dec 25 4€.
(Combined ticket with Troglodyte Tour).
The museum displays a permanent exhibition of the enigmatic, trance like, paintings, drawings et of the artist and medium Fernand Desmoulin (1853-1914).

EXCURSIONS

Château de Puyguilhem★

12km/7.5mi NE. Drive 3km/1.9mi along the D 78; left to Champagnac just before the bridge over the Dronne. ⏱*Opening times vary.* ⚫*5€.* ☎*05 53 54 82 18.*
This 16C château is typical of those built in and around the Loire Valley in the days of François I. The towers, balustrades, sculpted chimneys and mullioned windows create a graceful exterior impression. Inside, the **chimney-pieces**★ are particularly impressive.

Grottes de Villars★★

16km/10mi NE; 4km/2.5mi beyond Puyguilhem. ⏱*Open Jul-Aug,* 🚶*guided tour (1hr, last entrance 30min before closing), call for times.* ⚫*6.90€.* ☎*05 53 54 82 36. www.grotte-villars.com.*
The tour follows galleries linking several chambers dug out by an underground river. Among the most remarkable formations are yellow and ochre draperies (up to 6m/20ft long), two small rimstone pools, and very finely-wrought stalactites hanging from the ceiling. Halfway through the tour, a *son et lumière* show provides a dramatic overview of the main stages which led to the formation of the cave.
A video presentation, which can be viewed before or after the tour, provides a good insight into the local geological features.

Thiviers

26km/16mi E along the D 78.
This busy little town is known for its markets and fairs. The **Musée du Foie Gras** (♿⏱*opening times vary;* ⚫*1.50€;* ☎*05 53 55 12 50*), is to the right of the tourist office. Thiviers is one of the main production areas.

ADDRESSES

🏨 STAY

🛏🛏 **Chambre d'hôte Doumarias** – *Doumarias - 24800 St-Pierre-de-Côle. 12km/7.2mi E of Brantôme on the D 78* ☎*05 53 62 34 37. doumarias@aol.com. Closed 30 Sept–1 Apr* 🍴 *6 rooms.*
A charming house covered with Virginia creeper and a majestic lime tree reigning supreme over the inner courtyard. Quiet, unpretentious rooms and a pretty garden with a pool. Friendly welcome.

🛏🛏🛏 **Chambre d'hôte La Maison Fleurie** – *54 r. Gambetta .* ☎*05 53 35 17 04/ 05 53 05 16 58. www.maison-fleurie.net. Closed Feb school hols.* 🍴 *5 rooms.*
This 19C house, with its handful of attractive, comfortable rooms is right in the centre of town. Copious breakfasts, served in the courtyard.

🍴 EAT

🛏🛏 **Les Ondines Salon de Thé** – *13 bd de Coligny -* ☎*05 53 46 60 30. Closed 1 Nov–Easter except weekends.*
The summer terrace of this tea room overlooking the abbey enjoys a bird's-eye view of the Dronne.

🛏🛏 **Les Jardins de Brantôme** – *33/37 r. P.-de-Mareuil -* ☎*05 53 05 88 16. Closed Wed (except 15 Jul-Aug) and Thu. Reserv. required.* In the summer months, enjoy the terrace or sit under the trees in the garden of the former 18C stagecoach inn. Traditional regional cooking with vegetables fresh from the garden.

🛏🛏 **Au Fil du Temps** – *1, chemin du Vert-Galand.* ☎*05 53 05 24 12. www.fildutemps.com. Closed Mon and Tue lunch.* This elegant bistro occupies an attractively restored 14C posthouse. One dining room with a rotisserie, where the decor is kitchen inspired, the second is more elegant in feel.

🛏🛏🛏🛏 **Le Moulin de l'Abbaye** - *1, route de Bourdeilles, 24310 Brrantôme.* ☎*05 53 05 80 22. www.moulinabbaye.com.*
Located in the centre of town in an idyllic setting on the banks of the Dronne and overlooking the Monastery Garden. Gourmet cuisine and regional specialities.

EVENTS

Sinfonia en Périgord - ☎*5 53 09 51 30. http://festivals.aquitaine.fr .*
This Baroque music festival starts and finishes at Brantôme during the latter part of August and early September.

Abbaye de
Chancelade★

The abbey appears as a peaceful haven tucked into the foot of the green slopes overlooking the Beauronne: its role as a spiritual centre continues today.

ABBEY

Founded in the 12C by a monk who adopted the rule of St Augustine, the abbey was protected by the bishops of Périgueux and later answered directly to the Holy See. It therefore prospered and was accorded considerable privileges: asylum, safety and franchises. From the 14C the abbey's fortunes declined; the English captured it, sent the monks away and installed a garrison. During the Wars of Religion, the abbey buildings were partly destroyed. In 1623 Alain de Solminihac, the new abbot, undertook the reformation and restoration of Chancelade. He was so successful that he was named bishop of Cahors by Louis XIII. The abbey was able to function calmly

- ⓖ **Michelin Map:** 329: E-4
- ▷ **Location:** 7km/4mi NW of Périgueux
- ⓐ **Don't Miss:** The Sinfonia Baroque music festival that takes place in late August.

until the Revolution, when it became national property. The lower part of the **church** is all that remains of the original 12C church.

The Romanesque doorway features an elegant arcade, showing Saintonge influence.

The conventual buildings, added in the 17C, include the abbot's lodgings and the outbuildings around the courtyard and garden, which comprise the 15C pointed barrel-vaulted laundry room, stables, workshops and a fortified mill. A **museum** of religious art, housed in the basement of the abbot's lodgings, displays reliquaries, statues, altarpieces and paintings, including a Christ outraged believed to be the work of Georges de la Tour.

Château de
Hautefort★★

The proud outline of Hautefort Château dominates the skyline, reminiscent more of the royal palaces of the Loire Valley than of the fortresses of Périgord.

A BIT OF HISTORY

The strategic position of the Hautefort site on a hill in the middle of an immense amphitheatre was certainly exploited very early on: in the 9C the viscounts of Limoges are known to have built a stronghold here. During the Middle Ages several castles succeeded one another, leaving some traces (the courtayrd's west corner tower). The defensive position of the castle was strengthened in the 16C (barbican flanked by two crenellated bartizans and equipped

- ⓖ **Michelin Map:** 329: H-4
- 🛈 **Info:** Pl. Marquis J. Francois de Hautefort 24390 Hautefort, ✆05 53 50 40 27
- ▷ **Location:** 41km/25.5mi east of Périgueux.
- ⓐ **Don't Miss:** The superb timberwork in the north-west tower.

with a drawbridge) during the tumultuous years of the Wars of Religion. Complete reconstruction of the castle in the 17C led to a harmonious combination of architectural styles - Renaissance and Classical - which contributes to the building's original and elegant appearance.

In 1929, Baron Henri de Bastard and his wife bought the castle and decided to restore it; they also had the French-

Château de Hautefort

J. P. Clapham/MICHELIN

style gardens laid out. In 1968, fire swept through the main building but the two wings were spared. The fine interior has since been restored.

CASTLE

🕐 ☞ *Open Jun–Sept, guided tour (1hr, last entrance 1hr before closing), Open daily Jun–Aug, 9.30–7pm, Sept 10am–6pm, Apr & May, 10am–12.30pm and 2–6.30pm, Oct daily 2pm–6pm. Mar and Nov 1–Nov 11, Sat, Sun & public holidays 2pm–6pm.* ✆8.50€. *Garden:* ♿ *unaccompanied tour.* ✆05 53 50 51 23. www.chateau-hautefort.com. The terraces of the castle are laid out as French-style gardens, planted with flowers and box trees forming geometric patterns and offering views of the 30ha/74-acre English-style park where visitors can take a pleasant stroll.

Inside the castle, the northwest tower has beautiful chestnut **timberwork★★**, the work of the Compagnons du Tour de France guild.

It gives access to the watch-path dismantled in the 17C. The flower-decked gallery of the main building leads to a grand staircase giving access to various rooms, including Marie de Hautefort's bedroom furnished in Louis XV style.

ANCIEN HOSPICE

The former chapel of an almshouse stands on the village square, south of the castle. The edifice, shaped like a Greek cross, features a fine dome covered with slates and surmounted by a lantern. It houses the **Musée de la Médecine** which displays a reconstructed ward and presents an exhibition devoted to the progress of medicine in the 19C; another room illustrates dental care from 1870 to the present.

🕐 ☞ *Open daily Jun–Sep, 10am–7pm (guided tours possible - 1hr 15min); Easter–May 10am–noon, 2pm–6pm, Oct ,Mon–Fri, 10am–noon and 2–6pm.* ✆4.50€. ✆05 53 50 40 27 or 05 53 51 62 98.

Bertrand the Troubadour

The first castle of Hautefort was built by the Limousin family of Las Tours. In the 12C it passed by marriage to the house of De Born, of whom Bertrand, the very same mentioned by Dante in the Divine Comedy, is the most well-known member. **Bertrand de Born**, the famous troubadour who was much admired in the courts of love, became a warrior-knight when the need arose to defend the family castle against his brother Constantine. He succeeded in having Henry II acknowledge his rights in 1185. However, in 1186 Constantine returned to Hautefort and razed the castle. Renouncing everything, Bertrand became a monk.

ADDRESSES

🏠 STAY

🛏️🍽️💰 **Chambre d'hôte Villa des Courtissous** – *24210 St-Rabier 12km/8mi S of Hautefort on the D 704. ℘05 53 50 27 20 or 06 03 00 84 20. www.courtissous. com. Closed Dec & Mar ⏚4 rooms.*
This square, white house stands in the middle of a lovely park and a warm welcome by the new English-speaking owners awaits you. Breakfast is served by the fireside or on the terrace by the swimming pool.

🛒 SHOPPING

Les Abeilles du Périgord – *24210 La Bachellerie. ℘05 53 51 00 91. Open Jul–Aug, 10am–noon and 2.30–7pm; Mar–Dec, daily except Tue, 10am.* A visit to this honey farm will tell you all you need to know about raising bees and collecting their golden nectar. On Thursdays and Saturdays in July and August, you can even help extract the honey yourself. Honey products on sale here.

Neuvic

and the Forêt de la Double

This peaceful village lies on the south bank of the River Isle, which flows along the edge of the Forêt de la Double sprinkled with lakes and half-timbered clay houses.

- ▶ **Population:** 3 508
- **Michelin Map:** 329: D-5
- **Info:** Place de la Mairie. ℘05 53 81 52 11. www.paysdeneuvic24.com.
- **Location:** 24km/15mi southwest of Périgueux via the D1089/N89.
- **Kids:** Parc Botanique; the wild boar enclosure near the Grand Étang de la Jemaye.
- **Timing:** Allow a full day to explore the Forêt de la Double.
- **Also See:** Bergerac.

VILLAGE

Château de Neuvic

🕐🚶 *Open Jul–Aug, guided tours (1hr, last entrance 30min before closing) at 3pm and 5pm; Closed Thu. 👁5.50€ (château and botanical gardens). ℘05 53 80 86 60. www.chateau-parc-neuvic.com.*
Follow the rue Majoral Fournier from the centre towards the River. Take a walkway on the left lined with trees which leads to the castle; it is currently in use as a medical training centre. Built in 1530, the castle has retained its machicolated watch-path which is more of a decorative than a defensive feature; two main buildings surround a square keep erected at the beginning of the 16C. Inside, there are 16C and 18C frescoes.

Parc Botanique

🕐*Open Jul–Aug, 10am–7pm; Apr to Jun and Sept, 10am–noon and 2–6pm. 🕐Closed Thur.👁3.80€.(no charge Apr,May and Sept. Guided tour by prior arrangement. ℘05 53 80 86 65. www.chateau-parc-neuvic.com.*
🧒The castle grounds have been laid out as botanical gardens (6ha/15 acres) housing some 1 500 plant species (oak, dogwood, spindle tree, lilac, roses etc).

🚗 DRIVING TOUR

FORÊT DE LA DOUBLE

95km/59mi round-trip – allow one day. Drive north out of Neuvic, cross the River Isle then follow the D 3 to the right for **St-Astier**. Lying on the banks of the River Isle, the old town centre contains a few remaining Renaissance houses. It is overlooked by the church, supported by massive buttresses, and a magnificent 16C bell tower adorned with two tiers of blind arcades.
The D 43 climbs out of St-Astier on a series of steep hairpin bends to reveal

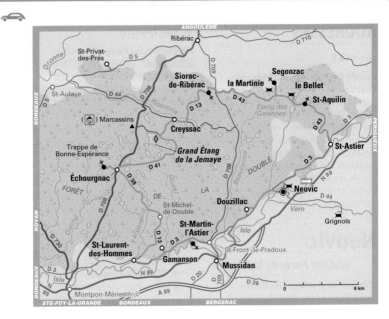

beautiful views of the town before descending into the forest. Next stop is **St-Aquilin**. The church, built in a transitional Romanesque Gothic style, contains a remarkable gilt-wood altarpiece.

From the church, drive 700m/766yd along the D 43 and turn right for **Château du Bellet**. The fine tiled roofs, massive round towers and separate dovecot of this castle, built on the side of a hill, come into view on the right.

Continue on the D 43; turn right onto the D 104 3km/1.9mi farther on for **Segonzac**. As you enter the village, note the **Château de la Martinie**, a 15C building remodelled several times. The village's Romanesque **church** (11C-12C) was altered and enlarged in the 16C.

From Segonzac, return to the D 43 (right) for **Siorac-de-Ribérac**. Overlooking a small valley, the fortified Romanesque church has a single nave partly surmounted by a dome.

Drive west from Siroac; turn left to the D 13, then right to the D 44 to St-Aulaye and **Creyssac**. Surrounded by the waters of a small lake, the elegant square dovecot makes a pleasant sight. 200m/220yd farther on, turn left towards **Grand étang de la Jemaye**. In the middle of

the Forêt de Jemaye, the lake has been set up as a water sports centre with a beach and facilities for fishing, windsurfing and a splashing good time. Nearby, at the intersection of the D 108 and the D 708, a **wild-boar and heron pen** (🐾) can be seen close to the road.

Return to the road and turn right for **Échourgnac**. Not far from this village (along the D 38) stands a **Trappist monastery** (Trappe de Bonne-Espérance). The monastery was founded in 1868 by Trappist monks from Port-du-Salut in Normandy. They set up a model cheese-making farm, collecting milk from the neighbouring farms. Their Trappe cheese is very similar to Port Salut.

Drive southeast out of Échourgnac along the D 38 to St-Michel-de-Double and turn onto the D 13 for **St-Laurent-des-Hommes**. This village boasts a few splendid traditional houses of the Double region.

Drive east on the D 3 for **Gamanson**. Set back slightly from the road, this hamlet constitutes the richest collection of traditional half-timbered and clay-walled houses of the Double region.

Turn back and continue along the D 3 (left) for **St-Martin-l'Astier**. The unusual outline of the Romanesque **church** is right at the extremes of most Double architecture. The **bell-tower** and **chancel** are octagonal; the latter is covered by a dome on eight engaged columns. Continue along the D 3 and cross the River Isle to see **Mussidan**. This old Huguenot city on the banks of the River Isle was besieged on several occasions during the Wars of Religion. The siege in 1569, which was particularly bloody, inspired one of Montaigne's famous Essays (*L'Heure des Parlements Dangereuse*). Mussidan is hoe to the **Musée des Arts et Traditions Populaires du Périgord André-Voulgre** (&⊙*Opening times vary; ⊛3€; ℘05 53 81 23 55*).

Displayed in the lovely Périgord mansion where Doctor Voulgre lived, this collection is rich and varied; it includes furniture, objects and tools, as well as a still, a steam engine and stuffed animals collected by the doctor during his lifetime.

Drive NE from Mussidan on N 89; turn left on D 3E5 3km/1.9mi farther on for **Douzillac**. Have a look at the town hall with its pepper pot and wooden balcony. The outline of the 16C **Château de Mauriac** situated near the D 3, on the way to Mauriac, is reflected in the calm waters of the River Isle.

Périgueux★★

and the Périgord Blanc

Périgueux is an ancient town built in the fertile valley of the River Isle. Its long history can be traced in its urban architecture and two distinctive districts, each of which is marked by the domes of its sanctuary: the Cité district, overlooked by St Stephen's tiled roof, and the Puy St-Front district, with the Byzantine silhouette of the present cathedral bristling with pinnacles. There is a good overall view of the town from the bridge beyond Cours Fénelon to the south-east. Périgueux's gastronomic specialities, with truffle and foie gras occupying prize position, have become famous around the world and attract many visitors.

A BIT OF HISTORY

The wonderful Vésone – The town of Périgueux owes its foundation to a sacred spring known as the Vésone. It was near the stream, on the Isle's south bank, that the Gaulish Petrocorii (Petrocorii, which meant the four tribes in Celtic, gave its name both to Périgueux and Périgord) built their main *oppidum* (defensive town). After siding with Vercingetorix against Caesar, the Petrocorii

- ▶ **Population:** 29,558
- **Michelin Map:** Michelin local map 329: F-4
- **Info:** 26 place Francheville. ℘05 53 53 10 63. www.tourisme-perigueux.fr
- **Location:** Périgueux is located on the banks of the River Isle, 48.5km/30mi north of Bergerac and 22km/14mi south of Brantôme.
- **Parking:** The town has three large underground car parks in place Montaigne, place Francheville and along the esplanade du Théâtre (first 35min free of charge). Free outdoor car parks can also be found along the river, along part of the allées Tourny and on place Mauvard.
- **Timing:** Once you have spent time exploring the town, allow a half day to explore the Périgord Blanc.
- **Don't Miss:** St-Front district; the cathedral; Musée du Périgord.
- **Also See:** Bergerac.

St-Front district by the Isle

©Nicolas Thibaut/Photononstop/Tips Images

finally had to accept Roman domination but in fact benefited greatly from the Pax Romana, which enabled the city to become one of the finest in all Aquitaine. Vesunna, as the town was then called, spread beyond the bend in the Isle; temples, a forum, basilicas and an arena were built and an aqueduct over 7km/4mi long was constructed to carry water to the baths. But in the 3C AD the city's prosperity was destroyed by the Alemanni, who sacked the town.

The unfortunate town – To avoid further disaster the Vesunnians shut themselves up in a narrow fortified enclosure; stones from the temples were used to build powerful ramparts and the arena was transformed into a keep.

In spite of all these precautions, the town suffered the alternate depredations of fire and pillaging by barbaric invaders such as the Visigoths, Franks and Norsemen. Such misfortune reduced Vesunna to the status of a humble village and finally even its name died; it was simply known as the city of the Petrocorii and *la Cité* eventually became the town's new name. St Front later established the town as an Episcopal seat and, in the 10C, it became the unassuming capital of the county of Périgord.

The ambition of Puy-St-Front – A little sanctuary containing the tomb of St Front, Apostle of Périgord, was built not far from the Cité. Initially the object of a pilgrimage, the sanctuary became a monastic centre. A busy market town, Puy St-Front, grew up round the monastery, soon eclipsing the Cité in size.

The townspeople of Puy St-Front joined the feudal alliances against the English kings, established an emancipated consular regime and then sided with Philip Augustus against King John of England.

Little by little, the expanding Puy St-Front annexed the Cité's prerogatives; there were more and more squabbles between the rivals. The Cité, unable to win against its neighbour which was under the protection of the king of France, was forced to accept union. On 16 September 1240, an act of union established that the Cité and Puy St-Front would now form one community governed by a mayor and 12 consuls, under the name of Périgueux.

Nevertheless, each town kept its distinctive characteristics; the Cité belonged to clerics and aristocrats whereas Puy St-Front belonged to merchants and artisans.

Périgueux becomes Préfecture – In 1790, when the Dordogne *département* was created, Périgueux was chosen over Bergerac as Préfecture. The town, which had slowly become dormant, suddenly found itself the object of a building boom. The old districts were enhanced by new avenues and squares.

🚶 WALKING TOURS
1 ST-FRONT DISTRICT★★★

The old artisans' and merchants' district has been given a face-lift. A conservation program for safeguarding this historic area was set up, and the area has been undergoing major restoration. Its Renaissance façades, medieval houses, courtyards, staircases and shops are being gradually brought back to life; the pedestrian streets have rediscovered their role as commercial thoroughfares.

Place du Coderc and place de l'Hôtel-de-Ville are colourful and animated every morning with their fruit and vegetable market, whereas place de la Clautre is where the larger Wednesday and Saturday market is held. During the winter, the prestigious truffle and foie gras markets held in place St-Louis attract hordes of connoisseurs.

In summer, the restaurants, overflowing onto the pavements, serve high quality Périgord cuisine in an atmosphere of days past.

▶ *Start at Tour Mataguerre (tower) opposite the tourist office.*

Tour Mataguerre

🚶*Part of a guided tour of the town.*

This round tower (late 15C) is crowned by a machicolated parapet and pierced by arrow-slits. It is the last of the 28 towers forming the defensive system of Puy St-Front in the Middle Ages. On the side of rue de la Bride part of the ramparts can be seen.

From the top (viewing table), there is a **view**★ of the old district with its tiled roofs, the towers of the noblemen's town houses, the domes of St-Front and the neighbouring hills, one of which is the well-known Écornebœuf Hill (*écorner* means to break the horns of an animal; *bœuf* means ox) so named because the hill was so steep that the oxen broke their necks... and lost their horns.

▶ *Follow rue de la Bride.*

Rue des Farges

At nos 4 and 6 stands the **Maison des Dames de la Foi** (House of the Women of Faith). The medieval (12C) layout of its façade is still visible: pointed arches on the ground floor, rounded arches on the upper storey and a loggia beneath the eaves. A small bell turret set in one corner brings to mind the fact that in the 17C the building was a convent.

▶ *Look down passage Taillefer before turning right onto the narrow ruelle des Farges which leads to place de Navarre. Walk up the stairs.*

Rue Aubergerie

At no 16, the **Hôtel d'Abzac de Ladouze** consists of great round arch, an octagonal tower and a corbelled turret, all characteristics of 15C architecture. At nos 4 and 8 the **Hôtel de Sallegourde**, also 15C, has a polygonal tower surmounted by a machicolated watch-path.

▶ *Turn left*

Rue St-Roch

At no 4 a small arcaded loggia is decorated with diamond-work. Farther on, on the corner of rue de Sully, note the restored half-timbered house.

▶ *Bear left.*

Rue du Calvaire

The condemned, on their way to be executed on place de la Clautre, came up this street, their road to Calvary. At no 3 there is a door ornamented with nailheads beneath a Renaissance porch. The street leads to place de la Clautre which offers an interesting view of the imposing St Front Cathedral.

Cathédrale St-Front★★

This cathedral, now on UNESCO's World Heritage List, is one of the largest in South-west France and one of the most curious.

A chapel was first built on the site of the saint's tomb in the 6C. In 1047 a larger church was consecrated but this second building was almost completely

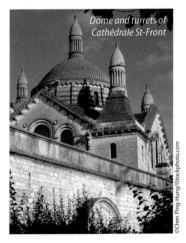

Dome and turrets of
Cathédrale St-Front

©Chen Ping-Hung/iStockphoto.com

saint's tomb destroyed. Restoration was carried out with little regard for the original design. It was largely reconstructed by Abadie from 1852 onwards in the style of Second Empire pastiche. He was to use this restoration later as the inspiration for the design of the Sacré Cœur Basilica in Paris.

Exterior - Stand in place de la Clautre to have an overall view. Before the restoration, the domes, covered in stones and tiles, had small end ornaments. The façade overlooking place de la Clautre and the open bays were part of the 11C church. The beautiful tiered bell tower is all that remains of the 12C church, and is preserved more or less as it was

PÉRIGUEUX

0   200m

originally. Abadie drew on its lantern as inspiration for the tall pinnacles which adorn the new domes.

Interior - *Enter the cathedral by the north door.*

In order to respect the chronological order of the building's construction, visitors should first of all see, near the base of the bell tower, the remains of the 11C church; two bays covered with domes perched on tall column drums.

From its prestigious Romanesque model, the church redesigned by Abadie appropriated its dimensions, the boldness of its domes on pendentives and the strength of its odd-looking pillars carved in places in the shape of a cross.

A visit to the cathedral is included in the guided tour of the "Medieval and Renaissance town".

Cloisters - The cloisters date from the 12C, 13C and 16C and are of a half-Romanesque, half-Gothic architectural style. The enormous pine-cone-like mass in the centre of the cloisters once crowned the bell tower; during the Revolution it was replaced by a weathercock which was later replaced by Abadie's angel.

Walk to the right of the building.

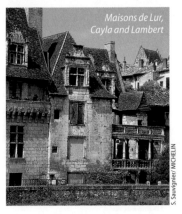

*Maisons de Lur,
Cayla and Lambert*

S. Sauvignier/ MICHELIN

Place du Thouin

The two bronze cannon with the inscription Périgueux 1588 were excavated at place du Coderc in 1979 on the site of the armoury in the old consulate.

▷ *Walk round the cathedral to place Daumesnil; then left on rue de la Clarté.*

Maison Natale de Daumesnil

This house, at no. 7, has an 18C façade. **General Pierre Daumesnil** was born here on 27 July 1776. This soldier followed Napoleon to Arcola, Egypt and Wagram, where he lost a leg. In 1814, while governor of the Vincennes fortress, he said to the enemy, who were laying siege, "I'll surrender Vincennes when you give me back my leg."

▷ *Continue along rue de la Clarté, turn left then right onto rue du Serment.*

Place de l'Hôtel-de-Ville

The town hall is located in the 17C and 18C **Hôtel de Lagrange-Chancel**. The 15C house at no 7 has a polygonal staircase tower characteristic of the period. Its machicolations are neo-Gothic.

▷ *Walk to the left of the town hall.*

Place du Coderc

Originally a field for keeping pigs, this square has become the geographic and administrative centre of the Puy St-Front district. In the early 19C the old consulate, the heart of municipal and legisla-

tive life, still had its square belfry, some 600 years old. The covered market was built on this site in c 1830.

▷ *Follow rue de la Sagesse opposite.*

Hôtel de la Joubertie

Visits as part of a guided tour of the town.
Located at no 1, this mansion contains an elegant **Renaissance staircase**★, of a square design, decorated with a coffered ceiling depicting mythological scenes including Venus putting down her weapons, which symbolises the young wife entering the household. The intertwined H and S represent the initials of the Hauteforts and Solminihacs.

Place St-Louis

This square is known locally as Foie Gras Square, as it is here that the foies gras are sold in late autumn.
It features a modern fountain, decorated with a bronze sculpture by Ramon.
Maison Tenant or the **Maison du Pâtissier**, opposite, used to be the Talleyrands' town house; it consists of a residential part set at right angles, with an adjoining corbelled turret. The façade on rue Eguillerie has a marvellous Gothic window. **No 5 rue Lammary** has an unusual superposition of mullioned corner windows.

▷ *Turn right.*

Rue Limogeanne★

In the past, this street led to Limogeanne Gate (Porte Limogeanne), which opened onto the Limoges road. The street is lined with numerous stores and several elegant Renaissance town houses.
In the courtyard of the **Hôtel de Méredieu** (no 12) there is a 15C carved doorway decorated with a coat of arms, which was added in the 17C.
At no 7, note the initials A C in the centre of the wrought-iron impost; these denote Antoine Courtois, the famous 18C caterer, whose partridge pâtés were the talk even of the Court of Prussia. His headquarters were in the cellars of this town house.

Maison Estignard (no 5) has an elegant Renaissance façade. The Regional Department of Architecture is to be found at no 3. Behind the heavy balustrade above the doorway, the inner courtyard has a lovely door decorated with grotesques on the lintel and François I salamanders on the tympanum. The huge staircase is remarkable. **Lapeyre House** (no 1), which is at the corner of place du Coderc, has a corbelled corner turret.

Retrace your steps and turn right onto impasse Limogeanne.

Galerie Daumesnil★
It consists of a network of courtyards and small squares linked by alleyways. The buildings, which were grafted on over the centuries, have been demolished, creating open spaces and revealing the fine 15C, 16C and 17C façades.

Come out onto rue de la Miséricorde and cross rue St-Front.

On the left along rue St-Front is an unusual Masonic Lodge (Loge Maçonnique) perforated by openings like arrow slits. The sculptures on the façade represent masonic emblems.

Rue de la Constitution
At no 3 is the **doorway of the Hôtel de Crémoux** with a crocketed arch between tall pinnacles.
At no 7, the **Hôtel de Gamanson**, also called Logis St-Front, consists of two 15C wings set at right angles, linked by a staircase tower, flanked by a corbelled turret and perforated by mullioned windows. A 17C well is sheltered by a Moorish dome.

Turn left onto rue du Plantier then turn right.

Rue Barbecane
The street owes its name to an old tower, now destroyed; all that remains is part of a wall. Before taking the stairs in rue de l'Abreuvoir, note the 19C façade of the Hôtel de Fayolle. Walk along the street then turn round to admire the 17C front of this mansion overlooking the river.

Turn right

Rue du Port-de-Graule
Just like rue Ste-Marthe which prolongs it, this street still has a medieval air about it with its large uneven paving stones, its low doors and the little staircase-alleyways that lead off it. In 1967, several scenes from the film of Jacquou le Croquant (based on local author Eugene le Roy's novel) were shot here.

Walk to boulevard Georges-Saumande on the left.

The Quays
Along the river there are several fine houses standing side by side.
Maison Lambert, on the left of Pont des Barris, is a fine Renaissance town house called the House with Columns because of its gallery. Next to it, **Maison Cayla**, also called the Consul's House, was built on the ramparts in the 15C. The roof is decorated with Flamboyant-style dormers. At the corner of avenue Daumesnil, the **Maison de Lur** dates from the 16C.
Continue along the quays; on the other side of avenue Daumesnil the half-timbered building, corbelled over the fortress wall, is a remainder of the **barn** attached to the cathedral, called the **Old Mill**, which once jutted out over the river.

Turn right onto rue de Tourville leading back to the cathedral.

② CITÉ DISTRICT★
This district, occupying the site of ancient Vesunna, has retained numerous Gallo-Roman ruins which testify to the town's importance under Roman occupation.

Leave from the tourist office, follow rue de la Cité then turn right onto rue de l'Évêché.

Arènes

A public garden occupies the space where the arena once stood. Built in the 1C, this amphitheatre, one of the largest in Gaul, had a capacity for 20 000 people. Great blocks of stone still mark the stairwells, the passages between banks of seating and the vaulting, but all of the lower part of the building is still buried. Demolition of the arena began in 3C, when the amphitheatre was turned into a bastion and became part of the city ramparts. The arena was next transformed into a quarry, its stone being used to build houses in the town.

On leaving the amphitheatre, take rue de Turenne on the left.

Porte Normande

This gateway formed part of the ramparts built in the 3C to protect the city from the hordes of barbarians sweeping across Europe. The story behind the name is that the gate is supposed to have played a part in the defence of the city against the Vikings who came up the River Isle in the 9C.

Maison Romane

This 12C (Romanesque) rectangular building is neighbour to the vestiges of a tower from the Gallo-Roman defence wall, jumbled up with bits of capitals, column drums and other architectural elements. An altar on which bulls were sacrificed was discovered here; it is now on display in the Gallo-Roman Museum (*see below*).

Château Barrière

This castle has a 12C keep rising above one of the towers of the ramparts. It was altered during the Renaissance period but kept the lovely, main entrance door in the staircase tower. Destroyed by fire during the Wars of Religion, it was not rebuilt.

Cross the bridge on the right.

Vesunna – Musée Gallo-Romain de Périgueux

Open daily Jul–Aug, 10am–7pm; Apr– Jun, & Sept , daily except Mon, 9.30am–5.30pm, Sat, Sun & Public Hols, 10am–12.30pm, 2.30–6pm; Oct–Mar, daily except Mon & Public Hols, 9.30am–12.30pm and 1.30–5pm, Sat–Sun, 10am–12.30pm, 2.30–6pm. 5.70€. 05 53 53 00 92. www.vesunna.fr

Designed by Jean Nouvel, this museum houses the remains of an opulent Gallo-Roman residence covering 4 000m2/4 784sq yd. Built in the centre of a garden, it is like a large glassed-in inner courtyard reflecting the surroundings and blending perfectly with them. On one side, a mezzanine on two storeys overlooks the ancient *domus*. This section of the museum is devoted to the ancient town of Vesunna: a scale model of the town in the 2C shows how extensive it was in Roman times – the residence can easily be located near the sanctuary and the forum.

Wooden footbridges enable visitors to wander through the house. Digs have revealed the presence of a 1C building, considerably extended in the 2C. Elaborate murals can be seen on the base of the walls of the primitive house. The frieze surrounding the central pond, on the other hand, was painted when the house was extended. Along the way, the daily life of the inhabitants is illustrated: hypocaust heating system, decoration, water distribution (oak water pump) and various handicrafts.

Temple de Vésone

This tower, 20m/65.5ft high and 17m/56ft in diameter, is all that remains of the temple dedicated to the titular goddess of the city. The temple, which was built in the heart of the old Cité in the 2C AD, originally had a peristyle, and was surrounded by porticoes and framed by two basilicas. The tower is still impressive despite being damaged.

Cross the bridge and turn left along rue Romaine where the remains of a Roman wall (Late Empire) can be seen.

St-Étienne-de-la-Cité★

🕐 *Open daily except Sun and holidays, 8am–7pm.*

Built in the 11C on the site of the ancient temple of Mars, this church, the town's first Christian sanctuary, was dedicated by St Front to the martyr Stephen and was the cathedral church until 1669.

It included a row of four domed bays, one after the other, preceded by an imposing belfry porch. When the town was occupied in 1577, the Huguenots demolished all but the two east bays. Restored in the 17C, ravaged again during the Fronde, secularised during the Revolution, St Stephen's was consecrated anew during the First Empire.

The church as it now stands is pure Périgord-Romanesque style.

Inside, it is interesting to compare the architecture of the two bays built within a 50-year interval. The first (11C) is archaic, primitive, short and dark. The second bay is more slender, its dome resting on pointed arches on square pillars.

Against the south wall of the first bay is an impressive 17C **altarpiece** in oak and walnut built for the seminary.

MUSEUMS

Musée du Périgord★

🕐 *Open 10am–5pm, Sat–Sun, 1–6pm; Closed Tue and public hols.* 💶4€. *No charge, noon–2pm, on Mon, Wed, Thu and Fri from Sept 15–June 15.* 📞05 53 06 40 70.

Located on allées de Tourny, on the site of what was an Augustinian convent, this museum has one of the most important **collections of prehistory** in France.

It contains, in particular, a remarkable collection of engraved objects of the Magdalenian period (15000-12000 BC), found in various sites across the Dordogne region, as well as the fossilized skeleton of the Regourdou man (Neanderthal man 70000 BC, 👣 *see LASCAUX*) and of the Raymonden man (*Homo sapiens*, 15000 years old).

The collection of **medieval exhibits** includes Limoges enamels, 11C capitals from the cathedral, the 13C Virgin altarpiece, the 13C Rabastens diptych,

Tour de Vésone

S. Sauvignier/MICHELIN

and a 15C liturgical cupboard. The **fine arts and decorative arts Department** (16C-20C), displays works by local artists next to works by French, European and Asian artists; note the portrait of Fénelon by F Bailleul (18C) and Sem by François Flameng (20C).

Musée Militaire du Périgord

🕐 *Open Jan–Mar & Oct–Dec, 2–6pm; Apr–Sept , 1–6pm, daily exc Sun and public hols, (last entrance 30min before closing). .* 💶3.5€. 📞05 53 53 47 36.

Arms and weapons of all sorts, standards and uniforms evoke the military history of Périgord from the Middle Ages to today. Particularly honoured is the 50th Infantry Regiment.

Musée du Trompe-l'œil

🕐👣 *Guided tours, Apr–Sep, 10.30am–12.30pm and 2.30–6.30pm, Sun, 3–6pm; Oct–Mar, daily except Mon and public hols, 2–5.30pm, Sun, 3–5.30pm.* 🕐*Closed Mon and public hols.*💶5€ 📞05 53 09 84 40. www.museedutrompeloeil.com

Located in the Gallo-Roman district, this museum relates the history of *trompe-l'œil* techniques from prehistoric times to the present, by means of panels illustrating each major period.

🚗 DRIVING TOUR

PÉRIGORD BLANC
56km/35mi round-trip – allow half a day

▷ *Leave Périgueux along the D 939 towards Brantôme.*

The region owes its name of Périgord Blanc to the colour of the local stone.

Abbaye de Chancelade★
⚓ *See Abbaye de CHANCELADE.*

▷ *Leave Chancelade on the D 2 travelling N. The road between Chancelade and Merlande rises through a wood of chestnut and oak trees.*

Prieuré de Merlande
In a deserted clearing in Feytaud Forest stand a small fortified chapel and a prior's house, as solitary reminders of the Merlande Priory founded here in the 12C by the monks of Chancelade. Both have been restored.

▷ *Return to the D 2, turning left then right 2.5km/1.5mi farther on.*

Château-l'Évêque
The village took its name from the Episcopal castle. The façades facing the Beauronne Valley have mullioned windows, and a machicolated watch-path runs around the line of the roof.

Château de des Bories

A. Cassaigne/MICHELIN

The parish church is where St Vincent de Paul, founder of missionary organisations to help the poor, was ordained in September 1600 at the early age of 20.

▷ *Leave the village travelling NE along the D 3E.*

Agonac
In a pleasant setting in the wooded hills of the area known as Perigord Blanc, the **Église St-Martin** (🕐*Open mid-Jul to mid-Aug;* ⚑*guided tours by prior arrangement, daily except Sat–Sun and public hols, 4–6pm;* ✆*05 53 06 36 71)* gives this town its character.
The square belfry and the buttresses (16C) were added to repair damage incurred during the Wars of Religion. The system of two-storey high defensive chambers encircling the 12C dome recalls the troubled times when churches were turned into fortresses.

▷ *Continue E along the D 106.*

Sorges
This pleasant village has a century-old reputation for producing truffles, and a museum to honour them. The **Musée de la Truffe** (⚓🕐*open daily Jul–Aug, 9.30am–12.30pm and 2.30–6.30pm (last entrance 30min before closing), Sept–Jun, daily except Mon, 10am–noon, 2–5pm;* ⚑*guided tours, Jul–Aug, Tue and Thu, 2.30pm;* 🕐*closed 1 Jan, 1 May, 1 Nov and 25 Dec;* ⚖4€; 05 53 05 90 11) in the tourist office is dedicated to this rare, delectable fungus and directs you to a walking tour (3km/1.9mi).

Château des Bories
On the way back to Périgueux along the N 21. 🕐*Open Jul–Aug.* ⚑*Guided tour (45min, château and park), daily except Sun, 3–6pm.* ⚖4€. ✆*05 53 06 00 01.*
A 15C-16C gem that boasts a splendid monumental staircase in the square tower, unusual vaulting over the guardroom and a fine Flemish tapestry in the long gallery.

ADDRESSES

🛏 STAY

🍽 **Comfort Hôtel Régina** – *14 r. Denis-Papin (opposite the train station). ℘05 53 08 40 44. 41 rooms.* Bedrooms are small, functional and colourful. Buffet breakfast. Friendly service and a good location.

🍽 **Hôtel Bristol** – *37 Rue Antoine Gadaud. ℘05 53 08 75 90. www.bristol france.com. 29 rooms.* A dull boxy exterior belies the cheerful interior of this modern centrally located 3-storey 3-star hotel, very close to the medieval heart of town.

🍽 **Etap Hôtel Périgueux** – *33, Rue du Président Wilson . ℘892 68 32 37 www.etaphotel.com. 49 rooms.* Centrally located cheerful simple budget chain-hotel accommodation.

🍽 **Hôtel Mercure Périgueux Centre** – *7 place Francheville. ℘05 53 06 65 00. www.mercure.com. 66 rooms.* Superior modern chain-hotel with smart bedrooms and business facilities.

🍽 **Chambre d'Hôte au Village** – *Au Bourg - 24220 Sorge. ℘05 53 05 05 08.* Closed Oct. 3 rooms. Simple rooms in an old stone maisonette abutting the Truffle Museum. Breakfast is served beneath the shade of a lime tree.

🍴 EAT

🍽 **Au Bien Bon** – *15 r. des Places. ℘05 53 09 69 91. Closed Feb school hols and early Nov; Jul–Aug Sat, Sun, Mon eve and public hols. Rest year, closed lunch Mon–Thur, Sat eve, Fri & Sun.* Dine on seasonal local products in the rustic interior or on the summer terrace.

🍽 **La Ferme-Auberge de Grande Maison** – *Vieux Bourg - 24750 Boulazac. ℘05 53 09 63 78. http://ferme-auberge-lassagne.com. Closed evenings and Mon out of season.* Reserv. required. Dine in a traditional beamed stone farmhouse on cuisine du terroir with périgourdines specialities. Impeccable service.

🍽 **L'Espace du Sixieme Sens** – *r. Francis Delpey. 6, pl. Saint Silain - 24000 Périgueux. ℘05 53 09 24 29. Closed Mon.* This epicerie fine is run by one of Perigord's top chefs. It stocks some of his finest creations which you can taste in the simple cafe.

🍽 **Au Petit Chef** – *5, Pl. du Coderc. ℘05 53 53 16 03.* Classic cheerful small bar (downstairs) and restaurant (upstairs) with few frills.

🍽 **Hercule Poireau** – *2 r. de la Nation. ℘05 53 08 90 76. Closed Jan 5–18, Tue eve in winter and Wed.* Set in a vaulted 16C cellar, this jokily-named place is popular with locals. Its varied menu includes several healthy options.

🍽 **Le Clos Saint-Front** – *5 r. de la Vertu. Closed Jan 28–Feb 10, Sun eve and Mon off season. ℘05 53 46 78 58. www.leclossaintfront.com.* Set in an old house, with exposed beams, fireplace and Louis XVI furniture, this elegant restaurant is devoted to Périgourdine cuisine with an inventive twist.

🍽 **La Taula** – *3 r. Denfert-Rochereau. ℘05 53 35 40 02. Closed 2–9 Mar, 6–13 Jul and Mon in low season.* Smart semi-formal city centre restaurant specialising in local cuisine.

🍽 **Le Grain de Sel** – *7 r. des Farges. ℘05 53 53 45 22. Closed 28 Jun–20 Jul, 20 Dec–4 Jan, Sun–Mon.* This traditional house, set in a narrow lane of old Périgueux, serves inventive modern dishes in a rustic setting.

🍽 **La Table du Pouyaud** – *rte de Paris - 24750 Champcevinel. ℘05 53 09 53 32. www.pouyaud.com.* Elegant semi-formal restaurant in a former farmhouse serving gastronomic regional cuisine.

🍽 **Auberge de la Truffe** – *sur N 21 - 24420 Sorges. ℘05 53 05 02 05. www.auberge-de-la-truffe.com. Closed Sun dinner and Mon lunch from 12 Nov– 30 Mar.* Spruce modern formal dining room serving local cuisine with truffles and foie gras in pride of place.

🛍 SHOPPING

Le Relais des Caves – *44 r. du Prés.-Wilson. ℘05 53 09 75 00.* The friendly proprietor, M. Aupert, sells a wide selection of wines from across France, including a few very special vintages.

La Poissonnerie Moderne – *Place Coderc. ℘05 53 08 00 70.* Pascale Mercier and Phillipe Ducreux offer an amazing array of fresh seafood brought in from St Malo, Roscoff, the Isle d'Oleron and Normandy.

Rocamadour, La Bouriane and the Causses are found just to the south of the Dordogne Valley, between the Cantal département and the Dordogne département. The region covers the northern Haut or High Quercy, the fertile Limargue in the east, and the Bouriane in the west. In its centre; the Causse of Martel, a vast, arid, stone covered plain, dissected by a relatively fertile zone and named after the medieval town of Martel; and the Causse de Grammat, an extensive limestone plateau, home to a number of natural sites, such as the Gouffre de Padirac, and of course the pilgrimage site of Rocamadour.

Rocamadour

Many visitors to both the Périgord and Quercy regions place the medieval pilgrimage site of Rocamadour, quite rightly, at the very top of their list of places to visit. Viewed from the belvedere at L'Hospitalitet in the early morning light, Rocamadour can be seen at its most impressive and followed up by a tour of its fascinating sights, its image will endure in memory. After falling into disrepair, Rocamadour once more attracts religious pilgrims, as well as the tourist variety.

Rocamadour
©Spectrumoflight/Dreamstime.com

La Bouriane

Blanketed in heath, coppices and woods, La Bouriane bears more resemblance to the Périgord than the Quercy. In this area, timber, chestnuts and walnuts are harvested, maritime pines are tapped for resin, and livestock is raised and sold. The capital of this area is the bustling town of Gourdon.

Causses

Aside from Rocamadour itself, the Haut Quercy is a varied region with much to see. The Causse of Gramat at its centre offers an opportunity to explore this, the wildest and largest causse (plateau) in Quercy, on foot, on a cycle, on horseback or even by car starting from the pleasant town of Gramat itself. The Gouffre de Padirac is an exceptional site – a 33m/108ft chasm is descended by stairs or lift and leads to an underground river where a boat trip takes you to the 94m/308ft high Salle du Grand Dôme. The Martel Causse is smaller and less wild but interesting nevertheless – there are rivers full of fish, walnut trees, truffles and lavender.

Several sights on the Causse, including Martel itself, (or close to it like Souillac and St. Céré), are incorporated in the section on the Upper Dordogne Valley.

Les **Arques**★

The tranquillity of this Bouriane village is undoubtedly the reason the sculptor **Ossip Zadkine** (1890-1967) chose to live here. Russian by birth and French by adoption, he arrived in Paris in 1909, where he was first influenced by Cubism, a style that he subsequently abandoned. In 1934 he bought a house in Les Arques where he created his most important works (Diana, **Pietà**, Christ).

VILLAGE
Musée Zadkine

46250 Les Arques. In the village.
Open Apr–Oct and school hols, 10am –1pm and 3–7pm; Nov–Mar, 2–6pm.
Closed Jan, May 1, Nov 1 and 11 and 25 Dec. ✏3€. *05 65 22 83 37.*
Three rooms display examples of the artist's work, including lithographs, tapestries, bronzes (Musical Trio, 1928) and monumental wood sculptures (Diana). An audio-visual presentation shows a lengthy interview with Zadkine.

Église St-Laurent★

In the centre of the village.
This church is all that is left of a priory-deanery founded in the 11C by the Abbaye de Marcilhac. When the nave was restored in the 20C, it was narrowed and shortened; however the apse and apsidal chapels have retained the purity of the Romanesque style. Several old features have been preserved such as the oculus in the south transept, a characteristic of the Carolingean style, and the tori at the base of the columns supporting the transverse arches. The most original part of the interior is the arches. Two moving works by Zadkine enhance the church's interior: the monumental **sculpture of Christ**★ (back of the façade) and **Pietà**★ (crypt).

Église St-André

Go down towards the River Masse, then cross the D 45. By request at the Musée Zadkine. *05 65 22 83 37.*
Set in a clearing, this church displays a remarkable series of **frescoes**★ from the late 15C, discovered in 1954 by Zadkine. The chancel window is framed by the Annunciation and on either side by the Apostles with either the instruments of their punishment – St Andrew and the X-shaped cross and St Matthew and the halberd – or the instruments with which they are symbolised in art: St Peter with his keys, St James with his pilgrim's staff and St Thomas with his architect's set square. On the vault, spangled with red stars, is Christ in Majesty seated on a rainbow-shaped throne with one hand held up in blessing and the other holding the globe. He is surrounded by the symbols of the four Evangelists. On the pillars of the apse, which are holding up a triumphal arch, are St Christopher and, on the other side, baby Jesus waiting for Christopher to help him cross the river.

♨ EAT

🍽 🍽 **La Récréation**. *05 65 22 88 08. Open Mar–Oct. Closed Wed and Thu.*
A pleasantsomewhat nostalgic restaurant housed in the old village school. Dine in the old classroom, or out in the playground. Schoolyard terrace and sculpted totem-chestnut tree! Reservation recommended.

Pietà by Ossip Zadkine, Église St-Laurent

S. Sauvignier/MICHELIN

Gourdon★

and La Bouriane

Gourdon is the capital of the green undulating countryside of Bouriane. The town, situated on the borders of Quercy and Périgord, is arranged in tiers up the flank of a rocky hillock, upon which the local lord's castle once stood. Follow the circular route of avenues that have replaced the old ramparts for pleasant views of the hills and valleys of Bouriane.

- ▶ **Population:** 4 858
- ◔ **Michelin Map:** 337: E-3
- ⊞ **Info:** 24 rue du Majou, 46300 Gourdon en Quercy. ℘05 65 27 52 50. www. tourisme-gourdon.com.
- ◔ **Location:**26km/16mi south of Sarlat; 44km/27.5mi north of Cahors.
- ◕ **Timing:** Allow half a day to explore the Bouriane.
- ◔ **Don't Miss:** Rue de Majou; the baptismal font in the Église des Cordeliers.
- ◔ **Also See:** Périgord Noir

TOWN WALK

Rue du Majou★

The 13C fortified gateway, Porte du Majou, leads to the street of the same name. This picturesque and narrow street was once the high street; all along it reside old houses with overhanging storeys and ground floors with large pointed arches. No 17, Anglars Mansion, has pretty mullioned windows.

◔ *The street leads to the esplanade, the town hall (right) and St Peter's Church.*

Hôtel de Ville (Town Hall)

This former 13C consulate, enlarged in the 17C, has covered arcades which are used as a covered market.

Église St-Pierre

The church (dedicated to St Peter), built in the 14C, used to be a dependency of Le Vigan Abbey. The doorway is decorated with elegant archivolts and is framed by two tall asymmetrical towers. The large rose window is protected by a line of machicolations, a reminder of former fortifications. The vast nave

has pointed vaulting; 17C wood panels, carved, painted and gilded, decorate the chancel and the south transept.

◔ *Go round the left of the church and go up the staircase leading to the esplanade where the castle once stood.*

Esplanade

A **panorama**★ unfolds from the terrace (*viewing table*): beyond the town and its roofs, which can be seen in tiers below the massive roof of the church (St-Pierre) in the foreground, one can see the churchyard, a forest of cypress trees, and then the plateaux stretching out around the valleys of the Dordogne and the Céou.

◔ *Return to place de l'Hôtel-de-Ville and go round the outside of the church starting from the right.*

There are some old houses opposite the east end, including one with a lovely early-17C doorway. Opposite the south door of the church take rue Cardinal-Farinié which goes downhill and contains old houses with mullioned windows and side turrets.
Below stands the Église des Cordeliers.

Église des Cordeliers

◕ *The former church is now used for concerts and exhibits in Jul–Aug. Tours by appointment.* ℘05 65 27 52 50.

The town was given to the **Gourdon family** by Count Raymond I of Toulouse in 961. Nearly all the Gourdons were killed by Richard Couer de Lion and local legend suggests that it was a surviving member of this same family who fired the fatal crossbow bolt which fatally wounded Richard at Chalus.

The church which used to be part of the Franciscan monastery is worth a visit, despite being slightly marred by a massive belfry porch which was added in the 19C. At the entrance, in the middle of the nave, stands a remarkable 14C **baptismal font**★. The outside is decorated with trefoiled blind arcades. The fine seven-sided apse is lit by 19C stained-glass windows.

EXCURSIONS

Grottes de Cougnac★

3km/2mi N on the D 704.

Open Jul 7–Aug 28, guided tour (1 hour) 10am–6pm; mid–Apr 5 to Jul 6 and Aug 29–Sept 30, 10–11.30am and 2.30–5pm; Oct 1–Nov 4, daily except Sun, 2–4pm. 6.50€. 05 65 41 47 54. www.grottesdecougnac.com.

These caves are fascinating for two reasons: their natural rock formations and their Paleolithic paintings similar to those of Pech-Merle (25000 to 18000 BC). The caves, consisting of two chasms about 200m/220yd apart, spread out beneath a limestone plateau.

The first cave consists of three small chambers; closely packed and sometimes extremely delicate stalactites hang in profusion. The second cave is bigger and has two remarkable chambers: the **Pillar Chamber**★ (Salle des Colonnes) is made particularly striking by the perspectives offered by columns reaching from floor to ceiling, and the **Hall of Prehistoric Paintings** (Salle des Peintures Préhistoriques) contains designs in ochre and black featuring ibex, mammoths and human figures.

Les Prades

7km/4.3mi NE.

Home to the **Musée Henri-Giron** (&⊙open Jun–Sept, daily except Mon, 10am–6pm; Oct–May by advance appointment; contact Monsieur Hoving. 2.30€; 05 65 41 33 78), whose collection includes about 40 of this Belgian painter's works. His style reflects a classic heritage and Flemish influence, all the while integrating remarkably modern subjects, including some unsettling interpretations of feminine forms.

Le Vigan

5km/3mi E on the D 673.

The Gothic **church** (⊙open weekday afternoons. For further information, contact the presbytery; 05 65 41 12 90), all that remains of an abbey founded in the 11C, became a regular chapter for canons in the 14C. The spectacular east end, overlooked by a tower rising from the transept crossing, has defensive turrets tucked in between the apsidal chapels. There is fine pointed vaulting over the nave.

Chapelle de Notre-Dame-des-Neiges

1.5km/1mi SE via rue des Nevèges from ave Gambetta. ⊙If the Chapelle is closed, the key can be obtained next door. Contact Gourdon Tourist Office for further information.

Set in the small valley of the Bléou, this 14C chapel, a pilgrimage centre which was restored in the 17C, has a 17C altarpiece. A miraculous spring flows through the chancel.

View of Gourdon from above

J. Damase/MICHELIN

DRIVING TOUR

LA BOURIANE

85km/53mi round-trip – allow half a day

The region known as La Bouriane extends from Gourdon to the Lot Valley and west of N 20. It is a region where the limestone formation disappears under a bed of sideritic sand (iron carbonate bearing), which is a lovely red and ochre colour. The rather infertile soil nevertheless allows the cultivation of chestnut, pine and walnut trees. There are vineyards on the south-facing slopes. A great number of rivers carve through the plateau creating a hilly, wooded countryside scattered with farms.

▷ *Leave Gourdon W on the D 673.*

Salviac

The Gothic church has some lovely 16C stained-glass windows depicting scenes from the life of St Eutrope.

Cazals

This old *bastide*, built in 1319 on behalf of the King of England, is designed around a large central square. An old castle overlooks a stretch of the River Masse offering recreation facilities.

▷ *Continue along the D 673.*

Château de Montcléra

The fortified entrance gate dates from the 15C. Behind it are a square keep and residential quarters flanked by round, machicolated towers.

▷ *Continue along the D 673 to Frayssinet-le-Gélat then turn left onto the D 660.*

Goujounac

There used to be a Romanesque priory around the church, but there are now only a few vestiges of this. On the south wall of the church, the Romanesque **tympanum**, depicting Christ in Glory giving the sign of God's blessing surrounded by the symbols of the four Evangelists, is the work of a Quercy artist who was probably influenced by the tympanum at Beaulieu-sur-Dordogne.

▷ *Continue on D 660; right on D 45.*

Villages of the Bouriane

The Bouriane countryside has a profusion of small villages which, while not in the guide books, have a certain appeal of their own. Visit St-Clair, Concorès St-Chamarand, Saint-Germain-du-Bel-Air, Peyrilles, Lamothe-Cassel and Montamel (all south) or Payrignac and Saint-Cirq-Madelon (both north)

Les Junies

The 15C castle flanked by round towers is decorated with elegant Renaissance windows. Set apart from the village, the 14C church, an austere building, is of massive proportions. It was part of a priory, which was attached to the Dominican order in 1345, and had been founded by one of the local lords, Gaucelin des Junies, Cardinal of Albano.

▶ *Leave Les Junies travelling N along the D 37.*

Lherm

This little village of white-limestone houses with steeply pitched roofs covered with small brown tiles is dominated by a bell-tower, a turret and several dovecotes. In a small isolated, wooded valley, the **church** (Notre-Dame-de-l'Assomption), once a priory, has a Romanesque apse and a plain barrel-vaulted nave of ashlar-stone. The chancel contains a profusely decorated altarpiece of gold and carvings against a blue background, a rather grandiose, local interpretation of the Baroque style. The building was altered in the 16C; there is a fine Renaissance-style door.

▶ *Continue N on the D 37.*

Les Arques★ ᕯ *See Les ARQUES.*

▶ *Leave SE on D 150; continue beyond Maussac; left onto D 47 2km/1.2mi farther on; the road leads to the D 25.*

LA BOURIANE

Rampoux

There is an interesting red and white stone 12C Romanesque church here, which used to be a Benedictine priory. Inside, the 15C frescoes illustrate the life of Christ in naïve style.

▶ *Continue E on the D 25. Turn left towards Concorès 2km/1.2mi beyond Lavercantière, then follow the D 12 back to Gourdon along the River Céou and River Bléou.*

ADDRESSES

🛏 STAY

🍴 **Chambre d'hôte du Syndic** – *Le Syndic, 46300 Payrignac. 6km/3.6m NW of Gourdon on the D 704 towards Sarlat, then a minor road the left. ℘05 65 41 15 70 . 6 rooms.* This family home is typical of the region and stands in an elevated position with views of the countryside and the Germaine Valley. The rooms are comfortable, spacious and calm, with some under the eaves. The fireplace in the dining room provides a welcome winter glow. Friendly atmosphere.

🍴 EAT

🍴 **Domaine du Berthiol** – *route de Cahors. ℘05 65 41 33 33. Closed 1 Jan –31 Mar.* Located on the outskirts of town in the middle of a beautifully maintained park. Two contemporary dining rooms where the menu shows a marked preference for local produce. *29 rooms* also available here.

🍴🍴🍴 **Hostellerie de la Bouriane** – *Pl. du Foirail. ℘05 65 41 16 37. hostellerielabouriane@wanadoo.fr. Closed Jan 20–Mar 15, Sun and Mon from Oct 25– Apr 30. 20 rooms.* Outside of the town centre, this hotel is a quiet retreat with a pleasant sheltered terrace. The rooms are traditional and bright, with those on the upper floor crowned by sloping ceilings. The dining room is adorned with reproductions of paintings and Aubusson tapestries. Good traditional French food at reasonable prices.

🛒 SHOPPING

Farmers' market - Thursdays in July and August, 8.30am–1pm.

🏃 ENTERTAINMENT

Les Médievales - *℘05 65 27 52 50.*

This festival is held in the streets of old Gourdon on the first weekend and Monday of August.

Les Enchantements de la Flûte - *℘05 65 41 20 06. cacgourdon@aol.fr.* This chamber music festival takes place in mid-July.

Labastide-Murat
and S. Causse de Gramat

Labastide-Murat, which stands at one of the highest points on the Gramat Causse, was originally called Labastide-Fortunière, but changed its name to Murat in honour of the most famous of its sons.

A BIT OF HISTORY

The miraculous destiny of Joachim Murat – Murat was born in 1767, the son of an innkeeper. He was destined for the Church, but at 21 decided instead to be a soldier. The campaigns in Italy and Egypt enabled him to gain rapid promo~tion under Napoleon, whose brother-in-law he became by marrying the First Consul's sister, Caroline; he was promoted to Marshal of the Empire, Grand Duke of Berg and of Cleves and King of Naples. His glory faded with that of his master, whom he abandoned in the dark days of the Empire. His miserable end in 1815 was in keeping with the diversity in his life: after the Bourbons had returned to Naples, he tried to reclaim his kingdom, but was taken prisoner and shot.

MUSÉE MURAT
Place de Tolentino
🕐 *Open Jul 15–Sept 15, guided tour (1hr), daily exc. Tue, 10am–noon and 3–6pm.* 🎫*3€ ℘05 65 21 11 39.*
The museum is in the house where Murat was born. The 18C kitchen and

- ▶ **Population:** 653
- 🚵 **Michelin Map:** 337: F-4
- ℹ **Info:** Grand'Rue, 46240. *℘05 65 21 11 39.*
- ▶ **Location:** 25km/15mi south of Rocamadour and 32km/20mi north of Cahors.
- 🕐 **Timing**: Allow a full day to explore the Parc Régional des Causses du Quercy and the Causse de Gramat.
- 👁 **Don't Miss**: The Sunday morning market in July and August and the regional fair on the second and fourth Monday of every month.
- 🚵 **Also See**: Périgord Noir.

the inn's saloon are on display to visitors. On the first floor there are mementoes of the King of Naples and of his mother.

PARC RÉGIONAL DES CAUSSES DU QUERCY
BP 10, 46240 Labastide-Murat. ℘05 65 24 20 50. www.parc-causses-du-quercy.org. Created in 1999, the nature park covers 1 760km2/680sq mi situated between Figeac and Cahors on the south bank of the River Dordogne. It includes 97 municipalities and over 25 000 inhabitants. The aim of the park is to safeguard this rural environment by stopping the population drain and installing long-term development.

🚗 DRIVING TOUR

SOUTHERN CAUSSE DE GRAMAT
60km/37mi round-trip – allow half a day

▷ *S. from Labastide-Murat on the D 32.*

St-Martin-de-Vers
In this small village the houses with brown-tiled roofs cluster round the old priory church and its asymmetrical bell-tower.

▷ *Drive E along the D 13 and turn left onto the D 10 3km/1.9mi farther on, then left again onto the D 17.*

Soulomès
The Knights Templars built a commandery here in the 12C. The chancel of the church contains interesting 15C and 16C frescoes depicting episodes of Christ's life.

▷ *Leave Soulomès S on D 17 and turn left onto the D 71 1km/0.6mi farther on.*

Désert de la Braunhie
Here, drystone walls seem to stretch forever into the distance, and the scrubby vegetation includes oaks, maples and stunted walnut trees, or stony heath with junipers and thorn bushes.

Caniac-du-Causse
Beneath the church, the **crypt** (*light switch at the bottom of the stairs to the right*) was built by the monks of Marcilhac-sur-Célé in the 12C to shelter the relic of St Namphaise, an officer in the army of Charlemagne who became a hermit.

Planagrèze Discovery Trail
An interesting brochure is available at the Maison de la Braunhie, beneath the town hall in Caniac-du-Causse and at the tourist office in Labastide-Murat.
℘05 65 31 16 03. 🚶 7.5km/4.6mi round-trip on foot.

▷ *Follow the D 42 towards Fontanes-du-Causse.*

This is the highest part of the Causse de Gramat. The trail reveals the local fauna and flora and offers an insight into the geology and history of the area.

▷ *Return to Caniac-du-Causse and continue along the D 71 to Quissac.*

The road runs across the most arid part of the Braunhie.

Quissac
Besides attractive farmhouses, the village of Quissac has retained its *travail à bœufs*, a farrier's sling used for shoeing oxen.

▷ *Drive W along the D 146. In Fontanes-du-Causse, turn left onto the D 2 and, 4.5km/2.8mi beyond Montfaucon, turn left onto the D 17.*

Château de Vaillac
The massive outline of the castle towers above the village. Built in the 15C and 16C, the stronghold comprises a large building flanked by four towers and a keep..

▷ *Return to Labastide-Murat along the D 10.*

Château de Vaillac

©DeAgostini/World Illustrated/Photoshot

ADDRESSES

🛒 SHOPPING

Fairs – The 2nd and 4th Monday of every month.

Market – A farmers' market is held from 9am–noon every Sunday in July and August.

Gouffre de
Padirac★★

The Padirac Chasm provides access to wonderful galleries hollowed out of the limestone mass of Gramat Causse by a subterranean river. A visit into the vertiginous well and a tour of the mysterious river and the vast caves adorned with limestone concretions leave visitors with a striking impression of this fascinating underground world.

- 🍴 **Michelin Map:** Michelin local map 337: G-2
- ▷ **Location:** 13km/8mi east of Rocamadour.
- 👁 **Don't Miss**: The guided tour inside the chasm.
- 🐾 **Guided tours:** (1.5hrs), Jul 6–Aug 2 9.30am–6pm; Aug 3–30, 8am–6.30pm; Apr 4 – Jul 5 9.30am– 5pm; Aug 31–Nov 8, 10am–5pm. 9€. ℘05 65 33 64 56. www. gouffre-de-padirac.com.

A BIT OF HISTORY

From legend to scientific exploration – The Padirac Chasm was a source of superstitious terror to the local inhabitants right up to the 19C, as people believed that the origin of this great hole was connected with the devil.
St Martin, so the tale went, was returning from an expedition on the causse where he had been looking unsuccessfully for souls to save. All at once his mule refused to go on; Satan, bearing a great sack full of souls which he was taking to hell, stood in the saint's path. Jeering at the poor saint, Satan made the follow-ing proposition: he would give St Martin the souls he had in his sack on condition that St Martin make his mule cross an obstacle that he, Satan, would create on the spot. Whereupon he hit the ground hard with his foot, and a gaping chasm opened up. The saint coaxed his mule forward and the beast jumped clear with such force that its hoof prints are still visible. Satan, defeated, retreated to hell by way of the hole he had created.
The chasm served as a refuge for the people living on the causse during the Hundred Years War and the Wars of Religion, but it would appear that it was towards the end of the 19C, following a violent flooding of the river, that a passage opened between the bottom of the well and the underground galleries. The speleologist, **Édouard A Martel**, was the first to discover the passage in 1892. He then undertook nine expeditions and finally reached the Hall of the Great Dome.
Padirac was opened for the first time to tourists in 1898. Since then, numerous speleological expeditions have uncovered 22km/13.5mi of underground galleries. The 1947 expedition proved by fluorescein colouring of the water that the Padirac river reappears above ground 11km/7mi away where the Lombard rises and at St George's spring in the **Montvalent Amphitheatre** near the Dordogne.
During the expeditions of 1984 and 1985, a team of speleologists, paleontologists, prehistorians and geologists discovered

Gouffre de Padirac

Gouffre de Padirac

PADIRAC CHASM AND UNDERGROUND RIVER

Chasm Cone of rubble · Grande Pendeloque · Grand Dôme · Lac Supérieur · Upstream siphon · Spring · CAUSSE DE GRAMAT · Lac de la Pluie · Calcareous rock · Galerie de la Source · Rivière Plane · Lifts · Impermeable layers · Pas du Crocodile · Salle des Grands Gours · 0 · 103

a prehistoric site, 9km/5.5mi from the mouth of the hole, on an affluent of the Joly, with bones of mammoths, rhinoceroses, bison, bears, cave-dwelling lions and deer, all of which were found to date from between 150 000 and 200 000 years ago. Copies of some of the bones are exhibited in the entrance hall.

CHASM

Two lifts and some staircases lead into the chasm, which is 32m/105ft in diameter, and to the pyramid of rubble, debris of the original caving-in of the roof. From the bottom of the lift (75m/247ft), there is a striking view of walls covered by the overflow from stalagmites and by vegetation and of a little corner of the sky at the mouth of the hole. Stairs lead down to the underground river, 103m/338ft below ground level. At the bottom, the 2km/1.25mi underground journey begins, 500m/547yd of which are by boat and 400m/438yd on foot.

Galerie de la Source – This chamber is at the end of an underground canyon, the roof of which gets gradually higher and higher; it is 300m/984ft long and follows the upper course of the river that hollowed it out. At the far end is the landing-stage.

Rivière Plane – A flotilla of flat-bottomed boats offers an enchanting journey over the astonishingly translucent waters of this smooth river. The depth of the river varies from 50cm/20in to 4m/13ft, but the water temperature remains constant at 11°C/51.8°F. The height of the roof increases progressively to reach a maximum of 78m/256ft; the different levels of erosion corresponding to the successive courses of the river can be seen from the boat. At the end of the boat trip admire the **Grande Pendeloque** (Great Pendant) of **Lac de la Pluie**

(Rainfall Lake). This giant stalactite, the point of which nearly touches the water, is simply the final pendant in a string of concretions 78m/256ft in height.

Pas du Crocodile – A narrow passage between high walls links the underground lake and the chambers to be visited next. Look to the left at the magnificent column known as the Grand Pilier, 40m/131ft high.

Salle des Grands Gours – A series of pools separated by gours, natural limestone dams, divides the river and the lake into basins; beyond them cascades a 6m/20ft waterfall. This is the end of the area open to tourists.

Lac Supérieur – This lake is fed only by water infiltrating the soil and falling from the roof; its level is 20m/66ft above that of the River Plane. Gours ring the lake's emerald waters.

Salle du Grand Dôme – The great height of the roof (91m/295ft) is most impressive in this, the largest and most beautiful of the Padirac caverns. The viewpoint, built halfway up, enables visitors to appreciate the rock formations and the flows of calcite decorating certain parts of the walls. The return trip (to the landing-stage) offers interesting views of the great pillar and the great pendant. From the end of the Galerie de la Source, four lifts lead back to the entrance.

Édouard A Martel

Édouard A Martel (1859-1938) is considered the father of modern speleology. His tours of the chasm were designed like Himalayan expeditions, with many local people employed to haul equipment.

Rocamadour ★★★
and N. Causses de Gramat

Rocamadour, with its slender castle keep towering above it, comprises a mass of old dwellings, oratories, towers and precipitous rocks on the rugged face of a causse cliff rising 150m/492ft above the Alzou Canyon. This is one of the most extraordinary places in France; a historic site, and a place of pilgrimage steeped in beliefs and legends.

A BIT OF HISTORY
The enigmatic St Amadour
The identity of St Amadour, who gave his name to the sanctuary village, has never been firmly established. A 12C chronicler reported that in 1166 "as a local inhabitant had expressed the wish to be buried beneath the threshold of the Chapel of the Virgin, men began to dig a grave only to find the body of a man already buried there. This body was placed near the altar so that it might be venerated by the faithful and from that time onwards miracles occurred".

Who was this mysterious person whose tomb appeared to be so old? Conflicting theories have been put forward but the most widely accepted view is that the body was that of the publican Zaccheus, a disciple of Jesus and husband of St Veronica, who were obliged to flee Palestine and set up home in Limousin. On the death of Veronica, Zaccheus retired to the deserted and wild Alzou Valley to preach. All this is hearsay, but one thing is certain; there was a hermit, and he often sought shelter at the rock. The Langue d'Oc expression – *roc amator*

▶ **Population:** 614

Michelin Map: 337: F-3

Info: Maison du tourisme, 46500 Rocamadour. ℘05 65 33 22 00. www.rocamadour.com.

Location: Northern Parc Régional du Haut Quercy. The best way to arrive in Rocamadour is along the L'Hospitalet road. From a terrace there is a marvellous **view**★★ of Rocamadour, with the Alzou winding its way through the bottom of a gorge, and the village clinging to the cliff face. The Cité Religieuse rises above the village, with the castle ramparts above it. There is another striking view of Rocamadour from the Couzou road (D 32).

Parking: There are several car parks in the valley as well as at L'Hospitalet.

Timing: Allow a full day to visit the village and Cité Religieuse and another half a day to explore the Causse de Gramat.

Don't Miss: The Cité Relig-ieuse; the ramparts; the view from L'Hospitalet.

Kids: Rocher des Aigles; Féerie du Rail; Forêt des Singes; Parc Animalier de Gramat.

Also See: Périgord Noir, Upper Dordogne Valley.

GETTING AROUND
BY CAR – The streets of Rocamadour are pedestrianised. Access for vehicles is only permitted for hotel and restaurant customers.

LIFT (ELEVATOR) – *Open Jul–Aug, 8am–8pm, May–Jun, 8am–7pm; Feb–Apr and Sep to mid-Nov, 10am–5pm. 3€ return, 2€ single (chidren under 8: no charge).*

℘05 65 33 62 44. Provides access to the village and the ecclesiastical city.

TOURS
Petit train de nuit – *Apr–Sept, departures evening only, every 15 mins from porte du Figuier. 5€.* ℘05 65 33 67 84 / 05 65 33 65 99 or 06 08 26 25 56. Guided tours by little train in seven languages (30min).

Rocamadour clings to the cliff face

E. Larribère/MICHELIN

(he who likes the rock) – was adopted as the name of this village sanctuary, later becoming Rocamadour.

The fame of Rocamadour

From the time that the miracles began until the Reformation, the pilgrimage to Rocamadour was one of the most famous in Christendom. Thirty thousand people would come on days of major pardon and plenary indulgence. Since the village was too small to house all the pilgrims, the Alzou Valley was transformed into a vast camp. Henry Plantagenet, king of England, was miraculously cured and among the first to kneel before the Virgin; his example was followed during the Middle Ages by the most illustrious people including St Bernard, St Louis and Blanche of Castille. Veneration of Our Lady of Rocamadour was established at Lisbon, Oporto, Seville and even in Sicily; the Rocamadour standard at the Battle of Las Navas at Tolosa, routed the Muhammadans and gave the Catholic kings of Spain victory.

Pilgrimage and penitents

Ecclesiastical, and in some cases, lay tribunals used to impose the pilgrimage on sinners. On the day of their departure, penitents attended Mass and then set forth dressed in clothes covered with large crosses, a big hat upon their head, a staff in their hand and a knapsack on their back. On reaching the end of their journey, pilgrims stripped off their clothes, climbing the famous steps on their knees in only a shirt, with chains bound round their arms and neck. Before the altar to the Black Virgin they pronounced their *amende honorable*. A priest recited prayers of purification and removed the chains from the penitents, who, now forgiven, received from the priest a certificate and a kind of medal in lead bearing the image of the miraculous Virgin, called a *sportelle*.

Decline and renaissance

Rocamadour reached its zenith in the 13C. Favours not even granted to Jerusalem were granted to it; the money poured in and the wealth brought greed with it. For 100 years the abbeys of Marcilhac and Tulle disputed who should own the church at Rocamadour; Tulle was finally awarded the honour after arbitration. During the Middle Ages, the town was sacked several times: Henry Short Coat, in revolt against his father Henry Plantagenet, pillaged the oratory in 1183; during the Hundred Years War, bands of English and the local soldiery plundered the treasure in turn; during the Wars of Religion the Protestant, Captain Bessonies, seized Rocamadour to desecrate it and lay it to waste; only the Virgin and the miraculous bell escaped. Rocamadour did not rise from its ruins; the abbey remained idle until it was dealt its final blow by the Revolution. In the 19C, the bishops of Cahors

Porte du Fort

D. Hée/MICHELIN

tried to revive the pilgrimage, and the churches were rebuilt. Though much of its splendour has vanished, Rocamadour has found again the fervour of its former pilgrims and is today a very respected pilgrimage centre.

ECCLESIASTICAL CITY

See green tour marked on cut-out map opposite. The ecclesiastical city is a pedestrian zone. It can be accessed from the plateau (P car park) on foot or by lift (charge), or from the Alzou Valley (P car parks) on foot or by a small train (charge) which runs to the village, and then from here to the ecclesiastical city either by the flights of stairs up the Via Sancta or by the lift. For guided tours (groups only), contact Le Relais des Remparts. 05 65 33 23 23.

Go through the **Porte du Figuier** at the northern end, which was a gateway to the town as early as the 13C, and enter the main street which is now cluttered with souvenir shops. Climb the 223 steps of the Great Stairway (Via Sancta). Pilgrims often make this ascent, kneeling at every step. Five flights of stairs lead to a terrace on which stand the former canons' quarters, now converted into shops and hotels. The terrace is called **place des Senhals** because of the pilgrims' insignia called *senhals* or *sportelles* made there. The **Porte du Fort**, which opens under the palace perimeter wall, is an old entrance way leading to the sacred perimeter wall.

Parvis des Églises

The parvis (open space in front of the churches), which is also known as place St-Amadour, is fairly small and has seven churches: St Saviour's Basilica opposite the stairway; St Amadour's Church below the basilica; the Chapel of Our Lady or Miraculous Chapel on the left; the three chapels of St John the Baptist, St Blaise and St Anne (*visit possible only as part of a guided tour of the Cité Religieuse*) on the right; and the Chapel of St Michael standing on a terrace to the left.

Basilique St-Sauveur

This 11C-13C Romanesque-Gothic sanctuary has three naves . One of the basilica walls is made out of the cliff's living rock, upon which the arches of the end bay are supported. The mezzanine was added in the 19C to enlarge the basilica during the great pilgrimages.

Above the altar stands a fine **16C Christ**, in polychrome wood, with a cross which resembles a tree.

Eglise St-Amadour

Included in the guided tour of the Cité Religieuse. Open Jun to mid-Sept, 9am–5.30pm; rest of the year, daily except Sat–Sun. 05 65 33 23 23.

This 12C crypt lying below the basilica consists of a flat chevet and two bays with quadripartite vaulting. It used to be a place of worship: the body of St Amadour was venerated here.

Chapelle Notre-Dame

From the parvis, 25 steps lead to the Miraculous Chapel or Chapel of Our Lady, considered the Holy of Holies of Rocamadour. It is here that the hermit is believed to have hollowed out an oratory in the rock. In 1476 the chapel was crushed by falling rocks and rebuilt in the Flamboyant Gothic style. This new chapel, sacked during the Wars of Religion and the Revolution, was restored in the 19C. On the altar, in the semi-darkness of the chapel blackened by candle smoke, is the miraculous Virgin, also called **Black Madonna**★. This rustic-style reliquary statue, carved in walnut, dates from the 12C. It is small in size (69cm/27in)and was covered with silver plating of which several fragments, blackened by candle smoke and oxidation, remain. The miraculous **bell**, made of jointed iron plates and most likely dating from the 9C, hangs from the roof. It rang out of its own accord to foretell miracles, for example when sailors lost at sea invoked Our Lady of Rocamadour. On leaving the chapel, stuck in the cliff face above the doorway, one can see a great iron sword, which legend identifies as **Durandal**, Roland's famous sword. The story goes that Roland, surrounded by the Saracens and unable to break his sword to prevent it falling into enemy hands, prayed to the Archangel Michael and threw him his sword, which in a single stroke implanted itself in the rock of Rocamadour, far from the Infidels.

To the right is St Amadour's grave, believed to have been dug out of the rock on the very spot where the saint's body was found.

Chapelle St-Michel

Included in the guided tour of the Cité Religieuse. 𝒫05 65 33 23 23.

This Romanesque chapel is sheltered by a rock overhang. The apse, which houses a small oratory, juts out towards the square. It was used for services by the monks of the priory, who had also installed a library there.

On the wall **outside** are two frescoes representing the Annunciation and the Visitation; the skill of the composition, the richness of colour and the grace of movement all seem to point to the works being 12C. Below them, a 14C fresco depicts an immense St Christopher.

Inside, the chancel is adorned with paintings: Christ in Majesty is surrounded by the Evangelists; farther down a seraph and the Archangel Michael are weighing souls.

Musée d'Art Sacré Francis-Poulenc★

Closed. 𝒫05 65 33 22 00.

The museum of sacred art is housed in the former palace of the bishops of Tulle, a vast military-style building once used to accommodate illustrious pilgrims. Erected in the 14C, it was restored in the 19C by one of Viollet-le-Duc's students. The museum is dedicated to the famous composer Francis Poulenc (1899-1963), who, having received a revelation during a visit to Rocamadour in 1936, composed *Litanies à la Vierge Noire de Rocamadour*. In the hallway various documents recount the history of Rocamadour and its pilgrimage, with the help of maps and a statue of St James as a pilgrim (Rocamadour was a pilgrims' stop on the way to Santiago de Compostela).

The vestibule displays objects from the sanctuary including the 17C reliquary casket of St Amadour, which once contained the relics of the saint's body (destroyed during the Wars of Religion).

The treasury contains fine items which came from the once fabulous treasure collection of the sanctuary. **Reliquary caskets** from Lunegarde and Laverhne

(both 12C) and Soulomès (13C), ornamented with enamelwork, demonstrate the craftsmanship of the Limousin artist. The next gallery contains 17C, 18C and 19C religious paintings.

On leaving the museum take the gallery (known as *the tunnel*) that passes beneath St Saviour's Basilica; than go down to the watch-path to the right.

PLATEAU
Stations of the Cross

A 19C shaded Stations of the Cross winds up towards the ramparts. After passing the caves (*grottes*) of the Nativity and the Holy Sepulchre, visitors will see the Cross of Jerusalem, brought from the Holy Land by the Penitential Pilgrims.

Ramparts

🕐*9am–6pm.* 2.50€. 𝒫05 65 33 23 23. These are the remains of a 14C fort which was built to block off the rocky spur and protect the sanctuary. Leaning against the fortress, the residence of the chaplains of Roc-Amadour was built in the 19C.

Rocher des Aigles

🕐*Open Apr–Sept. See website for times.* 8.5€ (under 16 5€). 𝒫05 65 33 65 45. www.rocherdesaigles.com. The Eagles' Rock is a breeding centre for birds of prey. Regular demonstrations showing how they fly and how they hunt are popular with visitors. A running commentary helps them to understand the behaviour of these birds, some of which are endangered species.

> *To return, go back to an esplanade on the same level as the Ecclesiastical City and take the lift to the main street near the Porte Salmon.*

VILLAGE WALK

The village is a pedestrian zone. It can be accessed from the plateau (P car park) on foot or by lift (charge), or from the Alzou Valley (P car parks) on foot or by a small train (charge) which runs to the village, and then from here to the ecclesiastical city either by the flights of stairs up the

Via Sancta or by lift. A tourist train offers visitors a view of the village by night.

▷ *At the end of the watch-path, walk to place des Senhals and turn left.*

Rue de la Mercerie

This former trading street is lined with tiered gardens. Note, on the right, the **Maison de la Pommette**, an old arcaded shop dating from the 15C and, slightly farther on to the left, a Romanesque house. The street leads to the 13C **Porte de Cabiliert**.

▷ *Return to place des Senhals; walk down the Grand Escalier; turn right.*

Le Coustalou

Once through the 13C Porte Hugon, one enters a picturesque medieval quarter. The half-timbered Maison de la Louve is the best preserved of the old houses, built on the slope down to the Alzou.

▷ *Return to Porte du Figuier.*

Hôtel de Ville

🕐*Opening times vary, usually 10am–12.30pm and 1.30–5.30pm.* 🕐*Closed 1 Jan and 25 Dec.* ▧*Exhibitions 2€. Hôtel de Ville free.* ☎*05 65 33 22 00.*
The town hall is located in a 15C house (restored), known as the Couronnerie or the House of the Brothers. In the council chamber there are two fine **tapestries**★ by Jean Lurçat which portray the flora and fauna of the causse.

MILL EXCURSION
Moulin de Cougnaguet

10km/6.2mi W along the D 673.
🕐*Open Apr–mid-Oct.* ☞*Tours 10am–noon and 2–6pm.* ▧*4€.*
☎*05 65 32 63 09. www.cougnaguet.com*
The rounded arches of this fortified mill span a derivation of the Ouysse in a cool, lush and charming **setting**. The current mill was built in the 15C at the foot of a sheer cliff, on the site of an earlier example. In the Middle Ages grain and flour were highly sought-after and needed to be defended, as illustrated here.

🚗 DRIVING TOUR

NORTHERN CAUSSE DE GRAMAT

70km/43.5mi round-trip – half a day. Named after the market town of Gramat the Northern Causse de Gramat lying to the south of the Dordogne Valley.

▷ *Drive N from Rocamadour on the D 32.*

The Gramat Causse, which stretches from the Dordogne Valley in the north to the Lot and Célé valleys in the south, is the largest and wildest *causse* in Quercy. It is a vast limestone plateau which lies at an average altitude of 350m/1148ft and contains a variety of natural phenomena and unusual landscapes.

L'Hospitalet

The name of this village, clinging to Rocamadour's cliff face, comes from the small hospital founded in the 11C by Hélène de Castelnau to nurse the pilgrims on the road from Le Puy (Auvergne) to Santiago de Compostela. Only a few ruins of this hospital remain; the **Romanesque chapel**, which is set in the middle of the churchyard, was remodelled in the 15C. L'Hospitalet is very popular with visitors for its **viewpoint**★★ which overlooks the site of Rocamadour. There is a large Tourist Information Centre (*syndicat d'initiative*).

Grotte des Merveilles

🕐☞*Open Jul 6–Aug 23 9.30am–7pm, guided tour (40min), Apr–Jun and Sep to early-Nov, 10am–noon and 2–6pm.* ▧*6€ (child 5-11: 4€).*
☎*05 65 33 67 92. www.grotte-des-merveilles.com*
Discovered in 1920, the Cave of Wonders is only 8m/24ft deep, but has some lovely formations: stalactites, stalagmites and natural limestone dams reflecting the cave roof and its concretions.
On the walls are cave paintings dating back, most likely, to the Solutrean Period (c 20 000 BC), depicting outlined hands, black spots, a few horses, a cat and the outline of a deer.

▶ *Leave L'Hospitalet E on D 36.*

▲▲ Féerie du Rail

On the road to Figeac. ♿🕐*Open mid-Jul to Aug 25, performances (45min) at, 11am, 1.30pm, 2.30pm, 3.30pm, 4.30pm and 5.30pm, Aug 26–Sept 11am, 1.30pm, 2.30pm, 3.30pm, 4.30pm and 5.30pm; Jun 11 to Jul 15, 11am, 2pm, 3pm, 4pm and 5pm; Apr to Jun 10 and Sept, 11am, 2.45pm, 3.45pm and 4.45pm; Oct, 3pm and 4.15pm; Nov school hols, 11am, 2.45pm, 3.45pm and 4.45pm.* 👓*8.5€ (child 4-11: 4.50€). ☏05 65 33 71 06. www.la-feerie.com*
▲▲ Visitors sit on bleacher seats which move, back and forth, alongside a giant scale model (85m2/915sq ft) including **animated miniatures**.
A fantastic **decor** represents city, country and mountainous landscapes, crisscrossed by a train network. Light and sound effects accent groups of automata playing out realistic scenes. Some of the animation is extremely detailed and unusual (hot-air balloons taking off).

▲▲ Forêt des Singes

On the road to Figeac. ♿🕐*Open Jul–Aug, 9.30am–6.30pm; Apr and first two weeks of Sep, 10am–noon and 1–5.30pm; last two weeks of Sep, 1–5.30pm, Sat–Sun, 10am–noon and 1–5.30pm; May–Jun, 10am–noon and 1–6pm; Oct, 1-5pm, Sat-Sun and public and school hols, 10am-noon and 1-5pm; Nov 1–11, 10am–noon and 1-5pm Sat–Sun only . 👓8€ (child: 4.50€). ☏05 65 33 62 72. www.la-foret-des-singes.com*
Living at liberty on 10ha/25 acres of woodland, the Monkey Forest, are 150 animals in an environment similar to the upper plateaux of North Africa, where they originated. The monkeys are Barbary apes and macaques, a species which is becoming extinct.

▶ *Continue along the D 36 to Rignac and turn left onto the D 20.*

Source Salmière
The beneficial properties of the Miers mineral water were discovered in 1624; rich in magnesium, it is used in the treatment of liver and urinary diseases and for its laxative properties.

Gouffre de Padirac★★
♿ *See Gouffre de PADIRAC.*

▶ *Drive S to Padirac and turn right onto the D 673, then left onto the D 11 2km/1.2mi farther on.*

Gramat
Capital of the causse that bears its name, Gramat is also a busy commercial centre attracting agricultural fairs. It is the ideal starting point for visits to Padirac, Rocamadour and the area that lies between the Lot and the Dordogne.
It was here that the French Centre de formation des maîtres-chiens de la Gendarmerie (Police Dog Handler Training Centre) was established in 1945.

▶ *Take the D 677 travelling SW and turn left onto the D 14 beyond the railway line.*

▲▲ Parc Animalier de Gramat
🕐*Open Easter to Sept, 9.30am–7pm; Oct to Easter, 2–6pm.* 👓*8.5€ (5-14 years old: 4.50€). ☏05 65 38 81 22. www.gramat-parc-animalier.com.*
This nature park extends over 40ha/99 acres. It was acquired by the local authorities so that animals and plants could be observed in their natural environment. A botanical park is home to trees and shrubs from the *causse* (durmast oak, dogwood, ash etc).
The animal park contains mainly European species living in semi-captivity in their natural habitat. Some of these animals – wild oxen, Przewalski's horses, ibexes, bison – are species which existed during prehistoric times.

▶ *Turn back and pick up the D 677 on the left. In Le Bastit, turn right onto the D 50 then right again in Carlucet onto the D 32, which takes you back to Rocamadour.*

ADDRESSES

🛏 STAY

🛏 **Le Camp'Hostel** – *Place De L'Europe.* ☎*05 65 35 73 50. www.hotelcompostelle.fr. Closed Dec–Feb. 15 rooms.* Set at the highest point of picturesque Rocamadour, some 3km (2 mi) from the centre, this 2-star hostel offers modern and cheerful, if rather spartan en-suite bedrooms, but with a beautiful panorama. There is also an outdoor swimming pool.

🛏 **Chambre d'hôte du Domaine de Lagardelle** – *Domaine de Lagardelle, 6km from Rocamadour L'Hospitalet via the D247.* ☎*05 65 33 44 03. www.lagardelle. com. Closed mid-Nov to mid-Mar. 3 rooms.* This farm is set in a quiet hamlet in the heart of the Parc naturel régional des Causses du Quercy with wonderful views. Bedrooms are simple and uncluttered and have real rustic charm. In addition to chambres d'hôtes they also offer a gîte. Ideal for horse-riding.

🛏🛏 **La Belvédère** - *L'Hospitalet, 46500 Rocamadour.* ☎*05 65 33 69 25. www.lebelvedere-rocamadour.com.* Despite its recent renovation this hotel has retained its family atmosphere. Guestrooms have a modern decorative touch and most have superb views.

🛏🛏 **Hôtel du Centre** – *Pl. de la République, 46500 Gramat.* ☎*05 65 38 73 37. www.lecentre.fr. 18 rooms.* The warm welcome in this family-style hotel in the town centre will charm you. Traditional fare.

🛏🛏 **Hôtel Le Panoramic** – *"Face à la Vallée".* ☎*05 65 33 63 06. www.logis-de-france.fr. 12 rooms.* This modern hotel may be short on cosy charm but it enjoys a splendid location. It is just a 10 minute- walk from the town centre but faces the Alzou Canyon with a superb view from its terrace of Rocamadour Castle. It also boasts an attractive 14m x 7m swimming pool.

🛏🛏 **Hôtel le Terminus des Pèlerins** – *Cité Médiévale.* ☎*05 65 33 62 14. www. logis-de-france.fr. Closed early Nov–early Apr. 12 rooms.* Set in a pedestrianised cobbled street in the Old Town (car access to hotel guests only) this charm-ing old hotel has been run by the same family since 1947. Bedrooms are modern and functional.

🛏🛏🛏🛏 **Hôtel Les Vieilles Tours** – *Rte de Payrac. 4km/2.5mi W of Rocamadour on the D 673.* ☎*05 65 33 68 01. www.vieillestours-rocamadour.com. Closed early Nov–Easter. 16 rooms.* The country house dates from the 16C and the hawk house from the 13C. The tower room is the nicest, if it's available, but the others are attractive too. Nice view of the valley from the garden. Pool.

🛏🛏🛏🛏 **Chambre d'hôte Moulin de Fresquet** – *46500 Gramat.* ☎*05 65 33 70 60. info@moulindefresquet.com. Closed Nov-Mar. 5 rooms.* This very agreeable guesthouse, a renovated mill in a pretty park, is just a short walk from the centre of town. The rooms are stylish and comfortable and look out over the garden. The welcome is warm and the food delicious.

🍽 EAT

🛏 **Le Roc du Berger** – *Bois de Belveyre, 2km (1.25mi) from Rocamadour.* ☎*05 65 33 19 99. www.rocduberger.com.* A terrace under truffle oaks, a busy atmos-phere, simple service and regional farm produce prepared over a charcoal fire.

🛏🛏 **Le Château** – *Rte du Château -* ☎*05 65 33 62 22. www.hotelchateauro-camadour.com. Closed Nov 8–Apr 4.* The traditional house is near the château, in a quiet setting. Oaks shade the large terrace and the dining area inside is embellished by a wooden sculpture of a shepherd. The rooms in the hotel are very comfortable whereas the annex offers simpler accommodation.

🛏🛏 **Jehan de Valon** – *Cité Médiévale.* ☎*05 65 33 63 08. www.bw-beausite.com. Closed Nov 11–Feb 9.* Dining room with a view of the valley and a pleasant terrace shaded by lime trees. The menu features traditional regional dishes.

🛏🛏 **Le Mas de Douze** – *Les Gîtes de Rocamadour. 4km/2.5mi E of Rocamadour on the D 673.* ☎*05 65 33 72 80. Closed Nov 7–Mar 21.* This country-style restaurant provides some quiet relief from the crowds offering hearty regional speciali-ties. Swimming pool..

This region stretches from the lush valley of the meandering River Lot in the North–namesake of the département in which most of the sights in this area are situated–to the Aveyron in the south. At its centre, on a loop in the River Lot, is the impressive old town of Cahors (pronounced ka-or), the largest town in the area and former capital of the Quercy.

Vineyards of Cahors

©A. J. Cassaigne/Photononstop/Tips Images

The Lot Valley

The River Lot, a tributary of the mighty Garonne, was once an important navigable waterway that linked the mountainous Auvergne region in the centre of France with the port of Bordeaux in the west. Its valley is dominated by Cahors, which gives its name to the famous red wine made from the malbec grape and enjoyed by wine lovers all round the world. The fabulous fortified Pont Valentré, or Devil's Bridge, across the Lot, is a sight unequalled anywhere and with its three towers (see if you can spot the Devil) and seven arches it is definitely a must see. Such was the impregnability of the bridge that it protected the town throughout the Hundred Years' War and only fell into English hands following the Treaty of Brétigny in 1360 when it was ceded to them. Upstream from Cahors the amazing perched village of St.Cirq Lapopie is one of France's *Plus Beaux Villages*. Downstream are vineyards that produce superb wine with such a deep red colour that many refer to it as the "black" wine of Cahors.

The Southern Quercy

The Southern Quercy includes the Quercy Blanc or White Quercy, situated to the southwest of Cahors, which is named after the tertiary white limestone that lends an unusual undulating landscape known as planhès. Lavender grows extremely well here, as it is especially suited to the soil conditions supporting a thriving oil industry, enabling it to compete with the better known lavender region of Provence. Here you will also find some bastides or small fortified towns, constructed during the Hundred Years War, during which time the area was heavily contested by both the English and the French. Castelnau-Montratier, founded during 13C by the Lord of Castelnau, is a good example of this type military architecture complete with a triangular town square.

Cahors Wine Road

The vineyards of the **Cahors** AOC follow the meanders of the Lot and climb up on to the plateaux stretching along the river between Cahors and Soturac. Explore both banks of the Lot and discover historic villages, impressive castles and numerous magnificent views of one of the most beautiful valleys in France. Cahors wines are all red.

◐ *Drive NW out of Cahors along D 8 towards Luzech.*

The **Cap Nature** Site in **Pradines** organises recreational activities up in the trees. The town's imprint vanishes from the landscape when you reach **Douelle**, a former stopover for inland water transport, where staves used for making barrels, known as *douelles*, were unloaded.

◐ *Turn right in Largueil.*

The ✍**Côtes d'Olt cooperative** in **Parnac** initiated the revival of Cahors wines after the severe frosts of 1956. The Château Saint-Didier, home of the ✍**Domaine Franck et Jacques Rigal**, is also well worth a visit.

◐ *Rejoin D 8 and turn right then left onto D 23. Drive through St-Vincent-Rivière-d'Olt and continue to Cambayrac.*

Cambayrac lies beyond the hamlet of Cournou, in a pleasant landscape of vineyards and arid plateaux. **Sauzet** is in truffle country, on the southern border of the Cahors vineyards.

◐ *Drive N to **Albas** along D 37. Follow D 8 to **Bélaye** on top of a high cliff towering over the Lot. Next is **Grézels**,*

which marks the boundary of the bishops of Cahors' old fief. Continue along D 8. Further on, the Pont de Courbenac offers the best overall view of the town of **Puy-l'Évêque**, a small town built on terraces on the north bank of the Lot. ◐ See LUZECH for descriptions of towns in bold in this paragraph.

✍**Clos Triguedina** is one of the fine wines of the Puy-l'Évêque area. If you follow the Lot Valley, west of Puy-l'Évêque, you will come across some of the famous estates of the Cahors region, such as ✍**Château Lamartine** in **Soturac** and the ✍**Château du Cèdre** in **Bru**.

◐ *Leave Puy-l'Évêque E along D 811.*

Lively in summer, the small town of **Prayssac** lying beneath Calvayrac castle overlooks one of the tighter meanders of the Lot, enclosing the **Domaine Cosse-Maisonneuve**, which produce good wines.

◐ *Drive to Luzech along D 9. Drive on to Cahors along D 9 and D 145.*

The narrow road follows the meanders of the Lot and goes through **Caix** with its splendid water sports centre offering swimming and various water sports. **Domaine de Lagrézette**, a handsome Renaissance building in **Caillac**, produces some of the finest (and most expensive) Cahors wines. The underground cellars and the barrel storehouse, which is 55m long and 19m high, can be visited *(46140 Caillac; ◐open by appt. 10am–7pm; ℘05 65 20 07 42).*

◐ *Rejoin D 145 and drive on to Mercuès.*

Château de
Bonaguil★★

This majestic fortress, standing on the borders of the Périgord Noir and the Quercy, is a perfect example of military architecture from the late 15C and 16C. One of the things that makes it unique is the fact that it appears to be a typical medieval defensive stronghold, but its design was actually adapted to the use of firearms.

A BIT OF HISTORY

A strange character – It was a strange quirk of character that made **Bérenger de Roquefeuil** enjoy proclaiming himself the "noble, magnificent and most powerful lord of the baronies of Roquefeuil, Blanquefort, Castelnau, Combret, Roquefère, Count of Naut." He belonged to one of the oldest families of Languedoc and was a brutal and vindictive man. However, extortion and other outrages he perpetrated incited revolt. In order to crush this, Bérenger transformed the 13C, Bonaguil Castle into an impregnable fortress from which he would be able to observe and quell any signs of an uprising. It took nearly 40 years to build this anachronism while his contemporaries were building renaissance châteaux along the Loire. However, his

Michelin Map: Michelin local map 336: I-2 Local map see LUZECH: Meanders of the Lower reaches of the river Lot.

Location: 8.5 km/5.3 mi north east of Fumel following the D673 and D158

castle was never attacked and was intact until the eve of the Revolution. Although partially demolished in the late 18C, it still evokes the absolute power it once represented.

CHÂTEAU

Open Jul–Aug: 10am–7pm (4pm early August during Festival); Jun to Sept: 10am–12.30pm, 2–6pm; Apr, May & Oct: 10.30am–12.30pm, 2–5.30pm; Feb–Mar: 10.30am–12.30pm, 2–5pm; Nov weekends & school hols (all zones): 10.30am–12.30pm, 2–5pm; Dec–Jan: school vacations all zones, 2–5pm, exc. Dec 25 & Jan 1 ☞6€. ℘05 53 71 90 33. www.bonaguil.org.

To reach the castle stronghold, you pass through the enormous **barbican**, which had an independent garrison, powder store, armouries and escape routes. The barbican formed part of the 350m/380yd-long first line of defence.

Château de Bonaguil

S. Sauvignier/MICHELIN

FORT DE BONAGUIL

0   20 m

1st line of defense
2nd line of defense

The second line of defence consisted of five towers of which one, known as the Grosse Tour, is among the strongest round towers ever to have been built in France. The tower is 35m/115ft high and is crowned with corbels; the upper storeys served as living quarters, the lower contained weapons, such as muskets, culverins and harquebuses etc. The **keep** overlooked both lines of defence; it served not only as a watchtower but also as a command-post and was the last bastion of defence. The castle garrison of about 100 men could easily withstand a siege, with a well sunk through the rock and vaulted tunnels that enabled the troops to move about quickly.

ADDRESSES

🍴 STAY

🏕 **Camping des Bastides** – 47150 Salles - Monflanquin. 19km/12mi W via Fumel, then the D 710 and D 162 - ✆ 05 53 40 83 09. www.campingdesbastides.com. Open Apr 25–Sept 13. Reserv. recommended. 91 pitches. Shop. The view across the Lède Valley from this terraced campsite is charming, and in the summer months the landscape is bright with sunflowers. Facilities here include a swimming pool with slides, volleyball court and children's play area. Mobile homes available.

🏕 **Camping Moulin du Périé** – 47500 Sauveterre-la-Lémance - 12km/7.5mi NW of Bonaguil on the D 440 and then the D 158 - ✆ 05 53 40 67 26. www.camping-moulin-perie.com. Open May 15–Sept 18. Reserv. recommended. 125 pitches. Restaurant. This campsite, laid out around a restored mill, is spacious and well-maintained. Small lake and pool, bikes and bungalows for hire, plus a restaurant serving regional cuisine.

Cahors★★

and the confluence of the Célé and the Lot

The town of Cahors, impressively enclosed by a meander in the River Lot, still retains precious vestiges of its glorious past. **Boulevard Gambetta**, a typically southern French avenue lined with plane trees, cafés and shops, is the town's main thoroughfare. The busy, bustling atmosphere here reflects the fact that Cahors remains an important commercial and administrative centre. The former capital of the Quercy is an excellent starting point for tours of the Célé and Lot valleys, where options include tours of the famous Cahors vineyards, boat trips along the River Lot, and visits to some of the region's famous underground caves.

▶ **Population:** 20 062
▶ **Michelin Map:** 337: E-5
▶ **Info:** Pl. F.-Mitterrand, 46004 Cahors. ☎05 65 53 20 65. www.tourisme-cahors.com.
▶ **Location:** 113 km/70 mi n. of Toulouse by A62, A20 & D820. 97km/60.5mi S. of Brive by A20 & D820. Train Station 500m W. of centre.
▶ **Kids:** Musée de Plein Air du Quercy, in Cuzals.
▶ **Parking**: A number of car parks are dotted around the centre.
▶ **Timing**: Allow a full day for the driving tour.
▶ **Don't Miss**: Pont Valentré; Cathédrale St-Étienne (north door and cloisters).

A BIT OF HISTORY

The Sacred Spring – A spring, discovered by Carthusian monks, led to the founding of Divona Cadurcorum, later known as Cadurca and later still as Cahors. First the Gauls and then the Romans worshipped the spring with a devotion which was confirmed by the discovery in 1991 of a great number of coins dating from the beginning of Christianity, which had been thrown into the fountain as offerings. The town grew rapidly in siñe: a forum, a theatre, temples, baths and ramparts were built. This spring still supplies the town with drinking water.

The Golden Age – In the 13C Cahors became one of the great towns of France and experienced considerable economic prosperity due in no small part to the arrival of Lombard merchants and bankers who also operated somewhat less reputedly as usurers. Cahors became one of the leading banking cities of Europe and the word cahorsin, as the people of Cahors were known, became synonymous with the word usurer.

War and Decline – At the beginning of the Hundred Years War, the English seiÑed all the towns in the Quercy. Cahors alone remained impregnable, in spite of the Black Death which killed

Cahors is tucked into a meander of the River Lot.

B. Kaufmann/MICHELIN

Pont Valentré

S. Sauvignier/MICHELIN

half the population. In 1360, under the Treaty of Brétigny, Cahors was ceded to the English and by 1450, when the English left the Quercy, it was a ruined city.

Cahors and the Reformation – After several decades of peace, Cahors was able to regain some of its past prosperity. By 1540 the Reformation reached the city and dissension among the population led in 1560 to the massacre of some Protestants Twenty years later the town was besieged and sacked by the Huguenots, led by Henri de Navarre.

Native Sons – These include Pope John XXII (1316-34), founder of the successful university in Cahors in 1332, the poet Clément Marot (1496-1544) and **Léon Gambetta** (1838-82), an outstanding lawyer and statesman. This ardent patriot played an active part in the downfall of Napoleon III and in the proclamation of the Third Republic on 4 September 1870.

PONT VALENTRÉ★★

Crosses the Lot to the west of the city at the foot of President Wilson.

The Valentré bridge is a remarkable example of French medieval military architecture. The three towers, with machicolations and crenellated parapets, and the pointed cutwaters breaking the line of the seven pointed arches, give it a bold and proud appearance. The bridge was originally an isolated fortress commanding the river; the central tower served as an observation post, the outer towers were closed by gates and portcullises. A guard house and outwork on the south bank of the Lot provided additional protection. The fortress impressed the English during the Hundred Years War and also Henri de Navarre at the time of the siege of Cahors (1580). It was, consequently, never attacked.

CATHÉDRALE ST-ÉTIENNE★

pl. Chapou

The clergy built this church as a fortress to provide a place of safety in troubled times, as well as to bolster prestige. At the end of the 11C, Bishop Géraud of Cardaillac began to build on the site of a former 6C church and much of his edifice remains standing to this day. The west front was built early in the 14C, and the paintings inside the domes and in the chancel were completed at the same time. The Flamboyant-style cloisters were commissioned at the beginning of the 16C by Bishop Antoine de LuÑech.

Exterior – The west front is made of three adjoining towers. The central one has a belfry above it and opens

CAHORS

0   200 m

with double doors. On the first floor, the rose window is surrounded by blind arcades. In spite of windows with twin bays completing the decoration, the appearance of the façade remains austere and military.

North doorway★★ – This Romanesque door was once part of the west front; it was transferred to the north side of the cathedral before the present façade was built. The tympanum depicts the Ascension.

Interior – Enter by the west door and cross the **narthex** which is slightly raised; the nave is roofed with two huge domes on pendentives.

There is a striking contrast between the nave, in pale-coloured stone, and the chancel, adorned with stained glass and paintings.

Northern doorway of
Cathédrale St-Étienne

J. Dumas/MICHELIN

The frescoes of the first dome were uncovered in 1872; these show the stoning of St Stephen in the central medallion, the saint's executioners around the frieze and eight giant-sized figures of prophets in the niches.

Cloisters★ – Dating from 1509, these Renaissance cloisters were built after those of Carennac and Cadouin, with which they have a number of stylistic similarities. Near the chancel door is a spiral staircase, and on the north-west corner pillar a graceful carving of the Virgin of the Annunciation.

WALKING TOUR
Chapelle St-Gausbert
Open Sat 3pm–5pm or by prior arrangement. Contact the Tourist Office ☎05 65 53 20 65.

16C paintings in the style of the Italian Renaissance decorate the ceiling of this former chapter house, whereas 15C paintings representing the Last Judgement adorn the walls. The chapel also contains the Cathedral Treasury. Enter the inner court of the former arch-deaconry of St John through the door in the north-east corner of the cloisters. Note the lovely Renaissance decoration.

▷ *On leaving the cathedral, follow rue Nationale past the covered market.*

Rue Nationale
This was the main thoroughfare of the active Badernes Quarter. At no 116, the panels of a lovely **17C door** are decorated with fruit and foliage. Across the way, the narrow **rue St-Priest** has kept its medieval appearance. It leads to place St-Priest which boasts a beautiful outside wooden staircase in Louis XIII style (no 18).

▷ *Turn right.*

Rue du Docteur-Bergounioux
At no 40 a 16C town house has an interesting Renaissance façade opened by windows influenced by the Italian Renaissance style.

▷ *Retrace your steps and continue straight on.*

Rue Lastié
Note the Rayonnant windows at no 35. At no 117, a 16C house has kept its small shop on the ground floor above which are twin bays.
At the far end of the street, the pretty brick houses have been recently restored.

▷ *Turn left.*

Rue St-Urcisse

The late-12C church of St-Urcisse is entered through a 14C doorway. Inside, the two chancel pillars are decorated with elegant historiated capitals.

Note the 13C half-timbered house (no. 68) with its *soleilho* (open attic), in which laundry was hung out to dry.

▷ *Turn right.*

Maison de Roaldès

The mansion is also known as Henri IV's Mansion because it is said that the king of Navarre stayed there during the siege of Cahors in 1580.

The house dates from the end of the 15C and was restored in 1912. In the 17C it became the property of the Roaldès, a well-known Quercy family.

▷ *Turn back then right onto rue Ñde la Chantrerie.*

La Daurade

This varied set of old residences around the Olivier-de-Magny square includes the Dolive House (17C), the Heretié House (14C to 16C) and the so-called Hangman's House (Maison du Bourreau), with windows decorated with small columns (13C).

▷ *Turn right then walk down the street on the right.*

Pont Cabessut

From the bridge there is a good **view**★ of the upper part of the city, the Soubirous district. The towers bristling in the distance are: Tower of the Hanged Men or St John's Tower, the bell tower of St-Bartholomew, John XXII's Tower, Royal Castle Tower and the Pélegry College Tower.

Tour du Collège Pélegry

The College was founded in 1368 and at first took in 13 poor university students; until the 18C, it was one of the town's most important establishments. The fine hexagonal tower above the main building was constructed in the 15C.

▷ *Follow the narrow lane to the left; it runs onto rue du Château du Roi. Turn right then right again past the prison.*

Tour du Château du Roi

Near Pélegry College stands what is today the prison and was once the governor's residence. Of the two towers and two main buildings erected in the 14C, the remaining massive tower is known as Château du Roi.

▷ *Return to the prison, follow the street opposite and turn right.*

Ilôt Fouillac

This area has undergone an extensive programme of redevelopment. By getting rid of the most run-down buildings, a square has been cleared. Its sides are decorated with **murals**, and it is brightened by a particularly interesting **musical fountain**.

▷ *Turn right towards rue des Soubirous.*

Tour Jean-XXII

This tower is all that remains of the palace of Pierre DuèÑe, brother of John XXII. It is 34m/112ft high and was originally covered in tiles. Twin windows pierce the walls on five storeys.

Église St-Barthélémy

This church was built in the highest part of the old town, and was known until the 13C as St-Etienne de Soubiroux, *Sancti Stephani de superioribus* (St Stephen of the Upper Quarter), in contrast to the cathedral built in the lower part of the town. The church was rebuilt to its present design in several stages. The belfry, the base of which dates from the 14C, has no spire, and it is built almost entirely of brick.

The nave, with its ogive vaulting, was designed in the Languedoc style. In the chapel nearest the entrance, on the left, a marble slab and bust call to mind that John XXII was baptised in this church. The cloisonné enamels on the cover of the modern baptismal font depict the main events in the life of this famous Cahors citiÑen.

▶ *Walk to boulevard Gambetta and head North.*

Barbican and Tour St-Jean★
The ramparts, constructed in the 14C, completely cut the isthmus formed by the meander of the River Lot off from the surrounding countryside. Remains of these fortifications can still be seen and include a massive tower at the west end, which sheltered the powder magaÑine, and the old gateway of St-Michel, which now serves as entrance to the cemetery. It is on the east side, however, where the N 20 road enters the town, that the two most impressive fortified buildings remain: the barbican and St John's Tower. The barbican is an elegant guard house which defended the Barre Gateway; St John's Tower or the Tower of the Hanged Men (Tour des Pendus), was built on a rock overlooking the River Lot.

MUSEUMS
Musée de la Résistance, de la Déportation et de la Libération
pl. Bessières, BP 294 46009 Cahors
🕐*Open 2–6pm (mornings by prior arrangement).* 🕐*Closed 1 Jan, 1 May and 25 Dec.* 🚫*No charge.*
☎*05 65 22 14 25.*
Housed in six rooms, this museum illustrates the birth of the Resistance movement in the Lot region, deportations and persecutions which followed, fighting for the Liberation of France and the epic journey of the Free French from BraÑÑaville to Berlin. Eighteen models of war planes are also displayed and newspapers dating from that period are available to visitors.

Musée Henri-Martin
792, rue Emile Zola, 46000 Cahors.
🕐*Open daily except Tue, 11am–6pm; Sun and public hols, 2–6pm.* 🕐*Closed 1 Jan, 1 May and 25 Dec.* 🚫*3€.*
☎*05 65 20 88 66.*

This museum is housed in the former Episcopal palace. One room is devoted to the works of the painter Henri Martin (1860-1943), a member of the pointillist movement.

VIEWPOINTS
La Croix de Magne Viewpoint★
5km/3mi. From the western end of the Valentré Bridge, turn right and then immediately left; take the first left after the agricultural school, and left again at the top of the rise.
Around the cross, a **view**★ extends in all directions over the plateau, to the River Lot, Cahors and the Valentré Bridge.

Viewpoint to the North of the Town
5km/3mi along rue du Docteur-J.-Ségala which turns right off the N 20 just beyond the Tour St-Jean.
This road offers fine views of the Lot Valley and the surroundings of Cahors, including the old town built like an amphitheatre, with its pinnacles, crenellated towers and Valentré Bridge.

Mont St-Cyr Viewpoint★
7km/4mi via the Louis-Philippe Bridge and the D 6 which you leave after 1.5km/1mi to reach the mount, keeping to the left.
From the top (viewing table) there is a good **view**★ of Cahors; the contrast between the old and the new quarters of the town, which are separated by boulevard Gambetta, Cahors' main artery, is striking. In the background the distinctive shape of Valentré Bridge can be seen.

EXCURSION
Château de Mercuès
6km/3.7mi NW along the D 911.
Once the property of the count-bishops of Cahors, the château is now a hotel. It occupies a remarkable site overlooking the north bank of the Lot. In 1212 the château was a fortified castle, it was then enlarged in the 14C, besieged several times and not restored completely until

the 19C. There is an outstanding **view**★ of the valley from the château

West of Mercuès the road leaves the valley for a short distance to cross a flourishing countryside of vineyards and orchards; then the road returns to the river, following it closely.

▶ **Château de Roussilon** – 9km/5.4mi N on the N 20 and **Château de Cieurac** – 12km/7.5mi S via the D 6.

🚗 DRIVING TOUR

CONFLUENCE OF THE CÉLÉ AND THE LOT★★
125km/78mi round tour – allow one day. Leave Cahors travelling NE along the D 653 towards Figeac.

Laroque-des-Arcs
This village's name is a reminder of the aqueduct which crossed the Francoulès Valley and supplied water to Cahors. A three-tiered bridge bore the 20km/12mi aqueduct from Vers to Divona (ancient Cahors).

▶ *Continue along the D 653.*

Notre-Dame-de-Vêles
This small pilgrimage chapel was built in the 12C and has a lovely square bell tower and a Romanesque apse.

▶ *From Vers, keep following the Dordogne along the D 662. Starting from Conduché, where the Célé flows into the Lot, D 41 goes up the valley. Many crops grow in the valley with maiÑe tending to replace tobacco.*

Cabrerets
Cabrerets, set in a rocky amphitheatre, occupies a commanding position at the confluence of the River Sagne and River Célé. There is a good overall **view**★ of Cabrerets and its setting from the left bank of the Célé, which is reached by crossing the bridge. Opposite stand the ruins of the **Château du Diable** (Devil's Castle), or Castle of the English, clinging to the formidable Rochecourbe cliff.

On the far left is the impressive mass of the 14C and 15C **Château des Gontaut-Biron**★ overlooking the valley. A big corner tower flanks the buildings that surround an inner courtyard.

▶ *Take the D 198 up the valley of the Sagne to Pech-Merle Cave.*

Grottes du Pech-Merle★★★
👁 *See Grottes du PECH-MERLE.*

▶ *Shortly after Cabrerets the cliff road crosses the face of high stone cliffs.*

Fontaine de la Pescalerie
This is one of the most attractive sights of the Célé Valley; a beautiful waterfall pours out of the rock wall close to the road. It marks the surfacing of an underground river that has cut its way through the Causse de Gramat.

▷ *Continue along the D 41, then 1.5km/0.9mi beyond LiauÑu, turn left onto a minor road.*

Cuzals
Musée de Plein Air du Quercy (Quercy Open-Air Museum)
All the aspects of life in the Quercy region, from before the Revolution until the Second World War, are illustrated in the park, covering 50ha/124 acres. Visitors are offered an authentic, scientific approach to the area's cultural heritage.
A 3km/1.9mi-long discovery trail offers an insight into man's impact on the local environment.

▷ *Return to the D 41 and turn left.*

Sauliac-sur-Célé
This old village clings to an awe-inspiring cliff of coloured rock. In the cliff face can be seen the openings to the fortified caves used in time of war as refuges by the local inhabitants.

▷ *As you leave Sauliac, turn right onto the D 24 which crosses the Célé.*

Beyond Sauliac the valley widens out. Crops and pasture land grow well on the alluvial soil of the valley bottom. The road climbs onto the causse, runs across it then down into the Lot Valley.

▷ *From St-Martin-Labouval, follow the north bank of the Lot.*

Larnagol
This village has retained some fine 16C and 17C façades. The castle and its buttressed keep overlook the upper part.

▷ *Leave Arnagol S and cross the river.*

Calvignac
This old village, where a few traces of its fortress may still be seen, is perched on a spur on the river's south bank.

▷ *Staying on the same bank take the D 8 which leads to Cénevières.*

Château de Cénevières★
This imposing castle perches on a sheer rock face overlooking the Lot Valley from a height of more than 70m/230ft.
As early as the 8C the dukes of Aquitaine had a stronghold built here and in the 13C the lords of Gourdon had the keep built. During the Renaissance Flottard de Gourdon completely remodelled the castle. His son, Antoine de Gourdon, converted to Protestantism and participated alongside Henri IV in the siege of Cahors in 1580. He pillaged the cathedral in Cahors and loaded the high altar and altar of the Holy Shroud onto boats returning to Cénevières Castle. The boat carrying the high altar sank in a chasm along the way. Before his death Antoine built a small Protestant church, which is in the outer bailey. He died childless, his widow remarried and a new lineage took over Cénevières. The château was pillaged during the French Revolution.
The outside of the castle has a 13C keep and 15C wings joined by a 16C Renaissance gallery. The gallery is held up by Tuscan columns and above it are dormer windows. The moat, once crossed

Château de Cénevières

©DeAgostini/Photoshot

211

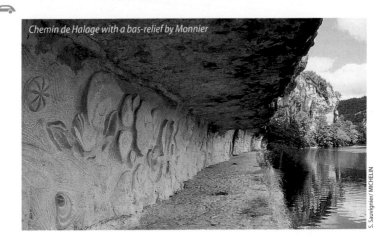

Chemin de Halage with a bas-relief by Monnier

S. Sauvignier/ MICHELIN

by a drawbridge, is now filled in. Inside, the ground floor includes the vaulted salt room and kitchen. The keep has a trap door, which permits a glimpse of the three floors of underground cellars. The adjacent chapel, still consecrated, houses the altar of the Holy Shroud.

On the first floor the great drawing room, with a lovely Renaissance painted ceiling and recently discovered murals, contains 15C and 16C Flemish tapestries and the shrine of the Holy Shroud brought back from Cahors. Various objects are displayed in the following room: a Spanish helmet, a mould for cannon balls and letters from famous people.

◐ *Cross the River Lot and pick up the D 662 towards St-Cirq-Lapopie.*

From Pont de Tour-de-Faure, admire St-Cirq-Lapopie in its remarkable setting on the river's south bank.

St-Cirq-Lapopie★★
See ST-CIRQ-LAPOPIE.

Beyond St-Cirq-Lapopie, the D 40, which is built into the cliff, has been designed as a tourist route. There is a good **view**★ of the confluence of the Lot and the Célé from the **Belvédère du Bancourel**.

Bouziès
On the bank opposite the village, the **Défilé des Anglais** (Englishmen's Gorge) is the most famous of the forti-

fied gullies constructed during the Hundred Years War in cave-like openings only accessible by a rope-ladder.

Towpath along the Lot★ (Chemin de Halage)
Take the GR 36 trail off to the right of the car park by the moorings.

After about 500m/547yd, the spectacular towpath comes into view, carved out of the rock because here, the cliff juts out over the river. In sections such as this, the barges coming up the Lot with their cargoes of salt, dried fish, spices or plaster could not be towed by the usual teams of horses or oxen, but had to be pulled along by hand This pathway is now a marvellous walk. At the top of the first lock there is a 15m/9ft-long bas-relief, the work of contemporary artist D Monnier, decorating the limestone wall with fish and shellfish.

◐ *Rejoin the D 8 and turn right. The road runs onto the D 911 at Arcambal.*

ADDRESSES

🏠 STAY

🛏 **Chambre d'hôte Les Poujades** – *Flaynac, 46090 Pradines. 5km/3/.1mi N of Cahors on the D 8.* ☎05 65 35 33 36. *2 rooms. Cottage available.* A flower garden and shady trees surround this typical Quercy house, from where you can enjoy a wonderful view of the Château de Mercuès, the Cahors vineyards and the outskirts of the town. The decor is a little on the sombre side, but is compensated by the warm welcome.

Chambre d'hôte Le Clos des Dryades – *46090 Vers. 19km/11.4mi NE of Cahors on the D 653. ℘05 65 31 44 50. www.closedryades.com. 5 rooms.* Nestled deep in the woods, this tiled-roof house is the perfect place to get away from it all. The rooms are comfortable and the large swimming pool is a great place to cool off on a hot summer's day. Two self-catering cottages are also available.

Chambre d'hôte Domaine de Labarthe – *46090 Espère. 8km/5mi NW of Cahors on the D 911. ℘05 65 30 92 34. Reserv. required. 3 rooms.* Guests at this manor house, complete with dovecote, are assured the warmest of welcomes. The rooms are pretty, and fresh flowers and biscuits await you on arrival. All the rooms open onto the garden and pool.

Chez Madame Lestrade Lola – *76, Rue Clémenceau. ℘ 05 65 35 25 93. 2 suites, 1 room.* Set on the second floor of a restored old house in the town centre these colourful contemporary accommodations enjoy fine views.

Jean XXII ((*Previously Hôtel A l'Escargot*) **–** *5 bd Gambetta. ℘05 65 35 07 66. Closed Feb school hols,Oct 20–31 and Sun Oct–May. 9 rooms.* 7€ Near the Tour Jean XXII, this hotel occupies the old palace built by the pontiff's family. Functional bedrooms with colourful furnishings, plus a renovated breakfast room.

Hôtel de la Paix – *30 place Saint-Maurice. ℘05 65 35 03 40. www. logis-de-france.fr. 17 rooms.* This small two-star hotel is set in the heart of the old town by the indoor market. It has recently been completely renovated but retains its original charm and the comfortable bedrooms all have en-suite facilities

Chambre d'hôte La Vayssade – *Lalbenque 16km/10mi S of Cahors. ℘05 65 24 31 51. www.lavayssade.com. Closed Oct-Dec & Mar. 5 rooms.* Very characterful rustic *grange* (renovated barn) set in its own grounds amid 10 hectares of truffle oaks with a highly

impressive monumental communal living room. Special truffle weekends.

EAT

L'Auberge des Gabarres – *24 place Champollion. ℘05 65 53 91 47. Closed Sun and Mon.* This inn is known for its simple tasty terroir cooking and its warm welcome. A meal on the shady terrace is a treat.

La Garenne – *Saint-Henri, 7km/4.5mi N towards Brive. ℘05 65 35 40 67. Closed Feb–Mar 15, Mon eve, Tue eve and Wed, except Jul–Aug.* Delicious regional cuisine is served in a cosy interior that was formerly a stable .

Auberge du Vieux Douelle – *46140 Douelle. 8km/5mi W of Cahors on the D 8. ℘05 65 20 02 03. www.aubergeduvieuxdouelle.new.fr. Closed Christmas week.* The dining room in the vaulted cellar of this popular inn, known locally as "Chez Malique", is decked out with bright red tablecloths. Meats are grilled over a wood fire; Terrace and pool in the summer.

L'Ô à la Bouche – *134 rue Ste-Urcisse. ℘05 65 35 65 69. Closed Easter hols, autumn half-term hol, Sun and Mon.* Old stone and exposed brickwork and beams plus a large fireplace lend undeniable character to this restaurant, renowned for its contemporary gourmet fare. There is a small side terrace for warm weather.

Le Rendez-Vous – *49 rue Clément-Marot. ℘05 65 22 65 10. www. le-rendez-vous-cahors.com. Closed 29 Apr–14 May, 28 Oct–12 Nov, Sun and Mon - reserv. recommended.* Near the cathedral, Le Rendez-Vous has developed a reputation for its modern cuisine. The mix of colourful contemporary decor and old stonework combine well in the dining room and mezzanine extension.

Au Fil des Douceurs – *90 quai de la Verrerie. ℘05 65 22 13 04. Closed Sun and Mon. 15 Jun–3 Jul, 2–25 Jan.* This boat-restaurant enjoys a romantic setting with a stunning view of the Lot and old Cahors near Le Pont Cabessut. Traditional fare is served in two dining rooms, one above the other. Leave room for the excellent dessert.

⊖⊜⊜⊜ **Vinois** – *Le Bourg, Caillac.* *℘05 65 30 53 60. www.levinois.com. Closed 5–19 Oct, 12 Jan–12 Feb . Mon (except dinner Jul–Aug) Sun dinner and Tue lunch.* In the heart of the Cahors vineyards, north of the city centre, don't miss this stunning inn that sports a minimalist contemporary style in keeping with the fashionable cuisine – expect creative twists on Quercy lamb, duck, foie gras and truffles, and of course a great choice of local wines Jazz usually plays softly in the background. Ten designer bedrooms (⊖⊜⊜⊜).

🛒 SHOPPING

Market – *Pl. Chapou*. A traditional market is held on Wed all day and Sat mornings, with numerous stalls run by farmers selling a range

EVENTS

Cahors Juin Jardins - *June* *℘05 65 53 20 65. www.tourisme-cahors.com.* **Festival de Blues** - *mid-Jul.* *℘05 65 35 99 99.* **Festival du Quercy Blanc** - *late-Jul to mid-Aug.* *℘05 65 31 83 12.*

Figeac★★
the Célé and Lot Valleys

Sprawled along the north bank of the Célé, Figeac developed at the point where the Auvergne meets Upper Quercy. A commercial town, it had a prestigious past as is shown in the architecture of its tall sandstone town houses.

A BIT OF HISTORY
From Abbots to King
Figeac began developing in the 9C around a monastery, which itself expanded in the 13C.

The abbot was the town's lord and governed it with the aid of seven consuls. All administrative services were located inside the monastery. Because Figeac was on the pilgrimage route running from Le Puy and Conques and on to Santiago de Compostela, crowds of pilgrims and travellers flocked through it.

Benefiting from the town's geographical situation between Auvergne, Quercy and Rouergue, local craftsmen and shopkeepers were prosperous.

In 1302, following a disagreement between the abbot and the consuls, Philip the Fair took control of the town, represented by a provost. He won the inhabitants' favour by allowing them the rare privilege of minting royal money.

The Hundred Years War and the Wars of Religion had an adverse effect on the town's development. From 1576 to 1623 Figeac was a safe stronghold for

▶ **Population:** 9,943
🕭 **Michelin Map:** Michelin local map 337: I-4
🛈 **Info:** Hôtel de la Monnaie, pl. Vival, 46102 Figeac. *℘05 65 34 06 25.* www.tourism-figeac.com
◗ **Location:** 70km/43.5mi W of Cahors via D653. Train station 600m S. of centre.
🅿 **Parking:** Parking in centre.
🔍 **Don't Miss:** The old town; Hôtel de la Monnaie; Chapelle Notre-Dame-de-Pitié; Place des Écritures.

the Calvinists, until Richelieu broke their fortifications up. Prosperity continued in the 18C and 19C as mills and tanneries settled along the canal.

🦶 WALKING TOUR
OLD FIGEAC★★
The old quarter, surrounded by boulevards which trace the line of the former moats, has kept its medieval town plan with its narrow, twisting alleys.

The buildings, built in elegant beige sandstone, exemplify the architecture of the 12C, 13C and 14C. Generally the ground floor was opened by large pointed arches and the first floor had a gallery of arcaded bays. Underneath the flat tiled roof was the *soleilho*, an open attic, which was used to dry

Jean-François Champollion

Champollion, the outstanding Orientalist, whose brilliance enabled Egyptology to make such great strides, was born at Figeac in December 1790. At the beginning of the 19C, Ancient Egyptian civilisation was still a mystery, since the meaning of hieroglyphics ('*sacred carving*') had not yet been deciphered.

By the time Champollion was 14, he had a command of Greek, Latin, Hebrew, Arabic, Chaldean and Syrian. After his studies in Paris, he lectured in history, at the youthful age of 19, at Grenoble University.

J. Damase/MICHELIN

He set himself the task of deciphering a polished basalt tablet, showing three different inscriptions (Greek, Egyptian hieroglyphics and demotic – a simplified Egyptian script that appeared around 650 BC), which had been discovered in 1799 by members of Napoleon's expedition to Egypt near Rosetta in the north-west Nile delta, from which it derives its name – the **Rosetta Stone**.

However, he was not able to carry out his research on the stone itself, which had been seized by the English while at war with France (it is now in the British Museum, London), but had to make do with copies. Drawing on the work of a predecessor, the English physicist Thomas Young (1773-1829), who had succeeded in identifying genders and proper nouns, Champollion gradually unravelled the mystery of hieroglyphics.

In 1826, he founded the Egyptology Museum at the Louvre Palace, Paris, and became its first curator. He left for Egypt on a two-year mission and deciphered many texts while he was there. In 1831, he was appointed professor of Archaeology at the Collège de France, however he gave only four lectures before dying a year later, worn out by his hard work.

food, laundry or even hand-crafted objects. Its openings were separated by columns or pillars in wood or stone, sometimes even brick, which held the roof up. The buildings were flanked by corbelled towers and their doorways were elaborately decorated; spiral staircases heralded the Renaissance style. Traditional crafts are still alive in Figeac, as you can see by walking down rue de Colomb, rue Émile-Zola and rue Baduel.

Hôtel de la Monnaie (Mint)★

Tourist Information Centre
This late-13C building, restored in the early 20C, exemplifies Figeac's secular architecture with its *soleilho*, pointed arches on the ground floor and the depressed arched windows placed either singly, paired or grouped in the façade. It is interesting to compare the façade, overlooking the square, which was rebuilt with the elements of the former consul's house of the same period, with the other plainer façades. The octagonal, stone chimney was characteristic of Figeac construction at one time, but very few examples remain.

The name *Oustal dé lo Mounédo* owes its name to the Royal Mint created in Figeac by Philip the Fair. It has since been established that the stamping workshop was located in another building and that this handsome edifice was the place where money was exchanged.

It now houses the Musée du Vieux Figeac (see Sights).

▷ *Take rue Orthabadial and turn right onto rue Balène.*

Rue Balène

At no 7 stands the 14C Palais Balène, which houses the community hall. Its medieval fortress-like façade is lightened by an ogive doorway and chapel windows with decorated tracery.

At no 1, the 14C Hôtel de Viguier d'Auglanat, once the home of an influential family, is decorated with a lovely basket-arched doorway and castellated turret.

Rue Gambetta

This is the old town's main street. The houses at nos 25 and 28 are half-timbered, with decorative brickwork, and have been beautifully restored.

◑ *Continue via rue Gambetta and place aux Herbes to place de la Raison.*

Église St-Sauveur

This used to be an abbey church, the oldest parts of which date from the 11C. It has kept its original cross plan: a high nave with 14C chapels off the aisles. The nave is unusual for the lack of symmetry between its north and south sides. The south side includes: in the lowest section, rounded arcades; in the middle section, a tribune with twinned bays within a larger arch; and in the upper section, 13C clerestory windows.

The chancel, surrounded by the ambulatory, was rebuilt in the 17C. Four Romanesque capitals, remnants of the earlier doorway, support the baptismal font.

Chapelle Notre-Dame-de-Pitié★

This former chapter-house became a place of worship after the departure of the Protestants in 1622. A sumptuous carved and painted **wooden decor**★ was added to it, apparently the work of the Delclaux, a family of master painters from Figeac. To the right of the altar there is a striking panel depicting the infant Jesus asleep on the cross, dreaming of his future Passion.

◑ *Walk northwards along rue Tomfort then turn right.*

Rue Roquefort

The house with the bartizan on a carved corbel belonged to Galiot de Genouillac, Grand Master of the Artillery of François I.

◑ *Follow rue du Canal to rue Émile-Zola.*

Rue Émile-Zola

The oldest street in the town still has ogival arcades and an interesting sequence of Renaissance doorways from no 35 to 37.

◑ *Turn right*

Rue Delzhens

No 3, the Provost's House (**Hôtel du Viguier du roy**) has a square keep and a 14C watch turret. It has been restored and converted into a hotel.

◑ *Walk up the street.*

Église Notre-Dame-du-Puy

The church is on a hill which gives a good view of the town and its surroundings. The Protestants used it as a fortress, strengthening the façade with a watch room.

This Gothic building underwent many alterations in the 17C; it has an enormous altarpiece carved in walnut dating from the end of the 17C, which frames two pictures representing the Assumption and the Coronation of the Virgin.

◑ *Go back down the hill along rue St-Jacques.*

Rue Malleville, Rue St-Thomas

Both these streets pass under a covered passageway painted with the coat of arms of the Hôtel de Laporte (17C).

Rue du Crussol

The courtyard of the 16C Hôtel de Crussol (no 5), now a terrace-bar, features a gallery over the courtyard stairway.

◑ *Take rue Laurière then rue Bonhore.*

FIGEAC

0   200 m   **N**

TOULOUSE, GAILLAC   VILLEFRANCHE-DE-R.

WHERE TO STAY	
Bains (Hôtel des)	①
Bastie d'Urfé (Hôtel la)	②
Champollion (Hôtel)	④
Pont d'Or (Hôtel Le)	⑨
Relais de la Tour (Hôtel du)	⑫

WHERE TO EAT	
Diège(Auberge de la)	④
Dînée du Viguier (La)	⑥
Domaine des Villedieu (Auberge du)	⑧

At the far end of **rue Caviale**, opposite no 35 (**l'Hôtel d'Ay-de-Lostanges**), starts the street leading to the **Maison du Roi**, so-called because Louis XI is supposed to have stayed there in 1463.

▷ *Walk along rue Caviale.*

Place Carnot

Formerly place Basse, this was headquarters to the wheat exchange, which was destroyed in 1888. In the northwest corner, with a small side turret, is the **house of Pierre de Cisteron**, Louis XIV's armourer.

▷ *From place Carnot, after crossing the narrow, medieval-looking rue Séguier, go through a porch to get to place des Écritures.*

Place des Écritures★

Surrounded by medieval buildings, this square has an enormous (14×7m/ 46×23ft) **replica of the Rosetta Stone** underfoot.

This was sculpted in black granite from Zimbabwe by the American conceptual artist Joseph Kossuth. Unveiled in 1991, this significant contemporary work of art is more clearly understood from the hanging gardens overlooking the square. The French translation of the inscriptions is carved on a glass plaque kept in a small neighbouring courtyard.

Place des Écritures, Figeac

J. Damase/MICHELIN

Place Champollion

Two contrasting buildings overlook the square: a 14C private mansion and the town's oldest house dating from the mid-12C, known locally as the Maison du Griffon.

▷ *Return to place Vival via rue Gambetta and rue du 11-Novembre.*

MUSEUMS AND TEMPLARS
Musée Champollion★

Place Champollion. ◷*Open Jul–Aug daily, 10.30am–6pm; Apr–Jun & Sept, 10.30am–12pm, 2pm–6pm,Oct–Mar, 2–5.30pm* ◷*Closed Mon and Jan 1, May 1, Dec 25.* ◈*4€.* ☎*05 65 50 31 08.*
Recently re-opened, the museum has been extended and the collections are now displayed in Champollion's birthplace and in the adjacent building. This new exhibition area, devoted to "signs and writing", illustrates the history of writing from its invention to the present.

Musée du Vieux Figeac - Hôtel de la Monnaie

Office de Tourisme, Place Vival. ◷*Open Jul-Aug, 9am–7.pm; May–Jun and Sep, 9am–12.30 and 2–6pm, Sun 10am–1pm; Oct–Apr, daily except Sun and May 1, 9am–noon and 2–6pm.* ◈*2€.* ☎*05 65 34 06 25.*
The museum displays sculpture from religious and secular buildings (the

door of the Hôtel de Sully), sarcophagi, grain measurements, old coins, the town seal originating from the period when the town had its seven consuls and furniture.

Commanderie des Templiers

41, rue Gambetta. ◷*Open Jun 15–Sept 15, 10.30am–7pm; Sept 16–Jun 14, 2.30–7* ◷*Closed Mon.* ◈*3€(Guided Visit.5€)* ☎*06 86 76 86 04.*
This group of buildings dating from the mid-14C boasts a beautiful Gothic façade. The first building consists of two roofed towers, the second building features a half-timbered structure. Inside, it was remodelled to present the interior of a Knights Templars commandery.
A remarkable 15C wooden staircase leads to the first floor where the guardroom, the chapter-house and the chapel are to be found. The latter are connected by oratory hatches. On the second floor a wooden balcony links the monks' dormitory with the commander's residence in which there is also a private chapel.

EXCURSIONS
Aiguilles de Figeac
See description for location.
These two octagonal-shaped, false obelisks to the south and west of the town measure (base included) respectively 14.50m/47ft and 11.50m/38ft. It is believed that they marked the boundaries of the land over which the Benedictine abbey had jurisdiction.
The **Aiguille du Cingle**, also known as Aiguille du Pressoir, can be seen from the D 922, south of Figeac. The more remote **Aiguille de Lissac** is located in a wooded area near the Nayrac district about 2km/1.25mi W of town centre. (*footpath*).

Cardaillac
11km/7mi N of town along the N 140 and then the D 15.
This village is the home territory of the Cardaillacs, one of the most powerful Quercy families. The district, where the fort stands, is located on a rocky spur above the town. Of this triangular shaped fortification, dating from the

12C, there remain two square towers: the Clock or Baron's Tower and Sagnes Tower (*only the latter is open to visitors*). The two tall rooms with their vaulted ceilings are reached by a spiral staircase. From the platform there is a lovely view of the Drauzou Valley and the surrounding countryside.

The **Musée Éclaté** on Place de la Tour (🕐 ☞ *open Jul–Sept 15, guided tour (2hrs) at 3pm (from Jul 14 –Aug 25 at 4.30 also), daily except Sat, Sept–Jun, by prior arrangement; ✆05 65 40 10 63*) consists of several different sites scattered (*éclaté*) around the village in a determined effort to integrate evidence of the past firmly into the modern life of the village. Exhibits represent the village school, local crafts and the rural way of life. A study of the manufacture of wine-growers' baskets, once a speciality of Cardaillac, is given pride of place.

Capdenac
7km/4.3mi SE.
Capdenac-le-Haut, perched on a promontory and enclosed by a meander in the River Lot, occupies a remarkable **site**★. This small town, which still looks much the way it did centuries ago, overlooks Capdenac-Gare, a busy railway junction which has developed in the valley.

The **ramparts** are vestiges of the 13C and 14C outer walls and the citadel as well as the Northern Gate (Comtale), the village entrance, and the Southern Gate (Vijane). The **keep**, a powerful square tower flanked by turrets (13C-14C), houses the Tourist Information Centre and a small **museum** which recounts Capdenac's history.

 DRIVING TOUR

CÉLÉ AND LOT VALLEYS★
95km/59mi round-trip – allow one day. Drive W out of Figeac along the D 41 towards Cahors.

Espagnac-Ste-Eulalie
In this delightful village built in the picturesque setting of a series of cliffs, the houses with their turrets and pointed roofs are grouped round the former priory known as the **Ancien Prieuré Notre-Dame-du-Val-Paradis**, founded in the 12C; during the Hundred Years War the convent suffered considerably; the cloisters were destroyed and the church was partly demolished. It was rebuilt in the 15C, however, and the community carried on until the Revolution. The buildings are now occupied by a rural centre and holiday rentals (*gîtes communaux*), managed by the local authorities.

The present Flamboyant-style **church** has replaced the 13C building (only the walls of the nave, a doorway and ruined bays remain). Note the unusual pentagonal east end and belfry-tower.

◗ *Return to the north bank and continue along the D 41.*

Brengues
This small village is in a pleasant setting, perched on a ledge overlooked by a vertiginous bluff.

St-Sulpice
The houses and gardens of this old village lie within the shadow of an overhanging cliff. The approach is guarded by a 12C castle which was rebuilt in the 14C and 15C. It is still the property of the Hébrard family of St-Sulpice.

Marcilhac-sur-Célé
ᒋ *See MARCILHAC-SUR-CÉLÉ.*
The D 17 runs round the Bout du Rocher cliff. The landscape is dotted with dolmens, ruins, caves and a few farms. The shaded road runs down the slopes offering fine views of the Lot Valley.

Cajarc
The town was brought into the public eye when President Pompidou had a house here. Near the church, the Hébrardie Mansion with Gothic windows is all that remains standing of a 13C castle. Inaugurated in 1989, the **Centre d'Art Contemporain Georges-Pompidou** (🕐 *open Jun–Aug, 10am–1pm, 3pm–7pm; Sep–May, daily except Mon, 2–6pm; ☞no charge. For annual closing*

and holiday periods, call ℘05 65 40 78 19) organises retrospective exhibits of the works of contemporary European artists: Hartung, Bissière and Soulages have been featured, ranking Cajarc among the foremost centres of contemporary art in the region.

▷ *Drive S out of Cajarc on D 24 towards Villefranche-de-Rouergue; cross river and turn left onto the D 127.*

The road, which follows the south bank of the Lot, overhangs the river to start with, then immediately after Saujac rises and winds round to overlook a wooded gorge, before reaching the top of the *causse.*

Saut de la Mounine★

There is a good **view**★ of the valley from the top of this cliff rising 155m/509ft above the river. The end of the spur overlooks a wide bend in the river as it encircles a mosaic of fields. Over on the left, on the far bank, stands Montbrun Castle.

The curious name, Saut de la Mounine – the little monkey's leap – comes from a rather strange legend. The lord of Montbrun decided to punish his daughter for her love of another lord's son and ordered her to be hurled from the top of the cliff; a hermit, appalled at this cruel

idea, disguised a small blind monkey in women's clothes and hurled it into the air. When he saw the object falling the father immediately regretted his brutal action; on seeing his daughter alive and well he was so overjoyed that he forgave her.

▷ *Return to Cajarc and drive E along the D 662 towards Figeac.*

Montbrun

The village of Montbrun rises in tiers on a rocky promontory encircled by steep cliffs. It looks down on the Lot and faces the Saut de La Mounine (see above). Towering over the village are the ruins of a fortress that belonged to one of Pope John XXII's brothers, and then to the powerful Cardaillac family.

▷ *Continue along the D 662.*

Château de Larroque-Toirac

Open Jul to early Sep, guided tour (45min), 10.30am–12.30pm and 2.30–6pm. ∞5€. ℘06 12 37 48 39 or 06 60 08 80 10. www.chateautoirac.com. This 12C fortress belonged to the Cardaillac family who, during the Hundred Years War, took an active part in the region's resistance to English domination. From the church square (*parking area*), a surfaced path leads to the castle.

CELE AND LOT VALLEYS

Saut de la Mounine

©Philippe Body/Hemis/Photoshot

The visit starts with a round tower built at the beginning of the Hundred Years War to withstand artillery fire, newly introduced in siege warfare. Note the charming heart-shaped opening. The 15C seigneurial residence is reached through two successive courtyards.

A spiral staircase, located in an adjacent tower, leads to the different levels; there is a Romanesque fireplace in the guard-room and a Gothic one in the great hall; the original kitchen can also be seen. To the east stands the enormous late-12C keep which was greatly reduced in height during the Revolution.

▶ *Continue along the D 662.*

St-Pierre-Toirac

This small village, on the north bank of the Lot, contains an interesting **church**,

its architecture dating from the 11C and 14C. The Romanesque apse alone belies the fortified appearance of this building which served as a defence point with its massive crenellated keep and upper floor. Recently discovered Merovingian sarcophagi have been placed behind the church.

▶ *Continue along the D 662.*

Faycelles

This village overlooking the Lot Valley once belonged to Figeac Abbey. A peaceful atmosphere pervades the old streets and the suburb of Les Carbes.

▶ *The D 662 leads back to Figeac.*

ADDRESSES

☞STAY

⊜☷ **Hôtel des Bains** – *1, rue du Griffoul.* ℘*05 65 34 10 89. www.hoteldesbains.fr. 19 rooms.* This recently renovated former public baths, dating from the end of the last century, is located near the historic center, in a beautiful setting on the banks of the river Célé. Most rooms are air conditioned and all have broadband connection and WiFi. Breakfast can be taken on the riverbank veranda

⊜☷ **La Bastie D'urfé** – *Bez De Naussac, 12 Naussac. 19km (12mi) SE of Figeac.* ℘*05 65 64 13 77. www.hotel-bastie-urfe-naussac.federal-hotel.com. 10 rooms.* Set in the peaceful heart of the Diege countryside, La Bastie D'urfé combines the charm of an 18C mansion with the comfort of a modern home with contemporary styling., Each room has been individually designed and equipped with *balnéothérapie* facilities.

⊜☷ **Hôtel Champollion** – *3 pl. Champollion.* ℘*05 65 34 04 37. 10 rooms.* This historic building was once the main meat market. Although its bedrooms are on the small side, they are modern and well-maintained.

🛏🍴 **Grand Hôtel du Pont d'Or** – 2, av Jean-Jaurès. ✆05 65 50 95 00. www.hotelpontdor.com. 35 rooms. ⌷12€. A welcoming stone house on the banks of the Célé, with some rooms offering balconies overlooking the river. A yellow and orange colour scheme, contemporary furniture and immaculate bathrooms. Fitness room and rooftop swimming pool. In summer, breakfast is served on the riverside terrace.

🛏🍴 **Hôtel du Relais de la Tour** – Place Lucter - 46100 Capdenac le Haut. ✆05 65 11 06 99. www.lerelaisdelatour.fr. 5 rooms. The outside of this Hôtellerie de Charme et de Caractère rather belies its modern bedrooms and restaurant though other areas retain its ancient character.

🍴 EAT

🍴 **Auberge la Diege** – Saint-Julien d'Empare12700 Capdenac Gare. t 05 65 64 70 54. www.logis-de-france.fr. The rustic dining room of this charming auberge (with modern extensions) features exposed beams and brickwork. You can work up an appetite beforehand (or maybe work off your meal afterwards), with a session in the swimming pool or on the tennis court (28 rooms €52-70).

🍴 **La Dînée du Viguier** – R. Boutaric. ✆05 65 50 08 08. Closed 23 Jan–15 Feb, 15–22 Nov, Sun eve out of season, Sat lunchtime and Mon. The restaurant in the Château Viguier du Roy combines medieval decor with contemporary cuisine.

🍴 **Ferme-Auberge Domaine des Villedieu** –46100 Boussac - 8km/5mi SW of Figeac on the D 13 and D 41. ✆05 65 40 06 63. www.villedieu.com Reservation required. An enchanting 18C farmhouse deep in the country. The owners serve their own produce in the wood-floored dining room and on the outdoor terrace. The restored farm buildings have been converted into attractive guest rooms (🛏🍴).

🏃 LEISURE ACTIVITIES

Domaine de Loisirs du Surgié – Chemin Moulin Surgie. ✆05 65 34 59 00. Open Jul–Aug, 11am–10pm exc Sun and Wed, 2–7pm. This large (14ha/34.5-acre) outdoor watersports and leisure area is on the banks of the River Célé to the northeast of Figeac.

🛒 SHOPPING

Market – The town's weekly market is held on Saturdays (the largest one is the last Saturday of the month). Evening markets are held on Thursdays in July and August.

Grottes de

Foissac★

Discovered in 1959, Foissac Caves have a total of 8km/5mi of galleries. The underground stream, which flows through the caves, is a tributary of the Lot, joining it near Balaguier.

VISIT

Note the gleaming white stalactites and the lovely rock formations in the Obelisk Chamber (Salle de l'Obélisque); and the reflections, the stalagmites and ivory tower-like formations in the Michel Roques Gallery. In one gallery, known as the Cave-in Gallery (Salle de

- 🦽 **Michelin Map:** 338: E-3
- ▶ **Location:** 15km/9mi S of Figeac.
- 🔍 **Don't Miss:** The view of the town, the Pistoule promontory and the Lot valley from the Pech de l'Impernal.
- 🕐 **Opening:** Guided tours 10am–11.30am, 2pm–6pm. 🌙Nov-Mar, by appointment. Closed 1 Jan, 1 and 11 Nov, and 25 Dec. 👛7.50€. ✆05 65 64 77 04. www.grotte-de-foissac.com.

l'*Éboulement*), there is a roof covered with round mushroom-like formations, thus proving that the stalactites were in the gallery well before earthquakes changed the aspect of the cave. Bulbous stalactites known as onions (*Oignons*) are also worth noting.

These caves were inhabited during the Copper Age (2700-1900 BC), when they were used as quarries, caves and a cemetery, as evidenced throughout: the hearth, copper utensils and large rounded pieces of pottery. Also visible are human skeletons, some of which are accompanied by offerings suggesting some sort of ritual burial, and the imprint of a child's foot, fixed here in the clay 4 000 years ago. A park illustrates the daily life of Copper-Age man.

Grottes de Foissac

J. Damase/ MICHELIN

Luzech
and Lower Reaches of the Lot

Luzech has grown up on the narrowest part of a tongue of land almost completely encircled by a loop in the River Lot. The isthmus at this point is some 100m/110yd wide.

The town is crowned by the old castle keep. To the north lies the Roman city of Impernal and to the south the Pistoule Promontory, washed by the waters of the river as it sweeps round the bend. A reservoir has been formed by the construction of a dam upstream from the peninsula, and a water sports centre has been set up there (*boat tours available*).

A BIT OF HISTORY
Pech de l'Impernal

A natural defensive position, this rise has been inhabited since prehistoric times; Gauls, recognising its potential, transformed the plateau into a powerful stronghold. A citadel was constructed during the Middle Ages and Luzech became the seat of one of the four baronies of Quercy. Much coveted by the English during the Hundred Years War it nevertheless resisted all attacks and became an important central strong-

- ▶ **Population:** 1 737
- ⏱ **Michelin Map:** Michelin local map 337: D-5
- ▤ **Info:** Maison des Consuls - rue de la Ville ✆05 65 20 17 27. www.ville-luzech.fr.
- ▶ **Location:** Luzech is situated 27km/17mi west of Cahors.

hold. During the Wars of Religion, it remained a faithful bastion of Catholicism under the bishops of Cahors.

WALKING TOUR
▷ *Start from the top of the Imperial.*

Viewpoint★
From the top of the Pech de l'Impernal, the view encompasses Luzech clustered at its foot, as well as the Promontoire de la Pistoule, slicing through the wide alluvial plain like a ship's prow, and the Lot winding between rich and fertile crops.

▷ *Follow the marked path (GR) down to the town.*

Keep
Entrance via place des Consuls.

The entrance used to be through the small, pointed-arched doorway opening onto the first floor. From the terrace of the 12C keep there is a bird's-eye view of the brown-tiled roofs of the town, tucked amid meadows and crops with a row of hills along the horizon.

Old Town
In the old district known as the *faubourg du Barry*, picturesque alleyways link rue du Barry-del-Valat with the quays.
Around place des Consuls, on the other side of place du Canal, several examples of medieval architecture are still to be seen: Penitents' Chapel (12C), Capsol Gateway with its brick pointed arch and Consuls' House with its elegant twinned windows.

MUSÉE ARCHÉOLOGIQUE ARMAND-VIRÉ
Maison des Consuls - Rue de la Ville
🕐*Open Daily exc Sun Jul–Aug, 10am–1pm, 2–6pm, Sept–Jun: daily except Sun 10am–1pm, 2–5pm.Oct–Apr Mon, Wed and Thur 10am–1pm, 2–5pm*🕐*Closed Christmas to Jan and holidays.* 🔖*3€.*
📞*05 65 20 17 27.*
Established in the fine vaulted cellar of the old Consuls' House (13C), now the tourist office, the museum retraces the history of the site of Luzech. The items displayed include the exceptional **scale model of the Column of Trajan**★, and an unusual Gallo-Roman hinged spoon, of bronze and iron.

EXCURSIONS
Notre-Dame-de-l'Île
1.2km/0.8mi S along the D 23.
The chapel, set in a calm landscape of vineyards and orchards against a backdrop of hills along the course of the Lot, stands at the furthest point of the isthmus. This Flamboyant Gothic sanctuary is a pilgrimage centre, dating to the 13C.

Église de Cambayrac
8km/5mi S along the D 23 and D 67.
The hamlet has an odd-looking church identifiable from afar by a belfry-wall with a shape like a French policeman's hat. Inside, the Romanesque apse and the side chapels were recovered in the 17C with an unusual marble and stucco decor in the Classical style

🚗 DRIVING TOUR

LOWER REACHES OF THE LOT
85km/52mi round-trip – allow one day
As the Lot flows between the tall limestone cliffs of the Quercy causse, its thousand curves provide a never-ending variety of magnificent views. Follow the south bank for views of the valley.

▷ *Drive W out of Luzech along the D 8.*

Albas
From its past as the seat of the bishops of Cahors, this small town has retained ruins of the Episcopal castle and a network of narrow streets with old houses.

▷ *Continue along the D 8.*

Anglars-Juillac
A Crucifixion adorns the church's Renaissance doorway.

▷ *Continue along the D 8 and turn left on to the D 50, 2.5km/1.5mi farther on.*

Bélaye
Once the fief of the bishops of Cahors, Bélaye stands on top of a hill. An extensive **view**★ of the Lot Valley unfolds from the top of the spur and from the upper square of this little village.

▷ *Rejoin the D 8 and turn left.*

Grézels
Overlooking the village is the feudal **Château de La Coste** (🕐*open Jul 10-Aug, lecture tour (1hr 30min) 4pm* 🔖*2€; wine museum: 3-6pm.* 🔖*2€.* 📞*05 65 21 34 18*), which was razed and rebuilt on several occasions. The bishops of Cahors, whose fief extended over the Lot Valley from Cahors to Puy-l'Évêque, built a stronghold here to mark the limits of their territory.

DE BONAGUIL AUX ARQUES

During the Hundred Years War, it was transformed into a fortress. Severely damaged and then restored in the 14C and 16C, it was abandoned after the Revolution. The curtain wall and corner towers are the castle's oldest parts.

▷ *Continue along the D 8.*

The Pont de Courbenac offers the best overall **view** of Puy-l'Évêque (& *see below*).

▷ *Continue along the D 8 to Touzac, cross the river and turn left onto the D 911 then right to Cavagnac. Drive N to the D 673, turn left then right 2.5km/1.5mi farther on (D 158).*

Château de Bonaguil★★
& See Château de BONAGUIL.

▷ *Return to Couvert (D 158) then turn left to St-Martin-le-Redon 500m/547yd farther on.*

Admire the **view**★ of Bonaguil Castle in its lovely green setting (*parking*).

St-Martin-le-Redon
This charming village is known for the St-Martial mineral spring, reputed to cure skin ailments.

▷ *Leave St-Martin on the D 673 towards Gourdon.*

Montcabrier
The *bastide* was founded in 1297 by Guy de Cabrier and was granted a charter of franchises by Philip the Fair. Overlooking the square, several old houses are laid out in the regular pattern of the original plan. The church, partly rebuilt in the 14C, has a Flamboyant doorway (restored) surrounded by a fine open-bayed bell-tower. Inside, a plain 14C statue of St Louis, the parish's patron saint, is surrounded by ex-votos. This statue was the object of a local pilgrimage.

▷ *Drive SE along the D 68 and turn right onto the D 58 1km/0.6mi farther on.*

Duravel
The 11C **church** (*keys available from the tourist office*) has historiated capitals decorating the chancel. There is an archaic crypt supported by columns with rough-hewn capitals. The bodies of St Hilarion, St Poémon and St Agathon lie buried at the back of the apse.
The ostension, or solemn exhibition of relics to the faithful, is held every five years.

▷ *Drive S along the D 911.*

Puy-l'Évêque
⟜*Guided tours of the church by advance appointment at the church office,*

pl. du Rampeau, L'Abbé Charpentier, 46700 Puy-l'Évêque.

This small town, which took its present name when it came under the lordship of the bishops of Cahors, occupies one of the most picturesque sites in the valley downstream from Cahors. From the bridge into town, admire the old houses in golden stone.

The **church** was built on the north-east side of the town, at the furthest point in the defence system of which it was itself a part. In front of the church stands a massive belfry-porch flanked by a turret and buttresses. The magnificent doorway is surmounted by a pediment adorned with statues. The nave was built in the 14C and 15C and ends in a polygonal apse. In the churchyard there are many old tombs, and on the left of the church stands a wayside cross ornamented with archaic-style sculpture.

▷ *Walk back towards place du Rampeau and place du Mercadiel. Beyond Grande-Rue is a maze of twisting lanes clinging to the promontory.*

The **keep**, all that remains of the Episcopal castle, dates back to the 13C.

From the **Esplanade de la Truffière**, next to the keep, admire the terraces and hillsides covered with vines, and the wide alluvial valley carpeted with fields.

▷ *Drive N out of Puy-l'Évêque along the D 28.*

Martignac

This small village boasts a fine rustic **church**, built of yellow stone and surmounted by a timber-framed bell-tower. The nave and chancel are decorated with 15C frescoes: realistic representations of the capital sins contrast with scenes depicting the Coronation of the Virgin Mary and the arrival of the chosen in Paradise, led by St Michael and welcomed by St Peter.

▷ *Return to Puy-l'Évêque then follow the D 911 back on the north bank.*

ADDRESSES

🏠 STAY

🛏 🛏 **Chambre d'Hôte La Maison Rose** *Niaudon 46220 Prayssac – 17.5k/11m W of Luzech on the D9 and D911 to Prayssac and 3.5k/2m N on the D67 N and D172. Tel: 05 65 20 08 27. www.lamaisonrosebb.com. Reserv. Required.* A former tobacco farmhouse in the quiet hamlet of Niaudon set in over 15 acres of pasture and woodlands. Four charming and newly refurbished rooms. Vegetarian and special dietary req. catered for. Swimming pool.

🛏 🛏 🛏 **Chambre d'hôte Château de la Coste** – *46700 Grezels. 16km/10mi W of Luzech on the D 8. ℘05 65 21 34 18. Closed Sep-Jun ⚑ Reserv. required. 4 rooms.* This B&B occupies an authentic medieval château in a delightful spot above the Lot Valley. The guestrooms, varying in size, each have their own individual feel.

🍽 EAT

🍴 **Auberge Imhotep** – *La Rivière Haute - 46140 Albas - 4km/2.5mi W of Luzech on the D 8 - ℘05 65 30 70 91. Closed Sun eve and Mon - reserv. recommended.* Imhotep is best-known as the great architect of ancient Egypt. But he also invented the method of gavage - force-feeding of geese to yield foie gras. This and other regional dishes are available, as well as a vegetarian menu.

🍴 🍴 🍴 **Le Gindreau** – *46150 St-Médard. 8.5km/5mi NE of Castelfranc via the D 911 and D 5. ℘05 65 36 22 27. http://perso. orange.fr/le.gindreau. Closed 5-18 Mar, 22 Oct-14 Nov, Mon and Tue - reserv. required Sun and public holidays.* Nestled among the chestnut trees on top of a hill, this restaurant was once the village school. The dining room is cosy, with its attractive woodwork and paintings on the walls. Elegant cuisine with a contemporary twist.

🛒 SHOPPING

Markets – *In Duravel*: Fête de Village Jul 13–14. Wine and regional produce fair weekend of August 15. *In Prayssac*: Pays du Lot farmers' market, Sun mornings in July and August and all day fair 3rd Tue of month. Foire des Rameaux (Palm Sunday) and Flea market last weekend June or first weekend July.

Château de Chambert – *Marc and Joël Delgoulet, Les Hauts-Coteaux - 46700 Floressas. ℘05 65 31 95 75. www.chateau dechambert.com. Open Mon-Fri, 8.30am-12.30pm and 2pm-6.30pm, Sat 10am–12.30pm and 3pm–6.30pm (in Summer telephone to make an appointment).* The wines produced here have won a number of prestigious awards. Tours of the cellars and tastings available.

Clos Triguedina – *Jean-Luc Baldès, 46700 Vire-sur-Lot. ℘05 65 21 30 81. www.jlbaldes.com. Open Mon-Fri, 9am–noon and 2–6pm.* The Baldès family is proud of its eight centuries of wine-growing on this 60ha/150-acre property. Their Clos Triguedina wine is considered one of the best wines produced in the Quercy. Visits of the cellars, winery and family museum.

🏃 LEISURE ACTIVITIES

Boat trips on the Lot – ♿ *Departures from the Base Nautique de Caix - Jul and Aug, 4.15-6.30pm. ℘05 65 20 18 19.* Cruises last 1hr 30min.

Marcilhac-sur-Célé

Marcilhac is built in the centre of an amphitheatre of cliffs in the enchanting Célé Valley. Interesting old houses surround the ruins of a Benedictine abbey.

A BIT OF HISTORY
An eventful past

In the 11C the modest sanctuary of Rocamadour was under the care of Marcilhac Abbey, which let it fall into ruins. Noticing this negligence some monks from Tulle installed themselves in the sanctuary. However, in 1166 the discovery of the body of St Amadour turned the sanctuary into a rich and famous pilgrimage centre. Marcilhac recalled its rights and expelled the Tulle monks. Soon afterwards the abbot of Tulle threw out the Marcilhac monks and again occupied Rocamadour.

Lawsuits followed and the bishop of Cahors, the papal legate, the archbishop of Bourges and even the Pope himself were all called on to give judgement, but avoided reaching a decision. Finally, after 100 years of squabbling, Marcilhac accepted an indemnity of 3 000 sols and relinquished its claim to Rocamadour.

▶ **Population:** 199
◉ **Michelin Map:** Michelin local map 337: G-4 – Local map see FIGEAC.
▯ **Info:** Maison du Roy - Le Bourg. ℘05 65 40 68 44/ 05 65 34 06 25.
◐ **Location:** 47km/29.5 W of Cahors via D653, D17 & D14.
◉ **Don't Miss:** The ruins of the Benedictine abbey.

Marcilhac Abbey flourished until the 14C, but during the Hundred Years War it was virtually destroyed. After the Reformation, the abbey, fell into the hands of the Hébrards of St-Sulpice and the monks were expelled. The abbey church was secularised in 1764.

OLD ABBEY TOUR

Romanesque section - The west porch and the first three bays of the nave are open to the sky. They are flanked by a tall square tower, which was probably fortified in the 14C. A round-arched door on the south side is topped with sculpture forming a **tympanum** depicting the Last Judgement: Christ in Majesty, with figures on either side thought to represent the sun and moon, appears above St Peter, St Paul and two thick-set angels with open wings.

◯ *Go through this doorway and enter the church to the right.*

Gothic section - This part of the church, closed to the west from the fourth bay on, dates from the 15C and is built in the Flamboyant style. A Baroque stall decorated with the Hébrard family crest has a fabulous **misericord** carved with the head of an angel. A chapel on the left of the chancel has 15C frescoes: Christ giving Blessing with the Twelve Apostles; under each Apostle is his name and a characteristic phrase. The coat of arms in the centre of each triad is that of the Hébrards of St-Sulpice.

◯ *Leave the church, turn right (from the second Romanesque bay) onto the path to the chapter-house.*

Chapter house - The 12C building has very delicate Romanesque capitals alternately made of grey-blue limestone and rose-coloured stalagmite stone.

◯ *Go towards an esplanade shaded by plane trees; a round tower marks the site of the abbot's house. By the banks of the Célé (right), the line of the rampart wall is interrupted by a postern. Return to the Romanesque ruins.*

Montpezat-de-Quercy★
and around

On the edge of Limogne Causse, this picturesque small Lower Quercy town, with its covered arcades and old half-timbered or stone houses, owes its fame to the 14C collegiate church of St Martin and to its artistic treasures.

A BIT OF HISTORY
The Des Prés family
Five members of this family from Montpezat became eminent prelates. Pierre Des Prés, cardinal of Préneste (now Palestrina in Italy), founded the collegiate church of St Martin, which he consecrated in 1344; his nephew, Jean Des Prés, who died in 1351, was bishop of Coïmbra in Portugal and then of Castres in France.
Three other members of the family were consecrated bishops of Montauban: Jean Des Prés (1517-39), who gave his famous Flemish tapestries to the collegiate church at Montpezat, Jean de Lettes (1539-56) and Jacques Des Prés (1556-89). Jacques was a warrior-bishop, and a committed persecutor of the Huguenots. He fought for 25 years,

▸ **Population:** 1413
◉ **Michelin Map:** Michelin local map 337: E-6
▤ **Info:** Bd des Fossés. ℰ05 63 02 05 55. www.montpezat-de-quercy.fr
◯ **Location:** Montpezat-de-Quercy is located 29km/18mi south of Cahors and 32km/20mi north of Montauban.
◉ **Don't Miss:** The 16C tapestries in the Collégiale St-Martin.

his diocese being one of the most ardent Protestant strongholds, and was killed in an ambush at Lalbenque, some 15km/10mi from Montpezat.

TOWN
The *bastide* is laid out in tiers above the ramparts. The central place de la Résistance is surrounded by arcades and half-timbered houses. The 19C town hall replaces an older building.
To the north, the 12C cloisters of the former Couvent des Ursulines were remodelled in the 20C and now house a school.

COLLÉGIALE ST-MARTIN

This church, dedicated to St Martin of Tours, was built in 1337 by an architect from the papal court at Avignon. It is comparatively small in size and has many of the characteristics of a Languedoc building.

Nave – Unity, simplicity and harmony make a striking impression as visitors enter the nave. The side chapels contain several notable religious objects: a 15C Virgin of Mercy in polychrome sandstone (first chapel on the south side), three 15C-16C Nottingham alabaster altarpiece panels depicting the Nativity, the Resurrection and the Ascension (second chapel on the south side) and 15C wooden caskets with gold inlay work (fourth chapel on the north side).

Tapestries★★ – These 16C tapestries were specially made to fit the sanctuary. Woven in the north of France and consisting of five panels, each divided into three pictures, depict the best-known historic and legendary events in the life of St Martin, including the dividing of his cloak. The excellent condition of these tapestries, the vividness and richness of their colouring and the fact that they are still hanging in the exact spot for which they were designed all contribute to their outstanding interest.

Recumbent figures★ – Although the body of Cardinal Pierre Des Prés lies beneath the paving before the chancel, his statue and tomb carved in Carrara marble were placed on the right of the chancel entrance in 1778. Opposite, making a pair, lies the recumbent figure of his nephew Jean Des Prés, which is a masterpiece of funerary statuary.

EXCURSIONS
Église de Saux

5km/3mi N. Leave Montpezat-de-Quercy along the D 20 towards Cahors, then turn left 2km/1.2mi farther on.
Once the centre of a large parish, this church now stands isolated in the middle of the woods. The plain interior consists of three domed bays decorated with beautiful 14C and 15C **frescoes**. The best preserved are in the chancel and show Christ in Majesty with the

J. Damase/MICHELIN

Tapestry depicting St Martin dividing his cloak, Collégiale St-Martin

symbols of the four Evangelists, the Crucifixion and scenes from the Childhood of Jesus.

Molières

13km/8mi W along the D 20.
The village grew during the 13C when Alphonse de Poitiers made it into a *bastide*. The covered market has gone, but Molières has retained its characteristic town plan and part of its ramparts, the bulk of which was destroyed during the Revolution.
Two 19C wrought-iron footbridges linking the ramparts to some houses testify to the town's past prosperity. Note the brick-built arch with a bell hanging from it: it stands to the north, where the clock tower used to be.

ADDRESSES

surrounding countryside. The spacious rooms have been superbly decorated by the owner - a painter and former theatre set designer.

℘/ EAT

⊜⊜ **Hotel Restaurant Orsay** – *29 rue Roger Salengro, 82000 Montauban Sud. Tue–Fri, noon–2pm and Mon–Sat, 7.30– 10pm. Closed Sun, 1 week in May, second and third weeks of Aug and Dec 23 –Jan 8. ℘05 63 66 06 66. www.hotel-restaurant-orsay.com.* Reputed to be the best restaurant in Montauban. The Chef of this refined yet unpretentious hundred year old hotel, Maître Cuisinier Alain Blanc, offers inventive regional cuisine and a splendid dessert trolley.

Grotte du Pech Merle★★★

Prehistoric people performed religious rites in this cave, which was only rediscovered thousands of years later in 1922. Not only is its natural decoration interesting, there are also wall paintings and carvings that are of great documentary value to prehistorians.

- ⓖ **Michelin Map:** Michelin local map 337: F-4 – Local map see CAHORS.
- ⓒ **Location:** The cave is located 7km/4.5mi north of St-Cirq-Lapopie and 32km/20mi east of Cahors.
- ⓐ **Don't Miss:** A guided tour inside the cave.

A BIT OF HISTORY
The underground explorers
Two boys of 15 and 16 were the heroes of the Pech Merle Cave rediscovery. Inspired by the expeditions and discoveries made throughout the region by Abbé Lemozi, the priest from Cabrerets who was also a prehistorian and speleologist, the boys explored a small fault and after several hours their efforts were rewarded by the sight of wonderful paintings.

Abbé Lemozi, who soon afterwards explored the cave scientifically, recognised the importance of the underground sanctuary. In 1949 the discovery of a new chamber led to the finding of the original opening through which men had entered the cave about 16 000 to 20 000 years ago.

Prehistoric painting in Grotte du Pech-Merle

E. Larribère/MICHELIN

PECH-MERLE CAVE
(HORIZONTAL PROFILE)

0   100 m

Entrée naturelle   OSSUAIRE

Silhouettes de chevaux

SALLE PRÉHISTORIQUE

Accès primitif

GALERIE DE L'OURS   **Tête d'Ours**

Chapelle des mammouths

SALLE DE COMBEL

Plafond des hiéroglyphes

Empreintes de pas   SALLE DES DISQUES

CAVE

🕐1hr 45min 🚶‍♂️Open early-Apr to early Nov, guided tour (1hr); tickets on sale from 9.30am–noon and 1.30–5pm. Access limited to 700 visitors per day (in July and August it is advisable to book 3 days in advance). 💶7.50€, combined ticket with the Musée Amédée-Lémozi. 📞05 65 31 27 05. www.pechmerle.com.

In addition to the interest it offers lovers of speleology who can marvel at the caverns of vast size communicating with each other through wide openings and decorated with beautiful concretions, the Pech Merle Cave offers prehistorians the sight of highly advanced paintings and engravings and material traces of prehistoric man's sojourn there.

The upper level of the **Chapelle des Mammouths** (Chapel of Mammoths or Black frieze) is decorated with drawings of bison and mammoths outlined in black and forming a frieze 7m/23ft long by 3m/10ft high.

The **Salle des Disques** is patterned with many strange concretions that look like discs. The footprints made by a prehistoric individual can be seen, petrified forever in the once wet clay of a *gour* (natural dam).

Further on the **Galerie des Ours** contains huge, impressive columns, eccentrics with delicate protuberances that defy the laws of gravity and cave pearls, with colours ranging from shining white pure calcite to red-ochre (clay and iron oxide in the limestone).

Beyond the Salle Rouge, visitors go down a narrow passageway, which contains an engraving of a bear's head, to the lower level of the **prehistoric gallery**, where one wall is decorated with the **silhouettes of two horses**, with dots patterning them and the surface around them, mysterious symbols and outlined hand prints, known as negative hands. These prints were made by stencilling in different pigments around the hands placed flat against the rock. The horses are depicted with distorted silhouettes (similar to those at Lascaux): a huge body and a tiny head. These prints and the roof of hieroglyphics once decorated a sanctuary older than that of the Chapel of Mammoths.

In the last cave to be visited, **Salle de Combel**, are the **bones of cave bears**.

Musée Amédée-Lémozi

♿🕐Same opening times and charges as the Grotte du Pech-Merle (combined ticket). 📞05 65 31 23 33.

This is a research and information centre on prehistory in Quercy. There is an attractive and informative display of bones, tools, weapons, utensils and works of art from 160 different prehistoric sites, dating from the Lower Paleolithic Era to the Iron Age. The visit ends with a film on Paleolithic art in Quercy.

Le Quercy Blanc★

Region

The region known as Quercy Blanc, so-called because of the white colour of the chalky soil, is characterised by low, long plateaux, arranged in rows (*serres*) with narrow, fertile valleys between them. The landscape and architecture are similar to that of the neighbouring Garonne region; red brick constructions, nearly flat roofs covered in pale-pink Roman tile. Vineyards (the noble Chasselas variety is grown in Moissac), plum trees, peach trees and melons thrive on the sunny hillsides; tobacco, sunflower and corn grow on the valley floors.

🚗 DRIVING TOURS

1 CHURCHES AND MILLS
60km/37mi round-trip from Castelnau-Montratier – allow one day

Castelnau-Montratier
Get a town map at the tourist office.
This hilltop *bastide* was founded in the 13C by Ratier, lord of Castelnau. It replaced a small village, Castelnau-de-Vaux, which was destroyed by Simon de

One of three mills at Castelnau-Montratier

S. Sauvignier/MICHELIN

😊 **Michelin Map:** Michelin local map 337: C/E-5/7

📍 **Location:** Between the Lot and Tarn valleys.

🕐 **Timing:** Allow two full days to explore this scenic region.

Montfort in 1214 at the time of the Albigensian Crusade. The town "**square**" is in the form of a triangle, surrounded by covered arcades and old houses. Note the **Église St-Martin** standing right at the end of the promontory. North of the promontory are three **windmills**, one working. These mills with rotating caps were once common in Quercy.

▷ *Leave Castelnau S along the D 659 and turn left 3km/1.9mi farther on.*

Église de Russac
The church has an oven-vaulted Romanesque east end decorated with carved modillions; the original north doorway was walled up. Inside, note the 16C fresco in the apse, particularly the central panel depicting St George slaying the dragon.

▷ *Rejoin the D 659, drive 1km/0.6mi towards Castelnau and turn right onto the D 26, then left onto the D 214 6km/3.7mi farther on.*

Flaugnac
This once fortified village occupied a picturesque position overlooking the Lupte Valley. In the 13C, a castle stood at the end of the promontory.

▷ *Leave Flaugnac along the ridge, turn left onto the D 19 then right onto the D 64 6km/3.7mi farther on.*

Moulin de Boisse
🎫 2€ 📞 05 65 21 84 39.
There are demonstrations five times a year in this well-preserved mill (built 1669).

▷ *Continue on the D 64 then the D 55.*

Montcuq

Main town of a castellany to which Raymond VI, count of Toulouse, granted a charter of customary law in the 12C. Montcuq was the centre of many a bloody battle during the Albigensian Crusade, the Hundred Years War and the Wars of Religion. All that remains of this once fortified village is a tall castle keep (12C), on a hillock overlooking the Barguelonnette river and a few old houses between place des Consuls (near the town hall) and place de la Halle-aux-Grains.

▷ *Leave Montcuq NW on D4, then D55.*

Château de Lastours

♿*See CHALUS, Excursion.*
The casle's towers on the defensive wall overlook the Séoune Valley. The main building is 16C.

▷ *Turn back then right onto the D 228 1km/0.6mi farther on.*

Ste-Croix

This village has retained many old houses nestling round the imposing church. Note the Romanesque doorway which once gave access to the cemetery.

▷ *Continue along the D 228; left on the D 953 to Montcuq. Drive S out of Montcuq along the D 28 and turn right onto the D 45 2km/1.2mi farther on.*

Église de Rouillac

The 12C church was remodelled in the 15C; several chapels and a bell-tower were added in the 19C. In the flat east end, there are traces of Romanesque frescoes depicting the Passion.

▷ *Continue on D 45; turn left to St-Laurent-de-Lolmie; drive on for 2km/1.2mi, turn left on D 28, left again on D 57, then follow D 104.*

Moulin de Brousse

🕐*Visits by prior arrangement.*
🎫*No charge.* ☎*05 65 21 95 81.*
This watermill dating from the 13C has been worked by a family of millers since 1917: locally grown wheat is ground in the mill.

▷ *Turn right to Castelnau-Montratier.*

② PAYS DE SERRES

▷ *70km/31mi round-trip from Lauzerte – allow one day*

Lauzerte

This *bastide* was built in 1241 by the count of Toulouse and was occupied at one time by the English.

Upper Town

The pale-grey stone houses with their almost flat roofs are clustered round the church of St Bartholomew and a square, place des Cornières. This square, named after its covered arcades (*cornières*), still has one half-timbered house.

Promenade de l'Éveillé, in the once wealthy middle-class district, has retained elegant residences, some half-timbered, some Gothic in style with twin windows and some Renaissance with mullioned windows. The ground floors of several 13C and 14C houses in rue de la Garrigue and rue de la Gendarmerie were occupied by busy shops.

The Via podiensis, which starts from Le Puy-en-Velay, runs through Lauzerte on its way to Santiago de Compostela. The landscaped **Jardin du Pèlerin** (Pilgrim's garden) laid out beneath the barbican is a kind of outdoor snakes and ladders (*ask for the dice at the tourist office*).

▷ *Leave Lauzerte travelling S along D 2; left on D 953, then right on D 81 and right again towards Sainte-Amans-de-Pellagal 2km/1.2mi farther on.*

Chartron

This place boasts a fine square dovecot built on pillars. These are topped with a kind of cap (*une capel*) designed to prevent various rodents from getting in. The half-timbered dovecot is covered with flat tiles and surmounted by a lantern.

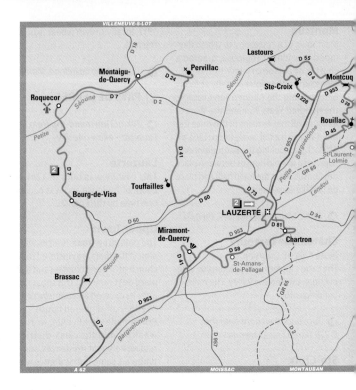

▷ *Turn left then immediately right 1km/0.6mi farther on and continue to Ste-Amans, then Miramont.*

Miramont-de-Quercy

From the watch-path of this small village, there is a fine valley view.

▷ *On leaving Miramont, turn left onto the D 41 then right onto the D 953; drive on for 8km/5mi then turn right onto the D 7.*

Château de Brassac

🕐 *Open Jul–Sept, guided tour of the château (1hr), 10am–8pm; Apr–Jun, 10am–noon and 2–8pm; Oct–Mar, by prior arrangement.* 🕐 *Closed Mon.* 💶 *4€.* 📞 *05 63 94 59 67.*

The 12C fortress, towers above the Séoune Valley. During the Hundred Years War, the stronghold fell successively into English and French hands. Besieged by Protestant troops during the Wars of Religion, burned down during the Revolution, Brassac was aban-

doned in the 19C. A fixed stone bridge, which replaced the original drawbridge, leads into the bailey. (*not open to the public*).

▷ *Continue on D 7 to Bourg-de-Visa.*

Bourg-de-Visa

The wrought-iron structure of a covered market surrounded by arcaded houses stands in the centre of the town hall square. A few ruins are all that remains of the castle. Note the dovecot tower.

▷ *Continue along the D 7 and turn left after 10km/6.2mi.*

Roquecor

This village, perched on a rocky spur, towers above the Petite Séoune. Walk along rue des Coutelets, which starts opposite the town hall; the street is lined with old houses.

Continue along rue du Barry and bear left towards the **wash-house**, past the ruined ramparts of the old town, to the 19C neo-Gothic church. Rue des Colombiers skirts the ramparts and rue des Anciens-Fours leads back to the town hall.

▷ *Drive NE out of Montaigu on D 24 and turn left 2km/1.2mi farther on.*

Pervillac

This hamlet boasts a Romanesque **church** (*ask for keys at the Maison Fournier foie gras and wine shop, ℘05 63 94 39 20) remodelled in the 19C, which houses well-preserved 15C murals depicting hell, purgatory and the virtues.

▷ *Turn back, then right to Montaigu and first left (D 41) to Touffailles.*

Touffailles

The late-15C **Église St-Georges** overlooks the village (*on the right past the town hall*). The nave vaulting is decorated with 12 scenes depicting Christ's childhood and Passion. ◷ *Guided tour by prior arrangement at the town hall, Mon, Tue and Thu, 2–6pm, Fri, 2–4pm.*

▷ *Continue along the D 41 and turn left onto the D 60 then right onto the D 73 leading back to Lauzerte..*

reach a troglodytic site known as the **Roc de la Nobis**.

▷ *Drive N out of Roquecor and turn right onto the D 7.*

Montaigu-de-Quercy

The village nestles round a promontory on which a castle once stood. Follow rue des Frères-Quémeré to place de la Mairie: note the wash-house and

ADDRESSES

♀/ EAT

◲◲ **Chez Bernadette** – 82190 Miramont-de-Quercy. 7km/4.3mi S of Lauzerte on the D 953. ℘05 63 94 65 57. Closed 2 weeks in Oct, Tue eve and Wed. Reserv. recommended. Enjoy a relaxing drink in the shade of the catalpa trees on the terrace of this typical country inn.

◲ **Le Quercy** – Fg d'Auriac - 82190 Miramont-de-Quercy - ℘05 63 94 66 36. Closed Mon. Popular with locals, this

bright and welcoming dining room offers regional produce and a few rooms.

⊨ SHOPPING

Markets – In addition to local Sunday markets around the area, in summer there are markets on Wed in Castelnau-Montratier and Thu in Montcuq.

EVENTS

National Windmill Day – Visits and activities at the Moulin de Boisse on 15 August. For further information, contact the tourist office. ℘05 65 21 84 39.

St-Cirq-Lapopie★★

St-Cirq-Lapopie (*Cirq* pronounced *Sear*), faces a semicircle of white cliffs and is itself perched (80m/262ft) on a rocky escarpment that drops vertically to the left bank of the Lot; it is a remarkable setting★. The present name of the site commemorates the martyrdom of the young St Cyr, killed with his mother in Asia Minor during the reign of Diocletian. It is said his relics were brought back by St Amadour. The La Popies, local lords in the Middle Ages, gave their name to the castle built on the cliff's highest point and, by extension, to the village that grew up at its foot.

A BIT OF HISTORY

A contested stronghold – This rock commanding the valley has probably tempted would-be occupiers since Gallo-Roman times.

The history of the fortress is a long series of sieges and obscure battles until 1580 when Henri de Navarre, the future Henri IV, ordered that the walls of the valiant fortress be knocked down.

▶ **Population:** 215
♿ **Michelin Local Map:** 337: G-5 – Local map *see CAHORS.*
ℹ **Info:** Place du Sombral. ℘05 65 31 29 06. www.saint-cirqlapopie.com.
◐ **Location:** 34km/21.5mi W of Cahors via D653 & D662. For a wonderful view of the River Lot, head to the top of La Popie Rock.
◷ **Timing:** Allow a full day to explore the Célé and Lot valleys.

The end of a craft – St-Cirq-Lapopie had a strong guild of woodturners dating back to the Middle Ages.

Until the late 19C, there were a considerable number of craftsmen still to be seen working their primitive lathes; their industry added a colourful note to the old-fashioned village alleyways.

Their shopfronts set small and large arched openings side by side. Nowadays there is only one woodworker left in St-Cirq.

St-Cirq-Lapopie rises above the Lot

S. Sauvignier/MICHELIN

VILLAGE

It is a perennial pleasure to wander along narrow, steeply sloping streets lined with houses with lovely brown-tiled roofs. The corbelled façades and exposed beams of some of the houses are further ornamented with Gothic windows, or bays with mullioned windows in the Renaissance style. Most of the houses have been carefully restored by artists, particularly painters and craftsmen who have been attracted by the beauty of St-Cirq-Lapopie and the Lot Valley. Among the most famous are the writer André Breton, who lived on place du Carol in the old sailors' inn, and the painters Foujita, Man Ray, Henri Martin and Pierre Daura; the latter lived in the house with carved beams (his own work) in ruelle de la Fourdonne.

La Popie – Take the path that starts on the right of the town hall (mairie), to reach the castle ruins and the highest part of the cliff. From the cliff top (telescope), on which once stood the keep of La Popie Fortress, there is a remarkable **view**★★ right over the village of

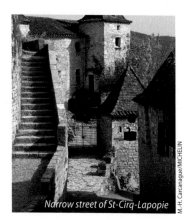
Narrow street of St-Cirq-Lapopie

M.-H. Carcanague/MICHELIN

St-Cirq, with the church clinging to the cliff face, to a bend in the River Lot, encircling a patchwork of arable fields and meadows delineated by poplars, and to the north, the foothills that border the Gramat Causse.

Fortified church – Village centre. This 15C sanctuary stands on a rock terrace overlooking the Lot. A squat belfry-tower, flanked by a round turret, stands at the front end.

ADDRESSES

🏠 STAY

🍽️🍽️ **Les Gabarres** – *Tour de Four. 2km E by D8.* ☎*05 65 30 24 57.* Modern hotel located on the banks of the Lot, at the foot of a picturesque hilltop village. Practical rooms and a swimming pool.

🍽️🍽️🍽️ **Auberge du Sombral "Aux Bonnes Choses"** ☎*05 65 31 26 08. www.lesombrai.com. Closed mid Nov–early Apr, Thur exc. Jul – Sept and evenings exc Fri and Sat. 8 rooms.* A country inn in the heart of the charming medieval hill village. Take a seat in one of the two dining rooms and admire the array of decorative objects. Country cooking. A few rooms available, under the eaves.

🍽️🍽️🍽️🍽️ **Hôtel La Pelissaria** – ☎*05 65 31 25 14. Closed 15 Oct–15 Apr. 10 rooms.* If you love the old stone houses of this region, check in to this hotel. The medieval building has a garden with an exceptional view, Nice rooms, small pool.

🍴 EAT

🍽️🍽️🍽️ **Le Gourmet Quercynois** – *R. de la Peyrolerie.* ☎*05 65 31 21 20.* A nice restaurant and an interesting wine museum have been set up in this village house owned by an oenologist. Naturally, the wine list is excellent and the choices go well with the regional cuisine on the menu. The decor of the dining room is a happy mixture of modern and old-fashioned styles.

🍽️🍽️ **L'Oustal** – ☎*05 65 31 20 17. loustal. restaurant@wanadoo.fr. Closed Mon and Dec–end Mar. Reserv. required.* This restaurant is small in size and big on quality. The menu features unpretentious regional dishes at reasonable prices. Afternoons, before dinner service starts, you can enjoy a drink on the terrace.

🏃 LEISURE ACTIVITIES

Kalapca – ☎*05 65 30 29 51 or 05 65 24 21 01. kalapca@wanadoo.fr.* On the River Lot and River Célé: recreational activities and canoe hire. Guide available.

Follow the course of the magnificent River Dordogne from near its source on Mont Dore in the Puy de Dôme département in the east, to just beyond Souillac and the border with the Périgord Noir in the west. To the north is the natural barrier of La Montagne in the Limousin, which is not really a mountain at all but a series of plateaux, including the Plateau de Millevaches and the Plateau de Gentioux, which stretch away into the distance. The Dordogne flows through a substantial part of the Corrèze département before entering the Lot to the south and curving inbetween some key sights of the Haut Quercy, such as Carennac, Martel, Souillac and St.Céré.

Starting in the far north east the Dordogne enters the Corrèze département north of Bort les Orgues and its enormous dam. It then flows along the border of the Corrèze with the Cantal département of the Auvergne.

The River turns west just beyond Bort passing the famous cliffs known as 'les Orgues' due to their similarity to the pipes of a huge organ. Turning south again the river is damned again at the Barage de Marèges still flowing along the border through magnificent gorges to yet another Barage at l'Aigle. The river turns west again through the Corrèze all the way to the Barage du Chastang until it reaches Argentat. From here the Dordogne used to be navigable and the Gabares took on their profitable loads of timber all the way to Bergerac.

The valley now opens up as the river flows sedately through Beaulieu sur Dordogne entering the Lot département on the way to its confluence with the Cère near the bastide town of Bretenoux.

To the south lies St Céré on the Rivière la Bave, a tributary of the Dordogne. Beyond here the river flows gently west through a wide valley past sleepy villages, several with much historical interest such as Carennac, until it reaches Souillac with its Byzantine inspired abbey church at the western boundary of the Lot.

Just north of the Dordogne Valley on the Causse de Martel can be found Martel itself with its seven towers and associations with the legendary Frankish ruler Charles Martel, the 'Hammer' of the Moors, and Henry Short Coat, the eldest son of King Henry II of England who died a rather unpleasant death here. It is well worth spending some time exploring this unspoiled market town.

🚗 DRIVING TOURS

DORDOGNE IN THE QUERCY★★

Round tour from Souillac – 85km/53mi – allow one day

Souillac★ 👋 *See SOUILLAC.*
▷ *Drive NE out of Souillac along the D 703.*

Martel★ 👋 *See MARTEL.*

▷ *Continue along the D 703 to Vayrac and turn N along the D 20 towards Brive-la-Gaillarde. Turn left onto the D 119 before leaving the town.*

Puy d'Issolud★

The plateau near Vayrac, of which the highest point is Puy d'Issolud with an altitude of 311m/1020ft, is bordered by steep cliffs overlooking little tributaries flowing into the Dordogne.

From the plateau there is an extensive **view**★ of the Dordogne.

Puy d'Issolud was surrounded, at the time of the Gauls, by such solid earth-works and dry-stone defences that it was one of the most redoubtable *oppida* of Quercy, and is said to have been the former **Uxellodunum**, site of the last Gaulish resistance to Caesar after Alésia. Some historians place Uxellodunum at

Capdenac or Luzech, but archaeological research suggests that it is more likely to be the Puy d'Issolud.

The battle, led by the Roman legionaries, was waged with unbelievable ferocity and, after a spring had been diverted through underground caverns, causing those defending Uxellodunum to believe that their gods had deserted them by cutting off their water supply, ended in another defeat for the Gauls.

▷ *Return to Vayrac*

Vayrac

Located in place Luctérius, the **Musée Uxellodunum** (🕐open Jul–Aug, 9am–noon and 3–6pm; 🕐closed Sun, public hols and the weekend after 15 Aug. ≈1€; ☎05 65 37 30 03) displays prehistoric and Gallo-Roman finds discovered in and around the Puy d'Issolud oppidum.

▷ *Continue on D 703 towards Puybrun. In Bétaille, turn right onto the D 20.*

Carennac★
👋 *See CARENNAC.*

▷ *Leave Carennac to the NW via the D 43 which runs alongside the south bank of the river.*

239

Beyond Carennac, the Dordogne cuts a channel between the Martel and Gramat *causses* before entering the beautiful area of the Montvalent Amphitheatre.

Floirac

A 14C keep is all that remains of the old fortifications. North of the village stands a lovely 15C chapel.

Cirque de Floirac★

The road is very picturesque, running for the most part beside the river, though sometimes running along a ledge above it. There are attractive views of the valley and the *causse* cliffs from every bend.

▷ *Take the D 140 towards Gluges then turn right on the D 32 after crossing the river.*

Belvédère de Copeyre★

There is a good **view**★ of the Dordogne, the Floirac Amphitheatre and Puy d'Issolud from a wayside cross standing on the edge of the cliff.

Gluges

This village lies in a beautiful **setting**★ beside the river at the foot of the cliffs.

▷ *Leave Gluges SW along the D 43 and continue along the D 23 carved out of the cliff.*

Creysse

The charming village of Creysse with pleasant, narrow streets, brown-tiled roofs, houses bedecked with climbing vines and flights of steps leading to their doors, lies at the foot of the rocky spur, on which stands a pre-Romanesque church, the former castle chapel, with its curious twin apses. The 12C church and the remains of the 15C castle are reached by a stony alleyway, which climbs sharply to a terrace. It is from a little square shaded by plane trees, near the war memorial, that you get the best overall view of the village.

▷ *Drive NW from Creysse along the D 114 and, in Sozy, turn left onto the D 15.*

Meyronne

From the bridge over the Dordogne, there is a pretty **view** of the river and the village – former home of the bishops of Tulle – with its charming Quercy houses built attractively into the cliffs.

▷ *Continue SE along the D 15 then turn right 1km/0.6mi farther on.*

Site du Moulin du Limon

The ruins of an old mill and a chasm overgrown with greenery form a charming setting.

Floirac

©bobroy20/Fotolia.com

Grottes de Lacave in black light

Grottes de Lacave

▶ *Return to Meyronne and turn left onto the D 23.*

The road subsequently follows the course of the Dordogne through beautiful countryside of rocks and cliffs, then crosses the River Ouysse near Lacave.

Grottes de Lacave★

Visits by guided tour only (1hr 20mins). Open Mar 10am–noon and 2pm–5pm, Apr–June 9.30am–noon and 2pm–6pm, Jul 9.30am–12.30pm and 1.30pm–6pm, Aug 1–25 9.30am–6pm, Aug 26–Sept 30 9.30am–noon and 2pm–5.30pm, Oct–early Nov 10am–noon and 2pm–5pm. Closed Nov school hols to mid-Mar. 7.80€. 05 65 37 87 03. www.grottes-de-lacave.com.
Near the valley of the Dordogne as it makes a deep cut through the Gramat Causse, a series of caves was discovered in 1902 by Armand Viré, a student of the geographer and speleologist EA Martel, at the foot of the cliffs beside the river. The galleries open to visitors are 1.6km/1mi long (*complete tour, on foot*) and divide into two: concretions and stalactites prevail in the first; in the second, underground rivers run in between natural rimstone dams (*gours*) and flood out into placid lakes. In the **Salle des Merveilles**, black light first shows up the "living" part of the stalactites; then normal lighting enhances the reflection of the concretions in the still water of the lake.

Château de Belcastel

A vertical cliff dropping down to the confluence of the Ouysse and the Dordogne is crowned by a castle standing proudly in a remarkable **setting**★. Only the eastern part of the main wing and the keep date from the Middle Ages; most of the other buildings were rebuilt later.

▶ *D 43 cuts across the meander of the Dordogne and runs towards Pinsac. Turn left just before the bridge.*

Château de la Treyne

Open Jul-Aug, 9am–noon and 2-6pm. no charge. 05 65 27 60 60.
The château stands perched on a cliff, which on one side overlooks the east bank of the Dordogne and on the other side a vast park. Burned by the Catholics during the Wars of Religion, the château was rebuilt in the 17C. The park and chapel (where exhibitions are held) are open to the public.

▶ *The D 43 leads back to Souillac. If you wish to enjoy the Dordogne a while longer, turn left at Port de Souillac and return to Souillac via Cieurac.*

Argentat★

La Xaintrie and Vallée de la Souvigne

The name of the town has evolved from the Celtic *Argentoratum*, meaning "the passage of the river." In the 17C and 18C, Argentat enjoyed great prosperity as a result of the transport of wood along the Dordogne by traditional, flat-bottomed "gabarres" to Bergerac, where it was used in the barrel-making industry. Many of the elegant buildings in the centre of town and along the river bank, with their turrets and pepper-box towers, date from this period.

🐾 WALKING TOUR

Built in 1844, the riverside embankment of **Quai Lestourgie** along the Dordogne is lined with fine houses crowned with turrets, gables and pepperbox towers. In olden days, it was here that the typical *gabares* were moored to load up their precious cargo. Walk onto the **bridge** for a pleasant view of the town, with its impressive houses fronted by wooden balconies jutting out over the river. Argentat's busy main street divides the town into two distinct districts. Note the unusual mix of **lauze** (roughly hewn slabs of stone of either schist or lava) and slate roofs. Beyond the bridge, continue along the riverside promenade as far as **rue des Contamines**, passing typical

- ▶ **Population:** 3 125
- 🕐 **Michelin Map:** 329: M-5
- 🗎 **Info:** Place de maïa, 19400. ✆05 55 28 16 05. www.tourisme-argentat.com
- 🌐 **Location:** 44km/27,5mi E of Brive via the D941. If possible, try to approach Argentat on the N120 from the south for a great view of the town.
- 🚫 **Don't Miss:** The view of the town from the bridge carrying the D1120 over the river.
- 🕐 **Timing:** Allow at least an hour to explore the town.
- 👪 **Kids:** For older children there is canoeing on the river and also a trip by Gabare.

narrow streets along the way. Continue towards the centre via **place Delmas**, surrounded by old houses such as the Manoir de l'Eyrial and the Maison Filliol. From the church of **St-Pierre**, head down the steps towards **rue Ste-Claire** to the privaHenry Short Coate Turenne. Cross rue Henri IV to **rue des Goudous**, where the construction date on several impressive houses has been chiselled into the lintels. Beyond the **Chapelle Jeanne d'Arc**, rue Ledamp returns to the car park.

Argentat

E. Larribère/MICHELIN

ARGENTAT CIRCUITS

🚗 DRIVING TOURS

1️⃣ LA XAINTRIE

Round trip of 55km/34mi – allow half a day. The name **Xaintrie** is a corruption of the word Saint-Trie. It consists of a granite plateau deeply cut by the gorges of the Dordogne, the Maronne and the Cère, where moorland and scrubland alternate with pine and silver birch woods. There is a marked contrast between the white Xaintrie in the north (St-Privat) and the black Xaintrie in the south (Mercœur).

▷ *Leave Argentat to the S towards St-Privat then turn left onto the D 129.*

Barrage d'Argentat

This is one of five dams with a hydro-electric power station on the Upper Dordogne. It was built 2km/1.2mi upstream from Argentat to maximise the use of the waters from the Le Chastang reservoir. It rises to a maximum height of 35m/115ft, with a crest spanning 190m/623ft long. Four sluices can empty 4 000m3/880 000 gallons per second. This power station has five hollow piles, three of which are equipped with hydroelectric generators.

🚶 Near the church of **St-Martial-Entraygues** on the west bank of the Dorgogne, a trail leads to the promontory of the **Roc Castel**, with its viewpoint over the river and dam.

Chapelle de Glény

The chapel, all that remains of the former church, has an attractive chevet and a bell gable (a high wall pierced with openings).

Barrage du Chastang★

🚇 *Visits are currently suspended for security reasons. The power station at this dam is the largest producer of electricity in the whole valley.*

🚶 Less than 1.6km/1mi beyond the dam, a narrow winding path (signposted) heads off to the right of the D 29, leading to a belvedere on the left bank of the Dordogne, from where there is an impressive view of the dam and reservoir.

Servières-le-Château

This former stronghold, owned in turn by the Turenne and Noailles families, enjoys a picturesque **setting**★ overlooking the deep gorges of the Glane. The stone *lauze* roofs of the village are encircled by jagged rocks and pine trees.

▷ *Head north out of Servières along the D 75.*

Lac de Feyt

Stop on the north side of the Barrage de la Glane to admire the splendid view of this 65ha/161-acre lake, a popular outdoor leisure and sailing centre.

▶ *Continue along the D 75 towards Darazac; turn right on D 75E1.*

St-Privat
The village's 13C and 16C church is crowned by an imposing square tower.

▶ *Leave St-Privat S along the D 13.*

Tours de Merle★★
♿*See Tours de MERLE.*

▶ *Leave the D 13 and drive towards St-Bonnet-les-Tours.*

Vallée de la Maronne
The D 136 climbs through a wooded landscape to a plateau with fine views of the Tours de Merle. The road passes through St-Bonnet-les-Tours, before skirting the foot of the **Château du Rieux** (13C and 16C).

▶ *Beyond Sexcles, the N 120 follow the east bank of the Maronne to Argentat.*

② VALLÉE DE LA SOUVIGNE★
Round-trip of 45km/28mi – allow 3hr.
A varied drive along the Souvigne Valley taking in a church, a calvary and a view before returning to Argentat.

▶ *Head northwest out of Argentat along the N 120 towards Tulle.*

The road climbs through the wooded hills of the Souvigne Valley.

Église de St-Chamant
The doorway of the church, fronted by a belfry-porch and wooden gallery, is particularly interesting. Note the doorway capitals and the tympanum.

▶ *Drive north out of St-Chamant along the D 11 to St-Bonnet-Elvert, then turn left towards Forgès.*

Calvaire d'Espargilière
15min round trip on foot.
🚶The view from the calvary extends over meadows to the wooded hillsides of the surrounding valleys.

▶ *Cross the N 120 to reach the west bank of the Souvigne. In Grandchamp, turn onto the D 113E.*

Cascades de Murel★
🚶Walk along the banks of the crystal-clear Valeine to reach this waterfall, situated in a delightful setting of greenery and rocks.

▶ *Return to Grandchamp. Turn left onto the D 113, which flanks the hillside and provides fine views of the Souvigne Valley, then continue to Albussac along the D 87 before turning right on the D 176 towards Sirieix.*

Roche de Vic★
🚶*15min walk. Alt 636m/2 087ft.*
This bare-flanked hill of granite blocks is crowned by a small chapel and a statue of the Virgin Mary. The **view**★ from here encompasses the Lower Limousin (*viewing table*). The hills roll northward as far as the Massif des Monédières, and south to the Causse de Quercy.

▶ *Follow the D 940 as far as La Grafouillère, then turn left onto the D 169 leading back to Argentat.*

ADDRESSES

Beaulieu-sur-Dordogne★★

and Gorges de la Cère

Built on the right bank of the Dordogne, Beaulieu is famous for its fine Romanesque church, once part of a Benedictine abbey.

A BIT OF HISTORY

Foundation and growth of the abbey – Raoul, archbishop of Bourges, visited this part of the country in 855 and, enchanted by the beauty of this particular site which he christened *bellus locus* – *beau lieu* (beautiful place) – decided to found a community here. The monastery rose to significance despite the warlike struggles for control waged by the lords of Turenne and Castelnau. The abbots became the equals of city merchants and, as their special privileges increased, became virtually independent.

The Benedictine reform – The monks gradually came to interpret the order's rule of discipline more and more liberally. During the Wars of Religion (1562-98), they deserted their monastery. In 1663 the Abbot of La Tour d'Auvergne called on the austere Benedictine Congregation of Maurists to undertake the necessary reforms and to repair the buildings. The community prospered until the Revolution took hold, and drove them out again.

OLD TOWN★

A maze of narrow streets and old houses is huddled around the church. Note the 16C tower, with its decorative shell motif, on rue Ste-Catherine, and the building known as the **Renaissance house** on place de la Bridolle, embellished with statues and medallions.

Église St-Pierre★★

Open Jul-Aug, guided tour, *10am-noon and 2.30-6pm. No charge.* The influence of both the Limousin and the Aquitaine are apparent in the architecture of this 12C abbey church, once an important place of pilgrimage.

▶ **Population:** 1 287
Michelin Map: 329: M-6
Info: 6 pl. Marbot, 19120 Beaulieu-sur-Dordogne, ℘05 55 91 09 94.
Location: 46km/28.75mi SW of Brive via the D921/ D940
Don't Miss: The Église St-Pierre and its south doorway; the old town.

The sandstone building is typical of Benedictine establishments which served as places of pilgrimage. The choir, transept and eastern bay of the nave were the first to be completed, from about 1100 to 1140. In the middle of the 12C, works were continued from the southern end of the nave to the northern parallel walls. The project was finished in the 13C, with the western bay of the nave and the façade.

The **south doorway★★** was carved in 1125 and is one of the great masterpieces of early Romanesque sculpture. The craftsmen who created it came from Toulouse and also worked on the carvings at Moissac, Collonges, Souillac and Carrennac.

The doorway is preceded by an open porch; the sculpture (which has been restored) is remarkable in its composi-

Romanesque tympanum of the south doorway, Église St-Pierre

tion and execution. The theme on the tympanum is the Last Judgement. In the centre, Christ in Majesty dominates all by his height and extends his arm in welcome to the chosen. On either side two angels sound trumpets, whereas above, four angels hold the instruments of the Passion – the Cross, the Nails and the Crown of Thorns. The Apostles are grouped left and right and above them the dead rise from their graves. Monsters line the upper part of the lintel. The lower part, as at Moissac, is decorated with rosettes from which emerge chimera, serpents and monsters.

The style and proportions of the graceful **east end** of the church are highlighted by the window mouldings typical of the Limousin region, and cornices with sculpted modillions.

As you walk around the outside of the chevet, note the vestiges of the cloisters where they once extended from the northern side of the church (sacristy).

There is no tympanum above the wide doorway of the **west front**. The tower rising up to the right was added in the 14C during the Hundred Years War. Raised higher in 1556, it served as the town belfry. Inside, the sanctuary was designed for pilgrimages and, like others so-dedicated, planned out to facilitate the movement of crowds, as evidenced in the wide aisles.

The nave has barrel vaulting. The tall, asymmetrical dome on pendentives rises above the transept from recessed columns. The chancel is lit by five rounded bays.

The decorative aspect is rather rustic compared to the intricate beauty of the south doorway. There are just a few sculpted capitals, at the entrance to the ambulatory and the transept chapels; with garlands and caryatids.

The other capitals bear geometrical designs typical of the Quercy region. In the northern arm of the transept, above the door to the stairway, an unsophisticated lintel carving of lions and a tree.

Trésor

🕐 *Open Apr-Sep, 8am-8pm; Oct-Mar, 8am-7pm.* 📞*05 55 91 18 78. Housed in the north transept, the treasury includes a remarkable 12C* **Virgin and Child**★ *in silver-plated wood and a chased enamel shrine (chest) from the 13C.*

Chapelle des Pénitents

For information, contact the tourist office, 📞*05 55 91 09 94. This delightful Romanesque chapel is reflected in the waters of the Dordogne downstream from the town. Built originally in the 12C but since restored, it now hosts temporary exhibitions in summer.*

GORGES DE LA CÈRE

The River Cère meets the Dordogne downstream of Bretenoux, at the foot of a promontory crowned by the Château de Castelnau. Along its course, it passes through wild gorges which can be best viewed from the Rocher du Peintrea (off the D 13, to the east of Beaulieu-sur-Dordogne).

ADDRESSES

🏠 STAY

😊 **Charme d'hôte La Maison** – *11 r. de la Gendarmerie.* 📞*05 55 91 24 97. Closed Oct to Mar.* 🍴 *6 rooms.* A friendly welcome awaits in this unexpected Mexican hacienda in the middle of Beaulieu. Arcades, a patio with flowers, walls in shades of red ochre and appealing rooms with original names.

😊😊😊 **Manoir de Beaulieu**– *4 pl. du Champs-de-Mars.* 📞*05 55 91 01 34. www.manoirdebeaulieu.com 25rooms.* This

solid regional-style building enjoys a central location. Ask for one of the renovated rooms - the others are more sober. Dine on tasty local recipes.

🍴 EAT

😊 **Au Beau-Lieu Breton** – *R. du Presbytère -* 📞*05 55 91 33 38. Open– May–Oct Close Mon exc Jul–Aug.* This crêpe and salad restaurant in the old town is a welcome stop for a simple yet pleasant meal. Take a table outdoors and tuck into house smoked magret or a buckwheat galette, complemented by a glass of Cahors wine or a bowl of cider.

Bort-les-Orgues
and around

The town of Bort, on a lovely site in the Dordogne Valley, is known for its huge dam (barrage) and for the cliffs rising above it. The cliffs are known as "les orgues", because the formation, seen from below, resembles the pipes of a massive organ.

TOWN
Church
Boulevard de la Nation
Dating from the 12C-15C, the plain architecture provides a frame for a 15C statue of St Anne, modern stained-glass windows and a bronze Christ sculpted by Chavignier. Next door, the former priory was built in the 17C.

Cascade du Saut de la Saule
2.5km/1.5mi SE, then 30min on foot there and back. Take the road which climbs towards the Institut médico-pédagogique, continue along the alleyway crossing the Rhue then turn left and follow the river.
The path reaches a small gorge and then continues to some rocks towering above the Saut de la Saule where the River Rhue flows over a 5-6m/17-20ft rocky shelf.

▶ **Population:** 3 260
Michelin Map: 329: Q-3
Info: place Marmontel, 19110 Bort-les-Orgues. ℘05 55 96 02 49. www.bort-artense.com.
Location: 120km/75mi E of Brive via A20/A89/D879
Don't Miss: The dam or the cliffs (orgues).
Timing: Allow a couple of hours to visit Les Orgues de Bort and a full day to explore the Dordogne Valley.
Kids: The Insects of the World exhibition in Ydes.

Barrage de Bort (Bort Dam)★★
Open May–Sept, 1hr boat trip taking in the Château de Val and the Dordogne Valley; Jul and Aug, departing from the Château de Val, every day at 11.15am, 14.30pm, 3.30pm, 4pm and 5pm. In May, June and September at 3pm only. Departing from the Barage, in July and August every day at 11am, 3pm and 4.30pm. 8€. Vedettes panoramiques. ℘04 71 40 30 14. There are car parks on either side of the dam, on the D 979 and D 922. 45min guided tours of the dam are also available by prior arrange-

Cliffs, Bort-les-Orgues
©A. Demotes/Photononstop/Tips images

ment from Mon am–Sat noon.
Contact the tourist office. ☎05 55 96 02 49.
☺ Passport/identity card required.
☜no charge.
From the road across the top of the dam (390m/1 280ft long), the upstream view encompasses the vast reservoir, crisscrossed by the wakes of **pleasure cruisers**.
The reservoir has a capacity of 477 cubic metres/16845 cubic feet and is 21km/13.1mi long
A **tour**, complete with video film and working model, starts at the base of the dam, illustrating the hydroelectric power system established along the River Dordogne and its tributaries.

🚗 DRIVING TOURS

1 LES ORGUES DE BORT★
Round trip of 15km/9mi – allow 2h.
This tour takes in the Orgues at close quarters and also affords panoramic views of the Dordogne Valley and the mountains of Cantal.

▷ *Leave Bort along the D 127 S, near the cemetery.*

The view to the left encompasses the Rhue Valley.

Along the Dordogne near St-Nazaire

E. Larribere/MICHELIN

▷ *Just beyond the last houses in Chantery, take a stairway to the right, which leads directly to the stone columns. Follow signs to the Grottes des Orgues and the Site d'escalade des Orgues.*

The 80-100m/262-328ft high organ pipes, spread over a distance of 2km/1.2mi, are composed primarily of phonolite rock, known also as clinkstone or soundstone.

▷ *Go back to the D 127, continue for 2km/1mi until the right turn-off marked Point de vue des Orgues, and drive a short distance to the car park and picnic area on the plateau (alt 769m/2 523ft). From the parking area, there is a 15min walk there and back to the scenic overlook.*

🚶 There is a wide **panoramic view**★★ over the Dordogne Valley, the Cantal region and the Mont Dore range. To the southwest, Lake Madic lies on the former course of the Dordogne.

▷ *Go back to your car and continue along the D 127 for 500m/0.3mi. A path on the left climbs to a rocky outcrop (15min round trip on foot).*

The panorama embraces the Puy de Sancy and the mountains of Cantal, the River Dordogne and its tributaries, the Monédières range and the Plateau des Mille Vaches.
From the D 979, as you travel towards Bort, keep an eye out for the pretty **Pierefitte Château** on the right, and more views of the lake and dam.

2 ALONG THE DORDOGNE
Round-trip of 95km/59mi – allow one day.

Here the Dordogne used to flow through narrow gorges. The dams and reservoir lakes, which now succeed one another down the valley, forming a gigantic water stairway 100km/60mi long, have altered the appearance of the countryside, but often fit remarkably well into the beautiful valley settings.

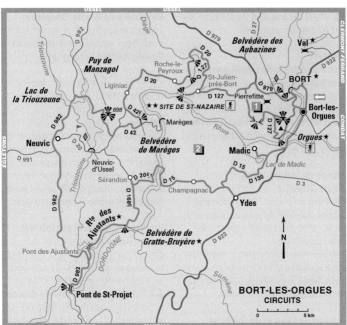

This tour offers a view of the Dam and Lake and also the Dordogne and Diège gorges from the Calvary at St.Nazaire. It includes a visit to the resort of Neuvic and a chance to see some insects!

▷ *Leave Bort-les-Orgues on the D 922 heading N then turn left onto the D 979.*

Belvédère des Aubazines

This viewpoint on the right side of the D 979 (picnic area) offers a view of the dam and its 1 400ha/3 460-acre lake.

▷ *Continue along the D 979 and turn left onto the D 127 2km/1.2mi farther on.*

Saint-Nazaire Site★★

30min round trip on foot.

After parking the car, bear right along the ridge on the slope and later follow a path to the Calvaire, lined with the Stations of the Cross. Pass a statue of St Nazarius and from the Calvary at the end of the promontory there is a fine view of the Dordogne and Diège gorges.

▷ *Drive to St-Julien-près-Bort and continue along the D 127.*

The road crosses the Diège, climbs wooded slopes and, as far as Roche-les-Peyroux provides views of the river.

▷ *After Liginiac take the D 42E on your left.*

Belvédère de Marèges

The road drops down to the **Marèges Dam** in a series of hairpin bends; 500m/550yd farther, a belvedere affords a view of the dam and its lake hemmed in by steep banks forming a picturesque wild setting.

▷ *The D 42 leads to the D 20; 2km/1.2mi farther on, turn right onto the D 183 towards Plage de Liginiac.*

Two beaches line the shores of Triouzoune Lake. The Neuvic d'Ussel Dam to the south contains this impressive reservoir covering 410ha/1 013 acres, ideal for water sports enthusiasts.

Puy de Manzagol

Alt 698m/2 290ft.

From the summit (*viewing table*) there is a vast panorama of the Triouzoune Lake and the Massif Central.

▶ *The D 183 and then the D 982 on the left skirt the beautiful lake.*

Neuvic

This attractive resort, built on the hillside has a beach with a sailing school and a centre for water skiing. The village has retained its narrow streets lined with granite houses, its fortified gate and its church with a characteristic belfry-porch.

Musée de la Résistance Henri-Queuille

🕐 *Open May–Oct, 10am–noon and 3-6pm; Nov–Apr, by prior arrangement.* ⌨3€. ℘05 55 95 96 87. www.musee-henriqueuille.com.
This museum is dedicated to the Resistance movement in Corrèze where, in 1944, fierce fighting prepared the way for the liberation of the region.

Maison de l'Eau et de la Pêche

Next to the church. 🕐*Open May to mid-Sept, daily except Sun, 9am-noon and 2–6.30pm; mid-Sept to Apr, daily except Sun and Mon, 10am-noon and 2-5pm.* 🕐*Closed public hols (except 1 May).* ⌨*No charge.* ℘05 55 95 06 76. *Near the church.*
This information centre presents an exhibition devoted to fishing methods, water treatment and fish species that are commonly found in rivers. Excursions are organised on the themes of fishing and nature.

▶ *Drive S out of Neuvic along the D 982 towards Mauriac.*

Pont de St-Projet

This suspension bridge provides a good view of the reservoir.

▶ *Turn back and follow the D 168.*

Route des Ajustants★

The Ajustants Tourist Road follows the Dordogne Valley with its rock-strewn wooded slopes, providing beautiful views of the L'Aigle reservoir.

Belvédère de Gratte-Bruyère★

This is a magnificent viewpoint (*picnic area*) from which to see the Sumène flowing into the Dordogne.

▶ *Shortly before Sérandon, turn right onto the D 20E1.*

Ydes

This small village lies on the banks of the Sumène, in an area dotted with basalt peaks. The 12C church is typical of the Haute-Auvergne Romanesque style; the east end is decorated with carved modillions representing lively young faces.

Insects of the World exhibition

Entrance behind the town hall. ♿ 🕐*Open every day Jul–Aug, 2-7pm and by arrangement from 15 - 30 June and 1–15 Sept.*⌨3€. ℘04 71 67 92 34
👪 This exhibition is mainly devoted to butterflies and moths. Note the size and colours of some of the remarkable specimens on display.

▶ *Return to the D 15 then bear left onto the D 130.*

Madic

This attractive village is the starting point of a pleasant walk round the lake of the same name.

▶ *The D 30 and the D 922 lead back to Bort-les-Orgues.*

ADDRESSES

Carennac★

Carennac is one of the most attractive sights along the Dordogne and is classified as one of France's 'Plus Beaux Villages'. Its picturesque tiled houses and turreted mansions clustering around the old priory were once occupied by the prelate and writer François de Salignac de la Mothe-Fénelon.

◄ VILLAGE WALK

This charming village, where some of the houses date from the 16C, has barely changed since Fénelon's day. The Île Barrade, in the Dordogne, was renamed Calypso's Island, and visitors will still be shown a tower in the village which is called Telemachus' Tower in which, it is maintained, Fénelon wrote his masterpiece. The deanery was suppressed by order of the Royal Council in 1788, and put up for auction and sold in 1791. Of the old ramparts there remains only a fortified gateway, and of the buildings, only the castle and the priory tower are left.

▷ *Go through the fortified gateway.*

Château

Next to the church of St-Pierre (see below), this 16C edifice consists of a main building flanked by corner turrets and a gallery built above the church's Gothic

▶ **Population:** 385
 Michelin Map: 337: G-2, or Dordogne in the Quercy.

chapels. The severe façade looks over the Dordogne and Calypso Island.

Espace Patrimoine

Open Jul–Sept, daily except Mon, 10am–noon and 2–6pm; Easterr to Jun and Nov 1, daily except Mon and Sat-Sun, 10am–noon and 2–6pm; public hols and weekends by prior arrangement. ℘05 65 33 81 36.

The three storeys of the château house a discovery area devoted to the River Dordogne where it passes through the Lot *département*. A **scale model** is enlivened by lights and sounds which create a picture of the Dordogne Valley from Biards to Souillac. The other rooms also use audio-visual programmes to explore various subjects: flora and fauna, regional arts, the history of navigation, prehistoric times (3-D projection).

Musée des Alambics et Aromathèque

Open 11am–7pm; ℘05 65 10 91 16.

Adjacent to the park of the château, this museum is devoted to stills and aromatic plants; it offers guided tours with a demonstration of how lavender is distilled.

Northern entrance to Carennac

S. Sauvignier/MICHELIN

François de Salignac de la Mothe-Fénelon

The priory-deanery at Carennac, which was founded in the 10C and attached to the famous abbey at Cluny in the following century, owes its fame to the length of time spent there by François de Salignac de la Mothe-Fénelon before he became archbishop of Cambrai. While he was still a student at Cahors, Fénelon used to enjoy spending his holidays at the house of his uncle, senior prior of Carennac. In 1681 Fénelon's uncle died and was succeeded by the young abbot, who remained at the priory for 15 years. Fénelon was greatly revered at Carennac; he enjoyed describing the ceremonies and general rejoicing that greeted his arrival by boat and his installation as commendatory prior. Tradition has it that Fénelon wrote *Télémaque* while living at Carennac. The description of the adventures of Ulysses' son was at first only a literary exercise, but was subsequently turned into a tract for the edification of the duke of Burgundy, Louis XIV's grandson, when Fénelon was appointed his tutor.

Église St-Pierre

In front of this Romanesque church dedicated to St Peter, stands a porch with a beautiful 12C carved **doorway**★.
It is well preserved and from its style would appear to belong to the same school as the tympana of Beaulieu, Moissac, Collonges and Cahors. Inside, the interesting archaic capitals in the nave are decorated with fantastic animals, foliage and historiated scenes.

◐ *On leaving the church, walk to the end of the priory courtyard.*

Cloisters

◷*Open Jui–Aug, 10am–12.30pm and 2–7pm (last entry 15min before closure of tourist office); Apr–Jun and Sept–Oct, daily except Sun, 10am–noon and 2–6pm; Jan–Mar and Nov–Dec, daily except Sun, 10am–noon and 2–5pm.* ◈*2.50€. ℘05 65 10 97 01. www.tourisme.carennac.com. The restored cloisters consist of a Romanesque gallery adjoining the church and three Flamboyant galleries. Stairs lead to the terrace.*
The chapter house, which opens onto the cloisters, shelters a remarkable **Entombment**★ (15C). Christ lies on a shroud carried by two disciples: Joseph of Arimathea and Nicodemus.

◐ *Leave the priory and walk alongside the castle overlooking the Dordogne and Calypso Island. Take the first street on the left.*

A small public park gives access to a charming **Romanesque chapel**. Opposite stands a 16C house with a corner window.

◐ *Turn right to walk round the former priory and return to the castle.*

A bartizan still towers over the Pont de Carennac. On the other side of the bridge, another four-storey, 16C tower overlooks a small pier.

ADDRESSES

⌂STAY

⊖⊖⊜ **Chambre d'hote L'Oustal Nau les Combes, Mme Lemant, 46110 Carennac.** ℘05 65 10 94 09/ 06 88 18 13 43. www.oustalnau-carennac.com. Quiet chambre d'hote, with beautiful garden, situated on a wooded hillside overlooking Carennac. Guest rooms, all en-suite, have lovely views of the surrounding Dordogne valley.

⊖⊜ **Hostellerie Fénelon, 46110 Carennac.** ℘05 65 10 96 46. www.hotel-fenelon.com. 15 rms. A large Quercy house with a family atmosphere where you may prefer the bedrooms with a view of the Dordogne. Beams, a fireplace and country ornaments give character to the dining room.

Château de Castelnau-Bretenoux★★

On the northern border of the Quercy stands Castelnau-Bretenoux Castle with the village of Prudhomat tucked beneath it. The great mass of the castle's red stone ramparts and the towers rise up from a spur overlooking the confluence of the Cère and the Dordogne. The scale on which the castle defence system was built makes it one of the finest examples of medieval military architecture. Seen from the countryside more than 5km/3mi round, the castle, as Pierre Loti wrote,

"...is the beacon... the thing you cannot help looking at all the time from wherever you are. It's a cock's comb of blood-red stone rising from a tangle of trees, this ruin poised like a crown on a pedestal dressed with a beautiful greenery of chestnut and oak trees."

A BIT OF HISTORY

Turenne's egg – From the 11C onwards the barons of Castelnau were the strongest in the Quercy; they paid homage only to the counts of Toulouse and proudly styled themselves the Second Barons of Christendom. In 1184 Raymond de Toulouse gave the suzerainty of Cas-

- ♿ **Michelin Map:** 337: G-2. Local map see St-Céré, Excursions
- ℹ **Info:** Av. de la Libération, 46160 Bretenoux. ℘05 65 38 59 53. www.ot-bretenoux.com.
- ▶ **Location:** 47km/29.5mi S of Tulle via D940.
- ⊘ **Don't Miss:** The view from the ramparts of the Château Fort.
- ♿ **Also See:** Rocamadour; Gouffre de Padirac; Beaulieu-sur-Dordogne

telnau to the viscount of Turenne. The baron of Castelnau refused to accept the insult and paid homage instead to Philip Augustus, king of France. Bitter warfare broke out between Turenne and Castelnau; King Louis VIII intervened and decided in favour of Turenne. Whether he liked it or not the baron had to accept the verdict. The fief, however, was only symbolic: Castelnau had to present his overlord with... an egg. Every year, with great pomp and ceremony a yoke of four oxen bore a freshly laid egg to Turenne.

CHÂTEAU FORT

⊙*Open Jul–Aug,* 👥*guided tour (30min, last entrance 1hr before closing), 10am–7pm; May 2–Jun, 10am–*

Château de Castelnau-Bretenoux

J. Damase/MICHELIN

12.30pm and 2–6.30pm; Sept and Apr 10am–12 pm and 2–5.30pm; Oct –Mar 10am – 12.30pm and 2pm –5.15pm. ©Closed 1 Jan, 1 May, 1 and 11 Nov, 25 Dec and Tue from Oct–Mar. ⊛7€. ℘05 65 10 98 00.

Round the strong keep built in the 13C, there grew up during the Hundred Years War a huge fortress with a fortified curtain wall. The castle was abandoned in the 18C and suffered depredations at the time of the Revolution. It caught fire in 1851 but was skilfully restored between 1896 and 1932.

The ground plan is that of an irregular triangle flanked by three round towers and three other towers partially projecting from each side. Three parallel curtain walls still defend the approaches, but the former ramparts have been replaced by an avenue of trees.

From along the ramparts there is a far-reaching **view**★ of the Cère and Dordogne valleys to the north; of Turenne Castle set against the horizon to the north-west; of the Montvalent Amphitheatre to the west; and of Loubressac Castle and the Autoire Valley to the south-west and south. A tall square tower and the seigneurial residence, a rectangular building still known as the *auditoire* (auditorium), suggest the vast scale of this fortress; the garrison numbered 1 500 men and 100 horses.

Inside the château, in addition to the lapidary depository, containing the Romanesque capitals of Ste-Croix-du-Mont in Gironde, other rooms should be visited on account of their decor carried out by the former proprietor, a singer of comic opera, Jean Moulierat, who bought the castle in 1896. The former chamber of the Quercy Estates General is lit by large windows; the pewter hall and the Grand Salon contain Aubusson and Beauvais tapestries.

▷ *Leave the castle and turn left, down to the collegiate church.*

Collégiale St-Louis

The church was built in 1460 by the lords of Castelnau in red-ferriferous stone, at the foot of the castle. A few canons' residences can be seen nearby.

▷ *Enter the church*

The lords' chapel has lovely quadripartite vaulting, the pendant of which is emblazoned with the Castelnau coat of arms.

Marcillac-la-Croisille

the Dordogne to L'Aigle

This small village, built on a granite plateau, grew at the point where Roman roads once converged. This peaceful holiday resort is situated near the Barrage de La Vallette and the Barrage de Meyrignac, both of which offer a range of leisure activities, including swimming and sailing.

VISIT

Barrage de La Valette

5km/3mi SW along the D 131E2.

The River Doustre goes through a gorge on its way to join the Dordogne near Argentat. Walk along the top of the dam

▷ **Population:** 827
◈ **Michelin Map:** 329: N-4
▣ **Info:** Mairie. ℘05 55 93 04 34. Open Jun 15–Sept 15.
▷ **Location:** 27km/17mi to the east of Tulle.
◷ **Timing:** Allow half a day to explore the nearby Dordogne valley.
◈ **Don't Miss:** A boat trip on the Dordogne; Barrage de l'Aigle.
◈ **Also See:** Upper Vézère and Corrèze Valleys

for a fine view of the reservoir framed by hills over a distance of 8km/5mi.

DORDOGNE VALLEY

Château de Sédières

7km/4.5mi W along the D 978 and D 135 E. ⏱*Open Jun–Sept, unaccompanied visit (last entrance 45min before closing), 10am–12.30pm and 2–6.30pm; rest of the year, please enquire.* ⊜*3€.* ☎*05 55 27 76 40. www.sedieres.fr*
This elegant Renaissance château stands in a pleasant setting near a waterfall. It comprises a fortified gatehouse, a main building and a high square keep. The main façade is crowned with machicolations in striking contrast with the large windows and their pediments decorated with scallops. Inside, note the carved fire-places of the reception rooms and the vaulting with pendentives of the guard-room.

 DRIVING TOUR

DORDOGNE VALLEY★

75km/47mi round-trip – allow half a day Leave Marcillac NE along the D 978.

Spontour

⏱*Excursions operate Apr–Oct (please enquire for times). Three departure points: Pont de Chambon, Pont du Sablier and Beaulieu sur Dordogne.* ⊜*6.50€ (Pont de Chambon, Pont du Sablier), 5.50€ (Beaulieu).* ☎*05 55 28 86 45.*
From the bridge, admire the village where you can still enjoy a taste of the

past by boarding a traditional *gabarre* for a trip on the river.

◯ *Cross the Dordogne; left on D 105.*

Aynes

The granite houses with their slate roofs are grouped round the chapel.
The road, which is now laid out as a corniche road, provides views from different angles of the L'Aigle Dam.

Barrage de l'Aigle★★

The dam impresses by its size and the boldness of concept. Two ski-jump flood control gates can let through 4 000m3/880 000gal per second.

Belvédère

Leave the car opposite the L'Aigle Dam and go on foot up the D 16 to the belvedere built below the dam (the path lies between two road tunnels).
From the belvedere there is a good **view**★ of the dam as a whole and the valley below it.

◯ *Turn back then left onto the D 75 just before the Spontour Bridge.*

The road climbs and offers fine glimpses of the River Dordogne and the village of Spontour.
🚶 As you come out of a bend, note the parking area and viewpoint, which is

Barrage de l'Aigle

E. Larribère/MICHELIN

the starting point of a pleasant walk (*1hr 30min there and back*) to the **Rocher de la Valette**.

Auriac
The church of this charming village contains a 17C carved-wood crozier.

▶ *Drive W on D 65 to St-Merd-de-Lapleau, then turn onto the road left of the calvary (opposite the cemetery).*

Redenat
This is the starting point of two pleasant woodland walks. The first leads to a prehistoric **standing stone**; the second (*to the east*) leads down to a **waterfall** near the Chambon Bridge.

▶ *Continue to the D 72 via Vaujour.*

Bassignac-le-Haut
Near the church stands a 16C limestone wayside cross; the four sides of the shaft are carved with scenes from Jesus' life. From the **belvedere**★ situated to the north of the village (D 13), you can appreciate a meander of the Dordogne; the road to Chapeloune offers other fine views.

Pont de Chambon
This is the ideal place for a break, particularly for anglers; boat trips aboard a traditional gabarre are available.

▶ *Continue along the D 13 on the opposite bank.*

La Chapeloune
Two walks offering fine views start nearby. To the south, 30min there and back from the D 13 is a **viewing table**. A forest road leads down to a clearing affording a splendid view of the Chastang reservoir and the Cantal mountain range.

Grotte des Maquisards
▶ *To the N, 1hr 30min there and back starting from the parking area (D 13).*
Enjoy this typical scrubland and the fine view but beware, the last 200m/220yd to the cave are only suitable for experienced hikers.

St-Merd-de-Lapleau
Note the shape of the belfry-porch of the church with its row of four bays, each fitted with a bell.

▶ *Continue along the road running alongside the church.*

Étang des Ramandes★
The ideal place for relaxing or a walk (*2hr*) through the 260ha/642-acre pine and spruce forest.

▶ *Rejoin the road back to Marcillac-la-Croisille.*

Martel ★

and around

Built on the Upper Quercy causse to which it has given its name, Martel is known as the town of the seven towers: it still contains many medieval buildings. Today fine foods are part of its reputation: it is a central market for walnuts, and cottage industries processing and preserving local produce.

- **Population:** 1 519
- **Michelin Map:** 337: F-2; or Dordogne in the Quercy.
- **Info:** Palais de la Raymondie, Place des Consuls. ℘05 65 37 43 44. www.martel.fr.
- **Location:** 15km/9.5mi E of Souillac; 20km/12mi N of Rocamadour.
- **Don't Miss:** Places des Consuls; Hôtel de la Raymondie.
- **Also See:** Upper Vézère and Corrèze Valleys; Rocamadour.

A BIT OF HISTORY
The three hammers

After stopping the Saracens at Poitiers in 732, **Charles Martel** chased them into Aquitaine. Several years later he struck again and wiped them out. To commemorate this victory over the infidels and to give thanks to God, Charles Martel had a church built on the spot.

A town grew up around the church and was named Martel in memory of its founder taking as its crest three hammers, which were the favourite weapons of the saviour of Christianity.

Martel and the Viscounty of Turenne

The founding of Martel by the conqueror of the infidels is probably based more on fiction than on fact. However, it is known that the viscounts of Turenne made Martel an important urban community as early as the 12C. In 1219, Viscount Raymond IV granted a charter establishing Martel as a free town – exempt from the king's taxes, and with permission to mint money. Very quickly Martel established a town council and consulate and thus became the seat of the royal bailiwick and of the seneschalship. It established a court of appeal which handled all the region's judicial matters; more than 50 magistrates, judges and lawyers were employed. It reached its peak at the end of the 13C and beginning of the 14C. Like the rest of the region, the town suffered during the Hundred Years War and during the Wars of Religion. In 1738, when the rights of Turenne were sold to the king (*see TURENNE*), Martel lost its privileges and became a castellany.

Village of Martel

J. Damase/MICHELIN

Place des Consuls

©Kate Duffell/Bigstockphoto.com

The rebellious son

At the end of the 12C, Martel was the scene of a tragic series of events which brought into conflict **Henry II Plantagenet**, king of England and lord of all western France, his wife **Eleanor of Aquitaine** and their four sons. The royal household was a royal hell. Henry could no longer stand the sight of Eleanor, and shut her up in a tower. The sons thereupon took up arms against their father, and the eldest, **Henry Short Coat**, pillaged the viscounty of Turenne and Quercy. To punish him, Henry Plantagenet gave his lands to his third son, Richard the Lion Heart, and stopped his allowance. Henry Short Coat found himself penniless and to pay his foot-soldiers he plundered the treasure houses of the provincial abbeys. He took from Rocamadour the shrine and the precious stones of St Amadour, whose body was profaned, and he sold Roland's famous sword Durandal. But as he was leaving Rocamadour after this sacrilegious act, the bell miraculously began to toll: it was a sign from God.

Henry fled to Martel and arrived there with a fever; he felt death to be upon him and was stricken with remorse. He confessed his crimes while Henry II was sent for, to come and forgive his son on his death bed; the King was at the siege of Limoges and sent a messenger with his pardon. The messenger found Henry Short Coat lying in agony on a bed of cinders, a heavy wooden cross upon his chest. Shortly afterwards he died, a last farewell to his mother Eleanor on his lips.

WALKING TOUR

Start at the **former perimeter walls**. Wide avenues, fossé des Cordeliers and boulevard du Capitani, have been built on the site of the old ramparts (12C-13C). The machicolated **Tournemire Tower**, which used to be the prison tower, and the Souillac and Brive Gateways (found at the end of Route de Souillac and rue de Brive; *not on the town plan*) hark back to the time when Martel was a fortified town, well protected by double perimeter walls. The second perimeter wall, built in the 18C, enclosed the suburbs.

▷ *Leave the car in the car park along the north wall. Pass between the post office and the Tournemire Tower to enter the old town.*

Rue du Four-Bas

There are still some Renaissance houses along this street, which is spanned by an archway.

▷ *Follow the street towards place de la Rode.*

MEYSSAC
BRIVE ⑤ LES QUATRE-ROUTES A B

Place Gambetta

MARTEL
0   50 m

Pl. de la Rode

R. Mercière
Maison Grise
Tour de Tournemire
des
Cordeliers
N 140

R. Noire

H. de la Monnaie
R. Tournemire
H. de la Raymondie
St-Maur

Pl. des Consuls
R. Senlis
R. du Four-bas
Pl. H.-Ramet
Rue
Droite

R. Henri Mantel
Rue
Droite
Maison Fabri

Capitani

H. Vergnes-de-Ferron
R. de la Bride
Pl. de la Bride
de l'Église

Pl. M. Meteye
Rue
de

Hôtel de Mirandol
②
du

R. de la Forge
R. du Font

Boulevard

D 703
D 23

N

LACAVE ⑦ A B

WHERE TO STAY	
Cabrejou (Chambre d'hôte)	①
Cour au Tilleul (Chambre d'hôte La)	②
7 Tours (Auberge des)	⑤
Relais Ste-Anne	⑦
WHERE TO EAT	
Moulin à Huile de Noix (Ferme-auberge Le)	①

Église St-Maur

This Gothic church (13C-16C) has some interesting defensive features; huge buttresses converted into defence towers, machicolations protecting the flat east end and a 40m/131ft-high bell-tower which looks more like a keep.

Beneath the porch is a fine historiated Romanesque **tympanum** depicting the Last Judgement. The width of the nave is striking. The chancel with its stellar vaulting is lit by a large 16C **stained-glass window** showing God the Father, the four Evangelists and scenes from the Passion.

▷ *Return to the centre via rue Droite.*

Rue Droite

There are old town houses all along this road, one of which, Hôtel Vergnes-de-Ferron, is adorned with a lovely Renaissance door.

▷ *From place de la Bride, take rue de la Bride.*

Hôtel de Mirandol

This 15C town house constructed by François de Mirandol features a great square tower with a spiral staircase.

▷ *Rue de la Bride leads to place M.-Meteye; turn right then left.*

Maison Fabri

The tower, called Court-Mantel after Henry Short Coat who died here in 1183, has windows with frontons decorated with balls at the intersections of their cornices on all five floors.

Place des Consuls★

In the centre of the square is the 18C **covered market** with timbering set on great stone pillars. On one side the old town measures can be seen.

Hôtel de la Raymondie★

Once the fortress of the viscounts of Turenne, built around 1280, this building was converted into a Gothic mansion in the 14C. The **façade**★ overlooking rue de Senlis has remarkable apertures; a row of ogive arches on the ground floor is surmounted by seven quatrefoil rose windows.

The main entrance on place des Consuls is decorated with the town's coat of arms, a shield with three hammers. In the first-floor rooms note the two carved wooden chimney-pieces and the Renaissance bas-relief.

259

Musée d'Uxellodunum

🕐Open Jul–Aug, 10am–noon and 3–6pm. Visit by prior arrangement. 🕐Closed Sun, public hols, weekend following 15 Aug and rest of year. ➡1€. This museum, essentially devoted to prehistoric and Gallo-Roman archaeology, also houses medieval objects and a collection of 17C-18C chemist's jars.

Rue Tournemire

This attractive little street leads off to the left of the Hôtel de la Raymondie. The 13C **Hôtel de la Monnaie** with intersecting turrets used to mint coins (écus and denier) for the viscounty of Turenne. The 16C **Maison Grise** is decorated with a carved bust and a heraldic shield with three hammers.

EXCURSION
Reptiland

2km/1.2mi along the N 140 towards Figeac. 🕐&.Open Jul–Aug, 10am–6pm; Sept–Jun, daily except Mon and public holidays, 10am–noon and 2–6pm. 🕐Closed Dec 23–Feb 6. ➡7.50€ (4–12yrs, 5€). 𝄞05 65 37 41 00. www.reptiland.fr.
👥 92 species of snakes, lizards, crocodiles, tortoises etc. Explanatory panels provide information about each species. The owner, Pancho Gouygou, tries to show the peaceful disposition of his guests rather than their dangerous or spectacular side. He even claims to be able to cure anyone suffering from a morbid fear of snakes!

ADDRESSES

🛏STAY

🍴 **Chambre d'hôte Cabrejou** – 46600 St-Denis-lès-Martel. 3km/1.9mi E of Martel on the D 703. 𝄞05 65 37 31 89. www.ferme-cabrejou.com. 7 rooms. This attractive farm, which grows tobacco and walnuts, offers plain but comfortable rooms. Pleasant garden.

🍴🍴 **Auberge de 7 Tours** – Av. de Turenne. 𝄞05 65 37 30 16. www.auberge7tours.com. 8 rooms. Rooms are fairly basic but have recently been renovated and are in an annexe of the main Auberge, which is a restaurant.

🍴🍴🍴 **Chambre d'hôte La Cour au Tilleul** – Av. du Capitani . 𝄞05 65 37 34 08. www.lacourautilleul.com.3 rooms. An attractive B&B whose façade dates from the 12C. Cosy rooms all have character. In fine weather, enjoy a hearty breakfast in the lovely inner courtyard

🍴🍴🍴🍴 **Le Relais Sainte-Anne** – Rue du Pourtanel. 𝄞05 65 37 40 56. www.relais-sainte-anne.com. A true Hôtel de Charme et de Caractère, this beautiful historic stone luxury house is set in glorious grounds with a lovely pool.

🍴 EAT

🍴🍴 **Ferme-Auberge Le Moulin à Huile de Noix** – Rte de Bretenoux. 3km/1.9mi E of Martel on the D 803.

𝄞05 65 37 40 69. Closed 11 Nov–25 Mar, Sun eve and Mon. Reserv. required. Enjoy a delicious meal in the unique setting of this 17C walnut-oil mill. On Tuesday and Thursday afternoons visitors can learn how oil was once pressed according to traditional methods. Small shop selling products made on the property.

🍴🍴 **Au Vieux Four** – Av. Augustin-Garcia - 46110 Les Quatre-Routes. 8km/5mi NE of Martel on the D 96. 𝄞05 65 32 01 98. Closed Mon Reserv. required Sat and Sun. A warm welcome awaits in this small, simply decorated restauran with a refined menu.

🛒 SHOPPING

Markets and fairs – Traditional market under the *halle* on Wednesdays and Saturday mornings. Truffle market in December and January. Wool fair on 23 July.

Chemin de Fer Touristique du Haut-Quercy "Le Truffadou" – Sun and public hols, Apr–Sept; Jul 1–14 Wed,Sun and Hols; Mon–Thur, Sun and Hols Jul 15–Aug 31. Departures at 11am, 2.30pm and 4pm; ➡9.50€. For diesel train timetable see website. 𝄞05 65 37 35 81. www.trainduhautquercy.info. This rail line runs from Martel to St-Denis-près-Martel, along cliffs 80m/250ft above the valley. A great way of discovering the Dordogne, its châteaux, and the history and culture of the area (approx. 1hr).

Tours de Merle★★

The remains of this 12 and 14C feudal fortress of the Lords of Merle stand on a spur surrounded by a meander of the River Maronne not far from Argentat.

A BIT OF HISTORY
An Impregnable lair
At the juncture of Auvergne and Limousin, the site was an obvious choice for defensive purposes. The promontory rises 30m/98ft above the river, and sits 150m/492ft below the high plateau. This type of border fortress takes best advantage of the lay of the land; it is, in theory, inaccessible, and commands a vast area around itself. The lords of Merle were the most feared in the region in the Middle Ages and the family jealously guarded this the surest of strongholds.

Alongside the 11C castle rose the castles of the younger sons until by the 14C the Merle domain was divided into seven. During the Hundred Years War the English managed to force the stronghold to surrender in 1371 but gave it back at the request of Pope Gregory XI. The advent of artillery changed the fortune of this fortress which could be bombarded from neighbouring heights; made vulnerable, the old fortresses were one by one abandoned.

- **Michelin Map:** 329: N-5 – Local map *see ARGENTAT*
- **Location:** 61km/38.1mi W of Brive via D921/D13E/ D136E. For a wonderful view of the **ruins★★**, approach the Tours de Merle from the north, park by the side of a bend in the road and walk along a path to the viewpoint, nestled amid lush vegetation.

TOWER TOUR
◷*Open Jul–Aug, 10am–6.30pm; May–Jun and Sept, 2–6pm; Feb–Apr and Oct–Nov, Sun, pub and school hols, 2–6pm.* ∞6€. ℘05 55 28 22 31 or 05 55 28 27 67. www.st-geniez-o-merle.com.
Merle is made up of a series of seven castles, like pearls on a rope, strung from north to south. On two terraces, three distinct units in various states of disrepair can be distinguished, made up of keeps, towers, and main buildings dating from the 12C through the 15C.

The entrance is on the northern side. After passing through the vestiges of the chapel of St-Léger, visitors enter the old castle of Hugues and Fulcon de Merle, which occupies the highest point of the site: Romanesque keep (*terrace access*) and main buildings. The second section is made up of two square tow-

Tours de Merle

B. Kaufmann/MICHELIN

ers with castellated crowns, on the far end of the platform: the Noailles and Pesteils towers. From the top of the second tower, there is a good view over the whole site. A mysterious and magical air floats around the impressive façades broken into pieces with fireplaces suspended in mid-air and stairways leading nowhere.

Château de
Montal★★

The Château de Montal is a harmonious group of buildings with pepperpot roofs camped on a wooded hillside near the charming Bave Valley. A nine-hole golf course has been laid at the foot of the castle.

A BIT OF HISTORY

The wonder of a mother's love – In 1523 Jeanne de Balsac d'Entraygues had a country mansion built on the site of a feudal stronghold for her eldest son, Robert, who was away fighting in Italy for François I. The chatelaine had the best artists and workmen brought to Quercy, and by 1534 the masterpiece begotten of a mother's loving pride was there for all to see.

Hope is no more – Everything was ready to welcome home the proud knight. She waited day after day for her eldest son's arrival but alas, Robert's

♥/ EAT

🍽 **La Vieille Auberge** – *19220 St-Geniez-Ô-Merle. 5km/3mi NW of Les Tours de Merle via D 111.* ✆*05 55 28 20 60. Closed Jan, Mon eve.* A few miles from the medieval site, this charming country inn built in the early 20C is a pleasant rural stopover. Simple decor and regional cuisine including cabécou (the local goat's cheese).

▶ **Population:** lot
🛈 **Michelin Map:** 337: H-2; or see St-Céré: Excursions
🌐 **Location:** 3km/2mi W of St-Céré.
🚩 **Visit:** May 2–Aug 31 guided tour (45min), daily except Sat, 10am–12.30 and 2–6pm Sept–Mar 10am–12.30 and 2–5.30pm Closed Mon, Tue and May 1. ✆05 65 38 13 72. ⬚7€
👁 **Don't Miss:** A tour inside the castle to admire the Renaissance staircase.
🛈 **Also See:** Rocamadour

body was all that returned to the castle. The beautiful dream crumbled. Jeanne had the high window from which she had watched for her son blocked up and she had carved beneath it the despairing lament Hope is No More (*plus d'espoir*). Jeanne's second son, Dordé de Montal,

Detail of the façade

S. Sauvignier/MICHELIN

a church dignitary, was absolved from his ecclesiastical duties by the Pope in order that he might continue the family line; he subsequently married and had nine children.

Death and resurrection– Montal was declared a national asset but became uninhabitable as a result of the spoliation it suffered during the Revolution; finally in 1879 it fell into the hands of a certain Macaire. This impecunious adventurer made a bargain with a demolition group and divided the palace into lots; 120t of carved stone were sent to Paris. The masterpieces of Montal were then auctioned and dispersed throughout the museums and private collections of Europe and the United States. In 1908 a new and devoted owner set about finding and buying back at ransom prices all the Montal treasures, until he had refurbished the castle. He donated it to the State in 1913.

CHÂTEAU

Exterior - Steeply pitched *lauzes* roofs and massive round towers with loopholes give the castle its fortress-like appearance. But this forbidding exterior contrasts with the inner courtyard, designed with all the graceful charm of the Renaissance.

Montal consists of two main wings set at right angles and linked at the corner by a square tower containing the staircase. The façade of the main building with all its rich decoration is one of the castle's most glorious features.

The frieze - Above the ground floor windows and doors, runs a 32m/105ft-long frieze. It is a marvel of ornamental diversity: cupids, birds and dream-like figures appear beside shields and a huge human head. There are also the initials of the founder and her sons: I (Jeanne), R (Robert) and D (Dordé).

The busts - On the first floor mullioned windows alternate with false bays with intricately carved pediments, which contain seven busts in high-relief, all masterpieces of realism and taste. Each statue is a likeness of a member of the Montal family; from left to right they are: Amaury with a haughty air,

Renaissance staircase

J. Damase/MICHELIN

wearing a hat; Jeanne, his wife and the founder of the castle, with the air of a holy woman transfixed in eternal sorrow; Robert, the eldest son killed in Italy, wearing a plumed hat in the style of François I; Dordé, the second son, as a young page.

The dormers - There are four, and their decoration brings to mind those of Chambord; the dormer gables have small supporting figures on either side and the niches contain statues.

Interior - The entrance is at the corner, where the wings meet, through a door flanked by pilasters and topped with a lintel supporting several niches.

Renaissance staircase★★ - The staircase is built in the fine gold-coloured stone from Carennac, beautifully proportioned and magnificently decorated. Admire the fine carving beneath the stairs: ornamented foliage, shells, imaginary birds, initials and little figures form a ceiling, with decoration which completes that of the lierne and tierceron vaulting of the vestibules.

The **guardroom**, vaulted with basket-handled arches, contains a lovely chimney-piece. The Stag Room (**Salle du Cerf**) and the other rooms house fine pieces of furniture (mainly in the Renaissance and Louis XIII styles), altarpieces, paintings and plates attributed to Bernard Palissy, as well as tapestries from Flanders and Tours, which constitute a marvellous collection.

Souillac★

At the confluence of the Corrèze and the Dordogne, in the centre of a fertile region, Souillac is a small town bustling with trade and tourists, bisected by the national route 20.

A BIT OF HISTORY

After the Benedictines settled in the plain of Souillès, (*souilh* meaning bog or marshland where wild boar wallow), they transformed the marsh into a rich estate. Souillac Abbey was plundered and sacked several times by the English during the Hundred Years War and the Wars of Religion, but rose from its ruins each time thanks to the tenacity of its abbots. During the Revolution, its buildings were used for storing tobacco.

ABBEY CHURCH

place de l'Abbaye

⏱*Open year. Summer 8am–7pm and Winter 8am–6pm.* ☎05 65 37 81 56
Dedicated to Mary, Mother of Christ, this church became a parish church to replace the church of St Martin, which was destroyed during the Wars of Religion. Built in the 12C, the church is related to the Romanesque cathedrals of Angoulême, Périgueux and Cahors with their Byzantine inspiration, but it is more advanced in the lightness of its columns and the height of its arcades than the others. From place de l'Abbaye

- **Population:** 3,970
- **Michelin Map:** 337: E-2; or see Dordogne in the Quercy.
- **Info:** Boulevard Louis Jean Malvy. ☎05 65 37 81 56. www.tourisme-souillac.com
- **Location:** Along the N 20, 29km/18mi east of Sarlat-la-Canéda and 39km/24mi south of Brive-la-Gaillarde.
- **Kids:** Musée National de l'Automate, Parc Aquatique Quercy Land.
- **Also See:** Rocamadour, Périgord Noir

one can admire the attractive east end with its five pentagonal, apsidal chapels and an unusual tower on the other side of the building.

The back of the doorway★ - This composition consists of the remains of the old doorway, which was badly damaged by the Protestants and had been placed inside the nave of the new church, when it was erected in the 17C.

Above the door, framed by the statues of St Peter on the right and St Benedict on the left, is a bas-relief relating episodes in the life of the monk Theophilus, deacon of Adana in Cilicia. On the right side of the door is a bas-relief of the prophet **Isaiah★★**. ⊙*The disfigured bell tower,*

East end of église abbatiale Sainte Marie

J. Damase/MICHELIN

which is all that remains of the church St Martin, is now the town hall belfry.

Musée National de l'Automate★

Enter by the parvis of the abbey church (Abbatiale St-Pierre). 🕐*Open Jul–Aug, 10am–7pm; Jun and Sept, 10am–noon and 3–6pm; Apr–May and Oct, daily except Mon, 10am–noon and 3–6pm; Nov–Mar, daily except Mon and Tue, 2.30–5.30pm.* ✆*5.50€ (child 5–12: 3€).* ✆*05 65 37 07 07.*

👥The museum contains some 3 000 objects, including 1 000 automata donated by the **Roullet-Decamps** family, who for four generations were

Virginia Woolf and Souillac

Virginia Woolf stayed here in 1937 and was moved to write "no tourists … England seems like a chocolate box bursting with trippers afterward." A little different today perhaps, but Souillac remains an everyday french provincial town.

leaders in the field. In 1865 Jean Roullet created his first mechanical toy: a small gardener pushing a wheel barrow. Note especially the **Jazz band** (1920), a group of electric automata with black musicians performing a concert.

ADDRESSES

🛏 STAY

😊😊 **Belle Vue** – *68 av. J.-Jaurès.* ✆*05 65 32 78 23. www.hotelbellevue-souillac.com. Closed Jan 8–31, Feb and Sat-Sun in Mar. 25 rooms.* Conveniently located near the train station, this hotel offers rooms, which are plain and clean. In the garden, you can enjoy the use of tennis courts and a pool. A shop on the premises sells regional products.

😊😊 **Grand Hôtel** – *1 allée Verninac.* ✆*05 65 32 78 30. www.grandhotel-souillac.com. Closed Dec 8–Mar 17. 30 rooms.* Go up to the rooftop terrace and enjoy a drink with a view. Modern rooms in the main building contrast with those in the 18C section. The dining room has a veranda and there is a nice terrace under the plane trees.

😊😊 **Chambre d'hôte et Gîte Le Manoir** – *La Forge. 5km/3.1mi NW of Souillac on the D 15.* ✆*05 65 32 77 66. www.lemanoir.net. Closed Nov 1–Easter. 5 rooms.* In need of a little R&R? You will be able to relax in this attractive guesthouse or in one of the five comfortable holiday cottages (up to six people). Non-smokers only. Pool.

😊😊 **La Vieille Auberge** – *1 r. Recège.* ✆*05 65 32 79 43. www.la-vieille-auberge.com. Closed Nov 12–Feb 11 and Sun from Feb 12–end of Mar. 19 rooms.* This inn is just around the corner from the church,

in a quiet neighbourhood. The 3rd floor rooms have sloping ceilings under the eaves. For a pick-me-up, dive into the pool – open air in the summer months – or use the exercise facilities.

🍽 EAT

😊😊 **Les Ambassadeurs** – *12 av. du Gén.-de-Gaulle.* ✆*05 65 32 78 36. www.ambassadeurs-hotel.com. Closed Jan 2–Feb 15 and Fri–Sat from Oct 15–Easter.* The façade of this restaurant features local stone, a red awning and a golden stew pot. The atmosphere is old-fashioned and the cuisine traditional French, with local highlights.

🛒 SHOPPING

Distillerie Louis Roque – *41 av. Jean-Jaurès.* ✆*05 65 32 78 16. www.lavieille-prune.com. Open Mon-Sat, 8.30am–noon and 2–5pm. Closed public hols.* The heirs of Louis Roque make regional liqueurs and apéritifs using traditional recipes that have proved their worth over the century. The most famous elixir is *la vieille prune*. Visit the distillery and the museum and sample the wares, all free of charge.

🏃 LEISURE ACTIVITIES

Parc Aquatique Quercy Land – *Open May–mid Sept, 11am–8pm.* ✆*7€* ✆*05 65 32 72 61. contact@copeyre.com* 👥 Canoe-kayak hire on the River Dordogne, go carts and water park.

St-Céré★

and Vallée de la Bave

The lovely old houses of St-Céré cluster in the cheerful Bave Valley, at the foot of St Laurence's Towers. St-Céré stands at the junction of roads from Limousin, Auvergne and Quercy, but has become a good place to stay in its own right because of its pleasant site. It is also an excellent starting point for walks and excursions in Upper Quercy, and its renowned festival is a popular rendezvous for music lovers.

A BIT OF HISTORY

A prosperous town – In the 13C the viscounts of Turenne, overlords of St-Céré, granted a charter with franchises and many advantages to the town. Other charters added to the wealth of the town by giving it the right to hold fairs and establish trading houses. Consuls and officials administered the town, which was protected by St Laurence's Castle and a formidable line of ramparts. Even the Hundred Years War left the town practically unscathed. With the 16C dawned a new period of prosperity.

Jean Lurçat and St-Céré – Born in 1892 in the Vosges *département*, Jean Lurçat, whose parents had planned that he would become a doctor, directed his talents instead to painting and other art

Maison de Jean de Séguirier

S. Sauvignier/MICHELIN

- ▶ **Population:** 3 540
- **Michelin Map:** 337: H-2
- **Info:** Pl. de la République. ℘05 65 38 11 85. www. tourisme-saint-cere.com.
- ○ **Timing**: Allow half a day to explore the Bave valley.
- **Don't Miss**: The Atelier-Musée Jean-Lurçat; Vallée de la Bave.

forms. He soon became interested in tapestry; it is for his work on tapestry design and technique that he achieved world renown (*see AUBUSSON*).

After a period spent in Aubusson, he participated in the Resistance movement and through this discovered the region of the Lot. He settled in St-Céré in 1945. It was in St Laurence's Towers that he set up his studio, and lived here until his death in 1966.

Lurçat had the Aubusson tapestry factory weave most of the tapestries for which he had painted the designs (cartoons).

WALKING TOUR
OLD TOWN

The 15–17C houses give St-Céré a picturesque character all of its own. Some houses still have half-timbered corbelled façades and brown tiled roofs.

Place de l'Église

The church of Ste-Spérie was rebuilt in the 17C and 18C in the Gothic style. **The Hôtel de Puymule** (15C), in the square near the east end, is a turreted town house, with doors and windows decorated with ribbed arches.

○ *From place de l'Église, follow rue Notre-Dame and rue de la République.*

Rue du Mazel

This street and surrounding area form one of the most charming districts in the old town, with old houses and fine doorways. At the corner of rue St-Cyr, note the 15C **Hôtel Ambert** with its corbelled turrets and Renaissance doorway.

TOURS DE ST-LAURENT, ATELIER-MUSÉE J.-LURÇAT

ST-CÉRÉ

WHERE TO STAY

Château de Gamot
(Chambre d'hôte)............①
Relais de Castelnau
(Hôtel Le)........................④
Villa Ric..........................⑥

WHERE TO EAT

Crêperie de Py..................①
De France.........................④
Victor Hugo (Le)...............⑧

CAHORS, FIGEAC, D 940

Farther along on the right, the narrow cobblestoned **passage Lagarouste**, with a stream down the middle, is overshadowed by tall corbelled houses.

▷ *Continue along rue du Mazel.*

Place du Mercadial

This was the market square where fishermen brought their catch to be displayed on the *taoulié*, a stone bench beside the 15C **Maison de Jean de Séguirier** at the corner of rue Pasteur. From this spot, there is a lovely view of the square surrounded by half-timbered houses against St Laurence's Towers. The **Maison des Consuls** has an interesting Renaissance façade overlooking rue de l'Hôtel-de-Ville.

▷ *Follow rue des Tourelles.*

Rue St-Cyr

On the corner of rue de l'Olie stands a lovely medieval house with three corbelled façades. Farther on, in rue de l'Olie on the left, is the 15C Hôtel de Miramon flanked with a corner turret.

▷ *At the end of rue de l'Olie, turn right onto boulevard Carnot.*

Maison Louis XIII

This mansion has an elegant façade.

▷ *Return to place de l'Église.*

MUSEUMS AND EXHIBITIONS
Atelier-Musée Jean-Lurçat★

ⓘ*Open mid-Jul to Sept and during the Easter school holidays (zone B), 9.30am–noon and 2.30–6.30pm.*
⊘*2.50€.* ☎*05 65 38 28 21.*

In the artist's studio, now a museum, the ground-floor rooms (studio, drawing room, dining room) exhibit Lurçat's works (tapestries, designs, paintings, ceramics, lithographs, gouaches, wallpaper).

Galerie d'Art le Casino

ⓘ*Opening times vary.* ⊘*No charge.*
☎*05 65 38 19 60.*

In addition to temporary exhibitions, this gallery displays a large collection of **Jean Lurçat's tapestries★**. Hung on the walls, the tapestries combine a variety of forms and colours, depicting fantastic animals and cosmic visions.

EXCURSIONS
Site de Notre-Dame-de-Verdale★

9km/5.6mi E. Leave St-Céré travelling E on the D 673. After 2km/1mi, turn right on the D 30. 1km/0.5mi beyond Latouille-Lentillac a narrow road branches off to the left and runs along the river. Park the car in the area provided and continue on foot.
🚶 *1hr round trip on foot.*

Walk up a path, which runs beside the Tolerme, as it falls in cascades over the rocks. After crossing the stream twice on primitive wooden bridges the path climbs steeply, in a hilly setting.

Shortly, the pilgrimage chapel of Our Lady of Verdale appears perched on a rocky crag. From the site, there is an extensive **view**★ of the Tolerme gorges and the chestnut-covered hills.

Lac du Tolerme

23km/14.5mi E. Leave St-Céré E on the D 673 and continue along the D 30.

The lake, at 530m/1 739ft, is surrounded by greenery and covers 38ha/94 acres. At the lake there is a **recreation centre** open to visitors (⏱*Parking fee in Jul-Aug.* ⬤*5€.* ☎*05 65 40 31 26).* A lakeside footpath (4km/2.4mi) is a pleasant place to stretch your legs.

🚗 DRIVING TOUR

VALLÉE DE LA BAVE

45km/28mi round-trip – allow 3hr

▷ *Leave St-Céré W along the D 30.*

The towers of Montal Castle soon come into view on the left, rising above fertile fields and meadows interspersed with lines of poplars.

Château de Montal★★

👣 *See Château de MONTAL.*

▷ *The road towards Gramat climbs above the Bave Valley, offering views of St Laurence's Towers. Join up with the D 673 via St-Jean-Lespinasse.*

Grotte de Presque★

⏱🚶*Open Jul 5–Aug 25, guided tour (45min), 9.30am–6.30pm; Feb 15–Jul 4 and Aug 26–Sept 30, 9.30am–noon and 2–6pm; Oct–Nov 1, 10am–noon and 2–5pm.* ⬤*7€.* ☎*06 88 04 47 04. www.grottesdepresque.com.*

The cave consists of a series of chambers and galleries that extend 350m/380yd into the rocks. Concretions, especially strange-shaped stalagmite piles and frozen falls along the walls, have built up in the different *salles* or chambers of the caves. Slender columns of aston-

ishing whiteness stand at the entrance to the **Salle des Merveilles**★ (Hall of Wonders).

▷ *Continue on D 673 for Padirac then turn right onto the D 38.*

Cirque d'Autoire★

Leave the car in a parking area.

Take, on the left of the road, the path that overlooks the River Autoire, which here forms a series of waterfalls.

Cross the little bridge and go up the steep stony path cut in the rocks. Very soon a wonderful **view**★★ of the natural amphitheatre, the valley and the village of Autoire unfolds.

Autoire★

Autoire in its picturesque **setting**★ is typical of the character of the Quercy region. Enchanting scenes are revealed at every street corner: a fountain at the centre of a group of half-timbered houses; old corbelled houses with brown-tiled roofs; elegant turreted manors and mansions.

From the terrace near the church, which has a fine Romanesque east end, there is a good view of the Limargue Mill and the rocky amphitheatre that lies to the south-west.

▷ *Drive N along the D 135.*

Loubressac★

This old fortified town stands on a rocky spur overlooking the south bank of the River Bave. From near the church, there is a good view of the valley and of St-Céré, marked out by its towers. Walk through the enchanting narrow alleys as they wind between brown-tiled houses to the castle's postern. This 15C manor house, which was rebuilt in the 17C, stands on a remarkable **site**★ at the very end of the spur on which the village was built.

▷ *D 118 and then the D 14 from the hamlet of La Poujade descend towards the Bave Valley, giving fine **views**★ of the Dordogne Valley dominated by the* *impressive outline of Castelnau-Bretenoux Castle.*

Château de Castelnau-Bretenoux★★
See CASTELNAU-BRETENOUX.

▶ *Leave north on D 14.*

Bretenoux

In its leafy riverside setting, this former bastide, founded in 1277 by a powerful lord of Castelnau, has kept its grid plan, its central square, covered arcades and parts of the ramparts. After visiting the picturesque **place des Consuls** with its 15C turreted town house, go through a covered alley to the old manor at the corner of the pretty rue du Manoir de Cère. Turn right and right again returning via the charming quay along the Cère.

▶ *Drive 4km/2.5mi along the D 940 towards St-Céré and turn left onto the D 43 then right onto the D 40 5km/3mi beyond Belmont-Bretenoux.*

Map: VALLÉE DE LA BAVE

Tours de St-Laurent

Traffic on the private road branching off to the right is allowed. 🚶1hr on foot there and back.

Perched on a steep hill which overlooks the town, the two, tall medieval towers and curtain wall are a familiar local landmark. They were acquired by Jean Lurçat in 1945.

▶ *The D 48 (left) leads back to St-Céré.*

ADDRESSES

🏠 STAY

◗◗🛏 **Chambre d'hôte Château de Gamot** – *46130 Loubressac. 5km/3.1mi W of St-Céré.* ℘*05 65 10 92 03. Closed Oct–Apr. 7 rooms.* B&B in a charming 17C family manor house, in a pastoral setting. Not all en-suite, but spacious and comfortable.

◗◗🛏🛏 **Inter-Hotel Le Relais de Castelnau** – *46130 Loubressac, route De Padirac Rocamadour.* ℘*05 65 10 80 90. www.relaisdecastelnau.com. 40 rooms* In a beautiful village setting, the hotel offers magnificent views over the Dordogne Valley and Castle; lovely swimming pool and gourmet restaurant.

◗◗🛏 **Logis Villa Ric** – *46400 Saint-Céré, Rte De Leyme, 2km (1.25mi) from town.* ℘*05 65 38 04 08. www.logis-de-france. fr. 5 rooms.* Set on a hill in lush parkland, with panoramic views and beautiful outdoor swimming pool.. Rooms are

characterful. The restaurant serves good regional cuisine.

🍴 EAT

◗◗🛏 **Crêperie de Py** –*46130 Loubressac.* ℘*05 65 38 52 09. www.creperie-py.fr.* With a beautifully located pool at guests' disposal and regular concerts, this is a popular summer hang out serving crêpes and grills.

◗◗🛏 **De France** –*av. François de Maynard.* ℘*05 65 38 02 16.www.lefrance-hotel.com. Closed 20 Dec–25 Jan and Fri dinner 15 Oct–8 Feb – dinner only except Sun.* Comfortable, rustic-style restaurant with a shaded terrace: traditional dishes, mostly Quercy cuisine.

◗◗🛏 **Le Victor Hugo** – *7 av. du Maquis.* ℘*05 65 38 16 15. www.hotel-victor-hugo.fr. Closed Mar 1–15 & Oct 20–Nov 10, Mon (and Sun eve low season) Reserv. recommended.* Half-timbered 17C house on the banks of the River Bave. Some of the pretty little rooms have a river view and there is an outdoor terrace.

The Upper Vézère and Corrèze Valleys stretch from the Puy-de-Dome *département* in the east to the Périgord Noir and the Périgord Vert in the west. The Corrèze *département* lies just north of the Upper Dordogne Valley, whose river rises on the slopes of Mont Dore, just a few kilometres from the Corrèze's eastern edge. Two other large rivers dominate this region; the Vézère and the Corrèze, both of which rise within the département. The Corrèze River is a tributary of the Vézère, the confluence being just a short distance downstream from Brive-la-Gaillarde, the largest town in the Corrèze *département*.

The depression of the Brive Basin is a sunken zone between the crystalline escarpments of the Uzerche plateau and the limestone ridges of the Causses du Quercy. It is an area of sandstone and schist, drained by the River Vézère and River Corrèze. In its green valleys,

Maison de la Sirène, Collonges-la-Rouge

Jacassi/MICHELIN

demarcated by screens of poplar, the gentle south-facing slopes given over to orchards.

Today, Brive on the River Corrèze is an important centre for the fruit and vegetable canning industries. It is also an important communications hub being at the centre of the north-south route from Paris to Toulouse connected by the A20 and east–west from Lyon to Bordeaux connected by the recently completed A89.

Further up the Corrèze valley lies Tulle, the capital of the Corrèze, which gave its name to the soft fine lace net used for veils and dresses. At the northern boundary lies the Plateau de Millevaches, now a National Park, which forms part of the Montagne region of the Limousin. Not particularly mountainous, the highest point is Mont Bessou at 977metres/3205ft. To the south, the Causse Corrèzien below Brive is covered with large farms devoted to the rearing of geese and sheep, and truffle oak plantations.

Arnac-Pompadour★

and the Upper Auvézère

These two villages in the Corrèze, just 2km/1.2mi apart, today form a single administrative area (*commune*). The château and title of Pompadour were given by King Louis XV to his favourite in 1745. In 1761, the king established a famous stud farm here which, in the 19C, saw the development of the Anglo-Arabian breed in France. A number of important horse races and other competitive events are held here regularly in summer.

▶ **Population:** 1 334
🕓 **Michelin Map:** 329: J-3
🛈 **Info:** 1, Place de la Poste 19230 Arnac-Pompadour. ℘05 55 98 55 47. www.pompadour.net
👁 **Don't Miss:** National Stud Farm (Haras National) and Château de Pompadour.

Château de Arnac-Pompadour

E. Larribère/MICHELIN

CHÂTEAU

BP5 19230 Arnac-Pompadour
🚹*Open all year - ⊚4€ For information on times, call ℘05 55 98 51 10 or visit www.les3tours-pompadour.com.*
This imposing 15C castle with its magnificent façade stands in a delightfully verdant setting. The château is home to the stud farm's administrative offices.

HARAS NATIONAL (NATIONAL STUD FARM)

BP5 19230 Arnac-Pompadour
🚹*Open all year - Stallion's Stables ⊚6€ and the Mare Farm ⊚6€. ℘05 55 98 51 10 or visit www.les3 tours-pompadour.com.*
The Puy-Marmont stallion farm, in a park opposite the château, is home to forty or so thoroughbreds, including pure-bred English, Arabian and Anglo-Arabian stallions. A number of other horses (draught horses from the French regions of the Ardennes, Brittany and Franche-Comté, Percherons etc) are also stabled here.

🚗 DRIVING TOUR

UPPER AUVÉZÈRE VALLEY

Lave Pompadour along the D 126.

Église d'Arnac

This church, with its severe appearance and imposing dimensions, was built in the 12C, and is an unusual mix of the Romanesque and Gothic styles.

The doorway, characteristic of the Limousin style, is decorated with capitals, medallions and pointed, hanging ornaments at the apexes of the vaults. Three statues are set into the façade above: from left to right, St Martial, the Virgin and St Pardoux – the two saints are patrons of the Limousin region.

Inside the nave, the keystones bear the arms of Pompadour, and the transept has preserved its Romanesque appearance. Interesting historiated capitals adorn the columns in the nave, including scenes of the Annunciation and Daniel in the Lion's Den.

🔾 *Continue on D 126; left on D 127.*

Ségur-le-Château★

Nestled in a deep gorge carved out by the River Auvézère, the charming village of Ségur is a maze of old houses crowning two steep hills. On top of one of these hills stand the ruins of a 12C-13C castle with its double curtain walls. It is possible that Ségur's origins may go back as far as Gallo-Roman times; it certainly played an important role in

271

the Middle Ages and under the Ancien Régime. Cradle of the first viscounts of Limoges, when feudalism was at its peak, this prosperous settlement was the birthplace, in 1470, of Jean d'Albret, first king of Navarre and grandfather of Jeanne d'Albret, the mother of Henri IV. However, Ségur's main claim to fame derives from the time (15C to mid 18C) when it served as the seat of the high court of appeal for hundreds of feudal jurisdictions in the Limousin and the Périgord. Ségur's charm lies in its beautiful residences built by the many court officials who lived here. These include the **Maison Febrer** (15C), with its Renaissance chimneys and turrets, and the **Maison Henri IV**, named in honour of the d'Albret family. Today the long robes and powdered wigs of magistrates are long gone, replaced by artists who paint the village's half-timbered houses embellished with turrets, crowned with characteristic pointed brown tiled roofs, and fronted by Gothic doorways opening onto narrow, winding lanes.

▷ *Head NE out of Ségur along the D 149.*

Lubersac

In the **Église St-Étienne** (*if the church is closed, contact the tourist office*) note the remarkable **historiated capitals**★ decorating the chancel and the delicately carved capitals adorning the north and south apsidal chapels. The village also boasts a fine arcaded house with Renaissance windows known as the **Maison des Archiprêtres.**

▷ *Leave Lubersac to the SE along the D 148. In St-Pardoux-Corbier, take the D 54E1 to Fargeas, and then the D 148 to Troche.*

Chartreuse de Glandier

For information, call ☎05 55 98 55 47.
A **Carthusian monastery** (*chartreuse*) was established in the heart of the Loyre Valley in the 13C. Destroyed during the Revolution, the order repurchased it in 1860 and rebuilt it over a period of 10 years. Nowadays the buildings serve as a medical centre, with an exhibition area

devoted to its history, including a scale model of the site. One of the **monk's pavilions** has been reconstructed; its two floors show a workshop on the ground floor, with a bedroom and library (for meditation and spiritual needs) on the floor above.

Jumenterie Nat. de la Rivière

🕭*For information, call* ☎05 55 98 55 47.
The Domaine de la Rivière, covering an area of 88ha/217 acres, was created in the 18C on the site of a ruined 15C castle (only the towers and a Gothic chapel remain), and became a national centre for breeding mares in the 19C - nowadays, some 40 mares are permanently based here. In the months of May and June, proud mothers can be seen gambolling in the fields with their colts. The riding centre also owns a dozen stallions.

▷ *Take the D 7E3, then the D7 which will take you back to Pompadour.*

ADDRESSES

🛏 STAY

◺ **Chambre d'hôte Ferme de la Petite Brunie** – *2km/1.2mi NE of Pompadour along the D 54E1 towards St-Pardoux-Corbier.* ☎05 55 73 34 17. 5 rooms. Closed 16 Nov-14 Mar. ⌂. This charming house, now a bed and breakfast, used to be the farm's pigsty! The bright, modern rooms overlook a secluded garden and meadows. The hearty breakfast includes cold meats, pastries and home-made jam. Dinner here is traditional family cooking.

◺ **Chambre d'hôte à la Ferme du Domaine de la Roche** – *19210 St-Julien-le-Vendomois. 7km/4.2mi NW of Arnac along the D 126.* ☎05 55 98 72 87. michel.souriou@wanadoo.fr. 4 rooms, reservation required. ⌂. Enjoy the peacefulness of this charming farm in the heart of the countryside. The simple attic bedrooms are housed in a separate 18C building. Home-made and regional products, including foie gras, confit, jams, etc, are also on sale here.

Aubazine★

The village of Aubazine and its Cistercian abbey, formerly known as Obazine, are pleasantly situated between the River Corrèze and River Coiroux, on a promontory set back from the main road.

▶ **Population:** 807
⚲ **Michelin Map:** 329: L-4. Local map see *Brive-la-gaillarde* and *Tulle:* Excursions
🛈 **Info:** Le Bourg -B.P. 2, 19190 Aubazine. ℘05.55.25.79.93. www.cc-beynat.fr.
▶ **Location:** 17km/11.25mi SW of Tulle via D1089/D130
🛈 **Don't Miss:** The 12C Abbaye d'Aubazine, a superb example of a Cistercian abbey.

A BIT OF HISTORY

At the beginning of the 12C a group of men and women, united by a common desire to lead a life of fasting and prayer, gathered together in the forest of Aubazine to join the hermit St Stephen. Having adopted the rule of St Benedict, this small community built a monastery at Aubazine, and then a convent, just 600m/656yd away in the Coiroux Valley. In 1147, both communities were admitted into the Cistercian Order and this dual monastery was preserved until the Revolution. The founder had decreed that the women take vows of complete enclosure, so they were totally dependent, both spiritually and materially, on the monastery. This no doubt gave rise to the local joke that anyone with a daughter at Coiroux gained a son-in-law at Aubazine.

ABBEY★

The abbey was built in the second half of the 12C and dedicated to the Blessed Virgin. In the 18C it was truncated, losing six of its nine bays, so it is easy to imagine how large the original was.

Bell tower★ – The bell tower crowning the transept crossing is of a very original design; the transition from a square shape to an octagonal one is a technical achievement unique to that time.

Interior – The central nave has a barrel vault and the huge square of the transept is crowned with an elegant dome. The stained-glass windows in grisaille are the only ones to have been permitted in a Cistercian church.

Furnishings★ – In the south arm of the transept there is the remarkable **tomb of St Stephen★★** made from limestone between 1250 and 1260. The face of the recumbent figure has been disfigured by the faithful flock (who believed that the dust they obtained by scraping at the stone held miraculous powers). The liturgical cupboard was made in the 12C from oak beams and its sides are decorated with blind arcades. The **Coiroux Entombment** is a piece of polychrome stonework rediscovered in 1895.

Conventual buildings

🕐*Jul 14–Aug 15, 🚶guided tour (1hr 15min) Tue–Sat at 10.30am, 3pm and 4pm, Sun 10am, 3pm, 4pm ; Jun 1–Jul 13 and Aug 16– Sept, Tue–Sat at 10.30am and 3pm, Sun 10am, 3pm; Apr, May, Oct, Tue–Sun 3pm; Feb, Mar, Nov–Dec, Sat–Sun 3pm.*🕐*Closed Mon, Jan, Easter and last week Aug.* ✆*5.00€.* ℘*05 55 84 61 12.*
Once part of the men's monastery, the conventual buildings are home to a community of Catholic nuns. The visit includes the large fish-breeding pond, its water sourced via the impressive 12C **Canal des Moines** (Monks' Canal).

Convent

600m/656yd from Aubazine along the road to Palazinges.
The church walls are all that remain of the convent, which was abandoned in 1791. However, recent excavation work has unearthed the irrigation system for drinking water and the arched doorway by which the monks and nuns communicated. This is designed like a lock chamber; one of the communities had the key to the outside door and the other the key to the inside door.

ADDRESSES

🛏 STAY 🍴 EAT

🍲🍲 **La Tour** – *Place de l'Église, 19190 Aubazine. 🖀 05 55 25 71 17. Closed Jan 2–20 (restaurant also closed Mon lunchtime in winter and Sun eve. exc. July and August) - 19 rooms (half board available) - ☲.* This hotel, standing opposite the abbey, consists of two attractive houses, the oldest flanked by a tower. Traditional bedrooms decorated with coloured wallpaper. The restaurant specialises in regional cuisine served in rustic-style rooms adorned with copper and pewter pots. The hotel bar is popular with locals.

🍲🍲 **Le Saut de la Bergère** – *2km/1.2mi E of Aubazine on D 48. . 🖀 05 55 25 74 09 www.le-saut-de-la-bergere.com.* *Closed Dec 24– Mar 15, Sun evening, Mon Sept–Apr and Wed from Sept 15–Dec 24. 7 rooms.* The name of this restaurant is also the name of a nearby escarpment that experienced climbers may tackle before settling down to enjoy regional specialities in this quiet country restaurant. A few simple rooms.

🏃 LEISURE ACTIVITIES

Parc du Coiroux – *4km/2.5mi E of Aubazine along the D 48 - 🖀 05 55 27 25 66 - www.golf-coiroux.com - Open Jun to early Sep: daily 7am-7pm; Sep-May: daily 9am-5pm - golf course open all year - Closed Christmas and New Year.* This 180ha/445-acre park offers a broad range of activities, including swimming in the lake, archery, tennis, volleyball, horse-riding and golf. The park also has a campsite and restaurant.

Brive-la-Gaillarde

Basse Vallée de la Corrèze, Turenne, Causse Corrèzien

Brive owes its suffix 'La Gaillarde' (the bold) to the courage displayed by its citizens during sieges in centuries past. This busy town stands in the alluvial plain of the River Corrèze: as a result of its fertile soil, the surrounding area is an important centre for market gardening and fruit growing. Located at the crossroads of the Bas-Limousin (Lower Limousin), the Périgord and the limestone plateaux of the Quercy, the town is an important railway junction with a thriving economy. Since 1982, an important annual book fair (the Foire du Livre) has been held in the town. No mention of Brive can be made without reference to its rubgy union team, one of the most respected in France.

A BIT OF HISTORY

A brilliant career –**Guillaume Dubois** (1656-1723), the son of an apothecary from Brive, took the Orders and

- ▶ **Population:** 50,009
- 🕭 **Michelin Map:** 329: K-5
- 🛈 **Information:** Place du 14 Juillet, 19100 Brive-la-Gaillarde. 🖀 05 55 24 58 24 www.brive-tourisme.com
- ▶ **Location:** 94km/58.75mi S of Limoges via the A20
- 👪 **Kids:** Lac de Causse, in the Vallée de la Couze.
- 👁 **Don't Miss:** Hôtel de Labenche; Basse Vallée de la Corrèze; Causse Corrézien; Gouffre de la Fage.

became tutor to Philip of Orléans. He became prime minister when Philip was appointed regent during the minority of Louis XV. Offices and honours were heaped upon him; he became Archbishop of Cambrai and then a cardinal. He made an alliance with England, which thus ensured a long period of peace in France.

A Glorious Soldier – **Guillaume-Marie-Anne Brune** (1763-1815) enlisted in the army in 1791 and rose to become a general commanding the army in Italy in 1798. Following victories in Holland and Italy he was appointed ambassa-

BRIVE-LA-GAILLARDE

WHERE TO STAY	
Collonges (Hôtel Le)	①
Coq d'Or (Le)	③
Truffe Noire (La)	⑤

WHERE TO EAT	
Francis (Chez)	③
Relais du Quercy (Le)	⑧
Table d'Olivier (La)	⑨
Toupine (La)	⑩

dor to Constantinople. Elected Maréchal de France in 1804, he was banished by Napoleon soon afterwards for his republican attitude. He became the symbol of the Revolution and died, a victim of a Royalist mob, in 1815 at Avignon.

WALKING TOUR
OLD TOWN

The old town located in the heart of the city, bounded by a first ring of boulevards, has been successfully restored. The buildings, old and new, create a harmonious ensemble of warm beige sandstone and bluish tinted rooftops.

▶ *Start from the tourist office (place du 14-Juillet). Follow avenue de Paris* then *rue de Toulzac across boulevard Anatole-France and turn immediately right onto rue de Corrèze.*

Chapelle St-Libéral

This Gothic chapel is the venue of temporary exhibitions throughout the year.

▶ *Continue along rue de Corrèze then follow rue Majour.*

Collégiale St-Martin

In this church, only the transept, apse and a few of the capitals are Romanesque, the traces of a 12C monastic community. Inside, over the transept crossing, is an octagonal dome on flat pendentives, characteristic of the Limousin style. The nave and side aisles are 14C. The chancel was faithfully rebuilt by Cardinal Dubois in the 18C; note the 12C baptismal font, decorated with the symbols of the Evangelists.

Archaeological Crypt

Vestiges of previous churches have been uncovered beneath the chancel, including the primitive construction dating from the 5C over the tomb of St Martin the Spaniard.

▷ *On coming out of the church, take rue des Échevins on the left.*

Tour des Échevins

In the narrow rue des Échevins stands a town house with a fine corbelled Renaissance tower with mullioned windows.

▷ *Retrace your steps and turn right.*

Place Latreille

This square was once the spiritual and commercial heart of the city and is still surrounded by old houses. The house known as **Tours St-Martin** dates from the 15C and 16C.

▷ *Continue straight on along rue du Docteur-Massénat then turn right onto rue Raynal.*

Positioned at the corner of rue Raynal and rue du Salan is the 18C Hôtel Desbruslys.

▷ *Walk along rue Raynal and enter the Hôtel de Labenche through the small door on the left.*

Hôtel de Labenche★

From the inner courtyard, the view encompasses the two buildings standing at right angles, which support the arcaded gallery. Built in 1540 by Jean II de Calvimont, lord of Labenche and the king's keeper of the seals for the Bas-Limousin, this mansion is a magnificent example of Renaissance architecture in Toulouse style and is the most remarkable secular building in town. Inside, it has been converted into a museum.

▷ *Continue along boulevard Jules-Ferry and turn left onto rue du Dr-Massénat.*

Logis de l'Abbesse des Clarisses

(Residence of the Mother Superior of the Order of St Clare). This Louis XIII building is distinguished by its dormer windows with semicircular pediments decorated with keel-shaped spheres.

▷ *Turn right onto rue Teyssier.*

Ancien Collège des Doctrinaires

This college was maintained by the Brothers of Christian Doctrine, who were as much open-minded humanists as men of faith, and its prosperity increased up until the Revolution. Today these 17C buildings house the town hall.

▷ *Turn right.*

Place Jean-Marie-Dauzier

On this large square, modern buildings (Crédit Agricole bank) and old turreted mansions form a harmonious architectural unit.
The 16C **Maison Treilhard** consists of two main buildings joined by a round tower, decorated by a turret.

▷ *Retrace your steps, walk back to the collegiate church across place de l'Hôtel-de-Ville, then turn right onto rue de Toulzac.*

MUSEUMS

Musée de Labenche★

&⊙*Open daily except Tue. Permanent collections open Apr–Oct, 10am–6.30pm; Nov–Mar, 1.30–6pm. Temporary exhibitions open Apl-Oct 10am–noon and 1.30–6.30pm, Nov–Mar 10am–noon and 1.30–6pm* ⊙*Closed 1 Jan, 1 May, 1 Nov and 25 Dec.* ⊛4.70€, *no charge last Sun of the month for the collections.* ℰ*05 55 18 17 70 www.musee-labenche.com .*
The Roman-style **main staircase** of the Hôtel de Labenche exudes the same

exuberance as the outside. Among the 17 rooms displaying the collections, pay particular attention to the Counts of Cosnac room decorated with a marvellous set of **tapestries**, known as the Mortlake tapestries, made in the 17C using the widely renowned techniques of English high-warp tapestry. In the Cardinal Dubois room, there is a wonderful 11C silver and bronze **eucharistic dove** hanging above the altar. One of the main attributes of this museum is the successful reconstruction of the various series of excavations.

Musée de la Résistance et de la Déportation Edmond-Michelet

⏱*Open daily except Sun, 10am-noon and 2-6pm.* ⏱*Closed public hols.* ✆*No charge.* ☎*05 55 74 06 08.*

The museum traces the history of the Resistance movement and deportation with paintings, photographs, posters and original documents relating to the camps, especially Dachau, where Edmond Michelet, former minister under General De Gaulle, was interned.

🚗 DRIVING TOURS

1 BASSE VALLÉE DE LA CORRÈZE★

Round tour of 45km/28mi – allow 3hr

▷ *Take the N 89 NE towards Tulle.*

Aubazine★ ⓘ *See AUBAZINE.*

▷ *Drive E along the D 48.*

Puy de Pauliac★

30min round trip. Altitude 520m/1 706ft. 🗻The footpath makes its way through heather and chestnut trees, leading upwards to reveal a splendid **view**★. A **viewing table** helps to identify the Roche de Vic to the south-east and to the north, the Monédières range.
The **Parc du Coiroux** has been developed around a large lake with swimming beaches and sailing, golf and tennis facilities.

17C Mortlake tapestry depicting the meeting of Hero and Leander, Musée de Labenche

Musée de Labenche, Brive

▷ *Return to Aubazine. Drive SE along the D 130 and the D 175 to Lanteuil, then drive back to Brive along the picturesque D 921.*

1 LES TERRES DE MONSIEUR DE TURENNE★

Round trip of 55km/34mi – allow 4hr
This trip crosses the central area of the old viscounty of Turenne, which was not united with the French crown until 1738 (ⓘ*see TURENNE*). Beyond Turenne, the wooded hills of the Limoges region give way to the first limestone plateaux of the Quercy region.

▷ *Leave Brive-La-Gaillarde travelling SE on the D 38 towards Meyssac.*

Château de Lacoste

This former stronghold, built of local sandstone, has a main building flanked by three 13C towers. It was completed in the 15C with an elegant turret and a polygonal staircase.

At **Noailhac** you enter the region of red sandstone, which is used to build the lovely warm-coloured villages of the area. Soon Collonges-la-Rouge, perhaps the best-known, can be seen against a backdrop of greenery.

Collonges-la-Rouge★★
ⓘ*See COLLONGES-LA-ROUGE.*

Meyssac

Meyssac is in the centre of hilly coun-tryside where walnut and poplar trees, vineyards and orchards prosper. Like Collonges-la-Rouge, the town is built of red sandstone.

The **church** is an unusual mixture of architectural elements: a Gothic inte-rior, a belfry-porch fortified by hoarding and a limestone doorway in the Roman-esque Limousin style. Near the church, is the **18C covered market**. The red earth, known as Collonges clay, is used in pot-tery manufacture here in Meyssac.

▶ *Leave Meyssac S on D 14, towards Martel. After 2km/1.2mi, turn right on the D 28.*

Saillac

The village nestles among walnut trees and fields of maize. Inside the small Romanesque church is a doorway, pre-ceded by a narthex, with a remarkable **tympanum**★ in polychrome stone, relatively rare in the 12C.

The village has retained its old mill (○*Open daily*, ∞*no charge*); walnut oil is pressed here every other year during the Walnut Festival on the first Sunday in October.

▶ *Leave Saillac travelling NW to reach the D 19, then turn SW towards the D 8.*

Turenne★
& *See TURENNE.*

▶ *Continue along the D 8. After 3km/1.8mi, turn left towards Lagleygeolles.*

Gouffre de la Fage★
○*Open daily Jul and Aug,*⚬ *guided tour (1hr, last entrance 30min before closing), 9.30am–1pm and 2–7pm; Apr–Jun, unaccompanied tour, 2–6.30pm exc. Wed; Sept 1 to Oct 10 2–6pm exc. Wed, unaccompanied tour, 2–6pm; Nov school hols, Tue and Thu, 3pm.* ∞*8€.* ℘*05 55 85 80 35.* www.gouffre-de-la-fage.com
The underground galleries in this chasm form two separate groups, which can be visited one after the other. A staircase leads into the chasm, which was created by the collapse of the roof section. The first group of chambers, to the left, contains fine draperies in the form of jellyfish in beautiful rich colours. In the Organ Hall (Salle des Orgues), the con-cretions are played like a xylophone.

The second group, with many stalagmites and stalactites, also has a forest of nee-dle-like forms hanging from the roof.

Return to Lagleygeolles, and take the left turn that will bring you to D 73.

Jugeals-Nazareth – The village of Nazareth was founded by Raymond I of Turenne on his return from the First Crusade. He built a leper-house which he entrusted to the care of the Knights Templars.

As you leave town to the N. on the D 8, a scenic overlook comes into view on the right. At the Monplaisir crossroads, D 38 goes back to Brive-la-Gaillarde.

③ LE CAUSSE CORRÈZIEN★
Round trip of 45km/29mi – allow 3hr

▶ *Leave Brive on the D 920 S, towards Cahors.*

The road rises above the Brive basin.

Grottes de St-Antoine
These caves, hollowed out of sandstone, were used as a retreat by St Antony of Padua. Follow the Stations of the Cross to the top of a hill for a view of Brive.

▶ *Take the small signposted road to the left.*

Grottes de Lamouroux
This group of caves arranged in five tiers was used by man in times of danger.

Noailles
Noailles, lying in a pleasant setting of green hills, is overlooked by its Renais-sance **château,** seat of the De Noailles family, and a church perched on a hill. The **church**, topped with a Limousin-style bell gable, has a Romanesque apse and chancel. There is a painting by Wat-

teau's teacher Claude Gillot (*Instruments of the Crucifixion*).

◗ *Leave Noailles on the D 158 heading W.*

The road climbs towards the lake and Corrèze Causse, an area of white limestone.

Lissac-sur-Couze

Set back from the lake, this elegant manor, flanked by battlemented turrets, was a military tower in the 13C and 14C.

Lac du Causse★

Also known as the Lac de Chasteaux, this superb stretch of water (90ha/222 acres), set in lush green countryside in the lovely Couze Valley, is a recreation centre.

◗ *Leave Lissac on the D 59 SW.*

The itinerary runs along the lake shore, revealing its extent and beauty.

◗ *Turn right off the D 19 onto the D 154 towards Chartrier-Ferrière.*

Le Maillet

The limestone walls of the houses in this hamlet are constructed in a traditional way using house martin mortar, that is lumps of clay pressed into cracks.

◗ *Continue along the D 154.*

Nadaillac

This charming country village is famous for its high-quality truffles. Some of the medieval houses have typical *lauzes* covered roofs.

◗ *Leave Nadaillac on the D 63.*

Farther on, scenic road D 60 weaves in and out of the départements of the Dordogne and Corrèze at their borders.

◗ *In Larche, take the N 89 back to Brive.*

The Brive Basin

Brive is situated in the Brive Basin which enjoys a sheltered climate free from extremes and excellent communications. As a result both industry and agriculture are well established here.

ADDRESSES

🛏 STAY

🍽 **Collonges** – *3 pl. Winston Churchill.* 📞*05 55 74 09 58. www.hotel-le-collonges. com. 24 rooms.* A family-run hotel set back slightly from the main boulevard encircling the centre of town. Cosy lounge-bar and modern, functional bedrooms.

🍽 **Le Teinchurier** – *Av. du Teinchurier.3km/1.8mi W of the centre on the Périgueux road.* 📞*05 55 86 45 00.ww.leteinchurier.com. 40 rooms & 3 apartments. Closed Dec 24–Jan 1.* On the outskirts of town with easy access from Clermont, Cahors and Bordeaux. Pastel shades in the contemporary dining room, where the focus is on unpretentious local cuisine. Spacious, functional bedrooms with good soundproofing.

🍽 **Chambre d'hôte** – *Mme Jacqueline Verlhac. Belveyre. 19600 Nespouls. 15km/9mi S of Brive. Take the A 20 (Nespouls exit), the D 19 and then turn right onto the D 920.* 📞*05 55 85 82 58.* 🛏 *5 rooms.* This bed and breakfast on the Causse Corrèzien is nestled amid a landscape of oak trees, meadows and typical stone huts. Pleasant rooms, tasty local cuisine and a friendly welcome.

🍽🍽 **La Truffe Noire** – *22 bd Anatole-France -* 📞*05 55 92 45 00. www.la-truffe-noire.com. 27 rooms.* The Black Truffle occupies a 19C regional-style house on the edge of the old town. Welcoming lounge with an imposing fireplace, and attractive guestrooms furnished with a contemporary feel. The pleasant dining room and shaded terrace are the setting for Corrèze specialities (including the trademark truffle).

🍴 EAT

🍽🍽 **Chez Francis** – *61 av. de Paris.* 📞*05 55 74 41 72. Closed Feb school hols, Tue in Aug, Sun, Mon and public hols. Reserv. required.* An authentic Parisian bistro in the centre of town. Simple but tasty traditional cuisine.

🍽🍽 **La Toupine** – *11 r. Jean-Labrunie -* 📞*05 55 23 71 58. - Closed Feb 23– Mar10 holidays, Aug 1–26, Wed evening and Sun.* *Reserv. required.* A popular local haunt in the old town serving good value-for-money cuisine.

🍽🍽 **La Potinière** – *6 bd de Puyblanc.* 📞*05 55 24 06 22 . Closed Sun eve (except Aug).* This old house with painted shutters is decorated in warm tones, with tables set out around an attractive bar counter. Traditional cuisine, including a number of grilled dishes. Attractive shaded terrace.

🍽🍽 **Taverne de Maitre Kanter** – *25, Bd Koenig, 19100 Brive -* 📞*05 55 17 62 30. Open every day exc. public holidays* Conveniently situated in the centre of town with an air-conditioned veranda and shady terrace. Excellent service and varied regional cuisine.

🍽🍽 **Le Relais du Quercy** – *19500 Meyssac -* 📞*05 55 25 40 31 - Closed first two weeks of Mar and Nov 15-30.* Choose between the comfortable dining room or attractive terrace to sample typical cuisine prepared using the best local ingredients A few guest rooms are also available. Piano-bar.

🍽🍽🍽 **Les Arums** – *15 av. Alsace-Lorraine.* 📞*05 55 24 26 55.Closed Mar, Sept 1-15, Sat lunchtime, Sun eve and Mon (excluding public hols).* A recently modernised restaurant in the heart of Brive serving contemporary dishes in an elegant dining room or private garden. Attractive choice of menus.

🛒 MARKETS

Marché Brassens - *place du 14-juillet. Open Tue & Sat, 8am–12.30pm.* This wonderful covered market, named after George Brassens who sang about Brive, sells a huge range of local products. ,

Duck and goose fairs - These typical markets are held four times a year between Dec and Feb.

🛒 SHOPPING

Distillerie Denoix – *9 bd du Mar.-Lyautey -* 📞*05 55 74 34 27 - www.denoix. com . - Tue-Sat 9am-noon and 2.30-7pm; Jul-Aug: daily.* Founded in 1839, this distillery produces and markets Le Suprême de Noix walnut liqueur and Le Quinquinoix, an aperitif also made of walnuts. Violette de Brive mustard is also sold here.

Collonges-la-Rouge ★★

Collonges the Red, built of red sandstone, is set with its small manor houses, old houses and Romanesque church, in a countryside characteristic of the Quercy, with juniper bushes, walnut plantations and vineyards. An historic atmosphere pervades this lovely old village.

A BIT OF HISTORY

The village developed in the 8C around its church and priory, a dependency of the powerful Charroux Abbey. In the 13C, Collonges was a part of the viscounty of Turenne and thus received franchises and liberties. In the 16C, Collonges was the place chosen by prominent denizens of the viscounty for their holidays. They erected charming manors and mansions flanked with towers and turrets, which give the town its unique image.

☜ WALKING TOUR

▶ *Start near the old station (ancienne gare); take rue de la Barrière (left).*

Maison de la Sirène

This 16C corbelled house, with a porch and beautiful lauze roof, is adorned with a mermaid holding a comb in one hand and a mirror in the other. The interior has been reconstructed as the inside of a Collonges house of olden days.

▶ **Population:** 450
🕙 **Michelin Map:** 329: K-5; or see Brive-la-Gaillarde
ℹ️ **Info:** Pl. de l'Ancienne-Gare, 19500. ℘ 05 55 25 47 57.
🧭 **Location:** 19km/11.9mi SE of Brive via the D38. For one of the best views of Collonges walk down rue de la Barrière into the village. Turn left and continue along rue de la Garde until the whole village can be seen from the west.
🅿️ **Parking:** Cars are not allowed during 10am–7pm Easter–Sept. There are three car parks off the main road above the village.
👁️ **Don't Miss:** Église St-Pierre, Castel de Vassinhac.

Farther along, the pointed gateway arch (Porte du Prieuré) marks the entrance of the former Benedictine priory, which was destroyed during the Revolution.

Hôtel des Ramades de Friac

The *hôtel*, crowned by two turrets, was once the town house of the powerful Ramades de Friac family. Go past the Relais de St-Jacques-de-Compostelle and through a covered passageway. Soon afterwards in an alley, on the right, there is an old turreted house.

COLLONGES-LA-ROUGE
0   100 m

WHERE TO STAY	
Diligence (Chambre d'hôte La)	①
Jeanne (Maison d'hôtes)	⑤
Relais de St-Jacques de Compostelle (Le)	⑪

WHERE TO EAT	
Cantou (Le)	①
Prieuré (Le)	⑥

Château de Benge

Set against a backdrop of poplar and walnut trees is this proud towered and turreted manor house with its lovely Renaissance window. The lords of Benge owned the famous Collonges vineyards, until these were decimated by phylloxera.

Porte Plate

This flat gateway, so named because it has lost its towers, was part of the town walls protecting the church, cloisters and priory buildings.

Halle

The covered market, with its massive framework supported by strong pillars, served as a central granary store and shelters the communal oven. The **Église St-Pierre**★ stands opposite.

Castel de Vassinhac★

This elegant manor house was owned by Gédéon de Vassinhac, lord of Collonges, captain-governor of the viscounty of Turenne. Built in 1583, the manor house bristles with large towers and turrets with pepper-pot roofs. Despite a large number of mullioned windows, its defensive role is obvious from its many loopholes and castellated turrets.

Église St-Pierre★

The church, which dates from the 11C and 12C, was fortified during the Wars of Religion in the 16C. It was at this time that the great, square keep was strengthened by a defence chamber communicating with the watch-path.
Tympanum★ – Carved in the white limestone of Turenne, the 12C tympanum stands out among all the red sandstone. The whole tympanum is outlined by a pointed arch ornamented with a fine border of carved animals.
Bell tower★ – The 12C bell tower is in the Limousin style: two lower square tiers pierced with round-arched bays are surmounted by two octagonal tiers flanked by gables.
Interior – In the 12C, the church had a cruciform plan around the transept crossing. The dome above the transept crossing rests on 11C pillars. Side chapels were added in the 14C and 15C, as well as a second, Flamboyant-style nave.

Chapelle des Pénitents

The 13C chapel was modified by the Maussac family during the 17C, during the Counter-Reformation.

Rue Noire

This street cuts through the oldest part of Collonges, where old houses can be seen set back one from the other, ornamented with turrets and towers and adorned with climbing plants.

Castel de Maussac

This building is embellished with a turret and a porch roof above the main door. A barbican projects from the square tower, which is overlooked by a dormer window. Continue farther south along the street to enjoy a pretty **view**★ of Collonges, Vassinhac Manor and the tower.

MUSEUM
Musée de la Sirène des Arts et Traditions Populaires
◷*Open Easter–Nov 1, 10.30am–12.30pm and 3–6pm. ◦2€. Visits by arrangement; Madame Faucher, ℘05 55 84 08 03.* A traditional local interior has been reconstructed inside.

ADDRESSES

▨ STAY
◍◍ **Chambre d'hôte La Raze** *19500 Collonges-la-Rouge. 5.5km/3.5mi SW of Collonges along the D 38 and D 19 (follow signs to La Raze). ℘05 55 25 48 16. ▱ 5 rooms.* This 18C farm is a 10min walk from Collonges. The main features here are the comfortable rooms decorated with stencilled designs, and an impressive English-style garden

⌾ EAT
◍◍◍ **Le Cantou,** *Le Bourg 19500. ℘05 55 84 25 15 www.lecantou.fr. Closed Jan and Mon Sept–June* This attractive 16C house built from purplish sandstone has kept its original charm. The menu is simple served in a room with a vaulted ceiling or on the shaded terrace.

Gimel-les-Cascades★★

Gimel stands in a remarkable **setting**★, one of the most picturesque of the Bas-Limousin, near Tulle and the Corrèze Valley. The Montane flows over the tumbling rocks of a wild ravine and hurls itself down waterfalls 143m/469ft high.

CASCADES★★

🚶*1hr round trip (strenuous). Follow marked pathways through the Parc Vuillier or Parc Blavignac.* 🕐*Open Mar–Nov 1, 10am–6pm (7pm, Jul–Aug); Wed, 11am–6pm.* 👓*5€.* 📞*05 55 21 26 49.*
The *Grande Cascade* (also known as the *Grand Saut*) tumbles down 45m/145ft; the next falls, *la Redole*, is 27m/90ft high. The two cascades, one above the other, are an impressive sight. The third one, with its amusing name of *Queue de Cheval* (Pony Tail), appears suddenly, spouting from a little rocky promontory; it plunges 60m/200ft into the deep ravine of Hell's Swallow Hole (le Gouffre de l'Inferno).

TRÉSOR DE L'ÉGLISE ST-PARDOUX★

The **Shrine of St Stephen**★★, a decorative chest from the late 12C, is embel-lished with Limoges enamels, the figures are in relief, with eyes of precious stones. The silver-gilt **reliquary bust** is a 14C homage to St Dumine, a soldier from Clovis' army who retreated to the Montane ravines as a hermit; note the 14C champlevé enamel **pyx** (receptacle for the Eucharist) and a 13C gilded copper **monstrance** (vessel in which the consecrated host is exposed for veneration).

▸ **Population:** 679
💧 **Michelin Map:** 329: M-4
ℹ **Info:** Le Bourg, 19800, www.gimellescascades.fr.

Grande Cascade

J. Malburet/MICHELIN

Meymac★

and Plateau de Millevaches

Perched on the edge of the Millevaches Plateau, Meymac is one of the prettiest villages in Corrèze, its streets and old houses clustered around the old abbey of St-André. In bygone days, the mountain folk came to town to trade their wool, cheese and chestnuts for products manufactured on the plains. Today, forestry is at the forefront of the local economy; a technical school trains future foresters. Rural and rustic, Meymac is an attractive tourist site, in lovely surroundings.

▸ **Population:** 2 661
💧 **Michelin Map:** 329: N-2
ℹ **Info:** Place de l'Hôtel de Ville. 📞05 55 95 18 43. www.ot-meymac.visite.org.
▸ **Location:** 49km/30.5mi northeast of Tulle via the D1089.
🕐 **Timing:** Allow half a day for Meymac and a full day to explore Plateau de Millevaches.
👁 **Don't Miss:** The Black Virgin in the abbey church.

OLD TOWN

The *vielle ville* is a charming place for a stroll. To the left of the church, an early-19C **covered market**, its framework resting on granite pillars, is set in a square formed by the buildings of the Hôtel-Dieu, erected in 1681.

Follow the street up towards the **clock tower**, which once guarded the castle gate, and discover the sculpted doorways (15C-16C), stair towers with pepper-pot caps, granite houses with steeply sloping slate roofs. Past the clock tower, a fountain embellishes a pretty little square.

Abbey Church

In 1085, Archambaud III founded a Benedictine abbey on the site of a church his forefathers had built. The church was under construction in the 12C, and was finished in the 13C after modifications to the initial plans were made.

There are some unusual aspects to the plans: a deviation of the transept arms, an irregular alignment of the apse and its chapels.

The belfry-porch has a multifoil doorway in the Limousin style, an arch on either side. The porch is adorned with Romanesque capitals carved in the archaic style.

The nave has ogive vaulting and continues into a chancel which is equally wide. Note a 12C **Black Virgin**★ on the pillar to the left of the chancel. Except for the turban on her head, the statue is typical of Auvergne in the posture and position of the long, protective hands.

Fondation Marius-Vazeilles

⏱*Open daily Jul–Sept, 10am–noon and 3–7pm; May, Jun and Oct,Mon,Wed and Fri, 2.30–6pm, Sat–Sun and public hols, 10am–noon and 2.30–6pm.* ▨*2.80€.* ✆*05 55 95 19 15.*

Established in a building beside the abbey, the foundation owns interesting archaeological collections illustrating human settlements and life on the Millevaches Plateau from prehistoric times (stone tools) and the Gallo-Roman period (funerary items, vestiges from habitations) to the Middle Ages.

Centre d'Art Contemporain

⏱*Open Jul–Aug, 10am–1pm and 2–7pm; Sept–Jun, 2–6pm.* ⏱*Closed Mon and mid-Dec to mid-Feb.* ▨*4€.* ✆*05 55 95 23 30.*

In the southern wing of the old cloisters of the abbey of St-André, the art museum presents one-person shows devoted to young artists as well as retrospectives (François Bouillon, 1990, Jesus Rafaël Soto, 1992, Gérard Garouste, 1996) and thematic exhibitions on trends in contemporary art. The monumental sculpture in front of the centre is by Robert Jakobsen.

EXCURSIONS
Lac de Sechemailles

2km/1.2mi SW via the D 76.

The road to Tulle goes to Sechemailles Lake (42ha/104 acres), where a large wooded shoreline and various amenities attract holidaymakers.

Douglaseraie des Farges

🚶 *3km/1.9mi NW via the D 109.*

A path starting near the Viaduc des Farges runs through a forest (20ha/49 acres) of conifers rising to a height of 40m/131ft!

🚗 DRIVING TOUR

PLATEAU DE MILLEVACHES★

98km/61mi round-trip – allow one day. The plateau of one thousand cows or, as some say one thousand springs, is now the 'Parc Naturel Regional de Millevaches en Limousin' and forms a kind of step into the Massif Central.

▷ *Leave Meymac travelling N along the D 36.*

Mont Bessou

With the Puy Pendu just across the way, this is the highest point on the plateau (977m/3 205ft). Above the forest, a television transmitter rises; the 67ha/165 acres are now a municipal park. An artificial lake offers a shady resting area. A road goes all the way round the mount.

Continue to the D 979 and turn towards Bugeat; 3km/1.9mi farther on, turn right onto the D 109 to Celle.

Tourbière du Longéroux★

Tourbière du Longéroux

S. Sauvignier/MICHELIN

The source of the Vézère is located in this 255ha/630-acre conservation area. At Le Longéroux, the average thickness of the peat is 2m/6.56ft and the study of fossilised pollen shows that the bog is 8 000 years old. The heath is home to a well-adapted fauna (lizards, vipers, meadow pipits) and the favourite hunting ground of the short-toed eagle. The discreet presence of otters is a sure sign of the quality of the area's fresh-water supply. Three marked paths offer nature lovers the opportunity of exploring this wild area: 200m/220yd there and back, 5km/3mi there and back (yellow markings), 20km/12mi round trip (blue markings).

○ *Continue to St-Merd-les-Oussines and turn right onto the D 164 towards Millevaches.*

Étang des Oussines★
This site is also the favourite haunt of otters. A path runs round the 15ha/37-acre lake filled with water from the River Vézère.

○ *Go back to the D 164 and turn right 1.5km/0.9mi farther on.*

Église de Chavanac
The small 13C-14C church houses a stone polychrome statue, known as **la Dansarelle**, said to represent Salomé, the bewitching biblical figure who charmed Herod into bringing her the head of John the Baptist on a platter.

○ *Continue along the D 36 towards Felletin.*

Millevaches
This little village (alt 912m/2 992ft) sits in the middle of the plateau of the same name, and is indeed characteristic of the region.

○ *Continue along the D 36 for 3km/1.9mi.*

Plateau d'Audouze
The streams that run down from the western and northern slopes of the Audouze Plateau provide the waters for the River Vienne; the streams from the eastern and southern slopes those for the Diège, a tributary of the Dordogne. The Ardouze Beacon (Signal d'Ardouze) which is out of bounds (*military area*) towers over the plateau.

○ *Continue along the D 36 then turn right onto the D 174.*

Arboretum de Saint-Setiers
&○*Open mid-May to mid-Sept, 10am–noon and 2pm–6pm; mid-Sept to mid-May, by prior arrangement.* ∞6€. ℘05 55 95 61 75.
The owner of a tree nursery has opened his park to the public. A stroll along alleyways lined with a variety of trees, enables visitors to discover more than 100 species, including a Douglas pine planted in 1895 and now more than 50m/164ft high. A former greenhouse contains an exhibition on the economical use of wood and offers a detailed study of 24 tree species.
Before leaving, make a detour via the D 174E3: the road starts climbing behind the town hall to a spot above the village which affords a magnificent **panorama**★★ of the Massif Central (*picnic area*).

○ *Turn back then follow the D 174E1.*

◐ *Leave Bugeat towards Meymac then turn left onto the D 164. In Fournol, turn right onto a minor road which joins the D 78 via Les Fargettes.*

Vestiges Gallo-Romains des Cars★

In the middle of nowhere, **Gallo-Roman vestiges** emerge from the greenery. The ashlar stone blocks now in a pile were once part of a temple and mausoleum.

The **temple** was rectangular, with a semicircular apse; visitors can still see the foundations, the podium and the monumental staircase.

The **mausoleum** was certainly very large, with a funeral urn in its centre.

The impressive **tank** above (it weighs about 8t) was a reservoir which supplied water to the building.

The so-called **thermes** were probably not public baths, but more likely a luxurious private residence built in the mid-2C and abandoned at the end of the 3C. Elements found on the site demonstrate the penetration of Roman civilisation in this hidden corner of the world: a hypocaust (a heating system: hot air circulated through brick pipes), a mosaic, marble panelling and fragments of painted walls.

◐ *Continue on D 78. Shortly before Pérols-sur-Vézère, turn left onto the D 979 towards Meymac, drive for 8km/5mi; turn right onto the D 979E.*

Belvédère de la Route des Hêtres

The panoramic **view**★ extends over the Vallée des Farges, with Mont Bessou to the east and Meymac and Sechemailles Lake to the south.

Peyrelevade

This attractive town with its slate-roofed houses welcomes tourists. The church and the Templar's Cross date from the 13C. If you like peat bogs, make a detour (3km/1.9mi N along the D 78) to Négarioux.

◐ *Continue along the D 21 for 2km/1.2mi then bear left onto the D 160.*

Tarnac

The **church** *(when the church is closed, contact Mme Banette, 2 r. du Four)* in this village is party Romanesque and partly Gothic. The northern doorway is adorned with sculpted covings and medallions; St George appears on the right, St Gilles on the left.

In the village, note the two ancient oaks and the lovely Fontaine St Georges.

◐ *Continue along the D 160.*

Bugeat

Near the source of the river, this sizeable town sits between the Millevaches Plateau and the Monédières hills. The Gallo-Roman vestiges reveal that people have lived here for a long time, despite the rugged climate. The proximity of the forest and rivers make Bugeat a centre for sports and recreation.

Treignac

and Les Monédières

Treignac lies in the upper valley of the Vézère, at the foot of the Monédières mountains and downstream from a dam across the river. From the D 16 to the north, there is a fine view of the village and its picturesque setting.

▶ **Population:** Corrèze 1 376
Michelin Map: 329: L-2 or 522 fold 15.
Info: 1, Place de la République ℘05 55 98 15 04.
Locaton: 37km/23mi northeast of Uzerche.
Kids: Maison de l'Arbre.
Don't Miss: Massif des Monédières; Suc-au-May.

LOWER TOWN

The old Gothic **bridge** spanning the fast-flowing Vézère affords a view of the castle ruins towering above the river, of the old slate-roofed houses and the church. The square **church** covered with slates has a hexagonal bell tower; inside, note the pointed vaulting on massive pillars and granite dolmen-shaped altar.

UPPER TOWN

This district, stretching between place de la République and place du Collège, comprises a number of turreted old houses with carved doorways (note the numerous shells reminding visitors that Treignac was once a stopover for pilgrims on the way to Compostela) and a 15C granite covered market.

MUSEUM

Musée des Arts et Traditions Populaires de la Haute et Moyenne-Vézère

Maison Marc Sangnier, 19260 Treignac
℘05 55 98 15 04.
Located in the house of Marc Sangnier, the founder of the Auberges de Jeunesse (youth hostels), this museum contains ethnographic collections.

EXCURSIONS

Rocher des Folles

45min round trip on foot; the path starts at the SW end of the village.
A pleasant marked stroll up to the Rocher des Folles – Crazy Women's Rock – affording fine views of Treignac, the gorge and wooded hills of the Vézère.

Lac des Bariousses

4km/2.5mi N along the D 940.

The road goes along the shoreline of this lake and provides a lovely drive. The wooded site (chestnuts, oaks and evergreens) has a recreation centre.

Chamberet

10km/6.2mi NW along the D 16.
On the outskirts of the village, along the road to Eymoutiers is an **arboretum** (free). Located in the municipal park, it consists of some 100 species of trees surrounding a pond (playground and picnic area). Next to the arboretum is the **Maison de l'Arbre** (*open daily Apr–Oct exc Wed; 3.50€ (6-18 years old: 2€); ℘05 55 97 92 14)*. This "tree centre" provides comprehensive information about trees, but also about other living species and ecosystems connected with them including. There are attractive interactive panels for children as well as guided discovery trails and workshops (*from three years upwards*).

Barrage de Monceaux-la-Virole

17km/11mi NE along the D 940 and D 160.
The first of the dams on the Vézère straddles Lake Viam, where waterfalls once tumbled. The view reveals the contrasts of the surrounding landscape.

🚗 DRIVING TOUR

LES MONÉDIÈRES★

50km/31mi round-trip – allow 3hr
Adjoining the Millevaches Plateau, the Monédières Massif, stretching between the upper valley of the Vézère and the River Corrèze, forms the southern bas-

LES MONÉDIÈRES

→ TREIGNAC

0   2 km

Lestards   D 16

△ 770
Puy Pantout   D 32

Puy-Messou
△ 907

Col des Géants

PARC   NATUREL   824   RÉGIONAL

D 128

Puy de la Monédière
△ 919   DE   MILLEVACHES

LES   Col du Bos   D 32
809   128

GR 46   D 128   Suc-au-May ★★
Puy de Chauzeix △ 893   908   D 325

Cirque de Freysselines   EN   LIMOUSIN
Chaumeil   869   △ Puy
Charrin

GR 46   Freysselines   le Mas Michel

Chauzeix   D 32

la Croix-sous-l'Arbre

D 121

MADRANGES   MONÉDIÈRES   ÉGLETONS   N

tion of the area known as the *montagne limousine*.

◆ *Leave Treignac travelling SE along the D 16 towards Égletons.*

Église de Lestards
Note the unusual thatched roof of the Romanesque church.

◆ *On leaving the village, turn right onto the D 32 then right again at Col des Géants onto the D 128 to Madranges.*

◆ *Turn left onto the D 128E.*

The road, lined with conifers, soon runs into the open, affording a wide view across the heath.

Heather and Bilberries

In late summer the slopes are covered with a carpet of pink heather. Slowly but gradually bilberries (known as blueberries in North America) are replacing the heather above 700m/2300ft, creating a new source of income and activity especially at harvest time. Picked with an adroit movement of the hand, the fragile berries are dispatched to markets, canning factories and pharmaceutical laboratories.

Suc-au-May★★

◆ *Leave the car in the parking area; then 15min round-trip on foot. Altitude 908m/2 979ft.*

From the viewing table there is a **panorama** of the Limousin countryside and the Millevaches Plateau to the north-east.
The Monédières Massif in the foreground has an undulating, severely eroded surface.
In fine weather conditions, it is possible to see the mountain ranges of the Auvergne.

◆ *Return to Col de Bos and take the D 128 to the left.*

The road runs down amid meadows and conifers. Note to the right the long ridge of the **Puy Pantout** (770m/2 526ft).

◆ *At the end of the road, turn left onto the D 121.*

The road winds along the south facing slope where arable crops alternate with rough grazing and chestnut groves.

Cirque de Freysselines
This natural amphitheatre surrounds a small hamlet of the same name. Drive east through the village (D 121) for a better view of the cirque.
🚶 A path (12km/7.5mi round-trip) runs round the cirque towards Suc-au-May.

La Croix-sous-l'Arbre
In a bend, to the right of the road, there is a fine view of Chaumeil (the main village in the area) and Puy de Sarran.

◆ *Continue along the D 121.*

Chaumeil
This attractive village, capital of the Monédières, with its sturdy granite houses roofed with slates or stones, is

clustered round the 15C **church** adorned with a fine 16C porch.
Local products can be found in the **Maison des Monédières**.

◐ *Continue N along the D 32.*

Le Mas Michel
At the crossroads take the narrow road leading to this hamlet, which lies at the foot of the Puy Charrin.

◐ *Turn back; continue along the D 32.*

Col des Géants
Beyond the pass, the road goes uphill amid conifers. There are fine glimpses of the **Puy Messou** (907m/2 976ft) to the right and the Suc-au-May to the left.

◐ *D 32 and D 16 lead back to Treignac.*

ADDRESSES

☒ SHOPPING

Ferme de la Monédière –
La Monédière.19390 Chaumeil.
℘05 55 98 20 48. Open late Jul–Aug. This farm sells a selection of cheeses, jams, fresh fruit and fromage frais.

Tulle

and the Upper Corrèze

Tulle extends over a couple of miles, its main street following the course of the narrow and winding valley of the Corrèze and its old houses rising in terraces on the hillsides overlooking the river. From the centre of the city rises the elegant stone steeple of the cathedral of Notre-Dame. The administrative seat of the département of Corrèze, although not its largest city, Tulle is a centre for the manufacture of armaments and lace.

- ▸ **Population:** 15,734
- ⚅ **Michelin Map:** 329: L-4
- ▤ **Info:** 2 pl. Émile-Zola, 19000 Tulle. ℘05 55 26 59 61.
- ◐ **Location**: 27km/17mi northeast of Brive-la-Gaillarde.
- ◷ **Timing**: Half a day for exploring Upper Corrèze.
- ◉ **Don't Miss**: Maison de Loyac; bell tower of the Cathédrale Notre-Dame.
- ⚅ **Also See**: Upper Dordogne Valley.

A BIT OF HISTORY
A Heavy Toll – During the Hundred Years War the town fell twice to the English, in 1346 and 1369. Each time, the invaders were driven away by the local militia. During the Wars of Religion, Tulle sided with the papists. The Protestant army under the viscount of Turenne failed to take the city in 1577 but in 1585 Turenne came back and with bloody vengeance sacked the city after first assaulting it.
On 8 June 1944 Tulle was liberated by the men of the *maquis*, but the next day the Germans retook the town. Several hundred townspeople were arrested: 99 were hanged in the streets, the others were deported; 101 never came back. South of town (*N 89, the road to Brive*), is a monument to the victims of Nazism.

☙ WALKING TOUR
OLD TOWN
This area, lying north of the cathedral and known as the Enclos (the Enclosure), retains a medieval atmosphere with alleys, stairways and old houses. A short walk starting at the cathedral (*15min round-trip*) offers a view of the edifice.

Cathédrale Notre-Dame
In 1103, Abbot Guillaume wished his abbey, which was then very prosperous,

Maison de Loyac

JACASS/MICHELIN

to have a worthy setting, so he undertook the reconstruction of the church and the cloistral buildings. The 12C saw the building of the nave, the porch and the first storey of the belfry.

The **belfry**★ is 73m/240ft high; the three storeys are surmounted by an elegant octagonal spire surrounded by bell turrets. The ogive-vaulted **porch** contains a tiers-point doorway, adorned with moulding and small columns in the Limousin style.

The interior decoration is plain, although the colours of the modern **stained-glass windows** by Jacques Gruber (1979) in the chancel are vivid: in the centre, Our Lady of Tulle; below, John the Baptist bearing the Lamb of God. The border shows: on the right, Bishop Dumoulin-Borie (a local missionary who suffered martyrdom in Tonkin) with St Sebastien below; on the left, St Jacques with, below, a hanged man commemorating the terrible events of 1944. A much venerated **16C wooden statue of St John the Baptist** stands in the north aisle. Since the 14C, the inhabitants of Tulle have celebrated his birth with a procession known as *la lunade* (23 June).

Cloisters – Built in the early 13C, the building has been greatly damaged over time. Still standing are the west gallery and two bays in the north and east galleries. The south gallery was destroyed in the 19C for the purposes of a municipal theatre project.

Many vestiges are displayed along the galleries: a collection of 16C-18C firebacks, statues, copies of recumbent figures representing popes from Limousin, various stone fragments.

Maison de Loyac★

This is the most outstanding secular building in Tulle. Built in the early 16C it has an attractive façade: the windows and door are framed by small columns and are topped by accolades adorned with sculptured foliage, roses and animals.

▷ *Take rue de la Tour-de-Maïsse, to the left of the building.*

Rue de la Tour-de-Maïsse

This street is a narrow stairway, where the roofs of corbelled houses almost meet above the alley.

▷ *Bear left again onto rue de la Baylie and yet again onto the sloping rue des Portes-Chanac.*

Rue des Portes-Chanac

Along this steep street, you will notice among a group of old houses on the left (at no 9), a sculptured doorway belonging to a late Renaissance mansion.

Rue Riche

Note the carved façade at no 13.

▷ *Rue Riche returns to the cathedral.*

MUSEUM
Musée du Cloître de Tulle

⊙*Open Jul–Aug Tue–Fri, 9am–6pm and Sat–Sun 9am–noon, 2–6pm; Apr–Jun and Sept 10am–1pm and 2–6.30pm (Oct–Mar, 5pm).* ⊙*Closed Mon and 1 Jan, 1 May, 1 Nov and 25 Dec.* ⊛*2.50€, no charge 1st Sun of the month.* ℘*05 55 26 91 05.*

The museum adjoins the west gallery of the cloisters. The ground floor is used for **temporary exhibitions**. The spiral staircase dates from the Middle Ages; it leads to the **first-floor** rooms, which display a collection illustrating the history, the **popular arts and traditions** of Tulle and its region. One of the rooms devotes pride of place to the **accordion**, whose manufacture Corrèze was once famed for. Those on display date from 1832 to 1950, and include the work of a local craftsman still in business. The second floor houses a collection of **swords and firearms**, a display of regional **ceramics** and of **religious art**.

🚗 DRIVING TOUR

UPPER CORRÈZE VALLEY

Round-trip of 140km/87mi – half a day
Surging forth to the west of Meymac, at an altitude of nearly 900m/2952ft, the River Corrèze crosses the Monédières range and digs a deep valley in the granite. It is the main artery of the *département* which bears its name, and passes through Tulle and Brive before joining forces with the Vézère.

▷ *Drive out of Tulle along N 89 towards Brive-la-Gaillarde.*

The road follows the west bank of the Corrèze and almost immediately runs by the **Champ des Martyrs**, a monument to the massacre of 99 young men in Tulle on 8 and 9 June 1944.

▷ *Continue on N 89 towards Brive.*

Cornil

A four-storey square tower above the village, all that remains of the castle, rises next to the Romanesque church. There is a scenic overlook of the bend in the river.

▷ *In the village, take the D 48E.*

Parc du Coiroux

This park has been developed around a large lake with swimming beaches and sailing, golf and tennis facilities.

▷ *Left on the D 48 outside Coiroux.*

Ste-Fortunade

Near a much-restored 15C **castle** stands a small Romanesque church containing, on the left at the entrance to the south chapel, the **reliquary-head**★ of St Fortunade. This is a delightful 15C work in bronze.

○ *Follow the D 940 for 1km/0.5mi, turn left onto the D 1 and follow the D 10 to Marc-la-Tour. Take the D 125E to St-Bonnet-Avalouze, continue along the D 61E to St-Martial-de-Gimel then drive along the D 53.*

Gimel-les-Cascades★★
○ *See GIMEL-LES-CASCADES.*

○ *Take the D 53 towards Touzac.*

The road runs alongside the southern shore of the Étang de Ruffaud. This lovely stretch of water with bathing beaches lies in a romantic setting. The **Étang de Brach**, 3.5km/2mi farther on, has boating facilities.

○ *Continue on D 26 to La Gare-de-|Corrèze; take N 89 (right) to Égletons.*

Égletons

The tour of the **Centre de Découverte du Moyen Âge** (Middle Ages Discovery Centre) begins with a short video presentation devoted to Bernard Ventadour, the 12C troubadour. Several workshops (illumination, stained glass, blacksmith's) are open in summer. ○*Open Jun 15–Sept 15, 10am–1pm and 2–7pm; Sept 16–Jun 14, Wed and Sun 10am–noon and 2–6pm, Thur 2–5pm,* ○*2.50€* ○*05 55 93 29 66.*

Sarran

President Jacques Chirac, a former MP for the Corrèze constituency, inaugurated his **Musée du Septennat** in the Village of Sarran in December 2000. The museum houses gifts and souvenirs collected by the president during his seven-year term of office. ○*Open Jul–Aug, 10am–12.30pm and 1.30–6pm; Mar–Jun and Sept–Dec, daily except Mon, 10am–12.30pm and 1.30–6.30pm; Jan–Feb, Sat–Sun and public hols, 10am–12.30pm and 1.30–6pm.* ○*Closed 1 Jan and 24-25 Dec.* ○*4€.* ○*05 55 21 77 77.*

Puy de Sarran

A narrow, bumpy road climbs steeply over 1.5km/1mi to reach the summit at 820m/2690ft. The wayside crosses form an impressive calvary, dominating the nearby mounts, bare of vegetation.

○ *From the village of Sarran, take the D 135 for 1km/0.5mi, then turn left on the D 142 towards St-Augustin.*

Le Tourondel

This charming little village has an attractive château (*not open to the public*) and a communal **bread oven**. The oven is in a thatched-roof shelter, where other local farming items are on display.

○ *At the end of D 142; left on D 26.*

Corrèze

In this old hamlet the granite houses are topped with slate roofs; they cluster around the massive 15C church, next to the **Margot gateway**, last vestige of the fortifications which once surrounded the village. The 15C **Église St-Martial**, surmounted by an English-style tower, contains a fine 18C altarpiece. A short distance away (*600m/660yd via rue Talin*), the **site**★ of the **chapelle Notre-Dame-du-Pont-du-Salut** offers a pleasant detour.

○ *Take the D 23 towards Bar.*

The village of **Bar** sits on a promontory overlooking the valleys of the River Vimbelle and the River Corrèze.

Naves

The 15C church, flanked by a fortified turret, contains a huge **reredos**★ in sculpted wood. The vertical imagery is centred around Christ; horizontally, the carvings detail the founding of the church (St Peter in chains).

○ *Follow D58; go right on N120 briefly before turning left to return to D58.*

The road winds down to the river, and follows its course as far as Tulle.

ADDRESSES

🛏 STAY

🍴 **Hôtel Bon Accueil** – *10 r. Canton.* 📞*05 55 26 70 57. Closed Dec 23–Jan 7. 12 rooms.* There's a medieval feel to this small, modest hotel thanks in part to the window and door frames dating from the 16C. Family ambience and cuisine at very inexpensive rates.

🍴 **Chambre d'hôte Chez M. et Mme Perrot** – *Gourdinot. 19460 Naves. 5km/3mi N of Naves via the N 120 and a side road.* 📞*05 55 27 08 93.* ⛔ *3 rooms.* Located in a pretty wooded valley, this old stone farm is run by convivial young owners. Pleasingly calm and cosy bedrooms. Regional dishes at the table d'hôte and home-made gingerbread served with a panoply of jams for breakfast.

🍴 EAT

🍴 **La Ferme du Léondou** – *19700 St-Salvadour. 12km/7.2mi N of Naves. Take the N 120, the D 53 towards Corrèze, then the D 173.* 📞*05 55 21 60 04. jlfauvert@ aol.com. Closed Feb and Wed except for lunch in Jul–Aug.* Leave the beaten path to discover this old barn with its handsome wood troughs and grand fireplace. Local traditions are taken seriously in this kitchen, which serves specialities such as *flognarde* (baked apple pudding), guinea fowl with veal sweetbreads, *la poux* (buckwheat cakes or gruel), blood pudding with chestnuts, stuffed cabbage and goose conserves with cepes.

🍴 **La Toque Blanche** – *Pl. M.-Brigouleix.* 📞*05 55 26 75 41. www.hotel-latoqueblanche.com. Closed Jan 20–Feb 3, Jun 30–Jul 4, Sun eve and Mon.* This downtown restaurant gives diners a choice between the rustic dining room and the veranda. The white chef's cap - la toque blanche - rides atop the head of the son of the family, who concocts tasty cuisine that's good value for the price. A few rooms upstairs.

🍴 **Le Central** – *2 r. de la Barrière.* 📞*05 55 26 24 46. Closed Jul 28–Aug 10 Sat and Sun eve.* This impressive house near the Corrèze is home to this first-floor restaurant with an attractive dining room with exposed beams, stonework, lace tablecloths etc. Le Central enjoys an excellent local reputation for the quality of its traditional local cuisine.

🍷 BARS AND 🍸 CAFÉS

La Taverne du Sommelier – *8 quai de la République -* 📞*05 55 26 57 63. www.restaurant-tulle.com. Open daily 8.45am–1am.* This traditional brewery proposes a wide range of wines by the glass. The owner, Didier Bordas, was chosen as best young sommelier of France in 1983. A handsome terrace overlooking the Corrèze.

🛒 SHOPPING

Maugein Accordéon – *Route de Brive - Zone Industrielle de Mulatet.* 📞*05 55 20 08 89. accordeon.maugein@wanadoo.fr. Open Mon–Thur 5am–noon and 2–5.30pm; tours by arrangement. Closed last week of Jul, 3 weeks in Aug and public hols.* This brand of accordions was established in 1919. The manufacturer, who has been in business longer than any other French accordion maker still in activity, was the first to introduce the MIDI system accordion nationally, in September 1984.

Le Jardin du Centaure – *Les Chaussades. 19300 St-Yrieix-le-Déjalat.* 📞*05 55 93 93 79. Open daily except Sun; Jul–Aug, guided tour (2hr) Mon, Wed and Fri at 10am Closed public hols in early-Nov. No charge.* Dominique Lepage, an organic farmer specialised in raising plants used for health and beauty aids or seasoning food, welcomes you to share his knowledge and passion for his aromatics: use in medicine and in cooking, origin of the names, mythology etc. You may visit the drying room; plants and herbal tea preparations for sale.

Le Poinct de Tulle (*Lace shop*) - *2 r. des Portes-Chanac.* 📞*05 55 26 71 75/06 85 18 16 25. Open daily except Sun & Mon, 9am–noon and 2–6pm. No charge.* Cathy Vedrenne is an experienced lacemaker who can demonstrate a rare needle technique.

Turenne★

"Pompadour pompe. Ventadour vente. Turenne règne." **This old French pun defies translation, but can be loosely construed as crediting Turenne with noble dignity, whereas the other cities mentioned are just full of hot air. Today the ruins of the proud castle, once the stronghold of the viscounts of La Tour d'Auvergne, rise above the picturesque town.**

▶ **Population:** 795
◔ **Michelin Map:** 329: K-5; or see Brive-la-Gaillarde.
▯ **Info:** Place du Belvédère.
✆05 55 24 08 80
▶ **Location:** 15km/9.5mi south of Brive-la-Gaillarde.
◉ **Don't Miss:** The castle; the view from the Tour de César.

A BIT OF HISTORY

A small town with a great past – The incapability of the last Carolingians to govern the whole of their territories and the aptitude of the lords of Turenne for resisting Viking invasion seems to have been the root of the fief's emancipation from royal power.

As early as the 11C, a fortress was set on the outlines of the Martel Causse. In the 15C, Turenne held sway over a third of Lower Limousin, Upper Quercy and the Sarladais region or 1 200 villages and a number of abbeys.

The viscounty, in its heyday, enjoyed enviable privileges; like the king of France, the viscounts ruled absolutely, ennobling subjects, creating offices and consulates, minting money and levying taxes.

⌁ WALKING TOUR
LOWER TOWN

At the foot of the hill is the Barri-bas Quarter, the old part of town.

Place du Foirail

The Hôtel Sclafer, with a loggia, was a residence for notaries in the 17C. Opposite, there is a small shop (15C) with a large arcade.

▷ *Follow rue du Commandant-Charolais.*

Place de la Halle

The town houses around this square reflect the wealth of its inhabitants, especially **Maison Vachon**, the residence of the consuls of Turenne in the 16C and 17C.

Rue Droite

This narrow street, lined with old corbelled houses and small shops, climbs towards the castle.

▷ *Turn right onto rue Joseph-Rouveyrol.*

Rue Joseph-Rouveyrol

Note the **Maison de l'Ancien Chapitre** (Old Chapter-house), the tower of which is decorated with a lovely Flamboyant-Gothic-style doorway.

▷ *Continue straight on along rue de l'Église.*

Église

The construction of the church in the form of a Greek cross. was decided upon by Charlotte de La Marck in 1593, the year Henri IV converted to Catholicism. After Charlotte's death, Elizabeth of Nassau took over the project.

La Tour d'Auvergne - Turenne Family

The name Turenne became famous through the family of La Tour d'Auvergne. In the 16C, Henri de la Tour d'Auvergne was leader of the Limousin Huguenots and the most valiant supporter of the Reformation. As a reward for his zeal, Henri IV allowed him to marry the heiress to the duchy of Bouillon, Charlotte de la Marck; the Turennes then went to live in Sedan and administered their viscounty, which remained sovereign, at a distance. Charlotte died three years after her marriage, leaving the titles of duke de Bouillon and prince of Sedan to her husband Henri, who remarried Elizabeth of Nassau.

His youngest son, also a Henri, was to become the great **Turenne** (1611-75). His eldest son, who inherited the viscounty and title of duke de Bouillon, participated in the Fronde (an aristocratic rebellion against Mazarin with which Turenne had associated himself in its early days – 1648). In 1650 he welcomed two supporters of the Fronde, the princess of Condé and her son the duke of Enghien. The meeting was celebrated with such pomp and magnificence that it was baptised 'Turenne's Wild Week', and in consequence the people of Turenne were taxed for two years to refill the impoverished coffers.

Just above the church, a vast building, the Maison Tournadour was once the town's salt storehouse.

Upper Town

Access is through the **fortified gateway** of the second of the three curtain walls which protected the castle.

On the right the **Seneschal's House** has an elegant tower. On the left the **Chapelle des Capucins** (1644) houses exhibitions.

Château

🕐Open Jul–Aug, 10am–7pm; Apr–Jun and Sept-Oct, 10am–noon and 2–6pm; Nov–Mar, Sun and public hols, 2–5pm. 👓3.80€. ☎05 55 85 90 68.

The castle was demolished by Louis XV after the viscounty became crown property. Only the Clock and Caesar's towers, at each end of the promontory, were spared. The **site**★ is remarkable.

Tour de l'Horloge

The Clock Tower was the castle keep, dating from the 13C. Only the guard-room with broken-barrel vaulting is open to visitors. Above it is the *salle du trésor* – the counting room or treasury.

Tour de César

This round tower with irregular stone bonding seems to date from the 11C. A staircase goes up to the top, from where there is a vast **panorama**★★ of

Tour de César

Jacass/MICHELIN

the region. In the foreground below are the village's slate roofs, in the distance, beyond a green valley landscape, appear the Monts du Cantal to the east and the Dordogne Valley directly southwards (*viewing table*). Go round the castle from the right. A series of manor houses, roofed with slate and flanked by squat towers have

names which evoke their past purpose – the Gold Foundry, for example.

▷ *Return to the lower town along the lane separating the second and third curtain walls then via rue Droite.*

Ussel

Built 631m/2 067ft above sea level on the edge of the Millevaches plateau, between the Diège and Sarsonne valleys, Ussel has kept a raiment of 15C-17C monuments, souvenirs of a prosperous past.

▶ **Population:** 10,250
Michelin Map: 329: O-2
Info: Place Voltaire.
℘05 55 72 11 50
Location: 17km/10.5mi E of Meymac; 31km/19mi NW of Bort-les-Orgues.

OLD TOWN
Follow rue de la Liberté, behind the church, to place Joffre, where a fountain flows, and wander around the narrow surrounding streets. Many of the old houses have been restored; admire the turrets and decorative doorways.
Behind place de la République, the **Maison ducale de Ventadour** is an elegant Renaissance residence built by the dukes of Ventadour at the end of the 16C, to replace the austere feudal castle.

Rue Michelet
The 17C building at no 18 houses printing works and an exhibition hall.

Aigle Romain
The Roman Eagle monument, carved in granite, was discovered in the Peuch mill on the banks of the River Sarsonne.

Église St-Martin
Only the chancel and flat east end are late 12C; the nave and side aisles were rebuilt in Gothic style; the west front and bell-tower (19C) are modern.

Musée du Pays d'Ussel
⏱*Open Jul–Aug, 10am–noon and 2–7pm.* ✍*No charge.* ℘*05 55 46 54 00/02.* This museum, devoted to local crafts and traditional trades which are slowly

dying out, is housed in the Hôtel Bonnot de Bay (early 18C). Old-fashioned workshops have been faithfully recreated, illustrating traditional crafts practised by the village smithy, the weaver (rare 18C loom), the clog-maker, the *galochier* (who made leather shoes with wooden soles), the milliner, the caner and basket-weaver, and the woodworker. On the floor above, a display case presents selected local writers.

Chapelle des Pénitents
The religious life of the region is addressed by themes, including the historical context, processions and brotherhoods, popular devotions and religion as practised cradle to tomb.
There are some remarkable pieces of local art, a gilded and wood altar screen made in 1711; a painting (1664) by the Cibille brothers, *Pentecost*; and several painted wooden statues.

Chapelle N.-D. -de-la-Chabanne
1km/0.6mi S, access by rue Pasteur.
From the esplanade near this pilgrims' chapel, there is an extensive **view**, reaching the Plateau des Millevaches (north-west), the Monts Dore (east), and the hills of Cantal (south-east).

Uzerche★★

Upper Vézère and Gorges

Uzerche, a charming small Limousin town, stands on a promontory encircled by a bend in the River Vézère. On this picturesque site a surprising number of buildings are crowned with bell-turrets, watchtowers and pepper-pot roofs. It is said that, "he who has a house in Uzerche, has a castle in Limousin".

A BIT OF HISTORY

In 732, the Saracens, after being beaten at Poitiers, attacked Uzerche. The town was protected by solid walls with 18 fortified towers and held out for seven years. Surrender seemed near until the besieged hit on a trick: they presented the emir with their last fatted calf, and their last ration of corn.

Amazed at such prodigality, the Saracens raised the siege. The Uzerche arms – two bulls – recall this trick. The old town was never taken by force during any of the many sieges of the Middle Ages. Charles V, when he authorised the town to add three gold lilies to its arms, also gave it the appellation Uzerche the

- ▶ **Population:** 3,182
- **Michelin Map:** 329: K-3
- **Info**: Pl. de la Libération, 19140, ✆05 55 73 15 71.
- **Location**: 30km/18.5mi NW of Tulle and 38km/24mi N of Brive-la-Gaillarde.
- **Timing**: A full day for the Upper Vézère valley and the Gorges de la Vézère.
- **Don't Miss**: Eglise St-Pierre; the view of the town from the Ste-Eulalie district.
- **Also See**: Limoges/Vienne.

maid, and its crest *non polluta* (never sullied) confirms the glorious epithet.

🐾 UPPER TOWN WALK

▶ *Leave from place Marie-Colein.*

Rue Gaby-Furnestin

On the left, you will see the 16C timbered house in which Alexis Boyer, surgeon to Napoleon I, was born. In this street which extends onto rue Jean-Gentet, note a group of renovated old houses with fine carved doorways.

UZERCHE

0   100 m

Porte Bécharie

This fortified gateway is the only one of the old city gates still intact. Adjoining the gateway is a building known as the Château Bécharie, which is flanked by a square tower and a pendant turret; in the left wall is a great stone emblazoned with the Uzerche arms.

▷ *Take Escalier-Notre-Dame on the right immediately beyond the Bécharie Gateway.*

Place des Vignerons

This little square, the Wine-Grower's Square, was formerly the fruit market. It is surrounded by old houses and the chapel of Notre-Dame, the oldest church in Uzerche. The covered La Perception passageway leads to a small terrace which affords a bird's-eye view of the Vézère and of part of the town.

Leave the **Tour du Prince Noir** (Black Prince's Tower) on your left and walk along rue St-Nicolas which brings you out onto place de la Libération. This square is dominated by the impressive mass of the church of St-Pierre.

Église St-Pierre★

This is an interesting Romanesque church, built in several phases. Fortified during the Hundred Years War, repaired in the 17C, the church was restored at the beginning of the 20C.

The 12C **bell tower** is Limousin in style. Three square tiers with paired

windows and gables are surmounted by a fourth, octagonal in shape; this, in turn, is topped with a short roof covered in shingles. To the south-west stands a massive **round tower**, erected as the defence point for the main door, built of rough-hewn stone with loopholes. Since restoration work on the church was undertaken last century, this tower is all that remains of the ancient defence system. The perimeter wall included 18 towers and five fortified gateways.

Beneath the chancel, the 11C **crypt** is believed to be the oldest in the region. The **nave** has broken-barrel vaulting and is flanked by narrow aisles. An octagonal dome rises above the transept crossing.

Esplanade de La Lunade

From this esplanade there is a **view** immediately below of the La Pomme district which rises in terraces along the N 20; of the Vézère meander and of the hills beyond encircling the town.

Rue Pierre-Chalaud

It is lined with old houses adorned with Gothic and Renaissance doors and timbered houses. At the end of the street the **Château Tayac** (12C-14C) is a fine house with turrets and a door surmounted by a shield.

Centre Régional de Documentation sur l'Archéologie du Paysage

🕐 *Open Jul–Aug, daily except Tue, 2.30–6.30pm; rest of year by arrangement.* ✆*No charge. Guided visit* ✆*3€.* 📞*05 55 73 26 07.*

Set up in the 17C **Hôtel du Sénéchal**, the regional centre documents recent archaeological research in the area, covering the period from the Iron Age to the late Middle Ages.

▷ *Return to place de la Libération.*

Walk along rue Jean-Gentet, where you will notice carved doorways, to the Bécharie Gateway and place Marie-Colein.

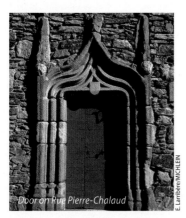
Door on Rue Pierre-Chalaud
E. Larribère/MICHELIN

EXCURSIONS
Masseret
16km/10mi N.
The village stands in a part of the Limousin countryside which is mostly woodland. In the centre of Masseret stands a modern tower with a viewing table as its top (104 steps).

There is a beautiful circular **panorama**★: to the north can be seen the Ambazac hills, to the east the Millevaches plateau, the Monédières massif and on a clear day the mountains of Auvergne.

The Romanesque **church**, largely restored in the 16C, has a shrine dedicated to St Valérie dating from the 13C (*key available from the chemist's opposite the church*).

Église de St-Germain-les-Belles
11km/6.2mi N of Masseret.
This building dating from the 14C is a fine example of a fortified church. Inside, to the right of the chancel, a spiral staircase gives access to the look-out points high above the tall pointed vaulting, and the watch-path. (*for guided tours, apply to the tourist office*)

🚗 DRIVING TOUR

UPPER VÉZÈRE VALLEY
55km/34mi round-trip – allow 3hr

▶ *At the Turgot Bridge, take the D 3, the Eymoutiers road, which climbs steeply and goes through the Ste-Eulalie suburb.*

Belvédère
Travel 800m/0.5mi from the bridge and before a turning on the left you get a good overall **view**★★ of Uzerche perched on top of a rock and the Vézère running below.

▶ *Continue along the D 3 and turn right onto the D 26 shortly after Eyburie.*

Chamboulive
The countryside is a pleasant mixture of volcanic *puys*, hills and meadows.

The **church**, a Romanesque edifice renovated in the 15C, has a raised, deep belfry-porch.

▶ *Take the D 142 towards Uzerche and turn left onto the D 920 just before reaching Uzerche.*

Vigeois
An abbey was founded in the 6C. The present **church** dates only from the 12C, although it has been much restored. ⏰*Open Jun–Sep, 9am–7pm. Key available from the café opposite the church.*
A street leads down to the **old bridge**, also 12C, which runs a quiet course here. Nearby, **Pontcharal Lake** and the recreation centre is spacious and welcoming.

▶ *Drive N out of Vigeois along the D 7 towards Arnac-Pompadour then turn right beyond Jargassou Bridge. Follow C 7 then V 1 to Baby.*

Cascades de Bialet
🚶 *Picnic area.* A footpath starts at the wooden bridge across the stream; other wooden bridges crisscross the water. (*take care that children do not fall in*).

▶ *Continue on the minor road, which goes steeply down to Uzerche.*

GORGES DE LA VÉZÈRE★
67km/42mi round-trip – allow 4hr

Downstream from Uzerche, the Vézère goes through deep gorges. There are some fine **views** from the Site de la Roche and from villages on both sides of the gorges.

▶ *Drive S out of Uzerche along the D 920 for 4km/2.5mi then turn right onto the D 3 to Vigeois, cross the Vézère and continue along the D 3. Shortly after Le Monteil turn left onto the D 9E to Estivaux.*

Belvédère de Comborn
The belvedere overlooks a meander of the Vézère and affords a view of the ruined **Château de Comborn**. The 18C

section houses a restaurant (open Fri-Sun), but only a few vestiges remain of the 11C keep. ⏲🕐*Open mid-Mar to mid-Nov, guided tour (45min), Sat–Sun, 2–6pm, Tue–Fri throughout the year by prior arrangement. ⏲Closed Mon. ⊜5€ ℘05 55 73 77 23.*

▷ *Continue along the D 9E3 to the end of the road and turn right onto the D 9.*

Site de la Roche★

A pretty little road leads to the edge of a precipice overlooking the Vézère gorges. To the right, a rocky trail leads to a **viewing table** (391m/1 283ft).

The view extends over the wooded **gorges du Saillant.**

To the left, a path leads to the **panorama**, where there is another spectacular view over the gorges.

▷ *Return to the D 9.*

Allassac

The distinctive houses of this town are built in black schist and roofed with slate; some have red-sandstone corner pieces (rue L.-Boucharel).

The **church**, commemorating the beheading of John the Baptist, is also built of black schist, except for the lovely **southern door**★, where various colours of sandstone are set in contrast. The nearby **Caesar's Tower** (30m/98ft)

is all that remains of the old medieval fortifications.

▷ *Leave NW on the D 134.*

Le Saillant

This hamlet is on a pleasant site at the mouth of the gorges. From the **old bridge** spanning the river, admire the Lasteyrie du Saillant manor, where the revolutionary orator Mirabeau (brother of the Marquis du Saillant) regularly came to visit. Do not miss the **six stained-glass windows**★ by Marc Chagall in the former castle chapel.

▷ *Continue on the D 134 and turn right.*

Vertougit

This charming village is beautifully located – overlooking the **gorges de la Vézère** and just across from the Site de la Roche. There is a good view from the viewing table.

▷ *Return to the D 134 and turn right to Voutezac.*

Voutezac

Built into the hillside, this agreeable village has a fortified church with a 15C square tower.

▷ *Drive N along the D 3 to return to Uzerche via Vigeois.*

ADDRESSES

🏠 STAY

🛏 **Camping Municipal la Minoterie** – *Left bank of the Vézère via quai Julian-Grimau. ℘05 55 73 12 75. Open May 1– Sep. 50 pitches.* Here, the gentle lapping of the Vézère will lull you to sleep at night. The campsites are set up around an old mill. Wide range of activities.

🛏🛏 **Hôtel-Restaurant Jean Teyssier** – *R. du Pont Turgot. ℘05 55 73 10 05. www.hotel-teyssier.com. Closed Dec 13–Jan 5 and Feb 21–Mar 9. 14 rooms.* The small, leafy terrace of this hotel near the town centre looks out over the Vézère.

🍴 EAT

🍽 **Chez Denise** – *8 r. Porte-Barachaude. ℘05 55 73 22 12. Closed Mon–Thu evenings out of season.* Cross the threshold of this modest house near the periphery of the old city and get a table on the balcony. You'll enjoy both the food and the view.

🏃 LEISURE ACTIVITIES

Base de Loisirs de la Minoterie – *℘05 55 73 02 84. www.vezerepassion.com. Open Jul–Aug 9.30am–12.30pm/1.30pm–6.30pm.* This recreation area on the banks of the Vézère offers canoeing, kayaking, rafting, climbing, mountain-biking and other outdoor activities.

Ruines de
Ventadour★

On a rocky spur high above the Luzège gorges, the ruins of the Château de Ventadour rise in an untamed natural site★. The name Ventador comes from the Occitan language and literally means exposed to the winds.

- **Michelin Map:** 329: N-3
- **Info:** Moustier Ventadour Tél : 05 55 93 04 34
- **Location:** 7km/4.5mi south-east of Égletons.
- **Timing:** Allow 60-90 minutes inc. walk from car park.
- **Don't Miss:** The view from the platform of the fortress.
- **Also See:** Bort les Orgues.

A BIT OF HISTORY

The fortress – Its location and formidable defences made Ventadour seem impregnable. However, it was captured and held by the English for 13 years as the Hundred Years War raged. During the Renaissance period, the viscounts left the cold fortress for the cosier rooms of an elegant manor in Ussel (*see USSEL*). Speaking with pride of his castle, the duke of Ventadour told Louis XIV: "All the straw in the kingdom would not be enough to fill the moats of Ventadour."

RUINS

To reach the ruins, take the footpath, 30min round-trip. Restoration work in progress; beware of falling stones.
The ruins can be admired from the narrow road leading out of Moustier-Ventadour. Two towers, high walls, old inner courtyards, vestiges of the main building and a barbican give an idea of what the medieval fortress must have been like. From the platform on the southern side, there is a dizzying **view** over ravines of the Luzège Valley.

Tour des Fossés

A tour of 7km/43mi starting from the castle's base; follow to the right.
Take the access road which turns into a narrow, but paved lane and dips sharply (hairpin curves) down into the *fossés* (natural moats) surrounding Ventadour Castle. Half way down, the road passes by the lowest part of the ruins, before leading to N 991. From that road, admire the picturesque **views**★ of the ruins and the bends in the River Luzège.

Bernard de Ventadour

Ventadour was a literary hotbed in the 12C. Generations of lords and ladies composed poetry there. In this rarefied atmosphere, Bernard was born (1125), son of a castle servant. As a youth, he revealed an extraordinary talent for versifying, and became a tender and passionate bard of courtly love. The viscountess willingly lent her ear to the clever young man's ardent words. Indeed, her jealous husband had the handsome but humble bard sent packing, and thereafter kept a close eye on his lady.

Bernard de Ventadour was welcomed into the household of **Eleanor of Aquitaine**, duchess of Normandy, then married to Henry II Plantagenet. Eleanor, credited as an inspiration for the ideals of courtly love, liked Bernard's verses so well that when she became queen of England, she took him with her court to London. Later, Bernard followed her to Poitiers, and when the Queen was carried back to England as a prisoner of her husband, Bernard retired to the home of the count of Niort for the next 10 years. Drawn to the monastic life, the ageing poet returned to his homeland and the abbey at Dalon, near Hautefort Château (*see Château de HAUTEFORT*). There he met another famous troubadour, Bernard de Born, and passed away at the end of the century.

Limoges and its region lie within the southern Haute-Vienne département of the Limousin, stretching from the Charente département in the west to the Corrèze and Creuse départements in the east. In the south the region shares its border with the Périgord Vert and, of course, the Parc Naturel Régional Périgord Limousin straddles this border. The undulating Plateaux of the Haut Limousin are dissected by the valley of the Vienne River, its bocage a patchwork of woods and fields. Trees thrive in this wet climate, with oak and beech on the uplands and chestnut trees at lower levels. Quickset hedges surround fields and meadows and the cattle-grazed pastures.

Limoges

Limoges, the regional capital, is a large city of more than 136,000 *Limougeauds*. The Limousin region derives its name from this city. Founded by the Romans around 10BC, it was then known as Augustoritum and was strategically placed on the right bank of the River Vienne on the main route between Paris and Toulouse. During the Middle Ages it became a centre for the arts. Despite being sacked by the Black Prince in 1370, from which It eventually recovered, by the nineteenth century Limoges was renowned for the quality of its porcelain. Limoges' most famous son, the Impressionist artist Pierre-Auguste Renoir , was born here in 1841 and spent his formative years working in the porcelain industry, where his artistic skill were much in demand for painting designs on fine china.

The Vienne and around

The River Vienne, which flows past Limoges, used to play a important role in the porcelain industry. Nowadays it passes peacefully along its 350km/217mi length from its source on the Plateau de Millevaches−near Peyrelevade in the Corrèze−towards the east.

After St-Junien the Vienne turns north widening as it flows through the Charente until it finally runs into the River Loire at Candes St-Martin near Chinon. The River Maulde, which flows into the Vienne just a short distance upstream from St.Léonard de Noblat, is dammed a few kilometres from Eymoutiers, forming one of the largest man-made lakes in France, and providing a valuable resource for water sports enthusiasts, fishermen and walkers alike.

Châlus★

and around

The old city of Châlus, dominated by its keep, recalls the memory of **Richard the Lion Heart's** tragic death. On every side are the densely wooded, solid granite masses of the Châlus Hills - last buttresses of the Massif Central.

▶ **Population:** 1 652

⚲ **Michelin Map:** 325: C-7

▤ **Info**: 28, Ave François Mitterand. ℘05 55 78 51 13.

◉ **Location:** 35km/21.9mi SW of Limoges via N21.

⊛ **Don't Miss**: Château du Haut-Châlu; Parc Naturel Regional Périgord-Limousin; Montbrun; Ch. de Brie.

A BIT OF HISTORY

A fatal siege – According to legend, in 1199 a serf belonging to Adhemar V, viscount of Limoges, discovered a fabulous treasure trove of "ninepins and large balls, all in solid gold" (these items now figure in the arms of Châlus together with a long bow). The viscount of Limoges hid the treasure in his castle at Châlus. Nevertheless rumours of the find reached Richard the Lion Heart, King of England and Lord of Western France.

Richard demanded his share of the booty as overlord, and when his vassal refused to give it up, it provided him with a pretext for punishing his vassal for siding with the King of France while he was a prisoner in Germany and he laid siege to Châlus. While he was directing the attack on the castle, he was struck on the shoulder by a quarrel from a prototype of a new crossbow. Richard refused to dress the wound, which turned black; the poison went to his heart and so he died, at 42, one of the greatest men of the Middle Ages. The castle defenders paid dearly for the death of the King: all were hanged except the sharp-eyed archer – he was flayed alive in spite of the fact that he was pardoned by the King on his death bed.

CHÂTEAU DU HAUT-CHÂLUS★★

The remains, known as Châlus-Chabrol, are privately owned and stand on rising ground in the upper part of the village.

Donjon

This cylindrical keep (25m/82ft high and 10m/33ft in diameter), an excellent illustration of feudal military architecture, dates from the 11C. Originally, it had four levels, but the highest one, crowned by machicolations, fell in 1870.

The keep's thick, smooth walls of gneiss stone, rising vertically, were a good protection against attack by battering ram, axe and fire.

A short distance from the keep are vestiges of the **chapel** where King Richard's remains were brought. At the time, the chapel was Romanesque; in the 15C a side chapel was added (one arch still stands).

Main building

Perhaps the most spectacular part of the tour is the exhibit on the discovery of architectural remains from the 11C and 13C. The main building opens onto a 13C room which contains a Romanesque column squeezed into a wall erected at a later date. In the next room, you can see the other side of it, as well as two Romanesque windows. The walls are hung with the coats of arms of the castle's different owners. A little corridor leads to the oldest sec-

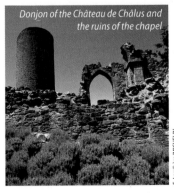

Donjon of the Château de Châlus and the ruins of the chapel

E. Larribère/MICHELIN

tion, dating from the 11C. Beyond an escape shaft tucked into a nook in the fortifications, a six-sided room forms the base of a corner tower; note the vaulted ceiling and the loopholes. Beside this tower room, a smaller room dissimulates another shaft, 16m/52ft high, and the entrance (walled off) to the watch-path. The lower level, once open to the air, was the ground floor.

The 17C wing features two drawing rooms furnished in 17C-18C style and an 18C oak staircase leading to a large exhibition hall where a collection of fancy dress for the Venice Carnival is displayed. The barn houses a small museum devoted to regional crafts.

Gardens

A medieval herb garden surrounding a central closed fountain has been laid out on the esplanade, in front of the castle, whereas the French-style garden with its rosemary maize, its rose trees and hornbeams, is laid out at the foot of the 17C building.

SIGHTS
Maison du Châtaignier

Along the N 21, next to the tourist office. &🕐*Open mid-Jun to mid-Sept, 10am–12 pm and 2–6.30pm (except Mon mid- Jun–mid-July and mid-Aug–mid-Sept); rest of the year, daily except Sat–Sun, 10am–noon and 2–5pm.* ✆*2.30€.* ✆*05 55 78 51 13.*
This exhibition centre, devoted to chestnut trees and their various uses, offers visitors interactive terminals and video presentations as well as a reconstructed hoop-wood maker's hut.

Château de Châlus-Maulmont

🕐*Open Jul-Aug, daily except Tue,* ⚬*guided tour (1hr), 3–6pm.* ⚬*No charge but donations to help with the restoration are welcome. Open Jul-Aug exc. Tue , 3pm – 5pm. Tourist office:* ✆*05 55 78 51 13.*
Located in the town centre, this castle is undergoing restoration work following the collapse of part of its 13C keep. It houses a small museum.

EXCURSIONS
Parc Naturel Regional Périgord-Limousin

24300 Abjat-sur-Bandiat. ✆*05 53 60 34 65.*
Created in 1998, this regional nature park covers 180 000ha/695sq mi within a triangle formed by the towns of Périgueux, Limoges and Angoulême. Its aims are to protect and enhance the natural and cultural heritage, to contribute to the economic and cultural development of the area and to attract new inhabitants and new activities to the Périgord-Limousin region. Various brochures are devoted to the local architectural heritage, traditional crafts, outdoor activities and accommodation available within the park.

Montbrun★

7km/4.3mi SW along the D 6BIS and the D 64A. ✆*05 55 78 51 13.*
This imposing castle stands deep in a valley, where it reflects in the waters of a pond surrounded by lawns and trees. Constructed in the late 12C, it once defended the borders of the ducal realm of Aquitaine, and still boasts a moat, high walls and an impregnable square keep surmounted by machicolations. Guided visits organised throughout the year.

Château de les Cars

8.5km/5.3mi NE. 🕐*Open Jul–Aug, daily except Tue 9am–noon, 2–6pm.* ⚬*2€.* ✆*05 55 36 90 22.* Mostly in ruins (13C - 16C); lapidary museum.

Château de Lastours

13.5km/8.5mi E. &🕐*Open mid-Jul to mid-Aug, daily except Mon 1–7pm; mid–Aug to mid-Jul, Sat-Sun and hols, 1–7pm. Preferably by prior arrangement.* ⚬*3€.* ✆*05 55 58 38 47.* Ruins of a 12C keep, 13C–16C buildings restored.

Château de Brie★

8km/5mi NW. 🕐*Open Apr–Oct,* ⚬*guided tour (45min), Jul–Aug daily 2–7, Apr-Jun and Sept–Oct Sun and public hols, 2–7pm.* ⚬*4.50€.* ✆*05 55 78 17 52.*

This fortified house was built around 1500; 16C-18C furnishings, Gothic granite stairway.

ADDRESSES

🎭 ENTERTAINMENT

Images, torches et lumières – *Late Jul- Aug, Tue and Fri, 10pm*. Evening tours of the Château de Lastours.

La Médiévale de Lastours – Medieval festivals, 3 times a year (*Easter, second weekend in Aug, and the third weekend in Sep*): Medieval camp, entertainment, street shows, archery etc.

International Circus School – ✆*05 55 58 34 71*. During the school holidays (except Christmas and February), some 250 students travel here from all over the world to learn circus skills including the trapeze, tightrope-walking and acrobatics.

Coussac-Bonneval★

The castellated towers of the Château de Bonneval rise on a height overlooking the village of Coussac in a typically Limousin countryside where fields divided by small streams alternate with hedges and chestnut coppices. It is the native hearth of the Bonneval family.

A BIT OF HISTORY

Achmet-Pasha – Claude-Alexandre de Bonneval was born in Bonneval Castle in 1675, he fought in the Italian Campaigns (1701-06) then offered his services to the Austrian Emperor, becoming a general in the army. After a personal quarrel he again became a soldier of fortune, this time with the Ottomans. He reorganised the Turkish Army and led it in decisive victories against the Austrians. He took the title of Achmet-Pasha, Pasha of the three tails, an honour which gave him precedence over ordinary pashas. He never returned to France and died in Constantinople at the age of 72.

CHÂTEAU★

🕐🚶|*Guided tour (45min, last entrance 30min before closing), Open daily Jul–Aug Daily 2.30–7pm; June 15 –30 and Sept 2–15 (exc Mon), 2.30–6pm* ◎*10€*. ✆*05 55 75 24 15*. www.bonneval.com.br.
The castle was built in the middle of the 14C and the inside was altered in the 18C and 19C. The plan is square with

- ▶ **Population:** Haute-Vienne 1379
- 🕐 **Michelin Map:** 325: E-7
- �ℹ **Info:** 11, Place aux Foires, 87500 Coussac-Bonneval. ✆05 55 75 28 46. www.coussac-bonneval.com.
- ◖ **Location:** 55km/34.4mi S of Limoges.
- 🖼 **Don't Miss:** The inside of the château; the Lanterne des Morts.

an inner courtyard: the corner towers are crowned with machicolations and topped with pepper-pot roofs; the keep and the Devil's Tower (Tour du Diable) adjoin another tower.

Inside the castle there are furnishings dating from the period of the Renaissance to the Directory (16C to the end of the 18C). Remarkable tapestries, portraits, engravings and contemporary documents recall the life of Bonneval-Pasha.

VILLAGE

Church

A small 12C building, renovated in the 15C, in which there are remains of a fresco (south transept) and a painting by Lebrun, *God the Father* (17C).

Lanterne des Morts★

This imposing Lantern of the Dead dates from the 12C and was restored in the 14C. The small door was used to insert a lamp, which was then raised up to the top of the structure, where light could shine through the openings.

ADDRESSES

⌂ STAY

⊜⊜ **Chambre d'hôte Le Moulin de Marsaguet** – *3.6km/2.2mi N of Coussac via D 17 towards La Roche-l'Abeille, then the D 57. ℰ05 55 75 28 29. Closed end Sept to mid-Apr ⌺ 3 rooms. Dinner Tue, Thu and Sat.* The hosts at this large 18C bed and breakfast property also

run the farm. Farm-produced cuisine, including duck, foie gras, veal and pork. The 13ha/32.5-acre lake is popular for fishing, swimming and boat trips.

⑨⁄ EAT

⊜ **Les Voyageurs** – *21 av. du 11-Novembre-1918. ℰ05 55 75 20 24. Closed last 2 weeks in Nov, Sun eve (except Jul–Aug) and Wed.* This old Limousin-style house is right by the château. The cuisine served in the rustic dining room is unpretentious and reasonably priced. Seven rooms, some overlooking the garden.

Eymoutiers
and Vallée de la Maulde

The only part of the Monastère d'Eymoutiers still standing is the collegiate church built from the 11C to the 15C. The village developed on a rise overlooking the River Vienne.

VILLAGE
Église
pl. du Chapitre.

The greatest part of the nave and the belfry-porch are Romanesque. The elegant chancel is lit by 15 remarkable stained-glass windows dating from the 15C. The church also contains a fine 13C reliquary **cross**★.

Espace Paul Rebeyrolle
route de Nedde
&⊙*Open Jun–Sept, 10am–7pm (last entrance 30min before closing); Oct–May, 10am-6pm.* ⊙*Closed Christmas hols and 1 May.* ⊜*4€ ℰ05 55 69 58 88. www.espace-rebeyrolle.com*

The building houses 43 works by the figurative artist born in 1926, obsessed by suffering. Rebeyrolles pastoral compositions are inspired by local landscapes.

Espace Minéralogique
Opposite the Espace Paul Rebeyrolle.
&⊙*Open Jun-Sept, 10am–noon and 2.30–7pm.* ⊜*3€. ℰ05 55 69 27 74, ℰ05 55 69 27 81.*

▶ **Population:** 2 115
⌖ **Michelin Map:** 325: H-6
▤ **Info**: 5/7 Avenue de la Paix, 87120 Eymoutiers. ℰ05 55 69 27 81.
▶ **Location:** 45km/28.1mi W of Limoges via the D879.
⊚ **Don't Miss:** The view from Mont Gargan; Vallée de la Maulde.
⚇ **Kids**: Cité des Insectes.

Guides inform visitors about their specificities, their different uses and the discovery of dinosaurs' eggs and enable visitors to see tiny minerals through special binoculars.

EXCURSIONS
Chaud
13km/8mi SE along the D 992. In Nedde, bear right onto the D 81 then, after crossing the river, right onto the D 81A.

Located on the edge of the Millevaches plateau, this village houses a centre devoted to the natural environment of the Limousin region.

A typical Auvergne barn houses the themed exhibitions of the **Cité des Insectes** (⚇⊙*Open daily Jul–Aug, 10.30am–7pm; Apl 4–Jun and Sept–Nov 4, Wed, Sat–Sun, school and public hols, 10.30am–7pm;* ⊜*6.50€(child: 5€); ℰ05 55 69 02 55).* The garden, which contains

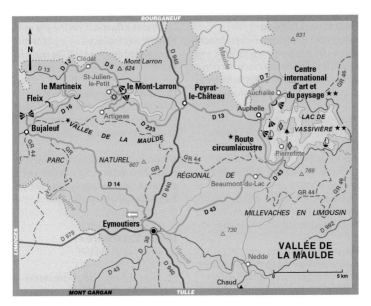

aromatic and melliferous plants, enables visitors to watch insects in their natural environment

Mont Gargan
23km/14mi SW along the D 30.

The road climbs steeply at first, leading to the summit, which is crowned by the ruins of a chapel. As you go round the chapel, you see a vast **panorama**★★, south-east over the Monédières Massif, north over the hills of Marche and west to the Limousin Mountains.

In July 1944, the mountain was the site of fierce fighting between German troops and the Resistance led by Georges Guingouin.

DRIVING TOUR

VALLÉE DE LA MAULDE
70km/44mi round-trip – allow half a day

▷ *Drive NW out of Eymoutiers along the D 14.*

Bujaleuf
Bear left to reach the bridge spanning the reservoir from which you can enjoy a good **view**★ of the two shores of the lake forming the recreation centre.

Beyond Bujaleuf, the D 16 descends into the valley affording lovely views. Barrage de Fleix

Set in a fine wooded site, the slim form of the dam (50m/164ft long and 16m/53ft high) is supported by buttresses.

Barrage du Martineix
A similar construction to the previous one, this dam stands in a wild but picturesque site.

▷ *Drive along the D 13 towards Peyrat.*

Shortly after Clédat, the D 5 runs past Mont Larron.

▷ *Turn right onto the D 5A1 towards St-Julien-le-Petit then left just beyond the cemetery.*

Usine et Barrage du Mont-Larron
This stark looking building is the control centre for the series of dams. To the right of it a path, leads to the foot of the massive dam. A path to the right climbs to the crest of the dam.

▷ *Turn left onto the D 233 just before Artigeas.*

Peyrat-le-Château

In this rolling landscape where broom and heather alternate with pine and beech, the remains of a castle stand by a lake; the square keep of this fortress was once the home of the Lusignan family.

Musée de la Résistance

Avenue de la Tour, Peyrat le Château
Open Jun–Aug, 10am-noon and 4-6.30pm; May and Sept, 3-5.30pm.
Closed Tue. 2.50€ 05 55 69 75 11 or 05 55 69 48 75.

This small museum is devoted to the local resistance movement, named Maquis Guingouin after its leader

Maison des Moulins

Maison de l'Eau. Guided tour *(1hr 15min, last entrance 1hr before closing), Jul–Aug, daily (except Sat), 2.30-6pm; May-Jun and Sept, Sun, 3.30-6pm.* 4.50€. 05 55 69 26 05.

There was a flour mill on the site until 1900; it was replaced by a paper mill which closed down in 1934. The museum has 13 working scale models (1:10).

▷ *Leave Peyrat to the E along the D 13 then turn left onto the D 7 towards Royère; 5km/3mi farther on, turn right to the Vassivière dam.*

A short distance beyond Auchaise, the **route circumlacustre**★, which skirts the west shore of Vassivière Lake via **Auphelle**, offers pleasant views of the lake and its islands.

Lac de Vassivière★★

👤 *See Lac de VASSIVIÈRE.*

▷ *Drive to Beaumont-du-Lac via the D 43 which leads back to Eymoutiers.*

ADDRESSES

🏠 STAY

 Chambre d'hôte Le Verrou – *Le Bourg, 87120 Nedde. 10km/6mi E of Eymoutiers along the D 992.* 05 55 69 98 04. *www.leverrou.com. Closed Jan 1–Feb 28. Reserve in winter. 4 rooms.*

You'll find delightful bedrooms with wood furnishings and embroidered linens in this bed and breakfast near the Lac de Vassivière, where the inner courtyard and its flower-filled garden exude tranquillity. For meals, you can choose between the crêperie and the family dining room.

EXCURSIONS

L'Escale – *7km/4.5mi E of Peyrat-le-Château along the D 13 and D 222. Rte circumlacustre, Lieu-dit Auphelle, 87470 Peyrat-le-Château.* 05 55 69 41 35. *contact@escale-limousin.com. Open daily mid-Mar–Nov, 8am–9pm.* The owners of this bar-restaurant organise regular excursions on Lac de Vassivière, including lunch on board. If you prefer to stay on dry land, enjoy a leisurely drink on the terrace.

GUIDED TOURS

Eymoutiers – During July and August *(Mon at 10am; 4€)*, the tourist office in Eymoutiers organises walking tours (1hr 30min) of the town's main sights, providing a fascinating insight into the town's history and architecture.

Pays Monts et Barrages – In July and August, you can enjoy a guided tour *(4€)* of this area of mountains *(monts)* and dams *(barrages)* covering 30 or so communes between Limoges and Vassivière in the company of a qualified local guide.

The summer programme for this area includes themed hikes, evenings with storytellers, and days in which you can help restore local buildings.
For further information, contact the Syndicat Intercommunal Monts et Barrrages in Bujaleuf, 05 55 69 57 60. *www.ville-saint-leonard.fr*

MARKET

According to locals, the weekly Thursday market has taken place here since 1270. If you miss it, you could make the drive to shop in Figeac on Tuesdays.

Limoges★

Limoges was sited for its defensive position by a ford across the Vienne and two stepped plateaus that could be put to defensive use. In the Gallo-Roman period, when the town was known as **Augustoritum**, it spread out in an amphitheatre along the right bank of the river. In the Middle Ages two separate and rival townships developed: the **Cité épiscopale** grouped round its cathedral built on a low shelf overlooking the Vienne, and the **Château**, the busy commercial town on the opposite slope in the shadow of the powerful abbey of St-Martial.

The city's industrial rise is largely due to its porcelain and enamel works and shoe factories. Limoges also boasts a university and is the administrative capital of Limousin.

▶ **Population:** 136 539
⬡ **Michelin Map:** 325: E-6
ℹ **Info**: 12, Boulevard de Fleurus. ℘05 55 34 46 87. www.tourismelimoges.com
▷ **Location**: Limoges extends across the north bank of the River Vienne.
🅿 **Parking**: A number of car parks are dotted around the centre (⬡see city plan).
🦅 **Don't Miss**: Musée Adrien-Dubouché; Cathédrale St-Étienne; Église St-Michel-des-Lions; Musée de l'Émail; Jardins de l'Évêché; Cour du Temple; Rue de la Boucherie; Chapelle St-Aurélien; Gare des Bénédictins.
👪 **Kids**: Aquarium du Limousin.

A BIT OF HISTORY

Limoges in Gallo-Roman days – The presence of the Roman military road, Agrippa's Way and the existence of a natural crossing point of the River Vienne, certainly contributed to the birth of the Augustoritum.

This new town followed a well-ordered grid plan and quickly acquired a number of significant structures including a stone bridge, a forum, baths, aqueducts, an amphitheatre and so on. The forum was located on the site of the current town hall. Despite the many facilities offered, research has shown Augustoritum was thinly populated.

At the end of the 4C, the barbarian invasions squeezed the town and people gathered around the St-Étienne hilltop thus forming the core of the *Cité*.

An enthusiastic reformer – In 1761, a young magistrate by the name of **Turgot** became general intendant of Limousin, one of the poorest regions in France. He was an admirer of the enlightened philosophers of his time and seized this opportunity to put his theories into practice and modernise the region. He

The White Gold of the Limousin

In Europe, **porcelain** was imported from China until the late 17C, when the Sèvres manufacture bought the secret of hard-paste porcelain, which required 50% of kaolin, a rare white form of clay. In 1766, kaolin of remarkable purity was discovered in various parts of Limousin and, after encouraging experiments had been carried out at the Royal Factory at Sèvres, Turgot, who was then general intendant of Limousin, set up a porcelain works in 1771. This was under the patronage of the count of Artois and marked the beginning, for Limousin ceramics, of an era of prosperity which was hardly interrupted even by the troubled years of the Revolution. After 1815 the industry concentrated round Limoges which, because of its position on the Vienne, could land the wood for the kilns from lumber rafts floated down river. Nowadays, more than 50% of all the porcelain made in France comes from Limoges, a world famous manufacturing centre.

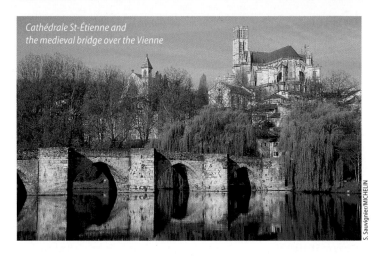

Cathédrale St-Étienne and the medieval bridge over the Vienne

S. Sauvignier/MICHELIN

built a network of modern roads, developed new industries (including the porcelain industry following the discovery of kaolin deposits), replaced Limoges' fortifications with wide boulevards and built a college and a hospital.

Famous citizens of Limoges – Many of the sons of Limoges have gained fame. Among the artists are **Leonard Limosin** (1505-76) enameller and painter in ordinary to the king's royal chamber. By his skill in engraving, painting and decoration he became one of the leaders of the great school of enamel artists of the 16C whose fame lasted until the 18C. The painter Auguste Renoir (1841-1919), worked here early in his career as a painter of porcelain.

Famous statesmen include, Pierre Vergniaud (1753-93), the orator of the Girondin Group and Sadi Carnot (1837-1894) who became president of the Republic.

LIMOUSIN PORCELAIN AND ENAMELS
Musée Municipal de l'Évêché - Musée de l'Émail★

◷*Open Jul–Sep, 10am–noon and 2pm–6pm; Oct–Jun, daily except Tue, 10am–noon and 2pm–5pm/6pm.* ☜*No charge.* ☏*05 55 45 98 10.*

The museum is housed in the elegant 18C former archbishop's palace.

The museum has some 500 **Limousin enamels**★ dating from the 12C to the 21C. The Middle Ages was an especially rich period for this type of art, which is well represented in the display cases.

Cloisonné enamels use an early technique where thin strips of metal are soldered to a metal base to outline the design. Although this process works well for gold, it is less effective for copper and was soon replaced by **champlevé**, where the lines of the design were cut away from the surface, and the enamel applied to the recesses.

The third technique is that of **painted enamels**; the design is painted on the enamel covering the copper plate.

In the series of painted enamels are two plaques by Monvaerni (late 15C), and a **Nativity triptych** (1515-20). Limoges is still an international centre of enamel art, as witnessed in the *Biennale International de l'Art de l'Émail*.

Egyptology - The two rooms in the Egyptology section present a particularly rich collection of terracotta figurines and bronze statuettes.

Lapidary museum - The fine vaulted cellars which were formerly the bishop's palace kitchens make a good setting for the ancient and medieval exhibits of the lapidary museum. These include Iron Age funerary items, stone lions, gravestones and statues characteristic of local Gallo-Roman works in granite. The Middle Ages are represented by a collection of sarcophagi, a 9C mosaic from the tomb of St Martial, and low-relief sculptures.

A Mini-Guide to Limoges Porcelain

True porcelain (hard-paste): resonant when struck, is translucent and made from ground feldspathic rock and the special white clay known as kaolin. Also called china, because that is where it was first made.

Artificial porcelain (soft-paste): made using clay and ground glass, it has a softer body and can be cut with a file, whereas true porcelain cannot. Dirt accumulated on an unglazed base is difficult to remove; on true porcelain it comes off easily.

Bone china: developed by Josiah Spode the Second, it contains calcined bones in a hard-paste formula, which makes it chip-resistant. Especially popular in England and the United States.

Earthenware: opaque and porous, this, the most common type of pottery, is made from clay baked at low temperatures.

Stoneware: fired at high temperatures until it is vitrified (glasslike and nonporous), it does not require a glaze; lead, salt and feldspathic glazes are used for decorative effects. Stoneware also originated in China, and came to Europe in the 17C, but by the early 19C its popularity had been superseded by porcelain.

Faience: tin-glazed earthenware made in France, Germany, Spain or Scandinavia. In Italy, it is called Faenza majolica (the town of Faenza, the origin of the name, was a major production centre in the Renaissance). Manufactured in the Netherlands or England, it is referred to as delft, after the Dutch city famous for its production.

Creamware: this fine white English lead-glazed earthenware (also produced briefly in France) is more durable and less expensive to produce than faience. Wedgwood and Leeds are the best-known manufacturers.

Ancient Limoges - Scale models illustrate the evolution of the city from its founding up to medieval times. A rare **fresco** (early 2C), discovered on the site of a villa gives a hint of the luxury of the residence.

French painting - This collection includes 17C-18C works (*Bataille de Constantin* by Charles Le Brun), landscapes of Limoges and the area by Courtot, and canvasses by Renoir (*Portrait de Mademoiselle Laporte*), Guillaumin, Pascin and Suzanne, Valadon.

Musée Adrien-Dubouché★★

🕐 *Open Jul–Aug, daily except Tue, 10am–5.40pm; Sep–Jun, daily except Tue, 10am–12.25pm and 2–5.40pm.*
🕐 *Closed 1 Jan, 1 May and 25 Dec.*
🎫 *4.50€, no charge 1st Sun of the month.* 📞 *05 55 33 08 50. www.museeadriendubouche.fr.*

The museum, founded in 1845, became a national museum in 1881 and is named after the director Adrien Dubouché, who provided it with the foundation of its collections. Today the collection, which includes items dating from the pottery of ancient times to porcelain from factories in production at Limoges today, shows the evolution of ceramics and glassware in France and throughout the world.

Ground floor - To the left of the vestibule and its bronze statue (1898 of Adrien Dubouché), eight display cases are given over to fine earthenware, popular in the 19C, and to clay pieces formed from slip (*Vase aux musiciennes* by Aube). A collection of pieces by **Théodore Deck** (1823-91) recalls his important role in ceramic arts in the 19C. One room provides explanations of the manufacturing techniques of the four major families of ceramics (pottery, earthenware, stoneware and porcelain).

The right-hand wing displays 19C porcelain. One thousand two hundred pieces of Limoges porcelain amply demonstrate the reason for the worldwide renown of porcelain manufactured here since 1771.

Salon d'honneur – This room houses Chinese porcelain. Tang earthenware,

Manufacture Bernardaud

©J.-C. & D. Pratt/Photononstop/Tips Images

Song porcelain, Yuan blue and white ware, 17C and 18C white China, and coloured ware known as *famille verte* and *famille rose* complete this collection of precious items from the Far East.

First floor - The history of ceramic manufacture, from its origins in the Middle East to Medieval times, is traced in the **right wing**. Ceramics arrived in Europe through Spain, reaching Italy by the end of the Middle Ages, where new techniques and artistic effects developed rapidly. During the second half of the 16C, the craft spread throughout France, Spain, Germany and the Netherlands. In France, the 17C and 18C were high points for ceramic design and manufacturing.

The **left wing** contains the 18C porcelain collection. The **soft-paste porcelain** technique (no kaolin), was perfected in the 17C. First produced in Rouen, major manufacturing began in Saint-Cloud in 1677. Several centres around Paris became famous for their wares: Chantilly, Mennecy, Vincennes and **Sèvres**.

The first **hard-paste** porcelains manufactured in Europe were made in the **Meissen** factory in Saxony in 1710. Kaolin was found near Limoges in 1768, enabling the development of hard-paste production in Sèvres, Paris, Lille, Bordeaux, Orléans and Valenciennes.

Manufacture Bernardaud

27 avenue Albert-Thomas (off map).
Guided tour (45min), Jun–Sept, 9.15–11.15am and 2.15–4.15pm; the rest of the year by prior arrangement. 4€.
05 55 10 55 91. www.bernardaud.fr
This porcelain manufacturer, founded in 1834, has become one of the leaders in the production of tableware. The bulk of the output today comes from Oradour-sur-Glane; the former works have been preserved and are open to visitors.

Four des Casseaux

Access via quai Louis-Goujaud or rue Donzelot. Open Jun–Aug, daily except Mon 2–6pm; Mar, May & Sept daily exc Sun 2–6; Nov–Feb daily exc. Sun 2–5. Closed public holidays.
Guided tour (1hr) by prior arrangement. 4€, unaccompanied tour 2€.
05 55 33 28 74.
Built in 1844, this round kiln was intended for firing porcelain. The kiln is 19.5m/64ft high. The lower part, heated to a temperature of 1 400°C/2 552°F, has 1m/3.28ft-thick brick walls reinforced with iron. The upper part, used for the first baking at 950°C/1 742°F, was surmounted by a high valve chimney. Today, gas-fired kilns allow continuous baking to take place.

LA CITÉ

Situated on a height overlooking the River Vienne, the Cité is Limoge's historic district. Built in 1210 to provide access to the Cité, the humpback **Pont St-Étienne** is made up of eight pointed arches. There is a good view from the bridge.

Cathédrale St-Étienne★

St Stephen's was successor to a Romanesque church of which only a part of the crypt and the lower storeys of the belfry remain. The Gothic cathedral was begun in 1273; the chancel and transepts were completed during the 14C and Jean de Langeac undertook the completion of the cathedral in 1537, but died in 1541. It was left to Monsignor Dusquesnay to complete the church between 1876 and 1888.

The **St John Doorway**★ is really the cathedral's main entrance. Made of very fine-grained granite, it was built in 1516–1530 when the Flamboyant style was at its peak. The square **belfry** is 62m/204ft high. The lower three storeys are Romanesque and the upper four storeys are Gothic. The top three are octagonal, a design often found in Limousin architecture. The belfry stood apart from the nave until last century when a modern narthex and three bays were added. The **nave** achieves a unity of style despite taking 600 years to build. The boldness and elegance of line of the roof vaulting are wonderful; the triforium acts as a base for the clerestory windows.

The rood screen★ (end of the nave under the organ-loft), built for Jean de Langeac by Touraine artists in 1533, once separated the chancel from the nave. The three **tombs**★ round the chancel are of considerable decorative interest:

- The tomb of Raynaud de la Porte (14C), bishop of Limoges;
- The tomb of Bernard Brun in the pure 14C French style, adorned with four low-relief panels and;
- The **tomb of Jean de Langeac**, built in 1544, an example of the Renaissance style at its most delicate.

Jardins de l'Évêché★ (Bishop's Palace Gardens)

These pleasant gardens rise in terraces above the Vienne and provide a good view of the cathedral and the palace. They include a themed garden and a "wild" garden featuring five natural environments typical of the region.

⚘ WALKING TOUR
CHÂTEAU DISTRICT WALK

The neighbourhood known as Le Château rose up long ago around the abbey of St-Martial and the château. Today it serves as Limoges' downtown, busy with shops and activity.

Église St-Pierre-du-Queyroix

The flamboyant façade dates from 1534. The well proportioned 13C bell-tower served as a model for two nearby churches, St-Michel and St-Étienne.

Jardins de l'Évêché

S. Sauvignier/MICHELIN

LIMOGES

0 — 200 m

> Walk west on rue St-Martial.

Abbey St-Martial remains

Once located outside the city walls, place de la République stands over the site of a Gallo-Roman necropolis where St Martial was buried. His tomb was highly venerated and a chapel was built above it in the 6C. The chapel's keepers adopted the Benedictine rule in 848, and the abbey grew, becoming affiliated with Cluny in 1063. During the Middle Ages, it was the site of intensive religious, cultural and artistic activity. Later the abbey declined and its buildings were destroyed during the Revolution.

Crypte St-Martial

🕒 Open Jul–Sept 9am–12.30pm, 2–7pm; for information on guided tours (1hr), contact the tourist office. ⚐No

charge (guided tours for groups only). 🕾 05 55 34 46 87.

The current stairway was added in the 13C to improve the flow of pilgrims. Martial and his two companions (Alpinien and Austriclinien) were laid to rest in the two big tombs measuring more than 2.80m/9ft long, still on view. In the 9C, Martial's remains were exhumed and placed in a gold reliquary on the main altar in the new basilica. The second room or sanctuary contains the enormous granite 4C tomb known by the name of Tève-le-Duc. Beyond, there is a large room which lies underneath and shores up the churches of St-Pierre and St-Benoît, installed on the Gallo-Roman ruins and on the site of an early Christian cemetery.

> Cross rue Jean-Jaurès and follow rue du Clocher; turn right on rue Gaignolle.

Place du Présidial

Note, at the corner of rue Haute-de-la-Comédie, the former **hôtel Maledent** built in 1639. Admire the pretty **place Fontaine-des-Barres** (16C) below. The north doorway of the church of **St-Michel-des-Lions** opens on to this square where the 17C-18C royal administrative buildings remain standing.

Église St-Michel-des-Lions★

Construction began in 1364 and continued until the 16C when a west bay was added. Outside near the belfry door on the south side can be seen the two lions carved in granite which have given the church its name. Behind the high altar, a monumental altar of carved stone supports a 19C gilded wooden reliquary shrine which contains relics of St Martial including the saint's head.

◗ *rue Ferrerie then rue du Temple.*

Cour du Temple★

Rue du Consulat, with its 18C buildings, is linked to rue du Temple by a narrow passage (at no 22), which opens onto 16C half-timbered houses and arcaded galleries, known as the temple courtyard.

◗ *Continue along rue du Consulat then rue des Halles.*

Les Halles

Built at the end of the 19C, the covered market stands on **place de la Motte**, probably named for the *motte*, or hillock, where the viscounts' castle stood.

Rue de la Boucherie★

This picturesque street is lined with half-timbered houses, some of which

315

still have the accoutrements of the 80 butchers' shops which once operated there. On the last Sunday in October, a regional festival known as the *Frairie des petits ventres* brings back the memory of bygone activities.

Maison Traditionelle de la Boucherie
See Abbaye St-Martial.
The butcher's stall at no 36 is now devoted to preserving the heritage of the meat trade in Limoges. In the kitchen (also a shop), visitors can admire the butcher's block and its accessories, a 19C icebox and a hearth. where tripe was prepared. Upstairs are the furnished rooms where about 25 people lived.

Place de la Barreyrrette
The name of this square comes from the fence (*barrière*) around the holding pen for animals awaiting slaughter. The pens disappeared when the municipal slaughterhouse was opened in 1832.

Chapelle St-Aurélien★
A 14C monolithic cross marks the entrance to this unusual little building dating from 1475. Founded to hold the relics of St Aurélien, the chapel was sold at an auction in 1795 and secretly purchased by the butchers' guild, which still maintains it today.

▷ *Walk across place des Bancs to rue Haute-Vienne.*

Aquarium du Limousin
Open 10.30am-6.30pm (last entrance 30min before closing).

6.50€. 05 55 33 42 11. www.aquariumdulimousin.com.
Set up beneath place Haute-Vienne on the site of an old reservoir, the aquarium has made use of the vaulted architecture to welcome European freshwater fish, tropical species, piranhas and more.

Boulevard Louis-Blanc
Take a stroll along the porcelain avenue. The square in front of the town hall is adorned with a porcelain fountain!

▷ *Place Wilson; left on rue du Collège.*

Pavillon du Verdurier
During exhibits, or included in the guided tours organised by the Office de tourisme.
Built after the First World War to store meat, this edifice looks rather unusual with its mosaics and floral friezes on a ceramic background.

▷ *Return to your starting point via place St-Pierre on the right.*

JARDIN DE L'ÉVÊCHE AREA
Cité des Métiers et des Arts
Open daily Jul–Aug, 10.30am–1pm and 2.30–7pm (last entrance 20 min before closing); June 2–6pm; Sept–Oct 2–6pm; Apl 11–May, 2–6pm Wed, Sat & Sun; Closed 1 Nov-Easter,and 1 May.
5€. 05 55 32 57 84.
www.cma-limoges.com
This centre, located in the Bishop's Palace gardens, presents the work of the **Compagnons du Tour de France** and of France's finest workers in the building trade. On the mezzanine are illustrated

---

The Butchers' Guild

Since 930, **Messieurs les Bouchers de Limoges** have administered a trade guild in the former rue Torte (now rue de la Boucherie). When the relics of St Aurélien (the bishop who succeeded St Martial) were discovered in 1315, the butchers of the city obtained the right to adopt the saint as their patron. They created a brotherhood which, in 1475, built the Chapelle St-Aurélien to receive the relics in a shrine. In the 16C, six families in the guild atook control of the brotherhood (today, members are still elected by a secret ballot for a seven-year term). Since the time of Henri IV, the brotherhood has had the privilege of offering the keys to the city to visiting dignitaries. At the dawn of the 21C, the millenary tradition persists.

the different stages a young *compagnon* has to go through to master his trade.

Musée de la Résistance

Ancien Couvent de la Providence
&⊘*Open Jul–mid-Sep, 10am–noon and 2–6pm; mid-Sep to Jun, daily except Tue, 2–5pm.* ✆*No charge.*
𝒫*05 55 45 63 40.*
During the Second World War, Limoges was hard hit by the numerous deportations and massacres in the region (&*see ORADOUR-sur-GLANE and TULLE*). In the series of rooms which make up the museum, posters, maps, documents and photos are among the items on exhibit, evoking the dark days of the war. Courageous women and men of Haute Vienne, led by Georges Guingouin, were some of the first in France to band together in the Resistance movement.

FURTHER OUT
Espace FRAC

From place Denis-Dussoubs, follow rue François-Chenieux then turn left onto avenue G.-et-V.-Lemoine and left again onto impasse des Charentes. &⊘*Open daily except Sun ,Mon and Public Holidays , 2–6pm.* ✆*1.50€.* 𝒫*05 55 77 08 98. www.fraclimousin.fr*
The Fonds Régional d'Art Contemporain (regional collection of contemporary art), created in 1982 is located in a former grocery warehouse.

Limougeaudes

52 rue de Belfort (not on map). From FRAC continue to place Sadi-Carnot.
&⊘*Open daily except Sun and Mon, 8.30–noon and 2–6pm.* ⊘*Closed public hols.* ✆*No charge.* 𝒫*05 55 77 23 57.*
The distillery museum is steeped in local traditions as well as the fragrance of the sweet liqueurs produced here. Tools and alembics, bottles and posters are among the items on display. Chestnut liqueur (*Feuillardier*) and other house specialities are on sale.

Gare des Bénédictins★

This is one of the landmarks of Limoges. Built from 1923 to 1929, it stands as a symbol of the town's prosperity

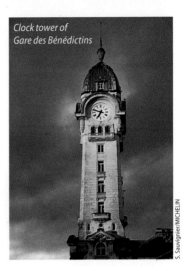

Clock tower of Gare des Bénédictins

S. Sauvignier/MICHELIN

and expansion between the two World Wars.

🚗 DRIVING TOURS

① VIENNE TO BRIANCE★
90km/54mi – allow 2hrs 30mins.Leave Limoges on the N 21 towards Périgeux.
This picturesque road along the valley of the Briance, winding its way through meadows. At **Pont-Rompu** hamlet, there is a view on the right of a picturesque old bridge with pointed cutwaters on which passed the ancient Roman way from Limoges to Bordeaux.

Église Abbatiale de Solignac★
& *See Église Abbatiale de SOLIGNAC.*

▷ *Follow the D 32 to Le Vigen then turn left onto the D 704. A short distance beyond the railway bridge, turn right onto the D 65 towards Boisseuil.*

Parc Zoologique et Paysager du Reynou
⊘*Open Apr–Sep, 10am–8pm (last entrance 2hr before closing); Oct & Mar 10am–7pm, Wed, Sat–Sun and public hols, School hols. 10am–7pm every day.; Nov–Feb, Wed, Sat–Sun, public and school hols , 12.30–5.30pm.* ✆*10.50€(child: 7.50P, 3–12yrs).* 𝒫*05 55 00 40 00. www.parczooreynou.com.*

Vallée de la Maulde

E. Larribère/MICHELIN

Laid out in 1870 for Haviland, the porcelain manufacturer, the landscaped park is planted with 150 different species of trees surrounding a castle.

In a nearby **zoo**, 120 species of animals from the five continents roam around relatively freely.

▶ *Return and continue along the D 32.*

Château de Chalusset

Access to the ruins is strictly forbidden for safety reasons; however, a footpath enables visitors to walk right round. It is also possible to visit the medieval village of Le Bas-Chalusset and the Tour Jeannette. Unaccompanied visits all year. No charge; possibility of guided tours daily mid-Mar to mid-Nov 9.30am–4.30pm. 3€. ℘05 55 00 96 55.
The impressive ruins of Chalusset Castle are a perfect example of medieval military architecture in their plan and position on a rock promontory, which juts forward to the point where the River Briance and River Ligoure meet. The castle was built in the 12C and in 1577 it fell into the hands of the Huguenots who used it as a base for their battles against Limoges. The troops of Limoges took the notorious castle by force and dismantled it (1593).
In Le Chatenet, the picturesque D 39, on the left (towards St-Léonard-de-Noblat), crosses the River Vienne. Turn left on reaching the confluence of the Vienne and the Maulde, overlooked by the **Château de Muraud** perched on a promontory.

Vallée de la Maulde

The road runs up the Maulde Valley through a rocky, wooded gorge. The river has been transformed by the French electric company into a giant, watery staircase, with remote-controlled dams.
The **Barrage de l'Artige**, the last dam of the series, serves to regulate the flow of water coming from the others upstream. The road overlooks the dam and affords a fine view of the valley and the ruins of the priory of Artige.

Ancien Prieuré de l'Artige

A narrow road opposite the dam to the left leads to the entrance of the Priory.
Founded in the 12C and secularised shortly before the Revolution, part of it was subsequently left to fall into ruin. From the road you can see the vast buildings with their round tiled roofs, the arcades between the chapter-house and the cloisters, and the remains of emblazoned doors.

▶ *The road (D 39) follows the Vienne, framed by overhanging rocks, then rises above the river.*

St-Léonard-de-Noblat★
See ST-LÉONARD-DE-NOBLAT.

Pont-de-Noblat

In the Vienne Valley, on the outskirts of town, this area has developed on both sides of the river. A 13C bridge spans the water; old houses line the time-worn path known as the *Pavé*.

Promenade du Chêne de Clovis

Between the bridge and the church, a steep path leads to a plateau where a castle once stood.

The the N 141 crosses the Vienne and follows the river valley before it rises up to a plateau. At St-Antoine, take the D 124 for a panoramic view of the Ambazac hills, then turn left on the D 39, a lovely country road.

St-Priest-Taurion

This town rests peacefully at the fork of the River Taurion and River Vienne, in a green valley cut across with dams.

After Le Palais, take the D 29 along the valley back to Limoges.

② LA VALLÉE TÉNÉBREUSE

Round trip of 90km/56mi – allow 3hr

Leave Limoges travelling W on the N 141 towards Angoulême.

Oradour-sur-Glane★★

See ORADOUR-SUR-GLANE.

St-Junien

See ST-JUNIEN.

Site Corot

See ST-JUNIEN: Excursions.

Église de St-Victurnien

The altar screen in the **church** has a 14C decorative painting illustrating the Passion and the Resurrection. Also worthy of note are the 13C enamel shrine, the 14C polychrome Virgin and Child, and, in the cemetery (*road to Oradour*), a lantern of the dead. The winding road follows the river and rises up above the valley.

Aixe-sur-Vienne

This town is a gateway of the Parc naturel régional Périgord-Limousin. Every seven years, during the *Ostensions* (see Introduction), 20 reliquaries are carried in a procession to Notre-Dame-d'Arliquet by representatives of different trades.

Maison de la Porcelaine

Open Jul–Aug daily except Sat–Sun, guided tour (30min) at 10am, 11am, 3pm, 4pm and 5pm; Sept–Jun, at 10am and 3pm except Sat–Sun. Closed 1 Jan, 1 May, 1 Nov and 25 Dec. No charge. ℘05 55 70 14 68. www.porcelaine-lys-royal.com.
A visit to this workshop provides an insight into porcelain making.

Return to Limoges via D 32 and N 21.

ADDRESSES

🏠 STAY

🛏️ **Hôtel de la Paix** – *25 pl. Jourdan .* 📞*05 55 34 36 00. www.phono.org./ limoges.html. 31 rooms.* This Napoléon III-style hotel in the heart of the city features an entertaining phonographic collection. Bright and airy bedrooms, some with wicker furnishings. Friendly atmosphere.

🛏️ **Hôtel Jeanne-d'Arc** – *17 av. du Gén.-de-Gaulle.* 📞*05 55 77 67 77. www.hoteljeannedarc-limoges.fr. Closed 21 Dec–7 Jan. 50 rooms.* This pleasant, well-located hotel is close to the city's famous train station. The well-mantained bedrooms and pleasant breakfast room have managed to retain their old French charm.

🛏️ **Chambre d'hôte M. et Mme Brulat** – *Imp. du Vieux Crezin - 87220 Feytiat. 5km/3mi E of Limoges. Take the A 20, exit 35, and head towards Feytiat; in Crézin follow signs to Le Vieux Crézin* 📞*05 55 06 34 41. 3 rooms.* Peace and quiet reign supreme in this large stone house in the middle of the country, yet just 10min from the centre of Limoges. Comfortable bedrooms, relaxing lounge, and a games room with billiards and darts.

🍴 EAT

🍽️ **Chez François** – *Halles Centrales.* 📞*05 55 32 32 79. Closed Aug 5–25, Sun and public hols.* Housed in the Halles de Limoges, a listed historical monument, this friendly bistro bases its menu on produce from the market. From the dining room, decorated with a fresco of sculpted wood, you can see the chef at work.

🍽️ **Chez Alphonse** – *5 pl. de la Motte.* 📞*05 55 34 34 14.Closed Jul 27–Aug 10 and Dec29–Jan 10, Mon eve, Sun and public hols.* Tucked away behind the *halles,* this bistro is a popular local haunt. Tables decorated with chequered tablecloths and a menu which is written up on the blackboard.

🍽️ **Le Pont St-Étienne** – *8 pl. de Compostelle.* 📞*05 55 30 52 54. www. lepontsaintetienne.fr. ClosedChristmas, Jan 1, Sun eve. Reserv. required at weekends.* Attractive bay windows with views of the old stone bridge and the river. The à la carte menu features a number of imaginatively named dishes. Summer terrace.

🍽️ **Les Petits Ventres** – *20 r. de la Boucherie.* 📞*05 55 34 22 90. www.les-petits-ventres.com. Closed Feb 8–22, Apr 20–May 3, Sept 5–20, Sun and Mon.* Classic French cuisine is to the fore in these two typical 15C houses, run by two young and enthusiastic owners. The cuisine is high on quality with traditional dishes based on liver, tongue, pig's trotters, tripe etc.

🍽️ **Le Bœuf à la Mode** – *60 r. François-Chenieux.* 📞*05 55 77 73 95. www.leboeuf-alamode.com/. Closed Aug, Sat lunchtime and Sun.* Excellent meaty cuisine served in a friendly and traditional ambience.

🍽️ **La Bibliothèque** – *7, rue Turgot.* 📞*05 55 11 00 47. www.restaurantla bibliotheque-limoges.com.* Attractive bar-pub-restaurant occupying what was the old library, serving beautifully presented carefully prepared traditional local and regional dishes.

🍽️ **Le Versailles** – *20, Pl. Aine. 05 55 13 39. www.restaurateursdefrance.com* Old French movie memorabilia fills the walls of this pleasnat brasserie.

🍽️ **Le Bistrot du Boucher** – *29 Bis, Boulevard Louis Blanc.* 📞*05 55 10 20 00. www.bistrotduboucher.com.* Bright cheery attractive modern chain restaurant specialising in top quality meat but also using seasonal and local produce.

🍷 BARS AND CAFÉS

La Parenthèse – *Cours du Temple - 22 r. du Consulat.* 📞*05 55 33 18 25. www.restaurant-tearoom-parenthese-limoges.com. Closed Sun, Public Hols and evenings*. This tea room sells home-made pastries and serves family-style meals at lunchtime. Either sit outdoors in the 16C courtyard or in the dining room painted with a mural of Montmartre.

Brasserie Artisanale St Martial – *8 pl. Denis-Dussoubs. ✆05 55 79 37 98. Open Mon–Sat, 3.30pm–2am; Closed Sun, Dec 25, Jan 1 and 15 Aug.* This brewery (in the true sense of the term), established over 10 years ago, perpetuates an old local tradition. Beer has been brewed in the region since the 18C; in the 19C there were no fewer than 50 brewers in the Limoges area.

Café des Anciennes Majorettes de la Baule – *27 r. Haute-Vienne. ✆05 55 34 34 16. Open Tue–Wed, 10.30am–1am; Thu–Sat, 10.30am–2am Closed mid-Jul to mid-Aug.* This renowned local bar is the venue for regular concerts and plays.

L'Irlandais – *2 r. Haute-Cité - ✆05 55 32 46 47. Open daily, 2pm–1am, Mon–Wed; 2pm–2am Thu–Sun.(Nov–Mar opens at 5pm).* This Irish pub is run by a fisherman from Brittany who has travelled the world and has already established a bakery and a pub in Ireland, and a concert violinist who has played in royal circles. They've hosted jazz, Celtic music and other concerts here.

🎭 ENTERTAINMENT

Cinemas - The main cinemas are in ave de Général de Gaule (Lido) and place Denis-Dussoubs (Grands Écrans). The Théâtre Municipal (rue Jean-Jaurès) hosts performances of ballet, opera, musicals and pop concerts. For theatre, head for La Limousine (rue des Coopérateurs) and Expression 7 (rue de la Réforme).

🛒 SHOPPING

Most of the city's shops are located in the area around the castle. The main boutiques selling porcelain are along boulevard Louis-Blanc and along the streets heading west from the city centre. Ali Babeth et les 40 couleurs (rue de la Boucherie) personalises your chosen piece. Discount shops selling seconds and end-of-line products include Michel Morel (boul. Louis-Blanc) and Cygne Bleu (place des Jacobins).

Le Pavillon de la Porcelaine - Musée Havilland – *Av. du Prés. John Kennedy. ✆05 55 30 21 86. www.haviland.fr. Open daily, 8.30am–7.30pm. Closed Sun in Jan, 1 Jan, 1 May and 25 Dec.* This factory out-

Rue de la Boucherie

let belongs to the Havilands, the American family which settled in Limoges in 1842 and began crafting prestigious porcelain sets for kings, queens and other famous names. The visit includes the museum and a demonstration of porcelain production, accompanied a film on a large screen. A wide choice of table and decorative ware is on sale in the boutique.

Paul Buforn – *4 pl. de la Cité. ✆06 37 25 62 62. Open Tue–Sat, 10am–12.30pm and 2–7pm. Closed Oct and public hols.* This impassioned enameller will delight in telling you all about his profession, its tradition and its techniques. He can also provide information about enamel-making workshops, as well as offer advice and appraisals on individual antique pieces. In the past, Limoges was home to a hundred or so enamel artisans, a number that has dwindled to just thirty today.

Buissières – *27, r. Jean-Jaurès. ✆05 55 34 10 44. Open Mon–Sat, 9am–7pm.* This chic confectioner, established in 1848, is one of Limoges' must-see places where the Art-Deco decor is almost worth a visit on its own. Evocatively named chocolates, pastries and desserts, including the house speciality black chocolate with chestnut cream.

🚶 GUIDED TOURS

The tourist office is able to provide information on guided, theme-based visits (2hr) of the old town, which take place during school holidays. *5€. ✆05 55 34 46 87.*

Oradour-sur-Glane★★

Ruined, fire-scarred walls and a cemetery stand in memory of 642 victims of a brutal attack by a detachment of SS troops, one of the cruellest events of the Second World War. An oddly peaceful impression seizes the visitor to this commemorative site, despite the fact that part of the horror of the massacre was that Oradour had been chosen for its very innocence and insignificance, the better to terrorise the French. The atrocity took place just four days after the announcement of the Allied landing in Normandy.

A BIT OF HISTORY

10 June 1944 – The people of Oradour, a large Limousin village, were going about their daily affairs on a busy Saturday morning. There were visitors from the city out for a day in the country, and visitors from the outlying farms had come to town for the day; a party of teenage cyclists was passing through. At 2 pm, as a cordon of German soldiers closed all the exits, a column of lorries and armoured cars entered the village. Curiosity soon gave way to fear. On Nazi orders everyone gathered on the fairground: men, women and 247 schoolchildren brought there by their teachers.

▶ **Population:** 2188
⚬ **Michelin Map:** 325: D-5; or see Limoges map.
⚑ **Info**: Pl. du Champ-de-Foire. ✆05 55 03 13 73.
⊙ **Location:** 24km/15mi northwest of Limoges.

The women and children were locked in the church, the men in the barns and garages. Grenade explosions and machine-gun bursts killed a great many; fire and dynamite completed the massacre. One woman managed to get out of the burning church through a window in the east end; a young boy and a few men were the only others to escape death.

VISIT

Centre de la Mémoire

Access to the ruins of the martyred village. ⏱*Open May 15–Sept 15, 9am–7pm (last entrance 1hr before); Mar–May 14 and Sept 16 –Oct, 9am–6pm; Feb, Nov to mid-Dec, 9am–5pm.* ☞*7€.* ✆*05 55 43 04 39. www.oradour.org.* This centre, located close to the ruins, houses a permanent exhibition about the rise of Nazism and 10 June 1944.

The ruins

Entrance via the Centre la Mémoire. Access via the Centre de la Mémoire. Go through the outer walls and along

Ruins stand to commemorate the victims

JACASS/MICHELIN

the streets of the ruined village. For a guide apply to the old church, where 500 women and children died. A visit to the Maison du Souvenir (contains objects that survived the flames), and to the cemetery (resting place of the victims), is a moving experience.

The New Oradour

Nearby, a new Oradour has been built. The modern church with its luminous stained-glass windows and square belfry may surprise at first, but it has been designed to blend harmoniously with the surroundings

Rochechouart

Rochechouart Castle rises above a rocky promontory. On the last day of the ostensions (see Introduction), held once every seven years (next in 2009), a unique procession takes place; the participants wear special costumes and carry precious shrines.

> **Population:** 3 808
> **Michelin Map:** 325: B-6.
> **Info:** 6, rue Victor Hugo.
> 05 55 03 72 73.
> **Location:** 42km/26.25mi W of Limoges via Ni41/ D941
> **Don't Miss:** The frescoes in the castle.

A BIT OF HISTORY

A distinguished family tree – The Rochechouart family can be traced back beyond the year 1000: their first castle rose up near the monastic settlement governed by the Charroux Abbey. A son of the viscount of Limoges became the lord upon his marriage to Ève d'Angoulême, whose dowry was the Rochechouart title and property.

Around 1205, Viscount Aymeric de Rochechouart married the beautiful Alix de Mortemart. The castle steward tried unsuccessfully to seduce her and in revenge the steward told his master that the viscountess had solicited him. The jealous and impulsive Aymeric had his wife thrown to a lion in the east tower. Two days later, he found the lion crouched docilely at his wife's feet. The guiltless woman was returned to favour, and the steward was thrown to the, by now, hungry lion.

In the struggle facing off Capetians and Plantagenets, the Rochechouart family sided with the king of France. One family member died at the battle of Poitiers protecting the king. In the centuries following the family tree branched out. The Mortemart line (see Château de MEILLANT) is also replete with history-making figures. The château was buffeted by wars and often threatened with ruin, but always saved – often with the help of Rochechouart wives who brought hefty dowries into their alliances. In 1836, the State acquired the buildings.

TOWN
Church
pl de l'Église

This is the former priory church, consecrated in 1067; only the western doorway, the northern wall, and part of the transept and chancel have survived.

Rue Jean-Parvy
Town centre

Note the 15C **Maison des Consuls**, and, farther on, a corner tower which stood within the medieval city wall.

Château★
pl du Château

The castle stands in a remarkable **setting**★ above the confluence of the Graine and the Vayres and is mostly late 15C. The 12C keep which flanks the entrance fort, was razed level with the rooftops in the 16C.

The second tower on the left end of the façade bears a lion carved in granite, perhaps in homage to the beautiful Alix, or more likely the crusading viscounts of Limoges. A drawbridge leads to the fort's entrance.

Château de Rochechouart

B. Kaufmann/MICHELIN

Cour d'honneur

The buildings lining the court on three sides were restored in the 18C and now house a museum.

Promenade des Allées

Leaving the château, the promenade is on the left, a shady terrace fragrant with age-old lime trees. From the site of the cross standing at the end of the walk, there is a good **view**★ of the Graine and Vayres valleys, and the castle.

SIGHTS
Musée Départemental d'Art Contemporain

pl du Château.

Open Mar–Sept, 10am–12.30pm, 1.30–6pm; Oct 10 to mid-Dec, 10am–12.30pm, 1.30–5pm. Closed Tue. 4.60€. 05 55 03 77 91. www.musee-rochechouart.com/musee_accueil.htm.

The Haute-Vienne General Council began building up the collection in 1985; today it is a significant centre for contemporary art. Raoul Hausmann, a major exponent of Dadaism, is particularly well represented.

Frescoes★ – Besides the main focus on contemporary art, the museum gives over two rooms to a remarkable group of 16C frescoes. The **salle d'Hercule** is decorated with rare murals painted in *grisaille*. Nearby, the **salle des chasses** has older frescos, which depict scenes from a royal hunt.

Espace Météorite

16, rue Jean Parvy

Open Jul 18–Sept 14, Mon–Fri, 10am–12.30pm & 1.30–6pm, Sat and Sun, 2–6pm; Apr, Mon–Fri, 10am–12.30pm and 1.30–6pm, Sun and public hols 2–6pm; May–Jun 17 & Sept 15–Oct, Mon–Fri & Sun, Nov & Dec, Mon–Fri 1.30–6pm Closed Sat, Apr–Jun 17 & Sept 15–Dec 21, Sun Nov & Dec and Dec 22– Mar. 4€. 05 55 03 02 70. www.espacemeteorite.com.

Rochechouart was built over a 20km/12mi-wide crater caused by a large meteorite which crashed in the area some 200 million years ago, releasing an energy 14 million times greater than the Hiroshima bomb.

EXCURSIONS
Cimetière de Rochechouart

NW, on the road to Chabanais.

The cemetery houses a novel funerary monument shaped like a large cask; it honours the memory of Léonce Chabernaud, whose profession - you guessed it - was that of a wine merchant.

Biennac

2km/1mi E via the D 10.

The church dating from the 12C and 13C, is topped by a hexagonal belfry and supported by buttresses. To reach the church pass a covered well and then go up the semicircular flight of steps.

Église Abbatiale de
Solignac★★

An interesting Romanesque church is all that remains of the once famous abbey founded in 632 by St Eligius near the green valley of the River Briance.

A BIT OF HISTORY

The great St Éligius – The legendary figure of St Éligius (St Éloi in French) dominated the Merovingian Age. This wise and saintly man was not only King Dagobert's chief minister but is also remembered as a man of great charity. Born at Chaptelat in 588 he trained as a goldsmith in the workshops at Limoges. He went to work in Paris; but soon rose to high office. Eventually, St Éligius felt the call of his native countryside and asked the king for land at Solignac on which to found a monastery where he could die in peace.

The abbey was built on a grand scale from the start, but in spite of its fortifications it did not escape the depredations of the Normans, the Saracens, the English and the Huguenots.

ABBEY CHURCH

🕐☞*Guided tours available. For information, contact the tourist office, ✆05 55 00 42 31.*

The present church dates from the first half on the 12C and is strongly influenced by the Périgord style of architecture.

Exterior – The big bell tower built at the same time as the abbey was replaced in the 19C by a belfry-wall. As you walk around the northern side of the church, admire the harmony of the construction: large buttresses and recessed columns reaching up to the ledge around the roof; on the lower part, groups of four arches falling alternately on plain pilasters and bases embellished with scrolling designs. A bas-relief of Christ in Majesty (1) rises above the north-transept doorway.

Interior – *Go in through the door in the porch.* The main body of the church is covered over with vast semicircular

▶ **Population:** Haute-Vienne
👠 **Michelin Map:** 325: E-6; local map see Limoges.
🔳 **Info**: Place Georges Dubreuil. 87110 Solignac ✆05 55 00 42 31. tourisme-solignac@wanadoo.fr
▶ **Location**: The abbey is located 8km/5mi south of Limoges.

Stalls, église abbatiale de Solignac

E. Larribère/MICHELIN

domes. The stalls (2), on each side of the nave, mostly date from the 15C, the carved misericords and arm rests depict foliage, animals and grimacing faces. The transept is asymmetrical. The south arm is roofed with barrel vaulting; note the 18C polychrome Virgin carved in wood (3). In the north transept a glass case (4) contains works of art including the 12C reliquary-bust of St Théau in gilded copper and silver.

The chancel is punctuated by seven arcades and three chapels. Two 17C frescoes represent the Temptation of Christ (5) and the Olive Garden (6). On the right pillar, note the restored distemper painting of St Christopher (7).

Monastery buildings
The buildings which were ravaged during the Revolution, are occupied by student missionaries.

The courtyard faces the south side of the church, which was connected to the cloisters by an archway leading from the second bay. The pointed arch (8), under which you pass as you go around towards the front of the buildings may have been another entrance to the cloisters.

St-Junien

St-Junien is a busy town, known for its paper mills, taweries (leather dressing works) and its glove factories. The collegiate church is Romanesque-Limousin in style.

A BIT OF HISTORY
St Junien, the miracle worker – In the early 6C, in a forest along the banks of the River Vienne, at Comodoliac, lived a hermit named Amand. Drawn to the hermit and his reputation for holiness, Junien joined him in his solitude. For some 40 years, Junien lived in this place, using waters from a sacred spring to cure those who came to see him, often from afar. His own reputation was so great that when he died, in 540, the bishop

▶ **Population:** 11605
◉ **Michelin Map:** 325: C-5; or see Limoges map.
▤ **Info:** Place du Champ de Foire. ℘05 55 02 17 93. www.saint-junien.net.
◗ **Location:** 12km/8mi NE of Rochechouart and 27km/17mi W of Limoges.

of Limoges personally presided over his funeral ceremonies and ordered the construction of a sanctuary above his tomb. A monastery grew up and soon a settlement formed around it.

The development of glove-making – St-Junien lies in the centre of a livestock rearing region and therefore had on hand the necessary raw materials – kid and lambskin. In addition the waters of the Vienne possess exceptional properties for tanning.

Glove-making began here in the Middle Ages and by the 15C had made the town famous. It is even said that Louis XI was received in great style at St-Junien and permitted the master glover makers to present him with pairs of gloves.

Expansion of the industry has brought about many changes but only handwork can ensure a good finish. Today, 300 workers in seven workshops produce over 480 000 pairs of gloves each year, 45% of all French production.

St Junien's tomb
B. Kaufmann/MICHELIN

The Ostensions of St-Junien

Every seven years, *Ostensions (next in 2009)* commemorate the memory of St Junien. When the ceremony is held the relics are shown and a picturesque spectacle unfolds: rich costumes are brought out, the main street is decorated with foliage and caged birds as a reminder of the forest in which the saint lived. The main events of the saint's life are evoked; music and ringing bells add an air of celebration.

COLLÉGIALE ST-JUNIEN★

pl Deffuas ⏰Open daily except Sun, 8am–noon.

The nave and transept of this remarkable Romanesque-Limousin building are late 11C; the main part of the building was completed when the façade was added at the end of the 12C; the plain, square chevet is 13C. The central bell tower was rebuilt after it had fallen down in 1922. The west doorway is divided into two bays and is framed by small columns. It is surmounted by a massive belfry-porch two storeys high, flanked by two stone bell-turrets.

Inside, the **nave** and the **chancel** are of equal length. The transept is punctuated by bays, one of which is quite narrow and extends the side aisle, and the chapels have primitive pointed arches. The crossing is surmounted by an octagonal cupola with flat pendants, pierced by four Limousin-style bays and a multifoil occulus. There are traces of 12C and 13C **frescoes** in several places, in particular on the vaulting of the second bay of the nave. The third bay on the north side houses an enamelled 13C reliquary.

Behind the main altar is **St Junien's tomb**★, a masterpiece of 12C Limousin sculpture. Two-thirds of the tomb is of limestone adorned with sculpture; the remainder is only a plaster covering added last century when the high altar was moved and no longer formed part of the sarcophagus. On the east side, Christ is shown in glory surrounded by the symbols of the Evangelists; medallions depict the theological and moral virtues. On the north face the Virgin, within a glory, holds the Infant Jesus; seated on one side are the figures of twelve Old Men of the Apocalypse.

On the opposite side the other twelve Old Men are portrayed together with a medallion of the Holy Lamb.

In the second bay on the northern side of the chancel is the **Chapelle St-Martial**. Of Gothic design, it once harboured the relics of the saint, whose life is depicted in the partly-visible 13C frescoes.

CHAPELLE NOTRE-DAME DU PONT

Quai des Mégisseries ⏰Open AprSep, 2-6pm. ☎05 55 43 06 90

Standing on the right bank of the River Vienne beside a 13C bridge equipped with cutwaters is the elegant Chapel of Our Lady of the Bridge.

There is a legend that the statue of the Virgin which now stands in the apse was originally found alongside the bridge on the river bank; the statue was immediately taken in solemn procession to the collegiate church, but the next day was found, once more, on the river bank. The people of St-Junien erected a chapel to the Virgin on the spot where the statue was found. The present church was built in the 15C on the site of the earlier sanctuary.

EXCURSIONS

Site Corot

2km/1.2mi NW along N 141. 15min round-trip on foot. As you leave town, take a sharp right turn at the bend in the road, then turn left immediately on a small road. Follow this road as far as the porcelain factory and park at the entrance of the lane.

Walk for a few minutes beside the river to reach the setting of the stream, flowing past rocks and trees, which inspired Corot and many other painters.

St-Léonard-de-Noblat★

Perched on a hilltop above a wide valley defined by the Vienne, Maulde and Taurion rivers, the bell tower of the old church in St-Léonard-de-Noblat is a remarkable example of Limousin-style Romanesque architecture. The main industry in town is the manufacture of porcelain and the valley is famed for its cattle. The distinctive, ruddy brown animals known as vaches limousines originate from the area around St-Léonard, which is an active export and breeding centre. For visitors with a sweet tooth, St-Léonard is memorable for its *massepain*, a speciality found in local pastry shops, made with sugary crushed almonds.

A BIT OF HISTORY
A hermit
Long before the Roman conquest, the road between Bourges and Bordeaux, crossing the Vienne near the village of Noblat, was well travelled. In the middle ages it was used by pilgrims on their way to Compostela.The town was named after the hermit **Léonard**, godson of Clovis, who early in the 6C chose the area as his place of retreat. His piety and the many miracles he performed made him one of the most popular saints in Limousin. A village was built alongside the retreat and took the name Noblat (derived from *nobiliacum*, meaning noble site). Léonard's help was invoked in protecting horses and seeking the release of prisoners. Because he was the patron saint of prisoners, it is the tradition in St-Léonard, in November to celebrate the *Quintaine*. A small wooden prison or *Quintaine* is trampled down by riders on horseback armed with clubs.

A great scholar
Joseph-Louis **Gay-Lussac** was born in St-Léonard in 1778 (d 1850). He distinguished himself in physics and chemistry: he discovered the law of expansion

▶ **Population:** 4 634
⏱ **Michelin Map:** 325: F-5; or see Limoges map
ℹ **Info**: Place du Champ de Mars ℰ05 55 56 25 06
◐ **Location**: 21km/13mi east of Limoges.
⊚ **Don't Miss**: The collegiate church and belfry.
👥 **Kids**: Historail.

of gases and made ascents in a balloon to examine whether the earth's magnetic attraction decreased as the altitude increased. In addition to his scientific achievements and awards, Gay-Lussac represented the Haute-Vienne in the French *Chambre des Deputés*.

MEDIEVAL TOWN
Two names are mentioned for every street: the present name in blue and the medieval name in red.

It is easy to imagine the layout of the medieval town: the ring of boulevards follows the path of the old defensive wall, whose vestiges can be seen on boulevard Carnot (south) and rue Jean-Jaurès (north-west). Some old houses date back to the 13C. In the days of the pilgrims, rue Georges-Perrin (then rue Aumônière) led from the Noblat Bridge to the centre of town; a 13C hospital gate still stands in this main street.

Start from **place Gay-Lussac** (commemorative monument and birthplace of the scientist). This was the centre of activities during the Middle Ages: the town's butchers had their stand here; note the corner house dating from the 13C and featuring a large bay surmounted by two storeys with twinned windows.

Follow rue Gay-Lussac to **place de la République**: no 18, known as the Maison de la Tour Ronde (16C), has a picturesque corbelled turret. On the corner of **rue de la Halle**, another 16C building, known as the Maison de la Tour Carrée, features a square bartizan. As you walk towards **place Noblat**, note the 13C house with its shop entrance surmounted by twinned windows.

SIGHTS

Ancienne Collégiale★

pl de la Collégiale Call tourist office.
This 12C former collegiate church (restored) remains a fine specimen of Romanesque architecture. It is said that Richard the Lion Heart contributed to the construction of the church on his release from prison in Austria.

Exterior – The **belfry**★★, built above a porch which is open on two sides and embellished with remarkable capitals, adjoins the third bay of the nave. The bell tower consists of four storeys built square, surmounted by two recessed storeys which are octagonal in shape. Each tier is adorned with beautiful blind arcades. The final touch of elegance is given by the stone spire which was constructed in the 12C.

Situated between the belfry and the transept, the **Rotonde du Sépulcre**, now restored to its original appearance, was probably built by a knight returning from the Holy Land.

The church's **west front**, built in the 13C, has a wide doorway flanked by small columns decorated with finely carved, crocketed capitals supporting the covings. The **east end** rises harmoniously in tiers and the chapels are roofed with rounded tiles.

Interior – The church went through several building stages (*see the scale model at the entrance*), which are apparent in the disunity of style within. The powerful **nave** has groined, barrel and broken-barrel vaulting, the **crossing** is roofed with a high dome on pendentives placed atop a drum pierced by eight windows and smaller and less ornate domes rise above the end of each transept arm.

In the 17C, a new vault, higher than the cupola in the transept, was added on and the church had to be shored up.

The 15C oak wood stalls (1) are sculpted with satirical motifs. On the gilded main altar (2), dating from the 18C, the relics of St Léonard are in a case below his statue. In the south transept, a wall niche

Ancienne Collégiale

B. Kaufmann/MICHELIN

holds the saint's tomb (3) and a revered lock bolt; the bolt is symbolic of St Léonard's power to intervene on prisoners' behalf (tradition also holds that it is effective in curing cases of sterility).

Musée Gay-Lussac

Rue Jean Giraudoux Open Jul–Aug, 3–6pm (last entrance 15min before closing); Closed Sept–Jun. Possibility of opening for group guided visits on reservation. No charge. 05 55 56 35 88 or 05 55 56 25 06.

The museum devoted to this man of science is located in a former convent. His memory and accomplishments are

Place Wilson

Ambulatory

N

CHANCEL

Chapelle St-Joseph

1 — 1

2

TRANSEPT

3

Rotonde du Sépulcre

★★ BELL TOWER

NAVE

Place Gay-Lussac

ST-LÉONARD-DE-NOBLAT

0   10 m

Place Denis Dussoubs

recalled in documents, objects (a hot air balloon basket; the re-creation of a 19C chemistry laboratory) and instruments (barometer, oven etc).

EXCURSION
Historail
On the D 39 S of town. ○*Open Jun 29– Aug, daily except Sat–Sun, 10.30–noon, 2.30–7pm; rest of the year by prior arrangement. Doors open exceptionally certain sundays and public hols. Ring* for details. ○*Closed on public hols.* ☞*4.50€ (children 8–16 years old: 3€).* ℘*05 55 56 11 12. www.historail.com.* The history of the iron horse is the subject of this museum's displays, which include genuine train parts as well as working models (six different scales; one of the models operates outdoors). Re-creations and simulations bring the heyday of rail back to life; in the yard, there are tracks, signals, a water tower, and engine motors.

ADDRESSES

☜ STAY ⨿ EAT

☞☞ **Hôtel Grand St-Léonard** – *23 av. du Champs-de-Mars.* ℘*05 55 56 18 18. www.hotelrestaurantlegrandsaint leonard-limousin.com. Closed Dec 20– Jan 20, Jun 15–Sept 15 Mon and Tue lunchtime. 14 rooms*. This old post house with an imposing façade is located in the centre of town. The pleasant rooms have been decorated with care, with the restaurant's dining room adorned with gleaming copper. Simple cuisine prepared from high-quality ingredients.

☞☞ **Le Gay Lussac** – *18 r. Victor Hugo.* ℘*05 55 56 98 45. Closed Christmas-Jan 1.* This bistro-style restaurant is housed in a former bakery. The upstairs dining room tends to be used by locals who appreciate the simplicity of the setting and the cuisine.

St-Yrieix-la-Perche

Bordering the Périgord Vert region, St-Yrieix (pronounced St-Irieh) stands at the centre of a rich stock rearing region and has a thriving cattle market. Nearby kaolin deposits are at the origin of Limoges porcelain.

A BIT OF HISTORY
The origins
A Gallo-Roman settlement named Att-anum was probably the first on the site. Around 530, Aredius, a noble from the court of King Théodebert inherited his father's house and came to stay there. A pious man, he founded a sanctuary which welcomed monks and, in 572, wrote his last will and testament (a document which tells us much about Merovingian society), leaving most of his property to the abbey of St-Martin de Tours.

▶ **Population:** 7 007
⏱ **Michelin Map:** 325: E-7
🏠 **Location:** 58 Boulevard Hôtel de Ville. ℘05 55 08 20 72.
☜ **Don't Miss:** Collégiale du Moustier; Musée de la Porcelaine.
⏱ **Also See:** Upper Vézère and Corrèze Valleys.

Near the monastery, a hamlet grew up, and took the name St-Yrieix, a transfor-mation of Aredius, to which La Perche was added in the 15C.
From 1307, the town was partly subject to royal authority, but was dominated by the powerful canons of the church at Moûtier. After the Hundred Years War, St-Yrieix and became a full-fledged municipality. Henri IV stayed here just before the Battle of La Roche-l'Abeille, and visitors are still shown the room he slept in.

Darnet and kaolin

Limoges owes its position as china capital of France to St-Yrieix, where kaolin deposits were discovered in the 18C. Experiments on this pure white clay had been conducted by manufacturers of the translucent soft-paste porcelain (☞see LIMOGES). Searches were being made all over South-west France, when, quite by chance, a surgeon by the name of Darnet who lived in St-Yrieix, met a chemist who was taking samples of clay and analysing them for the manufacturers. Darnet showed the chemist his wife's mixture for making her laundry snow white. Analysis revealed the pure kaolin content. In 1771 Darnet was charged by the king to supervise the mining of the kaolin.

Thanks to Turgot, the general intendant of Limousin, development was encouraged and St-Yrieix became the source of kaolin for Limoges and the whole region. Since 1774, a porcelain manufacture has been operating in Seynie, 1km/0.5mi from St-Yrieix.

The last gold mine

Gold mining in France and in particular in the St-Yrieix area goes back to Roman times. However, this lucrative activity disappeared for centuries and was only rediscovered in 1866 when an engineer revealed that ancient fortifications were in fact disused gold mines going back to the Gallo-Roman period. Le Bourneix near St-Yrieix-la-Perche was the last working gold mine in the European Union. Eighty-five persons were employed on the site and the mine yielded around 2t of gold every year until il closed down in 2001.

TOWN

Collégiale du Moustier★

pl Attane. The church stands on the site of the abbey founded by Aredius.

This vast edifice is a curious mix of Romanesque and Gothic styles. All that remains of the Romanesque church is the belfry-porch with its two narrow aisles. The nave has ogive vaulting and is very wide but the length is limited to

Capital of Collégiale du Moustier

E. Larribere/MICHELIN

two bays. A huge transept is followed by a long chancel.

Treasury –In a niche in the chancel, rests the 15C reliquary head of St-Yrieix made of wood plated with chased silver; the facial hair is picked out in gold.

A niche in the nave contains a small 13C reliquary of enamelled gilt copper, adorned with 20 medallions showing angels with outstretched wings; a Eucharistic dove in gilded copper, with wings which open to reveal the Host; and a fabric banner adorned with pearls which was used to cover the dove.

Tour du Plô – Near the collegiate church stands this 13C keep with twinned windows; it once formed part of the monastery's fortified precincts.

EXCURSION

Musée de la Porcelaine les Palloux

Head towards Limoges. After 2km/1mi, turn left towards the lake. ◷*Open Jul–Aug, 9am–noon and 2–6pm, Sun, 10am–noon, 2–6pm; Sept–Jun, daily except Sun, 9am–noon and 2–6pm.* ☞*No charge.* ☏*05 55 75 10 38.*

There is a rich collection dating from the 18C to the present day. Next to the soft paste porcelain from Vincennes, Arras and Strasbourg, are fine specimens in soft and hard paste from the count of Artois' factory.

Presented in a glass case are items from Germany and England and two other cases display French ceramics of the 19C, mainly from Limoges.

Lac de
Vassivière★★

The lake covers 1 000ha/2 471 acres, behind the Vassivière Dam over the River Maulde. Set in dark green hills, it is the site of many regular sporting and cultural events (sailing, motorcycle endurance trials, Tour de France bicycle race, contemporary art exhibits and more). The lakeside road (*route circumlacustre*) goes around the shoreline, offering beaches and coves for swimmers, fishing enthusiasts, sailors, and many footpaths for avid ramblers.

ÎLE DE VASSIVIÈRE

🕐 *Open all year.* 📞 *08 10 19 23 87. Access: take the lakeside road S, towards Beaumont-du-Lac. The road goes around Vassivière Island and the smaller Île aux Serpents. After 4km/2mi, turn left towards Pierefitte and park the car in the parking area. Take the little train or cross the bridge on foot to reach the island. Boat trips are also available.*

Sheltered in the western part of the lake, Vassivière offers visitors the combined attraction of its natural site and of its works of art displayed around the island. The path from the bridge leads to the **castle**, once the home of Mme de Vassivière, who owned most of the land which was submerged when the lake was created. Now the tourist centre and temporary exhibits have taken the

- 🦽 **Michelin Map:** 325: I-6; or see Eymoutiers map.
- ▶ **Location**: The lake is situated approximately 11km/7mi northeast of Eymoutiers.
- 🚲 **Don't Miss**: A boat trip on the lake; the outdoor leisure activities on offer here; the Centre National d'Art et du Paysage (CNAP).
- 🦽 **Also See**: Marche and the Upper Creuse.

place of footmen and chambermaids. Beyond, stands the **art museum**, and the surrounding woodland is home to the **sculpture park**, botany trails, a deer park and a farm with animals.

Centre National d'Art et du Paysage (CNAP)★★

🕐 *Open Apr–Sept, 11am–7pm; Oct–Mar, daily except Mon, 2–6pm.* 🕐 *Closed 1 Jan and 25 Dec.* 🎟 *3€.* 📞 *05 55 69 27 27.*

In 1991, a graceful new building rose up on the island in the middle of the lake, a centre for contemporary art which has since gained an international reputation.The distinctive structure housing the collection was designed by the Italian architect Aldo Rossi, in cooperation with the French architect Xavier Fabre. The design inspires an image of a ship **(galerie)** flanked by a lighthouse

Lac de Vassivière

S. Sauvignier/MICHELIN

(phare) 27m/89ft tall, and is well integrated in the landscape, pointing its prow up the hillside as though into a wave. Inside the **lighthouse**, a spiral stair leads past a monumental sculpture to the viewing platform above. From here, the visitor can appreciate the length and breadth of the gallery (80×10m/262×33ft). Inside the long **gallery**, wooden beams on a high, keel-shaped ceiling again recall the nautical theme.

Contemporary artists, both French and foreign, are often invited to exhibit their works in the museum and the **sculpture park** (☉ open to visitors year-round; there is also a 🚶 guided tour with the tour of the Centre d'Art Contemporain.

Along the path laid out for exploration of this outdoor extension of the museum are works by David Nash, Kimio Tsuchiya, Dominique Bailly and Jean-Pierre Uhlen.

ADDRESSES

🏠 STAY

🛏🍽 **Chambre d'hôte Villards - Bernard Blondel** – 87470 Peyrat-le-Château. 2km/1.2mi from Peyrat-le-Château towards the Lac de Vassivière and then Villards. ☎05 55 69 21 36 / 06 85 52 81 80. dusite@fermequestrevillards.com 🖂 5 rooms. Comfortable, calm guestrooms have been installed in this old stone farm. A billiards room, the living room fireplace or the nearby Lac de Vassivière provide ample opportunity for relaxation and leisure. Meals may be taken on the terrace.

🛏🍽 **Hôtel La Caravelle** – Lac de Vassivière - 87470 Peyrat-le-Château. ☎05 55 57 06 75. Easter –Nov 1. 21 rooms. Enjoy the view of the lake from your bedroom window. The breakfast room, living room and halls are adorned with reproductions of the famous Aubusson tapestries, Limoges enamels and works of art. The restaurant menu features regional cuisine prepared fresh.

🛒 SHOPPING

Ferme-Auberge Noëlle Digan - Lavergne – 23460 St-Martin-Château. 7km/4.2mi NE of Peyrat-le-Château via the D 68 and D 51. ☎05 55 64 72 69. The shop is open all year round, 10am–9pm; the inn is open Jul–Aug by prior arrangement. Closed Nov–Mar and Mon. This farm is devoted to raising a local breed of pig known as cul noir. The farmer is also a sculptor and his works are on display in the restaurant and for sale in the shop, along with local culinary specialities.

🏃 LEISURE ACTIVITIES

Base Nautique de Vauveix – Vauveix, 23460 Royère-de-Vassivière. ☎05 55 30 57 11/0685 47 00 83. Open Jul–Aug, daily, 9am–noon and 2–6pm. Sailing courses, boat and surfboard rentals.

Centre Équestre de Vassivière – Masgrangeas, 23460 Royère-de-Vassivière. ☎05 55 64 72 12 / 06 88 23 84 79. Open daily. This centre, a primary school for riding, offers outings ranging from trail rides to trips of several days (except in Jul–Aug).A children's hostel is also open during school holidays.

Vassivière-Club Tout Terrain – Route d'Aubusson, 23460 Royère-de-Vassivière. ☎05 55 64 75 33. www.vassiviereclubtout-terrain.com. Open Mon–Fri, 8am–5pm. Closed on public hols. This activity centre rents mountain bikes, quads, 4x4s, mini-motorcycles for children (Jul–Aug), and offers off-road vehicle excursions.

Ski Nautique Club Auchaise-Vassivière – Digue d'Auchaise (between Auphelle and Royère-de-Vassivière) - 23460 Royère-de-Vassivière. ☎05 55 64 72 79 (in season) Open Jun–Sept, daily Jul–Aug, 10.30am–1pm and 3–7pm. Weekends only Jun and Sept. This large lake is a great place to water ski and this club can provide you with all the necessary equipment.

🍷 NIGHTLIFE

La Galère – Broussas - 23340 Faux-la-Montagne. ☎05 55 67 98 07. Open Jul–Aug, daily; off-season, Fri–Sat and eve preceding public hols. La Galère is the most popular nightclub in the local area.

MARCHE *and the Upper Creuse*

As the name suggests, the Marche area was a marshland, which acted as a border territory between the Limousin and the Poitou. The region was known as the Marche Limousine and consisted of the stock-rearing area of the Haute-Marche and the arable farming area of the Basse-Marche. East of Marche, the Creuse valley winds down past Guéret to the Parc Naturel de Millevaches.

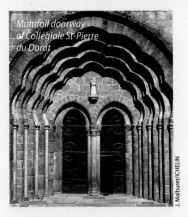

Multifoil doorway of Collégiale St-Pierre du Dorat

J. Malburet/ICHELIN

Haute Marche & Upper Creuse

The Upper Creuse, which flows through the Haute Marche, contains the northernmost part of the Parc Naturel de Millevaches en Limousin, which extends into the Corrèze and Haute Vienne. The Millevaches is a granite massif at an altitude of 400–1000m/1312–328ft, with gentle slopes and accessible valleys providing a perfect landscape for both summer and winter outdoor activities. Just north of the park is the world famous tapestry manufacturing centre Aubusson, which after a period of decline during the 19C and early 20C ,is now once again firmly established as a major centre of the industry, thanks in part at least to the painter and designer Jean Lurçat whose new designs revolutionised the industry. Further north again on a plateaus close to the Creuse Valley is the old capital of the Marche county and of the modern Creuse département, Guéret, which is an ideal base for exploring the local area.

Basse Marche

One of the least populated parts of the Limousin, the Basse Marche has been able to preserve much of its heritage. Dolmens, Roman remains, churches, windmills, and beautiful old villages stand testament to this. Bellac and Le Dorat, both featured in this guide, are classified as *Plus Beaux Villages de France*, as are Châteauponsac, Arnac la Poste, Magnac Laval, St.Pardoux, Blond and Razès. Bellac on the Basse Marche Plateau was the birthplace of author and playright Jean Giraudoux (1882). Just to the north of Bellac is the remarkable Collegiate Church of St. Peter at Le Dorat, which was once the capital of the Basse Marche.

Aubusson★

and Haute Vallée de la Creuse

Aubusson, situated in the upper valley of the Creuse, still manufactures the tapestries and carpets that have been world-famous for the past five centuries. A College of Decorative Arts, opened in 1884, offers courses aimed at keeping up this tradition. The Centre Culturel et Artistique Jean Lurçat was established to promote this exceptional craft.

A BIT OF HISTORY

Tapestry-making - It would appear that tapestry weaving was imported from Flanders in the 14C by Marie de Hainault, who was to become Countess of Marche, although it was only in the 15C that the tapestry weavers of Aubusson started to receive wider acclaim. The Lady and the Unicorn, a 15C masterpiece now in the Cluny Museum in Paris, is believed to have been woven by the craftsmen of Aubusson. Their fame peaked in the 16C and 17C with verdures (flower and foliage designs in shades of green) as well as sacred, mythological and historical themes. Colbert granted them the title of royal tapestry-makers in the 17C.

With the departure abroad of many of the weavers, following the Revocation of the Edict of Nantes in 1685, the industry faced ruin. It recovered only at the beginning of the 18C, thanks to the work of certain painters of that time,

- ▶ **Population:** 4 239
- **Michelin Map:** 325: K-5
- **Info:** rue Vieille, 23200 Aubusson. ℘05 55 66 32 12. www.ot-aubusson.fr.
- **Location:** 87km/60.6mi E of Limoges via the N141. Start from the Tourist Office in the old town.
- **Parking:** See town plan.
- **Don't Miss:** The Musée Départemental de la Tapisserie; the Château de Villemonteix.
- **Timing:** Allow half a day for Haute Vallée de la Creuse.

such as Watteau, Lancret and Boucher. The 19C was a period of decline, due in part to the aftermath of the Revolution but also to the development of a new source of competition: wallpaper. During the 1930s fresh impetus came when the artist Jean Lurçat played a decisive role in the rebirth of the art of tapestry weaving. A new generation of cartoon designers soon emerged including artists such as Prassinos, Tourlière, Picart-le-Doux and Wagensky.

Nowadays the town takes pride in maintaining its old weaving methods and tools. The great speciality of Aubusson is basse-lisse (low-warp) tapestry using horizontal looms; the same technique is used in Beauvais and Gobelins.

WHERE TO STAY	
Chambre d'hôte M. et Mme Dumontant	①
Chambre d'hôte Ourdeaux	③
Hôtel de France	⑤
Hôtel Villa Adonis	⑦

WHERE TO EAT	
Le Viaduc	②

OLD TOWN

Aubusson's old town straddles both sides of Grande-Rue, running east to west through the town from the Place de la Liberation to the Place du Marché, and behind which to the north lies the Rue Vieille. This cobbled pedestrianised street is lined with old houses which have been completely renovated and turned into art galleries, craft and antique shops. Above the Rue Vielle is the round medieval stone structure of the **Tour de l'Horloge**, with its open belfry which, due to its strategic location, was once used as a watchtower.

Below the Tour de l'Horloge is the **Pont de la Terrade**, the first bridge to be constructed at Aubusson. From this old bridge, an interesting 16C construction with pointed cutwaters, there is a pleasant view of the houses rising in terraces on the left bank of the Creuse.

Returning to the Place de la Libération at the foot of the Grande-Rue, there is a 16C turreted house known as the **Maison des Vallenet** and a fountain dating from 1718 which are the main attractions in this square. Take the Rue Barabant leading south from the Grande Rue to the Rue Châteafavier which leads to the **Église Ste-Croix**. This sturdy church with its centrally placed spire was built in the 13C and largely remodelled in the 19C. From the terrace near the church, a steep path climbs to the summit of the hill and the **Esplanade du Chapitre**, where the ruins (11C-13C) of the castle of the Counts of Aubusson still stand.

MUSEUMS AND EXHIBITS

Musée Départemental de la Tapisserie★

Avenue des Lissiers
🕙*Open Jul–Aug, 10am–6pm, Tue 2–6pm; Sep–Jun, daily except Tue, 9.30am–noon and 2–6pm.* *5€.* *℘05 55 83 08 30.*

The collection includes all types of tapestries and carpets from the 17C, 18C and 19C. The 20C is illustrated with various works by contemporary artists including Lurçat, Gromaire, Saint-Saëns, Picart le Doux, Tourlière and Julien. The modern works demonstrate the bril-

liance of the period of renewal inspired by Lurçat. A tour of the museum concludes with an exhibition on the history and technique of this art.

Manufacture de Tapis et de Tapisseries St-Jean

3, Avenue des Lissiers
🕙*Open May–Oct,* 🚶*Guided tour (1hr) by prior arrangement, 9am–noon and 2–5pm, Sat–Sun and public hols by prior arrangement; Nov–Apr, by prior arrangement.* *10€.* *℘05 55 66 10 08. www.aubusson-manufacture.com*

The workshops in the former royal manufactory work on commissions only. Carpets made by specialised weavers on high-warp looms are produced in the **savonnerie** workshop.

Other carpets (**ras**), with a rougher finished feel, are woven on a low-warp loom, with a cotton warp. The weavers work on one section at a time.

The restoration workshop handles carpets which have been damaged over time. After finding the right colours and materials, the tapestry workers rebuild the warp and weft.

L'Exposition – Tapisseries d'Aubusson, Felletin

Grande Rue. 🕙*Open July and Aug. 10am–noon and 1.30–5.30pm, Sun and public hols, 10am–noon and 2.30–5.30pm (last entrance 45min before closing); Sun and public hols, 2-5.30pm.* *No charge.* *℘05 55 66 32 12.*

The exhibit in the Hôtel de Ville comprises tapestries and carpets worked to traditional and modern designs.

Maison du Tapissier

Rue Vieille. 🕙*Open Daily 9.30am–12.30pm, 2–6pm (last entrance 45min before closing); Sun and Public Holidays 10am–noon and 2.30–5.30pm from Easter to end Sept.* *5€.* *℘05 55 66 32 12.*

In this lovely 16C house, pieces of local furniture and other objects evoke life in Aubusson in bygone days. On the upper floor, an old-fashioned workshop displays a low-warp loom, reels, wheels for preparing shuttles and bobbin stands, as well as several tapestries, cartoons and embroidered pieces.

 DRIVING TOUR

HAUTE VALLÉE DE LA CREUSE
Round trip of 90km/ 54mi – allow half a day.

▷ *From Aubusson, drive N along the D 990A, then the D 990 towards Montluçon.*

St-Maixant
A charming church and a late-14C castle stand on the village square.

▷ *Return to the D 990.*

Église de Chénérailles
Built in the 13C, this church contains a handsome **haut-relief**★ in memory of Barthélemy de la Place, the church's founder.

▷ *Follow the D 55 towards Ahun then turn right.*

Château de Villemonteix★
⟡*Open Jul–Sept,* ⟡*guided tour (1hr) 10am–noon and 2–7pm (last entry i hr before closing); Easter to Jun and Oct, 2–7pm; Nov to Easter, by prior arrangement.* ⟡8€. ⟡05 55 62 33 92 http://chateau.ville monteix.free.fr
The entrance yard to this 15C feudal stronghold is preceded by two corner towers. Strategically located, it was previously protected by a moat and drawbridge.
The watch-path, supported by corbels and two gargoyles, has a watchtower at each end. On the western side, two more towers fill out the defensive structure, safeguarding the rear of the central building. Tastefully restored, the castle contains a fine collection of

period furniture★★ and Aubusson, Felletin and Flemish **tapestries**★★ dating from the 16C to the 18C.

▷ *Leaving the château, turn left and go back to the D 53. Beyond Cressat, follow the D 50.*

Viaduc de Busseau
This 300m/328yd viaduct spanning the Creuse blends into the landscape.

▷ *Cross the viaduct; left on the D 16.*

Moutier-d'Ahun★
⟡*See MOUTIER-D'AHUN.*

▷ *Take the D 13.*

Ahun
This small town on the banks of the Creuse was once the brilliant *Acitodunum*, a major city on the map of the Roman Empire, and probably one of the first places to be evangelised by St Martial. It is home to the **Église St-Sylvain**. On the outside, between the arched bays of the chevet, the capitals crowning the columns of this church are carved

Frescoes, Église de Sous-Parsat

S. Sauvignier/MICHELIN

with animals and palmettos. Inside, the remarkable **woodwork**★ panels and columns date from the late 17C.

▶ *Take the D 13 towards Pontarion.*

Église de Sous-Parsat

The small church has some surprising **frescoes**★, the work of Gabriel Chabrat. Light filters through the windows, also designed by Chabrat, accentuating the unique ambience of the church.

▶ *Drive to Le Sec via the D 45, and then onto Chamberaud. Turn right onto the D 16 towards St-Sulpice.*

Masgot

🕐☞Guided tour (45min), Jul–Aug at 4pm, exhibition open in the afternoon. 🎫3€. ℘05 55 66 98 88.

The main attraction in Masgot are the stone sculptures by the artist François Michaud (1810–90). Using local granite, Michaud brought a new dimension to this traditional local craft. A **museum** has been opened in his home.

▶ *At the end of the path leading to the village, go back to Chamberaud and turn right onto the D 55 to reach La Rochette via Ars.*

Chapelle de la Rochette

Built in 1569 in Romanesque style and since restored, the chapel has a belfry topped with wooden shingles.

▶ *Drive to Aubusson along the D 18.*

ADDRESSES

🛏 STAY

🍴🍴 **Chambre d'hôte Ourdeaux** – *23200 Ourdeaux. 6km/3.6mi N of Aubusson on the D 942A. ℘05 55 66 98 58. www.ourdeauxholidays.com. 6 rooms.* A charming property with splendid views and a swimming pool. Evening meals served.

🍴🍴 **Chambre d'hôte M. et Mme. Dumontant** – *Les Vergnes, 23200 Les Vergnes. 7km/4.2mi E of Aubusson on the N 141. ℘05 55 66 23 74. Closed end Oct to early Apr. 6 rooms.* Quiet and relaxation await guests at this 18C farm in the heart of the countryside. The spacious rooms have all been renovated. Facilities include a covered swimming pool and fishing lake. Three holiday cottages are available for longer stays.

🍴🍴🍴 **Le France** – *6 r. des Déportés - ℘05 55 66 10 22. www.aubussonle france.com. 21 rooms.* This charming and characterful small luxury hotel offers lovely bedrooms and a gastronomic restaurant with summer dining in the courtyard.

🍴🍴🍴 **Villa Adonis** – *14, Av. de la République. ℘05 55 66 46 00 . www.villa-adonis.com.* Modern simple bedrooms close to the town centre in a renovated 19C building, albeit with little historic charm.

🍽 EAT

🍴🍴🍴 **Le Viaduc** – *23150 Busseau-sur-Creuse ℘05 55 62 57 20. www. restaurant-leviaduc.com. Closed Jan, Sun eve and Mon.* Located between Guéret and Aubusson, this country inn serves good honest simple cuisine The dining room's large bay windows open onto a green landscape with a view of the Busseau-sur-Creuse viaduct designed by Gustave Eiffel.

Bellac

and La Basse Marche

Bellac rises up on a spur overlooking the valley of the Vincou, which flows into the Gartempe. This picturesque green and undulating setting is situated on the borders of the Limousin plateaux and the plains of the Poitou. The town is associated with the novelist and playright, Jean Giraudoux.

- ▶ **Population:** 4 430
- **Michelin Map:** 325: D-4
- **Info:** rue des Doctrinaires ℘05 55 68 12 79
- **Location:** 45km/28mi NW of Limoges via N147. For a good view of the village head for the terrace 100m/110yd up rue Lafayette.
- **P Parking:** Leave your car on place de la République near the 16C town hall.
- **Timing:** Allow half a day to visit the sights and villages of the Basse-Marche area.

THE TOWN

Once you have enjoyed a view of the town, start your tour at no 29 rue Thiers, where a plaque commemorates La Fontaine's stay in the local inn, where he is said to have written one of his fables.

Église Notre-Dame

place de l'Église

The church, built on a terrace overlooking the Vincou, is built in a mix of Romanesque and Gothic styles. A huge square belfry surmounts the two naves, one 12C and Romanesque, the other 14C and Gothic. The two naves lead to the chancel which ends in a flat east end. The south doorway is adorned with small, serpentine capitals.

To the left of the entrance, in a chest set in the wall, there is a beautiful 12C **shrine★** (the oldest in Limousin), embellished with *cabochons* and medallions of *champlevé* enamel. Among the figurative decorations on the sacred receptacle are the symbols of the four Evangelists around the figure of Christ.

IN THE FOOTSTEPS OF GIRAUDOUX

Châteauroux may claim the glory of having educated **Jean Giraudoux** at its *lycée*, but it was in Bellac that he was born, in 1882 (d 1944). The countryside he knew as a child is depicted in an early work of poetic fiction, *Suzanne et le Pacifique*. He describes Bellac with the following words: "a countryside of streams and hills, a patchwork of fields and chestnut woods for it was a land with a long history, it was the region of Limousin."

Author of five novels, numerous short stories and influential political and literary essays, Giraudoux is best-known for his 15 plays. He created a new type of drama for the theatre, containing irony, poetry and magic. *Siegfried et le Limousin, Amphytrion 38, Intermezzo, Tiger at the Gates, Electra, Ondine, The Madwoman of Chaillot* and *The Apollo of Bellac* have been performed to appreciative audiences around the world. His style is sparkling, full of twists and innovations.

As a young man, he travelled widely in Europe and North America, and spent a year (1906-07) as an instructor at Harvard. Returning to France, he served in the First World War, was twice wounded, and became the first writer ever to be awarded the wartime Legion of Honour. In 1939-40, he was Commissioner of Information in Daladier's short-lived

Jean Giraudoux

government. Every year in July, a festival (theatre, music, dance) commemorates this talented native son.

Giraudoux's childhood home (Maison Natale)

4, rue Jean Jaurès. ⏰*Open Jul–Aug, daily except Tue, 2.30-6pm (5.30pm, Sat-Sun).* ⊘*3€.* ☏*05 55 68 03 77.*
The author's birthplace is now home to an exhibition of letters, photographs, set models and posters for his plays. In his room, the library includes a priceless collection of his books and manuscripts.
In 1951, a **monument** commemorating the author, by the sculptor Chauvenet, was erected beneath the magnificent trees of the town hall garden. On either side of his portrait are cameos of six heroines from his works: Ondine, Alcmène, Judith and Bella, Isabelle and Suzanne.

🚗 DRIVING TOUR

LA BASSE-MARCHE★
Round trip of 55km/33mi – allow 2hr 30min

▷ *Leave Bellac to the east along the D 1 towards Châteauponsac.*

Rancon
This peaceful hamlet in the Gartempe Valley is built into the hillside. The 12C Lantern of the Dead is surmounted by a cross with five foils (cusps).
The 13C **church**, built in the transitional Romanesque-Gothic style and fortified in the 14C, was formerly part of the town's defensive perimeter. Note the machicolations on the chevet and the openings for the archers; the belfry, a 16C square tower ends in an onion-shaped dome covered with shingles. In the chancel is a fine 13C wooden Christ.

Châteauponsac
The oldest part of this small town is huddled around the **church**, dating largely from the 12C, though the pointed vaulting was added in the narrow nave and aisles in the 15C. The tall transept is crowned with a dome on pendentives.

The chancel has fine round columns with carved capitals. Also of interest are the stone pulpit dating from 1642, a great 18C lectern and 16C-17C painted wooded statues.
Go around the church and walk to the promontory for a **view of the Gartempe**. From there the valley can be seen sloping steeply on the left bank. The Sous-le-Moutier quarter is in the foreground, with its busy pattern of old houses and terrace gardens.

Musée René-Baubérot
⏰*Open Daily Jul–Sept 15 and school hols, 2–6pm; Rest of year Sun and public hols, 2–6pm.* 👥*Guided tours possible by prior arrangement.* ⏰*Closed 25 Dec–1 Jan.* ⊘*5€ (child: 2.50€).* ☏*05 55 76 39 52. www.museechateauponsac. com.* Housed in a former Benedictine priory (1318), this museum recreates a dozen scenes of daily life, including a Limousin home, a young girls' bedroom, various workshops and a forge.
The impressive archaeological collections (prehistory, Gallo-Roman and medieval periods) include a quartz **polishing tool** used in the making of flint axes, Gallo-Roman chests, funerary urns, pottery and other items, most of which have been discovered in the local area.
The Maison du Terroir organises a number of annual exhibitions.

▷ *Follow the D 45 which wends its way through pleasant farmland.*

Magnac-Laval
This town is famous for a procession to St Maximus which travels more than 50km/32mi on Whit Monday (Pentecost). The pilgrims, wearing garlands of flowers around their necks, leave after midnight mass and return the following day after sunset.
The 12C **church** has a flat east end and a hexagonal belfry and contains the relics of St Maximus.

Collégiale St-Pierre du Dorat★★
👣 *See opposite.*

ADDRESSES

🛏 STAY

🍽🛏 **Auberge La Source** – *1 av. du Lac, 87250 Cieux. 7.5km/4.5mi S of Blond along the D 3. ℘05 55 03 33 23. www. lasource87.onlc.fr. Closed Jan9–Feb 9, Nov 6–13, Sun eve, Tue lunchtime and Mon. 8 rooms.* This former post house located in a village on the slopes of the Monts de Blond is a convenient stopover. The simply furnished rooms are reasonably spacious. Wooden beams crown the pleasant dining room located in the old stables.

🍴 EAT

🍽🛏 **Bellevue** – *2 av. de Limoges 87250 Bessines-sur-Gartempe. ℘05 55 76 01 99. Closed 10 Jan-10 Feb, Sat lunchtime and Fri from Oct–May- 12 rooms.* A typical regional house serving delicious traditional cuisine in a welcoming dining room. A dozen functional yet pleasant guest rooms.

Collégiale St-Pierre du Dorat★★

As the seat of the principal seneschalsy, or governorship of Basse-Marche from the 16C to the Revolution, Le Dorat prides itself on possessing one of the most remarkable buildings in Limousin, the Collegiate Church of St Peter. The Porte Bergère, complete with its machicolations, is all that remains of the fortifications built about 1420. Every seven years the Le Dorat ostensions give rise to unique ceremonies in which guards of honour take part – sappers and drummers in the uniforms of the First Empire (1804-14). Today, sheep and cattle raising are an important part of the local economy. The natural pastureland of the region is the ideal landscape for livestock breeding.

COLLEGIATE CHURCH

Construction began In about 1100 of a church of impressive proportions, (77m/253ft long, 39m/128ft wide at the transept), on the site of a 10C monastery which, after 50 years of work, bore the appearance we see today. A collegiate church is a church other than a cathedral that has a chapter of canons, or a church under the pastorate of more than one minister.

- ♿ **Michelin Map:** 325: D-3
- ▶ **Location**: 56km/35mi NNW of Limoges via N147 and D675 from Bellac
- 🛈 **Info**: 17 pl. de la Collégiale, 87210 Le Dorat. ℘05 55 60 76 81. www.ledorat.com.

Exterior

The collegiate church, which is built in fine grey granite, is striking in size and pleasing in proportion. The west front opens with a wide, **multifoil doorway** showing a Mozarabic influence which was perhaps inspired by the pilgrims who had journeyed to Santiago de Compostela.

An elegant **octagonal belfry** on three tiers of unequal height surmounted by a soaring spire topped with a 13C copper-gilt angel, rises above the transept. From below place de l'Église at a former churchyard where the roads from Guéret and Bellac meet, there is a good overall view of the **chevet**, the arrangement in tiers of the apse, the apsidal chapels and the stone belfries. The central apsidal chapel supports a semicircular tower which formed part of the 15C town's defence system. Two rectangular abutments shore up each apsidiole; each of the bays has a single Limousin-style arch. At the entrance, in the axis of the nave, the large granite baptismal font is pre-Romanesque, embellished on both sides with fancy tailed lions.

Interior

From the first bay which has a dome above, and is 12 steps above the level of the rest of the nave, one is struck immediately by the majesty of the building. The four bays following are broken barrel vaults on joists. Narrow aisles provide support for the central arching. The transept crossing, above which rises a tall dome on pendentives, is lit by Romanesque windows.

Crypt

Open Jun–Sept, guided tour, daily except Sun and public hols. Visits by prior arrangement at the tourist office. No charge. 05 55 60 76 81.

The crypt is reached from the south transept. It extends the length of the chancel and resembles it in plan and proportion. This fine 11C sanctuary, dedicated to St Anne, has columns whose primitive capitals are roughly hewn, one however is sculpted. The apsidal chapel contains fragments of 13C statues.

Sacristy

Open Jun–Sept, 2–6pm. For further information, contact the tourist office. No charge. 05 55 60 76 81.

It houses a small religious museum; this exhibits a multicoloured statue of St Anne and a Pietà dating from the 15C and a 13C reliquary cross with two cross-pieces, which belonged to the treasure of the collegiate church.

Crocq

and Le Pays de Franc-Alleu

This little medieval stronghold, its cobbled streets intact but its fortifications long since fallen, is located on a high point, surrounded by woodlands, meadows and lakes.

A BIT OF HISTORY

Formerly under the feudal wing of Auvergne, Crocq made up one side of a defensive triangle, with Auzanac to the north-east and Herment to the south-east. Facing the stronghold of St-Georges-Nigremont (*see below*) on high ground, Crocq was the leading line of defence against attacks from the Limousin region. The town gave its name to the peasant-rebels known as croquants.

TOWN

Chapelle Notre-Dame-de-la-Visitation

rue de l'Église

Founded at the end of the 12C, this small Romanesque edifice was thoroughly remodelled in the 15C and 16C, and restored in the 19C. It is surmounted by a belfry-gable and a lantern of the dead, removed to the top of the build-

- ▶ **Population:** Creuse 506
- **Michelin Map:** 325: L-5
- **Info:** 4 place Georges Hubert 05 55 67 4902.
- **Location:** 159km/99.4mi E of Limoges. Climb the towers of the castle for an impressive view of the surrounding area.
- **Don't Miss:** The triptych in the Chapelle Notre-Dame-de-la-Visitation.
- **Also See:** Plateau de Millevaches; Lac de Vassivière

ing. Inside, there is a remarkable **triptych**★ painted on wood, installed on the northern wall in 1995. This work, designed around 1530, relates the life of St Eligius in seven panels. An interesting feature on the representation of the Last Supper is the fork pictured on the back (this utensil was not in common use before the 17C)

Castle towers

rue de l'Église

Connected by a curtain wall, these towers are the only vestiges of the defensive 12C castle which fell in 1356 under assault by the troops of Edward, the Black Prince. Recently restored, the towers have been fitted with stairs making it possible to reach the orientation table in the eastern tower.

The table indicates the sites in the vast **panorama**★: the Combraille to the north; the Dôme range and the Puy de Dôme to the east; the Dore range and the Sancy peak to the south-east; the Millevaches plateau to the south-west.

View of the town of Crocq

S. Sauvignier/MICHELIN

🚗 DRIVING TOUR

LE PAYS DE FRANC-ALLEU★
Round-trip of 45km/27mi – allow 3hr

The name of this region recalls the Hundred Years War, which devastated it; in 1426, as compensation, an exemption from duties (*alleu*) was granted.

◗ *Leave Crocq on the D 996. Drive past the stadium, then turn left towards Dimpoux and park the car at Laval.*

 A pleasant lane bordered by beech and pine leads to a heath carpeted in fern. After 1km/0.5mi, in a little copse, stands the **Urbe dolmen**.
You can return to Laval by continuing down the lane, which shortly leads back to the road.
There is a good view of Crocq as you head back to the D 996.

◗ *At the crossroads, turn left on the D 996.*

After 2km/1.2mi through the heart of the Urbe Forest, look for a little road on the right which leads to the **church** (*Information at the town hall, ✆05 55 67 40 32*) of **Montel-Guillaume**, with its curious polychrome statues.

◗ *Return to the D 996 and turn right (1km/0.6mi) on the D 29.*

At St-Agnant-près-Crocq, follow the D 31 as it winds around ponds and lakes (Étang de la Motte is especially inviting). Nearby, the 15C **Château du Theil** (⊶ *not open to the public*) is well sheltered behind its wall.

◗ *At Magnat-l'Étrange, turn N on D 90.*

ST-GEORGES-NIGREMONT
Where the Limousin hills meet the Millevaches plateau, St-Georges-Nigremont is on a hill top (referred to as *Nigers Mons* in Latin texts) which faced a Gaulish *oppidum*. This hillside fort served as an important religious and administrative centre under the Merovingian and Carolingian dynasties.
From the terrace near the church, a wide **panorama** (*orientation table*) extends north-east to Crocq and beyond to the Combraille hills; to the south-east, the hills of Auvergne are visible.

◗ *Continue along the D 90 then turn right on the D 10. At Pontcharraud, take the D 21 SE for 7km/4.2mi, then turn left on the D 28. The road leads back to Crocq by way of the hamlet of Naberon, once home to a Knights of Malta commandery.*

Ruines de Crozant★

and around

The massive Crozant fortress, known as the key to the Limousin, rises, still impressive though in ruins, from a rocky promontory commanding the confluence of the Creuse and the Sédelle.

A BIT OF HISTORY

In the 13C, the Comte de la Marche, Hughes X de Lusignan, reinforced an existing wooden structure and the building began to take on the appearance of a fortress. Strong in his position, Hughes X revolted against Blanche de Castille and then St Louis. Crozant eventually fell to the royal troops and the Count and his father-in-law and ally Henry III of England were defeated at Saintes in 1242. Several thousand men could be garrisoned in the citadel which, a century later, was to resist the attacks of Edward the Black Prince.

In 1436, the castle changed hands, from the Bourbons to the Armagnacs. Restored to the Bourbons by Louis XI it was taken back after the treason of

- ⚲ **Michelin Map:** Michelin local map 325: G-2
- ⯐ **Info:** Mairie, 23160 Crozant. ℘05 55 89 80 12.
- ◐ **Location:** 85km/53mi NE of Limoges. The most spectacular view of Crozant, the castle ruins and the Creuse Valley, with the river cutting its way through the ravines, appears as you approach from the east along the D 30.
- ⬿ **Don't Miss:** A tour inside the ruined fortress; a boat trip on the lake.
- ⚲ **Also See:** Confluence of the two Creuse rivers; Argenton-sur-Creuse.

Constable Charles de Bourbon. The Wars of Religion and an earthquake brought calamity and by 1640 it was a ruin.

VISIT

◷*Open Jul–Aug, 10am–noon, 2–7pm, Sat–Sun and holidays: 10am–7pm; Apr to Jun and Sept: 2–6pm, Sat–Sun and holidays: 10am–noon, 2–6pm; Oct–11 Nov: Sat–Sun and holidays 2–6pm.* ⬭2€. ℘05 55 89 09 05.

In its heyday, visitors to the castle passed through the Charles VII gate to enter the first courtyard. The **square keep**, in the second courtyard, was the 12C castle.

A steep ramp leads to the third courtyard, the twin-walled section built by Hughes X. The base of the massive tower built by Isabelle d'Angoulême in the 13C stands on a rise 5m/16ft high. The line of towers continued to the end of the point, where the ground floor of the Tour Colin is intact.

EXCURSIONS
Fresselines
8km/5mi SE along the minor road skirting the cemetery.
Maurice Rollinat, the poet who was George Sand's godson, worked and

RUINES DE CROZANT
0   100 m
No longer exists

Sédelle
CREUSE
Tour Colin
Tour du Renard
Place d'Armes
Tour de l'Eau
Isabelle d'Angoulême keep
Donjon
Gateway
Hotel
VITRAT, LAC DE CHAMBON
CROZANT   ST. PLANTAIRE

died in this town. Painters still live and work here.

A rocky path leads from the church to the **confluence of the two Creuse rivers**★ (*1hr round trip on foot*), in picturesque surroundings. Claude Monet loved to set up his easel here.

Villejoint, les Jardins Clos de la Forge
From mid-Jun to mid-Sept: daily except Mon and Tue 2–5pm. Guided tour (2hr) 5pm, by prior arrangement 2 weeks in advance. 5€, 6.50€ guided tour. M. Allaert, 05 55 89 82 59 or M. Sautot, 05 55 8983 64. 5km/3mi S along the D 913 towards Dun-le-Palestel; turn right in Maisons.
Seven small -enclosed gardens planted around traditional Creuse houses, including a green theatre, small fruit garden, hardy plants garden, and a shade garden.

ADDRESSES

♉/ EAT

Le Lac – *At the Pont de Crozant - 23160 Crozant. 1km/0.6mi E of Crozant along the D 72 and D 30. 05 55 89 81 96. Closed Feb, 1–7 Mar, Sun eve, Wed eve and Mon.* Enjoy a meal in this pleasant restaurant before taking a boat trip on the lake. Traditional and contemporary cuisine. A few guest rooms are also available here.

BOAT TRIPS

L'hôtel du Lac - *23160 Crozant. 05 55 89 81 96. www.hoteldulac-crozant.com Apr–Oct, guided tours (1hr 30min) Jul–Aug, at 10.30am, 2.30pm and 4.15pm. Minimum of 15 people required. 9€.* These cruises on Lac d'Éguzon provide a different perspective of the ruins and the river.

Felletin

and La Montagne Limousine

This small industrial town, lying in hilly surroundings 10km/6mi south of Aubusson, owes its prosperity to tapestry weaving and claims to have woven the largest tapestry ever made (22×12m/72×40ft), which hangs in Coventry Cathedral. The city's oldest district, perched on an outcrop, has retained many 18C houses.

A BIT OF HISTORY

The birthplace of tapestry - Felletin owes its long-standing tradition to a group of Flemish weavers who settled there. In 1689 Felletin became a royal manufacturer, entering into fierce competition with the nearby town of Aubusson.
Today, the former rivals have joined forces and contribute to the renewal of tapestry weaving undertaken by Jean Lurçat. A new generation of talented cartoon designers soon followed Lurçat including artists such as Prassinos, Tourlière, nd Wagensky.

- ▶ **Population:** 1 912
- **Michelin Map:** 325: K-5
- **Info:** Place Quinault, 23500 Felletin. 05 55 66 54 60.
- **Location:** 97km/60.6mi E of Limoges and 10km/6mi S of Aubusson. Felletin is an excellent base for exploring the mountainous landscapes of the Limousin.
- **Timing:** Allow a full day to explore the Montagne Limousine region.
- **Don't Miss:** Felletin's tapestry workshops.

TOWN
Filature Terrade

Rue de la Papeterie. Open Jun–Sept, guided tour (1hr), Jul–Aug, Tue & Thu 3pm; Jun & Sept, Thu 3pm, rest of the year by prior arrangement with the tourist office (minimum 10 people). 4.50€. 05 55 66 54 60.
A guided tour of the tapestry workshops and of a wool mill gives an insight into the various stages of tapestry making.

Église du Moûtier

The three-tiered square bell-tower, dating from the 15C, dominates the whole town. The 15C frescoes decorating the nave are particularly noteworthy and there are traces of medieval murals in the transept.

Église Notre-Dame-du-Château

rue du Château
Themed exhibitions on tapestries; Jul–Aug 10am–noon and 2–6.30pm; May–Jun and Sept, 2–6pm.
05 55 66 54 60.

This Gothic church dates from the late 15C; its typical Languedoc style is unusual in the Limousin region.

Diamanterie

On the edge of the River Creuse.
Open Jul–Aug, guided tour (1hr), Wed and Fri, 3pm. 3€. For further information, contact the tourist office, 05 55 66 54 60.

These works belonged to a cooperative of diamond cutters who worked here until 1982.

DRIVING TOUR

LA MONTAGNE LIMOUSINE★
75km/47mi round-trip – allow one day.

Drive SW out of Felletin along the D 992.

The road winds pleasantly along the Gourbillon Valley, amid prairies and woodlands.

St-Quentin-la-Chabane

Surrounded by hilltops, this hamlet takes its name from one of them, the Puy de Cabanne. The 13C **church** has a Limousin-style door and bell gable. Beneath the chancel, an 11C crypt, harbours a Black Virgin.

Continue along the D 992 for 5km/3m, then take the D 59A to the right, towards La Nouaille

Domaine de Banizette★

Open Jul–Aug, last 2 weekends in Jun and the first 3 weekends in Sept, guided tour (1hr 15min) at 3pm, 4.15pm and 5.30pm; May–Jun and Sept–Oct, Sun and public hols, 3pm. 6€.
05 55 83 28 55.

This 17C lordly manor, which has been partially transformed into a museum of rural life, shows what a big farm must have been like at the beginning of the 20C. The flower garden featuring a central fountain and the three, marked forest trails are also interesting.

Leave the manor and turn right on the D 59. At St-Marc-à-Loubaud, turn left and take the D 16 towards Gentioux.

Site du Pont de Sénoueix★

This ancient Roman bridge over the Taurion has only one original arch left. The carefully mounted stones defy time, while the trickle of water at the river's source seems to mark it.

Gentioux

As of the 11C, Gentioux attracted stonemasons from around the Creuse. The 13C **church**, rebuilt in the 15C by the Knights of Malta is adorned with curious 16C sculptures. The town's monument to the fallen of the First World War is unique and moving in its pacifist expression.

Leave Gentioux on the D 8 towards Pigerolles. After 3km/1.8m, turn left on the D 35.

Maison des Chevaliers de Pallier

Open mid-Mar to mid-Nov, 10am–6pm; guided tours available in Jul–Aug. 5€. 05 55 67 91 73.

Built in the 12C by the Knights Templar, the chapel's façade is admirable. The doorway is flanked by two buttresses and crowned with a pointed arch and 14C sculpted tympanum.
Several displays relate the history of the Templars in the Creuse region.

Pont de Sénoueix

S. Sauvignier/MICHELIN

The **medieval garden**★ is particularly interesting since it illustrates the symbolic meaning of gardens during the Middle Ages:

◈ *1km/0.6mi before the town of Le Rat, take a small lane on the right, marked Chapelle. Park your car just beyond the turn-off and continue on foot.*

Site du Rat★

🚶 *1.2km/0.7mi on foot there and back (follow the path that climbs on the left).* The short walk leads to one of the loveliest **sites** on the plateau. A magnificent row of ancient trees shades the path to the 17C granite **Chapelle St-Roch**.

◈ *Continue along the same road and turn left in Malsagnes.*

Pigerolles

During winters when snow is plentiful, this village is an ideal cross-country ski resort. In summer, it offers pleasant hikes across the plateau.

◈ *Take the D 8 towards La Courtine.*

Féniers

Note yet another fine belfry-porch. Follow the D 26 along the Gioune gorge and admire the lovely views of the Auvergne mountain range.

Gioux

Granite table in the village and Gallo-Roman site (IC and 3C AD) in Maisonnière, 1.5km/0.9mi to the north.

◈ *Take D 35; then D 982 to Felletin.*

LA MONTAGNE LIMOUSINE

AUBUSSON
Felletin
D 10
★ Banizette
St-Quentin-la-Chabanne †
St-Marc-à-Loubaud
D 59
D 59A   D 992
la Nouaille
D 16
Pont de Sénoueix ★
Maisonnière ❖
Taurion
D 982
Gioux   D 35
PARC   NATUREL   RÉGIONAL
Pallier
Gentioux
D 8
Pigerolles
Maulde   D 16   D 164
DE   D 8
EYMOUTIERS   D 992
★ le Rat 🚶   D 78
Malsagnes   Féniers
D 85   D 36
MILLEVACHES   D 78   EN   LIMOUSIN
D 21
Gourbillon   Creuse
D 982
Gionne   D 26
D 19   D 982
N
LA COURTINE
MEYMAC

Guéret

Haute Vallée du Taurion,
Pays des Trois Lacs

Guéret stands on a plateau stretching as far as the Forêt de Chabrières, in close proximity to the Vallée de la Creuse. It is the capital of the Creuse département, the largest town and an excellent base from which to tour the Marche and Upper Creuse.

A BIT OF HISTORY

The town developed around a monastery founded there in the 8C by a count from Limoges, in a place known as Garactus, at the foot of a hill called Grandcher.

In 1514, Guéret became the capital of the county of La Marche, and has been an administrative centre ever since.

MUSÉE D'ART ET D'ARCHÉOLOGIE DE LA SÉNATORERIE

ave de la Sénatorie. ◎*Open Jul–Aug 10am–12noon, 2–6pm daily; May–June and Sept–Oct, daily except Tue, 10am–noon and 2–6pm; rest of the year, daily except Tue, 2nd and 4th and 5th Sun of each month, 2–6pm.* ◎*Closed on public hols.* ◎*2.80€.* ℘*05 55 52 07 20.*

The museum is in a fine 18C Classical building surrounded by a large flower garden. The collection of local **archaeological finds** ranges from prehistoric times to the Middle Ages. One room displays Chinese works of various periods as well as Japanese prints and objets d'art. Monumental **sculptures** depicting **Gaulish deities** and Gallo-Roman funerary stelae are exhibited in the basement.

Other works from the Middle Ages to the 20C, including *Eve* by Rodin and a *Bust of Rodin* by Camille Claudel, are displayed in various parts of the museum.

The museum houses a magnificent collection of Limousin **champlevé enamel work**★ from the 12C to the 15C. Note

▶ **Population:** 13,789

◔ **Michelin Map:** 325: I 3-4

▣ **Info:** 1, rue Eugène France, BP 52 23000 Guéret. ℘05.55.52.14.29. www.ot-gueret.fr

◖ **Location:** 66km/41mi W of Montluçon and 93km/58mi NE of Limoges.

▲▲ **Kids:** Parc Animalier des Monts de Guéret.

◔ **Timing:** Allow half a day to tour the Pays des Trois Lacs, and half a day for Haute Vallée du Taurion.

◈ **Don't Miss:** Enamel work in Musée d'Art et d'Archéologie de la Sénatorerie.

in particular a processional cross, pyxes (to hold the host) and the collection of shrines (chests and boxes). The vivid colours of the enamels harmonise with the gilding and polished stones. Scenes depicted include the Crucifixion (early 13C), the Adoration of the Magi (late 13C), the Stoning of St Stephen (late 12C), also known as the Malval Shrine, and the Martyrdom of St Thomas Becket (late 12C).

Several of the painted enamel pieces (15C-18C) can be attributed to great masters of the art, namely Limosin, Laudin and Nouailher. There are also

Malval shrine

Musée de la Sénatorerie, Guéret

Landscape around Guéret

©Authors Images/Photoshot

displays of glazed earthenware from Nevers, Moustiers, Rouen, Strasbourg and Delft as well as Italian majolica earthenware and glassware.

The painting section displays works by 17C French, Flemish and Dutch artists as well as more recent works by Guillaumin, Suzanne Valadon and Marinto, among others.

HÔTEL DES MONEYROUX

Château des Comtes de la Marche.

This Late Gothic-style building, contemporary with the Palais Jacques Cœur in Bourges (&see BOURGES), consists of two buildings joined by a corner turret. The right wing was built after 1447 by Antoine Alard, lord of Moneyroux; his successor, Pierre Billon, had the other wing built at the beginning of the 16C. The façade is pierced by many mullioned windows and is topped by dormer windows ornamented with finials and pinnacles.

EXCURSIONS

Forêt de Chabrières

Take the D940 S dir. Eymoutiers 2km/1.25mi.

The forest is dense with pine, oak, beech and birch trees; bracken forms a thick carpet underfoot. There are many marked footpaths and mountain-bike tracks offering various possibilities: one of them starting from the animal park runs past stones which have given rise to legends (10km/6.2mi, itinerary no 24, explanatory panels and brochure available at the tourist office). Stonemasonry works established along the road leading to Le Maupuy, testify to the importance of this activity in the past.

Les Loups de Chabrières, Parc Animalier des Monts de Guéret

Along the road to Bourganeuf. Open May–Sept 15, daily 10am–8pm, guided tours available. Dec 3– Dec 25.and Dec 31–Feb 9 8€ (4-12 years old: 5.50€). 05 55 81 23 23. www.loups-chabrieres.com

Located in the heart of the forest, this animal park offers (from the wooden watch-path) a fine panoramic view of the Puy de Dôme and Massif du Sancy, as well as a glimpse of the wolves in the pen below A trail later offers visitors the possibility of observing them more closely.

A tour of the museum provides information on popular beliefs, on myths connected with wolves and on their future. If you are keen to get to know them better, don't miss their feeding time at 4pm.

The park is also home to an **observatory** (*open Aug 10 only at 9pm; no charge; 05 55 81 23 23*).

Le Maupuy

Take the D914 W dir. La Brionne 2km/1.25mi.

A rocky plateau 685m/2 247ft high, its summit, together with its neighbour the Puy de Gaudy (621m/2 037ft), forms a natural barrier protecting Guéret. The view from the top provides surprising contrasts in landscape all around.

DRIVING TOUR

HAUTE VALLÉE DU TAURION
88km/55mi round trip – allow 3hr

▷ *Leave Guéret travelling S on the D 940 to Sardent.*

Sardent

The Chapel of St-Pardoux, 2km/1mi outside of the village, rises up on the right. The site is lovely, and popular with pilgrims who come for the virtues attributed to the water.

▷ *Drive E along the D 50 to Maisonnisses.*

Maisonnisses

Near the source of the River Gartemps, the village was once a headquarters for the Knights Templar. Only the church has survived; it contains a **recumbent figure**★ discovered in 1830 and replaced in its wall-niche tomb in 1955. It probably represents a 13C Knight.

▷ *Leave the village on the D 34, travelling S to St-Hilaire-le-Château.*

Pont Peri

🚶 A footpath leads to this Roman bridge spanning the Gosne. In the picturesque setting, admire the vaulting arch formed by massive hewn stones.

▷ *Return to St-Hilaire-le-Château, then take N 141 towards Bourganeuf.*

Pontarion

Settled along the banks of the Taurion, the salient feature of the hamlet is the 15C **château**, its corner towers and

battlements. The south façade faces the river and can be admired from the water's edge. Nature lovers will enjoy the arboretum, belvedere, garden and nature trail at the foot of the castle.

The **church** (13C) has a characteristic Limousin doorway, decorated with a frieze. Inside, the tombstones honour stonemasons.

▷ *After crossing the River Taurion, turn left on the D 13.*

Nécropole des Sagnes

🚶 A path leads through the woods (800m/875yd) to this Gallo-Roman site used for funeral ceremonies.

The burial grounds contained incinerated remains in 300 tombs, some in the form of funerary urns.

▷ *Continue along the D 13.*

Pierre aux Neuf Gradins

🚶 Walk under oak trees along a steep path to this mysterious and lovely site (there is an easier access from the north along a signposted path).

▷ *Continue on D 13 to Soubrebost.*

Soubrebost

Inside the church, note the interesting 13C **Virgin with Child**, a copper-clad wooden statuette.

▷ *Continue on D 13, turn right on D 37, then right on the D 8 to Bourganeuf. Return to Guéret along the scenic D 940A which runs onto the D 940.*

PAYS DES TROIS LACS★
75km/47mi round-trip – allow half a day

▷ *Drive W out of Guéret along N 145 towards La Souterraine.*

Église de St-Vaury

The church contains, at the back of the altar, a bas-relief cut in limestone, depicting scenes from the Passion. There are also two small 13C enamelled reliquaries.

le Bourg-d'Hem

BONNAT LA CHÂTRE

Lac de l'Age
Lac de Chézelles
Champsanglard

le Vignaud
Gorges
Anzême Chambon Jouillat

Lac de Champsanglard

N 145

St-Vaury
Longechaud

Glénic

Ajain

Etg de Courtille

49 48 47

GUÉRET

St-Laurent

685

le Maupuy

Ste-Feyre

LE PAYS DES
TROIS LACS

0 5 km

Puy de Gaudy

Forêt de Chabrières

PONTARION AUBUSSON

▶ *Continue NE along the D 48. The road veers to the left 3km/1.9mi beyond Longechaud.*

Le Vignaud

🚶 *1hr30min on foot there and back from a place known as Courtille*

A marked path leads to the Jupille meander where it is possible to see peregrines wheeling over the rocks, in search of some prey.

▶ *Continue along the D 48.*

Le Bourg-d'Hem

This village is picturesquely situated on a height overlooking the Creuse Valley; there is a fine **view** from the square behind the church.

Two nearby lakes, Lac de l'Age and Lac de Chézelles, offer swimming, fishing and hiking facilities.

▶ *Drive E along the D 33.*

Anzême

This pleasant little village boasts a fine bell-tower clad with chestnut-wood shingles. From the square in front of the church, there is a fine view over the gorge of the River Creuse and the **Pont du Diable**.

▶ *Turn back then right after the bridge.*

Lac de Champsanglard

This is the largest (55ha/136 acres) of the three reservoirs along the River Creuse. Water sports are available at Chambon, near the dam.

▶ *Drive on to Champsanglard then follow the D 14 which runs onto the D 6 and turn left 1km/0.6mi farther on.*

Jouillat

The local **church** (12C-13C) has a single nave which ends in an apse with five arcades (sculpted capitals).

A 13C **fresco** representing Christ decorates the chancel vaulting. Outside, on the southern side, a Carolingian tomb is embellished by a pattern of squares and rosettes, and a crouching lion in granite.

The **château** is an attractive 15C square building, flanked by corner towers.

▷ *Take the D 940 towards Guéret.*

Église de Glénic
Closed for restoration.
Perched on a promontory above the Creuse, the Romanesque **church** was fortified during the Hundred Years War. The east end is protected by towers; the other corners have corbelled turrets; the fourth bay and the chancel are elevated. In the 15C, the nave was lengthened and diagonal ribbed vaulting added. Beyond the 12C doorway, surmounted by a niche with a Romanesque statue of the Virgin, a 14C fresco faces the entrance, illustrating the fall of Adam and Eve.

▷ *Drive E along the D 63A.*

Église d'Ajain
The **church** (13C) was fortified with a watch-path atop the battlements, and buttressed watchtowers. In the nave with its diagonal rib vaulting, a cornice runs the length of the walls above expressive grimacing faces (mascarons).

▷ *Leave Ajain travelling S along the D 3.*

Ste-Feyre
🕑☎|*Guided tour of the château (1hr), mid-Jul to Aug, 2–7pm.* ✆5€.
℘*05 55 81 15 52.*
The town is dominated by the **château**, erected in the 18C. The **church**, built in the 13C and fortified in the 14C, has an elegant Limousin-style doorway on the west front. The single nave has four bays; the last of these forms the chancel. It is flanked with an aisle on the south side (16C) and has three chapels on the north side (15C).
In one of these chapels, note the polychrome stone statuary also dating from the 15C: St Anne, the Virgin and Child.

▷ *The D 942 takes you back to Guéret.*

Moutier d'Ahun★

The village of Moutier-d'Ahun (pronounced Moot-y-er da-un) lies between Guéret and Aubusson, near the upper valley of the Creuse, which is spanned by an old bridge bristling with cutwaters and called the Roman bridge although it was actually constructed during the 12C. The village clusters round the church, which contains remarkable 17C woodwork commissioned by the priors.

A BIT OF HISTORY
Fortune and misfortune – Shortly before the year 1000 Boson, count of Marche, gave a church on the banks of the Creuse to Uzerche Abbey as a first step towards founding a Benedictine monastery. The monastery became independent of its mother house and

▶ **Population:** 176
⬡ **Michelin Map:** 325: J-4
▷ **Location:** The village is located 20km/12mi SE of Guéret and 24km/15mi northeast of Aubusson.
⬡ **Don't Miss:** The woodwork and stalls in the village church.

took the name Moutier d'Ahun; in the 12C the monks replaced Boson's church by a larger building.
After a long period of prosperity, the abbey church was destroyed by the English during the Hundred Years' War and it had scarcely been restored when the nave was pillaged and set on fire during the Wars of Religion.
It was in 1610 that the woodwork to ornament the chancel was started and additions were made during the remainder of the the 17C . When the monks

Stall in the chancel

B. Kaufmann/MICHELIN

fled at the time of the Revolution, the woodwork was whitewashed but later regained its glory through patient restoration by the Abbé Malapert, priest of Moutier-d'Ahun. It was declared a national monument in 1889

CHURCH

South (top) end of village.
◷*Open mid-Jun to mid-Sept, 10.30am–12.30pm and 2.30–6.30pm; mid-Mar to mid-Jun and mid-Sept to mid-Nov, daily except Mon and Tue (except public hols), 2–5pm; mid-Nov to mid-Mar, daily except Mon and Tue, 2–4pm.* ◉*2.30€.* ℘*05 55 62 45 63.*

The church is now partly Romanesque, and partly Gothic. The western doorway, built in granite, is adorned with six covings embellished with little figures – prophets and angels jostle jugglers, musicians and dancers. The nave and the arms of the transept have been destroyed.

The crossing is surmounted by a square Romanesque belfry, pierced by three double bays on each side, supported by slender columns with smooth capitals. Pass below the grand cupola supported by squinches to reach the chancel under the arch made of three arcades in juxtaposition.

The chancel's eastern end is flattened, and the two chapels were embellished with ribbed vaulting in the 15C.
Outside, traces of the 14C fortifications can still be seen on the chevet.

Woodwork★★

The woodwork and the stalls entirely occupy the walls of the apse and chancel. All the carving was commissioned by Priors John Le Moyne, and later Etienne Le Moyne, and was carried out between 1673 and 1681 by the master-craftsman Simon Baüer.
Items from the old monastery may be seen in the sacristy. They include 12C statues in multicoloured granite of St Benedict and St Antony the hermit, 15C and 17C reliquaries and, above all, a wonderful Christ skilfully carved in boxwood (17C).

ADDRESSES

⏱ EAT

⊜⊜ **Les Touristes-Michel Roux** – *1 pl de la Mairie, 23000 Guéret. 20km/12.5mi NW of Moutiers via D942.* ℘*05 55 80 00 07. Closed Jan, Wed and Sun evening and Mon.* A regional building in the heart of the village, featuring a dining area with colourful and floral decor and a nice herb cupboard. Market Cuisine served.

BOISCHAUT AND LA BRENNE

The woods and rich pasturelands of the Boischaut and the marshes and lakes of the Brenne are part of the Berry Méridional, or southern Berry. The region occupies the southern part of the Indre département but it also extends into the southern tip of the Cher.

Boischaut

The southern Boischaut lies between the Cher and Creuse rivers, its clay soils overlapping the neighbouring Marche province. Here, undulating hedged pastureland and small farms in clearings are stocked with fine examples of Limousin and Charollais beef cattle along with sheep, goats and chickens. These animals, especially the chickens, feature heavily in the cuisine of the area and the delicious regional paté, which is available on most menus. This peaceful countryside, crisscrossed with many rivers and gardens, unspoiled by modern tourism. It is much the same as it was when described by the unconventional 19C novelist and playwright George Sand from Nohant. (see NOHANT).

Cloisters, Abbaye de Noirlac

©Thomas Pozzo di Borgo/Bigstockphoto.com

Brenne

Further west is the Brenne, a vast sand and clay depression, characterised by its abundant marshes, lakes and 'buttons', (small red sandstone hillocks. The Brenne is predominantly covered with heather, pine trees and broom. The River Creuse runs through the Brenne from east to west past the most important town of the area, Le Blanc, around which the richer soils are used for the production of cereals, fruit trees and the renowned Pouligny Saint Pierre goat's cheese. The central Brenne is characterised by traditional one roomed buildings of red sandstone with a loft, entered by an external ladder, especially at Preuilly la Ville, Lignac, Tilly, La Billarderie, Launeau and Lignac. Since 1989, the Brenne has been designated a nature park and is now popular with visitors interested in observing its exceptional flora and fauna. Once the exclusive haven of hunters and fishermen, the Brenne is an internationally important wetland that provides a home to many endangered species, both plant and animal. Here it is possible to see purple heron, black necked grebe, whiskered tern, short-toed eagle and the rare european pond tortoise. (see La BRENNE).

Abbaye de Noirlac★★

Between the River Cher and the Meillant Forest, this 12C-14C abbey, one of the best-preserved monasteries in France, is well worth a visit. In this exceptional setting, Gregorian chants, concerts and other cultural events take place.

▶ **Location**: South of Bourges.
 Michelin Map: 323; or *see St-Amand-Montrond*.
 Opening: Open Jul–Aug, 9.45am–6.30pm; Apr–Jun and Sep, 9.45am–12.30pm and 2–6.30pm; Oct–Dec and Feb–Mar, 9.45am–12.30pm and 2–5pm. Closed Dec 23–Jan 31. 6€. 02 48 62 01 01.

A BIT OF HISTORY

The foundation – This abbey was founded around 1130 by Robert of Clairvaux, St Bernard's cousin, on the right bank of the Cher and later came to be known as Noirlac. The first years were difficult and in 1149, Bernard himself went begging for a royal grant of wheat; but, the situation did improve: Ebbes V of Charenton made a significant gift that ensured the continuity of the community. The hard-working monks went to work on the land, clearing and building, and prosperity was just around the corner. By its fiftieth year, the abbey had a vast domain.

From destruction to restoration – After the surge of recruits in the 12C and 13C, fewer monks inhabited Noirlac in the 14C, and commercial activities there slowly came to a halt. From 1510: the abbot was appointed by the king, and managed the place in absentia. The Wars of Religion brought about further destruction and just before the French Revolution, only six monks were left. Declared national property, the abbey was sold and by 1820 it had become a porcelain factory. Prosper Mérimée discovered it in 1838, but not until 1909 did the Cher *département* acquire it. The buildings were still in use for humanitarian purposes until 1949, but by 1950, a vast restoration programme got underway.

ABBEY

The abbey buildings are set up in a typical Cistercian pattern.
Church – Work started in 1150 and lasted for 100 years, thus illustrating the passage from Romanesque to Gothic style. The sanctuary was built first, followed by the nave and the side aisles. The simplicity of line and the lovely pale stone add to the beauty of the architecture and to the sense of peace. In accordance with the rule of the order, sculpted ornamentation was barred: the capitals are plain and the windows uniformly grey in tone.

Abbey buildings – The other buildings were erected at various times: late 12C (east wing and lay brothers' building); first part of the 13C (refectory); second part of the 13C and early 14C (cloister galleries). Other works were carried out in the 18C (staircase with wrought-iron banister (1), dormitory rooms).

Cloisters and adjacent buildings – The rectangular buildings (38×33m/ 125×108ft) probably replaced an earlier construction. The east and south galleries have the most ornate carvings and all have fine ogive vaulting and rich ornamentation which contrasts with the simplicity of the church. The chapterhouse has a rounded doorway flanked

ABBAYE DE NOIRLAC

by twin windows; the six square bays are divided by polygonal columns. There is a great chimney-piece (2) in a corner of the heated common room which is roofed with flattened pointed vaulting. The refectory is lit by four large windows surmounted by two multi-lobed rose windows.

Only a portion of the **lay brothers' building** still stands. It was the economic centre of the monastery. The vast cellar is divided in two by a row of four pillars which support the vaults of the bays. On the upper floor, the lay brothers had their dormitory which today serves as an exhibit area.

ADDRESSES

♈/ EAT

◗◗ **Auberge de l'Abbaye de Noirlac** – *18200 Noirlac.* ℘*02 48 96 22 58.* *http://aubergeabbayenoirlac.free.fr.* After you've visited the abbey, enjoy a relaxing lunch in this small bar-restaurant. Attractive dining room embellished with wooden beams and a tiled floor.

Argenton-sur-Creuse★

Hills, Castles and the Creuse

Argenton is a pleasant provincial town with picturesque old houses lining the banks of the River Creuse. In the 19C, the town was a centre for the garment industry and still specialises in high-quality men's shirts.

A BIT OF HISTORY

The town of Argenton-sur-Creuse replaced the Gallo-Roman settlement of Argentomagnus which straddled a hill, the Colline de St-Marcel, 2km/1.2mi north of the town.

⟨⟨⟨ WALKING TOUR
Église St-Sauveur

The foundations of the church probably date from the settlement of the lower town in the 13C. The neo-Gothic belfry-porch in front of the church is crowned by a pierced stone spire (50m/164ft). The nave, rebuilt in the 19C, has groined vaulting with emblazoned keystones.

◗ *Head out of the church and turn left onto rue Grande.*

Impasse de Villers

Note the Hôtel de Scévole, a fine 17C-18C manor.

◗ *Turn right at the end of rue Grande.*

▶ **Population:** Indre 5 185
⚓ **Michelin Map:** Michelin local map 323: F-7
▯ **Info:** 13, place de la République BP 147 36200 Argenton-sur-Argenton. ℘02 54 24 05 30. www.ot-argenton-sur-creuse.fr
◗ **Location:** 92km/57.5mi N of Limoges via the A20. The Vieux Pont spanning the Creuse provides a perfect vantage-point from which to admire the River Creuse, Argenton's old quarter and the upper part of the town. For a view of the town's rooftops, head for the terrace of the Chapelle Notre-Dames-des-Bancs.
▣ **Parking:** Adequate parking in the east of the town (see map).
⊚ **Don't Miss:** The Musée de la Chemiserie, highlighting the history of the town's garment-making industry.

Vieux Pont

The old bridge (17C, but rebuilt in the 19C) provides a good **view**★ of the River Creuse, the old quarter and the upper part of town. To the left you can admire a fine stretch of the Creuse, with twin overflows to provide water for the mills, and houses with balconies, balustrades, wooden galleries and slate roofs, either overlooking the river or built into the now-overgrown cliff; to the right, the stone spire of St-Sauveur; and in the far distance the belfry of the Église St-Marcel. The imposing gilded statue of Notre-Dame of Argenton dominates the Chapelle Notre-Dame-des-Bancs. Beyond the bridge, note the old house with a small Renaissance door.

Rue Raspail

On the right, the **ancien collège**, now home to a regional archaeological restoration centre, was built in the late 15C in Renaissance style. It is crowned with a bell turret and adorned with a sculpted doorway. The building is also known locally as the old prison, for it served that purpose in 1782.

Chapelle St-Benoît

This former Gothic collegiate chapel (15C-16C) was restored and re-consecrated in 1873; the belfry was added in 1965. Outside, admire the fine doorway with wreathed columns; on the left is a statue (1485) of the Virgin and Child.

▷ *Cross rue Victor-Hugo*

Rue de la Coursière

This picturesque street opposite the chapel leads uphill, providing a good view of the town.

Chapelle Notre-Dame des Bancs

◷*Open daily, 10am–noon and 2pm–7pm exc Sat.*

This pilgrimage chapel, all that remains of a fortress dismantled in 1632, was erected in the 15C on the site of the ruins of a 2C sanctuary; is dominated by an enormous gilded statue of the Virgin Mary. The small statue that stands above the high altar is venerated under the name of the Good Lady of Argenton (Bonne Dame d'Argenton); it is said that she protected the town from the plague in 1632. The sanctuary was completely restored in the late 19C.

The monumental, gilded Virgin, unveiled in 1899, weighs around 3t and measures 6.5m/21ft in height.

From the **terrace**, the extensive **view**★ takes in the picturesque riverside quays, houses adorned with gables, turrets, and slate or brown tile roofs, the belfries of the Église St-Sauveur and Chapelle St-Benoît, as well as the valley of the Creuse encircling the town.

ARGENTON-SUR-CREUSE

WHERE TO STAY AND WHERE TO EAT

Hôtel
  Château de Bouesse.....①
Hôtel Le Cheval Noir.......②
Hôtel Le Prieuré.............③

▷ *Retrace your steps and turn left along rue Victor-Hugo.*

Pont-Neuf
Situated farther downstream, this bridge provides a panorama of the town.

Rue Charles-Brillaud
At the end of the street is the first machine-made garment workshop, founded in 1860 by Charles Brillaud; it houses the Musée de la Chemiserie.

Musée de la Chemiserie
& ⊙ *Open Jul–Aug, Tue-Sun, 9.30am-12.30pm and 2–6pm, Mon, 2–6pm; Sept–Jun, daily except Mon, 9.30am–noon and 2–6pm.* ⊙*Closed 23 Dec to mid-Feb.* ⊛*4€ (child 1.50 €).* ℘*02 54 24 34 69.*
This attractive museum, housed on several levels, provides an insight into the shirt *(chemise)* industry in Argenton and the local area. A production workshop exhibits several machines and accessories, with additional information provided by diagrams and plans explaining the various stages of manufacture.
The museum also displays shirts worn by stars such as Richard Burton, Charlie Chaplin and Frank Sinatra, and includes a simulation cabin with a virtual overview of men's fashion over the ages.

🚗 DRIVING TOUR

1 HILLS AND CASTLES
Round-trip of 50km/31mi – allow 3hr

St-Marcel★
📷 *See ST-MARCEL.*

▷ *Head along the D 927 and cross over the A 20 motorway.*

Le Pont-Chrétien-Chabenet
The 15C Château du Broutet now serves as the town hall. The Château de Chabenet, restored in the 19C, is visible above the limestone cliffs. The covered wooden bridge (1847) was built when the Paris–Toulouse railway opened.

▷ *Continue along the D 927.*

St-Gaultier
This village is nestled amid white chalky hills dotted with wooded groves. The **priory** dates from the 12C. After admiring the Romanesque capitals inside, follow the steep path that leads down to the river, where you will be rewarded with a fine view of the River Creuse.

▷ *Continue along the N 151.*

Lanterne des Morts de Ciron
This funerary lantern, crowned by a conical roof, dates from the 12C.

▷ *Cross the River Creuse via the D 44.*

Château de Romefort
Although the château is not open to visitors, it is worth stopping to admire its superb position perched above the river. The main building dates from the 14C; the square keep to one side from the 12C. It was once surrounded by three protective walls punctuated with towers, now forming rows of jagged ruins.

▷ *Follow the D 3 to Oulches, then continue along the D 927.*

Between Rivarennes and Thenay, enjoy scenic views of St-Gaultier, rising in tiers above the river, which is spanned here by an attractive stone bridge.

▷ *The D 48 leads back to Argenton.*

2 VALLÉE DE LA CREUSE★
Round-trip of 80km/50mi – half a day. Drive southeast out of Argenton along the D 48 towards Gargilesse.

Château du Courbat
This graceful manor is surrounded by a moat. The tower dates from the 13C, the building itself from the 17C. Restored in 1989, it now serves as the town hall.

▷ *Continue along the D 48.*

Le Menoux
This village overlooking the river (📷 *for the best views head for the Coline de Balicave*) was once famous for its wines, as

can be seen in the wine-growers' houses and cellar entrances.

The 19C church has been decorated by the Bolivian painter Jorge Carrasco. The artist's house, just a few doors away, is open to the public.

▷ *Return to the D 48.*

Barrage de la Roche-Bat-l'Aigue

Follow the road as it winds uphill and bear right onto a narrow road that runs close to the fast-flowing waters of the Creuse. A small dam (*barrage*), a spillway and a leisure area are enclosed between rocks and high wooded slopes.

▷ *Turn around, return to Badecon-le-Pin, then take the D 40.*

La Boucle du Pin★

As you come out of Les Chocats, you get a good **view**★ of the **Le Pin meander** (*boucle*) a wide bend made by the Creuse in a cirque of rocks and hills.

On the opposite side of the river, above a high promontory, stands the Romanesque church of Ceaulmont.

Gargilesse-Dampierre★

This is one of the most attractive villages in the valley, with its pleasant leafy setting, picturesque streets, old houses and church.

The village itself has an interesting literary history as **George Sand** (● *see NOHANT*) lived here and chose it as the background for several of her novels and accounts of rural legends and life. Claude Monet and Théodore Rousseau were among several painters of their time who stayed in Gargilesse, attracted by the village's natural beauty.

The **castle,** once the home of the former lords of Gargilesse, now houses art exhibitions.

Church

The 11C-12C Romanesque church stands within the walls of a medieval castle rebuilt in the 18C. The old keep and a door flanked by two towers are still standing. The church is well proportioned and has interesting historiated capitals portraying the Twenty-four Old Men of the Apocalypse.

A 12C Virgin and Child stands in the main chapel. The crypt is enormous and decorated with 12-15C **frescoes**: the Instruments of the Passion, St Gregory Celebrating Mass, the Apparition of Christ, Crucifixion, the Assumption, the Resurrection of the Dead, the Visitation and Three Kings.

George Sand's Retreat, Aligra

◐*Open Apr–Sept;* ⟶*guided tours (45min), 9.30am-12.30pm and 2.30–7pm.* ◐*4€ (no charge for children).* ℘*02 54 47 84 14.*

Mementos of the novelist, her son Maurice and her granddaughter Aurore are all on display in this small house.

▶ *Continue along the D 40. Beyond Cuzion, turn right onto the D 45 towards Éguzon. 2km/1.2mi farther on, turn right to the Moulin de Châteaubrun.*

Châteaubrun

The massive towers of Châteaubrun, a 12C fortress built in a picturesque setting overlooking the valley by Hugues de Lusignan, inspired George Sand to describe this wild country in two of her novels, *Le Péché de Monsieur Antoine* and *Les Maupras*.

▶ *Turn right onto the D 45E just before Pont-des-Piles.*

Belvédère du Barrage d'Éguzon★

This belvedere above the dam provides a superb view of the reservoir (Lac de Chambon) blending into a landscape of hills and rocks and, downstream, the valley of the River Creuse.

▶ *Head to the D 40, then turn right onto the D 40A.*

Plage de Bonnu

Before heading down to the Lac de Chambon, take a moment to admire an elegant castle surrounded by a moat on the right-hand side.

Ruines de Crozant★

Ⓖ *See Ruines de CROZANT.*

▶ *A narrow road skirting the foot of the ruins runs down to the lake.*

Chambon

This resort, set in beautiful surroundings, makes full use of the stretch of water contained by the Barrage d'Éguzon dam, with a full range of water sports available here. In season there is a regular boat service to the **Plage de Fougères**.

Éguzon

Éguzon was formerly a fortified town. On rue Athanase-Bassinet, daily life and traditional crafts of the region are brought to life in the **Musée de la Val-**

lée de la Creuse (Ⓖ ⚑ *guided tours (45min), Apr–Sept, daily except Tue, 10am–noon and 2–6pm, Sat–Sun and public hols, 2–6pm; Mar and Oct–Nov, Sat-Sun and public hols, 2-6pm;* ⊜3€; ☎02 54 47 47 75)*.

▶ *Continue on D 45 to Pont-de-Piles; left onto the D 72, then follow the D 913.*

Ruins of the Château de la Prune-au-Pot

The ruins of the castle are closed to visitors.

It was here that Henri IV stayed during the siege of Argenton in 1589.

Ceaulmont

The name of this town derives from its dominant position. In a meadow to the right of the road, note the charming little Romanesque church on the edge of a spur. Skirt it to the south side to enjoy a fine **view**★ of a loop in the Creuse, with the plateaux of the Marche and Combraille in the distance.

▶ *Return to the D 913 which leads back to Argenton-sur-Creuse.*

ADDRESSES

⊜ **Hôtel Le Cheval Noir** – *27 r. Auclert-Descottes.* ☎02 54 24 00 06. *www.le-chevalnoir.fr . 20 rooms.* This charming old post house is over a century old though bedrooms and restaurant reflect more modern tastes.

⊜⊜ **Hotel Restaurant Le Prieuré** – *44, rue Rio. 36200 Saint Marcel.* ☎02 54 24 05 19. www.restaurant-leprieure.com. This 2-star hotel occupies a plain 1970s building with good views. Traditional cooking.

⊜⊜⊜⊜ **Hôtel Château de Bouesse** – *1, Route d'Argenton 36200 Bouesse. 11km/ 6.6mi E of Argenton-surCreuse via D 927.* ☎02 54 25 12 20. www.relaisdusilence.com. *11 rooms.* Relive the past in the majestic towers of this 13C castle overlooking a wooded park.

La **Brenne**★★

Region

The northern limit of La Brenne
is marked by the River Claise, and
the eastern limit by the Fôret de
Lancosme. The Vallée de la Creuse
borders La Brenne to the west and
south. The region's main feature is
its 7 500ha/18 533 acres of lakes. At
the end of 1989, the **Parc Naturel
Régional de la Brenne** was created,
covering 1 660km2/640sq mi and
involving 47 different local governments and 32 000 inhabitants. For
information on tourist and cultural
activities here, head for the **Maison
du Parc**. The natural environment
is a haven for wildlife, in particular
some 100 species of birds. A good
observation point is the **Réserve
Naturelle de Chérine**.

- 🙂 **Michelin Map:** Local
  map 323: C/E-6/7
- ℹ️ **Info:** Maison du Parc,
  Le Bouchet, 36300 Rosnay.
  ℘02 54 28 12 13. www.
  parc-naturel-brenne.fr.
- ▶ **Location:** 102km/63.7mi
  N of Limoges via A20/
  D927/D134 to St Guatier
  on the edge of the Park.
- 👁 **Don't Miss:** Étang
  de la Mer Rouge.
- 🕐 **Timing:** Allow at least
  half a day to explore
  this fascinating area.

A BIT OF HISTORY

Land of a thousand lakes – La Brenne
is a land of legends: it has inspired painters and poets; fairies, elves and sorcerers
as well. The name recalls Geoffroy de
Brenne, lord of Mézières in the 13C. Once
neglected woodlands and moors, the
area was cleared out by monks
who engineered the ponds for
the purposes of cultivating fish
to enjoy on meatless fast days.
Later, in the 19C, the region
was further improved, remov-
ing the risk of malaria; roads
were laid and swampy lands
drained, opening the land to
agriculture. Today the area is a
patchwork of mixed uses.
The ponds and lakes mark
the landscape and symbolise
the close ties linking man and
nature in this region, in addition to providing a rich ecosystem and a lovely setting. The
waters are also a major factor
in the local economy, for over
1 000t of fish (carp, roach,
tench, pike, bass and eel) are
drawn out annually. There are
approximately 1400 lakes in
the Park which makes it one

of the largest wetland areas in France.
The lakes are inter-connected in series
and every year a sluice gate is opened
to drain the waters.

▶ DRIVING TOUR

LE PAYS AUX MILLE ÉTANGS
ROUND-TRIP
80km/50mi – allow half a day

Le Blanc

This busy burg is a commercial centre for the area, attracting fairs and markets, drawing regional inhabitants to its shops and cinemas. The upper town is a picturesque labyrinth of old houses, whereas the lower town gathers around the church of **St-Génitour.**

Écomusée de la Brenne

🕐 *Open Jul–Aug, 9.30am–6pm; May–Jun and Sep, daily except Mon, 9.30am–12.30pm and 2–6pm; Oct–Apr, daily except Mon, 10am–noon and 2–5pm.* 🕐 *Closed 1 Jan, 11 Nov and 25 Dec.* 🎫*3.50€ 📞02 54 37 25 20.*
This ethnographic museum, housed in Château Naillac, illustrates the history of the Brenne region and its population, bird life, the thousand lakes, the first settlers, smithies, local agriculture and architecture.

▷ *Leave Le Blanc north on D 975, then turn right after crossing the railway.*

Étang de la Mer Rouge

🚶 The Red Sea pond is believed to have been given its name by a former owner, Aimery Sénébaud, on his return from the Holy Land, where he had been imprisoned beside the Red Sea. It is the biggest lake in La Brenne, and has a surface area of 180ha/445 acres. It provides a natural refuge for migrating waterfowl. The church of Notre-Dame-de-la-Mer-Rouge, rebuilt in 1854, stands on a headland to the south and is the site of a yearly pilgrimage.

Château du Bouchet

🕐 *Open Jul–Aug,* 🚶 *guided tour (1hr, last entrance 30min before closing), Sun and Mon, 2.30–6.30pm; holidays in May, 2.30–6.30pm.* 🎫*5€ (guided tour); 2€ (exterior only). 📞02 54 37 80 14.*
This impressive medieval fortress, occupied by the English during the Hundred Years War, was restored in both the 15C and 17C. For 300 years it belonged to the Rochechouart-Mortemart family and for a while served as the residence of the Marquise de Montespan who was born a Rochechouart-Mortemart and was the daughter and sister of the lords of Le Bouchet (her portrait hangs inside the castle). From the keep and the terrace there is a view of the Brenne countryside and the Red Sea pond.

▷ *Drive past the Maison du Parc. Turn left at the intersection with the D 44 then right onto the D 17A at Le Maupas. There is a parking area a little farther on.*

Étang Massé

Le Blizon, Rosnay 🚶 *Guided tours.* 🕐 *Open Feb–Oct , 9am or 6pm, by prior arrangement.* 🎫*7€. Information and reservations 📞02 54 28 11 04 or go to www.parc-naturel-brenne.fr .*
In the early morning or late evening, the observation post overlooking the lake is the perfect spot to watch one of the richest natural spectacles in La Brenne, with wading birds such as bitterns and small bitterns and European pond turtles visible here.

▷ *Slightly farther on, the Blizon discovery trail branches off on the left.*

Sentier découverte de l'Étang du Blizon

1.5km/0.9mi, allow 30min.
🚶 Informative panels on the theme of "dragonflies and frogs" line this discovery trail which skirts the edge of the Blizon lake.

▷ *Turn left at the end of the D 17A. Leave the car in the Étangs Foucault parking area on the right.*

Étangs Foucault

A look-out post, located at the end of the marked path, offers good views of ducks, ospreys, herons, egrets etc.

▷ *Turn back and follow the D 15 to Mézières-en-Brenne.*

Mézières-en-Brenne

The most important town in Brenne is built on the banks of the Claise whose course is marked by a line of poplars. The **church** belfry, flanked by two stone

WILDFOWL OF THE BRENNE

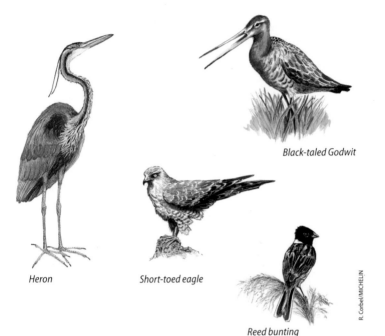

Black-taled Godwit

Heron

Short-toed eagle

Reed bunting

R. Corbel/MICHELIN

turrets, has a porch ornamented with sculpture. The nave has wooden vaulting with painted uprights and crossbeams. Note the beautiful stained glass of the Renaissance chapel to the right of the chancel.

Maison de la Pisciculture de Brenne

⏰ Open mid-Mar to Oct, daily except Su and Tue, 3-6pm (last entrance 30min before closing); Nov to mid-Mar, by prior arrangement with the tourist office. ⏰ Closed 1 Jan, 1 May and 25 Dec. 🎫 2.20€. 📞 02 54 38 12 24.
Established in one of the last vestiges of the 11C stronghold, this nature museum is one of the branches of the Écomusée de la Brenne. The exhibits displayed inside are related to fish and fishing in the region. In addition to aquariums, displays recount the history of the village and provide information on techniques for catching local fish.

Église de Paulnay

The **church** dating from the 12C and 13C has an interesting Romanesque **doorway**★. Three rows of finely sculptured covings are supported on elegant capitals.

▶ Drive S along the D 43 to St-Michel-en-Brenne then turn onto the D 44.

Réserve Naturelle de Chérine

Saint Michel en Brenne ⏰ Open Jul-Aug. 🚶 Guided tour (2hr), Thu 6-8pm, by prior arrangement; Apr to 28 Jun, 4pm-6pm and 5 July - 26 July, 6pm - 8pm, guided tour, see website for details of activities. 🎫 7€. 📞 02 54 28 11 02. www.parc-naturel-brenne.fr.
From the edge of a 26ha/64-acre lake, nature lovers can observe at leisure the amazing diversity of this unspoilt ecosystem, which shelters colourful bird life (including purple herons and ducks).

▶ Return to Le Blanc along the D 17.

ADDRESSES

🛏 STAY

Auberge Saint-Hubert – *8 pl. de l'Église. 36800 Migne.* ℘*02 54 37 99 84. Closed Christmas, New Year and Fri. 13 rooms.* Given the discreet façade, the interior of this inn is unexpectedly charming. The bedrooms, identical in size and comfort, have been tastefully personalised. A hunting scene embellishes one of the dining rooms. In winter, dine to the sound of live background piano music.

Chambre d'hôte La Presle – *Rte de Châteauroux. 36290 Mézières-en-Brenne - turn left after leaving the village.* ℘*02 54 38 12 36. Closed 15–30 Sept. 3 rooms.* This attractive small farmhouse dating from the 17C offers guests a choice of three comfortable bedrooms with Louis XV furniture, delicate English wallpaper, and views over the garden or surrounding fields. Communal breakfast around a large table.

🍽 EAT

Le Bellebouche – *Base de Loisirs de Bellebouche - 36290 Mézières-en-Brenne - 9km/5.5mi E of Mézières towards Châteauroux on the D 925.* ℘*02 54 38 30 77. Open weekends in May and every day in Jul-Aug.* This outdoor recreation centre has a restaurant on site. Located in a natural setting on the edge of the lake, its terrace is a pleasant place to relax, unwind and enjoy views of the neighbouring pine forest. Contemporary, reasonably priced cuisine.

Espace Dégustation de la Maison du Parc – *Hameau du Bouchet 36300 Rosnay. Open every day Jul–Aug 9–7pm and 10am–6pm rest oy year.* ℘*02 54 28 53 02. Closed 1 Jan and 25 Dec.* This renovated farmhouse, part of the old château, serves an interesting choice of copious, inexpensive local specialities (fried fish, cheeses, bread, rillettes etc). Terrace with views of the lake.

Auberge de la Gabrière – *2 La Gabrière. La Gabrière, 36220 Lingé .9km/5.5mi S of Mézières. Head towards Le Blanc, then La Gabrière along the D 15 and D 17 -* ℘*02 54 37 80 97. Closed Tue*

eve and Wed.-Reserv. recommended at weekends. This spacious, country restaurant is well-situated opposite the Étang de la Gabrière. The menu features a good choice of freshwater fish, as well as game in season. Very popular at weekends. Basic rooms.

$$ Au Bœuf Couronné – *9 pl. du Gén.-de-Gaulle, 36290 Mézières-en-Brenne.* ℘*02 54 38 04 39. Closed mid-Dec –Jan 31 and last week Jun, Sun eve and Mon except public hols.* A variety of harnesses adorn the dining room of this restaurant, a former 17C posthouse, on the village square. A good choice of fixed-price menus, including one for children. A few modest guest rooms are also available.

🏃 SPORT AND LEISURE

Base de Loisirs de Bellebouche – *10km/6mi E of Mézières-en-Brenne along the D 925. 36290 Mézières-en-Brenne* ℘*02 54 38 32 36. Open May–Jun and Sept, weekends 2–6pm; mid-Jul to mid-Aug, 10.30am–7pm; first 2 weeks of Jul and last two weeks of Aug, 2–6pm. Parking Jul–Aug: 4.50€. No dogs allowed.* A natural sandy beach (no lifeguards). Three nature trails for hikers, mountain bikes and horses, including a fitness trail. Discovery trail *(7.5km/4.5mi, 3hr)* around the lake, with three observation areas (the best views are from the southwest). Pedalos and kayaks available for hire.

Centre Équestre Poney-Club de la Virevolte – *Le Fresne - 9km/5.4mi E of Rosnay and 11km/6.5mi N of Le Blanc on the D 17. 36300 Douadic* ℘*02 54 37 10 28. Except for school holidays, daily except Tue; during school holidays, daily (Jul–Aug: daily except Sun)Closed first two weeks in Sept, Christmas and New Year's Day.* Isabelle and Jean-Charles Liva lead trips in the heart of the Land of a Thousand Lakes (Le Pays aux Mille Étangs), and offer riding lessons for children.

Domaine Ste-Marie – Éric Aphatie – *36290 Mézières-en-Brenne, open Mar-Nov, daily by prior arrangement -* ℘*02 54 38 01 18.* Take a horse-drawn carriage ride with Mr. Aphatie (father or son), who will tell you about the history of La Brenne, its local customs and point out the

La Châtre

*George Sand Country and the
Southwest Boischaut*

La Châtre is built on a hill overlooking the Indre Valley, in the centre of the area known locally as the Vallée Noire (Black Valley) beloved by George Sand (Tsee NOHANT). This is the dark green countryside of wooded farmland that the "good woman of Nohant" described in so many of her novels. Only the old castle keep recalls the fact that the town had a military origin and was a Roman encampment (castrum, which became Châtre over time).

- ▶ **Population:** Indre 4 488
- **Michelin Map:** 323: H-7
- **Info:** 134, rue Nationale - B.P.115 36400, La Châtre. ☎02 54 48 22 64. www. pays-george-sand.com.
- **Location:** 37km/23.1mi SE of Châteauroux via D943.
- **Timing:** Allow a full day to explore the rural backwaters of the Berry as described in the works of George Sand.
- **Don't Miss:** Musée George-Sand et de la Vallée Noire.

OLD TOWN

Around the church, and towards the river, the **old town** invites strolling. Start from square George-Sand and walk by the town hall, the former Carmelite abbey church (14C carved doorway) and the fine Villaines mansion (now the municipal library).

From there you have a choice of picturesque streets and several interesting old houses to admire: the **Maison Rouge**, a fine 16C timber-framed residence (place Laisnel-de-la-Salle) and private mansions in Classical style farther on along rue de **Bellefond**. A fine Gothic **statue** of the Virgin Mary stands on place Notre-Dame; it once decorated a fortified gate located here. From place de l'Abbaye, overlooking the River Indre, walk down the stairs lined with flower beds, which lead to the **Pont aux laies**, an old humpback bridge offering a charming view of the picturesque surroundings: at the river's edge, former tanneries with their typical sheltered porches are quiet today, and the water runs clear beneath them.

Donjon

rue Venôse. The prison at La Châtre, an old feudal fortress in the control of provincial lords, was then nothing more than a huge square tower, blackened by the centuries and standing straight upon the rock on the side of a narrow ravine where the River Indre flows amid luxuriant green" (George Sand, *Mauprat*). Built in the 15C by Guillaume III de Chauvigny, used as a prison from 1743 to 1934, it now houses a museum.

Musée George-Sand et de la Vallée Noire

71 rue Venôse. ◷*Open daily Jul–Aug, 9am–7pm; Apr–Jun and Sept, 10am–noon and 2–6.30pm; Oct–Mar, 10am–noon and 2–5pm.* ◷*Closed Tue(exc Jul and Aug) Jan and 25 Dec.* ◸*3€* ☎*02 54 48 36 79.*

The upper floor is devoted to George Sand and her guests at Nohant, including portraits, letters, first editions, novels and mementoes of her personal friends. Exhibits on the other floors evoke the folklore and art of the Black Valley.

Église St-Germain

pl. de l'Église
The porch and tower fell down in 1896, carrying the 12C nave with them. Inside, the pillars and Romanesque capitals have been reconstructed. A 14C *Pietà*, from the Carmelite convent, is in the Lady chapel on the left of the chancel; the *Pentecost*, is Jean Boucher's.

EXCURSIONS
Église de la Berthenoux

12km/7.5mi NE via the D 940 and the D 68.
The vast 12C edifice is surmounted by a powerful belfry crowning a fine dome

resting on squinches. The capitals in the transept have carved figures.

🚗 DRIVING TOUR

1 GEORGE SAND TOUR
60km/37mi – allow one day
This tour wanders through the countryside that served as backdrop for Sand's novels set in rural Berry. Their settings have changed but little in the past century. Still "vivid and sombre in colour… the melancholy far distant views".

▷ *Leave La Châtre travelling NE on the D 940 towards Bourges. Drive along the car-racing track and turn left.*

Château d'Ars
Surrounded by a large park, this 16C castle was chosen by George Sand as the setting for her novel *Les Beaux Messieurs de Bois-Doré*. It now houses the George Sand and Romanticism International Centre (exhibitions).

▷ *Drive to D 943; turn to Châteauroux.*

Château de Nohant★
&*See NOHANT.*

▷ *Turn back; continue on D 943.*

Fresques de Vic★
The village built along the Roman road (its Latin name Vicus means village), contains a small Romanesque church, **Église St-Martin**, decorated with interesting frescoes brought to light in 1849.
The **frescoes** adorn both sides of a wall that divides the chancel from the nave, as well as the walls of the chancel itself and the wall and vaulting of the apse. Though the faces lack expression, the composition is so skilled, the movement of the figures so alive and the detail so accurate, these paintings form a group whose technique was later copied in the pictorial and sculptural art of Limousin and the South-west.

▷ *Cross the D 943 (minor road opposite rue de l'Église).*

St-Chartier
Open Jun-Aug, 🔎 guided tour of the château (1hr), by prior arrangement (except mid Jul during "Les Rencontres du Festival" www.saintchartier.org.). ⮐ *2€.*
℘ *02 54 48 60 60.*
The interesting small church and château (restored in the 19C) can be admired as you go through the **park**.

▷ *Rejoin the D 943 via the D 69.*

Corlay
This inspired the landscapes described in *Fanchon the Cricket*; a rest area overlooks the green Indre Valley (*for a closer look, drive down the D 69*).

▷ *Turn left on D38 5kM/3mi farther on.*

La Mare au Diable
🚶 A forest clearing off the D 38 was probably the site of the marsh known as the haunted pool (*La Mare au Diable*), the title of one of Sand's novels.

Château du Magnet
The 15C castle stands surrounded by greenery, in a pastoral landscape.

▷ *D 19 on the left runs through charming countryside crisscrossed by hedges.*

Château de Lys-St-George
The château, whose towers rise straight up out of the moat, combines the architectural severity of a medieval fortress with the charm of the Renaissance. From the terrace you will see the 15C façade and the Gourdon Valley.

▷ *Continue along the D 19 and turn left 3km/1.9mi beyond Tranzault.*

Château de Sarzay
🕐*Open 9am to dusk.* ⮐*6€* ℘*02 54 31 32 25. www.sarzay.com.*
Blanchemont Castle in George Sand's novel *The Angibault Miller* is based on Sarzay. A proud feudal domain whose tall round towers have tiled roofs.

▷ *Drive N along the D 41.*

LA CHÂTRE
CIRCUITS

Moulin d'Angibault

Stop by the mill which stands on the Vauvre, a tributary of the Indre (*festivities, dancing, evening gatherings in summer*).

▷ *Take the D 49 back to La Châtre.*

2 SOUTHWEST BOISCHAUT
50km/31mi – allow 4hr.
Leave by D 73 SW towards le Magny.

Église de Chassignolles
Tour by prior arrangement.
Contact Mme Aussire, ☏02 54 48 31 77.
The **church** is crowned by a large belfry-tower. A small Renaissance door with an emblazoned pediment opens into the north transept.

▷ *Turn back; continue on D 72.*

St-Denis-de-Jouhet
The Gothic church has a shingle-covered steeple as well as 12C and 13C stained-glass windows.

▷ *Leave the village via the D 54.*

Cluis
The chancel of the 13C **church** ends with two apses bearing noteworthy capitals. One of the side chapels has a splendid 14C white-marble **Virgin and Child**★. Aubusson tapestries hang in the 16C town hall and the 17C covered market is surmounted by a pinnacle.

▷ *Drive NE along the D 38.*

Cluis-Dessous
Among the medieval castle's ruins you can see part of a curtain wall, a gate with two towers and a central building.

▷ *Continue on D 38 towards Mouhers.*

Neuvy-St-Sépulchre
🕐*Unaccompanied visit, daily 9–7pm.*
Guided tours possible end Jul–Aug Tue 3.30pm, other times by prior arrangement. ☏02 54 30 86 28.
This small town gets its name from the **basilica** modelled on the Holy Sepulchre in Jerusalem. It consists of a rectangular structure completed in 1049 joined to a vast **rotunda**★ 22m/72ft

across; the upper part was restored by Violet-le-Duc in the 19C.

▷ *Drive E from Neuvy on D 927.*

Abbaye de Varennes
🕐*Open Jul–Sept pm only.* 🎫*No charge.* 📞*02 54 31 30 59.*

ADDRESSES

🏠 STAY

🛏 **Camping Intercommunal le Val Vert** – *3km/1.8mi SE of La Châtre along the D 943 and the D 83A towards Briantes.* 📞*02 54 48 32 42. Open Jun–mid Sept. 77 pitches.* This simple but pleasant campsite stands in a verdant setting close to the town and the River Indre.

🛏🍽 **Hôtel Notre Dame** – *4 pl. Notre-Dame.* 📞*02 54 48 01 14. Closed Feb school hols. 19 rooms.* Located in a quiet neighbourhood in the heart of the old town, this small hotel offers guests simple yet well-maintained rooms, almost all of which overlook an inner courtyard.

🛏 **Chambre d'hôte et Ferme-Auberge Montgarni** – *36230 Sarzay. 1.5km/0.9mi S of Sarzay along the D 41 towards Chassignolles.* 📞*02 54 31 31 05. Reserv. recommended. 5 rooms.* Comfort-able bedrooms, delicious cuisine based on home produce and friendly hosts are the hallmarks of this 19C property in the middle of the countryside. Farm products are also on sale here.

🍴 EAT

🍽 **Le Duplex** – *22 r. Ajasson-de-Gransagne.* 📞*02 54 48 00 28. Closed Mon and Sun.* This recently restored 17C manor house has retained its original stones and beams. Two dining rooms decorated in attractive rustic style serving traditional cooking.

🍽🍽 **Ferme-Auberge de Poumoué** – *Poumoué, 36400 Le Magny. 7km/4.2mi SW of La Châtre along the D 72.* 📞*02 54 48 22 95. Closed Dec, Sat eve, Sun lunchtime, Tue-Thu from Sept–15 Jun - reserv. recommended.* An 18C farm-inn where the emphasis is on excellent local cheeses and *charcuterie*, both produced from the goats raised on the property.

The abbey, founded in 1148 is not far from the road, at the bottom of a dale. George Sand wrote of the abbey in her novel *Les Beaux Messieurs de Bois-Doré* (1857).

▷ *Rejoin the D 927 which leads back to La Châtre.*

Château de **Culan**★
and around

The powerful medieval fortress of Culan stands four square with its massive round towers looking straight down into the gorges of the River Arnon.

VISIT

👥👤🕐📷 *Guided tour of the château (45min) Jul–Aug 10am–8pm; Apr–Jun and Sept to 1 Nov: 10.15am–12.15, 2-6.15pm.* 🕐*Closed Nov 11–Mar.* 🎫*Gardens and château 8€(4-14 years old: 4.50P). Gardens and museum only, 6€* 📞*02 48 56 66 66. www.culan.net.* Captured by Philip Augustus in 1188, it was reconstructed in the 13C and con-

♿ **Michelin Map:** 323: K-7
📍 **Location**: 82km/51.25mi S of Bourges via A20/D951/D997. The best view of the castle **site**★ is from the place where the bridge crosses the river along the D 943 from Montluçon.

siderably altered during the 15C. Joan of Arc and Louis XI were guests here. in the 17C it passed into the hands of Michel Le Tellier, father of the Minister Louvois. The rooms reflect different periods of the castle's history and there is a diorama explaining the revolt known as *la Fronde*.

After the tour, go to the end of the terrace where there is a good view of the Arnon Valley.

EXCURSION
Épineuil-le-Fleuriel
19.5km/12mi E.

Located on the edge of the region known as the Bourbonnais, Épineuil was the childhood home of author **Alain-Fournier** from 1891 to 1898. Readers of his most famous work *Le Grand Meaulnes* will recognise the fictional Sainte-Agathe, where the story was set.

L'École du Grand Meaulnes
Open Jul–Aug, 10am–12.30, 2–6pm, closed Tue; Apr–Jun and Sept: 10am–noon, 2–6pm closed Mon and Tue; Oct 10am–noon, 2–5pm except Tue 10am–noon, 2–5pm. 6€ 02 48 63 04 82. http://grandmeaulnes.free.fr

The universe of the author, and of the young heroes of *Le Grand Meaulnes* is re-created here in the schoolhouse. Alain-Fournier is also remembered as a poet and a journalist.

Jardins du Prieuré Notre-Dame d'Orsan★★

Michelin Map: 323: J-6; or see St-amand-Montrond.

Location: 10km/6mi SE of Lignières.

On the border of the Cher and Indre *départements*, between St-Amand-Montrond and La Châtre, a former priory is home to a medieval garden; its design is loosely based on illuminations and miniatures created by monk s of the time.

A BIT OF HISTORY
Founded in the 12C by Robert d'Abrissel, the priory is said to possess a relic (the heart) of the founder, who died here in 1116. Pillaged and destroyed in 1569, the priory was rebuilt in the 16C and 17C, before the French Revolution brought about the end of its religious vocation.

GARDENS
Open Mar 28–Nov 1, 10am–7pm (exc Oct, 5pm). 9€. 02 48 56 27 50. www.prieuredorsan.com.

In medieval times, religious communities tended gardens planted to correspond to biblical themes. Generally, the plots were encompassed by buildings and a row of oaks. Gardeners provided for both earthly and spiritual nourishment in the choice of vegetables and the planning of green spaces appropriate for meditation. The garden in the middle of the monastery, was a natural cloister, a place of prayer and spiritual renewal. Marked out by four squares of grapevine, two grassy paths intersect; at the central point, a fountain symbolises the source of the waters of earthly paradise.

Eight gazebos provide access to the many adjacent gardens: herbs, small fruits, orchards, the **vegetable labyrinth**, the aromatic garden (near the kitchens), the **rose garden** (a harbour of peace dedicated to the Virgin), the pergola and the olive garden (symbol of mercy), the flower beds and the secret gardens. To the north of the gardens, a path (1.2km/0.7mi) passes through the gate and invites walkers to discover the typical Boischaut-Sud landscape.

Garden of Prieuré Notre-Dame d'Orsan
©Thomas Pozzo di Borgo/Bigstockphoto.com

♀/ EAT

⊜⊜⊜⊜ **La Table d'Orsan** – *In the priory - 18170 Maisonnais. ℘02 48 56 27 50. www.prieuredorsan.com. Open every eve (and lunchtimes except Sat–Sun and* public hols). *Closed Nov 2–Mar 31.* Fresh produce from the medieval garden and local markets are to the fore in this restaurant in a wing of the former priory.

Château de
Meillant★★

The Château de Meillant, constructed by Charles de Chaumont d'Amboise, governor of Italy, half-hidden by trees in its park, reveals the beauties of its architecture only a little at a time. The plain front seems, by contrast, to enhance the elegance and rich decoration of the east façade, which is adorned with all the beauty of line of the Late Gothic period graced by Italian influence.

- ◐ **Michelin Map:** 323: L-6; or see St-Amand-Montrond.
- ▷ **Location**: 7.5km/4.5mi N of St-Amand-Montrond and 39km/24mi S of Bourges.
- ◐ **Timing:** Open May 15– Sept 14, guided tours (45min), 9.30am–6pm; May 1–May 14 and Sep 15– Nov 14, 9.30am–noon and 2pm–5.30pm. ⊜7€. ℘02 48 63 32 05. www. chateau-de-meillant.com.
- ◐ **Also See**: Bourges.

CHÂTEAU
History
Pierre of **Amboise** obtained the Meillant lands by his marriage in 1453. His son, Charles I, decided to modernise the castle which was a massive structure flanked by high towers but following his death it was left to his grand-son, Charles II, to finish the work.

Charles II was to become grand-master, marshal and admiral of France. As governor of Milan, Charles II made such gains in Italy that he was able to complete the work planned for Meillant and also that for Chaumont in the Loire Valley.

Louis XII wrote to Charles II: "*I came to see you in your château of Meillant, but you were not home. I got bogged down in the mud, and the devil take me if I ever return.*" Fortunately, the roads in these wetlands have been upgraded since then!

In the 18C, the property passed on to the Béthune-Charost family, and in the 19C to the Mortemarts.

Among the famous Mortemarts in the 17C were Marie-Madeleine, abbess of Fontevrault and Françoise Athénaïs, Marquise de Montespan and mother of eight children by Louis XIV. The château was restored in 1842.

Exterior
The feudal character of the château can now only be seen in the southern front. The towers, though stripped of their watch-paths, still stand guard with narrow loopholes. The east façade is very different and approaches the château of the Loire in the richness of its decoration: two staircase turrets jut out from the main building and seem to have concentrated in them all the exuberance of the last blaze of the flowery Gothic style.

The pierced balustrade running at the base of the eaves, the carved dormer windows, the chimneys ornamented with flamboyant balustrades are all overshadowed by the incredibly intricate decoration of the Lion's Tower by Giocondo, one of Michelangelo's assistants. This tower, which owes its name to the lion, cast in lead, on its topmost lantern turret, strikes the onlooker by the close juxtaposition of contrasting carvings: twisted small columns, hearts entwined, monograms and crests with interlaced C's – the initials of Charles of Amboise – mountains on fire, the emblem of the château of Chaumont, and figures looking out of false windows as at Jacques Cœur's Palace in Bourges. A pretty 16C well and an elegant chapel of the same period, with buttresses topped by pinnacles, complete this harmonious group of buildings.

Interior

Among the rooms containing remarkable furniture and furnishings are: the main dining hall (*Grand Salle à manger*), where the walls are covered in Cordoba leather; the great salon (*Grand Salon*), where a beautiful chimney-piece is surmounted by a balcony once used as a musician's gallery.

Note the 17C tapestries brought from Bruges and a portrait of Charles VII, long attributed to Clouet, hanging next to one of *La Montespan*, Louis XIV's favourite, and the Smyrna carpet. Beyond the library, replete with rare books and overlooking the chapel, is the so-called **Cardinal d'Amboise Bed Chamber**, perhaps the loveliest room in the château.

Note the splendid 17C Flemish furnishings, tortoise shell encrusted with ivory; a wooden **statue** from Germany dated 1568, representing God the Father welcoming His Son. The Protestant origins of the statue recall the visit of Calvin in

Lion's Tower, Château de Meillant

E. Larribère/MICHELIN

1529. The final rooms on the tour are the Louis XII room with its chimney-piece and Aubusson tapestry and the guard-room, also hung with tapestries (17C Flemish) and arms. The recumbent figure represents François de Rochechouart-Mortemart.

In the courtyard, visit the **chapel**: interesting 16C stained glass; above the altar is an altarpiece of the Rhenish School on painted and gilded wood, depicting scenes from the Passion.

Nohant★

George Sand grew up in the manor here, near the Indre Valley in this quaint Berry village clustered round a little square, where century-old elms shade the village church and its rustic porch.

> ▶ **Population:** 477
> ⚙ **Michelin Map:**
>   323: H-7; or see La Châtre.
> ▶ **Location:** 6km/4mi N
>   of La Châtre.
> ◉ **Don't Miss:** The Maison
>   de George Sand.

A BIT OF HISTORY

The passionate life of George Sand (1804-76)

Amandine-Aurore-Lucile Dupin was born to scandal. Her father was an army officer and her mother, Sophie, was a camp follower, wed to the Lieutenant just before their daughter's appearance. The accidental death of her father did nothing to calm the stormy family atmosphere created by the circum-

stances of Aurore's birth. Her wealthy grandmother agreed to raise her, on the condition that Sophie stay out of sight. Thus, in her early childhood, Aurore developed a sense of rebellion, a sensitivity to injustice and social charade but also a deep attachment to nature and the Berry countryside which would later mark her work. She was married at 18 to Baron Casimir Dudevant and had two children, Solange and Maurice. Profoundly unhappy, she left her husband, established herself in Paris with Jules Sandeau in 1831, and out of financial necessity began writing for the satirical review *Figaro*. Her first independently written novel, *Indiana* (1832), was an immediate popular success. She thereafter kept up a prolific pace of literary production to support her family.

Her encounter with the poetic author Alfred de Musset and their trip to Venice fuelled her romantic works, most notably, *Lélia*, which amazed readers with its frank discussion of women's sensual feelings and a passionate call for the right to emotional satisfaction.

Sand's reputation for iconoclasm sprang from such themes and also from exaggerated reports of her unconventional behaviour: she smoked regularly and in public, occasionally dressed like a man and carried on love affairs with Musset, Prosper Mérimée and Frédéric Chopin. Yet she remained an idealist, convinced of the virtues of marriage between equals, and enraged at the prevalent social system which made such marriages impossible.

An uncommon woman

And yet, Sand was truly inhabited by the great ideas of moral progress that animated her times. France's leading woman author produced what are sometimes called socialist novels, including the *Consuelo* cycle. Dedicated to the advance of democracy, she put her pen to political pamphlets, created a local newspaper, and rejoiced when the French monarchy fell and the Second Republic was established. The return of Napoleon III so disappointed Sand that she withdrew to the estate at Nohant.

She continued to write successful plays and the ever-popular pastoral or rustic novels with their tender descriptions of the Berry countryside: *The Haunted Pool*, *The Country Waif*, and *Fanchon the Cricket*. Many readers enjoy her letters and journals, as well as her masterful autobiography, *Histoire de ma vie* (*My Life*,) and the travel essays collected under the title *Lettres d'un voyageur*

(*Letters of a Traveller*). In her final years, she undertook charitable works which earned her the affectionate title *la bonne dame de Nohant* (the good lady of Nohant).

With 70 novels, 50 volumes of other writing and 25 plays to her credit, George Sand has been an inspiration to many women writers, including Elizabeth Barrett Browning and George Eliot; her work has been praised by the likes of Turgenev and Flaubert.

MAISON DE GEORGE SAND★

🕐🎫 *Guided tour (1hr, last entrance 1hr before closing), Jul–Aug, 9.30am–6.30pm; Apr & Sept, 10am–12.30pm and 2–6pm; May and June 9.30–12.15pm and 2–6.30; Oct–Mar, 10am–12.30pm and 1.30–5pm;* 🕐*Closed Jan 1, May 1, Nov 1 and 11, and Dec 25.* 🎫*7€.* 📞*02 54 31 06 04.*

This country estate was built around 1760 on the site of an old château. Now a museum, it is devoted to the memory of George Sand and her many guests. The old-fashioned charm of Sand's home has remained unchanged since the 19C, and the visitor almost expects to find the author herself sitting at her desk.

The ground floor has eight rooms including the boudoir with its painted woodwork, where Sand's career began and *Indiana* took shape. "I was living in my grandmother's old boudoir … It was so small that with my books, my herbarium, and my rock collection, there was no room for a bed. I had a hammock installed instead. My table was made of a wardrobe which could fold out like a writing desk."

The theatre was built in 1849, for family entertainment. The salon, an inner sanctum, is the expression of family harmony, as suggested by the portraits on the walls. The upper floor consists of a vestibule, antechamber, George Sand's room, where she passed away on 8 June 1876, her writing room, which was Chopin's room until 1846, the library, and Aurore Lauth-Sand's room (the château's last resident, she died in 1961), which was once occupied by George Sand and her mother.

St-Amand-Montrond

and Grand Bois de Meillant

The original village developed around a monastery, founded in the 7C by St Amand, a disciple of St Colomban. Later a castle rose above it, on the hill known as Mont-Rond, and served to protect the growing town; it was destroyed in the 17C. St-Amand-Montrond is capital of the region known as Val de Germigny, where the fields are dotted with white Charollais cattle. A park, laid out on the hill top, offers a fine view of the town and its surroundings.

SIGHTS

Église St-Amand

rue Cornière. 02 48 96 16 19.
This interesting 12C Romanesque church with a Benedictine floor plan opens with a beautiful round arched doorway framed by two multifoiled bays. The nave with its barrel-vaulting, is rather dark. The transept crossing has pointed arches which certainly replaced an earlier cupola. In the 15C, side chapels were added. The capitals in the nave are interesting for their Romanesque design: birds with long, twining necks, monstrous faces and acanthus leaves.

Musée St-Vic

Cours Manuel Open daily except Tue Sat, Sun, 10am–noon and 2–6pm. Closed Jan 1, May 1, 3rd Sun Oct and Dec 25. 2.50€. 02 48 96 55 20.
The 16C St-Vic Mansion, set amid a pleasant garden, was the town residence of the commendatory abbots of Noirlac (see NOIRLAC). The exhibit area presents a wide panorama of this region, rich in history and vestiges.
There are rooms devoted to materials related to the old castle; to local ethnography (furnishings, pottery, headdresses); to the ceramic work of the potters of La Borne; to the work of the clog-maker Louis Touzet, as well as to landscapes by Brielman, Cals, Delavaux, Detroy, and Osterlind.

- **Population:** 11 642.
- **Michelin Map:** 323: L-6
- **Info**: place de la République. 02 48 96 16 86. www.st-amand-tourisme.com
- **Location**: The village is located 44km/27.5mi south of Bourges.
- **Don't Miss**: Château de Meillant; Abbaye de Noiriac.

Cité de l'Or

Open Jun 15–Sept 15, 10am–6.30pm (last entrance 1hr before closing); Apl–Jun 15, 10am–12.15pm and 1.45–6.30pm; Oct–Mar, 10am–12.15pm and 1.45–5.30pm exc. Closed Tue (Feb, Mar & Oct and weekdays Nov–Jan), 1 Jan and 25 Dec. 9€. 02 48 82 11 33.
This vast complex testifies to the importance of gold and jewellery in the town's economic development.

DRIVING TOUR

1 GRAND BOIS DE MEILLANT

25km/15mi – allow 3hr

Leave St-Amand along the D 10 towards Dun-sur-Auron. The road goes through the forest, Grand Bois de Meillant.

Château de Meillant★★

See Château de MEILLANT.

Leave Meillant SW on D 92.

La Celle

The 12C **church of St-Blaise**, originally a dependency of Déols Abbey has an impressive square belfry and an east end adorned with modillions and Romanesque capitals. The west front is adorned with unusual carvings, including roughly sculpted characters and bulls' heads. Inside, the apsidal chapels are separated from the chancel by massive columns with interesting capitals depicting mon-

Church of St-Blaise

B. Kaufmann/ MICHELIN

sters, bearded faces, birds, lions, masks etc. The church contains the tomb of St Silvanus, the legendary apostle of Berry, whose relics were moved from Levroux to La Celle in the 15C.

Bruère-Allichamps

A Gallo-Roman milestone was found in the town in 1757. It was erected in its present site at the junction of the N 144 and the D 92 in 1799. Since 1865, this point has been popularly held to mark the geographical centre of France. D 35 now follows the course of the picturesque Cher Valley rich in meadowland.

Abbaye de Noirlac★★
  See Abbaye de NOIRLAC.

▶ *The N 144 follows the north bank of the Cher to St-Amand-Montrond.*

2 LE BOISCHAUT
Round-trip of 75km/47mi – allow 4hr

▶ *Leave St-Amand S on the D 97.*

Drevant

This quiet village is infused with a feeling of timelessness. The ruins of a **theatre** and traces of a **forum, baths** and **temple**, were part of a Gallo-Roman rural sanctuary. The Berry canal runs through a park by the ruins.

▶ *Continue S, cross the River Cher and turn left in La Groutte.*

Ainay-le-Vieil★

The **castle**★ (guided tour (45min, last entrance 45min before closing) Jul–Aug 10am–7pm, Feb–Jun and Sept–Nov 10am–noon and 2–7pm or nightfall, Feb–Mar and Nov daily except Tue, (Feb mornings only); closed Jan–Feb; 7.50€; 02 48 63 50 03) is the town's proudest feature, its severe **medieval walls** (12C-14C) hiding a gracious Renaissance building within.

The **hexagonal tower** (early 16C) is reminiscent of Meillant, and from the watch-path visitors can admire the moat and crenellated ramparts. The interior is beautifully decorated and furnished.

▷ *Drive W along the D 1 then turn left onto the D 997 at the Fosse Nouvelle crossroads.*

Jardins Artistiques de Drulon

♿🕐*Open Apr 12–Oct 1, 10am–7.30pm; Weekends till Nov 1, 10am–7.30pm.* 👓*7.50€.* ☎*02 48 56 65 96.*

This extraordinary place, a 15ha/37-acre landscaped park surrounding a former 15C-17C hunting lodge, offers a variety of settings to about 100 sculptures by contemporary European artists: there is the flower garden, the greenery, the marsh skirted by footpaths and natural labyrinths and the secret garden with its fishponds.

▷ *Rejoin the D 997 on the left and drive to Loye-sur-Arnon to pick up the D 951 on the left.*

Le Châtelet, Abbatiale de Puy-Ferrand

🕐🚶*Open Easter to Nov 1, Sat–Sun and public hols, 3–6pm. Guided tours available.* ☎*02 48 56 29 35.*

The former abbey church of Puy-Ferrand, south of Le Châtelet, is a fine Romanesque building. The façade is ornamented with bays, finely carved capitals and geometrical designs.

▷ *Leave Le Châtelet travelling NW along the D 951 then turn right onto the D 65.*

Jardins du Prieuré Notre-Dame d'Orsan★

👣 *See Notre-Dame d'ORSAN.*

▷ *Follow the D 65 towards Lignières.*

Château du Plaix

🕐*Open Jun–Aug, daily except Tue, 2–6pm; Easter to May and Sept to early-Nov, Sat–Sun and public hols, 2–6pm.* 🚶*Guided tours available by prior arrangement.* 👓*5€.* ☎*02 48 60 22 14.*

This small castle, surrounded by a moat, houses the **Musée des Arts et Traditions Populaires**: temporary exhibitions on various themes are organised every three years. Nearby, stands a typical Berry house with its 1850 interior.

Lignières★

In the heart of a landscape of well-kept family farms and meadows neatly bordered by hedgerows, this small town was a centre of Calvinism when the famous protestant reformer was a student in Bourges. The classical **château** (🔒 *closed to the public*) was designed by François Le Vau brother of the more famous Louis. Near the bank of the River Arnon, there is a pretty 12C church.

▷ *Continue E along the D 925.*

Église d'Orval

🕐*For information on opening times, contact the town hall,* ☎*02 48 96 57 40.* The church in town has a 13C reliquary cross in gold-plated silver, its crosspieces embellished with enamel.

ADDRESSES

🛏 STAY

🍽🍽 **Chambre d'hôte La Trolière** – *18200 Orval. 4km/2.4mi W of St-Amand-Montrond towards Châteauroux then 500m after the last roundabout on the right.* ☎*02 48 96 47 45.* 🛏 *3 rooms.*

This large bourgeois family home offers comfortable rooms in pastel tones decorated with etchings and porcelain pieces. You'll appreciate the pervasive quietude and charm of the site.

🍽🍽🍽 **Chambre d'hôte Domaine de la Vilotte** – *Lieu-dit la Vilotte - 18170 Le Châtelet. 6km/3.6mi SE of Châtelet on the D 951 and a secondary road.* ☎*02 48 96 04 96. Apr–Sept* 🛏 *5 rooms.*

Hidden away in the Berry countryside, this 19C manor house is elegant and tasteful. The rooms are warm and welcoming, with attractive antiques. The grounds boast a lovely rose garden and a lake with a boat for guests.

St-Marcel ★

The medieval hamlet of St-Marcel stands on a hill overlooking the right bank of the Creuse, on the site of the Gallo-Roman town of **Argentomagus**, high above the River Creuse. An archaeological dig carried out on the site and in the surrounding area revealed traces of ancient monuments and a large number of items were excavated. Some of these are now in the local museum.

▶ **Population:** 1 647
⚙ **Michelin Map:** 323: F-7
▯ **Info**: 13, place de la République - BP 147 36 200 Argenton sur Creuse. ℘02 54 24 05 30.
◖ **Location**: Northern outskirts of the town of Argenton-sur-Creuse.
⊛ **Don't Miss**: Théâtre du Virou; Musée Archéologique d'Argentomagus.

A BIT OF HISTORY

Archaeological excavations – The site is remarkable for the preservation of its vestiges, which long slumbered beneath a vineyard. Several roads passed through the town, a pivotal point between the upper valley of the Creuse and the low wet lands of the Brenne; the river runs a regular course here and is navigable. The development of trade, ..the abundant game, the presence of water and wood, explain why this land was occupied so long ago, and the diversity of the archaeological discoveries. Magdalenian reindeer hunters dwelled in caves here (14000-8000 BC), whereas their Gallo-Roman successors built an *oppidum*, or fortified city, to live in.

Following the Roman conquest (50 BC), **Argentomagus** underwent spectacular demographic and economic growth, as trade, crafts and especially metal working – the Bituriges (⚙ *see BOURGES*) were specialists – developed. The site figures on a 15C reproduction of the road network of the lower Roman Empire known as the **Peutinger Table**, and is mentioned in a 4C text as the leading Gaulish arms manufactory.

For two centuries the site expanded beyond the bounds of the original oppidum although it did not become a major city.

ARCHAEOLOGICAL SITE

⊜*No charge.* ℘*02 54 24 47 31.*
In addition to the sections known as Mersans and Virou, other areas have been explored, including a necropolis, called Champ de l'Image (200m/220yd north-west of the museum).

Les Mersans

This plateau (27ha/67 acres), protected by cliffs and a moat, was the first urban core. The so-called Sergius Macrinus house is on the site, as well as a religious enclave made up of two **temples** and a square edifice.

Along with most of the rest of the town, these temples were destroyed during a Barbarian invasion in 276.

During excavations, archaeologists discovered some lovely bronze statuettes: a goat lying down, an eagle, and the famous Mercury. Some 40 sacrificial pits have been found in the sanctuary. To the east of the temple area, the forum and other ancient monuments are still buried. In 1967, a **monumental fountain** was discovered by chance. The exact purpose of this fountain (the largest of its kind from the period) is uncertain. It certainly played some cultural role, before it was filled in by metal workers, some time after 276.

Théâtre du Virou ★

Return down the hill towards Argenton; turn right just before the railway bridge, go along for about 200m/220yd, then take a steep path on the right which goes up to the theatre.

Until 1966, only a part of the outside wall was visible, and this gave the parcel of land its name: *Virou*, something which rotates or revolves. Now the building has been entirely uncovered, revealing the two successive stages of construction: the first, rustic period, from the early 1C, and a second 2C part. The way the works of two centuries have been superimposed creates an interesting study for archaeologists. The first theatre, with poor acoustics, was typical of Gallo-Roman times in its horseshoe shape, small stage area, and wide orchestra section. Mime and dance were commonly performed in such theatres, where the Greek influence is strongly felt. The 2C improvements brought the theatre into line with Roman design: the circular seating (84m/275ft in diameter) could accommodate up to 6 000.

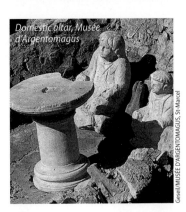

Domestic altar, Musée d'Argentomagus

Gesel/MUSÉE D'ARGENTOMAGUS, St-Marcel

Musée Archéologique d'Argentomagus★

♿ &Open Daily Jul–Aug, 9.30am–noon and 2–6pm; Sept–Jun, daily except Tue, 9.30am–noon and 2–6pm. ⊙Closed Dec 24–Jan 19. ⊛4€, no charge 1st Sun of the month. Tactile exhibits for the blind and some explanations in braille. ℘02 54 24 47 31. www.argentomagus.com

The **prehistoric collections** take visitors back in time to a million years BC, to the period known as the lower Palaeolithic. A hut from the **Lavaud** site, in Éguzon-Chantôme has been recreated. The prehistoric displays continue in chronological order and include: tools from a Solutrean find (18000-16000 BC) from Fressignes and the Roches shelter, in Pouligny-St-Pierre; and many items found in the **Garenne cave** (hills around St Marcel), dating from 14000 BC.

The **Gallo-Roman section** is organised around themes: the city and its monuments (scale models); work, daily life, and trade (an interesting display of pottery and household utensils); funerary rites (re-creation of part of the Roman cemetery at Champ de l'Image).

The final room, devoted to **religious practices**, illustrates, with statuary, the coexistence of gods of many origins in Gaulish civilisation. Native, Greek and Eastern divinities are depicted; the small bronzes are most remarkable.

Finish the visit with a walk through the **crypte archéologique**, 150m/492ft along the vestiges of the north moat and past an area devoted to crafts (leather and dye workers' tanks) and shelters, where a rare domestic altar has been left in place (& see photograph).

MEDIEVAL VILLAGE

At the town hall and in the museum, a map is available for an interesting self-guided tour.

Church★

rue de l'Ormeau.

To the left of the nave, the **massive 14C bell tower** was used as a keep. The severe, shingled tower differs from others in the region in its defensive allure. The **doorway** on the western façade has two rounded arches, topped by a band of mouldings with a diamond pattern. At the end of the nave, to the left above the door, a 15C **Fresco of Our Lady** (Notre-Dame-de-Pitié) shows St Louis in a fur coat presenting a priest to the Virgin, who holds the Infant Jesus in her arms.

The **treasure** contains several processional crosses (13C), a 15C sculpted shrine representing the martyrdom of St Marcel and St Anastase, a gilded copper shrine from the 13C adorned with Limoges enamel, the arm of St Marcel and a 14C reliquary.

Outside the church, the visitor can walk around the **medieval streets**: vestiges of the 15C fortifications, many entranceways surmounted by lintels, some with a tympanum bearing the arms of the household.

The Champagne Berrichonne covers the territory from the Nièvre *département* of Burgundy in the east to the Indre-et-Loire *département* of the Centre Region in the west. Bourges is the main city of the Berry and capital of the Cher département.

Château de Bouges, decorated with 18C furniture

A. Cassaigne/MICHELIN

Champagne Berrichonne

The Champagne Berrichonne in the Cher *département* is a region of plateaux and limestone soil extending between the River Loire to the east and the River Indre to the west, watered by the River Cher as it winds its way towards the Loire. Covered in the main by scattered woods and forests, manure and rich fertilisers have transformed the light, sandy soil into excellent farm land. In addition to grain crops, sheep and Normandy dairy cows are bred indoors and fed on beetroot pulp. Bee-keeping is also an important economic activity around Châteauroux.

Away to the east, the Val de Germigny is a long depression, formerly marshland, which runs along the foot of the escarpments crowned by the Bois de Meillant. The pastures here and in the Northern Boischaut, in the west of this region, are areas of rich pasture grazed by creamy white Charolais cattle.

Bourges

Bourges was once so important that it was the capital of France during the reign of Charles VII, whilst the Hundred Years' War was in its final stages. A fine city with many half-timbered houses and a magnificent cathedral, it is both an extremely interesting place to visit and an excellent centre from which to tour the Berry region. Although Joan of Arc wintered here in 1429, just before her arrest and subsequent execution, the most renowned person to be associated with the place, apart from Charles VII, is the financier Jacques Coeur who became so fabulously wealthy, thanks to his position as the King's Master of the Mint, that he engendered envy amongst members of the Court and provoked the monarch's wrath, which led to his subsequent trial and exile. A tour round the Palais Jacques Coeur with its boiler room, bathroom and latrines with running water, unique at the time, explains why the King became peeved about his employee's great wealth!

Bourges★★★

From whichever direction you approach the city, the magnificent cathedral, classified by UNESCO as a World Heritage Monument, soars above the Berry-Champagne countryside, a striking symbol of Bourges' rich medieval past. Built on the slopes of a hill, the city is dissected by the waters of the Yèvre and Auron and a network of rivers and marshes. The commercial and industrial centre of the Berry, the city is the capital of the Cher département.

▶ **Population:** 70,828

Michelin Map: 323: K-4

Info: 21 r. Victor-Hugo (near the Cathedral), 18000 Bourges. ℘02 48 23 02 60. www.ville-bourges.fr, or www.bourgestourisme.com.

▷ **Location:** 196km/122.5mi NE of Limoges via A20/N151. The city's tourist train provides a good introduction to the city. For a wonderful view of Bourges and its surrounding countryside, climb the 396 steps to the top of the cathedral's north tower. (see Ascent of the North Tower).

P **Parking:** There are several car parks dotted around the city (see city plan).

Don't Miss: Cathédrale St-Étienne; Palais Jacques-Cœur; Hôtel Estève; Les Marais.

Kids: Muséum d'Histoire Naturelle.

A BIT OF HISTORY

One of the loveliest towns in Gaul – Avaricum, town of abundant water, made its mark in history in 52 BC, during the tumultuous Gallic wars. The Bituriges, a powerful Celtic people (who gave their name to the town), took part in the resistance to Roman occupation. The celebrated warrior Vercingétorix had adopted a scorched-earth policy, destroying town and field before the invading army's advance. When he arrived in Bourges, the denizens begged him to leave their dwellings intact, and assured him that the town could never be taken, thanks to its strategic location atop a hill surrounded by rivers and marshland. Exception was made, Caesar's legions attacked, and the town, despite its bravest efforts, fell. Caesar estimated the population at 40 000: all were massacred. After a few days rest, the sated soldiers of the Roman empire moved on, leaving the shell of the looted, desolate city behind them.

Caesar reported that the town was "one of the loveliest in Gaul"; archaeological research has revealed that it was a busy iron craft and trade centre. Little is known of its history.

Bourges under Roman rule – Avaricum set about healing its wounds and once again rose to prominence as a capital city and trade centre. Prosperous and attractive, the town spread to the surrounding hillsides and monuments were erected. The town boasted a vast amphitheatre, a river port with harbour and wharves, and necropolises on the outskirts.

Jean de Berry: a patron of the arts – The young duke, Jean de Berry, third son of King John the Good of France, made Bourges the capital of his duchy and a centre of the arts of utmost importance. From 1360 to 1416 the Duke, an inspired lover of the arts, spent a fortune as, with mad prodigality, he commissioned work from painters, illuminators such as Pol de Limbourg, the author of the Très Riches Heures (The Rich Hours), now to be seen in the Chantilly Museum, and Jacquemart de Hesdin, the author of the Très Belles Heures (The Beautiful Hours).

"A vaillans cœurs, riens impossible" – "To a valiant heart, nothing is impossible" was the motto of **Jacques Cœur**, Master of the Mint to King Charles VII of France at a time when that kingdom

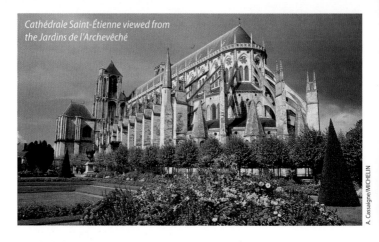

Cathédrale Saint-Étienne viewed from the Jardins de l'Archevêché

A. Cassaigne/MICHELIN

was largely occupied by the English. This man of humble origin, son of a furrier, had an extraordinary life: amazingly gifted in commerce and trade, he soon made a colossal fortune. Given charge of the finances of Bourges, he became, in 1442, counsellor to Charles VII and principal emissary for the kingdom's expansion of trade; finally he built a magnificent palace at Bourges, though he was to see little of it. Hated by many courtiers who were jealous of his political and diplomatic offices, the honours he had bestowed upon him and the king's favour, he fell into disgrace, a victim of his own advancement. He was arrested in 1451 and condemned to perpetual banishment, confiscation of all his property and a heavy fine.

But this was not the end for Jacques Cœur: he escaped from prison, sought refuge in Rome and was given command by the Pope of a fleet of ships. It was while he was on the Ninth Crusade, that he died in 1456 in Chios.

The University, a cradle of new ideas – The town of Bourges owes the foundation of its university in 1463 to Charles de Berry, Louis XI's brother. Its influence spread far beyond the duchy for over a century. The law school attracted many students some even from abroad. German students brought with them the new doctrines of Luther: Calvin, a student at Bourges, was influenced by these views which informed his *Institutes of the Christian Religion*. in spite of per-

secution, his ideas soon gained support in Bourges and throughout Berry.

The duchy was thus divided and became a battlefield during the period of the Wars of Religion; the prosperity of the city, which had been much reduced by a terrible fire in 1487, came to an end.

Decline and expansion – By the mid-17C, Berry was in a sort of stupor which lasted two more centuries. Off the main routes, it was by-passed while towns like Tours and Orleans, on the River Loire, underwent economic expansion. The bourgeoisie were not drawn into industry and trade, as elsewhere, but lived lives circumscribed by regional politics and religion.

The construction of the Berry canal (1819-42), the railway and the establishment of the armaments industry in Bourges under the Second Empire breathed new economic life into the region.

Since the end of the Second World War, Bourges has expanded rapidly. Many industries have arrived, creating thousands of jobs and the A 71 motorway has contributed to the lively dynamics of the town today.

A city of music – The cultural influence of Bourges is far greater than its small size might suggest. As well as the Maison de la Culture (👋 *see Address Book*). Bourges also hosts the renowned musical festival, **le Printemps de Bourges**, a yearly event drawing crowds of young fans of popular music.

CATHÉDRALE ST-ÉTIENNE★★★

The vigour of the architecture, the harmony of proportion and the richness of the decoration make one marvel before this cathedral.

Construction took place in two stages. From 1195 to 1215, the chevet and the chancel were built outside the fortifications standing at that time, due to lack of space. The second stage, which lasted 35 years (1225-60), concerned the nave, the west front and the final embellishments. The cathedral was consecrated on 13 May 1324.

Additions and restorations - The southern tower was consolidated during the 14C by a reinforced arcade. Once the west front had been remodelled, it was possible to install the great window above the central door.

Misfortune came in the 16C: at the end of 1506 the north tower collapsed and had to be rebuilt and in 1562 a Protestant army pillaged the cathedral and destroyed the statues adorning the west front.

Some restoration was undertaken in the 19C in the form of additional balustrades, bell-towers and pinnacles.

During the 20C, pollution has necessitated a preservation campaign to prevent further deterioration of the stone carvings.

CATHÉDRALE ST-ÉTIENNE

from 1195 to 1215	from 1225 to 1260
14C	15C
16C	

Outside

West front – Five **doorways** beneath individual gables stand in a line beneath the great stained-glass window, known as the *grand housteau* – the great western gable. The theme of the **central doorway** is the Last Judgement. Great vitality and realism make the doorway one of the masterpieces of 13C Gothic sculpture.

The tympanum of **St Stephen's doorway** is devoted to episodes in the life and the martyrdom of St Stephen, patron of the cathedral.

The story of St Ursinus, the first bishop of Bourges, and of St Justus is depicted on the tympanum of **St Ursinus' doorway**. The **Virgin's doorway** and **St Guillaume's doorway** had to be partly rebuilt after the collapse of the north tower in the 16C.

Two **towers** of unequal height frame the five doorways. On the right, the so-called Deaf Tower (*Tour Sourde* – because no bell was hung), never completed, is architecturally more sober in style than the flamboyantly decorated Butter Tower on the left (*Tour de Beurre*).

▷ *Go round the cathedral by the north.*

North side – This side is embellished by a 12C **doorway**, which was incorporated in the present cathedral. On the tympanum are scenes from the Vigin's life.
East end – Note the little turrets above the chevets radial chapels.
South side – This side is adorned with a 13C **doorway**. Christ appears in majesty on the tympanum, surrounded by the symbols of the Evangelists.

▷ *Enter the cathedral by the south.*

Inside

Nave – St Stephen's Cathedral, which is 124m/407ft long, 41m/135ft wide and 37m/121ft high to the top of the inner vaulting, is one of the largest Gothic cathedrals in France. There

Stained-glass window depicting Joseph's dream, Cathédrale Saint-Étienne

are no transepts and this gives the nave with its four side aisles a feeling of greater majesty; the five aisles correspond to the five doorways. The columns of the nave rise in a single thrust to a height of 17m/56ft and they are encircled by groups of smaller columns, some of which reach the vaulting. To extend the perspective the architect slightly increased the distance between the pillars in the chancel.

The building is original in having double side aisles of different height with windows on two levels; the five bands of light and shade thus created within the cathedral considerably enhance the architectural effect (see cross section). A double ambulatory continues the line of the twin aisles. Five small radial chapels, each semicircular in shape, open on to the apse.

 Turn right and enter the chancel via the second south aisle.

Chapelle St-Jean-Baptiste – This chapel contains two beautiful frescoes dating from the late 1460s, depicting the Crucifixion and the Resurrection.

Chapelle des Tullier – The chapel is lit by Lescuyer's fine Renaissance windows. **Stained-Glass Windows★★★** – Although they have incurred some damage over the years, the collection of

stained-glass windows in the cathedral is one of the most remarkable in France, dating from the 12C to the 17C.

The five apsidal chapels and the windows between them are adorned with windows shaped to fit the architecture, and medallion windows, most of which were made between 1215 and 1225.

First the **master of the Last Judgement and the New Alliance**, employs a style both exuberant and majestic, apparent in the bodies and clothing draped over them.

The Good Samaritan master is also supposed to be the artist responsible for the execution of the intermediate windows representing the Passion and the Apocalypse, the windows of St Mary the Egyptian, St Nicholas and the martyrdom of St Stephen (radial chapels).

The master of the St Stephen reliquaries illustrates some of the typical traits of Gothic representational art: over-long bodies on spindly legs, disproportionate heads, faces seeming to express displeasure, yet these windows are lively and evocative.

Crypt★★ – Guided tour (45min) Jul–Aug, 9.30am–12.30pm, 2– 5.30pm; May–Jun, 9.30–11.30am, 2–5.30pm; Apr and Sept, 9.45–11.45am, 2–5.30pm; Oct–Mar, 9.30–11.30am, 2–4.45pm. Closed Jan 1, May 1, Nov 1 and 11, Dec 25. 7€; combined ticket with the *north tower and Palais Jacques-Coeur: 9€. ℘02 48 65 49 44.*

A long sloping gallery leads down to the vast late-12C crypt. Twelve large windows light the sanctuary. Six massive pillars (2.10m/7ft in diameter) support the vaulted ceiling on diagonal ribs which, in turn, supports the cathedral above.

In the crypt, note the **recumbent white marble figure** of the Duke of Berry, the only vestige of a grandiose mausoleum (1422).

Ascent of the north tower –

Open Guided tour (45min) Jul–Aug, 9.30am–12.30pm, 2– 5.30pm; May–Jun, 9.30–11.30am, 2–5.30pm; Apr and Sept, 9.45–11.45am, 2–5.30pm; Oct–Mar, 9.30–11.30am, 2–4.45pm. Closed Jan 1, May 1, Nov 1 and 11, Dec 25. 7€; combined ticket with the crypteand Palais Jacques-Coeur: 9€. ℘02 48 65 49 44.

The attempt to complete the northern tower at the end of the 15C resulted in its collapse in 1506. Reconstruction lasted until 1540, carried out under the direction of architect Guillaume de Pelvoysin, who introduced new decorative elements in the Renaissance style. A spiral stair (396 steps) leads to the top (65m/213ft), where a **view**★★ rewards those who venture up.

Organ – The organ case dates from 1663. The old pipes are still in place but the mechanism has been changed many times.

Astronomical clock★ – Designed by mathematician and astronomer Jean Fusoris in 1424, this magnificent clock (6.2m/20ft high) is set in a square frame, surmounted by a concave roof and a bell. The decorative elements were designed by Jean Grangier.

PALAIS JACQUES-CŒUR★★

Guided tour (1hr). Open Jul–Aug, 9.30am–12.30pm and 2pm –6.15pm; May–Jun, 9.30am–12 noon and 2–6.15pm; Sept–Apr, 9.30am–12 noon and 2–5.15pm. Closed 1 Jan, 1 May, 1 and 11 Nov, and 25 Dec. 7€. Combined ticket with the crypt and the north tower: 9€. ℘02 48 24 79 41.

The architectural elegance, the richness and variety of decoration, make this one of the most beautiful and sumptuous secular buildings of the Gothic age.

This splendid mansion was commissioned in 1443 for Charles VII's famous Master of the Mint, and was intended no doubt, as the place to which he would retire.

Jacques Cœur fell into disgrace in 1451 and so never enjoyed his completed palace. In 1457 it was restored to his heirs and from then on knew many changes of fortune. In 1679 it belonged to Colbert (statesman: 1619-83); soon afterwards it was acquired by the city of Bourges. Since 1925, when it was bought by the State, it has been completely restored.

Palais Jacques-Cœur

S. Sauvignier/MICHELIN

Exterior

Jacques Cœur's Palace consists of four main buildings round a central court. Whereas the west face looks like the exterior of a fortress with massive towers and bare walls, the **east face** draws attention through the delicacy and richness of its decoration. This appears, in one instance, as a motif of hearts and shells – emblems from Jacques Cœur's coat of arms – adorning the mullioned windows of the top floor and the balustrade at the base of the eaves.

On either side of a balcony, note the amusing figures of a man and a woman. To the left of this wing, at the base of the octagonal staircase tower, Jacques Cœur's motto may be seen inscribed: *A vaillans cœurs, riens impossible* (To a valiant heart, nothing is impossible).

As you enter the **central court** there is a striking difference between the sober appearance of the galleries and the rich decoration of the main living quarters containing the banqueting and ceremonial halls and the private apartments.

Interior

A tour of the palace gives an idea of the luxury to which a wealthy burgher with a taste for beautiful things and practical sense could aspire.

On the ground floor, the taste for luxury produced the magnificence of the **dining hall** with its monumental chimneypiece (restored in the 19C) and a loggia to accommodate musicians; the practical sense comes out in the installation of running water, a **boiler room** and **bathroom** and the planning of staircases and corridors so that those wishing to take a bath could do so without going outside to adjoining buildings.

Of particular interest on the first floor are the **Salle des échevins** decorated with 17C murals depicting rural and hunting scenes; the **Treasury**, which has a heavy iron door closed with a secret lock; the **Attic** with its wooden vaulting in the shape of an inverted boat keel; the **Council chamber**, which houses a model of the original palace; the **Galleries** where Jacques Cœur used to receive the town's merchants; and the Chapel.

WALKING TOUR
OLD TOWN

The whole town centre comes under a preservation and renovation scheme which aims at restoring the **half-timbered houses**★ (many date from the 15C and 16C) to their former glory. The old district lying north of the cathedral offers a particularly pleasant stroll.

Jardins de l'Archevêché★

Designed in the 17C and extended in the 18C, these gardens feature splendid flower beds, fine shaded alleyways, ornamental ponds, bronze vases and a bandstand. From the garden's beautiful flower beds and shaded alleys, there is a good view of St Stephen's Cathedral.

Place Étienne-Dolet

As you walk across the square, note on your left the façade of the former **archbishop's residence** which now houses the Musée des Meilleurs Ouvriers de France (see below). Walk the length of the **cathedral**★★★ and admire the successive doorways.

Grange aux Dîmes

Opposite the cathedral's north doorway at the corner of rue Molière, this massive tithe barn with its buttresses and stairway designed as a half-timbered balcony was used to store the dues paid to the church.

Short walk down rue des Trois-Maillets then turn left through a porch.

Promenade des Remparts★

Visible in several places, the ramparts are clearly distinguished along the **Promenade des Remparts** behind and below the cathedral. Ingeniously integrated into the fabric of the contemporary town, the dressed stone wall dates back to the 3C, when it was erected for protection against barbarian invasions.

Take the George Sand stairs on the left.

This passageway, known as casse-cou (breakneck) – one understands why on

BOURGES

M Musée des Meilleurs
Ouvriers de France

N 151 LA CHARITÉ
D 940 MONTARGIS

Carref.
de Verdun

JARDIN
DES PRÉS-
FICHAUX

JARDIN
DES PRÉS-
FICHAUX

LES
MARAIS

Halle
St-Bonnet

N.-Dame

Maison de
Pelvoysin

HÔTEL DES
ÉCHEVINS

St-Bonnet

Pl.
Gordaine

HÔTEL CUJAS

PALAIS
JACQUES-CŒUR

HÔTEL
LALLEMANT

Coursarlon

R. Joyeuse

Escalier
G.-Sand

Pl.
du Berry

R. des
4-Piliers

REMPART
GALLO-ROMAIN

Maison dite
"de Jacques-Cœur"

Grange
des Dîmes

CATHÉDRALE
ST-ÉTIENNE

St-Pierre-
le-Guillard

PRÉFECTURE

Pl. É.
Dolet

JARDINS
DE
L'ARCHEVÊCHÉ

CITÉ
ADMINISTRATIVE

Pl. A.
Bardoux

Pl. A.
Malraux

Pl. du
8 Mai 1945

PALAIS DES
CONGRÈS

PARC DES
EXPOSITIONS

Rampe
Marceau

MUSÉUM D'HISTOIRE
NATURELLE

Pl.
Séraucourt

TOUR

MÉDIATHÈQUE

D 2144 MONTLUÇON, GUÉRET

BASE NAUTIQUE
DU VAL D'AURON

rainy days – runs through the ramparts and leads to place George-Sand. Cross **rue Porte-Jaune** and admire the massive cathedral towers on your left. Next, rue St-Michel-de-Bourges leads into the town centre's high street; note **Louis XI's statue** near the neo-Gothic post office dating from 1926.

▶ *Follow rue Moyenne and turn right onto rue Mayet-Genetry.*

The lovely **Fontaine Bourdaloue** adorns place de la Préfecture.

▶ *Walk along rue des Armuriers.*

Jacques Cœur's "Birthplace"

A half-timbered, corbelled house, standing at the corner of rue d'Auron and rue des Armuriers, bears an inscription describing it as the house in which Jacques Cœur was born (c 1395-1456).

In fact it was built early in the 16C on the site of a house that came to Jacques Cœur through his marriage.

▶ *Follow rue d'Auron and turn right onto rue des Arènes.*

Église St-Pierre-le-Guillard

According to legend, funds for building the church were provided by the Jew, Zacharie Guillard, whose mule knelt before the Holy Sacrament as it was being carried by St Antony of Padua through Bourges in about 1225.

A massive belfry-porch leads to the nave flanked by side aisles to which chapels were added in the 15C.

▶ *Continue along rue des Arènes then turn right.*

Rue des Linières

This steep street is attractively cobbled.

Place des Quatre-Piliers

Three splendid 17C and 18C mansions, Hôtel Témoin (the former library), Hôtel Bengy and Hôtel Méloizes, overshadow the fountain decorating the square.

▶ *Follow rue Jacques-Cœur.*

Palais Jacques-Cœur★★

Walk to place Jacques-Cœur to admire his statue and the remarkable façade of his mansion (restored 1998).

▶ *Retrace your steps and go down some stairs on your right, leading to the lower part of town.*

Place du Berry

Facing you is the west front of Palais Jacques-Cœur built on the remains of the Gallo-Roman ramparts: it looks like a fortress flanked with massive towers… quite a contrast to the earlier view.

▶ *rue des Arènes.*

Hôtel Cujas★

This elegant building was designed in about 1515 by Guillaume Pelvoysin for Durando Salvi, a rich Florentine merchant who had settled in Bourges.

▶ *Cross place Planchat to rue Pelvoysin.*

Maison de Pelvoysin

An interesting group of old, half-timbered houses stand at the corner of rue Pelvoysin and rue Cambournac. Next to these is the house of Pelvoysin, the cathedral architect. It is built of stone and now houses the savings bank.

The street was so narrow when it was being built, that the architect designed the front to stand at an angle to the street thus giving the house an appearance of greater width and dignity. The courtyard is best viewed from rue Cambournac.

Église Notre-Dame

The church was gutted by the fire of 1487. When it was rebuilt many modifications were made to the original plan including the addition of side aisles and the square tower which rises at the north end of the west front. In the south aisle, opposite the door, a **white-marble baptismal font** adorned with fleurs-de-lis bears an inscription from the *Romance of the Rose*, the French medieval poem which inspired Chaucer.

▶ *Walk across place de la Barre.*

Rue Mirebeau

This pleasant pedestrianised street is lined with timber-framed houses whose ground floor is often occupied by shops. Opposite passage casse-cou (yet another one) you can see the doorway of the former Augustine convent. Enter the courtyard to admire the trapezium-shaped cloisters.

▶ *Walk up the steep dark passage casse-cou (Mirebeau stairs); once at the top, turn right onto rue Branly.*

Hôtel des Échevins★

This former town hall now houses the Musée Estève. (*see Sights*). There is a striking difference in architectural style between the two parts of the building:

Place Gordaine

S. Sauvignier/MICHELIN

– the living quarters at the far end of the courtyard date from 1489 and were built in the Flamboyant Gothic style.
A fine **octagonal tower**★★ juts out from the façade and, rising to a height of three storeys, contains a circular staircase.

◐ *Continue along rue Branly to place Cujas then turn onto rue des Beaux-Arts.*

Rue Coursalon
There is a fine view of place Gordaine along this lively pedestrianised street. Turn right onto a narrow street with a 15C house on the corner. It leads to the elegant Hôtel Lallemant.

◐ *Return to rue Coursalon.*

Place Gordaine
Situated at the intersection of the pedestrianised streets, this flower-decked square is popular with strollers. Note the stone on which Calvin used to stand to advocate the reformation.

◐ *Turn right onto rue Bourbonnoux.*

Hôtel Lallemant★
Altered in the 17C this mansion has been converted into a museum of decorative art. The site straddles the town's Roman wall and certain parts of the house are on different levels.

City of Art and History

Even a short visit to the City will confirm the sentiments of author and art historian André Malraux who in 1962 dubbed Bourges ,the "City of Art and History"

◐ *Turn onto the street facing Hôtel Lallemant.*

Rue Joyeuse
Note the carved-wood pillar on the street corner; it supports the Maison des Trois-Flûtes (*now a bakery*). Walk up this peaceful street lined with private mansions.

◐ *Return to rue Bourbonnoux via place Louis-Lacombe.*

If you like cobblestones, walk along rue Moncenoux then turn right onto rue de la Thaumassière.

Rue Bourbonnoux
There are many craftsmen's workshops along this former high street lined with timber-framed houses. Farther along it reaches the east end of the cathedral.

◐ *A small flight of stairs located between the cathedral and the adjoining gardens takes you back to the starting point of this walk.*

387

Marais de Bourges

LES MARAIS

Before you take a stroll through the town's unusual wetlands, go into Église St-Bonnet, which somehow links the historic part of the city and the rural district known as Les Marais.

Église St-Bonnet

Open Jul–Aug, 10am–noon and 2–6pm; Sept–Jun, 2–5.30pm. Dating from 1510, the church was remodelled in the 20C by the addition of two bays and a neo-Flamboyant façade.
Inside, the most remarkable features are the **stained-glass windows** by Jean Lescuyer and a work by the 17C local painter Jean Boucher.

From place St-Bonnet, walk along rue Voltaire towards the Marais, then cross boulevard du Général-Chanzy.

Les Marais★

A pleasant walkway wanders through the wetlands and canals formed by the River Voiselle, winding among the many garden plots held by the residents of Bourges. A gate marks the border between the town and the Marais.

Go through the gate and walk along the narrow road on the left. At the end of the road, walk across the footbridge

(on your left) then bear right. A path skirting the **Voiselle** *and the Marais de Mariens leads to the River Yèvre.*

Digue de l'Yèvre

Flat-bottomed boats are moored beneath a willow tree.

Retrace your steps and take the first path on the right.

Rue de Babylone

There is a fine view of the cathedral to your left. On the right, beyond the Marais Hauts the horizon is barred by the town's northern suburb and the convent of the Sisters of Charity.

Follow avenue Marx Dormoy on the left then turn right beyond the bridge onto cours Beauvoir.

Jardin des Prés-Fichaux★

A beautiful garden has been laid out on marshland between the river and the close of St-Ambroise Abbey where the Protestants used to gather in the 16C to sing.

Return to place St-Bonnet along boulevard de la République. Note the lively covered market on your left, just before the square.

MUSEUMS

Musée des Meilleurs Ouvriers de France

Place Etienne Dolet 📞*02 48 57 82 45.* ♿🕐*Open Jul–Aug 10am–12.30pm noon and 2–6pm; Apr–Jun and Sept–Dec 10am–12 noon, 2–6pm; Mar 6–30 and Jan 6–25, 10am–12 noon, 2–5pm* 🕐*Closed Sun morning, Mon, Jan 1, May 1, Nov 1 and 11, Dec 25, Jan–Feb 20.* ✍*No charge.*

Housed in the former archbishop's residence, this unusual museum contains exceptionally fine objects made by gifted craftsmen.

Musée du Berry

4, rue des Arènes. 📞*02 48 70 41 92.* 🕐*Open daily except Tue, 10am–12noon and 2–6pm, Sun 2–6pm.* 🕐*Closed Jan 1, May 1, Nov 1 and 11 and Dec 25.* ✍*No charge.*

This quiet, unpretentious museum, housed in the Hôtel Cujas, contains **archaeological collections**★ (dating from prehistory to the end of the Gallo-Roman period), sculpture, furniture and pottery as well as a fine collection of **statues**★ including *The Prophets* (1382) by Jean de Cambrai and André Beauneveu and *The Weepers* from the Duke of Berry's tomb by Jean de Cambrai.

Musée Estève★★

Hôtel des Echevins, 13, rue Eduard Branly. 📞*02 48 24 75 38 musee-esteve@bourges.fr* ♿🕐*Open daily*

Musée Estève

©FORGET Patrick/SAGAPHOTO.COM/Alamy

except Tue, 10am–12noon and 2–6pm, Sun 2–6pm. 🕐*Closed Jan 1, May 1, Nov 1 and 11 and Dec 25.* ✍*No charge.*

Since 1987, this museum, located in the Hôtel des Échevins, has been home to a unique collection of 130 works in oil and on paper.

Born in Culan in 1904, **Maurice Estève** had no formal training as an artist. His work reveals a stunning evolution in technique, while themes from his native Berry are repeated over time: the home (curtains, window, table, other household objects), his grandmother (*Paysanne endormie aux rideaux verts*, 1924), the natural environment (*Châtaigneraie*, 1927).

In Paris, Estève was able to absorb the influence of Surrealism and later,

---

Le Printemps de Bourges

Created in April 1977, this musical event still aims to bring together not only the current headliners but also an increasing assortment of lesser known artists. The first year, 15 000 people flocked to hear such non-conformist French artists as Béranger, Font and Val, and Lavilliers. Two years later, ever more popular, the festival was extended to one week and welcomed other musical genres (rock, folk, jazz). Most of the spectators are young (75% between ages 15 and 25), and now number more than 100 000. Shows take place in a dozen different halls, and the street life is certainly as big an attraction as what goes on inside. Over the decades, some of the groups and individual artists who have won acclaim at Bourges are Téléphone, Charles Trenet, Claude Nougaro, Murray Head, Touré Kunda, Patricia Kass, Johnny Hallyday, Véronique Sanson, Joe Cocker, Miles Davis, Nina Simone, The Cure, U2, Frank Zappa, Juliette Gréco and Abd al-Malik. Now in its 34th year, the spring festival remains fresh and exciting. Play on!

Cézanne. Until 1947, his work shifted between the figurative (*La Toilette Verte*, 1934) and the abstract (*Embarquement pour Cythère*, 1929), before settling on the latter course. Most of his paintings are a subtle combination or a juxtaposition of masses of colour.

Hôtel Lallemant★

This magnificent Renaissance mansion has retained the name of Jean Lallemant, the rich cloth merchant who had it built. It now houses the **Musée des Arts Décoratifs** *(6, rue Bourbonnoux;* ◔ *open Jul–Aug, daily except Mon, 10am–12.30pm and 1.30–6pm, Sun 1.30–6pm; Mar–Jun and Sept–Dec, daily except Mon, 10am–noon and 2–6pm, Sun 2–6pm; Jan–Mar, daily except Mon, 10am–noon and 2–5pm, Sun 2–5pm;* ◔*closed Jan 1, May 1, Nov 1 and 11, and Dec 25;* ⊜*no charge;* ☎*02 48 57 81 17).*
A sloping ramp, covered with barrel vaulting and used to lead horses in and out of the building, goes through to the **main courtyard** which is on two levels.
The large main building shows the styles of different architectural periods: the mullioned windows and arcades are 15C, the doors to the corridors and the window-frames of the bays above the passageway are 16C and the entablature and round frontons bearing the arms of the Dorsannes who once owned the

mansion are 17C. An Italian-style loggia, has 17C frescoes representing hunting scenes and a polychrome bas-relief dedicated to St Christopher.
On the top floor, one room houses a notable **collection of miniatures**★*;* toys, master craft pieces all perfectly executed and together providing an unusual and thorough summary of the history of furniture from Louis XV to Art Nouveau.

▷ *Return to the main building and take the spiral staircase opposite the information desk.*

Displayed in elegant rooms are enamels, porcelains and ivories, as well as Renaissance and 17C French and Flemish tapestries.

Musée d'Histoire Naturelle★

Les Rives d'Auron. ☎*02 48 65 37 34. www.museum-bourges.net.* ▲▲& ◔*Open daily, 2–6pm; school hols, 10am–noon and 2–6pm.* ◔*Closed Jan 1, May 1, Nov 1 and 11 and Dec 25.* ⊜*4€ (child: 2.20€).*
The Natural History Museum was created in 1927 and renovated in 1989.
It is interactive, entertaining and educational, with an emphasis on the regional environment as well as the work of local naturalists and scientists.

ADDRESSES

🏠 STAY

⊜⊜ **Hotel Ibis Bourges** – *Rue VladimirJankelevitch Quartier du Prado.* ☎*02 48 65 89 99. www.accorhotels.com. 86 rooms.* Comfortable smart modern chain hotel in the centre of town.

⊜⊜ **Chambre d'hôte Château de Bel Air** – *Lieu-dit le Grand-Chemin, 18340 Arcay. 16km/10mi S of Bourges on the D 73.* ☎*02 48 25 36 72. 6 rooms.* Surrounded by spacious grounds, this 19C château is calm and comfortable. The vast entrance hall leads to the dining room with its massive fireplace. Large bedrooms on the upper floor.

⊜⊜ **Hôtel Christina** – *5 r. Halle.* ☎*02 48 70 56 50 . www.le-christina.com. 71 rooms.* Two categories of well-maintained bedrooms are available in this city-centre hotel: cosy and chic (⊜⊜⊜) or smaller and functional (⊜⊜).

⊜⊜ **Hôtel Les Tilleuls** – *7 pl. Pyrotechnie.* ☎*02 48 20 49 04 . www.les-tilleuls.com. 39 rooms.* Situated in a quiet part of town, this hotel offers guests accommodation in the main building and an annex, where the rooms are less spacious, more basic, but with the benefit of air-conditioning.

⊜⊜⊜ **Le Berry** – *3, Place Du Général Leclerc. 02 48 65 99 30. www.le-berry.com.* Modern five-storey hotel, close to the historic centre, with attractive colourful spacious bedrooms and a pleasant restaurant, both of which which belie its plain exterior.

Best Western Hôtel d'Angleterre – *1 pl. des Quatre-Piliers ℘02 48 24 68 51. www.bestwestern-angleterre-bourges.com. Closed 24 Dec-1 Jan. 30 rooms.* The city's former court of justice is located close to the Palais Jacques-Cœur. All necessary creature comforts in the bedrooms (most with air-conditioning), where the decor is sober yet modern. Buffet breakfast. Friendly staff.

🍴 EAT

Le Bourbonnoux – *44 r. Bourbonnoux - ℘02 48 24 14 76. Closed 11-21 Feb, 16-26 Apr, 16 Aug-3 Sep, Sun eve Nov-Jun, Sat lunchtime and Fri.* The restaurant is in a street lined with craft shops, just a few steps away from St-Étienne Cathedral. The welcome is warm and the dining room is pleasantly decorated with bright colours and exposed beams. Popular with locals.

Le Bistro Gourmand – *5 pl. de la Barre. ℘02 48 70 63 37. Reserv. recommended.* A delightful bistro specialising in regional and Lyonnais cuisine. The sober decor here is enhanced by gentle candlelight. The terrace looks onto the Église Notre-Dame.

Le Savoyard – *40 r. Bourbonnoux. ℘02 48 02 57 27. Closed 2 wks end June, 2 wks start Aug, Sat lunch, Sun dinner and Thu.* As the name suggests, the focus here is on the cuisine of Savoy, with a menu that includes cheese fondues, raclettes, tartiflettes etc. Wooden skis, clogs, cow bells and other typically Savoyard objects adorn the cool stone vaults of this former coal cellar.

La Courcillière – *R. de Babylone. ℘02 48 24 41 91. www.lacourcilliere.com. Closed Wed, Sun eve and Tue eve.* Located in the Les Marais district just a stone's throw from the city centre, this pleasant, rustic restaurant has a terrace by the water facing the gardens. Down-to-earth reasonably priced cuisine.

🍷 BARS AND CAFÉS

Pub des Jacobins – *Enclos des Jacobins 7, Rue Armuriers. ℘02 48 24 61 78. Open Mon-Sat, 9.30pm-2am. Closed Sun.* This

piano-bar is whole-heartedly devoted to jazz, as demonstrated by the photos of musicians covering the walls. Top-quality concerts are held here once a month. The pub specialises in cocktails.

Pub Jacques Cœur – *1 r. d'Auron. ℘02 48 70 72 88. Open Mon-Sat, 10am-2am. Closed Sun.* This 16C half-timbered residence, now a pub, was built on the site where Jacques Cœur, a wealthy and influential 15C merchant and councillor to King Charles VII, was born. Sloping and lopsided, this antique building is the most photographed of Bourges.

🎭 ENTERTAINMENT

Maison de la Culture de Bourges – *Pl. André-Malraux. ℘02 48 67 74 70. www.mcbourges.com. Ticket office open Tue-Sat, 2pm-7pm. Closed 13 Jul-20 Aug and 1 May. Ticket prices.* Opened by André Malraux, then Minister of Culture, this was the first Maison de la Culture in France. This lively and popular venue hosts plays, dance performances and classical music and jazz concerts. Cinema and café.

Les Nuits Lumières de Bourges – *℘02 48 23 02 60. Open every evening in Jul-Aug and during the Printemps de Bourges festival; May-Jun and Sep: Thu-Sat. No charge.* A walk through the historic city centre at night to view illuminated buildings (2hr 30min). Blue lanterns mark the way.

🚶 LEISURE ACTIVITIES

Base de Voile du Val-d'Auron – *23 chemin de Petit Mazières. ℘02 48 20 07 65 (part-time reception) or ℘02 48 20 49 46. Open 9am-noon and 2-6pm. Closed Oct-Apr and Mon.* This watersports centre at the Val d'Auron Lake covering 85 ha/210 acres offers a range of activities, including swimming, canoeing, fishing and rowing.

🛍 SHOPPING

The main shopping area is in the pedestrianised area that includes rue Coursarlor and rue Mirebeau (near the palais Jacques-Cœur), and rue Bourbonnoux and rue Moyenne (near the cathedral).

Markets – Every Saturday morning, the listed Halle au Blé comes to life with 200 stallholders selling all types of food. A permanent daily market is also held at the *Halle St-Bonnet* (Open 7.30am-1pm and 3-7.30pm), selling fresh seasonal produce, local cheeses and other regional specialities. On Sunday mornings, stalls selling bric-a-brac, inexpensive clothes etc add to the charm of this popular market.

La Maison des Forestines – *3 pl. Cujas. ℘02 48 24 00 24. Open Mon 3p–7pm; Tue–Sat 9.30am–12.15pm, 2pm–7.15pm.* This chocolate/confectionery business founded in 1825 occupies an attractive Haussmann-style building. The shop, with its coffered ceiling and superb Gien china, produces irresistible house specialities such as the *Forestine*, a chocolate praline with a satiny sugar coating created in 1879, the *Amandine* and *Noisette* (created in 1885) and the *Richelieu*, a nougatine filled with an almond and pistachio creme, created in 1890.

Domaine de Coquin –*18510 Menetou-Salon. ℘02 48 64 80 46. Open Mon–Sat 8am–noon, 2pm–6.30pm, Sun and public hols, by appointment.* Francis Audiot is a wine-producer whose family has been producing excellent white wines for the past 150 years.

TOURIST INFORMATION

Guided tours – Bourges, which has been officially designated as a *"ville d'art et d'histoire"*, offers guided tours (1hr 30min/2hr) with qualified local guides. *For information, contact the tourist office (℘02 48 23 02 60) or log onto www.bourges-tourisme.com*

P'tit train touristique – The city's tourist train provides a 45min overview of the city's history and architecture. Operates daily 10h15 à 18h15, Apr to early-Nov (departures every 15min from the tourist office). 6.50€. *For information, call ℘06 08 60 54 56.*

Château de Bouges★★

Set in the heart of the Berry-Champagne region, this 18C château was built in the Italian style on the site of a former stronghold. Because of the arrangement of its pediments and façades, it closely resembles the Petit Trianon at Versailles. The Château appeared in the 1994 version of the film "Le Colonel Chabert" starring Gerard Depardieu

CHÂTEAU

The château was built in 1759, restored from 1917 onwards by Henri Viguier, the director of a Parisian department store and finally bequeathed to the state in 1968. It contains an interesting collection of 18C **furniture**★, particularly sofas and chairs which was patiently assembled by the previous owners. Note in particular the small Louis XV salon, the games room with its fine furniture, the drawing room with its marble chimney-piece and astronomical clock, and the charming Louis XVI bedroom.

- **Michelin Map:** 323: G-4
- **Location:** 10km/6.2mi NE of Levroux
- **Timing:** Guided tour (45min) Jul–Aug at 11.15am, noon, 3pm, 4pm, 5pm and 5.45pm; Apr–Jun and Sept–Oct, daily except Tue at 11am, 3pm, 4pm, and 4.45pm; Mar and Nov, Sat–Sun at 11am, 3pm, 4pm and 4.45pm. Closed 1 May Nov 1 and 11and Dec-Feb. 6.50€, gardens 5€. ℘02 54 35 88 26.

The outbuildings are vast edifices with tall mansard roofs and include fine stables with aharness room containing an important collection of saddles, harnesses and riding boots. In the wing set at right angles, there are several horse drawn carriages dating from the beginning of the 20C. French style gardens and a 80ha/198-acre **park**★ planted with a variety of fine trees and with a pond bring the visit to an end.

Issoudun

and Forêt de Chœurs, Forêt de Bommiers

Issoudun dates back to Gallic times: Uxellodunum comes from a Celtic term meaning a high - and thus fortified - site. Later, during the Middle Ages, Issoudun was the stake in many a battle, the most famous being that between Philip Augustus and Richard the Lion Heart.

A BIT OF HISTORY

Honoré de Balzac (1799-1850) stayed at Frapesle Castle, near Issoudun, where he wrote most of *César Birotteau* and researched material for *La Rabouilleuse (The Black Sheep)*. Issoudun has retained the peculiar street names which appear in Balzac's works: rue du Boucher-Gris (Drunken Butcher Street), rue à Chercher (Hard to Find Street).

WALKING TOUR

▷ *Start from place St-Cyr.*

Église St-Cyr

There is a very fine 14C-15C **stained-glass window** in the nave. It is divided into five vertical sections and in addition to depicting the Crucifixion contains medallions illustrating scenes from the lives of St Cyran and St Juliet..

▷ *Walk up to place du 10 juin.*

Beffroi

The belfry, flanked by two round towers of unequal size, once served as a

- ▶ **Population:** Indre 13 930
- **Michelin Map:** 323: H-5
- **Info**: Place St Cyr, 36 100 Issoudun. ℘02 54 21 74 02. www.issoudun.fr.
- **Location**: 35km/22mi S of Vierzon; 37km/ 23mi west of Bourges.
- **Parking**: Car parks are dotted around the centre (*see town plan*).
- **Timing**: Half day to explore the Chœurs and Bommiers forests.
- **Don't Miss**: The Musée de l'Hospice St-Roch.

gateway (12C) through the castle wall to the town. Dismantled during the Wars of Religion, it was restored in the Renaissance style and used as a prison until 1914.

Place des Miroirs

The façade of the **Hôtel de Ville** (town hall) dates from 1731; it is attached to a modern building and fronted by a courtyard designed by Marin Kasimir. This work, known as La Place des Miroirs, is made of eight glassed-in spaces surrounded by steps and waterworks.

Tour Blanche

Open Jul–Aug, Mon–Sat 2–6pm, Sun and public hols, 2–7pm; Jun and Sept, daily except Mon, 2–6pm, Sun and public hols, 2–7pm. Apr–May, Thur–Sat 2-6pmm. Evening shows, Jul–Aug,

Place des Miroirs

S. Sauvignier/MICHELIN

ISSOUDUN

WHERE TO STAY		Hôtel Le Relais Issoldunois......................⑧
Camping municipal les Taupeaux............③		WHERE TO EAT
Hôtel Campanile......................................⑥		L'Augergeade...⑤

Thur-Sat 9pm;. ⊜3€ *for tour and show.*
℘*02 54 03 22 15.*

The tower, standing in the middle of the town hall gardens, was built at the end of the 12C by Richard the Lion Heart. The inside is octagonal, the outside nearly circular; it is 28m/92ft high and the walls are 3.5m/12ft thick.

The four floors in the tower may be visited: the 8m/26ft-high former cellars (audio-visual presentation about Richard the Lionheart and Philip-Augustus), a lofty vaulted hall where the original entrance was located (presentation of King Arthur's legends), a room devoted to the Hundred Years War and an exhibition area displaying a model of the 17C town.

From the top platform there is a view over the country that lies between the valleys of the Indre and the Cher.

Parc François-Mitterrand

Access via the panoramic lift built within the fortifications. This pleasant park is easily reached from all parts of town; it stretches across both sides of the river.

Musée de l'Hospice St-Roch★

&. ⏱*Open May 2–Sept, Wed–Sun 10am–noon and 2–7pm, Mon–Tue, 2–7pm; Oct–Apr, daily except Mon & Tue, 2–7pm, Sat–Sun and public hols, 10am–noon and 2–6pm.* ⏱*Closed Jan, 1 May, 1 and 11 Nov, 24-27 and 31 Dec.* ⊜*No charge.* ℘*02 54 21 01 76. www.issoudun.fr.*

The museum is housed in the former hospital (Hôtel-Dieu) which is built on piles over the River Théols in a picturesque setting. St Roch (St Rock) is legendary for healing victims of the plague in the 14C. Stricken himself, he was succoured by a dog, and is often pictured with one in paintings and statuary.

Sculpture – The sculpture collection gives an insight into past local monuments: capitals, statues of the Virgin Mary and columns dating from the 8C to the 15C. The men's ward (**salle des hommes**) gives access to the **chapel** built around 1500. The most outstanding items are two 15C carvings of the **Tree of Jesse**★★ showing the genealogy of Christ.

Ancient medecine – The last wing, the women's ward (**salle des femmes**), displays a collection of instruments used by surgeons, dentists and gynaecologists. The **Apothicairerie**★ (pharmacy), facing a garden where medicinal herbs are cultivated, houses a valuable pharmaceutical collection.

Basilique Notre-Dame-du-Sacré-Cœur

This late-19C neo-Gothic basilica is a popular place of pilgrimage as the numerous ex-votos testify. The stained-glass windows are particularly interesting: abstract designs in various hues of blue along the aisle, more classical designs in the nave and chancel.

🚗 DRIVING TOUR

FORÊT DE CHŒURS AND FORÊT DE BOMMIERS
Round trip of 60km/37mi – allow 3hr

Located in the *départements* of Indre and Cher, these lovely forests cover more than 7 500ha/18 525 acres; 75% of the trees are oaks.

▷ *Head east on the D 8 for St-Ambroix. In St-Hilaire, take the D 84E.*

Bordered by woods, the route goes along the picturesque Arnon Valley. Above the river bank rise the vestiges of the **Abbaye de la Prée** (*concerts in season*), founded in the 12C.

Moulin de Nouan

🕐🎟️ *Guided tour (15min mill + 45min tour) when the sails are unfurled or by appointment.* 🎟️*2.50€.* 📞*02 54 03 18 72. www.moulindenouan.fr.st*
👥 An unusual site in the region, this windmill mainly served to back up the many watermills, which are often stilled in summer when rivers and streams are low.

▷ *Return to the road; right, on the D 9.*

Mareuil-sur-Arnon

Snug among the copses, this village was one of the metallurgical centres of the upper Arnon Valley. All that remains of the old forge is a tall brick chimney alongside the lake. South-west of the town of Mareuil, this 3ha/7.5-acre lake now serves as a **recreation centre**.

▷ *Outside of Mareuil, take the D 18 to the right.*

Abbaye de Chezal-Benoît

Founded in 1093 by the monk André de Vallombreuse, this former Benedictine monastery, now a psychiatric hospital, has kept the 12C nave of the church and the community buildings.

▷ *Leave Chezal SW on the D 65E.*

Travel along the southern edge of the **Forêt de Chœurs**, where many forest roads and trails lead to the central point known as the Croix Blanche.

▷ *At Pruniers, turn right on the D 925.*

Bommiers

This 12C **Église St-Pierre** is representative of the lower Berry by the clearly Benedictine plan. The capitals, also 12C, create an admirable ensemble: Christ handing over the Keys to St Peter and the Law to St Paul.
The 48 magnificent **stalls**★ (1511-15) are from the chapel and the Minimes convent in Bommiers.

▷ *Take the D 925 towards Lignières. 1km/0.5mi before Pruniers, turn left on the D 68.*

The road back to Issoudun crosses the **Bommiers Forest** as far as **St-Aubin**, where the church shelters a 15C sculptural ensemble: St Anne, the Virgin and the Infant Jesus.
After crossing the Cousseron, the road crosses the ancient Roman road known as the **Levée de César**, which linked Argentonmagus (🌿 *see St-MARCEL*) to Bourges.

ADDRESSES

🏠 STAY

🛏 **Camping Municipal les Taupeaux** – *37 rte de Reuilly.* ℘*0253 03 13 46. www.issoudun.fr. Open Jun-Aug.* Flat, grassy site with basic facilities.

🛏 **Hôtel Le Relais Issoudun** – *88 Rte de Bourges. N E on the N 151.* ℘*02 54 03 04 05. 16 rooms.* Simple accommodation in an imposing historic building.

🛏 🛏 **Hôtel Campanile** – *Rte 151 (Bourges).* ℘*02 54 21 06 40. www.campanile.fr.* Chain-hotel with well-equipped rooms.

🍽 EAT

🍷 🍷 **L'Aubergeade 321, Rte d'Issoudun - 36260 Diou.** ℘*0254 49 22 28. Closed Wed dinne, Sun dinner.* This lively restaurant boasts a garden terrace where traditional local dishes are served.

Levroux

and local Châteaux

Set between the wooded landscape of the Boischaut and the rich farmlands of the area known as Champagne Berrichonne, Levroux is in the heartland of tradition: as well as producing savoury goat cheeses, it is also home to tawing (a form of leather processing using alum and salt) and parchment enterprises.

A BIT OF HISTORY

A land steeped in history – The area has been inhabited since prehistoric times; the settlement of Levroux appeared at the end of the Celtic period. It was certainly one of the *oppida* burned to the ground by the Gaulish leader Vercingétorix as Caesar's armies approached in 52 BC. Once the *Pax Romana* was established, Levroux grew quickly, spreading from the towers on the hill to the area where the city now stands.

The historical interest of this sector is such that the district of Levroux has become one vast archaeological site. Besides the Gallo-Roman theatre, several villas have been discovered and are now being carefully unearthed.

In the Middle Ages, the town grew around the feudal château of the princes of Châteauroux and the church of St-Sylvain, the site of pilgrimages. There are several well-preserved 15C and 16C buildings in Levroux.

▶ **Population:** 2 839
⚲ **Michelin Map:** 323: F-5
🛈 **Info:** Maison de Bois, pl E Nivet, ℘02 54 35 63 39
▶ **Locn:** 20km/12mi N of Châteauroux; 55km/34mi SW of Vierzon.
🔍 **Don't Miss:** Stalls and organ case of St-Sylvain.

TOWN

Collégiale St-Sylvain★

de l'Hôtel de Ville.

In the early 11C, Eudes de Déols founded a collegiate church in Levroux and made a special land grant to the canons.

Thus, part of the town took on a separate status and became a place of refuge.

The church was built in two stages beginning in the late 12C. The crypt, the apse and the large bell-tower came before the vaulting in the nave and the construction of the porch, undertaken around 1263.

The east end of the church is a heptgonal apse flanked by a square bell-tower. The main doorway bears a much-damaged tympanum; the sculpted imagery represents the Resurrection of the Dead and the Last Judgement. Inside, the nave and side aisles are impressive for their soaring height. The chancel was built in transitional Romanesque-Gothic style; note the keystone in the sanctuary, showing Christ bestowing blessings.

The restored late-15C **organ case★** is one of the three Gothic organ cases left in France.

Maison de Bois (Maison St-Jacques)

place Victor-Hugo.
This wooden house was built between 1536 and 1547. Located in a street which leads to the façade of St-Sylvain, it is decorated with angelic carvings and the blazons of François I and Henri de Valois (later to become Henri II), as well as curious figures in the angles (note the **"wild man"** covered with leaves). The house was once used as a hospice for pilgrims on their way to Santiago de Compostela.

Porte de Champagne

rue de Champagne.
Close to the church, this former town gate (1435-1506) was turned into a prison at the beginning of the 19C. It is framed by round towers and roofed with dark brown tiles.

Musée du Cuir et du Parchemin

31 rue Gambetta. Open May–Dec, *Mon 10am–12.30pm, 3–6pm,Thur, Fri, Sat, 3–6pm, Thu–Fri, 3pm–6.pm, Wed and Sun by reservation.* 2.50€ 02 54 35 48 90.
This small temporary museum in the tourist office is devoted to techniques of dressing hides by 'tawing', and to the manufacture of parchment.

CHÂTEAUX OF THE REGION

Around Levroux, several interesting châteaux are found in the Boischaut and Champagne Berrichonne areas.

Château de Bouges★★

9.5km/6mi NE. Château de BOUGES.

Château de Valençay★★

22km/13.7mi N. Château de VALENÇAY.

Palluau-sur-Indre★

25km/15.5mi W on D 28 and D 15.
Perched on a rocky crest above the Indre Valley, the **château** is set in a lovely park. The 12C keep is known as the Tour de Philippe Auguste, in memory of his visit in 1188. From the terrace, the view extends over the valley.

"Wild man" on the Maison de Bois
S. Sauvignier/MICHELIN

The former **St Laurence Priory** contains remarkable Romanesque frescoes; note, in particular, a magnificent **Virgin in glory**★ decorating the oven vaulted apse and a Christ in glory in the chancel.

Château d'Argy★

16km/10mi SW along the D 926 and the D 63. Open Jul–Aug, guided tour *(45min), daily exc. Wed, 10am–noon and 2–6pm; Apr–Jun and Sept–Oct, Sat–Sun and public hols, 2–6pm.* 4.50€ *(no charge on Indre heritage day in Jun).* 02 54 84 21 55. *www.clubduvieuxmanoir.asso.fr*
Fortified in the 12C, this impressive château, is set in a 40ha/99-acre park. The square, 15C keep is an excellent example of military architecture, with its trefoil machicolations and guard towers.
In the courtyard, the **Louis XII-style gallery**★, carefully restored, contrasts with the severity of the outer walls. Nearby, a mill and a building housing a museum devoted to rural traditions (*traditions paysannes*) date from the 19C.

Ancienne Abbaye de St-Genou

3km/2mi SE of Palluau.
The church was once part of a Benedictine abbey, founded in 828. The relics of St Genou, who was sent to evangelise Gaul by Pope Sixtus II, gave the church its name. Begun in 994, and consecrated

in 1066, the abbey went into decline in the early 16C, gradually falling into ruin. It was completely restored soon after being registered as a historic building (1882).Only the transept and the choir, in the Berry Romanesque style, give a clue to the church's past. Beyond the triumphal arc, the vast choir has an oven-shaped vault. The monumental columns have remarkable **capitals** with fantastic animal figures, and episodes from the life of St Genou.

Mehun-sur-Yèvre★

and Fôret d'Allogny, Reuilly-Quincy Vineyards

This charming old town on the banks of the River Yèvre and the Berry Canal is a centre of porcelain manufacture. Jean de Berry's castle, where Joan of Arc met the King of France, towers above the river.

A BIT OF HISTORY

The third son of King John the Good, **Duke Jean de Berry** (1340-1416) was a lavish patron of the arts and admirer of the art of manuscript illumination. He rebuilt Mehun Castle in 1386 and it was here amid a brilliant court that he welcomed writers such as Froissart, miniaturists like the Limbourg brothers and André Beauneveu. The latter, who was also a sculptor and architect, worked for a lengthy period at the castle. The Duke left the castle to his grand-nephew Charles VII, who received Joan of Arc here in the winter of 1429 and 1430.

TOWN

Porte de l'Horloge

rue Jeanne d'Arc
A 14C gateway standing at the top of the street.

Rue Jeanne-d'Arc

This street leads down to Yèvre between old houses (some with wells in front). No 87, the house where Joan of Arc stayed,

ADDRESSES

⧉/ EAT

⊜⊜ **Le Sommelier** – *5, pl Gambetta, Châteauroux ℘02 54 07 45 52. Closed Apr 27–May 12, Aug 3–18, Mon eve and Sun.* This old house has been tastefully renovated without losing its inimitable Berry chatacter. Modern interior and rustic furniture. Traditional cuisine.

▶ **Population:** *6,884*
   Michelin Map: 323: J-4
▫ **Info**: place du 14 juillet. ℘02 48 57 35 51.
▶ **Location**: 13km/8mi NW of Bourges; 17km/10.5mi SE of Vierzon.
◔ **Timing**: Allow an hour or two to explore the Fôret d'Allogny and half a day to tour the Reuilly-Quincy vineyards.

has elegant bays with trilobed arches; to the left is the esplanade to the castle.

Jardin du Duc-Jean-de-Berry

place jean Manceau.
Fine views can be had of the public washing boards and 12C watermill. A shaded promenade alongside the Berry Canal has views of the castle and church.

Pôle de la Porcelaine

rue des Grands Moulins. ⧉*Open Jul–Aug, 10am–noon and 2–6pm; May–Jun and Sept, daily except Mon, 2–6pm; Mar–Apr and Oct, Sat–Sun and public hols, 2–6pm.* ⧉*Closed Nov–Mar.* ⊜*4.60€.* ℘02 48 57 06 19.
Near the castle, a glass building displays fine porcelain items, both rare and unusual (china, a 1900 fountain, a pedestal table, a funerary plaque etc). A 10min *son et lumière* show illustrates the transformation of kaolin into porcelain.

Musée Charles VII

place Jean-Manceau. Guided tours. *Same opening times and charges as the Pôle de la Porcelaine.*

Of this marvellous fairy tale castle, visited and admired by Claus Sluter and Holbein, sculptor and painter respectively, there remain two round towers, one of which is named after Charles VII (extensively restored). The original plan of the castle is still visible – note the position of the bastion jutting out like a spur towards the river. A miniature of the duke of Berry's *Très Riches Heures* (Rich Hours) now in the Condé museum of Chantilly (north of Paris), executed by the Limbourg brothers, shows the castle as it existed in the 15C.

Dismantled in the 17C the castle slowly fell into ruins. Excavations have revealed that over 10 castles were built onsite (10C and 15C).

Collégiale Notre-Dame

rue des Grands Moulins.

The construction of this church, Romanesque in style with the exception of the chapel added in the 15C, started with the horseshoe shaped chancel (11C).

At the entrance to the nave, on the left beside the baptismal font, is a 15C relics cupboard, which was fitted in the 17C with a carved wooden door representing the Education of the Virgin. In the northern mart of the nave, there is a Crucifixion painted by Jean Boucher from Bourges, the master of Mignard.

DRIVING TOUR

FORÊT D'ALLOGNY

Round trip of 40km/25mi – allow 1hr

▷ *Leave Mehun along the D 79 N.*

Note *La Pierre de Lu*, a great conglomerate made up of flint nodules, to the right of the road.

▷ *Right to Allouis; left (D 20) to Allogny.*

This wooded massif, a dark mass on the plateau which acts as a watershed,

Ruins of the Château de Mehun

S. Sauvignier/MICHELIN

dominates the Cher and Barageon valleys. This densely forested area is mainly composed of oaks with isolated clumps of pines, hornbeams, birch and beech. The D 56 between Allogny and St-Martin-d'Auxigny traverses the forest. From the slope reaching down to St-Martin there is a fine view of the smiling and fertile Moulon Valley, a striking contrast to the dark and mysterious forest.

▷ *Return to Mehun via the D 68.*

REUILLY-QUINCY VINEYARDS

62km/39mi round trip – allow half a day

▷ *Drive S out of Mehun along the D 35 to Ste-Thorette; turn right onto D 23 then left onto the D 114 towards Plou.*

Jardin Conservatoire de Plantes Aromatiques et Tinctoriales du Prieuré de Manzay

Open Jul–Aug, daily except Tue, 3–7pm; May–Jun and Sept–Oct, Sat–Sun, 3–7pm. 5€ . 02 48 57 34 53.

Situated on the edge of the Font-Moreau woods, this garden occupies more than 1ha/2.5 acres of the grounds of St-Laurent-de-Manzay priory, founded in the 13C. It contains the main plants used for seasoning and dyeing since prehistory.

▷ *Continue along the D 114.*

Chârost

The origins of this hamlet go back to the Bronze Age. In Antiquity and the Middle Ages, Chârost enjoyed prosperity, as witnessed in the remains of its feudal castle, the defensive wall (northern gateway to the city) and especially its church. The **Église St-Michel** *(apply in advance to the town hall)* abbey church is a vast Romanesque edifice (12C), built of ferrous limestone. A wide nave, the timber framework dating from the 19C, leads to a hemispherical sanctuary: the transept and apsidal chapels have vanished. Outside, above the entrances, a large cross with an intertwining motif supports the Pascal Lamb.

Go round the building and into the **cemetery**. From there, observe the apse and the wealth of carved ornamentation. (among the admirable capitals, look for the harpy – half woman, half bird – bearing a wheel).

▷ *Leave Chârost W on the D 2.*

Diou

This well-groomed village on the banks of the Théols is a pleasant stopover. Near the pretty church of St-Clément (13C), a lawn rolls down to the water's edge, where a mill straddles the river, with a dovecot alongside.

▷ *Leave Diou travelling N on the D 918 towards Mehun.*

Château de la Ferté

⊶ *Not open to visitors.*

This is a lovely classical manor with four corner towers, dating from 1659.

Reuilly

This village is known for its wines (*Appellation d'Origine Contrôlée*), grown in vineyards spreading over the *départements* of Indre and Cher.

Along the banks of the Théols and the Auron, 132ha/326 acres from Lury to Diou (Preuilly alone is isolated to the east) produce mostly white wine from Sauvignon grapes.

▷ *Drive E on D 20 towards Mehun.*

Quincy

The vineyards of Quincy and Brinay spread over 180ha/445 acres on the west bank of the River Cher. They produce one of the most distinctive white wines of the Loire region: very dry, crisp without being sharp, with a fairly high alcohol content, it is at its best during the first two years.

ADDRESSES

STAY

⊜⊜ **Chambre d'hôte Villemenard** – *Vignoux-sur-Barangeon, 18500 Mehun-sur-Yèvre. 6km/4mi N of Méhun. Take the D 79 towards Vouzeron.* ✆*02 48 51 53 40/06 72 79 79 37. www.villemenard.com. 5 rooms.* The surrounding lakes, river and park add to the charm of this imposing 19C property. Spacious and comfortable rooms. Two gîtes.

ⵙ/ EAT

⊜⊜ **Le Modinum** – *1 rue Fernand Baudry.* ✆*02 48 57 38 52. Closed Mon.* The old Forum restaurant refurbished from Mar 2007. A good choice of reasonably priced dishes in pleasant surroundings.

🛒 SHOPPING

Magasin d'usine Pillivuyt – *Allée de la Manufacture.* ✆*02 48 67 31 63. www.pillivuyt.fr. Open Mon–Sat, 10am–noon and 2pm–6pm. Closed public hols and August.* This factory outlet sells white and coloured porcelain sets and kitchen items.

Domaine des Bruniers – *Rte de Lury - 18120 Quincy.* ✆*02 48 51 34 10. Open by prior arrangement.* Expressive and intense white wines produced on a plateau alongside the River Cher, sold under the Quincy appellation.

Domaine Bernard Aujard – *2 r. du Bas-Bourg. 4km/2.4mi outside of Reuilly 18120 Lazenay.* ✆*02 48 51 73 69.* Part of the Reuilly appellation. The estate's most renowned product is a fruity rosé.

Château de Valençay★★★

Valençay is geographically part of the Berry region, but the château can be classed with others of its kind that grace the Loire Valley, by virtue of the time of its construction as well as its enormous size.It resembles the Château de Chambord which was constructed a few years previously.

A BIT OF HISTORY

A financier's château

Valençay was built c 1540 by Jacques d'Estampes, the owner of the castle then existing. He had married the daughter of a financier, who brought him a large dowry, and he wanted a residence worthy of his new fortune. The 12C castle was demolished and in its place rose the present sumptuous building.

Finance has often been involved in the history of Valençay; among its owners were several Farmers-General and even the famous **John Law**, whose dizzy banking career was an early and instructive example of inflationary practices. **Charles-Maurice de Talleyrand-Périgord**, who had begun his career under Louis XVI as bishop of Autun, was foreign minister when he bought Valençay in 1803 at the request of Napoleon, who was seeking a place to receive important foreign visitors. Talleyrand managed his career so skilfully that he did not finally retire until 1834.

Michelin Map: 323: F-4

Info: 2, Avenue de la Résistance. ℘02 54 00 04 42. www.pays-de-valencay.fr

Location: 42km/26km north of Châteauroux.

Don't Miss: A tour inside the castle and a wander around the car museum.

CHÂTEAU

Open Jul–Aug, 9.30am–7pm; May and Sept, 10am–6pm; Jun 9.30–6.30pm; Mar 28–Apr 30 10.30am–6pm; Oct–Nov 8, 10.30–5.30pm. ⊚*9€ for admission to château and grounds.* ℘*02 54 00 15 74. www.chateau-valencay.com.*

The entrance pavilion is a huge building, designed like a keep only for show not defence, with many windows, harmless turrets and fancy machicolations. The steep roof is pierced with high dormer windows and surmounted by monumental chimneys.

Such architecture is also found in the Renaissance châteaux of the Loire Valley, but here we see the first signs of the Classical style: superimposed pilasters with Doric, Ionic and Corinthian capitals. The Classical style is even more evident in the huge corner towers: domes take the place of the pepper-pot roofs which were the rule on the banks of the Loire in the 16C.

Château de Valençay

B. Kaufmann/MICHELIN

Bedroom of Princess Bénévent

A. Cassaigne/MICHELIN

the great gallery and the great staircase. Something of the spirit of the festivities organised by Talleyrand and his master chef, Marie-Antoine de Carème, still lingers in the great dining room and the kitchens.

Park
Black swans, ducks and peacocks strut freely in the formal gardens near the château. Under the great trees in the park, deer, llamas, camels and kangaroos roam in vast enclosures.

Musée de l'Automobile du Centre
🕐♿ *Open Jul–Aug, 10.30am–12.30pm and 1.30–7pm; Jun 10.30am–12.30pm and 2–6.30pm; late Mar–May and Sept–early Nov, 10.30am–12.30pm and 2–6pm.* ✆*5.50€ (Combined ticket with the Château 12.50€).* ☎*02 54 00 07 74. musee.automobile.de.valencay@ wanadoo.fr*

The car museum, contains the collection of the Guignard brothers, the grandsons of a coachbuilder from Vatan (Indre). There are over 60 vintage cars dating from 1898, perfectly maintained in working order, including the 1908 Renault limousine used by Presidents Poincaré and Millerand; there are also road documents from the early days of motoring, old Michelin maps and guides from before 1914.

West wing
The west wing was added in the 17C and altered in the 18C. At roof level the mansard windows alternate with bulls' eyes (round apertures).

The tour of the ground floor includes the great Louis XVI vestibule; the gallery devoted to the Talleyrand-Périgord family; the Grand Salon and the Blue Salon which contain many works of art and pieces of Empire furniture, including the so-called Congress of Vienna table.

On the first floor, the bedroom of Prince Talleyrand is followed by the room occupied by Ferdinand, the future king of Spain; the apartments of the duke of Dino and those of Madame de Bénévent;

ADDRESSES

🍴 EAT

🍽 **Le Lion d'Or** – *14 pl. de la Halle.* ☎*02 54 00 00 87. Closed Jan–Feb, Sun evening and Mon.* This former coaching inn is delightfully old-fashioned and ideally located across from the covered market. The dining room, decorated with woodwork in the style of the 1930s, is charming and in the summer the shaded terrace is a nice place to eat.

🍽🍽 **Auberge St-Fiacre** – *36600 Veuil. - 6km/3.6mi S of Valencay. Take the D 15, then a side road.* ☎*02 54 40 32 78. Closed Jan 6–27, Sept 1–14, Sun and Mon except*

public hols. This low 17C building in the middle of a flowery village has set up its terrace by a stream, beneath several horse chestnut trees. In chilly weather, the warmth of the country-style hearth and the dining room with its imposing beams is most hospitable.

🏃 LEISURE ACTIVITIES
Sound and Light Show – This nightly show, based around the theme of Capitaine Fracasse, a swashbuckling novel by Théophile Gautier, takes place August 1, 3, 4, 5, 8, 10, 12, 14, 15, 17 & 19 at 10pm. ✆*15€. Reservations at the tourist office* ☎*02 54 00 04 42.*

Vierzon
and Champagne Berrichonne

Vierzon came to be in 1937, as four local administrative districts were joined (Vierzon-Ville, Village, Bourneuf, Forges). Vierzon is the gateway between the Champagne Berrichonne region and Sologne (whose forests begin just northwest of town). The town also has a strategic location at the confluence of the River Yèvre and River Cher, the intersection of major roads, and the railway junction for the Paris-Toulouse and Nantes-Lyon lines.

▶ **Population:** 38,147
⚲ **Michelin Map:** 323: I-3
⊞ **Info:** 11, rue de la Société Française. ✆02 48 53 06 14. www.officedetourismede vierzon.com.
▷ **Location:** 39km/24mi northwest of Bourges and 58km/36mi northeast of Châteauroux.
🧒 **Kids:** The Maison de l'Eau and Hameau des Automates in Neuvy-sur-Barangeon.
🕑 **Timing:** Allow half a day to explore the Champagne-Berrichonne.

A BIT OF HISTORY

Industrial heritage – The Comte d'Artois, brother of Louis XVI opened a forge in Vierzon in 1779, and in no time a number of industries began work, in particular ceramics and later, mechanical construction. The first porcelain manufactory went into operation in 1816. At the turn of the 20C, there were a dozen such enterprises in town, making it second only to Limoges.

The second field of production began in the mid-19C with the establishment of the Société Française de Matériel Agricole" (making farm machinery, today the company is called La Case-Poclain). The first mobile threshing machine in France was made there. This period is recalled by the iron architecture of the Grand Magasin de la Société Française, and by the presence of the canal, created in 1835 to link Vierzon to Montluçon. No traffic troubles its waters today, but strollers enjoy walks beneath the poplars on its banks.

OLD TOWN

This pedestrian area has been artfully developed around the winding streets and old, half-timbered houses up against a slope watched over by a Gothic **belfry**, formerly the gate to the city.

Église Notre-Dame

🕑Open 9am–7pm.
This church, built in the 12C, enlarged and renovated in the 15C, is fronted by a belfry-porch and a basket-handled arch above the doorway. Inside, admire the restored barrel-vaulting and the Renaissance windows representing the Crucifixion (south wall of the chapel of Ste-Perpétue). In the transept, a painting by Jean Boucher depicts John the Baptist.

Square Lucien-Beaufrère

🖙Guided tour available by prior arrangement, Hugues Flamment: ✆02 48 53 09 32. h.flamment@tourisme -paysdevierzon.fr.
This garden, designed in 1929 in the Art Deco style, replaced an abbey whose remaining buildings now house the town hall offices. At the entrance, the 1935 **Auditorium wash-house** by Eugène Karcher is decorated with enamelled tiles; dating from the same period, the monument to fallen heroes is embellished with low-relief sculptures representing the trades practised in Vierzon. From the banks of the Yèvre there is a pretty view over the old town.

EXCURSION
Neuvy-sur-Barangeon
19km/11.8mi NW along the D 926.

Maison de l'Eau
🕑Open Jul–Aug, 10am–noon and 2–6pm (last entrance 1hr before closing); Jun and Sept, daily except Tue, 2–6pm;

12C frescoes depicting Last Supper, Église Saint-Aignan, Brinay

A. Cassaigne/MICHELIN

Apr–May and Oct, Sat–Sun and public hols, 2–6pm. ⇔4€ *(5–14 years old: 2.50€).* ℘*02 48 51 66 65.*

👥This 16C watermill, standing on the edge of a lake, presents the story of "water" through the seasons (animated scenes and audio guides): from spring rain falling on the Auvergne to frozen waterfalls in the Alps. There is also a section devoted to Neuvy and local millers and another one to the fauna and flora of the Sologne lakes.

Musée d'Histoire Militaire, Historimage
Along the road to Bourges, within the Fédération Maginot complex.
🕐*Open Mar–Oct, daily except Mon and Tue, 2–6pm.* ⇔6€. ℘*02 48 52 64 00.*
This museum, which illustrates the uniforms and equipment of French and foreign soldiers from the First World War to the present, stages an amazing show entitled "Le Carrousel de la Paix" involving many automata and special effects.

Le Hameau des Automates★
Opposite Historimage, along the D 944. Open daily Jul–Aug, 2.30–7pm; Apr–Jun and Sept–Nov 7, Tue–Sun, Public Holidays and French School Holidays, 2.30–7pm. ⇔*11€(children aged 5–12: 8€; under 5 years old: no charge).* ℘*02 48 51 63 00. .*

👥Two separate shows present the technical and artistic aspects of automata and the poetic charm of doves and pigeons. There are also reconstructions of Renaissance scenes and a video presentation illustrating the making of automata.

🚗 DRIVING TOUR

CHAMPAGNE BERRICHONNE
75km/46.5mi – allow 2hr.

▷ *Leave Vierzon SE along the D 27 towards Quincy.*

Brinay
This village is tranquil on the banks of the Cher upstream from Vierzon. The Romanesque church is worth visiting for its 12C **frescoes**★.

▷ *Take the D 18E towards Méreau.*

Massay
The **church**, rebuilt between the 14C and the 16C, was once part of a Benedictine abbey founded in the 8C.
The vestiges of the abbey include the chapter-house, parts of the dormitory (13C), cellars (12C) and the tithe barns. The 12C abbot's chapel (also known as St-Loup) is well preserved; it stood in the centre of the cloisters. The abbot's lodging dates from the 17C.

▷ *Leave SW, towards Châteauroux.*

Vatan
Église St-Laurian
This restored church has retained a 16C chancel with windows from the same period, recounting the life of the saint. There are some interesting 8C paintings and sculpted door leaves dated 1498.

Musée du Cirque
🕐*open daily except Mon, 10am–noon and 2–6pm; Tue, 2–6pm;* 🕐*closed 1 Jan, 1 May, 1 Nov and 25 Dec;* ⇔*3.80€ (child: 1.50€).* ℘*02 54 49 77 78. www.musee-du-cirque.com.*

This museum displays an interesting collection of posters, accessories, models and costumes connected with the circus world.

▶ *Take the D 922, N of town.*

St-Outrille

This village has an interesting **collegiate church**. Romanesque and Gothic styles are both present: the nave is 15C, the chancel, side chapels (except one) and the transept from the 12C. The east end is surmounted by a curious twisted bell-tower covered with shingles. The western doorway dates from the 14C.

Graçay

This medieval town, separated from St-Outrille by the River Fouzon, has kept its ramparts and a few old houses. The interesting **Musée de la Photo** retraces the history of photography. ⏲*Open Jun–Sept, daily except Mon, 10am–noon and 3–6pm; rest of the year, Sat–Sun and public hols, 10am–noon and 3–6pm and by prior arrangement.* ⏲*Closed Jan and 25 Dec.* ∞*3€.* 𝒫*02 48 51 41 80. www. museephoto.com.*

ADDRESSES

🛏 STAY

⊜⊜ **Hôtel Le Chalet de la Forêt** – *143 av. Édouard-Vaillant.* 𝒫*02 48 75 35 84. chalet-foret@wanadoo.fr. Closed Jan 8–28, Sun eve Nov 16–Feb. 11 rooms.* This hotel at the northern gate of Vierzon is a pleasant stopover. The pool's terrace is a fine place to relax; the rooms are comfortable. Meals are concocted from fresh ingredients bought from local growers. Friendly reception.

⊜⊜ **Arche Hôtel** – *13 rue du 11 Nov 1918.* 𝒫*02 48 71 93 10. www.arche-hotel.fr. Closed Sun except Jun 15– Sep 15. 40 rooms.* The modern glass façade of this hotel just a minute from the arches of the old bridge across the Yèvre playfully catches the sun. Practical, soundproofed rooms. Straightforward meals with an accent on salads and grilled fare served in a contemporary dining room.

▶ *Leave the village E on the D 68.*

Nohant-en-Graçay

Inside the charming **Église St-Martin** *(Jun–Sep: 10am–6pm; the rest of the year: by appointment at the town hall,* 𝒫*02 48 51 40 65)*, the columns supporting the vaulting of the central tower bear remarkable 12C capitals. The unusual bell-tower with its spiral spire is similar to the one in St-Outrille.

▶ *Leave Nohant travelling N along the D 164.*

Genouilly

At the far end of town stands the **Église St-Symphorien**. This 12C edifice, with a handsome porch, has stained-glass windows made in 1536. The chancel is covered by a 13C vault, exceptional in Berry because it is in the *angevin* style typical of the region of Anjou. In the southern chapel, the mausoleum of the La Châtre family is from the turn of the 16C and 17C.

▶ *Return to Vierzon on the D19 and D90.*

🍴 EAT

⊜⊜ **Victor-Hugo** – *5 r. Victor-Hugo.* 𝒫*02 48 75 43 34. Closed Sun.* This restaurant in the centre of town owes its reputation to the irreproachable quality of the food. Both dining rooms have a subdued ambience. In fine weather, it is nicer to sit outside in the courtyard.

⊜⊜⊜ **Le Relais de Vouzeron** – *2 pl. de l'Église, 18330 Vouzeron. 15km/9mi NE of Vierzon via the D 926 and D 104.* 𝒫*02 48 51 61 38.* Situated in a tranquil village in the heart of the forest, this old post house is quite charming. The flowery façade hints of the intimate parlour, inviting dining room and lovely bedrooms to come. Distinctive cuisine.

SANCERROIS *and Around*

The Sancerrois occupies the northern half of the Cher département in the Centre Region, which we have combined in this guide with the eastern Sologne and the Pays Fort. The Sologne stretches from the Loire in the west and is characterised by woods and marshes much loved by hunters.
The Pays Fort just to the north of Vierzon is characterised by its marl and clay soils, sloping towards the Sologne, whereas the vine-covered, chalky slopes of the Sancerrois rise above the river banks. This once-forested landscape has been remodelled by man as bocage (wooded farmland) and is host to some of France's finest wines.

🚗 DRIVING TOUR

1 WINES OF THE CENTRAL LOIRE

Starting at Sancerre this route takes you around the town and then across the Loire to the vineyards that produce the world famous Pouilly wines. Re-crossing the Loire and heading west, the route eventually takes you to Bourges and then onto Mehun-sur-Yèvre before finally reaching the AOC Reuilly vineyards between Issoudun and Vierzon.

Sancerre★

📖 *See Sancerre*
(following pages)
Sancerre, perched above a sea of vineyards, takes in the Loire Valley and Nivernais towards the east, and Berry to the west. The **panorama**★★ from the esplanade of porte César (318m) affords a view of the little northern Sancerre villages dotting the route des Vignobles (Wine Route) from St-Satur to St-Gemmes (don't miss the *circuit* that goes down to St-Satur).
With regard to the wine, the surest bets in **AOC Sancerre** are the 🍷**Domaines Vacheron** and **Henri Bourgeois**, fami-

lies which have had roots here since time immemorial. Near the church, the restored Maison Farnault (14C) houses the **Maison des Sancerre** *(3 r. du Méridien, 18100 Sancerre;* 🕐 *open Jun–Sept 10am–7pm; Apr–May and Oct–mid-Nov 10am–6pm;* 📞*02 48 54 11 35; www. maison-des-sancerre.com).*
This is a wonderful place to inform yourself about wines in general and particularly the Sancerre region via interactive presentations, videos and a relief model.
Particularly interesting are interviews with men and women of the profession, which show the human side of the wine industry. This is also a good spot to pick up information about the various cellars and estates in the region. The visit concludes with a tasting.

▷ *Leave Sancerre heading W on D 7, then turn right on D 923.*

At the crossroads, don't miss the remarkable **view**★★ of Sancerre, the vineyards, St-Satur and the Loire Valley.
The road goes through a sea of grape vines, then winds down the high chalky-clay hills known as *terres blanches* (white ground) where the vineyards produce full-bodied wines.

▷ *Turn right towards Chavignol*

The road goes through **Chavignol** which produces the famous *crottin* – a goat's cheese that can be soft, hard or extra mature, and goes wonderfully with Sancerre.

Vineyards of Sancerre in autumn

©Janet Carr/iStockphoto.com

▶ *Continue on D 183 to St-Satur, then cross the Loire and turn right onto D 553.*

The road runs into the Appellation Pouilly-sur-Loire area, which includes 50ha of Chasselais which produce the actual **Appellation Pouilly-sur-Loire**, and 950ha of Sauvignon which produce the famous Pouilly-Fumé.

The ✦**Château de Tracy** (15C-16C) is not open to visitors, but you can taste and purchase wines on the estate and catch a glimpse of the magnificent grounds with cedar trees standing among the vine stocks and a view stretching all the way to Sancerre.

▶ *At Bois-Gibault, take a right onto D 243 towards Les Loges. Watch for the fork to the left towards Les Loges under the railway bridge.*

Les Loges is a winegrowing hamlet which owes its name to the *loges de vigne*, small buildings used as shelters in the vineyards. Note the typical 19C winemakers' houses with vaulted cellars beneath the staircase.

Pouilly-sur-Loire

To get off to a good start in your exploration of Central Loire wines, go to the ✦**Caves de Pouilly-sur-Loire**.

The **Pavillon du milieu de Loire** *(audioguides available;* 🕐 *open Jul–Aug 10am–12.30pm & 2–7pm; Apr–Jun Wed–Mon 10am–12.30pm & 2–6pm; Sept–Oct Wed–Mon 10am–12.30pm & 2–5.30pm; Christmas holidays Wed–Mon 2–5.30pm;* 🕐 *closed Jan–Mar, Dec 25;* 🎫*4.50€;* ♿ ☎*03 86 39 54 54; www. pavillon-pouilly.com),* on the banks of the river, has displays of valley wildlife

Vineyards in Sainte-Gemme-en-Sancerrois

©World Pictures/Photoshot

and a room devoted to wine-growing. It also has information about the **reserve naturelle du Val-de-Loire** (nature preserve) and brochures about the ▮**sentiers du Milieu de Loire**, two of which go through vineyards overlooking the Loire.

▷ *Cross the bridge over the Loire and take D 59. Turn right (towards Sancerre) onto D 10 at Vinon.*

After about 2km, turn left and head up the tiny steep road marked "route des Vignobles" which affords a magnificent **view**★ of the Sancerre hills. At the D 955, stop in **Bué** for a tasting at ▯**Domaine Pinard**.

▷ *Turn left onto D 955 toward Aix-D'Angillon, then right onto D 22. Stop in La Borne if you are interested in its world-famous ceramics. Leave La Borne heading SW on D 46.*

Morogues

The vineyards covering the slopes from Morogues to Menetou – the pride and joy of Berry viticulture – were among the most highly valued in France in the days of Jacques Coeur. Today they cover more than 400ha and produce fresh and spicy white wines, supple and fragrant reds, and fruity rosés. The **Château de Maupas** produces a good red Menetou,

while the **Château de Menetou-Salon** has an antique car collection in the outbuildings.

▷ *To reach Bourges, leave Menetou on the D 59 towards Saint-Martin-d'Auxigny.*

Bourges★★★
♿ *See Bourges section.*

▷ *Take N 76 out of Bourges towards the Quincy-Reuilly region.*

Mehun-sur-Yèvre★
♿ *See Bourges section*

Quincy
AOC Quincy, stretching between Quincy and Brinay, boasts 204ha planted in Sauvignon grapes which produce a dry, subtle and elegant white wine which is usually at its best within two or three years. During the last weekend in August, Quincy hosts the Fêtes de l'Océan celebrating the marriage of seafood and wine.

Brinay
The little **church** contains an interesting series of 12C **frescoes**★, including a rare calendar of each month's labours (for September – a man trampling grapes in a large vat), and a representation of the Wedding at Cana alluding to the theme of wine.

▷ *In Brinay, take a left onto D 18^{E} (route du Vignoble) towards Méreau. In Méreau, take a left onto D 918 in the direction of Lucy-sur-Arnon and Reuilly.*

Reuilly
The **AOC Reuilly** vineyards, spread over both sides of the Arnon, cover 167ha producing remarkable dry and fruity white Sauvignon wines, as well as excellent quality rosés and reds from Pinot Gris and Pinot Noir. And why not visit the little **Musée de la Vigne et du Vin de Reuilly** *(5, r. Rabelais; ◷open mid-May–mid-Oct Tue–Sun 10am–noon & 3–7pm, open Fri 9am; mid-Oct–mid-May Tue–Sun 10am–noon & 2–6pm, open Fri 9am; ☎02 54 49 24 94; www.ot-reuilly.fr)* devoted to winemaking materials.

Aubigny-sur-Nère★

and around

Situated on the borders of the Berry and the Sologne, Aubigny is a small yet bustling town on the banks of the River Nère, which flows partly underground here.

▶ **Population:** 5 775
◉ **Michelin Map:** 323: K-2
▤ **Info:** 1, rue de l'église BP 87 F-18700 Aubigny-sur-Nère. ℘02 48 58 40 20. www.aubigny.org.
◗ **Location:** 46km/28.75mi N of Bourges via the D940
☺ **Don't Miss:** A unique way of discovering the area is by cycle-rail (cyclodraisines) along old railway tracks. A fun activity for all the family!

A BIT OF HISTORY

City of the Stuarts – In 1423 **Charles VII** gave Aubigny to a Scotsman, John Stuart, his ally against the English. He was succeeded by Béraud Stuart and then by Robert Stuart, known as the Marshal of Aubigny, who fought in Italy under François I.

Craftsmen from Scotland settled here, either working as weavers - using white wool from the Sologne - or as glassmakers.

TOWN

Ramparts

The line of the old town wall, built originally by Philippe-Auguste, is marked by the streets enclosing the town centre and two round towers overlooking the mall.

Old Houses★

A number of half-timbered houses have survived from the early 16C. Several of these are along rue du Prieuré and its continuation, rue des Dames, two charming streets hung with shop signs from the town hall to the church, as well as in rue du Charbon and place Adrien-Arnoux. No 10 rue du Pont-Aux-Foulons is the only house to have survived the fire of 1512. In rue du Bourg-Coutant stands the **Maison du Bailli**★ with its carved beams, and almost opposite, at the corner of rue de l'Église, the pretty **Maison François I.**

Ancien Château des Stuarts

rue du Château

This 16C building was erected by Robert Stuart and modified by Louise de Keroualle, duchess of Portsmouth; it now serves as Aubigny's town hall. In the charming irregular courtyard, note the mullioned windows and round or polygonal turreted staircases.

EXCURSIONS

Château de Blancafort★

9km/5.6mi NE along the D 30.
☜◖*Guided tour (45min), Jun-Sep, 10am-7pm; Apr-May and Oct, daily except Tue, 10am-noon and 2-6.30pm.*

Witchcraft in the Berry Region

Ethnologists have an explanation for the prevalence of witchery and the supernatural in the Berry. They say that the flat landscape, often swathed in mist, and solitary trees, burned by lightning or twisted by the wind, create dark and menacing silhouettes in the lonely countryside.

Ask one of the Compagnons de Vin de Bué, a local wine-growers' association, and you may get a different answer. The members call themselves "birettes" and dress in appropriate costumes for festive occasions. A local "birette d'honneur" (who also works as a sommelier in a fine restaurant) has a word of advice: it is best to seek out spirits in the small hours, as in the daylight you can see right through them.

Château de la Verrerie

©David Hughes/Fotolia.com

This Witchcraft Museum is housed in a 19C barn at La Jonchère, in the north of the Berry, a region known for its strong connections with sorcery. Around 20 scenes, some involving video animation and special effects (courtesy of the resident sorceress), and many explanatory panels delve into the mysterious world of superstition, myth and legend.

Château de la Verrerie★

11km/7mi SE along the D 89. ⏰Open every day exc. Tue. Guided tour 45min, (11am, noon, 2pm, 3pm, 4pm and 5pm. Last entrance 1hr before closing), Daily Jul–Aug; Mar 15–Jun 30 and Sept–Easter, Sat, Sun and Public Hols. ⏰10€. ☎02 48 81 51 60. www.chateaux-france.com/verrerie.fr

The château standing in an isolated but beautiful **setting**★ near the Forêt d'Ivoy is thought to have inspired Alain-Fournier for one of the episodes in his famous novel *Le Grand Meaulnes*.

The château originally consisted of four buildings around a courtyard; the oldest part was built by Charles VII who gave it to John Stuart at the same time as Aubigny-sur-Nère. In 1672 the château reverted to the crown and given it to the Duchess of Portsmouth, the favourite mistress of Charles II of England.

The graceful **Renaissance gallery**★ was erected by Robert Stuart in 1525. The 19C wing added behind the Renaissance gallery contains some fine furniture from the Renaissance to the Louis XVI period, including four remarkable 15C alabaster **weeping figures**★ from the tomb of Jean de Berry.

Independent visit of the park and gardens ⏰9.10€. ☎02 48 58 60 56. www.chateaublancafort.com.

The visit to this 15C red brick château includes the library, with its Regency panelling, and the dining room, with its walls covered in painted, gilded and embossed Flemish leather. After seeing the interior, enjoy a pleasant walk through the park with its attractive French-style flower beds, or along the woodland paths beside the river.

Musée de la Sorcellerie

From Blancafort, take the D 8 towards Vailly-sur-Sauldre. ⏰Open Apr 2 –Nov 5, Jul–Aug 10am-7pm. Apl–May and Sept–Oct 10am–6pm. ⏰6.20€ (4-13, 4.70€) ☎02 48 73 86 11. www.musee-sorcellerie.fr.

ADDRESSES

🏠 STAY

💬💬 **Le Domaine des Givrys** – *18410 Clémont - 3 km/1.8mi SE of Clémont along the D 79 towards Ste-Montaine then 1.3km/1mi along a forest track to the left.* ☎02 48 58 80 74 🛏 *5 rooms.*

This typical Sologne farmhouse is a haven of peace and quiet in the middle of a forest bordered by a river and ponds (trout and black bass fishing). The rooms are spotlessly clean, with a mixture of country-style and modern furnishings. In the winter, enjoy dinner by the fire.

💬💬 **Les Aulnains** – *Rte Presly - 18380 La Chapelle-d'Angillon. 14km/8mi S of Aubigny along the D 940.* ☎02 48 73 40 09. *Closed in Mar.* 🛏 *2 rooms.* This 18C-19C manor house typical of the Sologne region is the perfect base for nature enthusiasts. Spacious rooms and a cosy, old-fashioned dining room. Animals roaming the grounds and plentiful fish in the nearby river and lakes.

Hôtel La Solognote – *34, Grande Rue,18410 Brinon-sur-Sauldre.* ℘*02 48 58 50 29 lasolognote@wanadoo.fr. Closed 6-23 Mar, 14-30 Apl. Tue, Wed and Thurs. am.* **P** *12 rooms.* Check into one of the neat and tidy bedrooms in this typically Sologne hotel, then reflect on your day's adventures over a drink by the cosy fireplace or over dinner in the renowned restaurant.

ⵜ EAT

Les Rives de l'Oizenotte – *Étang de Nohant, 18700 Oizon. 6km/3.6mi E of Aubigny along the D 923.* ℘*02 48 58 06 20 - oizenotte.g@infonie.fr. Closed Feb school hols, Nov half-term, Christmas, Mon eve, Tue and Wed - reserv. required.* This small lakeside restaurant serves simple, unpretentious and reasonably priced cuisine. Eat in the fishing-themed dining room or on the wood-floored terrace overlooking the water.

Le Lion d'Or – *1, Place de l'Église, 41300 Pierrefitte-sur-Sauldre. 21km/13mi W of Aubigny along the D 13.* ℘*02 54 88 62 14. Closed 3-19 Jan, 30 Aug-24 Sep, Wed eve and Thu eve in winter, Mon and Tue except for hols.* This charming traditional house stands opposite the church in the centre of the village. The exposed beams and dark wood in the dining room provide additional character, as does the small, flower-decked garden. Fixed-price menus featuring local specialities.

🏃 LEISURE ACTIVITIES

Les Cyclodraisines d'Aubigny (Cycle-railing) – *Rte de Clémont, lieu-dit "Gorgeot".* ℘*02 48 81 50 07 (weekdays) or 02 48 58 35 81 (weekends). Open 1 May-20 Sep, Sat-Sun and public hols, 9am-7pm. Closed 21 Sep-30 Apr. 5€/hr; 15€/half day; 25€/full day.* Enjoy day out cycle-railing through the countryside along old railway lines.

Nançay

This village in the Sologne region is home to many artists' studios, as well as one of Europe's most modern astronomical observatories.

VILLAGE
Grenier de Villâtre

18330 Nançay .
🕐*Open mid-Mar to mid-Dec, Sat–Sun and public hols, 10am–12.30pm and 2–7pm, Mon–Fri by prior arrangement (2 weeks in advance). 5€.* ℘*02 48 51 80 22. www.capazza-galerie.com.*
Established in the nicely restored stables of the château, the Galerie Capazza exhibits sculptures, pottery, drawing etc created by 65 different artists.
One of the rooms, the **Musée Imaginaire du Grand Meaulnes**, is full of memories of Alain-Fournier, evoked by the family memorabilia on display: photographs, models and small furnishings.

▸ **Population:** 784
🚗 **Michelin Map:** 323: J-2
Info: 5 rue du château. ℘02 48 51 80 31, or ℘02 48 51 11 41.
▸ **Location:** 15km/9.5mi northeast of Vierzon.
Kids: Planetarium; Ciel Ouvert en Sologne.

Station de Radioastronomie

2km/1.2mi north along the D 29 towards Souesmes. 🕐*Open daily Feb–Nov, guided tour (1hr 15min), weekends pub hols and school hols: 10.15am–12.30pm and 12.30–6.40pm; weekdays, 9am–12.15pm and 12.15–5.30pm. 8€. (child no charge)* ℘*02 48 51 18 16. www.cielouvert.obs-nancay.fr.*
Created in 1953 by the École Normale Supérieure, the station came under the authority of the Paris Observatory in 1956. The main field of study involves radio waves from around the universe, which provide useful information on the solar system and distant galaxies.

Radio telescope

S. Sauvignier/MICHELIN

👥 Ciel Ouvert en Sologne

Route de Souesmes (D29) ♿🕐*Open daily Feb–Nov, weekends pub hols and school hols: 10.15am–12.30pm and 12.30–6.40pm; weekdays, 9am–12.15pm and 12.15–5.30pm; Permanent and temporary exhibitions (length of visit:*

1hr). 👁*5€ (child: 3€) visit includes exhibition and Planetarium.* ☎*02 48 51 18 16. www.cielouvert.obs-nancay.fr.* Protected from interference by a Faraday cage, this building, dedicated to the stars, houses all the equipment necessary for the would-be astronomer. to make numerous experiments.

👥 Planetarium

Route de Souesmes (D29) ♿🕐*Open daily Feb–Nov Film (50min), week-days: shows at 9.30, 10.30am, 2.30pm and,3.30pm; Weekends: 10.30am,2.30pm, 3.30pm & 5.30pm .* 👁*5€ for planetarium and exhibitions (child: 3€).* ☎*02 48 51 18 16. www.cielouvert.obs-nancay.fr.* The planetarium is the ideal place to learn all about the stars and their location in our universe.

Sancerre★

High above the banks of the River Loire, Sancerre roosts above St-Satur and St-Thibault. From this vantage point★, a wide panorama embraces the river and the Nivernais to the east, and Berry to the west. This little city, reigning over a land of trim vineyards and frisky goats, is renowned for its delicious white wine, flinty in flavour, and its little round cheeses, especially those from Chavignol. This creamy and savoury goat's cheese is so well-loved in France, that no one is put off in the slightest by its amusing name, *Crottin* (roughly translated as something you'd rather not step on). The steep streets of the town are enticing for their tempting food shops, restaurants and wine merchants.

A BIT OF HISTORY
A strategic location

Sancerre, already well-known in Roman times as the site of an *oppidum*, has long stood watch over the Loire. It may have been the 9C residence of Robert le Fort, an early member of the Capetian

- ▶ **Population**: 1789.
- 🚲 **Michelin Map**: 323: M, N-3.
- 🏛 **Info**: Nouvelle Place. ☎02 48 54 08 21.
- 📍 **Location**: 46km/28.7mi NE of Bourges via D955. For a wonderful view of the surrounding area, head for the Esplanade de la Porte César.
- 🕐 **Timing**: Allow a full day to explore the Sancerrois region.
- 👁 **Don't Miss**: The village's renowned vineyards.

dynasty. Later, the city played an important role in the Hundred Years War, as the gateway to Berry, placed between the Burgundians and the English. Charles VII, the so-called king of Bourges, assembled 20 000 warriors there, personally commanding them for a time.

Sancerre became a stronghold of Protestantism, withstanding the assault of royal forces. The Treaty of St-Germain (1570) and the St Bartholomew's Day Massacre (1572) had no effect on those who held to their reformed views of religion, and refused to give in. Thus, on 3 January 1573, the Maréchal de La Châtre, accompanied by 7 000 men, laid siege to Sancerre.

After an intense artillery preparation, an assault took place on three fronts, but the local resistance was strong. Capitulation came after seven long months of struggle. The population's surrender was accepted with honour, and they were allowed the freedom of their religion.

Sancerre wine

"Wine," wrote Balzac in 1844 in *La Muse du Département*, "is the main industry and the most important trading item of this land, which produces many generous vintages of rich bouquet, so similar to those of Burgundy that an untrained Parisian palate cannot taste the difference. Sancerre wines are therefore popular in Parisian cabarets where they flow steadily, which is a good thing, as they cannot be kept more than seven or eight years."

Vineyards are planted on every hill where the sun shines. The Sancerre label is only applied to white Sauvignon wines, and to red and rosé wines made from the Pinot grape.

OLD TOWN

Visitors will enjoy strolling in the old neighbourhoods, where many of the interesting houses and vestiges are marked with informative signs. There are many architectural details to attract the eye; around the renovated Nouvelle Place, many shops sell local crafts and pottery.

Esplanade de la Porte César★★

NE edge of town - see map.
From this terrace, there is a great **view★★** over the vineyards, St-Satur and the viaduct, St-Thibault and the Val de Loire, and even farther afield to the Puisaye region of woods and lakes, between the Loire and the Loing, north-east of Sancerre.

Vineyards and hillside of Sancerre

Tours des Fiefs

Eastern edge of town - see map.
🕐*Open Daily 2pm–6pm.* 👛*1€ For further details, call* 📞*02 48 78 51 52.*
This 14C cylindrical keep is the only vestige of the château of the counts of Sancerre, a Huguenot citadel bitterly defended during the 1573 siege.
From the top, there is a wide **scenic view**★ of the Loire Valley and the hills of Sancerre.

Belfry

pl de Beffroi.
This old belfry, dating from 1509, serves the church of Notre-Dame de Sancerre.

🚗 DRIVING TOURS

1 LE SANCERROIS★

77km/48mi round-trip – allow 6hr

▷ *Leave Sancerre travelling SW on the D 955 towards Bourges. Shortly thereafter, turn right on the D 923.*

At the intersection with the D 7, there is a splendid **view**★★ over Sancerre high atop its bluff, the vineyards, St-Satur and, beyond, the Loire Valley.

Chavignol

This lovely little wine-growers' village is nestled in a hollow with vineyards all around.
The name is synonymous with one of France's tastiest and most popular cheeses, **Crottin de Chavignol**.

▷ *Just outside the village, take a little road on the right which leads to the hamlet of Amigny.*

On the Sens-Beaujeu road, near the intersection with the D 85, there is a nice **view**★ of the village of Bué and the rolling countryside.

Château de Boucard

🕐*Open Apr–Sept, guided tour (40min, last tour 30min before closing), daily except Mon & Tue, 10am–noon and 2–6.30pm.* 👛*7€.* 📞*02 48 58 72 81.*
The castle, surrounded by a moat and well-kept outbuildings, was built between the 14C and the 16C. The furnished interior has several impressive chimneys and a chapel which was specially redesigned to allow the Princesse de la Trémoille to attend Mass without leaving her bedroom.

▷ *Continue along the D 74.*

Jars

Visitors to this charming town will notice the manor house with its round towers, the 15C-16C church in pink and white stone and the mill.
🕐*Open by prior arrangement with the town hall.* 🕐*Closed Wed and Sat afternoons and Sun.* 📞*02 48 58 70 15.*

▷ *Return to Le Noyer and drive SW along the D 55.*

Henrichemont

In the early 17C, Sully, minister to Henri IV, decided to create a refuge for his fellow Protestants. As he already owned a château in Chapelle-d'Angillon, he decided to build a town nearby, in a sandy, deserted place, which he called Henrichemont in honour of the king. Never completed, the design for the town includes eight streets like spokes of a wheel, converging on a central square. A few 17C houses with arched doorways and the old well with its decorative moulding are intact. (& *see La Borne, below*)

▶ *Leave Henrichemont travelling E on the D 22.*

La Borne

Berry is a good place for potters because of the rich clay soil; the abundant timber was an important factor in the past, when wood-burning kilns were the rule. Gallo-Roman earthenware household objects are on display in the Berry Museum (& *see BOURGES*).

Here in La Borne, visitors can see more recent items in the **Musée de la Poterie** (🕐*open Easter to early-Nov, Sat–Sun and school hols, 3–7pm; ⊜3€; ℘02 48 26 98 31*), established in an old chapel; or purchase local ceramics in the **exhibition-sales room** (🕐*open mid-Mar to Oct, Sat–Sun, public and school hols (zones B and C), 3–7pm; Nov to early-Jan, Sat–Sun, public and school hols (zones B and C), 2-6pm. ⊜No charge. ℘02 48 26 96 21*).

Musée Vassil Ivanoff

🕐&*Open May–Sept, daily except Tue, 2.30–6.30pm. ⊜2.50€. ℘02 48 26 96 24.*
This Bulgarian ceramic artist came to Paris in 1922 and discovered a book on the *Art of Pottery*. He became interested in learning new techniques and was soon installed at La Borne, in a small house which doubled as his workshop. He built his own kiln and set to work, producing some 3 000 pieces before his death in 1973.
The museum houses a generous collection of the artist's work: vases, pots, cups, engraved plaques, pieces with tubular structures, some of them resembling figurative or abstract sculptures. The red enamels known as bull's blood

are especially eye-catching. *His workshop can be seen on request.*

▶ *Leave La Borne SE on the D 46.*

Église de Morogues

This 13C Romanesque church, fronted by an octagonal belfry-porch in reddish stone has a wonderful wooden dais inside, which was originally in the Sainte-Chapelle in Bourges.

▶ *Leave Morogues W on the D 59.*

Château de Maupas

&🕐*Guided tour (30min) Daily Jul –Sept, 2–6pm, ⊜8€. ℘02 48 64 41 71. www.chateaudemaupas.com.*
Set in a forest, on the edge of a lake, the castle partly dates from the 13C. It was rebuilt in the 15C, then transformed in the 17C and 18C, when it fell into the hands of the Maupas family.
The furnishings are attractive, and pride of place is given to the **collection of plates**★ (880 pieces) dating from the 17C-19C.

▶ *Return to Morogues; take D 185 NE.*

The ridge road which goes to La Borne runs by the **Motte d'Humbligny** (alt 431m/1414ft), the highest point in the Sancerrois region.

▶ *Leave Humbligny NE on D 74.*

This is a lovely route along the Grande Sauldre Valley, as far as Neuilly-en-Sancerre, where D 22 goes back to Sancerre by way of the vineyards beyond Crézancy.

2 ALONG LATERAL CANAL, EAST OF PAYS FORT

60km/36mi round-trip – half a day

▶ *Leave Sancerre SW on D 955, then turn left on D 10 towards Baugy.*

Cross the vintners' village of Vinon, and go on to St-Bouize to reach the road which runs alongside the **Loire lateral canal**. The canal, which is parallel to the river, has many locks; since 1836 it has been navigable from Roanne to Briare.

St-Satur

This village was once called Château-Gordon, until the relics of the African martyr Satyrus were brought here and it was renamed St-Satur. The village is home to the **Église St-Guinefort**. The first church went up in the 12C, and was later completely destroyed by the English. A new abbey church was begun in 1362, but only the chancel and apse were finished.

St-Thibault

This river port was bustling with activity until the mid-19C.

Saint-Thibault quays along the Loire

M. Guillot/MICHELIN

▷ *Continue on D 955.*

Bannay

Tucked between the northern edge of the Charnes wood and the canal, this village in the vineyards has a curious church with two pepper-pot roofs.

▷ *Continue along D 955.*

Facing the road which leads to Cosne-sur-Loire, the 15C Château de Buranlure has a lovely natural setting; the road then follows the canal for about 5km/3mi as far as the lock in the Houards.

Léré

On the border of the region known as the Pays Fort and the Val de Loire, this hamlet was once fortified, as the remaining round towers and curving rue des Remparts show.

Collégiale St-Martin

Heavily restored after the 16C, this edifice has kept its Romanesque apse, adjoining a 15C chancel; above the Gothic doorway, note the tympanum where a few sculpted figures remain intact. Despite the damage, one can still recognise St Martin sharing his cloak. ⏱*Open Wed–Fri, 10am–noon and 2–5pm; Sat, 9am–noon.*

▶ *Leave Léré travelling SW on the D 47.*

Following the Judelle Valley as far as Savigny, the road goes through eastern **Pays Fort**, a verdant landscape of mead-ows and hedgerows. The D 54 takes you back to the vineyard south of the typical village of Ste-Gemme.

▶ *Return to Sancerre on the D 86 (to Sury-en-Vaux) and the D 57.*

ADDRESSES

🛏 STAY

🏕 **Camping S I René Foltzer** – *chemin des Godibolles. 18300 St. Satur. ℘02 48 54 04 67. 85 pitches. Reservations advised.* This leafy campsite on the banks of the Loire is a lovely place to camp on the grass. Games areas.

🏠 **Chambres d'hote La Floroine** - *Le Floroine - 18300 Ménétéol-sous-Sancerre ℘02 48 54 02 74. www.le-floroine.com. 5 rooms.* Simply but cheerfully furnished comfortable rooms in an attractive and friendly family-run restaurant-bar-hôtel at the water's edge

🏠🏠 **Chambres d'hote Le Moulin du Grand Senais** – *18300 Crézancy-en-Sancerre. 7km/4.2mi SW of Sancerre via the D 955 and D 22. ℘02 48 79 06 64. http://moulin-grandsenais.com.* In a small park in the heart of the vineyards, this pretty inn is set in an enchanting spot Traditional cuisine, games room and small swimming pool in the lovely garden.

🏠🏠 **Hôtel France** –*2 r.St-Martin. ℘02 48 54 00 52. 6 rooms.* A warm welcome awaits in this former 18C post house. Simple well kept bedrooms, a pleasant salon de thé (12 varieties to taste) and generous breakfasts.

🏠🏠🏠 **Hôtel de la Loire** – *2 Quai de la Loire. 18300 Saint Satur - France. ℘02 48 78 22 22. www.hotel-de-la-loire.com.* This pretty three-star hotel is located by the banks of the Loire 2km/1mi from Sancerre. Bedrooms – themed African, Indian, Coloniale etc – are spacious and comfortable. The George Simenon bedroom is where the renowned author stayed for a year while writing.

🍴 EAT

🍽🍽 **Auberge Joseph Mellot** – *16 Nouvelle Place - ℘02 48 54 20 53. www.joseph-mellot.fr/fr/auberge.htm. Closed Feb 26–Mar 11, Wed and every evening, exc Sat, out of season.* This authentic country inn is run by a venerable family of wine-growers who serves generous portions of local specialities.

🍽🍽🍽 **Côte des Monts Damnés** – *18300 Chavignol. 4km/2.4mi W of Sancerre on the D 183 - ℘02 48 54 01 72. restaurantcmd@wanadoo.fr. Closed Feb, 22–30 Jun and Mon. Reserv. required.* Enjoy an appetizing selection of dishes, either on the terrace or in the dining room of this little village restaurant.

🍽🍽🍽 **Le Laurier** – *29 r. du Commerce – 18300 St-Satur. 3km/1.8mi NE of Sancerre on the D 955. ℘02 48 54 17 20. www.ldf-berry.com. Closed 3 weeks in Mar, 3 weeks in Nov, Sun eve and Mon all year.* This former coaching inn has a splendid exterior and a charming interior with exposed beams, woodwork, antique furniture and copperware. Simple bedrooms.Traditional cuisine, .

🍽🍽🍽 **La Pomme d'Or** – *Pl. de la Mairie ℘02 48 54 13 30. Closed Feb 25–Mar 5, public hol in early-Nov, Tue and Wed eve. Reserv. Required.* This little neighbourhood restaurant has the atmosphere of a bistro.

🍽🍽🍽 **La Tour** – *31 Nouvelle-Place. ℘02 48 54 00 81. www.la-tour-sancerre.fr Closed 19 Dec–13 Jan.* The eponymous14C tower of this restaurant presides over the village square. There are two dining rooms: one, with a fireplace, is situated in the old section, the other, upstairs, has a panoramic view.

INDEX

INDEX

INDEX

INDEX

INDEX

⌂ STAY

⅋ EAT

MAPS AND PLANS

MAP LEGEND

	Sight	Seaside resort	Winter sports resort	Spa
Highly recommended ★★★		♨♨♨	✳✳✳	⚜⚜⚜
Recommended ★★		♨♨	✳✳	⚜⚜
Interesting ★		♨	✳	⚜

Additional symbols

?	Tourist information
══ ══	Motorway or other primary route
❶ ❶	Junction: complete, limited
⊏══⊐ ══	Pedestrian street
I═════I	Unsuitable for traffic, street subject to restrictions
▦▦▦ ----	Steps – Footpath
🚆 🚉	Train station – Auto-train station
🚌 S.N.C.F.	Coach (bus) station
▬▬	Tram
Ⓜ	Metro, underground
P+R	Park-and-Ride
♿	Access for the disabled
✉	Post office
☎	Telephone
⬚	Covered market
⚔	Barracks
△	Drawbridge
∪	Quarry
✕	Mine
Ⓑ Ⓕ	Car ferry (river or lake)
⛴	Ferry service: cars and passengers
⛵	Foot passengers only
③	Access route number common to Michelin maps and town plans
Bert (R.)...	Main shopping street
AZ B	Map co-ordinates

Selected monuments and sights

◉ ⇨	Tour - Departure point
⛪ ✝	Catholic church
⛪ ✝	Protestant church, other temple
✡ ⬚ ☪	Synagogue - Mosque
▩	Building
■	Statue, small building
✝	Calvary, wayside cross
◎	Fountain
●━━━■►	Rampart - Tower - Gate
⋈	Château, castle, historic house
∴	Ruins
∪	Dam
☼	Factory, power plant
☆	Fort
∩	Cave
▣	Troglodyte dwelling
⊓	Prehistoric site
▼	Viewing table
⋎	Viewpoint
▲	Other place of interest

Special symbol

⦂⦂⦂	Fortified town (bastide): in southwest France, a new town built in the 13-14C and typified by a geometrical layout.

Map Legend continued overleaf

Abbreviations

A   Agricultural office
(Chambre d'agriculture)

C   Chamber of Commerce
(Chambre de commerce)

H   Town hall (Hôtel de ville)

J   Law courts (Palais de justice)

M   Museum (Musée)

P   Local authority offices
(Préfecture, sous-préfecture)

POL.   Police station (Police)

⛨   Police station (Gendarmerie)

T   Theatre (Théâtre)

U   University (Université)

Sports and recreation

Racecourse

Skating rink

Outdoor, indoor swimming pool

Multiplex Cinema

Marina, sailing centre

Trail refuge hut

Cable cars, gondolas

Funicular, rack railway

Tourist train

Recreation area, park

Theme, amusement park

Wildlife park, zoo

Gardens, park, arboretum

Bird sanctuary, aviary

Walking tour, footpath

Of special interest
to children

COMPANION PUBLICATIONS

REGIONAL AND LOCAL MAPS

To make the most of your journey, travel with Michelin maps at a scale Regional maps nos 521, 525, 526, 519 and 522 and the new local maps, which are illustrated on the map of France below.

MAPS OF FRANCE

And remember to travel with the latest edition of the map of France no 721, which gives an overall view of the Dordogne-Berry-Limousin region, and the main access roads which connect it to the rest of France. The entire country is mapped at a 1:1 000 000 scale and clearly shows the main road network. Convenient Atlas formats (spiral, hard cover and mini) are also available.

INTERNET

Michelin is pleased to offer a route-planning service on the Internet: **www.ViaMichelin.com**.

Choose the shortest route, a route without tolls, or the Michelin recommended route to your destination; you can also access information about hotels and restaurants from *The Michelin Guide*, and tourists sights from *The Green Guide*. There are a number of useful maps and plans in the guide, listed opposite.

Bon voyage!

Michelin Apa Publications Ltd

A joint venture between Michelin and Langenscheidt

58 Borough High Street, London SE1 1XF, United Kingdom

No part of this publication may be reproduced in any form
without the prior permission of the publisher.

© 2010 Michelin Apa Publications Ltd
ISBN 978-1-906261-77-1
Printed: November 2009
Printed and bound in Germany